A Modern Guide to Post-Keynesian Institutional Economics

ELGAR MODERN GUIDES

Elgar Modern Guides offer a carefully curated review of a selected topic, edited or authored by a leading scholar in the field. They survey the significant trends and issues of contemporary research for both advanced students and academic researchers.

The books provide an invaluable appraisal and stimulating guide to the current research landscape, offering state-of-the-art discussions and selective overviews covering the critical matters of interest alongside recent developments. Combining incisive insight with a rigorous and thoughtful perspective on the essential issues, the books are designed to offer an inspiring introduction and unique guide to the diversity of modern debates.

Elgar Modern Guides will become an essential go-to companion for researchers and graduate students but will also prove stimulating for a wider academic audience interested in the subject matter. They will be invaluable to anyone who wants to understand as well as simply learn.

Titles in the series include:

A Modern Guide to the Urban Sharing Economy
Edited by Thomas Sigler and Jonathan Corcoran

A Modern Guide to the Digitalization of Infrastructure
Edited by Juan Montero and Matthias Finger

A Modern Guide to Sports Economics
Edited by Ruud H. Koning and Stefan Kesenne

A Modern Guide to Labour and the Platform Economy
Edited by Jan Drahokoupil and Kurt Vandaele

A Modern Guide to Financial Shocks and Crises
Edited by Giovanni Ferri and Vincenzo D'Apice

A Modern Guide to Local and Regional Politics
Edited by Colin Copus, Richard Kerley and Alistair Jones

A Modern Guide to Food Economics
Edited by Jutta Roosen and Jill E. Hobbs

A Modern Guide to Post-Keynesian Institutional Economics
Edited by Charles J. Whalen

A Modern Guide to Post-Keynesian Institutional Economics

Edited by

Charles J. Whalen

Research Fellow, The Baldy Center for Law and Social Policy, University at Buffalo, Buffalo, NY, USA

ELGAR MODERN GUIDES

 Edward Elgar
PUBLISHING

Cheltenham, UK • Northampton, MA, USA

Published by
Edward Elgar Publishing Limited
The Lypiatts
15 Lansdown Road
Cheltenham
Glos GL50 2JA
UK

Edward Elgar Publishing, Inc.
William Pratt House
9 Dewey Court
Northampton
Massachusetts 01060
USA

Paperback edition 2023

A catalogue record for this book
is available from the British Library

Library of Congress Control Number: 2022931711

This book is available electronically in the **Elgar**online
Economics subject collection
http://dx.doi.org/10.4337/9781800885752

ISBN 978 1 80088 574 5 (cased)
ISBN 978 1 80088 575 2 (eBook)
ISBN 978 1 0353 2743 0 (paperback)
Printed and bound by CPI Group (UK) Ltd, Croydon, CR0 4YY

Economists' work is not yet done.
On the contrary, it is just beginning.
—John Kenneth Galbraith

Contents

Figures

Tables

Contributors

Avraham I. Baranes, Assistant Professor of Economics, Department of Business and Economics, Elmhurst University, USA

Asimina Christoforou, Assistant Professor, Department of Economic and Regional Development, Panteion University of Social and Political Sciences, Greece

Samba Diop, Associate Professor of Economics, Centre de Recherche sur les Institutions, l'Industrie et les Systèmes Economiques d'Amiens (CRIISEA), University of Picardie Jules Verne, France

Eduardo Fernández-Huerga, Associate Professor, Department of Economics and Statistics, University of León, Spain

Alicia Girón, Researcher, Economic Research Institute, and Director of the University Program Studies of Asia and Africa, National Autonomous University of Mexico

Emek Karakilic, PhD Student, Department of Public Policy and Public Affairs, University of Massachusetts Boston, USA

Anna Klimina, Associate Professor of Economics, St. Thomas More College, University of Saskatchewan, Canada

Marc Lavoie, Professor Emeritus, University of Ottawa, Canada, and University of Sorbonne Paris Nord, France

Oren M. Levin-Waldman, Research Scholar, Global Institute for Sustainable Prosperity, USA

Yan Liang, Peter and Bonnie Kremer Chair, Professor of Economics, Willamette University, USA

Faruk Ülgen, Associate Professor of Economics, University of Grenoble Alpes, France

Christian E. Weller, Professor of Public Policy, University of Massachusetts Boston, and Senior Fellow, Center for American Progress, USA

Charles J. Whalen, Research Fellow, Baldy Center for Law and Social Policy, University at Buffalo, USA

Timothy A. Wunder, Clinical Professor of Economics, The University of Texas at Arlington, USA

Anna Zachorowska-Mazurkiewicz, Associate Professor of Economics, Jagiellonian University, Poland

David A. Zalewski, Professor Emeritus, School of Business, Providence College, USA

PART I

Introduction

1. Introduction to the history, contours, and frontiers of Post-Keynesian Institutional economics

Charles J. Whalen

This book advances Post-Keynesian Institutional economics—most often called Post-Keynesian Institutionalism (PKI)—a branch of the Institutionalist school that builds on common ground with Post Keynesianism. PKI was foreshadowed in the first half of the twentieth century by similarities in the views of John R. Commons and John Maynard Keynes; it was conceived in the mid-1970s, and began to take shape in the 1980s. The tradition proved its worth during the global financial crisis of 2007–2009, by analyzing and addressing that period's tumultuous events far better than standard economics. Additional and more recent Post-Keynesian Institutionalist research demonstrates that PKI remains ahead of the economic mainstream in shedding light on contemporary problems, especially by analyzing long-term trends in capitalist development, including financialization, spreading worker insecurity, and rising inequality.[1]

Today, PKI is a robust tradition with secure foundations and broad methodological, analytical, and policy contours. This *Modern Guide* extends PKI's recent analyses; explores pressing contemporary problems; highlights important concepts and methods; sketches out new theories; and integrates PKI with ideas from other research traditions. To set the stage, we begin with an overview of the history, contours, and frontiers of PKI, including an introduction to the chapters that follow.

A SHORT HISTORY OF PKI

Since PKI is a branch of Institutional economics, its history starts with Institutionalism's beginnings.[2] At the end of the nineteenth century, Thorstein Veblen (1898) provided a foundation for Institutionalism in an essay that called for replacing conventional economics with an evolutionary science grounded in the study of history, socioeconomic interrelations, and real-world institutions. Commons, another early Institutionalist, added a focus on achieving social and economic reform. While Veblen envisioned socioeconomic change as driven by pragmatic adaptation to the world of "matter-of-fact" reality, Commons saw it as an unending process of conflict and resolution, which he sought to channel away from exploitative outcomes and toward "reasonable" solutions.[3]

Institutionalism's science-building and problem-solving dimensions were both present when the tradition was part of the economic mainstream in the United States (US) between the two world wars. In that era, Institutionalists constituted the majority of the faculty in two of the top American economics departments: the University of Wisconsin (home of Commons, Harold Groves, and Edwin Witte) and Columbia University (home of Wesley Mitchell, John M. Clark, and Rexford Tugwell). During the Great Depression, many of those economists, their students, and like-minded scholars and practitioners helped shape the New Deal, some holding government posts even into the administration of President Lyndon Johnson.[4] While the most recent Institutionalist to hold a high-level position in the US government was Ray Marshall, who crafted an ambitious public service employment program as Labor Secretary for President Jimmy Carter, contemporary Institutionalists, including those affiliated with think tanks such as the Center for American Progress and the Economic Policy Institute, continue to shape legislative proposals.

Heading Toward PKI

Although Post Keynesian economics did not emerge until the 1970s (and PKI came a short time later), PKI was foreshadowed several decades earlier by the fact that Commons and Keynes held similar views on economic theory and policy. For example, Commons and Keynes both approached economic theory from the premises that markets are not self-adjusting and that economic activity and outcomes are shaped by history, institutions, and expectations about an uncertain future. They also aimed for a stabilized form of capitalism that would smooth business cycles (in the interests of economic efficiency, social justice, and individual liberty) by making use of a combination of direct public action, an effective civil service, and semi-autonomous bodies operating within the context of representative democracy. Corresponding with Commons about economic policy in the 1920s, Keynes ([1927] 1982) wrote: "There seems to me to be no other economist with whose general way of thinking I feel myself in such genuine accord."[5]

When Post Keynesianism materialized in the early 1970s, it began as a professional network and eclectic movement with footholds in both the UK and US. At the center of that emerging network was Joan Robinson of the University of Cambridge, who had been Keynes's colleague, and American economist Alfred Eichner, who was introduced to Institutional economics at Columbia University and considered himself an Institutionalist and Post Keynesian. The Post Keynesian movement developed out of dissatisfaction with mainstream economics for a variety of reasons, including the mainstream's inability to shed light on stagflation and other important economic problems, and its failure to appreciate many of Keynes's core insights.[6]

Despite Post Keynesianism's eclecticism and even heterogeneity, a number of Institutionalists saw much in it that they recognized. Acknowledging that affinity, Wallace C. Peterson (1977) used his presidential address before the Institutional economists' Association for Evolutionary Economics (AFEE) to highlight several core ideas that he saw as the foundation of both Post Keynesianism, which he called "the economics of Keynes," and Institutionalism. In particular, Peterson's address identified the following as key elements of a useful starting point for economic theory and policy analysis: (1) uncertainty is an inescapable part of the backdrop of economic life; (2) institutions and power relations not only influence human behavior and economic performance, but also underscore the need for economists to give serious attention to income distribution; (3) money and finance are among capitalism's key institutions; (4) economies change continuously and organically (in irreversible, historical time), and advanced capitalist economies are inherently prone to cyclical instability; and (5) public action is essential to addressing excessive concentrations and abuses of private power, even as private power is acknowledged to often have a grip on public power. Peterson concluded by calling for Post Keynesians and Institutionalists to collaborate by using those ideas to build and apply a shared analytical framework as a way to better understand and address real-world problems.

PKI Emerges

In the early 1980s, Charles Wilber and Kenneth Jameson adopted Peterson's starting point. The result was the first book to outline and use a synthesis called PKI—*An Inquiry into the Poverty of Economics* (Wilber and Jameson 1983). Drawing on a number of Institutionalist and Post Keynesian analyses of the US economy, the book emphasized an economic structure that John Kenneth Galbraith (1977), who identified himself as an Institutionalist and Post Keynesian, described as "bimodal." In particular, Galbraith's conception of the economy was one in which many industries were led by a few, oligopolistic firms with considerable economic power—firms that Alfred Eichner (1976) described as "megacorps"—while millions of smaller firms operated without such power. According to Wilber and Jameson (1983), understanding the bimodal economy was essential to accounting for the simultaneous occurrence of inflation and high unemployment.[7]

In many ways, Wilber and Jameson's book was a success. It demonstrated the coherence of Institutionalist methodology (with its focus on holism, systemic thinking, social institutions, and socioeconomic evolution) as well as that approach's usefulness as a research starting point consistent with the core ideas outlined by Peterson. It showed the compatibility of Institutionalist and Post Keynesian work on the structure and operation of the US economy. It also presented a unified perspective on the way social forces (via culture and socioeconomic institutions) influence all aspects of the economy, from the functioning of real-world markets to economic policymaking.

However, the influence of *An Inquiry* was limited by its focus on stagflation at a time when high inflation was abating. Wilber and Jameson's book was, ironically, a casualty of the economic change process they placed at the heart of PKI. To advance further in the late 1980s and beyond, the analyses of PKI would need a more dynamic focus.

PKI Turns to Minsky

Institutional economists looking for a new way to connect with Post Keynesianism found that dynamic focus in the work of Hyman Minsky, who considered himself a "financial Keynesian" but was accepted by (and felt equally at home among) Institutionalists and Post Keynesians. Institutions and the evolution of economic systems were important elements in all of Minsky's work; in fact, he once wrote that "monetary economics cannot escape being institutional economics" (Minsky 1982, 280). In 1996, upon receiving AFEE's Veblen-Commons Award, that association's highest honor, Minsky (1996, 357) began his acceptance remarks by highlighting the affinity between Keynes and the Institutionalists and stressing the continuing relevance of that affinity.

Minsky (1975; 1986a) is perhaps best known for his *financial instability hypothesis*, which argues that capitalist financial systems evolve endogenously from being robust to fragile, and that, as a consequence, such economies are susceptible to financial crises and deep recessions. That hypothesis—which rests on a monetary theory of production and an accompanying endogenous approach to money—not only provides an alternative to conventional economists' efficient market hypothesis (which argues that financial markets are efficient and stable), but also serves as the cornerstone of an investment theory of business cycles. In addition to exploring financial instability, Minsky, who died in 1996, devoted much of the last decade of his life to analyzing the emergence (in the early 1980s) of what he called *money manager capitalism*, which he saw as the latest stage of capitalist development.[8] What placed Minsky's contributions at the center of PKI was that his work on money, finance, cycles, and capitalist development consistently underscored themes (such as endogenous cycles and socioeconomic evolution) that had long been—and remain—common ground in the research of Institutionalists, Keynes, and Post Keynesians.[9]

PKI During and After the Global Financial Crisis

PKI proved its worth during the global financial crisis of 2007–2009, which blindsided mainstream economics but was anticipated by several Post-Keynesian Institutionalists.[10] While conventional economists struggled for an explanation of the financial meltdown after having denied such a crisis was possible, Post-Keynesian Institutionalists applied their evolutionary and institutionally grounded perspective not only to analyze what happened, but also to sketch a policy agenda for both recovery and reform. Throughout the crisis, the ideas of Minsky—who by then had been dead for over a decade—received much attention from journalists, practitioners, and policymakers because he had been the most prominent economist working from such a perspective and because he was well known to (despite having often been ignored by) many in the mainstream.[11] But what the crisis really demonstrated was that PKI had become a distinctive branch of Institutionalism, composed of an international group of scholars who not only stood on the shoulders of Minsky (and other Institutionalists and Post Keynesians) to peer more deeply into the workings of the real-world economy, but also adapted and extended his insights into areas that Minsky rarely examined, such as consumer finances, global markets, and developing economies.[12]

Additional and more recent Post-Keynesian Institutionalist research has analyzed long-term trends in capitalist development, including financialization, spreading worker insecurity, and rising inequality.[13] Minsky's own work on such trends—which stressed the emerging dominance of institutional investors and their relentless push for maximization of shareholder value— provides a point of departure for Post-Keynesian Institutionalist research on capitalist development. In fact, like his work on cyclical instability, Minsky's scholarship on capitalist development serves as the key to an expansive anteroom, not a closet in which it's "all Minsky (and nothing but Minsky) all the time." That's because Minsky's work on the rise of money manager capitalism puts us in touch with two features of Institutionalist research that are as old as Institutionalism itself: the study of stages of economic history, and the aim of understanding the economy as an ever-evolving whole.[14] Minsky provides a point of entry into the world of Veblen, Commons, Keynes, Peterson, Wilber and Jameson, Galbraith, Eichner, and more—and his work serves as an invitation for us to join their "grand adventure" of economic research and discovery.[15]

THE CONTOURS OF PKI

The contours of today's PKI can be organized into three categories: methodology, analysis, and public policy.[16] The first category includes essential preconceptions (pre-analytic foundations) involving society, the economy, human behavior, values, and science (for a summary, see Table 1.1). The second category includes key research themes and analytical constructs (for a summary, see Table 1.2). The third category includes shared perspectives on the role of government and public policy (for a summary and comparison to conventional economics, see Table 1.3).[17]

Methodology

As a branch of Institutional economics, PKI adopts the Institutionalist definition of economics as well as its underlying methodology (or pre-analytic vision). According to most contemporary Institutionalists, economics is "the science of social provisioning," a definition that originated with Allan Gruchy (1987, 21). This definition reflects an effort by Institutionalists to offer a broader conception of economics than conventional economists, who focus on the allocation of scarce resources—most often through market mechanisms (in fact, market allocation is the preferred method)—in a world populated by maximizing agents (individuals, firms, etc.) with unlimited wants.

The Post-Keynesian Institutionalist conception of society emphasizes interrelatedness and ongoing social change. The first of these emphases is referred to as *holism* (or *organicism*); it views social reality as a unified whole and holds that boundaries between the economy and other social spheres are always imprecise. Thus, while mainstream economics rests on an *atomistic* conception of society, which treats different social spheres as analytically separable and as operating according to their own laws and forces, PKI instead adopts the Institutionalist view described by Gunnar Myrdal (1969, 10): "In reality, there are not economic, sociological, or psychological problems, but simply problems, [all of which] … are complex." Meanwhile, the Institutionalist emphasis on ongoing social change is referred to as an *evolutionary* or *processual* perspective. In other words, while conventional economics focuses on conditions leading to a state of equilibrium, PKI views social systems as dynamic, ever-developing entities (owing to internal and external sources of change), and its economists are keenly aware that all social activity occurs in irreversible historical time.

By focusing on social provisioning, PKI casts a wider net than conventional economics when considering what constitutes "the economy." While the economic mainstream focuses heavily on the allocation of goods and services via market mechanisms, PKI encompasses such allocation but usually gives more attention to macroeconomic stabilization and distribution. PKI also goes further, not only by making room for analyses of production, social reproduction, and want creation, but also by recognizing that the market is only one type of human institution involved in shaping provisioning decisions (such as what is to be produced, how, and for whom), along with others institutions, including households, governments, and indeed all the institutions that determine culture in its totality.[18]

In contrast to the conventional economic presupposition that market mechanisms are self-regulating, PKI rejects the notion that economic systems have any inherent tendency. Instead, PKI sees social institutions, not impersonal forces or universal laws of nature, as the balancing wheel of the economy. To be sure, Post-Keynesian Institutionalists accept that the price system may sometimes exhibit equilibrating tendencies, but they recognize that market dynamics can also involve cumulative causation (such as a tendency toward increasing fragility), path dependence, and hysteresis. As a result, real-world markets may not rapidly or fully correct themselves, particularly in a downturn. In fact, like both Post Keynesian economics and Institutionalism, PKI emphasizes economic disequilibrium and instability, along with the fact that economies can stall at far below potential for extended periods.

PKI also has a broader and fundamentally different view of human behavior than does conventional economics. Competition is the driving force in conventional economics: the coordinating function of prices at the heart of such economics requires workers to compete with other workers, companies to compete with other companies, and consumers to compete with other consumers. Competition even lurks behind the "voluntary" market transactions that are the showpiece of conventional economics; the two main parties in every transaction are driven by a competing motivation (buyers want the lowest price and sellers want the highest price). In contrast, by building on the methodology of Institutionalism, PKI recognizes the full range of human motivation and interaction, including competition, conflict, compromise, cooperation, dependence, care, and nurturing. PKI also recognizes both that power is rarely distributed equally, and, as Peterson noted in his AFEE presidential address (discussed above), that power relations have a significant influence on human behavior and economic performance; thus, attention to power must be part of the work of PKI.

Moreover, what makes the Post-Keynesian Institutionalist view of human behavior fundamentally different from that of conventional economics is rejection of the extreme conception of rationality upon which the economic mainstream rests. As Marc Lavoie (1992, 11) writes, conventional economics is based on "a very peculiar type of rationality," which he calls *substantive* rationality. According to that rationality, humans maximize utility (or enterprise profits) in a manner consistent with an ability to predict all future events and fully assess all possible alternatives and consequences. In contrast, PKI—rooted in an extensive Institutionalist and Post Keynesian literature—is based on what might be called *bounded* rationality (also called *procedural* rationality) (Lavoie 1992, 12, 51): people act on the basis of imperfect knowledge, using expectations shaped by culture and formed in a world of uncertainty; they rely heavily on habits and social conventions; lessons are learned through experience (which often involves unmet expectations); and ends and means are subject to constant reconsideration.[19]

Turning to values, we find that conventional economics rests on a contradictory approach to values. On the one hand, mainstream economics asserts it is a *positive*—value free—science. On the other hand, it equates the market price of a good or service with economic value, and treats economic allocation via competitive markets—a state of "optimal" allocation that the mainstream calls "economic efficiency"—as the gold standard for economic activity.

The Post-Keynesian Institutionalist approach to values is multifaceted. It begins with a recognition that all economics is value laden. As Myrdal (1978, 778–779) wrote: "Valuations are always with us. Disinterested research there has never been and can never be. Prior to answers there must be questions. There can be no view except from a viewpoint. In the questions raised and the viewpoint chosen, valuations are implied." Robinson (1970, 122) also rejected the notion of positive economics, and her approach to dealing with the matter is an essential part of PKI: "[An economist's attempt] to be purely objective must necessarily be either self-deception or a device to deceive others. A candid writer will make his [*sic*] preconceptions clear and allow the reader to discount them if he does not accept them."[20]

Another facet of the Post-Keynesian Institutionalist approach to values is recognition that, depending on the circumstances, individuals and groups make value judgments by using one (or more) of a variety of valuation standards. For example, we can value things on the basis of *scarcity* (platinum, for example), *usefulness* (either because the item in question—water, for instance—is needed to sustain life, or because it—perhaps a hammer, or even a particular public policy—is the right tool for a particular job), *expected utility* (which could be based on either a whim or a careful consideration of the happiness to be gained through acquisition and/or consumption), or *embodied labor or skill* (that is, the time, effort, and talent we or others put into constructing something). Market prices also serve as a valuation standard; prices are often in large part a measure of scarcity value, but they are actually cultural products that may not fully reflect any of the various measures of value just mentioned. In addition, individual and group values can diverge, and there are a variety of ways to determine group or social values.[21] PKI recognizes these many different individual and group valuation standards and methods.[22]

Table 1.1   *The methodology of Post-Keynesian Institutional economics:*
              categories and content

Category	Content
Definition of economics	The science of social provisioning
Scope of economics	Encompasses all human culture relevant to providing the goods and services that satisfy human needs and wants Includes market and non-market institutions, as well as production, distribution, macroeconomic stabilization, want creation, and social reproduction
Conception of society	Emphasizes social interrelatedness (holism) and ongoing change (incessant evolution)
Image of the economic process	Economic coordination stems from social institutions (markets are not self-regulating) Pervasiveness of cumulative causation, path dependence, and hysteresis Macroeconomic activity is prone to financial crises, business cycles, and extended periods at less than full employment
View of human behavior	Recognizes the full range of human motivation and interaction (such as cooperation and nurturing, not merely marketplace competition) Underscores the significance of power relations Emphasizes bounded rationality and uncertainty: humans rely on habits, conventions, changeable expectations, and provisional judgments in a world characterized by imperfect knowledge and an uncertain future
Approach to values	All economics is value laden Market values reflect one of many approaches to valuation Economists should state their value premises and take a stand on policy matters
Philosophy of science	Strives to understand economic reality by using realistic assumptions and reevaluating theories to keep up with an ever-changing reality Theories are constructed via pattern modeling

Source: Created by the author.

But PKI doesn't merely recognize such standards and methods. It also underscores the need to study them: to discover what are the operative values in a given situation; to learn how those values were formed and are evolving; and to identify the way values affect economic outcomes. In short, another facet of the Post-Keynesian Institutionalist approach to values is that the entire valuation process is part of the subject matter of economics (as are social influences on wants and human behavior).[23]

A final facet of the Post-Keynesian Institutionalist approach to values comes from the recognition that PKI is a policy science—aimed at "making the world a better place in which to live" by means of social and economic reform

(Mitchell, quoted in Ramstad 1989, 762). Thus, PKI encourages economists to take a normative stance on matters of public policy. The only stipulation, of course, is that the value premises of such policy work should be stated "clearly and explicitly" (Myrdal 1978, 779).

The last methodological category involves preconceptions about economics as scientific endeavor. In conventional economics, *prediction* is the preeminent goal, and much less attention is paid to the realism of assumptions (indeed, some mainstream economists argue that realistic assumptions are unimportant). In contrast, PKI joins Institutionalists and Post Keynesians in holding that economics should focus on contributing to an *understanding* of actual processes of social provisioning, and in believing that the best way to achieve that end is to strive for theories grounded in realistic assumptions (recognizing, of course, that all theories are an abstraction from reality) as well as to regularly reevaluate theories to keep up with an ever-changing economic reality. Conventional economists often call their scientific methodology *instrumentalism* (Caldwell 1980); the approach of PKI (as just described) is a mix of Post Keynesian *realism* (Lavoie 2014, 12–13) and Institutionalist *pragmatism* (Gruchy 1947, 268–269; Whalen 1992, 63–64).

Consistent with Post-Keynesian Institutionalism's holistic conception of society, the scientific methodology of PKI can also be called systems thinking. When thinking in terms of interrelated systems and subsystems, Post-Keynesian Institutionalists often look at real-world cases and construct a theory by fitting individual cases into a larger pattern based on similarities and differences. This is sometimes described as pattern modeling (see, for example, Wilber and Harrison 1978). In conventional economics, a high degree mathematical formalism is often possible because economic institutions are downplayed as either troublesome (and thus, undesirable) "frictions" or inessential details. In contrast, in the course of pattern modeling, the economists of PKI are willing to forego some formalism in pursuit of greater realism because they recognize that understanding the economy's institutional makeup (including, for example, key features of the economy's structure, as well as the institutionally determined processes that shape wages and prices) is essential to understanding real-world economic activity.[24]

Analysis

At the level of economic analysis, we can further sketch the contours of PKI by identifying some main themes of Post-Keynesian Institutionalist research as well as the key analytical constructs (concepts and theories) used in that work. PKI began in the United States and focused initially on the workings of capitalism in that country and other advanced industrial democracies. Since the mid-1990s, however, analyses grounded in PKI have been used to study economies around the world as well as to examine questions involving inter-national economics. In fact, while Minsky's own work focused mainly on the United States, he stressed that capitalism comes in many varieties, even as the current stage of advanced capitalist development (money manager capitalism) was becoming increasingly global.[25]

Most PKI focuses on macroeconomic issues. In fact, *the* dominant, overar-ching theme of PKI has always been an effort to understand how economies operate for the purpose of achieving and sustaining broadly shared prosperity at the national level and extending that prosperity more widely. But that has not meant ignoring microeconomics; indeed, PKI has sought to incorporate, update, and extend the microeconomic insights of Institutionalism and Post Keynesianism.

Thus, one Post-Keynesian Institutionalist theme involves an effort to draw on psychology and other disciplines to better understand the determinants of human economic behavior, both in general and with respect to particular economic issues. For example, Fernández-Huerga (2008; 2013) builds on psy-chology and neurosciences to highlight the influence of habits and social insti-tutions upon human cognition, reasoning, and decision-making, and to outline Post-Keynesian Institutionalist models of human economic behavior and markets that are more realistic than those offered by conventional economics. Other examples of close examinations of human behavior by such economists include work by Brazelton (2005; 2011) and Harvey (2006; 2012), who draw on the research of psychologists (in addition to sociologists and neuroscientists in the case of Brazelton) to shed light on how the formation of expectations affects financial crises and exchange rates, respectively.[26]

Another theme focuses on the structure of industry. In that research, PKI builds on Galbraith's notion of a bimodal economy characterized by oligopo-listic megacorps and countless small businesses. Of course, the details of today's industrial structure differ greatly from those of the early 1980s when PKI emerged, but contemporary Post-Keynesian Institutionalists continue to find Galbraith's characterization full of relevant insights and useful as a point of departure for investigations of subsequent industrial evolution. For example, Galbraith's conception of a broadly bifurcated industrial landscape and his emphasis on the administered pricing practices of large corporations remain relevant, while his attention to corporate governance (which focused on the separation of ownership from control) provides a useful starting place for examinations of the rise of money manager capitalism.[27]

Post-Keynesian Institutionalist attention to the bimodal structure of industry is also part of a larger theme involving the question: to what extent do product markets, labor markets, and financial markets—indeed, all markets—operate without a conventional, market-clearing price mechanism? Addressing that question shines a light on the role of price markups and other types of administered pricing used in product markets, but also on the broader reality of "imperfect markets with significant monopolistic elements" (Eichner and Kregel 1975, 1309). It also highlights the stratified nature of labor markets, as well as the important role of social norms, institutions, and aggregate demand in determining employment, wages, and other aspects of the employment relationship.[28] In a similar manner, a look at financial markets highlights the fact that credit is a social institution, which depends heavily on culturally influenced expectations and the institutional details of a given regulatory setting. Moreover, no matter where we look, the economy is always evolving, so the answers today will often be quite different from those of a few decades ago. To be sure, there has been an overall trend over the past several decades toward greater price, wage, and interest-rate flexibility—owing to mounting pressure on corporations to maximize shareholder value, as well as increased globalization of production, decreased unionization, and new forms of financial intermediation (combined with a move away from relational financing)—but social and institutional determinants of market outcomes are often still more important than conventional economics acknowledges.[29]

Three other themes place an emphasis on finance: the centrality of money and finance; the evolution of finance; and the integration of finance and macroeconomics. The centrality of money and finance has been central to both Institutionalism and Post Keynesianism from the start. PKI inherits a view of capitalism as a monetized economy, in which money and financial institutions play vital roles and the financial accumulation motive is the key driver of economic activity. Minsky described this view as a Wall Street paradigm, which emphasizes not only that production precedes marketplace exchange but also that finance precedes production.[30] In PKI, that paradigm manifests itself in the effort to offer a *monetary theory of production*, a theory in which "money plays a central and indispensable role in explaining the process of production" (Dillard 1980, 265). (The notion of the monetary circuit, the process by which debt is created, circulates, and is destroyed, corresponds to the dynamics of a monetary theory of production; see Chapter 9; see also Tymoigne 2003.)[31]

A focus on the evolution of finance is important to PKI in recognition of the fact that economic change is often driven by developments and innovations in financial markets.[32] Some of this evolution is cyclical in nature, and is reflected in Post-Keynesian Institutionalists' use of the financial instability hypothesis. It assumes that, over the course of a period of economic prosperity, conservative "hedge" financing gives way to riskier forms that Minsky called "speculative" and "Ponzi" financing (the latter is named after financial swindler Charles Ponzi), a development that increases financial instability and ultimately ends with a financial crisis, a resetting of economic expectations, and an eventual return to hedge financing.[33] Other financial evolution is longer term in nature and is reflected in Post-Keynesian Institutionalists' attention, for example, to innovations such as shadow banking (including off-balance-sheet financing) and the shift from relational ("lend and hold") financing to securitized ("originate and distribute") and arms-length financing.

Attention to the integration of finance and macroeconomics also builds on the analytical construct of the financial instability hypothesis, which provides a foundation for Post-Keynesian Institutionalist analyses of business cycles. Recognizing Mitchell's (1941, ix) observation that "each new cycle presents idiosyncrasies," PKI does not offer a single explanation for all cycles. Still, such economists often find it useful to draw insight from the financial instability hypothesis, which leads most directly to an investment theory of endogenously generated cycles and gives attention to the challenges of coordinating short-term financing (and position taking) with expensive and durable capital assets (Minsky 1975).

As a result of many decades of Institutionalist and Post Keynesian research on finance and macroeconomics, PKI has inherited not just a perspective oriented toward endogenously generated business cycles, it has also assimilated three presuppositions, which are related both to that cycle perspective and to each other: (1) the money supply responds to credit creation, which means (as mentioned in the previous section) the money supply is endogenous; (2) aggregate demand is the main force determining output and employment in both the near and long term, since the economy's near-term path affects the supply-side determinants of long-run growth (this is what Post Keynesians call the principle of effective demand; see Lavoie 2014, 35); and (3) investment—which is heavily influenced by business expectations—determines saving, rather than the reverse (again, see Lavoie 2014, 35). Moreover, since the run-up to the global financial crisis of 2007–2009, a considerable amount of Post-Keynesian Institutionalist research has used insight from the financial instability hypothesis to highlight household financial insecurity as well as to bring household financing and consumer indebtedness into analyses of the relationship between finance and macroeconomics. Much of this work stresses that widening income inequality is a driving force behind household indebtedness, and that such inequality is both a consequence of and contributor to macroeconomic instability.[34]

A final theme involves examination of long-term trends in capitalist development. Today, this is perhaps the central focus of PKI—one that (as mentioned above, in the discussion of the tradition's history) not only connects PKI with some of Institutionalism's oldest themes (including attention to stages of history, the legal foundations of economic systems, and overall socioeconomic evolution), but also focuses its attention on some of the most pressing issues today (including financialization, worker insecurity, and rising inequality). Moreover, what has emerged through attention to this theme is an analytical construct—a (finance-driven) theory of capitalist development

Table 1.2   *Post-Keynesian Institutional economic analysis: key themes,
aims, and analytical constructs*

Theme	Aim and analytical constructs
Macroeconomic performance	Understand how economies operate, with the aim of achieving and sustaining broadly shared prosperity at the national level, but also internationally
Human behavior	Draw on psychology and other disciplines to better understand determinants of human behavior, both in general and with respect to particular economic issues
Structure of industry	Explore the bimodal structure (megacorps vs. small enterprises) of post-World War II advanced capitalism and its evolution
Institutional coordination versus market-clearing prices	Shed light on administered prices, monopolistic and oligopolistic features of markets, labor market stratification, and the importance of social norms and institutions in determining social provisioning
Centrality of money and finance	Explore the vital role of money and financial institutions in shaping economic activity Analytical constructs: monetary theory of production; monetary circuit
Evolution of finance	Analyze financial-system evolution as a driver of economic change in the near and longer term; includes attention to financial innovation, fragility, crises Analytical construct: financial instability hypothesis
Integration of finance and macroeconomics	Incorporate finance into macroeconomic theory to analyze and better understand endogenously generated business cycles Analytical constructs: endogenous money supply; Minsky's investment theory of business cycles (but more recent work focuses on household indebtedness); principle of effective demand
Capitalist development	Examine long-term trends in capitalist development (with special attention to the co-evolution of law, finance, and industry) and their consequences for economic performance and human well-being Analytical construct: A finance-driven theory of stages of capitalist development, with a focus on the transition from managerial capitalism to money manager capitalism in the United States as well as on the national and international consequences of the current era (which began around 1980)

Source: Created by the author.

rooted in compatible aspects of work by Veblen, Commons, Schumpeter, and Minsky (see, for example, Whalen 2001)—that has been used to study and explain various facets of the contemporary socioeconomic system in an integrated manner.[35] In fact, while there is more analytical work to be done to better connect capitalism's cyclical and long-term trends—and, indeed, helping to encourage and point the way forward for such research is a key aim of this book—Post-Keynesian Institutionalists researching cyclical issues have increasingly drawn upon Post-Keynesian Institutionalist work on capitalist development, and vice versa.

Public Policy

There are two sides to government and public policy in both conventional economics and PKI. In conventional economics, the typical view of the state is that government tends to interfere with market mechanisms. Thus, mainstream economists often argue against minimum-wage laws, fiscal policies designed to boost the economy, and other forms of government protections and policy activism. The general view among conventional economists has long been that public action, even when driven by good intentions, only disrupts the market system's ability to allocate goods and services efficiently, and, therefore, laissez faire is usually the best approach to public policy.

The other side to government and public policy in conventional economics is a view of the state as an entity that can take corrective action in instances of market failure. For example, government action may be warranted to address negative externalities such as pollution and positive externalities such as the social benefits associated with educating children. It might also become necessary to provide certain ("public") goods—which can range from a legal framework and courts to national defense—that markets do not deliver reliably.

The two sides to government and public policy in PKI center on the notion of the creative state and the notion of the predator state. Each is discussed in turn.[36]

PKI rejects both laissez faire and the mainstream notion of the *corrective* state. Instead, PKI rests on the notion of the *creative* state. According to that view, laissez faire is impossible: there is no such thing as a free market. PKI views the government as deeply and unavoidably involved in shaping the economy by fashioning property rights and institutions, and by making and enforcing rules that are always evolving.[37] Moreover, it is not enough to say that government must foster competitive markets; in the real world, market economies can take a variety of forms—government is regularly called on to determine the appropriate nature and scope of competition.[38] In fact, PKI recognizes that government's creative effort can be constructively directed toward any of a number of conceptions of efficiency (including, for example, allocative, macroeconomic, or adaptive efficiency) and that public policy is often shaped by other considerations as well (such as social justice).

From the perspective of PKI, market mechanisms are not inherently self-regulating and state action is so interwoven into an economy that prices have no meaning independent of their politico-cultural context. Thus, as mentioned in the earlier discussion of methodology, institutions are the true balancing wheel or coordinating mechanism of an economy, not the price system. As Minsky (1986a, 7) writes, this means that economic policy "must be concerned with the design of institutions as well as operations within a set of institutions." Moreover, policy can change an economy, but economies also evolve as a result of other internal and external forces. Given the reality of an ever-changing economy, "There is no magic economic [policy] bullet; no single program or particular reform that will set things right forever" (Minsky 1986a, 293).

PKI stresses the need to study existing policy institutions and government practices so as to understand how they function and evolve. But PKI also calls on economists to reimagine those institutions and practices with the aim of achieving socioeconomic reform that improves economic performance and advances the public interest. In other words, Post-Keynesian Institutionalists should study *what is*, but should also incorporate into their work a vision of *what ought to be* (as long as they are explicit about that vision and the values upon which it rests). And, of course, the two types of research are not mutually exclusive; indeed, as stressed already, PKI emphasizes that understanding things *as they are* provides a vital starting point for reform initiatives.[39]

Starting with the aims of understanding how economies operate and contributing to achieving and sustaining broadly shared prosperity, Post-Keynesian Institutionalists devote much attention not only to existing public policies and practices, but also to innovative proposals and policy options. For example, their policy work often focuses on issues such as:

- Achieving and sustaining full employment;
- Reducing economic insecurity;
- Addressing income inequality;
- Establishing and maintaining effective supervision and regulation of financial markets;[40]
- Shoring up automatic economic stabilizers;
- Attending to societal needs by looking at not only the *level* but also the *composition* of public expenditures;[41]
- Fostering technological economic progress;
- Curbing corporate power and extending workers' rights; and
- Promoting social objectives in the face of financialization.[42]

In conducting such work, Post-Keynesian Institutionalists use a variety of empirical techniques, including statistical and comparative methods, system dynamics, and scenario analysis.[43]

Of course, as Peterson (1977, 209) recognized, the state can be used for good or ill, and private power often has a hold on public power. In fact, drawing on the work of John Kenneth Galbraith, Peterson suggested that large corporations and other groups with economic power have long sought "to capture state power and subvert it to their private aims." This leads to the dark side of the creative state, which James K. Galbraith (in a work written at the suggestion of his father, John Kenneth Galbraith) calls the predator state.

Table 1.3   *The state and public policy in Post-Keynesian Institutional economics: Post-Keynesian Institutionalism versus conventional economics*

Post-Keynesian Institutionalism	Conventional economics
Considers the state an essential, creative entity that shapes socioeconomic activity	Considers the state, at its best, a corrective entity (which corrects for market failures)
Emphasizes the vital role of the state to promote and protect public well-being	Emphasizes that markets are largely self-regulating
Often highlights the state as a predatory force that shows little regard for the public purpose	Often highlights the "failure" of state action, arguing that public policies tend to interfere with market-based allocation

Source: Created by the author.

According to James K. Galbraith (2008, 147), public-sector predation is a situation in which economic and political pressure from the private sector results in government officials who do not recognize the public interest and instead manage the public sector to serve private interests. In a predatory regime, he explains, the people in charge "have friends, and enemies, and as for the rest of us—we are the prey." Of course, it comes as no surprise that decades of financial-sector deregulation constitute one illustration of public-sector predation offered by Galbraith: money manager capitalism didn't just emerge and spread on its own; it was helped along as financial elites used their influence to shape public policies in ways that furthered their own private interests.[44] Recognizing, exploring, and devising ways to curtail the predatory side of the state, which has become more visible and consequential in the money manager era, are essential elements of contemporary PKI.[45]

FRONTIERS: AN OVERVIEW

The methodological, analytical, and policy contours of PKI demonstrate that the tradition has accomplished much over the past few decades. But the purpose of this book is to advance PKI by adding to its contributions, which includes exploring and even expanding its frontiers. To accomplish that objective, the chapters that follow—which feature a stellar group of scholars from around the world—are organized into three sections.

Extending Analyses and Explorations of Money Manager Capitalism

Part II extends existing Post-Keynesian Institutionalist analyses and explorations of money manager capitalism. David Zalewski (Chapter 2) focuses on the transition from the early post-World War II era of US managerial capitalism to the era of money manager capitalism. In particular, he draws on work by John Kenneth Galbraith, Hyman Minsky, and others to highlight how corporate leaders have shifted uncertainty from enterprises to workers in an effort to secure profits and achieve other objectives. Because that risk shifting is enabled by power imbalances, Zalewski stresses that restorative collective action—especially a broad range of worker-oriented public policies—is necessary to ensure economic justice.

Avraham Baranes (Chapter 3) argues that the US productivity-pay gap of the past several decades can be explained by the rise of the financialized corporations of money manager capitalism. He demonstrates how corporations' focus on the maximization of shareholder value has profoundly transformed work and employment relations, resulting in less stable jobs and more economic insecurity for most workers. Recognizing that there is no simple solution to the pay gap and the underlying employment insecurity, Baranes concludes by discussing a variety of public policy proposals—involving taxes, public spending, expanded worker rights, and government regulation—that could help move the United States (and, presumably, other economies as well) in the direction of more broadly shared prosperity.

Yan Liang and Charles Whalen (Chapter 4) examine the economic experience of the United States to show that the coronavirus pandemic has exposed fundamental shortcomings in money manager capitalism. After a brief overview of the origins, development, and key features of that form of capitalism, Liang and Whalen identify four dimensions of the coronavirus crisis—inadequate industrial capacity, working families' financial distress, corporate vulnerability to sudden economic changes (owing to a culture of debt financing), and a dysfunctional public-sector safety net—and trace each to inherent shortcomings of the current system. The chapter closes by identifying not only possibilities for reform, but also challenges that must be confronted as the United States seeks to craft a robust and sustainable prosperity for the post-pandemic era.

Christian Weller and Emek Karakilic (Chapter 5) describe how the shifting of risk from corporations to individuals has increased US wealth inequality as well as financial insecurity among many households, and how those trends, in turn, slow economic growth and increase economic instability. While emphasizing that the COVID-19 pandemic has highlighted the widespread problem of household exposure to economic risk, the authors also demonstrate that such exposure has been growing throughout the era of money manager capitalism. In addition, they identify some of the policy interventions that are needed to achieve a more equitable distribution of wealth, greater economic security for households, and a more secure foundation for economic growth.

Oren Levin-Waldman (Chapter 6) argues that money manager capitalism in the United States has not only resulted in greater income inequality, rising worker insecurity, and erosion of the middle class, but also contributed to political polarization. In particular, he attributes at least part of that polarization to more adverse economic consequences of money manager capitalism for workers in what political analysts call "blue" states (which tend to favor the Democratic Party) than in "red" states (which tend to favor the Republican Party). Levin-Waldman concludes that the task ahead is to craft and build support for policy changes that could unify red and blue voters, and that the proper goal of such changes is to shore up labor market institutions that improve worker well-being.

Sharpening Concepts and Methods

Part III seeks to advance PKI by augmenting and sharpening its concepts (Chapters 7, 8, and 9) and methods (Chapters 10 and 11). Asimina Christoforou (Chapter 7) focuses on the interrelated concepts of social capital and civil society, explaining their role not only in developing the social values and institutions that hold markets and governments accountable to the public, but also in promoting public policies in the interest of social welfare. She also introduces research on the practice of participatory and deliberative democracy to further explore how social capital and civil society can build values and institutions to promote justice and participation in society. Christoforou concludes by stressing that attention to social capital and civil society enables PKI to more thoroughly explore the institutions capable of defining and enhancing social welfare. A deeper appreciation of social capital, civil society, and the social processes that accompany them can only enhance PKI's ability to understand and shed light on social values, public policy, and the socioeconomic impact of nongovernmental institutions ranging from informal community groups to formal entities such as labor unions and religious organizations.[46]

Anna Klimina (Chapter 8) focuses on economic democracy and explores that concept as it could be used to shape reform in the former Soviet Union, a region dominated today by oligarchical-bureaucratic state capitalism. In particular, she constructs a framework for economic democracy that builds on the work of Veblen, Commons, John Kenneth Galbraith, and contemporary contributors at the intersection of Post Keynesianism and Institutionalism. But Klimina's framework also incorporates ideas that emerged in the work of reform economists of the Soviet Union in the 1960s–1980s, ideas in touch with the region's institutional history as well as with the experiences and vision of the region's residents. Thus, the resulting framework, developed and presented by Klimina in historical perspective, is a hybrid of ideas from within and outside the region. According to Klimina, economic democracy is essential to reducing worker insecurity, protecting labor empowerment, and consolidating political democracy in society.

Alicia Girón (Chapter 9) offers a Post-Keynesian Institutionalist perspective from Latin America. Her chapter highlights the monetary circuit across stages of economic development. The chapter shows that heterodox Latin American scholarship has long contained elements compatible with Institutional and Post Keynesian economics, and that such scholarship has recently converged with—and enhanced—PKI by focusing on financialization as well as financial crises.

Timothy Wunder (Chapter 10) stresses the vital work of Post-Keynesian Institutionalists and other heterodox economists as translators of mainstream economists' pronouncements on the economy and public policy. His chapter looks at the privileged place of conventional economists in policy discussions and then explores three mainstream concepts that clearly call for translation: rationality, scarcity, and small government. In each case, Wunder finds a vast gulf between what the concept means to mainstream economists and what it means to other people. Thus, he concludes that exposing the mainstream's hidden premises is an important first step toward fashioning a better world.

In addition to training a critical eye on the hidden assumptions of conventional economics, PKI must offer superior analyses and help policymakers achieve constructive economic reform. Marc Lavoie (Chapter 11) contributes to advancing Post-Keynesian Institutionalist analyses with a technique called stock-flow consistent (SFC) modeling. SFC models, which derive mainly from the work of Wynne Godley, are usually considered part of the branch of Post Keynesianism associated with Nicholas Kaldor; but Lavoie explains that such models use flow-of-funds analysis and thus also have a strong connection to Institutionalism and PKI. In fact, a key feature of SFC modeling is the consideration of balance-sheet matrices and transaction-flow matrices. Through the use of examples, Lavoie shows that such matrices are closely associated with the description and assigned role of the various institutions and agents present in an economy, and that various SFC models take institutions into account in different ways.

Constructing Theories and Syntheses

Part IV advances Post-Keynesian Institutionalist efforts to craft economic theories (Chapters 12 and 13) and synthesize ideas across research traditions (Chapters 14, 15, and 16). Eduardo Fernández-Huerga (Chapter 12) outlines a Post-Keynesian Institutionalist framework for analyzing labor markets. His chapter presents the essential elements of a Post-Keynesian Institutionalist conception of labor supply and demand, giving particular attention to the underlying behavior of individuals and businesses, and then uses those elements to point toward a unified theoretical framework. A main conclusion is that decision-making processes associated with labor supply and demand involve far more than the regulatory force of wages; rather, they are conditioned by the socio-institutional environment. Thus, Fernández-Huerga's theorizing about the labor market—which is, in fact, many different markets—focuses on explaining diverse and complex relations between human beings and social institutions.[47]

Samba Diop (Chapter 13) builds on Minsky's work concerning both financial instability and stages of capitalism to provide a theoretical explanation for not only the endogenous nature of business cycles, but also the cyclical nature of financial regulation. At the heart of that explanation is Minsky's notion of an ever-evolving barrier of "financing orthodoxy," driven both by a systemic evolution traceable to the psychological effects of memories of economic crises and by the less predictable outcome of power struggles between competing economic interests. Thus, the evolution of financial regulation—as demonstrated by an examination of three real-world crises—is a consequence of the combination of systemic tendencies and the unique characteristics of a particular time and place. As a result, Diop's theoretical explanation offers not merely an analysis of business cycles and institutional dynamics, but also a broad analytical perspective on the political economy of financial regulation.

Faruk Ülgen (Chapter 14) connects PKI to a reconsideration of Public Choice economics. His chapter highlights both the propensity of today's capitalist economies to generate recurrent systemic instabilities and the need for regulatory institutions to fight against such a tendency in the interest of achieving a more stable and prosperous society. To that end, Ülgen demonstrates that PKI provides a valuable, holistic understanding of contemporary cyclical and structural economic dynamics; he also shows how insight from the Public Choice literature can be reframed to make it relevant to the macroprudential sort of financial regulation that PKI argues is needed to achieve macroeconomic coherence.[48]

Anna Zachorowska-Mazurkiewicz (Chapter 15) links the research traditions of PKI and Feminist economics to analyze the connection between women's unpaid work and the remuneration of women's paid labor, including the fact that women tend to earn less than men.[49] Such an integrated (Feminist and Post-Keynesian Institutionalist) analysis of work and gender relations is possible because both traditions emphasize the importance of examining culture and socioeconomic institutions for the purposes of understanding the economy and addressing economic problems. Zachorowska-Mazurkiewicz stresses not only that the gender wage gap is connected to the gender division of labor, but also that the gap has social as well as economic significance: Paying women less sends a message that society regards women as having less economic and social worth than men. Thus, finding ways to close that gap is a matter of economic and social justice.

Charles Whalen (Chapter 16) closes the book by aiming to make PKI more relevant to the issue of environmental sustainability. In particular, he explores how PKI can incorporate insight from Ecological economics. Although PKI has not devoted much attention to such sustainability, it should be well-positioned to do so: Institutionalism has long been better able than conventional economics to recognize and accommodate the issue of sustainability, and the relentless and single-minded drive for shareholder value at the heart of money manager capitalism represents perhaps the greatest challenge to moving toward sustainability. Because climate change represents a serious threat to life on Earth, the chapter concludes that environmental sustainability must be among PKI's top concerns.

A LOOK AHEAD

Confronted with the reality of an ever-changing world, PKI must always be a work in progress. But Post-Keynesian Institutionalists embrace that inevitability. To date, they have shown adeptness in the face of socioeconomic evolution. Moreover, the concepts, methods, theories, analyses, and insights offered in this book demonstrate that PKI has an ambitious agenda for future research.[50]

Although PKI began in the United States, it has quickly become a research tradition with global reach. In part, that reflects a recognition of the global scope of money manager capitalism. It also reflects worldwide concerns about issues central to PKI, including financialization, financial instability, economic inequality, and worker insecurity.

The coronavirus pandemic and global warming have exacerbated socioeconomic challenges in all regions of the world. And the challenges were already serious. For example, some months before the pandemic hit, Raghuram Rajan, an economist at the University of Chicago, warned that capitalism "is under serious threat" in all parts of the globe because it currently fails to provide opportunity for most people (BBC News 2019).

In some quarters, contemporary economic problems might trigger fierce debates over capitalism versus socialism.[51] But most Post-Keynesian Institutionalists understand that capitalism comes in many varieties and that a focus on labels such as "capitalism" and "socialism" obscures what is really important, which is, as Minsky (1985, 221) stressed, for society to be "democratic and humane."[52]

Economic systems are social entities, not natural systems.[53] Thus, the future, with regard to both economics and the economy, is in our own (collective) hands. By studying real-world social provisioning and the avenues available for institutional reform, Post-Keynesian Institutionalism contributes constructively to our fashioning of that future.

ACKNOWLEDGMENTS

The author thanks Glen Atkinson, Jim Peach, and Linda Whalen for reviewing and offering suggestions on this introduction. He also wishes to thank the chapter authors for excellent contributions, and the entire team at Edward Elgar for outstanding editing and production work.

NOTES

1. For consistency, this book capitalizes Institutionalism, Post Keynesianism, Post-Keynesian Institutionalism, and other varieties of economic thought. For the same reason, we do not hyphenate Post Keynesian economics, though some of this volume's contributors are partial to both the lower case and the hyphen ("post-Keynesian" economics). (An exception is Chapter 11, where Post-Keynesian is used at the contributor's request.)
2. For a concise look at various strands of the Institutionalist tradition, see Waller (1999); for an extended and more recent look, see Whalen (2022).
3. For further discussion on the beginnings of Institutionalism, see Mayhew (1987).
4. For more on Institutionalism in the interwar years and its fall from prominence after World War II (when, in many ways, economics returned to its earlier detachment from reality), see Rutherford (2011); and for an examination of the Wisconsin Institutionalist influence on public policy from the Progressive Era to the War on Poverty, see Chasse (2017).
5. For more on Commons and Keynes on the matter of foreshadowing PKI, see Whalen (2008, 44–46). Also, see Gruchy (1950, 125–126), who anticipated PKI by envisioning a synthesis of Institutional economics and the economics of Keynes. In Gruchy's view, Institutionalism contributed insight on microeconomics and capitalist development, while Keynes contributed insight on macroeconomics. However, while Gruchy stressed complementarity, there was already much compatibility, and the "sphere of compatibility" expanded as Post Keynesianism emerged and evolved, thereby helping to pave the way for PKI (see Keller 1983, 1091; O'Hara and Waller 1999, 530–531; and Whalen 2022, chapter 4).
6. For a history of Post Keynesian economics, see Lee (2000).
7. For a similar analysis of stagflation, see Eichner (1980).
8. In the mid-1960s and early 1970s, Minsky also devoted considerable attention to the role of public employment in ending poverty (see Minsky 2013, which was published posthumously), a policy notion that further ties Minsky to the Institutionalists and that he later incorporated into his work on macroeconomic stabilization (see, for example, Minsky 1986a).
9. Another economist working at the intersection of Institutional and Post Keynesian economics in the 1980s was Eichner (see, for example Eichner 1985). Eichner made valuable contributions on labor markets, endogenous money, administered pricing, large corporations (which he called "megacorps"), and macroeconomic dynamics. Unfortunately, a fatal heart attack in early 1988 (at age 50), brought

a tragic, premature end to Eichner's effort to fashion all of that into a formidable alternative to conventional economics and to further advance the work of Institutionalists and Post Keynesians. Eichner's legacy—including the effort to build on Institutionalist and Post Keynesian insight—is perhaps most evident in the work of his student, Frederic Lee (1996; 2018), and in that of Lee's student, Tae-Hee Jo (2016). Jo's work also demonstrates the complementarity in the lines of research of Eichner, Lee, and Minsky (see, for example, Jo and Henry 2015).

10. For a discussion of how conventional economics was blindsided by the global financial crisis, see Whalen (2013: 13–14). For evidence that PKI had long anticipated an international crisis involving mortgage securitization and other financial derivatives, see, for example, Minsky (1986b) and McClintock (1996).

11. See, for example, Lahart (2007); Yellen (2009).

12. For examples of this literature, see Brown (2008); Kaboub, Todorova and Fernandez (2010); Prasch (2010); Tavasci and Toporowski (2010); Todorova (2009); Tymoigne and Wray (2014); Whalen (2007; 2010; 2011); and Zalewski (2007; 2011; 2012). For recent evidence of the global reach of PKI research on the economic crises, see Bahtiyar (2020).

13. See, for example, Jo and Henry (2015); Liang (2011); Prasch (2014); Whalen (2020a); Zalewski (2002; 2003; 2005) and Zalewski and Whalen (2010).

14. Minsky's theory of capitalist development opens the door to understanding the economy as a whole because studying money manager capitalism requires examining not only the microeconomics of finance, labor, and product markets, but also the system's legal foundations (see Atkinson 2010) as well as its macroeconomic and global consequences. This broad scope of economic analysis (with micro, macro, and historical or developmental components) is reminiscent of the sort of Institutionalist-Keynes synthesis envisioned many decades ago by Gruchy (see note 5 above).

15. For Minsky's conception of economics as a "grand adventure," see Whalen (2020a, 196–197). For more on the history of PKI, see Whalen (2022, chapter 4).

16. The elements of PKI are interrelated and do not always fall neatly into a single category. Nevertheless, the categorization presented above is useful as an expository device.

17. The contours presented here are intended to be illustrative, not comprehensive. A comprehensive sketch would require at least a chapter of its own.

18. For perspectives on wants, want creation, and consumer choice consistent with PKI, see Brazelton and Whalen (2011, 32–33); Dugger (1996, 38–39); Lavoie (1994); and Waller (2008).

19. The type of rationality embedded in economic analyses can have major consequences. For example, the rationality embedded in PKI is consistent with unsustainable booms, financial crises, and severe downturns. In contrast, the rationality embedded in conventional economics is what led mainstream economists to reject as unimaginable the possibility of an event such as the global financial crisis of 2007–2009. The type of rationality embedded in PKI also leads to an approach to consumer choice that differs significantly from that of conventional economics; see Lavoie (1994). Also, see Lavoie (2014, 15–16), which uses the term "model-consistent" rationality in place of substantive rationality and "environment-consistent" rationality in place of bounded rationality, and emphasizes that the former is associated with optimizing behavior, while the latter is associated with satisficing; and see Chapter 10 (by Timothy Wunder), which stresses that acting rationally is not the same as engaging in optimization.

20. In the last dozen or so years of her life, Robinson highlighted a number of themes that fall within the common ground shared by Post Keynesians and Institutionalists. In addition to the value-laden nature of economic analysis, those themes include the economic importance of uncertainty, historical time, institutions (especially money and financial institutions), and the need to focus economics on addressing real-world problems. For example, see Robinson (1972; 1977; 1978; 1980).

21. The discussion of various types of valuation draws on Whalen (1992, 63; 1996a, 86) and on the concluding section of Waller (2022), which refers to usefulness as "instrumental" valuation.

22. Commons's "reasonable value" approach offers one approach to social valuation; see Whalen (2022, chapter 2).

23. For a further discussion of the valuation process, see Gordon (1984).

24. For more on the methodology of PKI, see Whalen (2008, 52–54; 2013, 16–17). For compatible discussions of the methodology of Institutionalism, see Atkinson and Oleson (1996); and Whalen (1992; 1996a). For compatible discussions of Post Keynesianism, see Dow (1991); and Lavoie (2014). The discussion of methodology above draws inspiration from these works.

25. This section's discussion of the analytical contours of PKI is based on Whalen (1996b; 2020b; 2022, chapter 4). The discussion also draws inspiration from Dow (1991, 205–206); Lavoie (2014, 33–37); and Whalen (1996a, 88–95).

26. For more on the importance of expectations in PKI, with special attention to the link between expectations and Commons's notion of "futurity," see Atkinson and Whalen (2011).

27. Galbraith's work on industry structure, pricing, and corporate governance was built on an extensive Institutionalist literature, which was later complemented by much Post Keynesian research.

28. PKI also recognizes that labor market outcomes are shaped by an underlying (and sometimes not so hidden) struggle for income shares, a struggle which underscores the importance of power in economic life. (Indeed, all market outcomes are income struggles.) In addition, PKI observes that market economies tend to operate at less than full capacity (which suggests that insufficient demand is a persistent problem).

29. On the matter of price flexibility at the macroeconomic level, PKI also stresses that even fully flexible wages and prices would not guarantee full employment because of the effects of wage and price reductions on consumer demand and business expectations.

30. Minsky (1975, 57–58) contrasted his Wall Street paradigm with what he called the barter paradigm of conventional economics, an approach that assumes the central features of capitalism can be grasped without attention to finance, capital assets, and production.

31. The centrality of money and finance in PKI also has implications for analytical tools and methods of economic research. From PKI's Wall Street perspective, much of the economy can be examined as a set of interconnected financial liabilities, cash-flow commitments, and balance sheets. For example, such a perspective is implicit in the "financial balances" model used by economists at Goldman Sachs to examine the US economic outlook. That model is constructed on a framework championed by the late Wynne Godley, a Cambridge University economist and Levy Economics Institute colleague of Minsky during the 1990s, which focuses on the gaps between income and spending within the different

sectors of the economy. Thus, the centrality of finance links PKI to the stock-flow consistent modeling pioneered by Godley and Lavoie (2007); see Chapter 11 (by Lavoie) below. A balance-sheet focus is also found in the Neo-Chartalist economics that some today call Modern Monetary Theory. According to Lavoie (2014, 41), at least some of the work of Neo-Chartalists overlaps with that of PKI owing to a shared interest in detailed analyses of monetary institutions and processes (see, for example, Fullwiler 2003).

32. Indeed, as Minsky often stressed, financial structures are features of the economy especially prone to innovation—in response to both the demands of businesses and the entrepreneurialism of financing organizations.

33. It is with the financial instability hypothesis in mind that Post-Keynesian Institutionalists often echo Minsky's pithy statement, "Stability is destabilizing."

34. See, for example, Brown (2008); Kaboub, Todorova, and Fernandez (2010); Scott and Pressman (2019); Tymoigne (2007); and Wunder (2020). Also, on inequality and instability, see Galbraith (2012); and Chapter 5 (by Weller and Karakilic) in the present volume.

35. In particular, according to PKI, money manager capitalism is an era driven by institutional investors and the pursuit of shareholder value, which has hollowed corporations, contributed to the globalization of supply chains, slowed techno-logical progress, fueled increasing worker insecurity, intensified income and wealth inequality, contributed to financial fragility, and exacerbated macroeco-nomic instability (see, for example, Whalen 2020a). On the co-evolution of law, industry, and finance that produced money manager capitalism (and the stages preceding it), see, for example, Atkinson (2010) and Whalen (2001).

36. This discussion of government and public policy in PKI draws on Whalen (2013, 21–22; 2020b, 79–80, 85–86), which offer further details and references. For more on public policy from the perspective of PKI, see Whalen (2011); and Zalewski (2019).

37. As Institutional economist Warren Samuels (1989) stressed, making and enforc-ing an ever-evolving set of rules (in response to competing claims and interests) is a creative, not a corrective, endeavor. Allan Schmid (1999, 233), Samuels's colleague, added that the notion of government versus markets is misguided; it's always "government, property, markets … in that order." The Institutionalism of Samuels and Schmid—which provides a foundation for PKI—rests on the work of Commons (1924; 1934, 882), who emphasized that American capitalism is governed by "judicial sovereignty" in that the Supreme Court ultimately decides the constitutionality of law and public policy: "The Constitution is not what it says it is—it is what the Court says it is" (Commons 1934, 697).

38. This is a key message of Commons (1924). In addition, the state shapes more than just institutions; it also plays a role in shaping—and then determining and acting upon—community preferences.

39. For an important recent work on the evolution of law and corporate governance and its broad economic consequences, see Atkinson, Hake, and Paschall (2021). It offers a thoughtful starting point for considering the possibilities of (and chal-lenges to) corporate reform in the face of financialization.

40. For PKI, financial regulation aims not only to protect consumers, but also to offset the tendency toward financial instability and crises.

41. For a forceful case for the need to consider the content, not just the level, of output and employment, see Robinson (1972).

42.   Attesting to the global significance of PKI is the fact that the policy issues listed above reflect problems facing economies worldwide.

43.   On system dynamics, see Radzicki (2008).

44.   For an extensive discussion of the policy-driven dimensions of wage suppression and inequality in the United States, see Mishel and Bivens (2021).

45.   The tension between the constructive potential of the creative state and the dark forces of predation is inescapable; the state is inevitably a terrain in which competing groups "assert the legitimacy of their rights and freedoms" (Brown 1992, 13).

46.   Until now, the concepts of social capital and civil society have usually been incorporated only implicitly in the work of Post-Keynesian Institutionalists and their Institutionalist forerunners—in discussions, for example, of the importance of community organizations, labor unions, and other non-governmental groups; see, for instance, Wilber and Jameson (1983, 230–263) and Commons (1934, 876–903). Christoforou's chapter advances PKI by making explicit the important role of these concepts in socioeconomic life.

47.   As discussed in several of this book's chapters, many aspects of labor markets in advanced and emerging economies have undergone tremendous change in recent decades. Fernández-Huerga's contribution provides a framework for considering how and why such change has occurred.

48.   To be sure, efforts to achieve macroprudential regulation must grapple with the challenges highlighted in Diop's chapter (the evolving psychology of the market and the power struggles between economic interests), but Ülgen's macroeconomic vantage point—grounded in a vision of collective rationality and the public interest as well as in a recognition of the endogenous nature of financial cycles—aims to do just that.

49.   In her chapter, Zachorowska-Mazurkiewicz reports that research published by the United Nations finds 67 percent of women's work is unpaid, in contrast to only 25 percent of men's work.

50.   To be sure, this book is not comprehensive. For example, both the economic consequences of venture capital financing and the growing problem of job loss from automation also warrant attention from Post-Keynesian Institutionalists. In addition, although a chapter addresses the oligarchical-bureaucratic state capitalism found in the region of the former Soviet Union, there is also a need for analyses of the more formidable variety of state capitalism found in China. Post-Keynesian Institutionalists would also likely benefit from incorporating into their work the insights and findings of other research traditions beyond those considered in this volume, such as Legal Realism, which shares much in common with Institutionalism.

51.   Indeed, there are many countries and communities in which such debates have already begun.

52.   As Minsky (1985, 221) wrote: "As I see it, the socialism of [Oskar] Lange had more in common with the capitalism of [Henry] Simons than with the socialism of Stalin, and the capitalism of Simons had more in common with the socialism of Lange than with the capitalism of Hitler." In other words, we must look beyond labels—and focus on the values and institutions that shape socioeconomic life.

53.   See Minsky (1986a, 7).

REFERENCES

Atkinson, Glen. 2010. "The Legal Foundations of Financial Capitalism." *Journal of Economic Issues* 44 (2): 289–299.

Atkinson, Glen, Eric R. Hake, and Stephen P. Paschall. 2021. *Evolution of the Corporation in the United States: From Social Control to Financialization.* Cheltenham, UK: Edward Elgar.

Atkinson, Glen and Ted Oleson. 1996. "Institutional Inquiry: The Search for Similarities and Differences." *Journal of Economic Issues* 30 (3): 701–718.

Atkinson, Glen and Charles J. Whalen. 2011. "Futurity: Cornerstone of Post-Keynesian Institutionalism." In *Financial Instability and Economic Security after the Great Recession*, edited by Charles J. Whalen, 53–74. Cheltenham, UK: Edward Elgar.

Bahtiyar, Görkem. 2020. "Theories of Crisis and the Great Recession: An Argument in Favor of Post-Keynesian Institutionalism." *Gazi İktisat ve İşletme Dergisi* 6 (2): 130–146. https://dergipark.org.tr/tr/pub/gjeb/issue/54884/658430. Accessed January 27, 2021.

BBC News. 2019. "Raghuram Rajan Says Capitalism Is 'Under Serious Threat.'" *BBC News*, March 12. https://www.bbc.com/news/business-47532522. Accessed December 12, 2019.

Brazelton, W. Robert. 2005. "Selected Theories of the Business Cycle in Terms of 'Econsochology.'" *Journal of Economic Issues* 39 (2): 527–533.

Brazelton, W. Robert. 2011. "Neuroscience, Psychology, Sociology with Relevance to Economic Analysis." Working Paper, Department of Economics, University of Missouri, Kansas City. Prepared for the annual meeting of the Association for Institutional Thought.

Brazelton, W. Robert and Charles J. Whalen. 2011. "Towards a Synthesis of Institutional and Post Keynesian Economics." In *Financial Instability and Economic Security after the Great Recession*, edited by Charles J. Whalen, 28–52. Cheltenham, UK: Edward Elgar.

Brown, Christopher. 2008. *Inequality, Consumer Credit, and the Saving Puzzle.* Cheltenham, UK: Edward Elgar.

Brown, Douglas. 1992. "The Capitalist State as a Terrain of Rights." In *The Stratified State*, edited by William M. Dugger and William T. Waller, 13–34. Armonk, New York: M.E. Sharpe.

Caldwell, Bruce J. 1980. "A Critique of Friedman's Methodological Instrumentalism." *Southern Economic Journal* 47 (2): 366–374.

Chasse, John D. 2017. *A Worker's Economist: John R. Commons and his Legacy from Progressivism to the War on Poverty.* New York: Transaction Publishers.

Commons, John R. 1924. *Legal Foundations of Capitalism.* New York: Macmillan.

Commons, John R. 1934. *Institutional Economics: Its Place in Political Economy.* New York: Macmillan.

Dow, Sheila C. 1991. "The Post-Keynesian School." In *A Modern Guide to Economic Thought*, edited by Douglas Mair and Anne G. Miller, 176–206. Aldershot, UK: Edward Elgar.

Dillard, Dudley. 1980. "A Monetary Theory of Production: Keynes and the Institutionalists." *Journal of Economic Issues* 14 (2): 255–273.

Dugger, William M. 1996. "Redefining Economics: From Market Allocation to Social Provisioning." In *Political Economy for the 21st Century*, edited by Charles J. Whalen, 32–43. Armonk, New York: M.E. Sharpe.

Eichner, Alfred S. 1976. *The Megacorp & Oligopoly: Micro Foundations of Macro Dynamics*. Cambridge: Cambridge University Press.

Eichner, Alfred S. 1980. "The Post-Keynesian Interpretation of Stagflation: Changing Theory to Fit Reality." In *Special Study on Economic Change, Volume 4, Stagflation: Causes, Effects, and Solutions*. Washington, DC: US Government Printing Office.

Eichner, Alfred S. 1985. *Toward a New Economics: Essays in Post-Keynesian and Institutionalist Theory*. Armonk, New York: M.E. Sharpe.

Eichner, Alfred S. and Jan A. Kregel. 1975. "An Essay on Post-Keynesian Theory: A New Paradigm in Economics." *Journal of Economic Literature* 13 (4): 1293–1314.

Fernández-Huerga, Eduardo. 2008. "The Economic Behavior of Human Beings: The Institutional/Post-Keynesian Model." *Journal of Economic Issues* 42 (3): 709–726.

Fernández-Huerga, Eduardo. 2013. "The Market Concept: A Characterization from Institutional and Post-Keynesian Economics." *American Journal of Economics and Sociology* 72 (2): 361–385.

Fullwiler, Scott T. 2003. "Timeliness and the Fed's Daily Tactics." *Journal of Economic Issues* 37 (4): 851–880.

Galbraith, James K. 2008. *The Predator State*. New York: The Free Press.

Galbraith, James K. 2012. *Inequality and Instability*. New York: Oxford University Press.

Galbraith, John K. 1977. "The Bimodal Image of the Modern Economy." *Journal of Economic Issues* 11 (2): 189–200.

Godley, Wynne and Marc Lavoie. 2007. *Monetary Economics: An Integrated Approach*. Basingstoke, UK: Palgrave Macmillan.

Gordon, Wendell C. 1984. "The Role of Institutional Economics." *Journal of Economic Issues* 18 (2): 368–381.

Gruchy, Allan G. 1947. *Modern Economic Thought: The American Contribution*. New York: Prentice-Hall.

Gruchy, Allan G. 1950. "Keynes and the Institutionalists: Important Contrasts." In *Economic Theory in Review*, edited by C. Lawrence Christenson, 106–126. Bloomington: Indiana University.

Gruchy, Allan G. 1987. *The Reconstruction of Economics*. New York: Greenwood Press.

Harvey, John T. 2006. "Psychological and Institutional Forces and the Determination of Exchange Rates." *Journal of Economic Issues* 40 (1): 153–170.

Harvey, John T. 2012. "Exchange Rate Behavior During the Great Recession." *Journal of Economic Issues* 46 (2): 313–322.

Jo, Tae-Hee. 2016. "What If There Are No Conventional Price Mechanisms?" *Journal of Economic Issues* 50 (2): 327–344.

Jo, Tae-Hee and John F. Henry. 2015. "The Business Enterprise in the Age of Money Manager Capitalism." *Journal of Economic Issues* 49 (1): 23–46.

Kaboub, Fadhel, Zdravka Todorova, and Louisa Fernandez. 2010. "Inequality-led Financial Instability: A Minskian Structural Analysis of the Subprime Crisis." *International Journal of Political Economy* 39 (1): 3–27.

Keller, Robert. 1983. "Keynesian and Institutional Economics: Compatibility and Complementarity?" *Journal of Economic Issues* 17 (4): 1087–1095.

Keynes, John M. (1927) 1982. Letter to John R. Commons. April 26, 1927. Reproduced in John R. Commons Papers, microfilm edition. Madison: State Historical Society of Wisconsin.

Lahart, Justin. 2007. "In Time of Tumult, Obscure Economist Gains Currency." *Wall Street Journal* August 18.

Lavoie, Marc. 1992. *Foundations of Post-Keynesian Economic Analysis*. Cheltenham, UK: Edward Elgar.

Lavoie, Marc. 1994. "A Post Keynesian Approach to Consumer Choice." *Journal of Post Keynesian Economics* 16 (4): 539–562.

Lavoie, Marc. 2014. *Post-Keynesian Economics: New Foundations*. Cheltenham, UK: Edward Elgar.

Lee, Frederic S. 1996. "Pricing and the Business Enterprise." In *Political Economy for the 21st Century*, edited by Charles J. Whalen. Armonk, New York: M.E. Sharpe.

Lee, Frederic S. 2000. "The Organizational History of Post Keynesian Economics in America, 1971–1995." *Journal of Post Keynesian Economics* 23 (1): 141–162.

Lee, Frederic S. 2018. *Microeconomic Theory: A Heterodox Approach*, edited by Tae-Hee Jo. London: Routledge.

Liang, Yan. 2011. "Money-Manager Capitalism, Capital Flows, and Development in Emerging Market Economies: A Post-Keynesian Institutionalist Analysis." In *Financial Instability and Economic Security after the Great Recession*, edited by Charles J. Whalen, 179–201. Cheltenham, UK: Edward Elgar.

Mayhew, Anne. 1987. "The Beginnings of Institutionalism." *Journal of Economic Issues* 21 (3): 971–998.

McClintock, Brent. 1996. "International Financial Instability and the Financial Derivatives Market." *Journal of Economic Issues* 30 (1): 13–33.

Minsky, Hyman P. 1975. *John Maynard Keynes*. New York: Columbia University Press.

Minsky, Hyman P. 1982. *Can "It" Happen Again? Essays on Instability and Finance*. Armonk, New York: M.E. Sharpe.

Minsky, Hyman P. 1985. "Beginnings." *Banca Nazionale Del Lavoro Quarterly Review* 38 (September): 211–221.

Minsky, Hyman P. 1986a. *Stabilizing an Unstable Economy*. New Haven: Yale University Press.

Minsky, Hyman P. 1986b. "Global Consequences of Financial Deregulation." *Marcus Wallenberg Papers on International Finance* 2 (1): 1–19.

Minsky, Hyman P. 1996. "Uncertainty and the Institutional Structure of Capitalist Economies." *Journal of Economic Issues* 30 (2): 357–368.

Minsky, Hyman P. 2013. *Ending Poverty: Jobs, Not Welfare*. Annandale-on-Hudson, New York: Levy Economics Institute of Bard College.

Mishel, Lawrence and Josh Bivens. 2021. "Identifying the Policy Levers Generating Wage Suppression and Wage Inequality." Economic Policy Institute Report. May 13, 2021. Washington, DC: Economic Policy Institute. https://www.epi.org/215903. Accessed July 11, 2021.

Mitchell, Wesley C. 1941. *Business Cycles and Their Causes*. Berkeley: University of California Press.

Myrdal, Gunnar. 1969. *Objectivity in Social Research*. Middletown, Connecticut: Wesleyan University Press.

Myrdal, Gunnar. 1978. "Institutional Economics." *Journal of Economic Issues* 12 (4): 771–783.

O'Hara, Phillip A. and William Waller. 1999. "Institutional Political Economy: Contemporary Themes." In *Encyclopedia of Political Economy, Volume 1*, edited by Phillip O'Hara, 528–532. Abingdon, UK: Routledge.

Peterson, Wallace C. 1977. "Institutionalism, Keynes, and the Real World." *Journal of Economic Issues* 11 (2): 201–221.

Prasch, Robert E. 2010. "Bankers Gone Wild." In *Macroeconomic Theory and Its Failings*, edited by Steven Kates, 184–206. Cheltenham, UK: Edward Elgar.

Prasch, Robert E. 2014. "The Rise of Money Manager Capitalism and Its Implications for Economic Theory and Policy." *Journal of Economic Issues* 48 (2): 559–566.

Radzicki, Michael J. 2008. "Institutional Economics, Post-Keynesian Economics, and System Dynamics: Three Strands of a Heterodox Braid." In *Future Directions for Heterodox Economics*, edited by Robert F. Garnett and John T. Harvey, 156–184. Ann Arbor: University of Michigan Press.

Ramstad, Yngve. 1989. "'Reasonable Value' versus 'Instrumental Value:' Competing Paradigms in Institutional Economics." *Journal of Economic Issues* 23 (3): 761–777.

Robinson, Joan. 1970. *Freedom and Necessity*. London: George Allen and Unwin.

Robinson, Joan. 1972. "The Second Crisis of Economic Theory." *American Economic Review* 62 (1/2): 1–10.

Robinson, Joan. 1977. "What Are the Questions?" *Journal of Economic Literature* 15 (4): 1318–1339.

Robinson, Joan. 1978. "Foreword." In *A Guide to Post-Keynesian Economics*, edited by Alfred S. Eichner, xi–xxi. White Plains, NY: M.E. Sharpe.

Robinson, Joan. 1980. "Time in Economic Theory." *Kyklos* 33 (2): 219–229.

Rutherford, Malcolm. 2011. *The Institutionalist Movement in American Economics, 1918–1947*. Cambridge, UK: Cambridge University Press.

Samuels, Warren J. 1989. "Some Fundamentals of the Economic Role of Government." In *Fundamentals of the Economic Role of Government*, edited by Warren J. Samuels, 167–172. Westport, CT: Greenwood Press.

Schmid, A. Allan. 1999. "Government, Property, Markets … In that Order … Not Government versus Markets." In *The Fundamental Interrelationships between Government and Property*, edited by Nicholas Mercuro and Warren J. Samuels, 237–242. Stamford, Connecticut: JAI Press.

Scott, Robert and Steven Pressman. 2019. "Financially Unstable Households." *Journal of Economic Issues* 53 (2): 523–531.

Tavasci, Daniela and Jan Toporowski, eds. 2010. *Minsky, Crisis and Development*. Basingstoke, UK: Palgrave Macmillan.

Todorova, Zdravka. 2009. *Money and Households in a Capitalist Economy: A Gendered Post Keynesian-Institutional Analysis*. Cheltenham, UK: Edward Elgar.

Tymoigne, Eric. 2003. "Keynes and Commons on Money." *Journal of Economic Issues* 37 (3): 527–545.

Tymoigne, Eric. 2007. "A Hard-Nosed Look at Worsening US Household Finance." *Challenge* 50 (4): 88–111.

Tymoigne, Eric and L. Randall Wray. 2014. *The Rise and Fall of Money Manager Capitalism*. London: Routledge.

Veblen, Thorstein B. 1898. "Why is Economics not an Evolutionary Science?" *Quarterly Journal of Economics* 12 (4): 373–397.

Waller, William. 1999. "Institutional Political Economy: History." In *Encyclopedia of Political Economy*, Volume 1, edited by Phillip A. O'Hara, 523–528. London: Routledge.

Waller, William. 2008. "John Kenneth Galbraith: Cultural Theorist of Consumption and Power." *Journal of Economic Issues* 42 (1): 13–24.

Waller, William. 2022. "Institutions, Technology, and Instrumental Value: A Reassessment of the Veblenian Dichotomy." In *Institutional Economics: Perspectives and Methods in Pursuit of a Better World*, edited by Charles J. Whalen, 1–16. London: Routledge.

Whalen, Charles J. 1992. "Schools of Thought and Theories of the State." In *The Stratified State*, edited by William M. Dugger and William T. Waller, 55–85. Armonk, New York: M.E. Sharpe.

Whalen, Charles J. 1996a. "The Institutional Approach to Political Economy." In *Beyond Neoclassical Economics*, edited by Fred E. Foldvary, 83–99. Cheltenham, UK: Edward Elgar.

Whalen, Charles J., ed. 1996b. *Political Economy for the 21st Century*. Armonk, New York: M.E. Sharpe.

Whalen, Charles J. 2001. "Integrating Schumpeter and Keynes: Hyman Minsky's Theory of Capitalist Development." *Journal of Economic Issues* 35 (4): 805–823.

Whalen, Charles J. 2007. "The US Credit Crunch of 2007: A Minsky Moment." *Public Policy Brief*, No. 92. Levy Economics Institute of Bard College.

Whalen, Charles J. 2008. "Toward 'Wisely Managed' Capitalism: Post-Keynesian Institutionalism and the Creative State." *Forum for Social Economics* 37 (1): 43–60.

Whalen, Charles J. 2010. "An Institutionalist Perspective on the Global Financial Crisis." In *Macroeconomic Theory and its Failings*, edited by Steven Kates, 235–259. Cheltenham, UK: Edward Elgar.

Whalen, Charles J., ed. 2011. *Financial Instability and Economic Security after the Great Recession*. Cheltenham, UK: Edward Elgar.

Whalen, Charles J. 2013. "Post-Keynesian Institutionalism after the Great Recession." *European Journal of Economics and Economic Policies: Intervention* 10 (1): 12–27.

Whalen, Charles J. 2020a. "Understanding Financialization." In *Alternative Approaches to Economic Theory*, edited by Victor A. Beker, 185–206. London: Routledge.

Whalen, Charles J. 2020b. "Post-Keynesian Institutionalism: Past, Present, and Future." *Evolutionary and Institutional Economics Review* 17 (1): 71–92.

Whalen, Charles J., ed. 2022. *Institutional Economics: Perspectives and Methods in Pursuit of a Better World*. London: Routledge.

Wilber, Charles K. and Robert S. Harrison. 1978. "The Methodological Basis of Institutional Economics: Pattern Models, Storytelling, and Holism." *Journal of Economic Issues* 12 (1): 61–89.

Wilber, Charles K. and Kenneth P. Jameson. 1983. *An Inquiry into the Poverty of Economics*. Notre Dame: University of Notre Dame Press.

Wunder, Timothy A. 2020. "Financial Insecurity in a World of Plenty." *Journal of Economic Issues* 54 (2): 510–516.

Yellen, Janet L. 2009. "A Minsky Meltdown: Lessons for Central Bankers." *FRBSF Economic Letter* Number 2009-15. Federal Reserve Bank of San Francisco.

Zalewski, David A. 2002. "Retirement Insecurity in the Age of Money Manager Capitalism." *Journal of Economic Issues* 36 (2): 349–356.

Zalewski, David A. 2003. "Corporate Objectives: Maximizing Social Versus Private Equity." *Journal of Economic Issues* 37 (2): 501–508.

Zalewski, David A. 2005. "Economic Security and the Myth of the Efficiency/Equity Tradeoff." *Journal of Economic Issues* 39 (2): 383–390.

Zalewski, David A. 2007. "Should the Oracle Have a Moral Compass? Social Justice and Recent Federal Reserve Policy." *Journal of Economic Issues* 41 (2): 511–517.

Zalewski, David A. 2011. "Too Important to Fail: A Reconsideration of the Lender of Last Resort Function." *Journal of Economic Issues* 45 (2): 373–380.

Zalewski, David A. 2012. "Collective Action Failures and Lenders of Last Resort: Lessons from the US Foreclosure Crisis." *Journal of Economic Issues* 46 (2): 333–342.

Zalewski, David A. 2019. "Uncertainty and the Economy of Exclusion: Insights from Post-Keynesian Institutionalism." *American Journal of Economics and Sociology* 78 (4): 955–972.

Zalewski, David A. and Charles J. Whalen. 2010. "Financialization and Income Inequality: A Post-Keynesian Institutionalist Analysis." *Journal of Economic Issues* 44 (3): 757–777.

PART II

Money manager capitalism

2. The transition from managerial to money manager capitalism: the role of risk and its distribution

David A. Zalewski

INTRODUCTION

Economic historian Barry Eichengreen (2019) notes that frequently cited theories of capitalism are either Marxian, centering on conflicts between profit-seeking owners of capital goods and the workers they employ in the production process, or neoliberal, emphasizing the importance of individual agency and unfettered markets in the exchange process. Despite their popularity, Eichengreen (2019, 20) finds both types of theories unsatisfactory: "Both conceptions are of ideal types. Both are ahistorical since they treat capitalism as a disembodied system detached from time and place." This is not the case, however, for Post-Keynesian Institutionalism (hereafter PKI).[1] For example, David A. Reisman (1990, 735) quotes Institutionalist and Post Keynesian John Kenneth Galbraith, who once remarked:

> We have a certain number of people who call themselves scholars of capitalism, who insist that it had a virgin birth in 1776 with Adam Smith, and it has not changed since. But I would urge that we must see capitalism, as we have seen socialism, as
> . being in a constant process of transformation.

Similarly, Post-Keynesian Institutionalist Hyman P. Minsky (1991, 10) observed that because of institutional diversity across places and time, "Capitalism comes in at least as many varieties as Heinz has of pickles."[2]

Minsky's comment reflects his work integrating the insights of Joseph A. Schumpeter (1934) and John Maynard Keynes ([1936] 1964) into a theory of capitalist development that assigns a key role to bankers and other financiers in Schumpeter's process of "creative destruction." Minsky (1993) argues that it is the dynamic interaction among financial and industrial innovations that drives economic progress. To illustrate how this relationship shapes the evolution of capitalism, he divides the economic history of the United States

(US) into several periods. According to Charles J. Whalen (2001, 809), what differentiates these stages are changes in answers to three questions: What is being financed? What is the pivotal source of external financing? What is the balance of economic power between those in business and banking? For example, during the *merchant capitalism* era of the early nineteenth century, banks provided trade credit to merchants by discounting commercial bills. This differs from today's *money manager capitalism* (MMC) in which powerful institutional investors have developed creative ways to fund large-scale capital projects and mergers by nonfinancial corporations. Given that capitalism is always evolving, key additional questions are: when will a new stage begin; and what will be the dominant characteristics of that new variety of capitalism?

This chapter addresses these questions by examining factors that help explain the passage of one capitalist era into another. As Whalen (2001, 815) points out: "Providing insight into the transition from one stage to another is an important aspect of any valuable theory of capitalist development. A deeper understanding of the economy is likely to be achieved by fleshing out [Minsky's] theory in this manner." An example of research on capitalist transitions is James R. Crotty's (1990a) analysis of the institutional factors underlying Keynes's methodology. Crotty explains how the relationship between *rentiers* and industrialists changed from a "patient capital" regime in the nineteenth century to a more myopic, speculative economy beginning in the interwar period, or as Crotty notes, the Age of Abundance described by John R. Commons was transformed into the Age of Stabilization. That dynamic relationship is a key factor in this chapter, which expands the analyses of Crotty and Minsky by adding another class—labor—to financiers and managers and focusing on how changes in relative power enables such groups to shift risk to others.[3] Drawing from the insights of sociologist Ulrich Beck (1992), Engelbert Stockhammer (2006–2007, 41) argues that "social conflicts in modern societies are not conflicts over the distribution of income, but over the distribution of risk."[4] The next section shows how the microeconomic foundations of Minsky's theory of investment, which are derived from Institutionalist and Post Keynesian theories of the firm, help explain intra-class transfers of risk.

The discussion of risk shifting is followed by a case study of that process by examining the transition of the US economy from *managerial capitalism* to the current MMC. The focus of the earlier period is Galbraith's (1971) *The New Industrial State* (*TNIS* hereafter), which was first published in 1967 and chronicles the development of what James Ronald Stanfield (1996, 69) calls the "administered sector," comprised of the largest, most powerful US corporations.[5] Galbraith details how most of those companies sought growth and power, at the expense of profit maximization, to manage uncertainty and maintain autonomy. The managerial era ended, however, after a series of economic developments threatened corporate dominance. As Barry Bluestone (1988, 377) concludes: "*TNIS* had the misfortune of being written precisely on the cusp of postwar economic history," after which American corporations lost much of their ability to control their own destiny. Consistent with Mark Blyth's (2002) theory of institutional change, which emphasizes the importance of ideas in response to events that disrupt the established order, neoliberal thinkers reacted to postwar developments by reshaping their theories (that promoted the primacy of shareholder interests) to appeal to nonacademic audiences and gain political support. The result was changes in corporate governance whereby both managers and shareholders shifted risk to workers and governments.[6]

The chapter concludes by considering whether recent social, political, and economic developments—especially those related to the COVID-19 pandemic—will generate a reexamination of research on economic inequality and pressure for significant changes in US public policy. Although both the Federal Reserve and President Joseph R. Biden's administration have made noteworthy strides towards mitigating economic insecurity in the first several months of 2021, it is premature to predict whether this will be the beginning of a new capitalist regime.[7]

A POST-KEYNESIAN INSTITUTIONALIST THEORY OF RISK SHIFTING

What differentiates the Minsky/Schumpeter/Keynes vision of capitalist development from mainstream theory is the important role played by finance. Schumpeter's process begins with a monetary theory of production—central to the work of both Institutionalists and Post Keynesians—in which capitalists borrow to acquire productive resources before commencing operations in pursuit of monopoly profits.[8] Although bankers are essential in Schumpeter's theory of money, Minsky adds that innovations in financial contracting are critical for providing funds to unleash "creative destruction."

According to Keynes and Minsky, entrepreneurs will purchase capital goods if they predict profitable differences between the supply and demand prices for these assets. Minsky (1993, 106) concludes: "This Keynesian theory in which investment is the outcome of the relative values of items in the two distinct price levels of a capitalist economy is the construct that Schumpeter needed to complete the vision of *The Theory of Economic Development*, a construct that he sought but never achieved." The supply price of capital has two components: (1) the price of the asset itself, which is what an additional unit of capital can be sold for and is determined by markup pricing; and (2) the explicit (interest rate) or implicit (cost of retained earnings) cost of financing the purchase. Capitalists then compare this value with the demand price, which is the estimated cash flow to be generated by the project, discounted by the opportunity cost of capital.[9] If the demand price exceeds the supply price, investment is justified; however, this decision rule is conditional since it must account for a foundational element in Keynesian theory: uncertainty. Because of uncertainty, Minsky explains that when capital projects are financed externally, both lenders and borrowers insulate themselves from unforeseen outcomes by imputing margins of safety in their expected cash flow, and the size of these buffers varies throughout the business cycle.

James Crotty (1990b) argues that Minsky's theory of investment is similar to James Tobin's "q" theory in the way that it helps explain aggregate fluctuations, except that it lacks Tobin's (Neoclassical) microeconomic foundations. However, he also points out that Tobin's model assumes there is no separation of ownership from control—i.e., managers and shareholders are the same people. Because that separation is an important factor in the arguments to be presented below, the Post Keynesian theory of the firm as summarized by Marc Lavoie (1992) is more appropriate as a foundation for Minsky's theory and for this chapter.[10]

According to Lavoie (1992, 99), power is the "ultimate objective" sought by firms. The reason for this choice is the ubiquity of uncertainty, which renders the Neoclassical goal of profit maximization untenable. The exercise of power enables firms to control their economic, social, and political environments. As Robert Dixon (1986, 588) wrote,

> [D]ecision makers attempt to control the consequences of their own decisions in order to prevent their desires being thwarted by others. They do this by attempting to influence the decisions by others (or the outcomes of their decisions) in order to prevent the decisions of others from having unfavorable or uncontrollable consequences for them.

According to Lavoie, capitalists must possess power, which they acquire through increasing their volume of economic activity.

Obviously, growing firms need cash to finance capital accumulation. Past earnings not distributed to shareholders are an internal source of finance, and companies requiring external finance will find both the supply and cost of funds more favorable if they have recently been profitable. Thus, the combination of internal and external funds available to firms is what Lavoie (1992) calls the "finance frontier," which increases arithmetically as a function of the firm's profit rate. Lavoie next describes the "expansion frontier," which relates the growth of the firm—measured by revenues—to its profit rates. Initially, growing firms generate increasing profits as they are better able to control their environments and can exploit economies of scale and new technology. At some point, however, the firm becomes too large to manage effectively, and profits begin to decline.

Combining the two frontiers leads to the following results: firms that seek to maximize profits do not grow as large as those that target growth; and relatedly, those that favor expansion often have lower profit rates. Stockhammer (1994) extends this model by adding utility functions for shareholders (who prefer profits) and managers (who prefer growth) to explain the recent slowdown in capital accumulation. Finally, Thomas Dallery (2009) contributes to this line of research by showing that in financialized economies both managers and shareholders seek to expand profits and, in pursuit of that end, attempt to shift risk to others, especially workers.

The next section provides an extended example of how firms in the administered sector of the US economy used their power to manage risk during the period of managerial capitalism. These companies generated steady earnings and dividends that were able to satisfy the demands of managers, shareholders, and workers. As described in the following section, continuing their success became more challenging in the 1970s, which sparked a shareholder revolt and contributed to the arrival of the age of MMC, during which managers and shareholders shifted risk to workers. Whether this arrangement is sustainable will be considered in the concluding section.

THE ADMINISTERED SECTOR AND ITS MANAGEMENT OF UNCERTAINTY

Like many PKI economists, John Kenneth Galbraith understood the forces that shape and transform capitalist economies. He observed that from the end of World War II until the publication of the revised edition of *TNIS* in 1971, the US economy evolved into two distinct structures: the administered sector, which encompassed the approximately 2,000 largest firms that produced about half of the total private sector output, and the "market system" of about 12 million smaller businesses. Galbraith consistently instructed his readers that mainstream theory is relevant only in the sphere he called the market system, since conventional theory ignores how corporate giants exploit their size and power. Galbraith also decided to focus on these firms in *TNIS* to provide a more realistic explanation of the dominant economic conditions of the time.[11]

A key factor that differentiates the two sectors is the type of technology employed, which Galbraith (1971, 31) defined as "the systematic application of scientific or other organized knowledge to practical tasks." According to Galbraith, large organizations needed to acquire, process, and coordinate massive quantities of specialized information (from myriad sources) to design, produce, and distribute goods and services successfully. In contrast, most market system companies used nonproprietary technology that did not require advanced scientific training and organizational skills to be employed profitably.

To illustrate the evolving relationship between commercial technology and uncertainty, Galbraith (1971, 32–36) compared the strategies of the Ford Motor Company at its beginning in 1903 with those it developed for the introduction of the Mustang in 1964. Three important points emerge:

1. The use of cutting-edge technology and reliance on complex processes lengthen the time span between acquiring financing to begin projects and realizing cash inflows from operations. This often results in an increased need for funds. Unlike the Mustang, which required several years of development and an investment of millions of dollars, the original Ford Model A needed only several months and approximately $28,000 (about $99,000 in 1964) before its launch.
2. Modern companies are likely to invest in specialized equipment and to develop narrowly-defined labor skills, both of which may have little value if the project fails. Galbraith (1971, 33) writes:

    > With increasing technology the commitment of time and money tends to be made ever more inflexibly to the performance of a particular task. The task must be precisely defined before it is divided and subdivided into its component parts. Knowledge and equipment are then brought to bear on these fractions and they are useful only for the task as it was initially defined. If that task is changed, new knowledge and new equipment will have to be brought to bear.

    By contrast, Ford utilized widely-available tools and techniques to manufacture early Ford models, and these could have been redeployed to produce unrelated products as necessary.
3. Because of the enormous task of managing advanced specialized resources, effective planning and coordination are critical. Galbraith noted that this required groups of decision-makers that he called the technostructure, not entrepreneurs like Henry Ford who oversaw their entire operation.

Because poor decisions under conditions of uncertainty may threaten the existence of large organizations, the benefits from controlling potential outcomes is obvious. Despite this, Stephen P. Dunn (2001) argues that although uncertainty is a central theme in Post Keynesian economics, more research is needed on how businesses react to this condition:

> While many post-Keynesians acknowledge the pivotal role of money as an institution for coping with uncertainty, they have written little on the fact that the firm is also an institution that deals with, and provides a flexible response to, uncertainty …. This is a big task and one which will undoubtedly occupy post-Keynesian minds for some time to come.

Galbraith (1971, 43) addressed this issue by noting that some executives merely ignore risk and proceed with their plans, especially if negative outcomes are tolerable. However, this is unlikely for most firms in the administered sector for which there could be dire consequences from failed programs. Unlike companies in mainstream theory that merely react to adverse market conditions, large corporations possess the power to take proactive steps to plan and control their environments. Galbraith (1971, 120) writes:

> When planning replaces the market this admirably simple [mainstream] explanation of economic behavior collapses. Technology and the companion commitments of capital and time have forced the firm to emancipate itself from the uncertainties of the market. And specialized technology has rendered the market increasingly unreliable. So the firm controls the prices at which it buys materials, components, and talent and takes steps to ensure the necessary supply at these prices. And it controls the prices at which it sells and takes steps to ensure that the public, other producers, or the state take the planned quantities at these prices. So far from being controlled by the market, the firm, to the best of its ability, has made the market subordinate to the goals of its planning.

As noted earlier, Galbraith claims that the profit-maximization goal of entrepreneurs in the market sector differs from the aims chosen by the technostructure, which is driven more by self-preservation and autonomy than pecuniary interests. To achieve those goals, corporate leaders in the administered sector must manage insecurity in several key areas:

1. *Prices and Quantities of Goods and Services to be Sold:* Uncertainty about future revenues can be controlled at both the microeconomic and macroeconomic levels. One of Galbraith's better-known ideas is the *revised sequence*, in which companies actively influence and shape preferences rather than respond to the wants of "sovereign consumers." By doing so, marketing experts create a persistent, gnawing sense of insecurity in many people. Echoing Thorstein Veblen, Galbraith (1971, 265) explains why: "[T]hough the need for food and shelter, especially in benign climates, is rather readily satisfied, the pressures of emulation and competition in adornment and display have no clear terminal point." Also, some companies—especially those in the defense industry—receive federal government guarantees that their investments will be profitable. Moreover, the ability of policymakers to stabilize aggregate demand and the overall price level instills an essential sense of confidence in the minds of corporate planners.
2. *Costs and Quantities of Production:* According to Galbraith (1971, 234), the technostructure "seeks certainty in the supply and price of all the prime requisites of production. Labor is a prime requisite. And a large blue-collar workforce, especially if subject to the external authority of

a union, introduces a major element of uncertainty and danger." Regarding labor, he notes that the value of collective bargaining to workers is gradually reduced by the ability of firms in the administered sector to replace workers with machines, maintain wage and employment levels, and align worker values with corporate goals. As for other resources like raw materials, sources of supply can be secured through vertical integration and acquisitions, long-term contracts, and the exercise of power to obtain needed resources on favorable terms.

3. *Sources of Finance:* Galbraith (1971, 53) considers this particularly important to the technostructure: "Control of the supply of savings is strategic for industrial planning. Capital use is large. No form of market uncertainty is so serious as that involving the terms and conditions on which capital is obtained." For this reason, it was essential that retained earnings, which are cash flows from operations that are not distributed to shareholders, be maintained as the primary source of funds since they shield the technostructure from any external interference in its decision-making. Moreover, the ability to generate steady cash flows also placated shareholders, whom Galbraith (1971, 64) dismissed as being irrelevant: "The power of the stockholders, as noted, has seemed increasingly tenuous. A small proportion of the stock is represented at stockholders' meetings for a ceremony in which banality is varied chiefly by irrelevance."

4. *Protection from Destructive Competition:* The secondary importance of stockholders suggests that few corporations sought to maximize share values. Instead, the goals of the technostructure centered on technological virtuosity and organizational growth. Accomplishing those goals raised barriers to potential entrants in the form of economies of scale and first-mover advantages, among other distinctive competencies, and provided companies in the administered sector with an absence of rivalry that helped secure returns from investment.

From the end of World War II until about the time Galbraith published the first edition of *TNIS*, most large companies in the United States successfully attenuated uncertainty and achieved the levels of autonomy and rates of growth that they sought. As described in the next section, however, a confluence of threatening factors emerged in the late 1960s that gave rise to changes in ideas about desirable corporate objectives and how enterprises should go about attaining them. Perhaps the most significant consequence of this revolution was the transition from an era of relatively shared prosperity to one during which the most powerful individuals and organizations insulated themselves from the vagaries of the market at the expense of those who were comparatively defenseless.

FROM MANAGERIAL CAPITALISM TO MONEY MANAGER CAPITALISM

During the age of managerial capitalism, administered sector companies sustained their autonomy by appeasing groups that could threaten their independence. At the end of 1971, in his presidential address to the Association for Evolutionary Economics, Daniel R. Fusfeld (1972, 2) observed:

> The corporate state in this country involves an economic and political compromise between those who hold power and those who do not. As long as the economic system provides an acceptable degree of security, growing material wealth, and opportunity for further increase for the next generation, the average American does not ask who is running things or what goals are being pursued. The system and those in power remain unchallenged as long as the material payoff is sustained.

In retrospect, however, we now know that several significant economic and political problems were emerging at that time and increasingly vexing many economists, politicians, and executives.

Summarizing many of the developments that disturbed business leaders during that period, Blyth (2002, 152) writes:

> The policies and practices of the late 1960s and early 1970s created a new sense of uncertainty among American business. Inflationary pressures, regulatory initiatives, hostile tax legislation, and general policy paralysis combined to convince business that it was under siege within the institutions of economic governance that business itself had designed.

Moreover, unease among corporate leaders was exacerbated by several factors related to globalization, including the collapse of the Bretton Woods monetary framework in 1971, increased foreign competition, and the 1973 Middle East oil embargo. Taken together, these factors created an economic environment that posed a challenge to corporate growth and profitability and that threatened the interests of both shareholders and the technostructure; institutional change was imminent.

According to Blyth, ideas play a key role in the process of institutional adjustment to significant shocks. Not only do they help people understand the circumstances they face, but ideas also suggest how to adapt to change as well as provide ways to gain acceptance of proposed courses of action. Although Blyth presents a detailed case study of how conservative interest groups in the United States rallied support for neoliberal policies addressing inflation and high taxes, problems that many people considered critical issues in the 1970s, his approach can also be used to understand how reactions to uncertainty may change the relationships among industry, finance, and labor.

Where do these ideas come from? Galbraith's reflection on *TNIS* in the 1980s, in light of the changed global order since its original publication, provides insight into this process. In 1987, to commemorate the twentieth anniversary of the book's first edition, the American Economic Association (AEA) sponsored a panel discussion to assess the volume's relevance.[12] Galbraith (1988) began the session by noting the persistent separation of administered and market sectors, with large corporations continuing to seek autonomy by using their power to prevent outside interference and avoid risk. He then prefaced his account of where *TNIS* fell short by noting the impermanence of ideas—especially economic theory:

> A willing recognition, if not of error, at least of obsolescence is, in fact, implicit in the view of economics that I avow in *TNIS*. I see economics as a subject in constant accommodation to social, political and institutional change and not, certainly, as a search for, and expression of, unchanging truth. (Galbraith 1988, 373)

However, Galbraith did not discuss whether "new" ideas should be original or adapted versions of existing thought. As noted below, the transition to MMC was driven by revitalizing old ideas with new theoretical insights.

Joshua Gans (2017) notes that a critical development Galbraith ignored was the conversion of complacent shareholders into a force for corporate change. Last year marked the fiftieth anniversary of the publication of Milton Friedman's (1970) pathbreaking piece in *The New York Times Magazine* that declared maximizing shareholder wealth is the only appropriate goal for corporations since he considered business efforts to improve the welfare of other stakeholders to be "socialism." Justin Fox (2009) notes that although Friedman made this point earlier in his *Capitalism and Freedom* (Friedman 1969), Ralph Nader's efforts to expand the board of directors of General Motors to include social activists motivated him to address a wider audience.

Friedman argued that managers, as agents representing the interests of shareholders, should focus only on the well-being of the owners; however, he did not specify how to achieve this objective.[13] Michael C. Jensen and William H. Meckling (1976) resolved that problem by focusing on the use of equity values as an incentive device. By granting executives stock options and awarding shares, corporate boards ensured that firms would maximize shareholder wealth, since both investors and managers would benefit from higher returns on equity. Moreover, failure to maximize such wealth would be punished by the market—often inviting hostile takeovers that threatened managerial job security.

Later, Jensen (1986) expanded that line of research by recommending the delegation of executive monitoring to capital markets. He argued that free cash flows, which are defined as the amount of funds remaining from net profits after all positive net present-value projects are financed internally, are often used by self-serving executives to expand the size of the enterprise and increase their power, rather than to reinvest efficiently. Although Jensen supported using excess cash to pay dividends, the fact that they could be legally reduced or eliminated provided executives with the opportunity to misuse free cash. Instead, he recommended that companies borrow in capital markets and use the proceeds to repurchase their shares. This clever scheme allocates free cash flows to shareholders in a legally binding manner since defaulting on debt obligations can lead to bankruptcy. In short, the use of external financing for most new investments in combination with the threat of bankruptcy would motivate creditors to monitor firm performance and take remedial action when necessary. The historical record suggests that corporate directors embraced Jensen's approach; the net value of new equity issues by US firms has been overwhelmingly negative due to share buybacks, and the aggregate increase in corporate leverage has been significant.

Viewed from the perspective of the PKI theory of the firm, these ideas and the innovations they inspired in corporate finance and governance transformed the relationship among managers, financiers, and labor. As Dallery (2009) concludes, Stockhammer's (1994) claim that managers and shareholders possessed separate and distinct utility functions disappears in this type of financialized economy: both groups seek to maximize profits, which, in the long run, requires corporate growth.[14] To help accomplish these objectives, many large firms have dismantled their conglomerate structures and have concentrated on exploiting narrowly-defined competencies. The result is that many companies have embarked on programs to boost share values by shifting risk from management/stockholders to labor.

Such programs have created fissured workplaces, which industrial relations scholar David Weil (2014) defines as those found in companies that focus on core competencies and that outsource peripheral tasks—that had previously been performed by employees—to outside contractors who provide minimal pay and benefits (since such contractors often operate in highly competitive markets). Interestingly, the result is the emergence of hybrid operations that combine administered- and market-sector firms. Another consequence, highlighted by Institutionalists Tae-Hee Jo and John F. Henry (2015), is a shift in business behavior from promoting social provisioning to targeting pecuniary goals, as evinced by the slowdown in capital accumulation beginning in the 1970s.[15]

Further consequences of the turn toward shareholder value and risk shifting have been identified by Post-Keynesian Institutionalists including Christopher J. Niggle and Avraham I. Baranes. Niggle (1986) shows that many companies moved from producing and selling goods and services to borrowing funds to finance business acquisitions, speculate in financial markets, and provide credit to customers and other borrowers. Thus, rather than consider long-term investments in irreversible assets that could generate cash flows for decades of uncertain possibilities, nonfinancial companies were drawn to shorter-term, liquid assets, especially after a combination of financial innovations and deregulatory initiatives enabled companies to exploit them.

Similarly, Baranes (2017) shows that large firms in the US pharmaceutical industry have increasingly relied on intangible assets rather than productive capital to generate profits. In fact, echoing William Lazonick's (2014) criticism of share repurchases, he concludes that such firms "*extract* value rather than *create* it" (Baranes 2017, 357, emphasis in original). Although critics may argue that generating such rents are necessary to finance the development of new drugs, this may not be the case. For example, David Blumenthal (2021) reminds us of the endemic public underfunding of US biomedical research, despite the many innovations like COVID-19 vaccines that required significant government investment. Besides congressional inaction on requests for budgetary expansion, Blumenthal mentions the cash hoard amassed by American drug companies as a primary reason for the reliance on privately funded research. Meanwhile, Standard and Poor's provides evidence supporting the points made by Baranes and Lazonick: the value of share buybacks by US pharmaceutical firms has ranged from almost $16 billion to $70 billion per year from 2010 through 2020 (Gibney and Woleben 2021).

As the term "money manager capitalism" implies, many executives reacted to pressure from institutional investors by ruthlessly cutting expenses to maximize stock values. That pressure was especially intense because portfolio and mutual fund managers faced stiff competition from their industry rivals and from pension funds that promised to pay fixed annuities to retirees (and, in the process, ran the risk of becoming underfunded if their portfolio returns were inadequate). As David A. Zalewski and Charles J. Whalen (2010) show, inequality increased in the United States and in other financialized countries after shareholders benefitted from lower labor costs resulting from their pressure on managers to downsize, outsource, or terminate segments of business operations.[16]

Moreover, Whalen (2008) argues that the single-minded focus on shareholder value contributed to the emergence of an "anxious society" in which economic insecurity has become widespread and is growing.[17] Anthropologist Katherine S. Newman (1994, 344) summarizes this development:

> Security is not easy to come by these days; it is a concern that looms very large in the lives of those who were raised in the prosperous, stable 1950s and the roaring, expansive 1960s. Contractions, leveraged buyouts, bankruptcies, layoffs, and general despair over the state of American competitiveness—these are the watchwords of today's business pages. Nothing in the boomers' upbringing, schooling, or early experience in the labor market prepared them for what we all must confront

now: the fact that the US economy cannot provide the type of job opportunities or personal security that the country took for granted in earlier generations.

Although many upper-level managers also felt less secure about their jobs, Zalewski (2004) notes that many of them were assuaged with pensions, health insurance, and severance packages that were both generous and guaranteed.

Clearly, the growing and autonomous technostructure that so occupied Galbraith's attention in the 1960s reached its zenith by the mid-1970s and is now considered a historical artifact. Perhaps more important, however, was the end of the goal, if not the reality, of widely-shared prosperity and a widely (but certainly never universally) perceived sense of economic security. As Minsky and Whalen (1996) conclude, because tolerance for uncertainty is limited, collective action addressing the distribution of risk and uncertainty should be—in Minsky's words (1996, 357)—one of the "institutional prerequisites for successful capitalism." Whether recent events like the pandemic may create the impetus for the development of a new stage of capitalism will be considered in the concluding section.

POSTSCRIPT: WHITHER A NEW TRANSITION?

Charles K. Wilber and Kenneth P. Jameson (1990, 188) provide an excellent summary of the driving force behind Minsky's PKI theory of capitalist development, which centers on the changing relationships between financiers and industrialists:

> Social reality is seen as more than a specified set of relations; it is the process of change inherent in a set of social institutions which we call an economic system. The process of social change is not purely mechanical; it is the product of human action, which is shaped and limited by the society in which it has roots.

This chapter extends that view by explaining that people formulate ideas to understand and react to significant socioeconomic shocks and then use those ideas to build support for institutional change. As this is being written in mid-2021, the question is whether recent events may generate a similar process resulting in the transition from MMC to a new stage of capitalism.

Because of the persistence of widespread economic inequality and insecurity since the early 1980s, the initial sense of displacement has been transformed into despair and resignation for some, and a spur to action for others.[18] To some extent, both reactions are partly reflected in the growing embrace of right-wing populism and nationalism, as illustrated, for example, in former President Donald Trump's promise to "Make America Great Again," which alluded to times preceding the Reagan Revolution.[19] According to CNN's Gregory Krieg

(2016), Trump revealed in an interview that he considered two periods of US history to be "great"—the first two decades of the twentieth century, and from the late 1940s through the 1950s—because of the country's military and economic strength.[20] Of course, Trump ignored the fact that many—especially woman and people of color—failed to prosper during those earlier times, but even more troubling than Trump's distorted view of history is that throughout the era of MMC many workers voted for candidates who supported policies that ran counter to their economic interests.[21]

However, the pandemic that developed in early 2020 may be the type of shock that sparks more progressive institutional and political change. The groups in the United States most adversely affected are those that also did not prosper during Trump's preferred periods, such as low-wage workers in nursing homes, meatpacking plants, and grocery stores. While many white-collar employees maintained their earnings, worked remotely, and bene-fitted from soaring stock market returns, countless essential workers continued to interact with the public despite inadequate protective gear and millions of others lost their jobs as much of the US economy shut down for about a year.

The pandemic is unusual since uncertainty plagued many people—capitalists and workers alike—in what Beck (1992) earlier described as the democratiza-tion of risk. Would this shared experience instill a greater awareness of the unequal exposure to economic risk? Emily Badger (2020) received mixed responses to her survey of several historians about this question. On the one hand, some noted that the coronavirus crisis increased the separation between members of economic classes, since people from affluent and middle-income households were often working from home and no longer mingled with those from lower-income households in restaurants, on buses and trains, and in other public settings. On the other hand, Cornell University's Louis Hyman argued (in response to Badger's survey) that the privileged had more exposure to "gig" workers delivering food and packages to their homes, increasing their under-standing of the precarity of such service jobs. The unanswered question is whether these conditions will lead to increased empathy for struggling workers and to support for policy changes that lessen their economic uncertainty.

As in earlier eras, new ideas may be critical for transforming this new awareness into collective action. Heather Boushey (2020) argues that changes in economic frameworks and methods, including the development of measures to better gauge the effectiveness of public policies, are vital to achieving government interventions that promote economic well-being. She recounts how Keynesian policy innovations helped lift the US economy out of the depths of the Great Depression, and how the work of economists like Simon Kuznets (who developed national income accounts) provided measurable standards to assess economic progress.[22] Boushey also claims that aggregate output measures have failed to convey the economic status of most Americans since at least the early 1980s, when MMC ushered in a new era of economic inequality.[23] Similar to the theoretical and empirical innovations of the 1930s and 1940s, innovative contemporary research by Boushey, Thomas Piketty, Emmanuel Saez, Gabriel Zucman, and others has not only established how inequality negatively impacts economic growth and stability, but also devised new measures such as distributional national income accounts, which offer a more detailed view of how US workers and households are faring today.

Some Neoclassical economists have criticized these efforts. In an op-ed piece in *The Wall Street Journal*, Alexander William Salter (2021) laments the fact that an increasing number of economists have moved from developing theoretical models to "collecting and analyzing data." He argues that although empirical work may be important, its value is questionable if analysts do not use mainstream price theory to form hypotheses and test them econometrically. Salter (2021, A17) writes:

> The heights of the economics profession are increasingly inhabited by people who disdain price theory. Reliance on the economic way of thinking in solving problems is viewed as obsolete and unscientific. The data jockeys think they're cutting edge, but they're merely repeating old mistakes. In the late 19th and early 20th centuries, economists of the German Historical and Old Institutionalist schools thought they could make do with history and statistics alone, unconstrained by theory. In the end, they got so bogged down in details that they came up with very little that lasted.

Salter also claims that the economists noted above are "particularly susceptible to the technocratic pretensions of the center-left," and that they "don't realize they have been politically compromised." Meanwhile, what "compromises" Salter's own judgement is that mainstream theory has failed to explain phenomena like the disconnect between public budget deficits and inflation, and the fact that minimum wage increases are not always "job-killers." Conventional economics also has nothing to say about the incessant evolution of capitalism and the far-reaching economic, social, and human consequences of that constant change.[24]

Despite critics like Salter, the new research on growth and inequality has helped to draw attention to distributional issues among top US policymakers. For example, Federal Reserve Chair Jerome Powell cited the benefits of stronger labor markets in narrowing income and wealth inequality at a speech before the Economic Club of New York in early 2021. Powell (2021) observed that although pre-COVID employment conditions had improved, approximately 10 million jobs had been lost during the pandemic to that date. He also noted that employment declines have not been evenly distributed, with only a 4 percent drop among those in the highest income quartile compared with a 17 percent decline among those in the lowest quartile.[25] To restore vitality in the labor market, Powell promised that the central bank would continue its accommodative policies by downplaying its previous concerns about potential inflation after economic conditions improve. Specifically, Fed leaders plan to wait until after prices rise before implementing restrictive measures, rather than engineering "preemptive strikes" on inflation as in the past.[26]

Within the administration of President Joe Biden, there is also a commitment to policies that emphasize equality, employment, and the well-being of workers. Indeed, the Biden administration might have the strongest commitment to such ends since the emergence of MMC. For example, Biden's team includes: labor economists Boushey, Cecilia Rouse, and Jared Bernstein at the Council of Economic Advisers (CEA); former Fed Chair Janet Yellen as Treasury Secretary; and former Boston Mayor Martin J. Walsh as Labor Secretary. Speaking about Boushey, Rouse, and Bernstein, Kevin A. Hassett (the first to chair the CEA under President Trump) remarked: "They have put together a very strong team of experienced policymakers and smart economists. At this difficult time, it is great to know that a strong CEA will be helping to guide policy."[27] Meanwhile, Yellen is notable for her rejection of conventional economists' belief in a strict inverse (Philips Curve) relationship between inflation and unemployment, and Walsh, who was raised in a working-class family, has blue-collar employment experience and served as head of the Boston Metropolitan Building and Construction Trades Council.[28] Responding to the Administration's planned labor reforms, Heidi Shierholz of the Economic Policy Institute remarked: "It's a world of difference from where we were under Trump … . Walsh will prioritize workers over corporate executives and shareholders, which was the absolute opposite under Trump."[29] Similarly, incoming US Trade Representative Katherine Tai (quoted in Hayashi 2021) proclaimed in a speech to the National Foreign Trade Council: "The president-elect's vision is to implement a worker-centered trade policy. What it means in practice is that US trade policy must benefit regular Americans, communities, and workers. And that starts with recognizing that people are not just consumers. They are also workers and wage earners."[30]

As of mid-2021, it remains to be seen whether central bank and federal government programs will successfully restore the economy and help put the nation on a path to more broadly shared prosperity. The Biden administration did not receive an overwhelming mandate from voters (having received 51.3 percent of the votes cast, while Donald Trump received 46.9 percent of the votes), and the Democratic party, which is not fully unified on economic policy, faces significant opposition from Republicans (which creates an especially difficult challenge in the Senate). Will the Federal Reserve continue to address inequality and labor market conditions after the pandemic ceases to be a drag on the economy? How current events play out will determine whether the COVID-19 pandemic will be a watershed event in the evolution of capitalism in the United States or just a temporary shock that will not disturb the recent trajectory of inequality and economic insecurity.

ACKNOWLEDGMENTS

The author thanks Glen Atkinson, Carol Heim, Oren Levin-Waldman, and Charles Whalen for comments and suggestions on a draft of this chapter.

NOTES

1. See Whalen (2013) for a comprehensive overview of PKI.
2. See Hall and Soskice (2001) for a detailed account of the "varieties of capitalism."
3. Vail (2008) provides precise definitions of the concepts of uncertainty, risk, and insecurity. Technically, executives pondering investment projects are more likely to encounter fundamental uncertainty, while insecure workers often experience risk (uncertainties that can be transformed into probabilities). However, because this chapter does not consider factors like the availability of information and cognitive limitations that often differentiate these concepts, "uncertainty" and "risk" will be used synonymously.
4. Stockhammer (2006–2007, 39) concludes that although his own work and most other studies of social conflicts in modern societies examine the shifting of uncertainty between capitalists and workers, other groups should also be considered. While this chapter also considers financiers, Stockhammer's article suggests that an even more complete picture of reality would emerge from using his approach to examine other fault lines of society as well.
5. Galbraith used several terms over the years such as the "planning system" and the "industrial system" when referring to the administered sector. Stanfield argues convincingly that the former sometimes refers to macroeconomic stabilization by the state, and the latter often describes the economy as a whole.
6. As Whalen (2008) notes, heterodox economists established the foundations for PKI as MMC emerged, in part to argue that these types of transitions are part of an evolutionary process of conflicts and their resolution. Furthermore, it is crucial to recognize that ideas and actions from earlier periods also shape transitions. For example, Glen Atkinson (2010, 295) argues that court decisions validating the establishment of the exchange value of property during the nineteenth century were necessary for the development of MMC nearly a century later.
7. This chapter is being completed in mid-June 2021.
8. Other economists, such as Richard M. Goodwin (1991), also examine ideas shared by Keynes and Schumpeter. Goodwin even includes Marx, but does not elaborate on the importance of the monetary theory of production emphasized by these three scholars.
9. The opportunity cost of capital is the expected return from the best alternative use of funds, adjusted for differences in risk.
10. In more recent work, Lavoie (2014) stresses that the Post Keynesian theory of the firm draws upon Institutionalist scholarship. Moreover, what Lavoie calls the Institutionalist strand of Post Keynesian economics aligns with what others (such as Whalen 2020) call PKI.

11. Again, *TNIS* was originally published in 1967 (see Galbraith 1967).
12. Galbraith's biographer Richard Parker (2005, 451) notes that this was part of the AEA's one-hundredth annual meeting, and that *TNIS* was the only book published during the preceding century to which an entire session was dedicated. Besides Galbraith, the panelists were Barry Bluestone, Robert M. Solow, and F.M. Scherer.
13. Attention to the separation of ownership from business control originated with the work of Berle and Means (1932).
14. Strictly speaking, of course, profit maximization remains untenable from the PKI perspective; in practice, it has (as discussed in this chapter) come to mean working to raise share values and to shift risk away from the corporation as much as possible. As Lavoie recognized (discussed above), power remains the ultimate objective of firms; and, as a consequence of MMC, that power has for decades been used to advance the common interests of money managers, stockholders, and top corporate executives.
15. Minsky actually warned of this slowdown, a consequence of capital development taking a back seat to short-term financial returns, in the early 1990s (see Whalen 2001, 820, n. 19).
16. Jeffrey T. Brookman, Saeyoung Chang, and Craig G. Rennie (2007) found that between 1993 and 1999, corporate chief executives (CEOs) and shareholders of firms that laid off employees for cost-saving reasons (rather than as an adjustment to lower sales volumes) were significantly rewarded, and CEO benefits were enduring. Stock-based pay packages for CEOs from layoff firms were 19.6 percent higher during the downsizing year than those for counterparts in non-layoff companies, 42.6 percent higher in the following year, 44.9 percent higher after two years, and 77.4 percent higher afterwards. Furthermore, they estimate that an average of $71 million per year (1992 constant dollars) in additional shareholder wealth resulted from the layoffs in their sample. Similarly, Greenwald, Lettau, and Ludvigson (2021) find that 44 percent of the $34 trillion in real equity growth generated by US corporations between 1989 and 2017 resulted from increased profit shares at the expense of labor compensation. Put differently, shareholders captured a larger portion of a slowly growing "pie" (relative to the earlier postwar years) at the expense of other groups.
17. Despite all of these consequences from the neoliberal emphasis on maximizing shareholder wealth, some University of Chicago economists continue to support Friedman's arguments. For example, Rajan Raghuram (2020) argues:

    Yet there is a deeper argument for Friedman's view, based on the recognition that managers will not necessarily squeeze everyone else to favor shareholders. Because shareholders get whatever is left over after debt holders are paid their interest and workers their wages, management can maximize shareholders' "residual claim" only if it expands the size of the corporate pie relative to these prior fixed claims on it. To the extent that management must satisfy everyone else before looking to shareholder interests, it already does maximize value for all those who contribute to the firm.

    Although Raghuram admits that too many executives unjustifiably benefitted from the use of stock options as an incentive to accomplish the Friedman ideal, he concludes that this has been a failure of corporate governance rather than the result of an inappropriate goal. However, why he does not link the size of "residual claims" to lower real wages and benefits provided to many workers, instead of considering them to be "fixed claims," is puzzling.

18.   For a look at how economic conditions have led to despair and resignation, see Case and Deaton (2020).

19.   Trump claimed that because of President Ronald Reagan's support for a trade agreement with Mexico, which led to the passage of the North American Free Trade Act during the Clinton administration, he does not consider the 1980s to have been all that great.

20.   A prescient Galbraith (1971, 243) predicted the rise of populist politicians like Trump in his observation that social conflict would not be between capital and labor, but between the highly-educated members of the technostructure and blue-collar workers left behind:

Politics also reflects the new division. In the United States suspicion or resentment is no longer directed to the capitalists or the merely rich. It is the intellectuals—the effete snobs—who are eyed with misgiving and alarm. This should surprise no one. Nor should it be a matter for surprise when semiliterate millionaires turn up leading or financing the ignorant in struggle against the intellectually privileged and content. This reflects the relevant class distinction in our time.

21.   For an examination of voters supporting candidates whose policies run counter to their economic interests in the age of MMC, see Frank (2004).

22.   Glen Atkinson (2008) recounts that the earliest efforts to measure economic well-being and progress were made by Institutional and heterodox economists like Scott Nearing, who, in the early decades of the twentieth century, sought to better understand economic inequality. Atkinson also notes that Department of Commerce economists Milton Gilbert and George Jaszi first developed measures of gross domestic product in the 1940s.

23.   Although Boushey does not cite them, Minsky and Whalen (1996, 159–161) make similar points about postwar changes in the adequacy of measures of economic well-being.

24.   For a contrary view on what Salter describes as the Old Institutionalist school, see Whalen (2022); the PKI presented throughout this volume is also evidence that runs counter to Salter's conclusion on Institutionalism.

25.   In addition, Powell (2021) highlighted the fact that people of color and workers in service industries, such as leisure and hospitality which employ more women than men, have disproportionately experienced economic losses (and, of course, restoration of those service jobs is likely to be slow and many are not expected to return).

26.   In more recent testimony before a congressional committee, Powell stated, "There is a growing realization, really across the political spectrum, that we need to achieve more inclusive prosperity." He also stressed that the Fed considers maximum employment a "broad and inclusive goal" (quoted in Smialek 2021).

27.   Quoted in Rappeport and Tankersley (2020).

28.   From the vantage point of PKI, it is worth noting that Yellen was also willing to re-read and draw on Minsky when addressing the global financial crisis of 2007–2009 (see Yellen 2009).

29.   Quoted in Johnston (2021).

30.   As of June 2021, the Biden administration proposed changes to the tax code to generate revenue from corporations and *rentiers* to fund programs addressing inequality. These include raising taxes on corporate profits, eliminating the carried-interest loophole, and increasing personal taxes on capital gains and high incomes. In contrast, most tax and other regulatory changes in the era of MMC have primarily benefitted large corporations and affluent households.

REFERENCES

Atkinson, Glen. 2008. "Purpose and Measurement of National Income and Product." *Journal of Economic Issues* 42 (2): 303–316.

Atkinson, Glen. 2010. "The Legal Foundations of Financial Capitalism." *Journal of Economic Issues* 44 (2): 289–299.

Badger, Emily. 2020. "Inequality Was Never So Visible as in 2020. What did We Learn?" *The New York Times*, December 29, 2020.

Baranes, Avraham Izhar. 2017. "Financialization in the American Pharmaceutical Industry: A Veblenian Approach." *Journal of Economic Issues* 51 (2): 351–358.

Beck, Ulrich. 1992. *Risk Society: Towards a New Modernity.* Newbury Park, CA: Sage Publications.

Berle, Adolf and Gardiner Means. 1932. *The Modern Corporation and Private Property.* New York: Macmillan.

Bluestone, Barry. 1988. "Time and the New Industrial State: Discussion." *American Economic Review Papers and Proceedings* 78 (2): 377–378.

Blumenthal, David. 2021. "Restore a Better Balance to Public-Private Funding of Biomedical Research." *Stat.* May 20, 2021. https://www.statnews.com/2021/05/20/better-balance-public-private-funding-biomedical-research. Accessed May 23, 2021.

Blyth, Mark. 2002. *Great Transformations: Economic Ideas and Institutional Change in the Twentieth Century.* Cambridge, UK: Cambridge University Press.

Boushey, Heather. 2020. "Unbound: Releasing Inequality's Grip on Our Economy." *Review of Radical Political Economics* 52 (4): 597–609.

Brookman, Jeffrey T., Saeyoung Chang, and Craig G. Rennie. 2007. "CEO Cash and Stock-Based Compensation Changes, Layoff Decisions, and Shareholder Value." *The Financial Review* 42 (1): 99–119.

Case, Anne and Angus Deaton. 2020. *Deaths of Despair and the Future of Capitalism.* Princeton, NJ: Princeton University Press.

Crotty, James R. 1990a. "Keynes on the Stages of Development of the Capitalist Economy." *Journal of Economic Issues* 24 (3): 761–780.

Crotty, James R. 1990b. "Owner-Manager Conflict and Financial Theories of Investment Instability: A Critical Assessment of Keynes, Tobin, and Minsky." *Journal of Post Keynesian Economics* 12 (4): 519–542.

Dallery, Thomas. 2009. "Post-Keynesian Theories of the Firm Under Financialization." *Review of Radical Political Economics* 41 (4): 492–515.

Dixon, Robert. 1986. "Uncertainty, Unobstructedness, and Power." *Journal of Post Keynesian Economics* 8 (4): 585–590.

Dunn, Stephen P. 2001. "Galbraith, Uncertainty and the Modern Corporation." In *Economist with a Public Purpose: Essays in Honor of John Kenneth Galbraith*, edited by Michael Keaney, 157–182. London: Routledge.

Eichengreen, Barry. 2019. "Financial History, Historical Analysis, and the New History of Finance Capital." *Capitalism: A Journal of History and Economics* 1 (1): 20–58.

Fox, Justin. 2009. *The Myth of the Rational Market: A History of Risk, Reward, and Delusion on Wall Street.* New York: Harper.

Frank, Thomas. 2004. *What's the Matter with Kansas? How Conservatives Won the Heart of America.* New York: Metropolitan Books.

Friedman, Milton. 1969. *Capitalism and Freedom.* Chicago: University of Chicago Press.

Friedman, Milton. 1970. "The Social Responsibility of Business Is to Increase Its Profits." *The New York Times Magazine*, September 13, 1970.

Fusfeld, Daniel R. 1972. "The Rise of the Corporate State in America." *Journal of Economic Issues* 6 (2): 1–22.

Galbraith, John Kenneth. 1967. *The New Industrial State*. Boston: Houghton Mifflin.

Galbraith, John Kenneth. 1971. *The New Industrial State*, Second Edition, Revised. New York: Mentor.

Galbraith, John Kenneth. 1988. "Time and the New Industrial State." *American Economic Review Papers and Proceedings* 78 (2): 373–376.

Gans, Joshua. 2017. "50 Years Ago an Economist Worried About Unchecked Corporate Power. Here's What His Theory Got Wrong." *Harvard Business Review*. August 22, 2017. Available at https://tinyurl.com/553yhfmp. Accessed January 7, 2021.

Gibney, Michael and Jason Woleben. 2021. "Big Pharma Rallies on Share Buybacks as Most Companies Cut Back During Pandemic." *S&P Global Market Intelligence*, February 25, 2021. https://tinyurl.com/2c9jya9z. Accessed May 23, 2021.

Goodwin, Richard M. 1991. "Schumpeter, Keynes, and the Theory of Economic Evolution." *Journal of Evolutionary Economics* 1 (1): 29–47.

Greenwald, Daniel L., Martin Lettau, and Sydney C. Ludvigson. 2021. "How the Wealth Was Won: Factors Shares as Market Fundamentals." National Bureau of Economic Research Working Paper 25769. http://www.nber.org/papers/w25769. Accessed June 21, 2021.

Hall, Peter A. and David Soskice. 2001. "An Introduction to the Varieties of Capitalism." In *Varieties of Capitalism: The Institutional Foundations of Comparative Advantage*, edited by Peter Hall and David Soskice, 1–68. Oxford: Oxford University Press.

Hayashi, Yuka. 2021. "Trade Pick by Biden to Focus on Jobs." *The Wall Street Journal*, January 13, 2021, A7.

Jensen, Michael C. 1986. "Agency Costs of Free Cash Flow, Corporate Finance, and Takeovers." *The American Economic Review Papers and Proceedings* 76 (2): 323–329.

Jensen, Michael C. and William H. Meckling. 1976. "Theory of the Firm: Managerial Behavior, Agency Costs, and Ownership Structure." *Journal of Financial Economics* 3 (4): 305–360.

Jo, Tae-Hee and John F. Henry. 2015. "The Business Enterprise in the Age of Money Manager Capitalism." *Journal of Economic Issues* 49 (1): 23–46.

Johnston, Katie. 2021. "Big Tasks, High Hopes Await Walsh in New Post." *The Boston Globe,* January 19, 2021.

Keynes, John Maynard. (1936) 1964. *The General Theory of Employment, Interest, and Money.* New York: Harcourt Brace Jovanovich.

Krieg, Gregory. 2016. "Donald Trump Reveals When He Thinks America Was Great." *CNN Politics*. March 26, 2016. https://tinyurl.com/vt3p5xzx. Accessed August 29, 2020.

Lavoie, Marc. 1992. *Foundations of Post-Keynesian Economic Analysis*. Northampton, MA: Edward Elgar.

Lavoie, Marc. 2014. *Post-Keynesian Economics: New Foundations*. Northampton, MA: Edward Elgar.

Lazonick, William. 2014. "Profits Without Prosperity." *Harvard Business Review* 92 (9): 46–55.

Minsky, Hyman P. 1991. "The Transition to a Market Economy: Financial Options." The Jerome Levy Economics Institute, Working Paper No. 66.

Minsky, Hyman P. 1993. "Schumpeter and Finance." In *Markets and Institutions in Economic Development*, edited by Salvatore Biasco, Alessandro Roncaglia, and Michele Salvati, 103–115. London: Macmillan.

Minsky, Hyman P. 1996. "Uncertainty and the Institutional Structure of Capitalist Economies." *Journal of Economic Issues* 30 (2): 357–368.

Minsky, Hyman P. and Charles J. Whalen, 1996. "Economic Insecurity and the Institutional Prerequisites for Successful Capitalism." *Journal of Post Keynesian Economics* 19 (2): 155–170.

Newman, Katherine S. 1994. "Troubled Times: The Cultural Dimensions of Economic Decline." In *Understanding American Economic Decline*, edited by Michael A. Bernstein and David E. Adler, 330–357. Cambridge: Cambridge University Press.

Niggle, Christopher J. 1986. "Financial Innovation and the Distinction Between Financial and Industrial Capital." *Journal of Economic Issues* 20 (2): 375–382.

Parker, Richard. 2005. *John Kenneth Galbraith: His Life, His Politics, His Economics*. Chicago: The University of Chicago Press.

Powell, Jerome. 2021. "Getting Back to a Strong Labor Market," February 10, 2021. https://www.federalreserve.gov/newsevents/speech/powell20210210a.htm. Accessed June 14, 2021.

Rajan, Raghuram G. 2020. "What Should Corporations Do?" *Project Syndicate*, October 6, 2020. https://tinyurl.com/3h2v2jze. Accessed October 7, 2020.

Rappeport, Alan and Jim Tankersley. 2020. "Expected to Pick 2 More Women for Leading Roles on Economic Team." *The New York Times*, November 30, 2020.

Reisman, David A. 1990. "Galbraith on Ideas and Events." *Journal of Economic Issues* 24 (3): 733–760.

Salter, Alexander William. 2021. "How Economics Lost Itself in Data." *The Wall Street Journal*, January 28, 2021.

Schumpeter, Joseph A. 1934. *The Theory of Economic Development*. Cambridge: Harvard University Press.

Smialek, Jeanna. 2021. "Powell Says US Needs 'Inclusive Prosperity.'" *The New York Times* June 23, 2021.

Stanfield, James Ronald. 1996. *John Kenneth Galbraith*. New York: St. Martin's Press.

Stockhammer, Engelbert. 1994. "Financialization and the Slowdown of Accumulation." *Cambridge Journal of Economics* 28 (5): 719–741.

Stockhammer, Engelbert. 2006–2007. "Uncertainty, Class, and Power." *International Journal of Political Economy* 35 (4): 31–49.

Vail, John. 2008. "Insecurity." In *The Elgar Companion to Social Economics*, edited by John B. Davis and Wilfred Dolfsma, 44–56. Northampton, MA: Edward Elgar.

Weil, David. 2014. *The Fissured Workplace: Why Work Became So Bad for So Many and What Can Be Done About It*. Cambridge, MA: Harvard University Press.

Whalen, Charles J. 2001. "Integrating Schumpeter and Keynes: Hyman Minsky's Theory of Capitalist Development." *Journal of Economic Issues* 35 (4): 805–823.

Whalen, Charles J. 2008. "Post-Keynesian Institutionalism and the Anxious Society." In *Alternative Institutional Structures: Evolution and Impact*, edited by Sandra S. Batie and Nicholas Mercuro, 273–299. New York: Routledge.

Whalen, Charles J. 2013. "Post-Keynesian Institutionalism after the Great Recession." *European Journal of Economics and Economic Policies: Intervention* 10 (1): 12–27.

Whalen, Charles J. 2020. "Post-Keynesian Institutionalism: Past, Present, and Future." *Evolutionary and Institutional Economics Review* 176 (1): 71–92.

Whalen, Charles J. 2022. *Institutional Economics: Perspectives and Methods in Pursuit of a Better World*. London: Routledge.

Wilber, Charles K. and Kenneth P. Jameson. 1990. *Beyond Reaganomics: A Further Inquiry into the Poverty of Economics.* Notre Dame, IN: University of Notre Dame Press.

Yellen, Janet. 2009. "A Minsky Meltdown: Lessons for Central Bankers." *FRBSF Economic Letter* No. 2009-15.

Zalewski, David A. 2004. "Wealth and Power: Ethical Implications of Executive Compensation Since the 1980s." In *The Institutionalist Tradition in Labor Economics*, edited by Dell P. Champlin and Janet T. Knoedler, 286–296. Armonk, NY: M.E. Sharpe.

Zalewski, David A. and Charles J. Whalen. 2010. "Financialization and Income Inequality: A Post Keynesian Institutional Analysis." *Journal of Economic Issues* 44 (3): 757–777.

3. Financialization and employment: a Post-Keynesian Institutionalist understanding of the transnational corporation under money manager capitalism

Avraham I. Baranes

INTRODUCTION

A troubling development in the post-World War II economy of the United States (US) is the well-documented productivity-pay gap: between 1973 and 2018, productivity increased by 73 percent, while labor compensation only increased by 12 percent (Economic Policy Institute 2019).[1] Post-Keynesian Institutionalism (PKI) argues that this divergence can be explained through the changing institutional arrangements in which the "megacorp" enterprises of managerial capitalism gave way to the financialized corporations of money manager capitalism. A hallmark of this new structure is what William Lazonick and Mary O'Sullivan (2000) refer to as the "maximizing shareholder value" theory of corporate governance. Based on Milton Friedman's shareholder doctrine (1970), this approach argues that the end purpose of enterprise activity is to generate as much value as possible for shareholders, defined by the stock value of the corporation. As William Lazonick (2008) and David Weil (2014) have argued, labor relations have changed drastically as a result of this new form of corporate governance.[2] The stable, long-term employment characterized by managerial capitalism has given way to more job hopping and less stable employment. It is increasingly common for workers to be hired as independent contractors or work in some form of alternative or contingent arrangement—hired for a temporary time with a known end date, rather than as a traditional, "permanent" worker.

This chapter argues that the development of these alternative employment arrangements and the resulting productivity-pay gap must be understood in the context of the financialized business enterprise under money manager capitalism.[3] These arm's-length arrangements offer enterprises an easy way to cut costs and improve their liquidity positions so as to increase shareholder value through a process of predatory value extraction—enterprises cut costs and outsource production-based activities and distribute the resulting gains to shareholders through stock repurchases, rather than reinvest in their operations (Lazonick 2015). Policy to correct these problems must then emphasize transforming this institutional structure into one that promotes shared prosperity.

This chapter is divided into three main sections. The first discusses the development of the financialized transnational corporation (TNC) through the lens of PKI. Building on Minsky's stages of capitalist development (Minsky 1988; Minsky 1990; Minsky and Whalen 1996–1997) and the Institutionalist approach to the business enterprise (Baranes 2020; Baranes and Hake 2018; Commons [1924] 2007; Dean 2018; Hake 2007; Veblen [1904] 2013; Veblen 1908a; Veblen 1908b), I recognize the development of financialization as a fundamental shift in the social relations that govern economic activity, especially with regard to who dictates the direction and purpose of that activity. The second section discusses labor and distribution in the context of the TNC, emphasizing what Weil (2014) refers to as the "fissured workplace." As argued here, the new forms of labor relations and distributional outcomes are not accidental or simply by-products of the new institutional arrangements. Rather, they are intentionally developed to strengthen and develop the value-extracting activities of the TNC. The final section discusses several policy changes that could begin to provide progressive structural change. Recognizing that there is no one "magic bullet" solution, the focus is on policies that can begin to move the American economy beyond money manager capitalism.

CAPITALIST DEVELOPMENT AND THE MODERN BUSINESS ENTERPRISE

Understanding the effect of financialization on labor first requires an understanding of the structural transformation of the business enterprise with the development of financialization. In this section that transformation is understood through a Post-Keynesian Institutionalist lens in a way that blends the Institutionalist theory of the business enterprise with Hyman Minsky's theory of capitalist development. In doing so, I recognize that money manager capitalism and the financialized business enterprise are the result of a historical process and must be understood within this historical context. As such, financialization is understood as the regime of accumulation under money manager capitalism and recognized as a fundamental shift in the social relations that govern economic activity within the business enterprise.

Charles Whalen (2001, 815) argues that there are three questions to ask in the context of Minsky's stages of capitalist development: "What is the distinctive activity being financed? What is the pivotal source of financing? And what is the balance of economic power between those in business and banking/finance?"[4] While these questions focus on the financing arrangement in each stage, we may also apply them to an analysis of the business enterprise. As Whalen (2008), Dean (2018), and Baranes (2020) have all shown, different stages of capitalism are marked by different forms of dominant enterprise organization, each with its own internal balance of power and financing relations. Recognizing that the business enterprise in the PKI approach is viewed through the lens of the "going concern" (Commons [1934] 2009), we may add two more questions that specifically emphasize the role of enterprise evolution in the context of capitalist development: How does the enterprise reproduce itself as a going concern? And to what extent is the community separated from its capital, defined in Institutionalist terms?

The business enterprise in the PKI approach is viewed through the lens of the going concern—its purpose is to engage in sequential acts of production through historical time (Lee 2012). Central to this concept is the Institutionalist theory of capital, capital accumulation, and capital appropriation (Baranes and Hake 2018; Ranson 1987). In *The Theory of Business Enterprise*, Thorstein Veblen ([1904] 2013) discussed the development of the corporation as an outgrowth of transformations in credit and the financing of capital development. As part of this development, Veblen traced how the institution known as the business enterprise has transformed within the context of transformations in the way in which capital is understood. This is extended upon in two articles published in 1908 (Veblen 1908a; Veblen 1908b), in which he argues that the concept of capital emerges from the community's knowledge stock and is appropriated by the business enterprise through tangible and intangible property rights.[5] Understanding the business enterprise from the PKI perspective, then, requires an understanding of that emergence and appropriation.

The theory of capital from an Institutionalist perspective emerges out of the Institutionalist theory of technology, "a process that itself is defined by the nature of social relations within the community" (Baranes and Hake 2018, 432). Clarence Ayres (1952) defines technology in the context of tool-skill combinations. The development of these tools depends on the size and accessibility of the joint stock of knowledge, and the skills developed to use these tools depends upon the value structure of the underlying social institutions (Lower 1987; Munkirs 1988). Capital development occurs when new additions to the joint stock of knowledge are made that allow for the development of new tool-skill combinations (Ayres 1944). As such, capital accumulation from the Institutionalist perspective is the result of a socially and community driven process where new knowledge is created and added to the existing institutional structure (Bush 1983; Bush 1987). From this perspective, the productivity of all assets depends on the community's joint stock of knowledge, and the primary focus is on the degree to which ownership of capital assets and the community itself are separated within the enterprise's structure.

In a capitalist economy, the community's capital is embedded within, and its use dictated by, the business enterprise. However, just as capitalism is dynamic and changes over time, so too does the dominant form of enterprise and the social relationships embedded in the community's capital. Of key interest in the PKI perspective are the relationships between the community, capital users, capital managers, and capital owners at various stages in capitalist development.[6] At different stages, the relationships between these four agents change based on access to the joint stock of knowledge (Dean 2018). As such, PKI answers the five questions above at each stage of capitalist development—with its unique form of dominant enterprise—in the context of the relationships between these four agents.

Merchant capitalism, the initial stage in Minsky's theory, was dominated by the sole proprietorship or partnership model.[7] Under this form of organization, the owner of the enterprise was the capital owner, capital manager, and often the capital user—though additional labor could be hired—and the life of the enterprise was tied to the life of the owners (Chandler 1977). A key aspect of this stage was the use of intangible and tangible property rights that allowed owners a mechanism for capturing economic returns generated by the community's joint stock of knowledge.[8] As such, owners were able to "lock out" the community from its joint stock and demand a monetary return for use of productive assets (Baranes and Hake 2018). As a result, production occurred for the purpose of market transactions, rather than final consumption as in pre-capitalist societies, and enterprise strategy emphasized the creation and maintenance of bargaining transactions (Commons [1934] 2009; Heilbroner and Milberg 2012).[9] Rather than large machinery, production activities required specialized tools (Heilbroner and Singer 1994; Whalen 2001), and financing for this activity was provided either internally through retained earnings or in the form of merchant and commercial banking, the purposes of which were to finance the transport of goods and "vouch for the legitimacy of distant trade partners" (Minsky 1990, 67). Ultimately, enterprises under merchant capitalism reproduced themselves as going concerns through a successful sales effort and the community was separated from its joint stock of knowledge in the form of bargaining transactions (Commons [1934] 2009; Dean 2018).

New innovations in production and transportation during the industrial revolution—most importantly, the development of the railway system—expanded both production capabilities and the size of the market, giving rise to industrial capitalism.[10] As small owner/operators could not afford the high fixed costs of industrial capital, the industrial corporation took hold as the dominant enterprise, supported by "financial organizations that could mobilize the resources needed for factory manufacturing, capital-intensive transportation, mills, and mines" (Whalen 2001, 810). Key to this new indus- trial enterprise is the internal separation of the production-based activities and control over the production process. The former includes the tangible assets and capital users, while the latter embodies the capital managers and owners in charge of ensuring an ongoing flow of funds to the enterprise and interacting with capital users in the form of managerial transactions (Commons [1934] 2009). As such, the enterprise's reproduction as a going concern in industrial capitalism depends less on the technical ability to produce and sell output than on whether or not that output can be sold at a high enough price to cover costs, including the costs of servicing debt undertaken to finance expansions of plant and equipment (Keynes [1936] 1964; Veblen [1904] 2013).[11]

Financing for these expansions came primarily from investment bankers and sales of equity, with investment bankers obtaining power to influence the direction of the enterprise (Chandler 1977; Minsky 1988; Whalen 2001). These bankers exerted this influence to generate combinations and reduce the cutthroat competition that threatened the ability of industrial corporations to operate as going concerns. "They [investment bankers] sought to protect cash flows that the firms they financed generated by forming trusts, cartels, and monopolies. Entry was the great villain which can destroy asset values and therefore the foundations of secure financing: barriers to entry had to be erected" (Minsky, quoted in Atkinson and Paschall 2016, 74). This develop- ment of banker capitalism—and with it a robust financial system and credit market—fully separated capital managers in charge of the activities of the enterprise and the capital owners, and generated the separation of ownership and control that is a hallmark of modern business enterprise (Berle and Means [1932] 2009; Veblen [1904] 2013; Veblen [1923] 2009).[12]

Stock ownership, what Commons ([1934] 2009) refers to as incorporeal property, represents both the wealth of the owner and a promise of payment in the form of profit distributions. As such, the primary focus of capital owners is the increase in value of this incorporeal property, which depends not on the productive capacity of the enterprise but its perceived earning capacity. To reproduce itself as a going concern, the enterprise must maintain its valuation and revaluation of incorporeal property at higher rates. A revaluation at a lower rate—or even a less than expected increase—may cause shareholders to panic, leading to a sell-off (Keynes [1936] 1964; Minsky [1975] 2008; Veblen [1904] 2013). Under this joint-stock organization, the community, capital users, capital managers, and capital owners are all separate entities and engage in different parts of the provisioning process.[13] As Baranes and Hake (2018) argue, capital is not accumulated under this form of organization; rather it is appropriated in that the enterprise capitalizes upon its ability to lock out the community from its joint stock of knowledge for the purpose of new debt and equity issuances and to swell its expected valuation.

Banker capitalism ended with the Great Depression and the New Deal legislation, which gave rise to the era of managerial capitalism dominated by the megacorp enterprise—a large conglomerate with corporate/capital managers dictating the direction of economic activity (Eichner 1976). These managers were at the top of a rigid managerial hierarchy and could be thought of as "organization men" who "tended to act in the interests of the organizations, rather than of just themselves; their own career success depended on the success of the whole enterprise" (Lazonick 2010b, 682). Economic activity emphasized long-term macroeconomic growth, with financing of that activity occurring through a retain-and-reinvest strategy for profits, aided by government financial assets accumulated as a result of wartime deficits (Eichner 1983; Minsky [1986] 2008; Lee 1999). At the industry level, a bifurcated (core and periphery) type of structure developed, with a group of megacorp enterprises taking the dominant central decision-making role and smaller enterprises—franchises, small businesses, and subsidiaries—forming the periphery to carry out the actions and decisions of the core (Galbraith 1967; Munkirs 1985; Munkirs and Knoedler 1987). While the megacorp is characterized by the separation of capital users, managers, and owners, as under banker capitalism, the balance of power rests with the capital managers, who view the going concern of the enterprise in the context of long-run growth. Issuances of stocks and debt financing were secondary to the internal generation of funds for investment, and, as such, short-term fluctuations in the stock prices were less of a concern (Eichner 1976).

Money manager capitalism began to emerge in the 1970s during a period of political and economic turmoil.[14] As a result, enterprises underwent a transformation of governing principles, led by what Lazonick and O'Sullivan (2000) refer to as the shareholder primacy theory of corporate governance. Rather than retain cash when no new investment opportunities were available, enterprises were restructured to incentivize managers to "disgorge the cash rather than investing it at below the cost of capital or wasting it on organizational inefficiencies" (Jensen 1986, 324). Shareholders were seen as the principal claimants on corporate profits and managers needed to act as their agents (Friedman 1970; Jensen and Meckling 1976). New institutional arrangements linked management pay to enterprise performance, measured by shareholder value in the form of return on equity and earnings per share (Fama and Jensen 1983). The shareholder revolution that spurred the fourth major merger wave—comprised of leveraged buyouts, corporate breakups, and hostile takeovers—put financial motives, incentives, and institutions firmly at the center of economic activity (Greer 1992; Krippner 2011; Lazonick 2010a). Institutional investors began to dominate financial markets and the business enterprise. "The aim of money managers, and the sole criterion by which they are judged, is the maximization of the value of investments made by fund holders. As a result, business leaders became increasingly sensitive to short-term profits and the stock market valuation of their firms" (Whalen 2001, 814). It is this increased focus on short-term financial gains and the increased power and importance of financial markets, motives, institutions, and elites in economic decision-making that defines enterprise activity under money manager capitalism and what is meant by a financialized business enterprise (Admati 2017; Epstein 2002; Haldane 2016; Lapavitsas 2013).

As a concept, financialization refers to this structural shift in economic organization that recognizes the importance of financial valuation in corporate governance and the changing strategy, organization, and financing of the business enterprise as a result (Lazonick 2008). Greta Krippner (2005, 174) refers to financialization as "a pattern of accumulation in which profits accrue primarily through financial channels, rather than through trade and commodity production." With this in mind, the dominant form of enterprise under money manager capitalism is the financialized TNC.

As described by Claude Serfati (2008), the TNC is better understood not as a unique producer, but as a financial center—it is a network where commands are delivered from a central node, the capital manager, and carried out by peripheral nodes, called special purpose entities (SPEs). These SPEs are subsidiaries and independent contractors that carry out various production and value-creation activities; in the grand scheme of the TNCs, these are the capital users. The value created by the SPEs is then appropriated by the capital managers at the core and used in ways to swell the enterprise valuation in the best interests of the capital owners, generally through stock repurchases (Jo and Henry 2015; Lazonick 2014a; Lazonick 2017; Jo 2019). Further, because these SPEs are generally subsidiaries and independent contractors, it becomes easier to liquidate the activity if needed, and the costs of maintenance and depreciation may be shifted to third parties (Froud et al. 2000), with the savings distributed to shareholders. David Peetz (2018) refers to this phenomenon as "not there" capitalism. Through clever contracting, the TNC is able to maintain control over economic activity while minimizing its exposure to costs and accountability:

> The key methods of "not there" contracting are: the retention of control by a central capitalist entity ("core capital"—these are, for example the lead firms in supply chains); production is undertaken within smaller entities ("peripheral capital") which is formally separated from core capital; peripheral and core capital are linked by contract; and labor is ostensibly and directly controlled by peripheral capital. In turn, that labor may be classed as "employees" or as "contractors," depending on the context. (Peetz 2018, 48–57)

Maintaining liquidity and arm's-length relationships is a hallmark of the TNC. Production-based activities for nonfinancial corporations are pushed off balance sheets in favor of increasing liquidity arrangements and financial assets that can more easily increase shareholder returns (Davis 2016; Davis 2018). Data from the integrated macroeconomic accounts supports this view of an increasingly "financial" nonfinancial corporation, as seen in Figure 3.1. Between 1960 and 1984, nonfinancial assets comprised at least 70 percent of the total assets for US nonfinancial corporations. However, in the 1980s and 1990s, this began to change. From 1984 to 1994, nonfinancial assets as a percent of total assets fell from 70 percent to 60 percent. By 1999, nonfinancial assets composed approximately 55 percent of total assets and this 55:45 ratio has been largely maintained ever since.

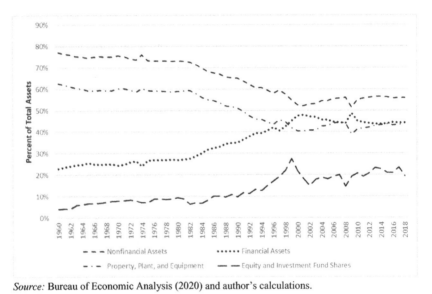

Source: Bureau of Economic Analysis (2020) and author's calculations.

Figure 3.1   *Breakdown of assets for US nonfinancial corporations,*
                 1960–2018

The main driver of the declining share of nonfinancial assets has been the reduced importance of property, plant, and equipment (PPE). Indeed, the decline in PPE follows closely the decline in nonfinancial assets, falling from approximately 60 percent of total assets prior to 1984 to 41 percent of total assets in the years since. Meanwhile, ownership in various types of equities and investment funds has become a more prominent feature of nonfinancial corporations' balance sheets.[15] Prior to 1984, these assets represented less than 10 percent of total assets. Between 1984 and 1999, they climbed to 27 percent of total assets before falling after the bursting of the dot-com bubble. Since then, these assets have represented approximately 20 percent of total assets for nonfinancial corporations.

The financialized TNC, then, represents the dominant form of enterprise under money manager capitalism. The organization of such an enterprise emphasizes the loose ties between the financial core and productive periphery, prioritizing the ability to quickly downsize, shed costs, and improve its liquidity position (Davis 2018; Froud et al. 1996; Froud et al. 2000; Lazonick 2013). Managerial strategy emphasizes distributing these gains to shareholders, rather than reinvesting in productive capacity or improving wages, even if doing so threatens the long-run viability of the enterprise and giving rise to what Lazonick and Shin (2020, 217) refer to as "predatory value extraction." The following section examines the effect of this new enterprise organization, a central institution under money manager capitalism, on labor relations and the distribution of income and wealth.

THE FINANCIALIZATION OF EMPLOYMENT

The evolution of business described above makes clear that, as the productive capabilities of the industrial system became more advanced, new methods of organization became necessary to maintain the value of intangible property and other assets, resulting in new modes of financing and new industrial relationships. From a Post-Keynesian Institutionalist view, there has been a split between the technical capabilities of the industrial system and the value system governing the use of those productive capabilities.[16] Rather than recognize that new technical capabilities require different economic governance systems, modern economic and social institutions have re-established the finance capitalist (banker capitalist) principles of maximizing the value of incorporeal property. Financialization, from this lens, is but the latest form of this type of structural change—a sort of old wine in a new bottle.

In this section, I discuss the changing labor relationships that have emerged as a result of the financialization of the economy. Of key interest, in line with Peetz's (2018) view of "not there" capitalism, I emphasize contingent labor as a key feature of a financialized economy and the distributional effect this has had. Ultimately, this section advances the notion of what I am calling the financialization of employment, in which labor relations function to improve enterprise liquidity and allow for predatory value extraction without affecting the productivity of the enterprise as a whole. The culmination of these changes is the well-documented productivity-pay gap, presented at the start of this chapter. Understanding the financialization of employment will go a long way in illuminating what has caused this division and what policy can do about it.

This section begins with an investigation into the structural transformation of labor, emphasizing what Weil (2014) refers to as the fissured workplace. This builds on the discussion of the TNC above and its emphasis on contracting and keeping production activities at arm's length compared to the in-house production of the traditional megacorp during managerial capitalism. Then, I discuss the effect that financialization and changing labor relations have had on income and wealth distribution, giving deeper context and meaning to the financialization of employment.

The Transformation of Employment Relations

The development of the TNC as the dominant form of enterprise brings with it a transformation in employment relations. Gone are the traditional labor relationships of managerial capitalism, in which corporations were characterized by rigid hierarchies, linear promotion, and lifetime employment. In its place are job hopping, long hours, job uncertainty, and low wages (Golden 2009; Lazonick 2010a; Lazonick 2010b). This change is not accidental, nor simply an unfortunate by-product of financialization—it is a key feature of the new institutional arrangements.

In a 2017 survey, the Bureau of Labor Statistics (BLS) found that alternative work arrangements accounted for 10.1 percent of total employment in the United States.[17] Contingent workers represented 3.8 percent of total employment.[18] Compared to noncontingent and traditional workers, contingent workers and those with alternative arrangements had lower median weekly incomes, were less likely to have employer-sponsored health insurance, and were less likely to be eligible for employer-provided pension or retirement plans (BLS 2018). Work by Skalski (2002) found that the gap between contingent and noncontingent labor was primarily due to differences in training and worker productivity, emphasizing that contingent workers receive less on-the-job training than their noncontingent counterparts.

In his study of new institutions surrounding labor markets, Weil (2014) describes the fissured workplace as the prevalence of third-party labor arrangements, contracted gig work, and other alternative work arrangements in the TNC. His argument is that "the fissured workplace is not simply the result of employers seeking to reduce wages and cut benefits. It represents the intersection of three business strategies, one focused on revenues, one on costs, and one on providing the 'glue' to make the overall strategy operate effectively" (Weil 2014, 8). The first strategy, emerging from the economic crises in the 1970s, was a focus on core competencies, effectively ending the conglomerate form of organization. In its place strategies evolved to refocus on brand building and economies of scale and scope in core production (Chandler 1990). "As a result, companies outsourced customer relations to third-party call centers; manufacturers shifted production to networks of subcontractors for subassemblies; and private, public, and nonprofit organizations contracted out everything from cleaning and janitorial services to payroll and human resource functions" (Weil 2014, 11).

As part of enterprise restructuring, employment activities were outsourced to third parties as well, composing the second key strategy of shedding costs by reducing employment (Weil 2014). The decisions to hire labor became largely separated from the core enterprise, with periphery entities in control of this process (Peetz 2018). As such, core enterprises cut costs by shifting the burden of employment onto third parties. This allowed management to show higher profits to satisfy shareholders and, if need be, quickly shed these contracts as needed. As Whalen (2008) and Froud et al. (1996) have argued, financialized labor effectively operates in a spot market, where it is bought and sold as necessary.

The ability for enterprises to engage in these strategies hinges on the ability to develop institutions that govern the relationship between the core and periphery nodes of the TNC. In other words, the core must be able to develop organizational structures that allow it to monitor standards of performance "and impose real costs if the affiliated companies fail to live up to them" (Weil 2014, 12). These structures ensure that standards surrounding quality and service are met. As a result, there has been a rise in different forms of monitoring, tracking, product identification, and shipping and delivering processes that have emerged with the rise of the TNC and the prevalence of globalized supply chains (Serfati 2008; Serfati and Sauviat 2019; Weil 2014). Enterprises are able to focus on their core competencies and expand their margins and markets while simultaneously ridding themselves of the costs of other "nonessential" activities. This includes employment activities, which have "been split off, shifted to a range of secondary players that function in more competitive markets and are separated from the locus of value creation" (Weil 2014, 14). These new employment relations are not an accident—they are a key feature of money manager capitalism and the financialization of the business enterprise.

Contributing to this financialization of employment has been the development of globalization and the offshoring of production-based activities. Bronfenbrenner and Luce (2004) showed that outsourcing was becoming increasingly common among United States corporations, with white-collar and service industry jobs among those increasingly likely to be offshored. They also found that unionized workers were "disproportionately affected by U.S. production shifts" (Bronfenbrenner and Luce 2004, 27). As Bronfenbrenner (2000) found, enterprises used plant closings and offshoring as a threat in union negotiations, even when the threat was not followed through. The primary argument for this offshoring is maintaining competitiveness in the face of higher labor costs domestically compared to abroad. However, it should be noted that it is primarily large, profitable, and well-established publicly held companies that are outsourcing production (Bronfenbrenner and Luce 2004). Further, the gains from this offshoring, as shown by Lazonick (2015) and highlighted later in this section, have been primarily used to increase short-term profits through stock repurchases, rather than to reinvest in pursuit of productivity gains. As a result, labor has found itself on a more uncertain footing, with fewer protections and less stability in the face of recessions and economic downturns, and, as will be shown later in this section, receiving less when the economy grows.

This is made more problematic by the increased influence of private equity in enterprise activity. In a financialized economy, private equity firms represent "financial 'intermediaries' ... that raise large pools of capital from wealthy individuals and institutions for investment funds, which they use to buy out companies" (Batt and Appelbaum 2015, 197). This is done through a leveraged buy-out process, where the company is purchased primarily through taking on high levels of debt, which is then put on the balance sheet of the purchased firm—indeed, Batt and Appelbaum (2015, 200) find that "private equity funds typically acquire companies using about 30 percent equity, while loading the companies with 70 percent debt." The equity partners themselves, further, invest less than 2 percent of the equity, meaning they are responsible for less than 1 percent of the purchase price (Covert 2018). After the company is taken over, the new managers shed costs by selling off business units, restructuring various labor and retirement contracts, and downsizing employment. Given the high debt that the company is saddled with as a result of the buyout, however, these savings are generally devoted to interest payments, rather than innovations or improvements in production. If the equity firm can sell the company at a profit, the gains are magnified—general partners receive approximately 20 percent of the returns (Batt and Appelbaum 2015). However, if the company fails, "the costs of bankruptcy do not fall on private equity, but on the portfolio company and other stakeholders—employees, retirees, suppliers, creditors, and others" (Batt and Appelbaum 2015, 197). Effectively, private equity funds participate in a low-risk, high-reward process whereby gains are disproportionately distributed to financialized interests and losses are disproportionately shouldered by labor and other production-based activities.[19]

Under the network organization of the TNC, independent contractors, staffing and temp agencies, on-call workers, and the gig economy in general should be thought of not as labor in the normal sense, but as their own branch of the network. This new structure has had detrimental effects on the standing of labor that contributes to various distributional problems. For one, such a structure has reduced upward mobility: as employees of staffing agencies or independent contractors, these workers do not have access to the same training and promotion opportunities that traditional employees have, which limits potential earnings, especially for low-wage workers (Weil 2017). Contracted cleaners and security guards, for example, have been found to earn 15–17 percent less than their in-house peers and are less likely to receive benefits. In general, contingent workers earn 10.6 percent less per hour than traditional workers and are about two-thirds less likely to have work-provided retirement savings plans (Kessler 2018). Deborah Goldschmidt and Johannes Schmieder (2015) find that these losses stem from a loss of firm-specific rents, which implies a strong cost-saving incentive to outsource these employment relations and rid the enterprise of the responsibility for making certain social contributions a part of labor compensation, allowing for greater distributions to shareholders.[20]

It is true that as a percent of value added for nonfinancial corporations, social contributions made by employers—health insurance, retirement matching, job training, etc.—have increased since 1960, from approximately 6 percent to just over 11 percent. Despite the increase, there are several problematic factors with this increase in the context of a financialized economy. First, as will be discussed below, wages as a percent of value added for nonfinancial corporations have fallen over the same time period from approximately 65 percent to 59 percent; as a result, total labor compensation as a percent of value added has not changed all that much. However, these social contributions represent an additional cost in hiring workers, especially full-time workers. As such, when increased demand necessitates an expansion of employment, it is more likely that enterprises will bring on contingent or part-time labor, or extend the hours of those already employed (Golden and Figart 2000).

There is also the question of who is responsible for ensuring not only that alternative work arrangements meet federal guidelines on fair labor standards, but also that the appropriate social contributions are made. As Goldman and Weil (2020) point out, laws that regulate employment typically assume a straightforward relationship between employer and employee—a relationship that does not exist under alternative work arrangements. Companies are able to distance themselves from social contributions and violations of labor standards, claiming that, because these workers do not officially work for the company, they are either independent contractors or employees of temp/ staffing agencies; thus, companies argue, labor violations, training, and other social contributions are not their concern or responsibility (Mojtehedzadeh 2018; Rohan and Musuraca 2018; Weil 2014).

These new institutional arrangements are directly linked to the primary activity of the business enterprise—what Lazonick and Shin (2020) refer to as predatory value extraction. Under managerial capitalism, with its emphasis on long-term economic growth and traditional labor relations as a means of being a going concern, enterprises generally followed a retain-and-reinvest strategy, where accumulated profits were used to generate new value-creating capabilities, retain workers, and generate shared economic prosperity (Lazonick 2010b; Minsky 1990; Minsky and Whalen 1996–1997; Wray 2009). As a financialized enterprise operating to maximize shareholder value, however, the going concern depends upon its ability to create value for shareholders. While traditional value-creation activities can and do generate these returns, they generally do so over a long time horizon. Shareholders—with their easily liquidated positions—may not have the patience necessary to wait for these projects to be completed (Haldane 2016).

The new structure of the TNC leads to value created by the peripheral nodes being extracted by core financial capital (Admati 2017; Serfati 2008; Zingales 2017). Rather than reinvest this value in capacity expansion, new employment, and other value-creating activities, the TNC uses it to reinforce its position through acquiring SPEs and intangible assets (to expand its extraction capabilities) and repurchasing shares to increase returns to absentee owners. Effectively, the TNC operates on a "downsize and distribute" model, shifting production activities to contracted third parties that are more easily shed and liquidated than if they were in house, and distributing the gains to shareholders rather than reinvesting in production:

> Even in blue-chip companies, whose management once built factories and market share, operating management becomes an endless series of cheap financial dodges: this year's target is met by ending the defined benefit pension scheme, which saves labor costs, and next year's dodge is leasing the trucks so that the capital appears on somebody else's balance sheet. (Froud et al. 2000, 19)

This institutional transformation has had an important impact on distribution. As shown below, falling capital investment, stagnant real wages, and increased income and wealth inequality are not simply side effects of financialization. They are a result of intentional decisions made by the TNC to swell shareholder value by engaging in predatory value extraction (Baranes 2017; Lazonick 2014a; Tulum and Lazonick 2018).

Distribution in a Financialized Economy

The changing structure of the business enterprise and the associated changes to labor relations have brought with them a change in income and wealth distribution, with the outcome favoring those at the top. Since 1980, median household income has lagged behind economic growth. While GDP per household has increased over 60 percent, real median household income has increased by approximately 20 percent, with much of this increase occurring from 1994 to 1999. In 1999, real median income peaked at $61,526; nearly 20 years later, it has increased to only $63,179, or an increase of 0.14 percent per year (Pressman and Scott 2020).[21] This stagnation is consistent with the trend of wages as a percent of value added for US nonfinancial corporations, shown in Figure 3.2. In 1960, wages comprised 65 percent of net value added. In 2013, after the Great Recession, they had fallen to 56 percent of value added. Since then, they have recovered as the economy recovered, reaching 59 percent in 2018, but are still below the levels reached in managerial capitalism. Shareholder distributions, however, have seen an opposite trend. In 1960, dividend payments were approximately 5.5 percent of net value added. By 2018, these had increased to approximately 9.6 percent.

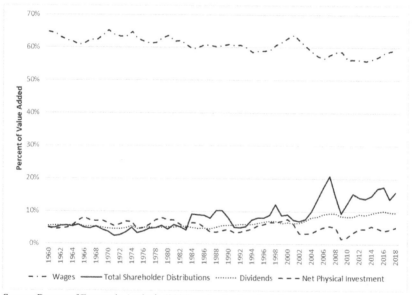

Source: Bureau of Economic Analysis (2020) and author's calculations.

Figure 3.2   *Distribution and investment as a percent of value added for US nonfinancial corporations, 1960–2018*

Dividend payments are only part of the distribution to shareholders; it is also important to address the rise of share repurchases. In 1982, the Securities and Exchange Commission (SEC) authorized Rule 10b-18, which allowed companies to repurchase their own common stock on the open market (SEC 2016). Since then, nonfinancial corporations have become net purchasers of equity, rather than net issuers (Lazonick 2015; Rubio 2019). If we combine dividends and share repurchases, as seen in Figure 3.3, we see that distributions to shareholders, while volatile, have increased throughout money manager capitalism, with much of the increase coming after the bursting of the dot-com bubble. In 2002, US nonfinancial corporations distributed 7 percent of net value added to shareholders. These distributions peaked at 20 percent, just before the Great Recession in 2007, but have since then comprised approximately 15 percent of net value added. It is worth noting that prior to 1984, distributions to shareholders were generally around 5 percent of net value added.

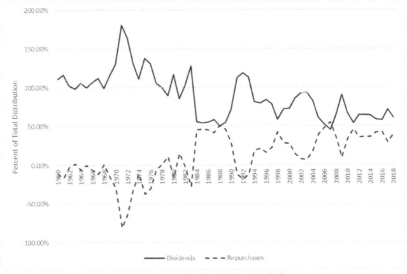

Source: Bureau of Economic Analysis (2020) and author's calculations.

Figure 3.3   *Breakdown of distributions to shareholders between dividends and share repurchases, 1960–2018*

The increased importance of share repurchases can be seen in the pattern of distributions to shareholders as well, seen in Figure 3.3. Between 1984 and 1990, stock repurchases accounted for approximately 43 percent of funds distributed to shareholders of US nonfinancial corporations before dipping during the recession of the early 1990s. Repurchases remained fairly low during the 1990s expansion, but saw a rise during the housing boom: between 2004 and 2007 share repurchases increased from 18 percent of distributions to 55 percent. Since 2010, share repurchases have comprised approximately 38 percent of distributions to shareholders. This prevalence of stock repurchases as a means of distributing funds to shareholders has important consequences for economic stability. An enterprise choosing to devote funds to share repurchases is simultaneously choosing not to devote those funds to wage increases, employment increases, or long-term growth-generating expansion.

The above is what is meant by predatory value extraction (Lazonick and Shin 2020). Enterprises divest themselves and reduce their investments in productive, value-generating capabilities, and use these savings to repurchase stock and swell shareholder value. This type of activity benefits primarily those who own stock, and this ownership is not evenly distributed. Edward Wolff, in his study of concentration in stock ownership, found that "despite the fact that almost half of all households owned stock shares, either directly or indirectly through mutual funds, trusts, or various pension accounts, the richest 10 percent of households controlled 84 percent of the total value of these stocks" (Wolff 2017, 19). As a result, income distribution has shifted to benefit top income earners while the bottom has suffered. Emmanuel Saez and Gabriel Zucman (2019) found that between 1978 and 2018, the bottom 50 percent of income earners saw their share of pre-tax national income fall from 20 percent to 12 percent; meanwhile, the top 1 percent of income earners saw their share rise from 11 percent to 20 percent in the same time period. Further, Saez and Zucman found that the bottom 50 percent of income earners—122 million adults—earned a pre-tax-and-transfer average income of $18,500 in 2019. That same year, the middle class, defined as including the 50th to 90th income percentiles, earned $75,000, while the upper-middle class and rich earned $220,000 and $1.5 million in average income, respectively. In the view of Saez and Zucman (2019, 5), "The striking fact about the American economy is not that the middle class is vanishing. It's how little income the working class makes."

Pavlina Tcherneva (2017) found that, prior to 1980, the majority of income growth (including capital gains) during business cycle expansions had gone to the bottom 99 percent of income earners. However, starting in the 1980s, the top 1 percent saw their size of the economic pie grow at a much larger rate, earning approximately 45 percent of income gained during the 1982–1990 and 1991–2000 expansions. During the 2001–2007 and post-Great Recession recoveries, approximately 75 percent and 55 percent of income gained (respectively) went to the top 1 percent. This supports research from Lonnie Golden (2012), who found that between 2002 and 2007, the top 1 percent of income earners saw a 10.1 percent annual income growth, while the other 99 percent saw 1.3 percent growth. Further, Tcherneva found that over the course of the business cycle, measured peak to peak, incomes for the bottom 90 percent of income earners actually fell in four of the last five cycles.[22] In other words, recovery and expansion are not being felt by the vast majority of households— they are unable to regain their incomes lost during the recession before the next one hits. "The rising tide no longer lifts most boats. Instead, the majority of gains go to a very small segment of the population" (Tcherneva 2017, 3).

Financialization, money manager capitalism, and the structure of the TNC may be recognized as a massive wealth and income redistribution from bottom to top. Value is created by the SPEs and appropriated by core capital, to be distributed to shareholders through share repurchases. The new labor relations that have emerged reflect this new form of enterprise organization and strategy and, as such, are not accidental or simply by-products—they are part and parcel of a financialized enterprise. In the next section, several policy proposals that could potentially move towards a solution are discussed.

PUBLIC POLICY FOR FINANCIALIZED LABOR

We now turn to what policy can do to begin to address the financialization of employment, and money manager capitalism in general. Goldman and Weil (2020) describe what they call a "concentric circle" approach—the main problem is that many workers in a financialized economy are treated as employees but classified as independent contractors. This allows the enterprise to cut them off from benefits and rights tied to employment, and reduces the bargaining power of labor in general. At the core of their proposed solutions— the innermost ring of the circle—are rights and benefits that should not be tied to employment, but to work itself. "These are workplace protections that have been recognized in both laws and judicial interpretations as fundamental and feasible to provide to all workers" (Goldman and Weil 2020, 3). This includes the right to be compensated for work, freedom from discrimination and retaliation, access to safe working environments, and other similar basic rights. The middle circle represents rights that are associated with the legal characteristics of employment. Under this approach, employment is the default position, "so unless employment is disproven for a particular set of workers, this set of workplace protections would apply" (Goldman and Weil 2020, 3). The goal of this circle, then, is to do away with the ability for employers to keep workers in their company at arm's length and push the responsibility of following workplace standards to third parties. Finally, the outer ring represents policies that make it easier for workers to access benefits that promote mobility and welfare. This involves making the same kinds of social contributions and providing the same kinds of benefits for all workers—including family leave and medical leave, retirement savings, job training, worker's compensation, and unemployment insurance—including those in alternative work arrangements.

The above framework recognizes the transformation of employment relations and focuses on bridging the gap between alternative and traditional arrangements. Incorporating the issues of financialization and the development of the TNC, a number of other policies can be implemented to recognize the structural reality of money manager capitalism and move beyond it. One important set of policies, discussed by Saez and Zucman (2019), would be changes to the tax code to incentivize production-based—rather than financial—activities. In their work, they show how changes to the tax code—primarily increases in the payroll tax, sharp cuts to tax rates paid by the top income bracket, and cuts to the corporate income tax—have disincentivized labor and promoted wealth hoarding through different treatments of capital gains and incomes. Rewriting the tax code to reverse this trend is an important part of correcting financialization.

One change would be to eliminate the cap on the payroll tax while lowering the rate at the bottom to promote a more equitable distribution of burdens and income.[23] Second, the imposition of a financial transactions tax could potentially curtail stock repurchases. Given the volume of these transactions, such a tax would not need to be especially large to be effective. For example, in 2018 and 2019, companies spent $806 billion and $727 billion respectively in stock repurchases (S&P Global 2020). Even a 1 percent tax would go a long way to incentivize enterprises to devote those funds to other means. Finally, a change to the capital gains tax, to recognize how company stock is used as a means of payment for upper management, is warranted. As mentioned above, the shareholder primacy theory of corporate governance required bringing shareholder and managerial interests in line, achieving this through stock-based compensation. As a result, stock-based compensation has become an important part of managers' pay.[24] When that stock is sold, the seller pays the capital gains tax on the income received, with the top tax rate on capital gains being less than the top tax rate on income (Saez and Zucman 2019). Therefore, a redesign of the capital gains tax—either by increasing the top tax rate or extending the length of time between the short-term and long-term capital gains tax—is necessary to change incentives.[25] Failure to do so is a failure to recognize the way in which incomes are earned at different income levels; any attempt to address income inequality without addressing this will be doomed to failure.

Many Post-Keynesian Institutionalists have pushed for the implementation of a job guarantee program, modeled after the Works Progress Administration of the New Deal.[26] At the most basic level, the job guarantee involves hiring anyone willing and able to work at a predetermined wage to complete public investment projects such as infrastructure rebuilding, creating public artwork, provide care work, and more. The funding for the program is federally granted, but implementation is conducted locally, as the community itself is most likely to know what it needs. While these proposals generally emphasize the way in which such a policy can be used in conjunction with policies to tackle issues such as climate change, I argue here that one of the key benefits of such a program is the way in which it addresses the effect of financialization on labor. Labor relations under the TNC operate as a branch of a larger network, where value is extracted by core capital and employment depends on the ability to generate returns to shareholders. A job guarantee program could detach labor from this TNC network and realign the labor process with the needs of the community as a whole.

Finally, a restructuring of the enterprise in a way that diminishes the shareholder primacy view of corporate governance is needed. William Lazonick (2010a; 2014b; 2016) has proposed his theory of innovative enterprise to directly challenge the financialized corporation. In this view, enterprises are social structures embedded within an institutional environment. As such, there is more investment in an enterprise than simply investment from shareholders. Workers, for example, invest when they undergo enterprise-specific training and have an interest in the reproduction of the enterprise as a going concern insofar as their livelihood is tied to the enterprise. The general public also invests in enterprises through the financing of scientific research and other public investment projects that allow the enterprises to generate profits by building on such investments, which Marianna Mazzucato refers to as "patient capital" that is often too costly and risky for an enterprise to undertake by itself (Mazzucato 2015; Mazzucato 2016). However, neither workers nor the general public have a say in the enterprise's use of retained earnings. "Financialization ... may be advancing the short-term interests for financial organizations and institutions, with only limited checks and balances available to other stakeholders in society" (Cutcher-Gershenfeld et al. 2015, 33). The theory of innovative enterprise proposes—at least as a first step—that boards of directors for public corporations include labor and public representatives to ensure that funds are directed toward long-run productive ends.

These proposals are not meant to be all encompassing or once-and-for-all fixes, but would go a long way to generating a new structure that lessens the influence of financialization in economic activity. For public policy to be successful in empowering labor and improving its standing, it must recognize the new enterprise structure of the financialized TNC under money manager capitalism, and the prevalence of financial motives and incentives therein.

CONCLUSION

From a Post-Keynesian Institutionalist approach, each stage of capitalism answers differently the questions of what is the distinctive economic activity being financed; what is the pivotal source of financing; where is the balance of power between business and banking; what is the dominant method of enterprise reproduction as a going concern; and who controls the community's capital? Under money manager capitalism, with its dominant form of enterprise as the TNC, these questions are answered to emphasize the power of shareholders as well as financial interests, motives, and institutions in governing economic activity. This chapter discussed the development of money manager capitalism from the perspective of PKI and emphasized the effect that it has had on labor relations. As argued here, the new institutional setting has transformed labor relations into a branch of the general network of the TNC organizational structure. This alternative arrangement allows value created by labor to be extracted by the TNC through alternative work arrangements, sub-contracting, and gig work—all designed to generate increased returns to shareholders.

This chapter fits within the broader literature on the impact of financialization upon global supply chains, as seen in Froud et al. (1996; 2002), Serfati (2008), and Baranes (2017), though the focus here has been on labor in this financialization process. It also fits within the broader literature on public policy, emphasizing the importance of structural improvements and the view that there is no "magic bullet" policy that will solve all problems forever: as institutions change, so too do appropriate policies for generating shared prosperity. Future research should expand upon these issues, developing more fully the issues of predatory value extraction as it pertains to global income and wealth inequality and potential productivity and innovation slowdowns. In doing so, solutions to help generate a new economic structure can be developed that will move the American economy beyond money manager capitalism and, ideally, into an era of broadly shared prosperity.

ACKNOWLEDGMENTS

The author would like to thank Glen Atkinson, Dave Zalewski, John Henry, and Charles Whalen for their helpful comments and feedback.

NOTES

1. The Economic Policy Institute measures productivity as net productivity, or the growth of output of goods and services less depreciation. Worker compensation is measured as the inflation-adjusted hourly compensation of the median worker (Economic Policy Institute 2019).
2. For an early examination of rising worker insecurity as a consequence of the drive for shareholder value, see Minsky and Whalen (1996–1997).
3. In this chapter, "financialization" refers to "a pattern of accumulation in which profits accrue primarily through financial channels, rather than through trade and commodity production" (Krippner 2005, 174). As a result, financial interests, motives, and institutions come to dominate economic decision-making (Palley 2007).
4. See Whalen (2001), Whalen (2008), Minsky (1988), Minsky and Whalen (1996–1997), and Wray (2009) for a more complete explanation of the stages of capitalism in Minsky's theory of capitalist development.

5.   The concept of the joint stock of knowledge refers to "The requisite knowledge and proficiency of ways and means ... of the life of the community at large" (Veblen 1908a, 519). While a full discussion of the topic is outside the purview of this chapter, more on the concept may be found in Ayres (1944), Lower (1987), Munkirs (1988), Hake (2007), and Baranes and Hake (2018).

6.   Capital owners represent the final claimants on the output produced by capital assets. Capital managers dictate how such assets will be used, though they may not be the final claimants on the output produced. Capital users represent those who operate the asset, though they may not be the ones dictating the use of those assets.

7.   It should be noted that while other forms of enterprise existed—such as joint-stock corporations—economic activity in the era of merchant capitalism was largely conducted by smaller merchants.

8.   Intangible property was legally recognized as property as a result of the Minnesota Rate Case in 1890, in which the Supreme Court ruled that the definition of property referred to the exchange-value of the physical thing in question, rather than the use-value (Commons [1924] 2007, 15–21). For more detailed discussions of the process whereby property rights provide owners with a way to capture economic returns generated by the community's joint stock of knowledge, see Baranes (2020); Commons ([1924] 2007); Commons ([1934] 2009); Dean (2018); Veblen ([1904] 2013); and Veblen (1908b).

9.   Commons identified three types of transactions: bargaining, which occurs between agents absent any form of hierarchical structure; managerial, which occurs between legal superiors and legal inferiors in the form of commands; and rationing, which occurs between collective action—such as the law or state—and members of the collective in the form of setting parameters within which economic activity may take place. In his own words: "Bargaining transactions transfer ownership of wealth by voluntary agreement between legal equals. Managerial transactions create wealth by commands of legal superiors. Rationing transactions apportion the burdens and benefits of wealth creation by the dictation of legal superiors" (Commons [1934] 2009, 68).

10. In 1800, it took six weeks to travel from New York to Chicago. In 1830, it took three weeks. By 1857, the trip could be done in two days (Chandler 1977).

11. As Veblen ([1904] 2013, 87) succinctly puts it:
     Under the old regime of handicraft and petty trade, dearth (high prices) meant privation and might mean famine; under the new regime low prices commonly mean privation and may on occasion mean famine. Under the old regime the question was whether the community's work was adequate to supply the community's needs; under the new regime that question is not seriously entertained.

12. Building on Commons and Minsky, Whalen (2001, 811) distinguishes an era of industrial capitalism from banker capitalism in that industrial capitalism first emphasized industrial expansion, whereas banker capitalism emphasized industrial consolidation.

13. The community consumes output; the capital users engage in production-based activities; the capital managers dictate the use of capital; and the capital owners act as the final claimants on output produced.

14. This included two oil shocks, heightened tensions between the United States and Soviet Union, and the emergence of Japanese competition (Snowdon and Vane 2005; Lazonick 2010a; Chang 2014).

15. This category includes money market fund shares, corporate equities, mutual fund shares, direct investment abroad, equity in government-sponsored enterprises, and investment in finance company subsidiaries.

16. Thorstein Veblen, John Commons, and John Maynard Keynes, at various points in their writings, have demonstrated this view. As mentioned above, when discussing industrial capitalism, Veblen ([1904] 2013, 87) claims: "Under the old regime [of handicraft and petty trade], the question was whether the community's work was adequate to supply the community's needs; under the new regime, that question is not seriously entertained." In a similar manner, Commons ([1934] 2009) discusses the transformation from what he calls the Age of Scarcity to the Age of Abundance, in which due to a lack of technical capabilities the physical control of output gives way to the legal control resulting from combinations and monopolizations in the marketplace. Keynes ([1930] 2015, 84) adds that the biggest problem of modern economic society is "the love of money as a possession—as distinguished from the love of money as a means to the enjoyments and realities of life." As he explains, this emerges out of a mindset in which the accumulation of wealth was paramount for social survival, which is not the society in which we currently live.

17. Of that 10.1 percent, 6.9 percentage points are independent contractors, 1.7 percentage points are on-call workers, 0.9 percentage points are temporary help agency workers, and 0.6 percentage points are workers provided by contract firms (BLS 2018).

18. The BLS has several ways of defining contingent labor. The 3.8 percent refers to workers who do not expect their jobs to last. This measure includes wage and salary workers who have held their job for more than one year and expect to hold their job for an additional year; BLS analyses of labor markets and contingent labor focus on this definition (BLS 2018).

19. A prime example of the effect of private equity on economic activity is the Toys 'R' Us experience. Purchased by private equity in 2005, it was immediately saddled with more than $5 billion in debt, with interest payments consuming 97 percent of their operating profit by 2007. As a result, the company was unable to innovate or adapt in the face of the Great Recession and declared bankruptcy in 2017, leading to 7,000 stores closed and 50,000 jobs eliminated (Covert 2018).

20. In their survey of workers with contingent or alternative work arrangements, the BLS found that independent contractors seemed to prefer the alternative arrangement (BLS 2018). Indeed, research has found a link between the amount of flexibility one has in one's work schedule and one's overall happiness (Okulicz-Kozaryn and Golden 2018). From this perspective, gig work and alternative work arrangements seem like a trade-off—the pay is lower, but the workers make up for it in terms of flexibility and control over scheduling. However, it is important to qualify these results in two important ways. Mas and Pallais (2017) found that when workers are given a choice between jobs, they place little value on flexible options—they are willing to take a $0.48-per-hour pay cut to set their own schedule, but are not willing to give up any pay at all to set their own number of hours. Lonnie Golden (2001) found, furthermore, that there were inequities in terms of who is actually able to set their own schedule. Workers in higher skilled, lower unemployment occupations and industries were more likely to have access to flexible schedules, while those with less education and training were less likely to have these options. Without accounting for differences in preferences or controlling for skills, the blanket claim that alternative

work arrangements are preferred due to schedule flexibility seems to be a stretch (Skalski 2002; Kessler 2018).

21. Pressman and Scott (2020) argue that, given how the government measures real median income, these numbers are actually overstating incomes. Rather than increasing, they argue that real median incomes and household living standards have actually fallen since 1999.

22. The exception was the 1990–2000 cycle.

23. In 2019, the payroll tax was capped at $132,900, meaning any dollar earned above that amount was not subject to the tax—a benefit to only the top 5 percent of income earners.

24. This helps explain the prevalence of $1 salaries for CEOs of large companies—their compensation comes from the stock options and other forms of stock-based compensation they receive (Herbst 2007; Mayerowitz 2008).

25. The time to switch between the short-term and long-term capital gains tax is one year, at which point the top tax rate falls from 35 percent to 20 percent.

26. For a sampling of this literature, see for example Minsky (1965; [1986] 2008), Wray (2015; 2016), Spross (2017), Nersisyan and Wray (2019), Whalen (2019), Tcherneva (2020), and Kelton (2020).

REFERENCES

Admati, Anat R. 2017. "A Skeptical View of Financialized Corporate Governance." *Journal of Economic Perspectives* 31 (3): 131–150.

Atkinson, Glen and Stephen P. Paschall. 2016. *Law and Economics from an Evolutionary Perspective*. Northampton, MA: Edward Elgar Publishing.

Ayres, Clarence E. 1944. *The Theory of Economic Progress*. New York: Schocken Books.

Ayres, Clarence E. 1952. "The Role of Technology in Economic Theory." *The American Economic Review* 43 (2): 279–287.

Baranes, Avraham I. 2017. "Financialization in the American Pharmaceutical Industry: A Veblenian Approach." *Journal of Economic Issues* 51 (2): 351–358.

Baranes, Avraham I. 2020. "Intangible Assets and the Financialized Business Enterprise: A Veblen-Commons Approach." *Journal of Economic Issues* 54 (3): 692–709.

Baranes, Avraham I. and Eric R. Hake. 2018. "The Institutionalist Theory of Capital in the Modern Business Enterprise: Appropriation and Financialization." *Journal of Economic Issues* 52 (2): 351–358.

Batt, Rosemary and Eileen Appelbaum. 2015. "Investors as Managers: How Private Equity Firms Manage Labor and Employment Relations." In *Inequality, Uncertainty, and Opportunity: The Varied and Growing Role of Finance in Labor Relations*, edited by Christian Weller, 197–224. New York: Cornell University Press.

Berle, Adolf A. and Gardiner C. Means. (1932) 2009. *The Modern Corporation and Private Property*. New Brunswick: Transaction Publishers.

Bronfenbrenner, Kate. 2000. "Raw Power: Plant-Closing Threats and the Threat to Union Organizing." *Multinational Monitor* 21 (12): 24–29.

Bronfenbrenner, Kate and Stephanie Luce. 2004. "Offshoring: The Evolving Profile of Corporate Global Restructuring." *Multinational Monitor* 25 (12): 26–29.

Bureau of Economic Analysis. 2020. "Integrated Macroeconomic Accounts." https://www.bea.gov/data/special-topics/integrated-macroeconomic-accounts. Accessed October 27, 2020.

Bureau of Labor Statistics (BLS). 2018. "Contingent and Alternative Employment Arrangements Summary." June 7, 2018. https://www.bls.gov/news.release/conemp .nr0.htm. Accessed October 27, 2020.

Bush, Paul D. 1983. "An Exploration of the Structural Characteristics of a Veblen-Ayres-Foster Defined Institutional Domain." *Journal of Economic Issues* 17 (1): 35–66.

Bush, Paul D. 1987. "The Theory of Institutional Change." *Journal of Economic Issues* 21 (3): 1075–1116.

Chandler, Alfred D. 1977. *The Visible Hand: The Managerial Revolution in American Business*. Cambridge: Harvard University Press.

Chandler, Alfred D. 1990. *Scale and Scope: The Dynamics of Industrial Capitalism*. Cambridge: Harvard University Press.

Chang, Ha-Joon. 2014. *Economics: The User's Guide*. London: Bloomsbury Publishing.

Commons, John R. (1924) 2007. *Legal Foundations of Capitalism*. New Brunswick: Transaction Publishers.

Commons, John R. (1934) 2009. *Institutional Economics: Its Place in Political Economy*. New Brunswick: Transaction Publishers.

Covert, Bryce. 2018. "The Demise of Toys 'R' Us Is a Warning." *The Atlantic* (July/August). https://www.theatlantic.com/magazine/archive/2018/07/toys-r-us -bankruptcy-private-equity/561758/>. Accessed October 27, 2020.

Cutcher-Gershenfeld, Joel, Dan Brooks, Noel Cowell, Christos A. Ioannou, Martin Mulloy, Danny Roberts, Tanzia S. Saunders, and Soren Viemose. 2015. "Financialization, Collective Bargaining, and the Public Interest." In *Inequality, Uncertainty, and Opportunity: The Varied and Growing Role of Finance in Labor Relations*, edited by Christian Weller, 31–56. New York: Cornell University Press.

Davis, Leila E. 2016. "Identifying the 'Financialization' of the Nonfinancial Corporation in the U.S. Economy: A Decomposition of Firm-Level Balance Sheets." *Journal of Post Keynesian Economics* 39 (1): 115–141.

Davis, Leila E. 2018. "Financialization, Shareholder Orientation and the Cash Holdings of US Corporations." *Review of Political Economy* 30 (1): 1–27.

Dean, Erik. 2018. "The Going Enterprise Paradox: Stability and Instability Under Money Manager Capitalism." *Journal of Economic Issues* 52 (4): 1084–1108.

Economic Policy Institute (EPI). 2019. "The Productivity-Pay Gap." *Economic Policy Institute*. https://www.epi.org/productivity-pay-gap/. Accessed October 27, 2020.

Eichner, Alfred S. 1976. *The Megacorp and Oligopoly: Micro Foundations of Macro Dynamics*. New York: Cambridge University Press.

Eichner, Alfred S. 1983. "The Micro Foundations of the Corporate Economy." *Managerial and Decision Economics* 4 (3): 136–152.

Epstein, Gerald A. 2002. "Financialization, Rentier Interests, and Central Bank Policy." Political Economy Research Institute, University of Massachusetts, Amherst. https:// www.peri.umass.edu/publication/item/77-financialization-rentier-interests-and -central-bank-policy. Accessed October 27, 2020.

Fama, Eugene F. and Michael C. Jensen. 1983. "Separation of Ownership and Control." *Journal of Law and Economics* 26 (2): 301–325.

Friedman, Milton. 1970. "The Social Responsibility of Business is to Increase its Profits." *The New York Times Magazine* (September). https://www.nytimes.com/ 1970/09/13/archives/a-friedman-doctrine-the-social-responsibility-of-business-is-to .html. Accessed October 20, 2020.

Froud, Julie, Colin Haslam, Sukhdev Johal, and Karel Williams. 2000. "Shareholder Value and Financialization: Consultancy Promises, Management Moves." *Economy and Society* 29 (1): 80–110.

Froud, Julie, Colin Haslam, Sukhdev Johal, and Karel Williams. 2002. "Cars after Financialisation: A Case Study in Financial Under-Performance, Constraints, and Consequences." *Competition and Change* 6 (1): 13–41.

Froud, Julie, Colin Haslam, Sukhdev Johal, Jean Shaoul, and Karel Williams. 1996. "Stakeholder Economy? From Utility Privatisation to New Labour." *Capital and Class* 20 (3): 119–134.

Galbraith, John K. 1967. *The New Industrial State*. Boston: Houghton Mifflin.

Golden, Lonnie. 2001. "Flexible Work Schedules: What Are We Trading Off to Get Them?" *Monthly Labor Review* 124 (3): 50–67.

Golden, Lonnie. 2009. "A Brief History of Long Work Time and the Contemporary Sources of Overwork." *Journal of Business Ethics* 84 (2): 217–227.

Golden, Lonnie. 2012. "Becoming Too Small to Bail? Prospects for Workers in the 2011 Economy and 112th Congress." *Indiana Law Journal* 87 (1): 11–42.

Golden, Lonnie and Deborah Figart. 2000. "Doing Something About Long Hours." *Challenge* 43 (6): 15–37.

Goldman, Tanya and David Weil. 2020. "Who's Responsible Here? Establishing Legal Responsibility in the Fissured Workplace." *Institute for New Economic Thinking Working Paper* No. 114. https://www.ineteconomics.org/uploads/papers/WP_114 -Goldman-Weil.pdf . Accessed October 27, 2020.

Goldschmidt, Deborah and Johannes F. Schmieder. 2015. "The Rise of Domestic Outsourcing and the Evolution of the German Wage Structure." *NBER Working Paper* No. 21366. https://www.nber.org/papers/w21366. Accessed October 27, 2020.

Greer, Douglas F. 1992. *Industrial Organization and Public Policy*, 3rd edition. New York: Macmillan.

Hake, Eric R. 2007. "Capital and the Modern Corporation." In *Thorstein Veblen and the Revival of Free Market Capitalism*, edited by Janet T. Knoedler, Robert E. Prasch, and Dell P. Champlin, 31–61. Northampton, MA: Edward Elgar Publishing.

Haldane, Andrew G. 2016. "The Costs of Short-Termism." In *Re-Thinking Capitalism: Economics and Policy for Sustainable and Inclusive Growth*, edited by Michael Jacobs and Mariana Mazzucato, 66–76. West Sussex: Wiley-Blackwell.

Heilbroner, Robert L. and William Milberg. 2012. *The Making of Economic Society*, 13th edition. London: Pearson.

Heilbroner, Robert L. and Aaron Singer. 1994. *The Economic Transformation of America: 1600 to the Present*. New York: Harcourt Brace.

Herbst, Moira. 2007. "The Elite Circle of $1 CEOs." Bloomberg News, September 17. https://www.bloomberg.com/news/articles/2007-09-14/the-elite-circle-of-1 -ceosbusinessweek-business-news-stock-market-and-financial-advice. Accessed October 27, 2020.

Jensen, Michael C. 1986. "Agency Cost of Free Cash Flow, Corporate Finance, and Takeovers." *American Economic Review* 76 (2): 323–329.

Jensen, Michael C. and William H. Meckling. 1976. "The Theory of the Firm: Managerial Behavior, Agency Costs, and Ownership Structure." *Journal of Financial Economics* 3 (4): 305–360.

Jo, Tae-Hee. 2019. "The Institutionalist Theory of the Business Enterprise: Past, Present, and Future." *Journal of Economic Issues* 53 (3): 597–611.

Jo, Tae-Hee and John F. Henry. 2015. "The Business Enterprise in the Age of Money Manager Capitalism." *Journal of Economic Issues* 49 (1): 23–46.

Kelton, Stephanie. 2020. *The Deficit Myth: Modern Monetary Theory and the Birth of the People's Economy.* New York: Public Affairs Books.

Kessler, Sarah. 2018. *Gigged: The End of the Job and the Future of Work.* New York: St. Martin's Press.

Keynes, John M. (1930) 2015. "Economic Possibilities for our Grandchildren." In *John Maynard Keynes: The Essential Keynes*, edited by Robert Skidelsky, 75–86. London: Penguin Books.

Keynes, John M. (1936) 1964. *The General Theory of Employment, Interest and Money.* New York: Harcourt Brace and Company.

Krippner, Greta R. 2005. "The Financialization of the American Economy." *Socio-Economic Review* 3 (2): 173–208.

Krippner, Greta R. 2011. *Capitalizing on Crisis: The Political Origins of the Rise of Finance.* Cambridge: Harvard University Press.

Lapavitsas, Costas. 2013. "The Financialization of Capitalism: 'Profiting Without Producing'. *City* 17 (6): 792–805.

Lazonick, William. 2008. "The Quest for Shareholder Value: Stock Repurchases and the U.S. Economy." *Louvian Economic Review* 74 (4): 479–540.

Lazonick, William. 2010a. "The Chandlerian Corporation and the Theory of Innovative Enterprise." *Industrial and Corporate Change* 19 (2): 317–349.

Lazonick, William. 2010b. "Innovative Business Models and Varieties of Capitalism: Financialization of the U.S. Corporation." *Business History Review* 84 (4): 675–702.

Lazonick, William. 2013. "The Financialization of the U.S. Corporation: What Has Been Lost, and How It Can Be Regained." *Seattle University Law Review* 36 (2): 857–909.

Lazonick, William. 2014a. "Profits Without Prosperity." *Harvard Business Review* 92 (September): 47–55.

Lazonick, William. 2014b. "The Innovative Enterprise and Shareholder Value." *Law and Financial Markets Review* 8 (1): 52–64.

Lazonick, William. 2015. "Labor in the 21st Century: The Top 0.1 percent and the Disappearing Middle Class." In *Inequality, Uncertainty, and Opportunity: The Varied and Growing Role of Finance in Labor Relations*, edited by Christian Weller, 143–196. New York: Cornell University Press.

Lazonick, William. 2016. "Innovative Enterprise and the Theory of the Firm." In *Re-Thinking Capitalism: Economics and Policy for Sustainable and Inclusive Growth*, edited by Michael Jacobs and Mariana Mazzucato, 77–93. West Sussex: Wiley-Blackwell.

Lazonick, William. 2017. "The New Normal is 'Maximizing Shareholder Value': Predatory Value Extraction, Slowing Productivity, and the Vanishing American Middle Class." *International Journal of Political Economy* 46 (4): 217–226.

Lazonick, William and Mary O'Sullivan. 2000. "Maximizing Shareholder Value: A New Ideology for Corporate Governance." *Economy and Society* 29 (1): 13–35.

Lazonick, William and Jang-Sup Shin. 2020. *Predatory Value Extraction: How the Looting of the Business Corporation Became the US Norm and How Sustainable Prosperity Can be Restored.* New York: Oxford University Press.

Lee, Fred S. 1999. *Post Keynesian Price Theory.* New York: Cambridge University Press.

Lee, Fred S. 2012. "Competition, Going Enterprise, and Economic Activity." In *Alternative Theories of Competition: Challenges to the Orthodoxy*, edited by Jamee K. Moudud, Cyrus Bina, and Patrick L. Mason, 160–173. London: Routledge.

Lower, Milton D. 1987. "The Concept of Technology Within the Institutionalist Perspective." *Journal of Economic Issues* 21 (3): 1147–1176.

Mas, Alexandre and Amanda Pallais. 2017. "Valuing Alternative Work Arrangements." *American Economic Review* 107 (12): 3722–3759.

Mayerowitz, Scott. 2008. "The Other Side of the $1 Salary." ABC News, November 28. https://abcnews.go.com/Business/Economy/story?id=6378775andpage=1. Accessed October 27, 2020.

Mazzucato, Mariana. 2015. *The Entrepreneurial State: Debunking Public vs. Private Sector Myths*. New York: Anthem Press.

Mazzucato, Mariana. 2016. "Innovation, the State, and Patient Capital." In *Re-Thinking Capitalism: Economics and Policy for Sustainable and Inclusive Growth*, edited by Michael Jacobs and Mariana Mazzucato, 98–118. West Sussex: Wiley-Blackwell.

Minsky, Hyman P. 1965. "The Role of Employment Policy." *Hyman P. Minsky Archive*, Paper 270. https://www.bard.edu/library/archive/minsky/. Accessed October 27, 2020.

Minsky, Hyman P. (1975) 2008. *John Maynard Keynes*. New York: McGraw Hill.

Minsky, Hyman P. (1986) 2008. *Stabilizing an Unstable Economy*. New York: McGraw Hill.

Minsky, Hyman P. 1988. "Schumpeter, Finance, and Evolution." *Hyman P. Minsky Archive*, Paper 314. https://www.bard.edu/library/archive/minsky/. Accessed October 27, 2020.

Minsky, Hyman P. 1990. "Schumpeter: Finance and Evolution." In *Evolving Technology and Market Structure*, edited by Arnold Heertje and Mark Perlman, 51–74. Ann Arbor: University of Michigan Press.

Minsky, Hyman P. and Charles Whalen. 1996–1997. "Economic Insecurity and the Institutional Prerequisites for Successful Capitalism." *Journal of Post Keynesian Economics* 19 (2): 155–170.

Mojtehedzadeh, Sara. 2018. "This Temp Agency Worker Shows Up at the Same Office Every Day. But His Agency Says He's Not a Real Employee." *The Star*, May 11. https://www.thestar.com/news/gta/2018/05/11/this-temp-agency-worker-shows-up -at-the-same-office-every-day-but-his-agency-says-hes-not-a-real-employee.html. Accessed October 27, 2020.

Munkirs, John R. 1985. *The Transformation of American Capitalism: From Competitive Market Structures to Centralized Private Sector Planning*. Armonk, NY: M.E. Sharpe.

Munkirs, John R. 1988. "The Dichotomy: Views of a Fifth Generation Institutionalist." *Journal of Economic Issues* 22 (4): 1035–1044.

Munkirs, John R. and Janet T. Knoedler. 1987. "The Existence and Exercise of Corporate Power: An Opaque Fact." *Journal of Economic Issues* 21 (4): 1679–1709.

Nersisyan, Yeva and L. Randall Wray. 2019. "How to Pay for the Green New Deal." *Levy Economics Institute of Bard College Working Paper* No. 931.

Okulicz-Kozaryn, Adam and Lonnie Golden. 2018. "Happiness is Flextime." *Applied Research Quality of Life* 13 (2): 355–369.

Palley, Thomas I. 2007. "Financialization: What It Is and Why It Matters." *Levy Economics Institute of Bard College Working Paper* No. 525.

Peetz, David. 2018. "The Labour Share, Power and Financialisation." *Journal of Australian Political Economy* No. 81 (Winter): 33–51.

Pressman, Steven and Robert Scott. 2020. "Debt and the Well-Being of United States Households." Paper Presented at the Allied Social Sciences Association Annual Meeting, January 5, 2020. Available at https://tinyurl.com/d7s63p6d. Accessed July 26, 2021.

Ranson, Baldwin. 1987. "The Institutionalist Theory of Capital Formation." *Journal of Economic Issues* 21 (3): 1265–1278.

Rohan, Shannon and Mike Musuraca. 2018. "Accounting for Fissured Workforces: Why We Need Disclosure that Accounts for the Entire Employment Footprint." Responsible Investor, June 14. https://www.responsible-investor.com/articles/share -article. Accessed October 27, 2020.

Rubio, Marco. 2019. *American Investment in the 21st Century: Project for Strong Labor Markets and National Development.* https://www.rubio.senate.gov/public/_cache/files/9f25139a-6039-465a-9cf1-feb5567aebb7/4526E9620A9A7DB74267AB EA5881022F.5.15.2019.-final-project-report-american-investment.pdf. Accessed October 27, 2020.

S&P Global. 2020. "S&P 500 Buybacks Up 3.2 percent in Q4 2019; Full Year 2019 Down 9.6 percent from Record 2018, as Companies Brace for a More Volatile 2020." S&P Global, March 24. http://press.spglobal.com/2020-03-24-S-P -500-buybacks-up-3-2-in-Q4-2019-Full-Year-2019-down-9-6-from-record-2018-as -companies-brace-for-a-more-volatile-2020. Accessed October 27, 2020.

Saez, Emmanuel and Gabriel Zucman. 2019. *The Triumph of Injustice: How the Rich Dodge Taxes and How to Make Them Pay.* New York: W.W. Norton and Company.

Securities and Exchange Commission (SEC). 2016. "Division of Trading and Markets: Answers to Frequently Asked Questions Concerning Rule 10b-18 ("Safe Harbor" for Issuer Repurchases)." *U.S. Securities and Exchange Commission.* https://www.sec .gov/divisions/marketreg/r10b18faq0504.htm. Accessed October 27, 2020.

Serfati, Claude. 2008. "Financial Dimensions of Transnational Corporations, Global Value Chain, and Technological Innovation." *Journal of Innovation Economics* 1 (2): 35–61.

Serfati, Claude and Catherine Sauviat. 2019. "Global Supply Chains and Intangible Assets in the Automotive and Aeronautical Industries." *International Labour Organization Working Paper* No. 43. https://tinyurl.com/4p5x6jrs. Accessed July 27, 2021.

Skalski, Nicole. 2002. "Explaining the Wage Gap Between Contingent and Non-Contingent Workers." *The Park Place Economist* 10 (1): 21–29.

Snowdon, Brian and Howard R. Vane. 2005. *Modern Macroeconomics: Its Origins, Development, and Current State.* Northampton, MA: Edward Elgar Publishing.

Spross, Jeff. 2017. "You're Hired!" *Democracy* 44 (Spring). https://www .democracyjournal.org/magazine/44/youre-hired/. Accessed October 27, 2020.

Tcherneva, Pavlina R. 2017. "Inequality Update: Who Gains When Income Grows?" *Levy Economics Institute of Bard College Policy Note*, 2017/1. Annandale-on-Hudson, NY: Levy Economics Institute.

Tcherneva, Pavlina R. 2020. *The Case for a Job Guarantee.* Hoboken, NJ: John Wiley and Sons.

Tulum, Oner and William Lazonick. 2018. "Financialized Corporations in a National Innovation System: The U.S. Pharmaceutical Industry." *International Journal of Political Economy* 47 (3–4): 281–316.

Veblen, Thorstein B. (1904) 2013. *The Theory of Business Enterprise.* Mansfield Centre: Martino Publishing.

Veblen, Thorstein B. 1908a. "On the Nature of Capital." *Quarterly Journal of Economics* 22 (4): 517–542.

Veblen, Thorstein B. 1908b. "On the Nature of Capital: Investments, Intangible Assets, and the Pecuniary Magnate." *Quarterly Journal of Economics* 23 (1): 104–136.

Veblen, Thorstein B. (1923) 2009. *Absentee Ownership*. New Brunswick: Transaction Publishers.

Weil, David. 2014. *The Fissured Workplace: Why Work Became So Bad for So Many and What Can Be Done to Improve It.* Cambridge: Harvard University Press.

Weil, David. 2017. "Millennials Aren't the Problem. The Transformed Workplace Is." *Huffington Post*, December 14. https://www.huffpost.com/entry/millennial -employees-arent-the-problem_b_5a317838e4b091ca2684ed54. Accessed October 27, 2020.

Whalen, Charles J. 2001. "Integrating Schumpeter and Keynes: Hyman Minsky's Theory of Capitalist Development." *Journal of Economic Issues* 35 (4): 805–823.

Whalen, Charles J. 2008. "Post-Keynesian Institutionalism and the Anxious Society." In *Alternative Institutional Structures: Evolution and Impact*, edited by Sandra S. Batie and Nicholas Mercuro, 273–299. London: Routledge.

Whalen, Charles J. 2019. "Institutional Economics and Chock-Full Employment: Reclaiming the 'Right to Work' as a Cornerstone of Progressive Capitalism." *Journal of Economic Issues* 53: 321–340.

Wolff, Edward N. 2017. "Household Wealth Trends in the United States, 1962 to 2016: Has Middle Class Wealth Recovered?" *NBER Working Paper* No. 24085. https:// www.nber.org/w24085. Accessed October 27, 2020.

Wray, L. Randall. 2009. "The Rise and Fall of Money Manager Capitalism: A Minskyan Approach." *Cambridge Journal of Economics* 33 (4): 807–828.

Wray, L. Randall. 2015. *Modern Money Theory: A Primer on Macroeconomics for Sovereign Monetary Systems*, 2nd edition. New York: Palgrave Macmillan.

Wray, L. Randall. 2016. "The Reality of the Present and the Challenge of the Future: J. Fagg Foster for the Twenty-First Century." *Journal of Economic Issues* 50 (1): 245–268.

Zingales, Luigi. 2017. "Towards a Political Theory of the Firm." *Journal of Economic Perspectives* 31 (3): 113–130.

4. Money manager capitalism and the coronavirus pandemic

Yan Liang and Charles J. Whalen

INTRODUCTION

The COVID-19 pandemic has shaken the world economy and triggered one of the worst economic downturns in United States (US) history. As of writing this (May 2021), the pandemic has sickened 33 million people in the United States and claimed 587,000 lives across the country; cases continue to rise at a rate of over 25,000 per day (Johns Hopkins University 2021). At the height of the pandemic and economic lockdown, 40 million American workers filed for unemployment benefits (*New York Times* 2021). Total nonfarm employment fell by a staggering 20.5 million jobs in April 2020, largely erasing the gains from a decade of job growth (US Bureau of Labor Statistics 2020). The pandemic ended a record-setting 128-month economic expansion, and gross domestic product (GDP) contracted by 3.4 percent in 2020 (US Bureau of Economic Analysis 2022). While federal financial assistance helped keep the economy afloat and a rollout of vaccines facilitated the recovery, there were still 8.2 million fewer jobs on private and government payrolls in April 2021 than in February 2020 (US Bureau of Labor Statistics 2021a). The US economy is far from out of the woods.

It is shocking how the United States was so ill prepared to prevent and combat the pandemic and its economic fallout. Although a lack of competent leadership exacerbated the severity of the economic crisis, fundamental short-comings of the current economic era have been major contributing factors to the overall problem. That era is described by Post-Keynesian Institutionalists as money manager capitalism (MMC).

The chapter begins with an overview of MMC, including its origins, development, and key features. We explain that although MMC is now largely a global phenomenon, it originated in the United States, evolving from the economic framework in place during the early decades following World War II—a period often called the era of managerial capitalism—and emerging in the early 1980s. MMC's features include: (1) institutional investors (money managers) dictate the processes of finance and industry with the objective of maximizing short-term stock-market values; (2) the flip side of attention to shareholder value is rising worker insecurity and inequality; and (3) money managers influence policymaking in ways that not only intensify the underlying economic trends but also contribute to the emergence of what James K. Galbraith (2008) describes as the "predator" state. That section of the chapter will also highlight the compatibility of MMC and what many scholars call financialization.

The chapter then identifies four dimensions of the coronavirus crisis as experienced in the United States—and traces each to fundamental shortcomings of MMC. One is inadequate industrial capacity, which can be traced to a single-minded focus on shareholder value, a preference for financial innovation over technological capabilities, and relentless cost cutting (leading, for example, to downsizing, outsourcing, offshoring, and just-in-time production). Another is working families' financial distress, which is associated with the spreading economic insecurity and inequality that has accompanied the pursuit of ever-expanding shareholder value (which appears in various forms, including the so-called gig economy and the profit-driven healthcare system). A third dimension is corporate vulnerability to sudden economic changes, which is linked to MMC's tendency toward debt financing (used increasingly to beef-up stock values) and financial fragility. Finally, the dysfunctional public-sector safety net (including the federal government's inability to plan for and effectively manage the coronavirus crisis) is attributable to the influence of financialization upon policymaking and public administration.

The chapter closes by stressing that it will not be easy to fix the shortcomings of MMC that the pandemic has exposed. That's because (as was the case with the 2007–2009 global financial crisis and subsequent Great Recession) the revealed shortcomings are actually core features of the system. Thus, we conclude not merely by identifying some important aspects of an agenda for public-policy reform, but also by addressing some of the challenges that must be confronted on the road from MMC to an age of broadly shared prosperity.

MMC: ORIGINS, DEVELOPMENT, AND KEY FEATURES

From the mid-1980s, Hyman Minsky keenly investigated the stage of capitalist development in which institutional investors—holders of the largest share of US corporate stocks and bonds by the end of that decade—began to exert their influence on financial markets and business enterprises. This stage of capitalism began to take shape in the United States in the decades after World War II and emerged in the 1980s as what Minsky (1990, 60) called the era of managed money. Minsky was concerned about the fragile financial structure in MMC that made the economy susceptible to financial crises. Further, he believed that the level of private investment would not be sufficient to consistently (or even regularly) produce full employment, and that the composition of that investment would not be conducive to generating dynamic technological development (Minsky 1990; 1992; 1993). The past three decades of MMC's development in the United States—and its spread worldwide—have demonstrated Minsky's foresight (Whalen 2012; 2020a).[1]

Over the past several decades, institutional investors have accounted for a large and increasing share of financial assets in the United States. In 2017, institutional investors' share of ownership of total financial assets accounted for 78.1 percent of the Russell 3000 and 80.3 percent of the Standard & Poor's (S&P) 500 (Pensions&Investments 2017).[2] Moreover, the oversized ownership share of institutional investors elevates their power and influence in the financial and non-financial sectors, and in the realm of public policy. For example, money managers have promoted financial innovations and financial-market deregulation, which eventually caused the global economic crisis of 2007–2009 (Wray 2009).[3] Some observers argued that the 2007–2009 crisis would result in the fall of MMC, but money managers are alive and well; they continue to dominate the financial system and exert great influence on the "real" (productive) side of the economy.

As emphasized in the research of Minsky and his followers, when institutional investors become the effective owners of listed companies, their financial incentives drive corporate governance and business behavior (Minsky 1993; Whalen 2020a). Institutional investors compete (and are compensated) on the basis of short-term performance; thus, they are "especially sensitive to the current stock market valuation of a firm" (Minsky 1996). Describing the emergence of MMC, Charles Whalen (2020a, 186) writes:

> Money managers certainly felt the pressure of the near term—as investors' resources migrated to the most successful fund managers—but so did corporate executives. The growing influence of money managers forced business leaders to become increasingly focused on quarterly profits and the stock-market value of their corporations—in other words, on shareholder value.[4]

The influence of institutional investors has several major consequences for the governance and behavior of corporations. First, corporations tend to shorten their investment horizons, as long-term investments generally do not boost short-term stock valuations.[5] Second, corporations exhibit "an almost chronic need" to downsize and pursue workplace flexibility (Minsky 1996, 363); means to this end have included outsourcing and offshoring as well as the introduction of "alternative" work arrangements characterized by unstable schedules and income volatility. Third, corporations are "addicted" to mergers and acquisitions, corporate breakups, leveraged buyouts, and stock buybacks, all of which aim to boost short-term portfolio values. Fourth, corporations tend to rely more on debt financing than equity issuance, as debt financing is less costly and does not dilute ownership benefits. Fifth, managed money provides the financing resources that corporate raiders need to secure corporate control (Atkinson and Whalen 2011; Whalen 2020a).

Such corporate behavior has, in turn, resulted in rising insecurity among workers. As corporations take on various cost-cutting strategies, jobs become increasingly scarce and precarious; wages and benefits are cut; and unions and other worker organizations are disempowered. Income and wealth inequality widen, and household debt mounts (Whalen 2020a).[6]

Another consequence of the rise of managed money is a reshaped public sector. Institutional investors exert influence on government policymakers that often results in business tax cuts and deregulation—of financial markets, corporations, and entire industries (such as electric power)—at the expense of the general welfare. Moreover, a fear of "bond market vigilantes" is used to justify cuts to public spending for the purpose of offsetting tax cuts and balancing government budgets (or at least reducing budget deficits) (Galbraith 2008; Whalen 2008, 286).

From the perspective of Post-Keynesian Institutionalism, these public-sector developments are evidence of "predatory" policymaking that has little regard for the public interest and instead caters to those seeking to use the state to advance private interests. In the era of MMC, those with financial power have not merely reshaped corporations; they have also exerted power on both Republicans and Democrats to refashion public policy (and policy discussions) to their own ends. Instead of the "new industrial state" that supported industrial growth and development in the era of managerial capitalism, the current era is characterized by the largely finance-driven "predator state" (Galbraith 2008, 126–148).[7]

While Minsky and Post-Keynesian Institutionalists have written about MMC since it first emerged, many other economists and social scientists have been writing for a couple of decades about what they call *financialization*. That literature describes a trend that has much in common with the features and consequences of what we call MMC. For example, Gerald Epstein (2005, 3) defines financialization as "the increasing role of financial motives, financial markets, financial actors, and financial institutions in the operation of the domestic and international economies;" and Thomas Palley (2007, 3) argues that the principal effects of financialization are to "elevate the significance of the financial sector relative to the real sector; transfer income from the real sector to the financial sector; and contribute to increased income ine-quality and wage stagnation."[8] All of this is consistent with Post-Keynesian Institutionalists' conception of MMC.[9]

MMC AFTER THE GLOBAL FINANCIAL CRISIS

Since the global financial crisis of 2007–2009, the aforementioned economic changes and consequences have accelerated, placing the US economy in a highly vulnerable position when the pandemic hit in 2020. This section provides a closer look at those aspects of MMC and explains how each contributed to the economic fallout triggered by the coronavirus pandemic.

Corporate Behavior: Outsourcing and Offshoring, Stock Buybacks, and Mergers and Acquisitions

As described above, MMC is characterized by the rise of managed money that influences all sectors of the economy. Managed money investment firms are often highly leveraged, pursue maximum total returns (income flows plus capital gains), and do so in an environment that systematically underprices risk (Wray 2009). Moreover, their motives are passed from the investment world to the broader corporate sector where they shape business behavior.

The key to institutional investors' influence on corporate governance and enterprise behavior is that money managers control a major share of corporate equities. Through such ownership, fund managers affect corporate investment and other enterprise decisions. Further, institutional holdings are more prominent among large companies. A short time before the pandemic hit, institutional investors owned between 70 percent and 85.8 percent of the 10 largest US companies (Pensions&Investments 2017).

The rise of equity ownership by managed money is tightly connected to observed changes in corporate governance, especially the pivot from a "retain (profits) and reinvest (in physical capital and human resources)" business model to a "downsize and distribute" model. Because the performance of managed money operations is evaluated on a quarterly basis, money managers have an incentive to focus on the short-term performance of corporations, and they, in turn, exert such pressure on corporate managers (Whalen 2020a). As William Lazonick and Mary O'Sullivan (2000, 27) write, the rise of institutional investors has encouraged corporate managers "to align their own interests with external financial interests rather than with the interests of the productive organizations" over which they exercise control.

In pursuit of downsizing and cost saving, many corporations engage in outsourcing and the offshoring of production. Globalization is often blamed for the "hollowing out" of US productive capacity. However, as Gerard Dumenil and Dominique Levy (2005, 17) note, "It is finance that dictates [capitalism's] forms and contents in the new stage of internationalization; it is not internationalization or globalization that creates the insuperable necessity for the present evolution of capitalism."[10] William Milberg (2008) concurs that globalization and financialization should be analyzed as interrelated tendencies, given that offshoring allows firms to reduce their input and operating costs.[11]

An interesting case study of the retail industry by Celine Baud and Cedric Durand (2012) shows that the continued push for returns by investors has led to increasing consolidation and globalization of supply chains. As they put it, "[G]lobalization of supply chains has increased retailers' market power and consequently allowed them to increase their profitability, as they can obtain lower prices from their suppliers" (Baud and Durand 2012, 255). Milberg (2008) and Milberg and Deborah Winkler (2010) further demonstrate that most of the gains associated with offshoring were used to sustain financialization rather than to invest in productive assets.

While offshore outsourcing (usually combined with just-in-time production and delivery) helps cut costs and boost returns to corporate shareholders, it also weakens domestic manufacturing capacity, a problem laid bare during the coronavirus pandemic. At the onset of the pandemic, the US economy failed to churn out basic personal protective equipment—including masks, gloves, and gowns—and other essential medical equipment and devices like test kits and ventilators (breathing assistance machines).[12] The Trump administration was quick to blame China for taking away production and jobs; but the truth is that US corporations face incentives favoring investments in financial products that promise rapid and large returns, not investments in plant, equipment, and production.[13] As mentioned above, research shows that offshoring allows firms to reduce the scope of productive activities and redirect profits to financial assets and dividend payments that raise shareholder value (Milberg 2008).

Related research by Özgür Orhangazi (2008) reveals that increased corporation payouts and financial profits are correlated with lower real investment. The "crowding out" effects are based on two channels: the diversion of internal funds toward dividend payouts, which reduce funds available for real investment, while the relatively quick returns from financial activities discourage corporations from focusing on productive activities. Orhangazi's work lends support to Minsky's (1993) arguments that technological development usually demands a longer time horizon than money managers are willing to accept, and that MMC often deprives corporations of financial resources for such development. In short, outsourcing and offshoring are part of the broader diversion of US corporate attention from production and trade to profits generated through financial channels.[14]

Given that stocks and options now make up two-thirds of pay for corporate executives, managers have every incentive to focus on short-term stock values. One sure way to quickly boost a firm's stock value is through share repurchases—also known as stock buybacks—because they reduce the outstanding shares of a company. Buybacks accounted for about 4.5 percent of corporations' assets in 2016, up from only 1 percent in 1994 (Marshall, Seretis, and Grunfeld 2018, 4). Just prior to the pandemic, the percentage of S&P 500 companies engaging in buybacks reached 85 percent (Smith 2020).

The amount of corporate cash devoted to buybacks since the global financial crisis has been enormous. For example, the companies in the S&P 500 spent $4.3 trillion on buybacks between 2009 and 2018, which amounts to 52 percent of their net income. They also spent another $3.3 trillion on dividends, an additional 39 percent of net income (Lazonick, Sakinç and Hopkins 2020). Research by S&P Global (2021) estimates that the sum of stock buybacks and dividend payouts was about the same as total operating earnings for S&P 500 companies (just over $1 trillion) in 2020.[15]

The draining of a corporation's internal funds leads to a reduction in capital investment. Capital spending as a percentage of US corporate net income dropped from 7.4 percent in the 1990s to only 4 percent at the start of the pandemic. Spending for research and development also decreased, from 3 percent to 2.3 percent (Smith 2020). In fact, between 2009 and 2018, only 43 percent of companies in the S&P 500 recorded *any* R&D expenses (Lazonick, Sakinç and Hopkins 2020). Thus, it's not surprising that the productive capacity of the United States has eroded.

Another way to give a quick boost to the value of corporate stock is through mergers and acquisitions (M&A). Summarizing Minsky's view, Whalen (2020a, 186) states that the rise of money managers "fueled the trend toward mergers, acquisitions, corporate breakups, leveraged buyouts and stock buybacks, since fund managers have a strong incentive to support whatever initiatives promise to boost near-term portfolio value; managed-money funds often provided the resources raiders needed to secure corporate control." Figure 4.1 shows the rising trend of corporate M&A, in terms of both the number and value of deals, over the past two decades.[16] These M&A are mainly driven by speculative motives, coupled with financial innovation, deregulation, and globalization (McCarthy 2013). Acquiring financially weak companies that have promising technologies and products provides enterprises with a cost-effective way to boost potential earnings and shareholder value. As Lazonick et al. (2017) report in a study of the pharmaceutical industry, many leading drug companies do not invest in their own research and development; instead, they acquire companies that have "blockbuster" products or other valuable intellectual property (see also Klinge, Fernandez and Aalbers 2020).[17]

The failed attempt of the US government to stockpile ventilators since 2006 is a direct result of M&A driven by maximization of shareholder value. In 2008, the federal government initiated Project Aura to purchase 40,000 portable ventilators, at $3,000 each, for the nation's stockpile. It offered the job to Newport Medical Instruments, a small, nimble, and specialized company based in California. After collaborating with US government officials, Newport delivered three working prototypes in 2011, and was on schedule to begin pro-duction in 2013. But then Newport was acquired (in mid-2012) by Covidien, a publicly traded medical device company with annual sales of $12 billion. Analysts suspect the acquisition was designed to prevent Newport from cutting into earnings from Covidien's existing ventilator business (Kulish, Kliff, and Silver-Greenberg 2020).

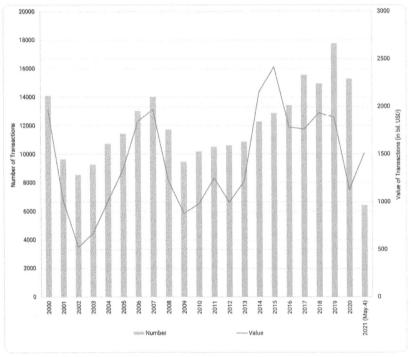

Source: Institute for Mergers, Acquisitions & Alliances (2021).

Figure 4.1   Mergers and acquisitions in the United States, 2000–2021

After acquiring Newport, Covidien demanded additional government devel-opment funding and a higher price per ventilator. Although the government gave the company an additional $1.4 million, no ventilators were delivered to the government by 2014. Instead, Covidien executives told the government that the portable ventilators were not "sufficiently profitable" and arranged to terminate the production contract (Kulish, Kliff, and Silver-Greenberg 2020). This case illustrates one way that M&A, aimed at protecting short-term profits, sabotage industrial production in the era of MMC.[18]

In sum, US economic experience demonstrates that MMC not only fails to generate enough private investment to create a full employment economy, but also doesn't deliver the types of investment needed to ensure dynamic technological development. Corporate behavior, driven to maximize shareholder value, has focused on outsourcing and offshoring, stock buybacks, and M&A, not on what Minsky called the (real) capital development of the economy. What the coronavirus pandemic has revealed is that the failure to ensure such development and strengthen industrial capacity can severely undercut economic resiliency and security.

"Lean and Mean" Workplaces and Worker Insecurity

The rise of MMC marked the end of "shared prosperity;" instead of seeking mutual gains for workers and other corporate stakeholders, companies enriched their shareholders and top managers while simultaneously eroding the economic security of their employees (Whalen 1997).[19] The coronavirus pandemic has exacerbated this divide. For example, Megan Neely and Donna Carmichael (2021) find that institutional investors have not only profited from the COVID-19 crisis, but also prompted predatory corporate behavior that has worsened inequality and created economic hardship for workers. By focusing on the COVID-19 pandemic, Neely and Carmichael (2021, 2) demonstrate that managed money—including private equity, hedge funds, and venture capital—plays an "instrumental role in how executives manage companies, which has important ramifications for societal responses to crises, the well-being and livelihoods of workers, and inequality throughout the labor market."

Minsky argued that companies in the era of MMC exhibit a seemingly relentless need to downsize and pursue workplace flexibility at the expense of worker security (Minsky 1996, 363; Minsky and Whalen 1996; Whalen 2008). Minsky's insight is supported by Jiwook Jung (2015), whose work is based on a sample of 714 US firms between 1981 and 2006. Jung finds that financial investors have pressured companies to downsize, de-unionize, outsource, and automate jobs (Jung 2015). That study is consistent with evidence of the long-term trend of job losses in the productive sector of the economy since the advent of MMC (Charles, Hurst, and Schwartz 2019). Moreover, research by Adam Goldstein (2012) shows that workforce downsizing does not make business operations more cost-effective and globally competitive; instead, it serves to redistribute earnings from workers to shareholders and executives.

Manufacturing job loss has been a serious and persistent problem in the United States since the late-1970s. The incidence of such (net) job loss in the first half of the 1990s stood at about 14 percent, even higher than the already high rate of about 10 percent in the 1980s. From 2000 through 2019, manufacturing job losses reached 4.5 million and durable goods manufacturing lost 2.9

million jobs. At the same time, finance and insurance industry added 712,000 jobs (US Bureau of Labor Statistics 2021b; 2021c; 2021d).

While much job loss in the past several decades was associated with business reorganizations and offshoring, automation has increasingly played a role. According to Carl Frey and Michael Osborne (2017, 268), nearly one half of total employment in the United States is at risk of automation within a decade or two. More recently, Dalia Marin (2020) estimated that the United States has about 200 robots for every 10,000 workers, and that the ratio is even higher in the automotive industry, once the bedrock of well-paying, blue-collar jobs. Marin also observed that low interest rates resulting from the pandemic make robots even more affordable, and projected that such interest rates would speed up robot adoption by more than 75 percent.

In addition to cutting their workforce, firms have also clamped down on wages and benefits (such as healthcare and retirement programs) to extract even more value for shareholders.[20] This continued even during the expansion that followed the Great Recession. Between 2009 and 2019, average inflation-adjusted worker compensation per hour rose 0.6 percent per year, half the rate of growth in output per hour (Center on Budget and Policy Priorities 2021a). Replacement of defined-benefit pensions with defined-contribution retirement plans (a development accompanying the rise of MMC) has meant not only greater risk borne by individual workers, but also increased overall retirement insecurity—and the pandemic has only further increased that insecurity for most Americans (Bond, Doonan, and Kenneally 2021; Davis, Radpour, and Ghilarducci 2020; Ghilarducci 2006; Morrissey 2019; Polivka and Luo 2015).

Corporations' quest for a lean and flexible workforce has also led to increased reliance on alternative work arrangements (including part-time and temporary work)—epitomized by work in the so-called gig economy, where workers of various service platforms are considered self-employed contractors, not employees, and do not receive the overtime pay and benefits that companies must provide to other workers. With such arrangements, companies may adjust their employment needs on a daily or even hourly basis, off-loading uncertainty and volatility to their "contractors."[21] As a result, workers' hours and earnings are more variable and less predictable than when hired via more traditional work arrangements.[22]

In addition, workers suffer from corporate failure to invest in employees. Part of this stems from shrinking investments by corporations in skill- and career-related human capital, which not only undercut the long-term prospects of corporations, but also deprive workers of career advancement opportunities (Foroohar 2016). But companies driven by shareholder value have also increasingly failed to supply workers with the equipment required to do their jobs safely and effectively. During the coronavirus pandemic, this was particularly evident in the healthcare industry, where years of industry consolidation and cost cutting to satisfy money managers (especially private equity firms) left frontline healthcare workers overburdened and under-protected in the face of a deadly virus.[23] Many other workers also faced—and continue to face—similar problems, including those working in grocery stores and the retail sector as well as those in occupations involving food processing, meatpacking, delivery, and hospitality.[24]

In short, MMC has fueled worker insecurity through workforce reductions, attacks on unions and collective bargaining, sluggish wage growth, erosion of benefits, less stable work arrangements, and corporations' failure to invest sufficiently in their workers. In addition, other research has found that the rise of MMC is associated with longer job searches, increased family dependence on multiple job holdings, reduced household savings, widening income and wealth inequality, declining income mobility, a shrinking middle class, persistent poverty, and increased despair among workers facing decreased economic opportunities (often leading to drug abuse, alcoholism, and suicide) (Whalen 1996; 2008; 2021).[25] This means average Americans were already in a vulnerable position before the pandemic hit.

Here are some indicators of economic insecurity among American households on the eve of the pandemic. Fifty-three million workers (44 percent of all workers between the ages of 18 and 64) were employed in low-wage jobs (Ross and Batemen 2019, 6). Nearly half of all households lived paycheck to paycheck (Gabler 2016). About six million people (3.8 percent of the workforce) worked in jobs that were contingent (not permanent) or involved alternative work arrangements, such as independent-contractor or on-call positions (US Bureau of Labor Statistics 2017). Close to 34 million workers did not have employer-provided sick leave (Desilver 2020).

The pandemic and economic lockdown subsequently forced many Americans to risk their personal safety to support themselves and family members, while others found themselves out of work and struggling to pay ordinary living expenses. Women and people of color have been particularly affected by these difficult challenges. Women account for 74 percent of those employed in high-contact occupations, such as hospitality and retail trade, which experienced heightened risks during the pandemic (Alon et al. 2020).[26] When the pandemic hit, 52 percent of the workers deemed "essential" by the US Department of Homeland Security were women—and most were frontline workers.[27] In the early months of the crisis, the Centers for Disease Control reported that women accounted for almost three out of four of the nation's infected healthcare workers (Robertson and Gebeloff 2020).[28] At the same time, between February and April of 2020—the initial months of the pandemic—women experienced a significantly higher percentage of job loss than men (Gogoi 2020). In April 2020, the unemployment rate was 13.2

percent for men and 16.2 percent for women; it was even higher for Black and Latina women—16.4 percent and 20.2 percent, respectively (Holder, Jones, and Masterson 2020, 2–6).[29]

The COVID-19 crisis—the brunt of which has fallen mainly on low- and middle-income households—has also exacerbated income and wealth inequality. In 2019, the bottom 50 percent of US households (ranked by wealth holdings) owned just 1 percent of the country's total wealth, while the top 10 percent held 76 percent. Then, during the first year of the pandemic, the country's 664 billionaires saw their wealth increase 44 percent, or $1.3 trillion (Elis 2021). By contrast, in April 2021—a year after the pandemic began—9.4 million persons reported that they had been unable to work that month because of the pandemic, down from 11.4 million in the previous month and 49.8 million in May 2020 (US Bureau of Labor Statistics 2021a; 2021e). At about the same time, a US Census survey reported that 27 percent of the nation's adults found it was "somewhat or very difficult" for their household to cover usual expenses such as food, rent or mortgage, car payments, medical expenses, or student loans (according to data collected between April 28 and May 10, 2021) (US Census Bureau 2021; Center on Budget and Policy Priorities 2021b).[30] After a year of dealing with COVID-19, the United States is even further from the broadly "shared prosperity" that is the central aim of Post-Keynesian Institutionalists and other progressive economists.

The "Cult of Debt" Culture and Financial Vulnerability

The pandemic has also revealed the financial vulnerability of many businesses, owing to what observers such as Palley (2007, 18) call a "cult of debt" culture adopted by corporations in MMC. A heavy debt burden can have both near-term and long-term adverse effects on firms in a period of economic and financial turmoil.

Prior to the pandemic, the US economy experienced an exceptionally long expansion, yet corporate debt kept mounting, continuing a long-term trend toward financial fragility that emerged with MMC (Minsky 1986). By the end of 2019, US corporate debt neared $10 trillion—47 percent of GDP—and BBB-rated bonds (the lowest investment-grade category) accounted for over 50 percent of the investment-grade bond market. In the era of MMC, a main reason for heavy reliance on debt financing (rather than selling equities or avoiding debt by using retained earnings for business spending) is that such financing increases leverage, which gives firms an opportunity to increase their return on equity (Palley 2007, 18).[31] In fact, much of the corporate leverage is not to finance fixed-asset investment, but to buy back stocks. For example, as much as 30 percent of stock buybacks in 2016 and 2017 were funded by credit (Lazonick, Sakinç, and Hopkins 2020).

When the pandemic hit, corporations had to pile up even more debt to cover operating costs. The total debt held by US non-financial corporations surged in 2020 to a record high of $17.5 trillion, or 83.5 percent of GDP (Brennan 2021). This borrowing binge has weighed greatly on the credit ratings of corporations. Speculative, non-investment grade issuers now make up 58 percent of corporations, an all-time high. Non-investment grade issuance reached $435 billion in 2020, up from $272.6 billion in 2019.

While debt service and refinancing costs remain low, thanks to the Fed's monetary easing, the sheer size of the debt overhang, especially the high risk-premium type, could wear on corporations' capacity to repay or invest over time. Even if massive defaults are unlikely to occur, the long-term effects of corporate over-indebtedness are still pernicious. For example, Kristian Blickle and João Santos (2020, 1) find that companies with high liabilities to cash flow experienced a 2 percent lower asset growth rate during ordinary times and up to 3 percent lower asset growth during the Great Recession than comparable firms without a debt overhang. Moreover, on the basis of the historical record, they warn that the increase in debt overhang caused by the COVID-19 pandemic could result in an up to 10 percent decrease in growth for firms in industries most affected by the economic downturn (Blickle and Santos 2020, 2).

It is also noteworthy that money managers do not merely play a major role in encouraging the debt culture (through their focus on near-term shareholder value); they also stand to profit from corporate failures resulting from that debt. For example, Bill Ackman, CEO of the hedge fund Pershing Square Capital Management, took a $27 million position on various bond indexes on March 3, 2020, betting that the debt bubble would burst and US equity and credit markets would subsequently tumble (Cohan 2020). Ten days later, when the US Federal Reserve announced new measures to bolster the economy, Ackman sold his positions and made a $2.6 billion profit. Ackman is certainly not alone. Money managers favor market volatility and have the incentive and means to create such volatility. Alas, this is just the latest example of the wide gap between financial gain and economic serviceability: The corporate debt cycle has long been found to severely undermine corporations' ability to employ, produce, invest, and innovate.

The State's Retreat from Serving the Public Interest

While Minsky did not extensively address the role of government in shaping MMC, his collaborators and followers have investigated the interplay of post-World War II capitalist development and public policy. According to Whalen (2008, 286), "Money-manager capitalism was not merely a product of endogenous changes. Its emergence was also facilitated or complemented by a number of public policies." These include restrictive monetary policy, generous depreciation allowances and tax credits, tax cuts for higher income earners, reductions in federal social spending, industry deregulation, tightened restrictions on personal bankruptcies, legalization of stock buybacks, and trade liberalization.[32] As L. Randall Wray (2009, 809) writes, "By dismantling rules, regulations, institutions, and safety nets, the predator state assisted the rise of money managers."[33]

Although Donald Trump presented himself as a pro-worker populist during the 2016 presidential campaign, the policies of the Trump administration consistently took the side of money managers and corporations aimed at maximizing shareholder value. For example, the Tax Cuts and Jobs Act of 2017 provided large, permanent corporate tax cuts and modest, temporary cuts for individuals. Those cuts are projected to increase the federal deficit by $1.9 trillion through 2028 (Congressional Budget Office 2018, 129), and, as expected, Republicans now point to deficits to justify their opposition to public investments and expenditures that benefit workers. The legislation also retained and even created incentives for moving tangible assets and jobs offshore, despite policymakers' public statements that they were aiming for just the opposite (Kitroeff 2018).[34]

It was the same story time and again throughout the Trump era.[35] On the one hand, President Trump signed legislation in 2018 that scaled back important regulatory aspects of the Dodd-Frank financial reform act of 2010, which was meant to protect the public from another global financial crisis (Werner 2018). On the other hand, his administration undertook dozens of actions—on issues such as wages, workplace safety, collective bargaining, and retirement programs—that undermined workers' rights and well-being (McNicholas, Rhinehart, and Poydock 2020).[36] It also supported repeal of the Affordable Care Act and undercut that legislation by effectively eliminating (via a provision in the Tax Cuts and Jobs Act) the individual mandate that required Americans to obtain health insurance for themselves and their dependents, resulting in an increase in the number of uninsured people and increasing health insurance premiums (Gee 2020; Jost 2017).[37]

During the coronavirus pandemic, managerial incompetence and self-dealing within the Trump administration intersected with the consequences of decades during which policymakers put financial and corporate interests before the well-being of workers and the general public. The COVID-19 response was marred not only by denials of the virus's severity, but also by failures in pre-pandemic planning, development of a federal strategy to address the crisis, and procurement and coordination of supplies (including reluctance to use the Defense Production Act).[38] In addition, throughout the Trump presidency the administration consistently ignored the public interest in pursuit of cuts to government spending on the environment, science, and health; in fact, existing federal pandemic response systems were gutted early in the Trump era, and a budget proposal submitted to Congress at the start of the pandemic aimed to trim the Centers for Disease Control (CDC) budget by almost 16 percent (Achenbach et al. 2020; Tracy 2020).

To be sure, the federal government provided $4 trillion in economic relief (in the form of grants, loans, and tax breaks) in response to the pandemic as of early October 2020, but only about one fifth of it went to help workers and families; much of the money went to companies that were not required to keep workers employed or even show they were adversely affected by the pandemic (Whoriskey, MacMillan, and O'Connell 2020). Moreover, while attempts to eliminate the Affordable Care Act were a main reason that 2.3 million Americans (including 726,000 children) became uninsured between 2016 and 2019, at least 1.9 million additional people became uninsured in the early months after the pandemic hit (Gee 2020). In addition, although about a dozen states responded to the crisis by enabling the unemployed to enroll in state-sponsored health insurance plans, most states rely on a federally sponsored service and the Trump administration refused to provide a helping hand to the newly uninsured by opening the service's enrollment period (Gee 2020).[39]

While workers in many occupations were put in a difficult situation because of the pandemic and the public sector's lackluster response, teachers (most of whom are public employees) and people employed in meatpacking plants were among those facing unique challenges because of action taken at the federal level. For example, teachers found that concerns for their safety were overshadowed by public statements from President Trump and Education Secretary Betsy DeVos that dismissed educational institutions' need to follow CDC guidance and that demanded schools reopen or risk losing federal funds (Cole 2020; Sargrad and Calsyn 2020; Sprunt and Turner 2020).[40] Meanwhile, meatpacking workers were caught between an executive order that kept meat and poultry plants open and an industry that took few precautions to protect employees from the coronavirus. Even worse, punitive attendance policies, a lack of sick leave and health benefits, and limited savings mean that many employees at processing plants work even when sick, which, of course, only further spreads the virus (Narea 2020; Yearby 2021).[41]

CONCLUSION

This chapter has shown that the coronavirus pandemic exposed structural flaws in the US economy and exacerbated the socioeconomic woes associated with the era of MMC. That era ushered in a sea change in corporate strategy and behavior, the treatment and well-being of workers, and the aims and administration of public policy. Those changes elevated the interests and power of money managers and corporate executives at the expense of American workers. A stock-market obsession, precarious jobs, stagnant and unstable worker incomes, high corporate debt, and a fraying social safety net have long threatened the well-being of American households and increased the vulnerability of the US economy to adverse events. The COVID-19 pandemic brought the system's underlying shortcomings to the surface, but it also intensified the associated, long-simmering problems, especially worker insecurity. Even worse, the surging disparity between society's "haves" and "have-nots" does not merely impede economic recovery; it also undermines democracy and social stability.

It will not be easy to fix the shortcomings of MMC that the pandemic has exposed, but that's not because Post-Keynesian Institutionalists and other progressives are at a loss for policy recommendations. For years, they have proposed an array of tax, regulatory, and other policy changes to bring corporate objectives and business practices closer in line with the interests of workers, communities, and the nation. They have also advocated labor-law reform to restore workers' rights to organize and bargain collectively, stronger fiscal stabilizers and economic security policies to bolster economic well-being (including a job guarantee, living wages, retirement supports, and healthcare for all), and a technology-driven industrial policy to secure prosperity by focusing on "brainpower" industries (thereby complementing, not substituting for human labor), resilient infrastructure, and environmental sustainability (see, e.g., Figart 2021; Whalen 2010; and Whalen 2020b, 85–86).[42] A recent proposal by Senator Elizabeth Warren (2020) and Representative Ro Khanna—aimed at protecting essential workers during the pandemic—also included provisions (such as health and safety protections, paid sick and family leave, support for child care, and safeguards for whistleblowers) consistent with the sort of pro-worker agenda envisioned by Post-Keynesian Institutionalists. In addition, many elements of the policy vision of President Joe Biden (2020) (as outlined during the 2020 presidential campaign) would contribute to moving the country in the direction of more broadly shared prosperity.

What makes fixing our economic problems so difficult is that the revealed shortcomings are actually core features of MMC (this was also true in the case of the global financial crisis and Great Recession of 2007–2009)—and, as this chapter indicates, the beneficiaries of the current system exert a powerful influence on both corporate behavior and public policy. The good news is that economic systems are not natural systems (rather, they are shaped by human institutions and policies; see Minsky 1986, 7); capitalism can be structured in a variety of ways, and there are plenty of constructive policy ideas to adopt that would enable us to engage in thoroughgoing economic reform and move constructively beyond MMC.[43] The bad news is that seeking to make the changes we need presents a direct challenge to our era's most powerful vested interests, and those interests are not inclined to yield without a fight.

Thus, a key challenge that must be confronted on the road from MMC to capitalism conducive to more broadly shared prosperity is the fact that conventional politics won't work; instead, those seeking genuine reform must, over the course of multiple election cycles, build a progressive political movement with broad appeal. Conventional politics requires candidates—Republicans and Democrats—to place a priority on campaign fundraising, which almost always means jettisoning a commitment to progressive ideas in order to win the approval of institutional investors and other donors with deep pockets (see, e.g., Calhoun 2018). In contrast, seeking genuine progressive reform requires a vision of America that can inspire working people—a vision that resonates with their experiences, highlights the common ground in their struggles (across regions and demographic divides), and offers a meaningful path to rewarding work, economic security, and robust opportunities. Then, building on that vision, the movement must press for constructive change day after day, month after month, and year after year. Realizing the promise of America requires constant effort, not merely a few weeks of political engagement every few years in advance of an election.[44]

Another major obstacle on the road to broadly shared prosperity is a Republican Party that demonizes its political opponents and most often chooses direct confrontation and unrelenting opposition over good-faith negotiations, joint problem solving, and authentic compromise. According to political scientists Steven Levitsky and Daniel Ziblatt (2017), democracies are fragile; a key norm that serves as their cornerstone is "mutual toleration, or accepting one's partisan rivals as legitimate (not treating them as dangerous enemies or traitors)." In the 1990s, William Greider (1993, 411) made a similar observation: "At its core, the idea of democracy ... [rests] on mutual respect."

Today, we are a long way from a political environment characterized by mutual respect.[45] In late 2010, both Senate Minority Leader Mitch McConnell and incoming House Speaker John Boehner announced that their driving aim was to stop every aspect of the agenda of President Barack Obama and make him a one-term president (Barr 2010). More recently, Senator McConnell—who prevented Obama's legitimate appointment of a Supreme Court nominee in 2016—told reporters he is "one-hundred percent" focused "on stopping" President Joe Biden's administration, which McConnell (quoted in Smith 2021) claims is working with House and Senate Democrats "to turn America into a socialist country." A short time later, McConnell and other members of his party blocked Democrats' proposed formation of a bipartisan commission to investigate the violent attack on the US Capitol that occurred on January 6, 2021 (Naylor 2021).[46]

As this chapter is being written, there are daily news stories and opinion essays warning that American democracy is in danger (see, e.g., Collinson 2021; Friedman 2021; and Riccardi 2021). The few members of the Republican Party who have bucked its "cultish devotion" to Donald Trump (such as Senator Mitt Romney, Representative Liz Cheney, and radio host Joe Walsh) have been ostracized, stripped of leadership positions, or ousted from their jobs.[47] Meanwhile, a statement recently signed by more than 100 scholars maintains that democracy in America "is now at risk" as a result of Republican-led efforts in several states to restrict voting and politicize electoral administration (Nietzel 2021). Columnists Michael Gerson (2021) and Frida Ghitis (2021) go further and warn that the threat of serious violence across the nation now infuses Republican Party politics.

To make matters worse, MMC itself contributes to the erosion of democracy. In part, this happens by making the political playing field more unequal—that is, rising worker insecurity and inequality disadvantage ordinary citizens by leaving them with a lack of time and money for politics and lobbying (Levin-Waldman 2010). But MMC also undermines democracy by causing millions of workers to become disaffected and angry, which enables demagogues (seldom interested in real solutions and often authoritarian in disposition) to acquire power by stoking workers' resentments (Feder 2020; Wallach 2020).[48]

All of these challenges to democracy provide another reason why a broad and genuinely progressive political movement is essential. Putting the United States back on the road to more broadly shared prosperity requires more than institutional changes to the economy; it also requires reinvigorating democracy. Bold and practical political progressivism—which some might even call progressive populism—is not only an essential foundation for constructive economic policy; by offering the realistic chance of achieving a genuinely pro-worker economy, such progressivism may also be the only way for democracy to prevail in the face of today's anti-democratic trends.

We close by recalling that Winston Churchill is said to have argued that Americans can always be counted on to do the right thing—after they've tried everything else. In the era of MMC, Americans have *tried* everything else: Ronald Reagan's supply-side conservatism, George H. W. Bush's "compassionate" conservatism, Bill Clinton's politics of triangulation, George W. Bush's neo-conservatism, Barack Obama's technocratic detachment, Donald Trump's populist authoritarianism, and now Joe Biden's moderate liberalism.[49] The challenges posed by MMC are formidable and require transformational economic and political change guided by the aim of broadly shared prosperity. It's time for the United States to do the right thing.

ACKNOWLEDGMENTS

The authors wish to thank Avi Baranes, Tae-Hee Jo, and Linda Whalen for providing valuable comments and suggestions on a chapter draft.

NOTES

1. For illustrations of the global reach of MMC, see, for example, Liang (2011) and Tavasci and Toporowski (2010). Also, for a look at three decades of the growing concentration of ownership by money managers not only in the United States, but also in Australia, Canada, and Germany, see Peetz, Murray, and Nienhuser (2013).
2. Looking back at the early post-World War II era, we find that the share of US corporate equities controlled by managed money increased from 8 percent in 1950 to 60 percent in 1990 (Porter 1992, 69). More recently, Peetz, Murray, and Nienhuser (2013) show the overwhelming ownership of the largest US industrial corporations by "finance capital" (that is, banks, insurance companies, mutual and pension funds, trusts, and private equity firms) before and after the global financial crisis.
3. For an early look at the crisis from a Minskyan perspective (emphasizing financial innovation, securitization, and unregulated practices and institutions), see Whalen (2007).
4. According to Michael Useem (2015, 1–2), institutional owners "are more demanding and less patient than individual [share]holders; they look for company competitiveness and clamor for change when firms fall short .... Individual shareholders had been relatively powerless to change underperforming company management, but professional investors acquired the clout and mastered the strategies for doing so." See also Useem (1996).
5. See, for example, Haldane (2015), which shows that firms seeking to boost the value of their stock avoid long-term investments.
6. Evidence of the strong link between the corporate pursuit of shareholder value and rising worker insecurity is provided by Greenwald, Lettau and Ludvigson (2021), which finds that 44 percent of the $34 trillion in real equity growth generated by US corporations from 1989 to 2017 was attributable to a reallocation of rewards to shareholders, primarily at the expense of labor compensation.
7. Of course, corporations also have—indeed have long exhibited—a predatory side, and it has become only more pronounced in the era of MMC; for more on the long evolution of corporations toward becoming "profit pirates," see Jo and Henry (2015).
8. In a similar manner, Greta Krippner (2005, 174) defines financialization as "a pattern of accumulation in which profits accrue primarily through financial channels rather than through trade and commodity production."
9. For more on the relationship between MMC and financialization, see, for example, Zalewski and Whalen (2010) and Whalen (2020a).
10. Minsky (1990, 56) acquired a similar view from Joseph Schumpeter, his dissertation adviser.
11. Krippner (2005, 196–197) adds that non-financial firms do not simply keep financial activities at home and offshore productive activities abroad. In fact, she

finds that US non-financial corporations actually generate more portfolio income from foreign sources than from domestic sources in the era we call MMC.

12.   For discussions of supply shortages during the pandemic, see, for example, McMullan (2020); Morris (2021); Pfeiffer, Anderson and Van Woerkom (2020); and Rose (2020).

13.   Imports of Chinese medical equipment to the United States increased by 78 percent between 2010 and 2018 (US-China Economic and Security Review Commission 2019, 251–252).

14.   For more on how finance has eroded US manufacturing, see Berger (2014); and for an early warning of the dangers of an economy driven by a short-term financial focus, see Hayes and Abernathy (1980). MMC's erosion of capital development is at the heart of what James Crotty (2003) calls the "neoliberal paradox," which is that investors' relentless pursuit of financial gains undermines the ability of corporations to sustain the investments and innovations essential for capitalism's long-term survival.

15.   After the Trump-era corporate tax cuts of 2017, billions of dollars were repatriated from overseas tax havens and funded an extraordinary buyback binge: stock buybacks among the S&P 500 surged by 55 percent to a record $806 billion in 2018 (Smith 2020). (It should also be noted that corporations are permitted to borrow external funds to finance buybacks, which means that buybacks are not constrained by the availability of internal funds.) Although the COVID-19 pandemic slowed the buyback boom, US corporations announced $484 billion in buybacks through the first four months of 2021. Analysts anticipate that 2021 will be not merely another record-setting year, but also the start of a new, multi-year buyback "bonanza" (Sozzi 2021).

16.   For the upward trend of M&A since the mid-1980s, see Institute for Mergers, Acquisitions, and Alliances (2021).

17.   For a recent article showing that the "Big Four" tech companies (Amazon, Apple, Facebook, and Google) have grown tremendously in size and scope by way of M&A, see Alcantara et al. (2021).

18.   For a broader discussion of how contemporary finance sabotages industrial production, see Nesvetailova and Palan (2020).

19.   While it is often said that the rise of MMC marked the end of shared prosperity, it is more accurate to say that MMC marked the end of the *pursuit* of shared prosperity. In fact, prosperity in the managerial era was far from broadly shared.

20.   For a discussion of wage stagnation in the United States since the mid-1970s, see Shambaugh et al. (2017, i).

21.   All too often, companies also deprive workers of pay and benefits to which they are legally entitled, and estimates suggest that as many as one in five employers have misclassified workers as independent contractors (Cooper and Kroeger 2017).

22.   Research by analysts at the US Treasury Department provides evidence of the growth in nonstandard employment. For example, the number of individuals with self-employment income increased by 29 percent between 2000 and 2014. According to the authors of that study, "[W]orkers who earn their living outside of the formal employee-employer relationship earn less, are less likely to have health insurance coverage, or to participate in or contribute to a retirement account" (Jackson, Looney, and Ramnath 2017, 22). For more on the rise of precarious work, see Kalleberg (2011) and Weil (2014).

23. For discussions on how a relentless pursuit of earnings endangered healthcare workers and patients during the pandemic, see, for example, Gold and Evans (2020) and Pattani (2021). For earlier discussions on the focus on profits over people in healthcare and related services, see Appelbaum (2019); Ivory, Protess and Bennett (2016); and Pasquale (2014). For a perspective outside the United States, see Garcia-Gomez, Maug, and Obernberger (2020).

24. For challenges faced by workers in the grocery and retail sectors, see, for example, MacGillis (2021) and Neely and Carmichael (2021).

25. For more on the consequences of financialization on workers and employment relations, see Weller (2015).

26. According to Campbell Robertson and Robert Gebeloff (2020), "More than two-thirds of the workers at grocery store checkouts and fast food counters are women."

27. Robertson and Gebeloff (2020) report that women "make up nearly nine out of 10 nurses and nursing assistants, most respiratory therapists, a majority of pharmacists and an overwhelming majority of pharmacy aides and technicians." They also report that 33 percent of women workers were deemed essential; in contrast, 28 percent of male workers were deemed essential (Robertson and Gebeloff 2020).

28. For a look at COVID-19 deaths among healthcare workers in the United States at the end of 2020, see Jewett, Lewis and Bailey (2020).

29. See Falk et al. (2021) for an examination of unemployment rates during the pandemic.

30. According to the same survey (conducted by the US Census Bureau), "Black and Latino adults reported difficulty covering expenses at higher rates: 42 percent and 36 percent respectively, compared to 23 percent for Asian adults and 21 percent for white adults" (Center on Budget and Policy Priorities 2021b).

31. Palley (2007, 18) also identifies two other reasons for the cult of debt financing. One is that the tax code favors such financing over equity financing because interest payments are tax deductible. The other is that debt can be used as a tactic to drain free cash flow from firms, thereby putting pressure on workers and leaving less income available for other income-stream claimants.

32. Prior to 1982, stock buybacks were considered stock manipulation and were prohibited in the United States. For details on many of the policy changes mentioned above (and additional references), see Whalen (2008); for Institutionalist analyses of bankruptcy reform that illustrate how such policy changes serve financial interests at the expense of US households, see Waller (2001) and Scott (2007).

33. Wray (2009, 816) also identifies a variety of ways that neoconservative policymakers (mostly Republicans) in the nation's capital sought to advance even further the interests of money managers, such as: privatizing Social Security, replacing income and wealth taxes with consumption taxes, transferring healthcare burdens to patients, substituting private training accounts for unemployment benefits, and supporting school voucher systems. The common thread of all these efforts is the aim of reducing government responsibility for public welfare and shifting economic risks from government and corporations to workers and households. In most cases, those particular efforts failed, but proponents of that agenda have not always been unsuccessful, as shown by Galbraith (2008), who surveys the record in a number of policy areas. Galbraith (2008, 14) also identifies financial deregulation as "the most complex and damaging example" of the predator state at work: "Here we see ..., in pure and unalloyed form, the

consequences of market power, of asymmetric information, and of regulatory capture, leading to rampant predation against both a public system and the public itself, and on a colossal scale." See also Mishel and Bivens (2021), who examine the policy-driven sources of wage suppression and inequality.

34. According to William Gale et al. (2018, II), under the most plausible scenarios, the Tax Cuts and Jobs Act will "end up making most households worse off" than if the legislation had not been enacted. For more on the Trump era tax cuts, see Cary and Holmes (2019), Desai (2018), Dickinson (2020), and Gleckman (2017).

35. In 2008, Galbraith (2008, 135–136) illustrated the predator state's disregard for the public interest by describing how the federal government contracted with private loan-servicing firms to handle university loans that were previously administered by government workers. During the Trump era, thousands of teachers were surprised to find that their university tuition grants were converted to loans by a servicing firm that stood to gain from the conversion. In the end, public outrage eliminated those loans, but the incident shows how privatization and predatory behavior have continued to undermine the public interest (Turner and Arnold 2018; Turner 2020).

36. The Trump administration also failed to support a bill to increase the federal minimum wage to $15 an hour by 2025, which passed the House of Representatives in 2019. That minimum wage, which was last raised in 2009, currently stands at $7.25 per hour; it has lost more than 30 percent of its purchasing power since its real-value peak in 1968 (Cooper 2019; McNicholas, Rhinehart, and Poydock 2020, 12).

37. According to an analysis by the Kaiser Family Foundation (Kamal et al. 2018), insurance premiums purchased through state health exchanges were expected to be about 16 percent higher in 2019 than would otherwise be the case because of the repeal of the individual mandate and other changes that weakened the Affordable Care Act.

38. A lack of federal coordination forced states to compete with each other for vital supplies and medical equipment during the pandemic (Soergel 2020). At the same time, to the extent that the administration was engaged, the record shows that the president and his top aides played favorites in awarding contracts and allocating scarce resources, often insisting that governors praise the president publicly (later used in campaign ads) and even relax state stay-at-home rules in exchange for federal assistance (Allen, McCausland, and Farivar 2020; Mackey 2020; Sarkis 2020).

39. Several other indicators of economic insecurity among American households at the start of the pandemic (such as the large number of workers without sick leave) have already been discussed in a previous section of this chapter.

40. DeVos also tried to force public school districts to divert an outsized portion of federal coronavirus relief funds to private schools (Bryant 2020).

41. Employees at such facilities are required to work even when experiencing COVID-19 symptoms or awaiting test results, since companies excuse absences for COVID-19 only when a worker has tested positive for the virus. However, meat- and poultry-processing workers often find tests expensive and difficult to access, so many sick employees forgo the tests and just continue to work (Yearby 2021).

42. For a broad strategy that remains relevant, see Minsky and Whalen (1996). Also, see the other chapters in Part II of this book for constructive policy ideas.

43. On the many varieties of capitalism, see Minsky (1991, 10).

44.   Of course, in addition to recognizing and addressing the political challenges that stem largely from the resistance of vested interests, Post-Keynesian Institutionalists and other progressive economists must also seek to advance the discipline of economics so as to improve academic and public understanding of contemporary economic challenges. In fact, contributing to that end by fleshing out Post-Keynesian Institutionalist analyses of today's capitalism is a key aim of this entire volume. Beyond that, we thoroughly endorse pluralistic efforts that seek to strengthen ties across heterodox traditions for the purpose of better understanding socioeconomic reality.

45.   Actually, this problem has been building throughout the era of MMC; see Whalen (2020c), which includes some ideas, based on the work of John R. Commons, to address this situation by means of institutional changes. In addition, it must be acknowledged that some members of the Democratic Party have also chosen to demonize their opponents and reject compromise; the difference is that Republicans have elevated such members to leadership positions; to date, Democrats have largely avoided doing so. As congressional scholars Thomas Mann and Norman Ornstein ([2012] 2016) demonstrate in *It's Even Worse than It Looks*, both parties participate in tribal warfare, but both sides are not equally culpable; instead, there is "asymmetric polarization," owing to a Republican Party that refuses, at all costs, to allow anything that might help Democrats politically.

46.   Meanwhile, most Republicans, accepting a narrative repeatedly presented on Fox News and other right-wing media outlets, falsely insist that Biden's election was illegitimate (Reuters 2021).

47.   For an interview with Joe Walsh, who was fired from his conservative radio show for speaking critically of Trump, see CNN Newsroom (2021).

48.   Moreover, when such anger threatens the interests of elites, the affluent look to the state for anti-democratic solutions to contain it (Parramore 2018).

49.   Although candidate Biden positioned himself as a moderate liberal, there is room and time (as of this writing, a little more than 100 days into his presidency) for him to evolve in the direction of progressive populism.

REFERENCES

Achenbach, Joel, Laurie McGinely, Amy Goldstein, and Ben Guarino. 2020. "Trump Budget Cuts Funding for Health, Science, Environment Agencies." *Washington Post*. February 10. https://tinyurl.com/489rnm7y. Accessed June 1, 2021.

Alcantara, Chris, Kevin Schaul, Gerrit De Vynck, and Reed Albergotti. 2021. "How Big Tech Got So Big: Hundreds of Acquisitions." *The Washington Post*. April 21. https://tinyurl.com/ymyd5xwu. Accessed June 18, 2021.

Allen, Jonathan, Phil McCausland, and Cyrus Farivar. 2020. "Want a Mask Contract or Some Ventilators? A White House Connection Helps." NBC News. April 24. https://tinyurl.com/8p7sfbzs. Accessed June 1, 2021.

Alon, Titan, Matthias Doepke, Jane Olmstead-Rumsey, and Michèle Tertilt, M. 2020. "This Time It's Different: The Role of Women's Employment in a Pandemic Recession." Working Paper No. 27660, National Bureau of Economic Research. https://tinyurl.com/m86y6zht. Accessed May 27, 2021.

Appelbaum, Eileen. 2019. "How Private Equity Makes You Sicker." *The American Prospect*. October 7. https://tinyurl.com/xdsbumhc. Accessed May 27, 2021.

Atkinson, Glen and Charles J. Whalen. 2011. "Futurity: Cornerstone of Post-Keynesian Institutionalism." In *Financial Instability and Economic Security after the Great Recession*, edited by Charles J. Whalen, 53–74. Cheltenham, UK: Edward Elgar.

Barr, Andy. 2010. "The GOP's No-Compromise Pledge." *Politico*. October 28. https://tinyurl.com/49dvbjp7. Accessed June 4, 2021.

Baud, Celine and Cedric Durand. 2012. "Financialization, Globalization and the Making of Profits by Leading Retailers." *Socio-Economic Review* 10 (2): 241–266.

Berger, Suzanne. 2014. "How Finance Gutted Manufacturing." *Boston Review* 39 (2): 12–17.

Biden, Joe. 2020. "Joe's Vision." https://joebiden.com/joes-vision. Accessed June 4, 2021.

Blickle, Kristian and João A. C. Santos. 2020. "The Costs of Corporate Debt Overhang." SSRN Research Paper. https://tinyurl.com/3288j7zk. Accessed May 30, 2021.

Bond, Tyler, Dan Doonan, and Kelly Kenneally. 2021. *Retirement Insecurity 2021: America's Views of Retirement*. Washington, DC: National Institute on Retirement Security. https://tinyurl.com/2bpnmxyw. Accessed May 27, 2021.

Brennan, Peter. 2021. "Corporate America Not Likely to Unwind COVID-19 Debt Buildup Despite Credit Hits." S&P Global. February 22. https://tinyurl.com/3fj82248. Accessed May 30, 2021.

Bryant, Jeff. 2020. "Betsy DeVos Using Pandemic to Strip Funding from Public Schools." The National Memo. June 15. https://tinyurl.com/23b4rzst. Accessed June 1, 2021.

Calhoun, Ben. 2018. "It's My Party and I'll Try If I Want To," Act One. This American Life. June 22, https://tinyurl.com/3jzm4r5m. Accessed June 4, 2021.

Cary, Peter and Allan Holmes. 2019. "The Secret Saga of Trump's Tax Cuts." Center for Public Integrity. https://tinyurl.com/2xamkzp2. Accessed May 31, 2021.

Center on Budget and Policy Priorities. 2021a. "Chart Book: Tracking the Post-Great Recession Economy." May 7. https://tinyurl.com/y3e6f5rt. Accessed May 25, 2021.

Center on Budget and Policy Priorities. 2021b. "Tracking the COVID-19 Recession's Effects on Food, Housing, and Employment Hardships." May 20. https://tinyurl.com/3kkrpsu8. Accessed May 27, 2021.

Charles, Kerwin Kofi, Erik Hurst, and Mariel Schwartz. 2019. "The Transformation of Manufacturing and the Decline in US Employment." In *NBER Macroeconomics Annual 2018, Number 33*, edited by Martin Eichenbaum, Erik Hurst, and Jonathan A. Parker, 307–372. Chicago: University of Chicago Press.

CNN Newsroom. 2021. "'Authoritarian Embracing Cult': Former Republican Lawmaker on State of GOP." CNN Videos. May 31. https://tinyurl.com/tjajcx2w. Accessed June 4, 2021.

Cohan, William D. 2020. "Inside the Greatest Trade of All Time—and What Bill Ackman Is Investing in Now." *Barrons*. September 21. https://tinyurl.com/2sxf3nsk. Accessed May 30, 2021.

Cole, Devan. 2020. "Education Secretary Won't Say If Schools Should Listen to CDC Guidelines on Reopening." CNN Politics. July 12. https://tinyurl.com/34z4x7ms. Accessed June 2, 2021.

Collinson, Stephen. 2021. "The GOP's Devotion to Trump Threatens to Destroy American Democracy." CNN Politics. May 4. https://tinyurl.com/bm8m43xc. Accessed June 4, 2021.

Congressional Budget Office. 2018. *The Budget and Economic Outlook: 2018 to 2028*. Washington, DC: Congressional Budget Office. https://tinyurl.com/3snb9w8y. Accessed May 31, 2021.

Cooper, David. 2019. "Congress Has Never Let the Federal Minimum Wage Erode for This Long." Economic Policy Institute. June 17, 2019. https://tinyurl.com/dvjfd7zr. Accessed May 31, 2021.

Cooper, David and Teresa Kroeger. 2017. "Employers Steal Billions from Workers' Paychecks Each Year." Economic Policy Institute. May 10. https://tinyurl.com/ 5e6b69pw. Accessed May 25, 2021.

Crotty, James. 2003. "The Neoliberal Paradox: The Impact of Destructive Product Market Competition and Impatient Finance on Nonfinancial Corporations in the Neoliberal Era." *Review of Radical Political Economy* 35 (3): 271–279.

Davis, Owen, Siavash Radpour and Teresa Ghilarducci. 2020. "Chartbook: Retirement Insecurity and Falling Bargaining Power Among Older Workers." New York: Schwartz Center for Economic Policy Analysis, The New School. https://tinyurl .com/ymnww8xw. Accessed May 27, 2021.

Desai, Mihir A. 2018. "Tax Reform Round One." *Harvard Magazine* (May–June): 57–61.

Desilver, Drew. 2020. "As Coronavirus Spreads, Which U.S. Workers Have Paid Sick Leave—And Which Don't?" Pew Research Center. March 12. https://tinyurl.com/ vxwfatax. Accessed May 27, 2021.

Dickinson, Tim. 2020. "How Trump Took the Middle Class to the Cleaners." *RollingStone*. October 16, 2020. https://tinyurl.com/yrsphxy9. Accessed June 4, 2021.

Dumenil, Gerard and Dominique Levy. 2005. "Costs and Benefits of Neoliberalism: A Class Analysis." In *Financialization and the World Economy*, edited by Gerald A. Epstein, 17–45. Cheltenham, UK: Edward Elgar Publishing.

Elis, Niv. 2021. "How the Pandemic Turbocharged Inequality." *The Hill*. March 11. https://tinyurl.com/j36wucrp. Accessed May 27, 2021.

Epstein, Gerald A. 2005. "Introduction." In *Financialization and the World Economy*, edited by Gerald A. Epstein, 3–16. Cheltenham, UK: Edward Elgar Publishing.

Falk, Gene, Paul D. Romero, Jameson A. Carter, Isaac C. Nicchitta, and Emma C. Nyhoff. 2021. "Unemployment Rates During the COVID-19 Pandemic." Congressional Research Service Report R46554. Washington, DC: Congressional Research Service. https://tinyurl.com/ztujdu7s. Accessed May 27, 2021.

Feder, Sandra. 2020. "Stanford Scholar Says Major Reforms are Needed to Save Our Democracy." Stanford News. https://tinyurl.com/48ct5eev. Accessed June 4, 2021.

Figart, Deborah M. 2021. "Good Work." *Journal of Economic Issues* 55 (2): 271–292.

Frey, Carl Benedikt and Michael A. Osborne. 2017. "The Future of Employment: How Susceptible are Jobs to Computerisation?" *Technological Forecasting and Social Change* 114 (C): 254–280.

Friedman, Thomas L. 2021. "The Trump GOP's Plot Against Liz Cheney—and Our Democracy." *New York Times*. May 11. https://tinyurl.com/hvhtrdtw. Accessed June 4, 2021.

Foroohar, Rana. 2016. *Makers and Takers: The Rise of Finance and the Fall of American Business*. New York: Crown Business.

Gabler, Neal. 2016. "The Secret Shame of Middle-Class Americans." *The Atlantic*. May. https://tinyurl.com/dar36dt6. Accessed May 27, 2021.

Galbraith, James K. 2008. *The Predator State*. New York: Free Press.

Gale, William G., Hilary Gelfond, Aaron Krupkin, Mark J. Mazur, and Eric Toder. 2018. *Effects of the Tax Cuts and Jobs Act: A Preliminary Analysis*. Washington, DC: Tax Policy Center.

Garcia-Gomez, Pilar, Ernst G. Maug, and Stefan Obernberger. 2020. "Private Equity Buyouts and Employee Health." Finance Working Paper No. 680/2020, European Corporate Governance Institute. Social Science Research Network. https://tinyurl .com/82s848yr. Accessed May 27, 2021.

Gee, Emily. 2020. "Less Coverage and Higher Costs: The Trump's Administration's Health Care Legacy." Center for American Progress. September 25. https://tinyurl .com/47tuw8sf. Accessed May 30, 2021.

Gerson, Michael. 2021. "The Threat of Violence Now Infuses GOP Politics. We Should All Be Afraid." *Washington Post*. May 20. https://tinyurl.com/3apfn9nt. Accessed June 4, 2021.

Ghilarducci, Teresa. 2006. "The End of Retirement." *Monthly Review*. May 1. https:// tinyurl.com/2f84vp4w. Accessed May 27, 2021.

Ghitis, Frida. 2021. "The Republican Party is Building a Political Bomb." CNN Opinion. May 28. https://tinyurl.com/wsz33b3j. Accessed June 4, 2021.

Gleckman, Howard. 2017. "The Final Tax Bill Falls Far Short of President Trump's Campaign Promises." Tax Policy Center. December 18. https://tinyurl.com/ 47hm5vvy. Accessed May 31, 2021.

Gogoi, Pallavi. 2020. "Stuck-At-Home Moms: The Pandemic's Devastating Toll on Women." NPR. October 28, 2020. https://tinyurl.com/ybfsz2n4. Accessed May 27, 2021.

Gold, Russell and Melanie Evans. 2020. "The Covid Storm: Yearslong Drive for Efficiency Left Hospitals Overwhelmed." *Wall Street Journal*. September 18.

Goldstein, Adam. 2012. "Revenge of the Managers: Labor Cost-Cutting and the Paradoxical Resurgence of Managerialism in the Shareholder Value Era, 1984 to 2001." *American Sociological Review* 77 (2): 268–294.

Greenwald, Daniel L., Martin Lettau, and Sydney C. Ludvigson. 2021. "How the Wealth Was Won: Factor Shares as Market Fundamentals." National Bureau of Economic Research Working Paper 25769. https://www.nber.org/papers/w25769. Accessed June 22, 2021.

Greider, William. 1993. *Who Will Tell the People? The Betrayal of American Democracy*. New York: Touchstone.

Haldane, Andrew G. 2015. "The Costs of Short-Termism." *Political Quarterly* 86 (S1): 66–76.

Hayes, Robert H. and William J. Abernathy. 1980. "Managing Our Way to Economic Decline." *Harvard Business Review* 58 (4): 67–77.

Holder, Michelle, Janelle Jones, and Thomas Masterson. 2020. "The Early Impact of COVID-19 on Job Losses among Black Women in the United States." Working Paper No. 963, Levy Economics Institute. https://tinyurl.com/j7rku2tj. Accessed May 27, 2021.

Institute for Mergers, Acquisitions and Alliances. 2021. Dataset on Mergers and Acquisitions in the United States. https://imaa-institute.org/m-and-a-us-united -states/. Accessed May 24, 2021.

Ivory, Danielle, Ben Protess, and Kitty Bennett. 2016. "When You Dial 911 and Wall Street Answers." *New York Times*. June 25. https://tinyurl.com/h5e6yetj. Accessed May 26, 2021.

Jackson, Emilie, Adam Looney, and Shanthi Ramnath. 2017. "The Rise of Alternative Work Arrangements: Evidence and Implications for Tax Filing and Benefit Coverage." Office of Tax Analysis, Working Paper 114. US Department of the Treasury: Washington D.C. https://tinyurl.com/uyw4kdsz. Accessed May 25, 2021.

Jewett, Christina, Robert Lewis, and Melissa Bailey. 2020. "More Than 2,900 Health Care Workers Died This Year: And the Government Barely Kept Track." Kaiser Health News. December 23. https://tinyurl.com/yfzx88bu. Accessed May 27, 2021.

Jo, Tae-Hee and John F. Henry. 2015. "The Business Enterprise in the Age of Money Manager Capitalism." *Journal of Economic Issues* 49 (1): 23–46.

Johns Hopkins University. 2021. Coronavirus Resource Center. http://coronavirus.jhu.edu. Accessed May 20, 2021.

Jost, Timothy. 2017. "The Tax Bill and the Individual Mandate: What Happened, and What Does It Mean?" *Health Affairs* Blog. December 20. https://tinyurl.com/3map8sz5/ Accessed May 31, 2021.

Jung, Jiwook. 2015. "Shareholder Value and Workforce Downsizing, 1981–2006." *Social Forces* 93 (4): 1335–1368.

Kalleberg, Arne L. 2011. *Good Jobs, Bad Jobs: The Rise of Polarized and Precarious Employment Systems in the United States, 1970s to 2000s*. New York: Russell Sage Foundation.

Kamal, Rabah, Cynthia Cox, Rachel Fehr, Marco Ramirez, Katherine Horstman, and Larry Levitt. 2018. "How Repeal of the Individual Mandate and Expansion of Loosely Regulated Plans are Affecting 2019 Premiums." Kaiser Family Foundation. October 26. https://tinyurl.com/7j2xvu8d. Accessed June 1, 2021.

Kitroeff, Natalie. 2018. "Tax Law May Send Factories and Jobs Abroad, Critics Say." *New York Times*. January 8. https://tinyurl.com/76bbusjf. Accessed May 31, 2021.

Klinge, Tobias, Rodrigo Fernandez and Manuel Aalbers. 2020. "The Financialization of Big Pharma." *Revista Internacional de Sociología* 78 (4): e174. https://tinyurl.com/4wch3ynp. Accessed May 26, 2021.

Krippner, Greta R. 2005. "The Financialization of the American Economy." *Socio-Economic Review* 3 (2): 173–208.

Kulish, Nicolas, Sarah Kliff, and Jessica Silver-Greenberg. 2020. "The U.S. Tried to Build a New Fleet of Ventilators. The Mission Failed." *New York Times*. March 29. https://tinyurl.com/4prtypm9. Accessed May 26, 2021.

Lazonick, William, Matt Hopkins, Ken Jacobson, Mustafa Erdem Sakinç, and Öner Tulum. 2017. "US Pharma's Financialized Business Model." Working Paper No. 60, Institute for New Economic Thinking. https://tinyurl.com/ry9vj784. Accessed May 25, 2021.

Lazonick, William and Mary O'Sullivan. 2000. "Maximizing Shareholder Value: A New Ideology for Corporate Governance." *Economy and Society* 29 (1): 13–35.

Lazonick, William, Mustafa Erdem Sakinç, and Matt Hopkins. 2020. "Why Stock Buybacks Are Dangerous for the Economy." *Harvard Business Review*. January 7, 2020. https://tinyurl.com/vs22cy9s. Accessed May 26, 2021.

Levin-Waldman, Oren M. 2010. *Wage Policy, Income Distribution, and Democratic Theory*. London: Routledge.

Levitsky, Steven and Daniel Ziblatt. 2017. "How a Democracy Dies." *The New Republic*. December 7. https://tinyurl.com/y7e7zo9h. Accessed June 4, 2021.

Liang, Yan. 2011. "Money-Manager Capitalism, Capital Flows and Development in Emerging Market Economies: A Post-Keynesian Institutionalist Analysis." In *Financial Instability and Economic Security after the Great Recession*, edited by Charles J. Whalen, 179–201. Cheltenham, UK: Edward Elgar Publishing.

MacGillis, Alec. 2021. *Fulfillment: Winning and Losing in One-Click America*. New York: Farrar, Straus and Giroux.

Mackey, Robert. 2020. "In Exchange for Aid, Trump Wants Praise from Governors He Can Use in Campaign Ads." The Intercept. March 28. https://tinyurl.com/hab6k8nh. Accessed June 1, 2021.

Mann, Thomas E. and Norman J. Ornstein. (2012) 2016. *It's Even Worse Than It Looks: How the American Constitutional System Collided with the New Politics of Extremism*, 2nd edition. New York: Basic Books.

Marin, Dalia. 2020. "How COVID-19 is Transforming Manufacturing." Project Syndicate. April 3. https://tinyurl.com/5yrx8jt8. Accessed May 27, 2021.

Marshall, Ric, Panos Seretis, and Agnes Grunfeld. 2018. "Taking Stock: Share Buybacks and Shareholder Value." MSCI Research Paper. https://tinyurl.com/3budbhts. Accessed May 24, 2021.

McCarthy, Killian J. 2013. "The Business Environment—Mergers and Merger Waves: A Century of Cause and Effect." In *Understanding Mergers and Acquisitions in the 21st Century*, edited Killian J. McCarthy and Wilfred Dolfsma, 11–36. Basingstoke, UK: Palgrave Macmillan.

McMullan, Matthew. 2020. "The Great American PPE Shortage of 2020." Alliance for American Manufacturing. December 11. https://tinyurl.com/ypx6d3fc. Accessed May 25, 2021.

McNicholas, Celine, Lynn Rhinehart, and Margaret Poydock. 2020. "50 Reasons the Trump Administration is Bad for Workers." Economic Policy Institute Report. September 16. https://www.epi.org/publication/50-reasons/. Accessed May 31, 2021.

Milberg, William. 2008. "Shifting Sources and Uses of Profits: Sustaining US Financialization with Global Value Chains." *Economy and Society* 37 (3): 420–451.

Milberg, William and Deborah Winkler. 2010. "Financialisation and the Dynamics of Offshoring in the USA." *Cambridge Journal of Economics* 34 (2): 275–293.

Minsky, Hyman P. 1986. *Stabilizing an Unstable Economy*. New Haven: Yale University Press.

Minsky, Hyman P. 1990. "Schumpeter: Finance and Evolution." *In Evolving Market Technology and Market Structure: Studies in Schumpeterian Economics*, edited by Arnold Heertje and Mark Perlman, 51–74. Ann Arbor: University of Michigan Press.

Minsky, Hyman P. 1991. "The Transition to a Market Economy: Financial Options." Working Paper Number 66, Levy Economics Institute of Bard College. https://tinyurl.com/dvpuanxs. Accessed June 3, 2021.

Minsky, Hyman P. 1992. "The Capital Development of the Economy and the Structure of Financial Institutions." Working Paper Number 72, Levy Economics Institute of Bard College. https://tinyurl.com/yw8zys9u. Accessed May 28, 2021.

Minsky, Hyman P. 1993. "Schumpeter and Finance." In *Market and Institutions in Economic Development: Essays in Honour of Paolo Sylos Labini*, edited by Salvatore Biasco, Alessandro Roncaglia, and Michele Salvati, 103–116. New York: St. Martin's Press.

Minsky, Hyman P. 1996. "Uncertainty and the Institutional Structure of Capitalist Economies." *Journal of Economic Issues* 30 (2): 357–68.

Minsky, Hyman P. and Charles Whalen. 1996. "Economic Insecurity and the Institutional Prerequisites for Successful Capitalism." *Journal of Post Keynesian Economics* 19 (2): 155–170.

Mishel, Lawrence and Josh Bivens. 2021. "Identifying the Policy Levers Generating Wage Suppression and Wage Inequality." Economic Policy Institute Report. May 13, 2021. Washington, DC: Economic Policy Institute. https://www.epi.org/215903. Accessed July 11, 2021.

Morris, David Z. 2021. "COVID Exposed Global Supply-Chain Flaws. Can Biden Bring Manufacturing Back to the U.S.?" *Fortune.* April 23. https://tinyurl.com/2fbrvjbs. Accessed May 25, 2021.

Morrissey, Monique. 2019. "The State of American Retirement Savings." Washington, DC: Economic Policy Institute. https://epi.org/136219. Accessed May 27, 2021.

Narea, Nicole. 2020. "Trump is Keeping Meatpacking Plants Open—But Employees are Scared to Show Up for Work." Vox.com. April 30. https://tinyurl.com/3u2bh9za. Accessed June 1, 2021.

Naylor, Brian. 2021. "Senate Republicans Block a Plan for an Independent Commission on Jan. 6 Capitol Riot." NPR. May 28. https://tinyurl.com/tr5hd8. Accessed June 4, 2021.

Neely, Megan Tobias and Donna Carmichael. 2021. "Profiting on Crisis: How Predatory Financial Investors Have Worsened Inequality in the Coronavirus Crisis." *American Behavioral Scientist* March 24, OnlineFirst. https://doi.org/10.1177/00027642211003162. Accessed May 26, 2021.

Nesvetailova, Anastasia and Ronen Palan. 2020. *Sabotage: The Hidden Nature of Finance.* New York: Public Affairs.

New York Times. 2021. "US Jobless Claims Pass 40 Million." May 28. https://tinyurl.com/4mxhrhxu. Accessed May 20, 2021.

Nietzel, Michael T. 2021. "More than 100 Scholars Issue Warning that American Democracy Is in Danger, Call for Federal Reforms." June 1. https://tinyurl.com/wmrtysz8. Accessed June 4, 2021.

Orhangazi, Özgür. 2008. "Financialization and Capital Accumulation in the Non-Financial Corporate Sector: A Theoretical and Empirical Investigation of the US Economy, 1973–2004." *Cambridge Journal of Economics* 32 (6): 863–886.

Palley, Thomas. 2007. "Financialization: What It Is and Why It Matters." Working Paper Number 72, Levy Economics Institute of Bard College. https://tinyurl.com/4ynr4yma. Accessed May 28, 2021.

Parramore, Lynn. 2018. "Meet the Hidden Architect Behind America's Racist Economics." Institute for New Economic Thinking. May 30. https://tinyurl.com/y5kdjnlk. Accessed June 4, 2021.

Pasquale, Frank. 2014. "The Hidden Costs of Health Care Cost-Cutting: Toward a Postneoliberal Health-Reform Agenda." *Law and Contemporary Problems.* 77 (4): 171–193.

Pattani, Aneri. 2021. "For Health Care Workers, the Pandemic is Fueling Renewed Interest in Unions." Health News from NPR. January 11. https://tinyurl.com/83d9jv3w. Accessed May 27, 2021.

Peetz, David, Georgina Murray, and Werner Nienhuser. 2013. "The New Structuring of Corporate Ownership." *Globalizations* 10 (5): 711–730.

Pensions&Investments. 2017. "80 Percent of Equity Market Cap Held by Institutions." April 25, 2017. https://tinyurl.com/n2dmn7y8. Accessed May 20, 2021.

Pfeiffer, Sacha, Meg Anderson, and Barbara Van Woerkom. 2020. "Despite Early Warnings, U.S. Took Months to Expand Swab Production for COVID-19 Test." NPR Special Series: The Coronavirus Crisis. https://tinyurl.com/hxw876x5. Accessed May 25, 2021.

Polivka, Larry and Baozhen Luo. 2015. "The Neoliberal Political Economy and Erosion of Retirement Security." *The Gerontologist* 55 (2): 183–190.

Porter, Michael E. 1992. "Capital Disadvantage: America's Failing Capital Investment System." *Harvard Business Review* 70 (5): 65–82.

Reuters. 2021. "53 Percent of Republicans View Trump as True U.S. President— Reuters/Ipsos." May 24. https://tinyurl.com/8xyrpc3h. Accessed June 4, 2021.

Riccardi, Nicholas. 2021. "Trump's Grip on GOP Sparks Fears about Democratic Process." *Washington Post*. June 3. https://tinyurl.com/4766m844. Accessed June 4, 2021.

Robertson, Campbell and Robert Gebeloff. 2020. "How Millions of Women Became the Most Essential Workers in America." *New York Times*. April 18. https://tinyurl.com/rn26pru8. Accessed May 27, 2021.

Rose, Joel. 2020. "NPR Probes Why Personal Protective Equipment Is Still in Short Supply." NPR Health. September 16. https://tinyurl.com/3ddm2vew. Accessed May 25, 2021.

Ross, Martha and Nicole Bateman. 2019. *Meet the Low-Wage Workforce*. Washington, DC: Metropolitan Policy Program at Brookings. https://tinyurl.com/wd5rkf5v. Accessed May 27, 2021.

S&P Global. 2021. "S&P 500 Buybacks Increase 28.2 Percent in Q4 2020 from Q3 2020; Full Year 2002 Down 28.7 Percent from 2019." S&P Dow Jones Indices, Press Release. March 24, 2021. https://tinyurl.com/hm6wr3yp. Accessed June 18, 2021.

Sargrad, Scott and Maura Calsyn. 2020. "Three Principles for Reopening Schools Safely During the COVID-19 Pandemic." Center for American Progress. July 2020. https://tinyurl.com/vk7xxp2s. Accessed June 1, 2021.

Sarkis, Stephanie. 2020. "Trump's Narcissistic Punishment of Withholding Michigan Aid." *Forbes*. March 28. https://tinyurl.com/8hdwzr8. Accessed June 1, 2021.

Scott, Robert H. 2007. "Bankruptcy Abuse Prevention and Consumer Protection Act of 2005: How the Credit Card Industry's Perseverance Paid Off." *Journal of Economic Issues* 41 (4): 943–960.

Shambaugh, Jay, Ryan Nunn, Patrick Liu, and Greg Nantz. 2017. *Thirteen Facts about Wage Growth*. Washington, DC: The Hamilton Project. https://tinyurl.com/w5jfet78. Accessed May 27, 2021.

Smith, Allan. 2021. "McConnell Says He's '100 Percent' Focused on 'Stopping' Biden's Administration." NBC News. May 5. https://tinyurl.com/4xwe4t4x. Accessed June 4, 2021.

Smith, Randall. 2020. "The Battle over Buybacks." *Wall Street Journal*. December 7.

Soergel, Andrew. 2020. "States Competing in 'Global Jungle' for PPE." *US News & World Report*. April 7. https://tinyurl.com/pntu3dh4. Accessed June 1, 2021.

Sozzi, Brian. 2021. "Here Comes the Stock Buyback Explosion: Goldman Sachs." Yahoo Finance. May 7. https://tinyurl.com/ymjjj32d. Accessed May 24, 2021.

Sprunt, Barbara and Cory Turner. 2020. "White House Stumbles Over How Best to Reopen Schools, as Trump Blasts CDC Guidance." NPR. July 8. https://tinyurl.com/5yhmz3xn. Accessed June 1, 2021.

Tavasci, Daniella and Jan Toporowski. 2010. *Minsky, Crisis and Development*. Basingstoke, UK: Palgrave Macmillan.

Tracy, Abigail. 2020. "How Trump Gutted Obama's Pandemic-Preparedness Systems." *Vanity Fair*. May 1. https://tinyurl.com/2ppdx2h3. Accessed June 1, 2021.

Turner, Corey. 2020. "More Than 6,500 Teachers Have Had Unfair Student Debts Erased." NPR. August 22. https://tinyurl.com/vb5f9t44. Accessed May 31, 2021.

Turner, Corey and Chris Arnold. 2018. "Dept. of Education Fail: Teachers Lose Grants, Forced to Repay Thousands in Loans." NPR Morning Edition. March 28. https://tinyurl.com/2sv6ukvp. Accessed May 31, 2021.

US Bureau of Economic Analysis. 2022. National Income and Product Accounts. https://tinyurl.com/2p89ra69 January 27, 2022. Accessed on February 8, 2022.

US Bureau of Labor Statistics. 2017. "Contingent and Alternative Employment Arrangements—May 2017." News Release. https://tinyurl.com/nehs22xc. Accessed May 27, 2021.

US Bureau of Labor Statistics. 2020. "Payroll Employment Down 20.5 Million in April 2020." The Economics Daily. May 12. https://tinyurl.com/3r4kmzra. Accessed May 20, 2021.

US Bureau of Labor Statistics. 2021a. "The Employment Situation—April 2021." May 7. https://tinyurl.com/bwzadzwj. Accessed May 20, 2021.

US Bureau of Labor Statistics. 2021b. All Employees, Manufacturing. Retrieved from FRED, Federal Reserve Bank of St. Louis. https://fred.stlouisfed.org/series/MANEMP. Accessed May 26, 2021.

US Bureau of Labor Statistics. 2021c. All Employees, Durable Goods. Retrieved from FRED, Federal Reserve Bank of St. Louis. https://fred.stlouisfed.org/series/DMANEMP. Accessed May 26, 2021.

US Bureau of Labor Statistics. 2021d. All Employees, Finance and Insurance. Retrieved from FRED, Federal Reserve Bank of St. Louis. https://fred.stlouisfed.org/series/CES5552000001. Accessed May 26, 2021.

US Bureau of Labor Statistics. 2021e. "Labor Force Statistics from the Current Population Survey: Supplemental Data Measuring the Effects of the Coronavirus (COVID-19) Pandemic on the Labor Market." Table 3. https://tinyurl.com/4wz5ydnv. Accessed May 29, 2021.

US Census Bureau. 2021. "Week 29 Household Pulse Survey: April 28–May 10." https://www.census.gov/data/tables/2021/demo/hhp/hhp29.html. Accessed May 26, 2021.

US-China Economic and Security Review Commission. 2019. *2019 Report to Congress*. Washington, DC: US Government Publishing Office. https://tinyurl.com/r7357sey. Accessed May 22, 2021.

Useem, Michael. 1996. *Investor Capitalism: How Money Managers Are Changing the Face of Corporate America*. New York: Basic Books.

Useem, Michael. 2015. "Investor Capitalism." In *Wiley Encyclopedia of Management, Volume 11: Organizational Behavior*, edited by Patrick C. Flood and Yseult Freeney, 2 pages. https://tinyurl.com/ees24y5a. Accessed May 20, 2021.

Wallach, Philip. 2020. "'Presidents, Populism, and the Crisis of Democracy' Review: A Big-Thinking Executive." *Wall Street Journal*. December 1. https://tinyurl.com/4cskt3e2. Accessed June 4, 2021.

Waller, William. 2001. "Kickin'em While They're Down: Consumer Bankruptcy Reform." *Journal of Economic Issues* 35 (4): 871–888.

Warren, Elizabeth. 2020. "Elizabeth Warren and Ro Khanna Unveil Essential Workers Bill of Rights." Press Release. https://tinyurl.com/yknewtzc. Accessed June 4, 2021.

Weil, David. 2014. *The Fissured Workplace: Why Work Became So Bad for So Many and What Can Be Done to Improve It*. Cambridge, MA: Harvard University Press.

Weller, Christian, editor. 2015. *Inequality, Uncertainty, and Opportunity: The Varied and Growing Role of Finance in Labor Relations*. Champaign, IL: Labor and Employment Relations Association.

Werner, Erica. 2018. "Trump Signs Law Rolling Back Post-Financial Crisis Banking Rules." *Washington Post*. May 24. https://tinyurl.com/2pxvdcep. Accessed May 30, 2021.

Whalen, Charles J. 1996. "The Age of Anxiety: Erosion of the American Dream." *USA Today: The Magazine of the American Scene* 125 (September): 14–16.

Whalen, Charles J. 1997. "Money-Manager Capitalism and the End of Shared Prosperity." *Journal of Economic Issues* 31 (2): 517–525.

Whalen, Charles J. 2007. *The U.S. Credit Crunch of 2007: A Minsky Moment.* Levy Economics Institute Public Policy Brief, No. 92. Annandale-on-Hudson, New York: The Levy Economics Institute of Bard College.

Whalen, Charles J. 2008. "Post-Keynesian Institutionalism and the Anxious Society." In *Alternative Institutional Structures: Evolution and Impact,* edited by Sandra S. Batie and Nicholas Mercuro, 273–299. London: Routledge.

Whalen, Charles J. 2010. "Economic Policy for the Real World." *Policy Note,* No. 2010-1. Annandale-on-Hudson, NY: Levy Economics Institute of Bard College.

Whalen, Charles J. 2012. "Money Manager Capitalism." In *Handbook of Critical Issues in Finance,* edited by Jan Toporowski and Jo Michell, 254–262. Cheltenham, UK: Edward Elgar Publishing.

Whalen, Charles J. 2020a. "Understanding Financialisation: Standing on the Shoulders of Minsky." In *Alternative Approaches to Economic Theory,* edited by Victor A. Beker, 185–206. London: Routledge.

Whalen, Charles J. 2020b. "Post-Keynesian Institutionalism: Past, Present, and Future." *Evolutionary and Institutional Economics Review* 17 (1): 71–92.

Whalen, Charles J. 2020c. "The 'Middle Way' of John R. Commons: Pursuing Reasonable Value in the Age of Unreason." *Journal of Economic Issues* 54 (4): 1161–1173.

Whalen, Charles J. 2021. "Post-Keynesian Institutionalism and the Failure of Neoliberalism: Returning Realism to Economics by Highlighting Economic Insecurity as the Flip Side of Financialization." *Journal of Economic Issues* 55 (2): 477–484.

Whoriskey, Peter, Douglas MacMillan, and Jonathan O'Connell. 2020. "'Doomed to Fail': Why a $4 Trillion Bailout Couldn't Revive the American Economy." *New York Times.* October 5. https://tinyurl.com/yh4h88hy. Accessed June 4, 2021.

Wray, Randall L. 2009. "The Rise and Fall of Money Manager Capitalism: A Minskian Approach." *Cambridge Journal of Economics* 33 (4): 807–828.

Yearby, Ruqiijah. 2021. "Meatpacking Plants Have Been Deadly COVID-19 Hot Spots—But Policies that Encourage Workers to Show Up Sick are Legal." The Conversation. February 26. https://tinyurl.com/5ekab26w. Accessed June 1, 2021.

Zalewski, David A. and Charles J. Whalen. 2010. "Financialization and Income Inequality: A Post-Keynesian Institutional Analysis." *Journal of Economic Issues* 44 (3): 757–777.

5. Wealth inequality, household debt, and macroeconomic instability

Christian E. Weller and Emek Karakilic

INTRODUCTION

A growing number of households in the United States (US) face current and future financial insecurity due to rising wealth inequality and increased exposure to economic risks. As the COVID-19 pandemic made abundantly clear, many households find it difficult to weather economic emergencies, such as a layoff or unexpected medical expenses. In addition, households often cannot adequately prepare for the future because of current financial insecurity. For example, many households took out new loans or borrowed from friends or family members just to pay daily expenses during the recession of 2020. Such indebtedness contributes to future financial insecurity for those households. It often comes at the expense of borrowing for investments (in higher education or in starting a business, for example) that could enhance household economic security in the future. And, households need to pay down that debt, cutting the resources households will have available to make security-enhancing investments for some time to come.

Although the COVID-19 pandemic starkly illustrates widespread household exposure to economic risks, that exposure is not new. For decades, US households have increasingly faced large economic risks on their own. Jobs have become less stable; wage growth has lagged behind productivity gains; and many employers have not provided workers with adequate retirement and health benefits (Weller and Newman 2020).

This greater risk exposure happened amid rising wealth and a growing economy. For more than a decade prior to the start of the pandemic, the US economy expanded steadily, causing corporate profits and stock-market values to reach record highs. The US economy generated more wealth, but it also distributed that wealth in an increasingly unequal manner. For example, at the end of 2019, just before the pandemic began, the top 1 percent of income earners owned 25.4 percent of all wealth in the United States, and the top 10 percent of income earners owned 70.5 percent; those wealth shares for high-income earners were the highest on record, going back to September 1989 (Board of Governors 2020a). The problem of increased exposure to economic risk is rooted in wealth inequality, not wealth creation.

Moreover, wealth inequality creates a problem for the overall economy. The rising household indebtedness caused by increased risk exposure threatens not only individual well-being but also economic growth and stability. Such indebtedness adversely affects the macroeconomy through a number of key channels, as we discuss below.

The purpose of this chapter is to explore these problems, linkages, and channels. The investigation is organized as follows. We begin by summarizing the evidence on rising wealth inequality in the United States. Then we consider the increased exposure to economic risk faced by individuals and households, especially the rise of precarious jobs, highlighting the costs of that increased exposure and the impediments to increased saving by households. That analysis is followed by an examination of how the growth of household debt represents a key link between wealth inequality, mounting economic risks, and the macroeconomic problems of slower growth and greater instability. A final section offers a brief discussion and conclusion, including some attention to our investigation's implications for public policy.

WEALTH INEQUALITY

Wealth in the United States is unequally distributed. As Figure 5.1 illustrates, wealth has become increasingly concentrated among the richest families for decades, but especially in the years after the Great Recession of 2007–2009 (Bricker et al. 2020; Piketty, Saez, and Zucman 2017; Wolff 2017). Wealth inequality even increased during the more recent recession: from December 2019 to September 2020, the average real wealth of households in the top two income quintiles grew faster than the average wealth for households in the bottom three quintiles.

In addition, Figure 5.1 does not tell the whole story because it shows only the average wealth for each income quintile. Before the crisis hit in 2020, even many middle- and upper-income households had little wealth (Wolff 2017). Moreover, a large fraction of US households have seen their real (inflation-adjusted) wealth shrink since the eve of the Great Recession, which began at the end of 2007. The median wealth of non-retired households in 2019 was $91,540, or 22.2 percent below the $117,627 (in 2019 dollars) recorded in 2007.[1] Similar differences held for all income quintiles, other than the bottom quintile, where median wealth in 2019 was the highest since 1995.[2] The typical wealth of all middle-income groups lagged far behind the levels recorded before the Great Recession. As a result, many households were more badly prepared for the economic risks associated with the COVID-19 pandemic than they were for that earlier recession.[3]

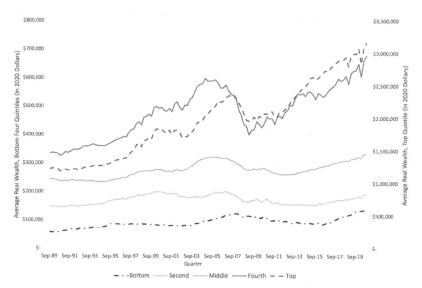

Notes: Population sizes based on Federal Reserve Research (Board of Governors 2020b) for the third quarter of survey years of the Survey of Consumer Finances. All other quarters up to June 2019 are linear interpolations. Population growth after December 2019 is assumed to be the same as from September 2016 to September 2019. Real dollar values deflated using the Bureau of Economic Analysis' (2020) price index for personal consumption expenditures. All dollar figures expressed in September 2020 dollars.
Source: Authors' calculations based on Federal Reserve research (Board of Governors 2020a; 2020b).

Figure 5.1   *Average real per household wealth by income quintile, 1989–2020*

Wealth inequality is especially pronounced by race and ethnicity (Hanks, Solomon, and Weller 2018; Solomon and Weller 2018; Weller and Thompson 2018). For example, research using various data sets and time horizons finds that Black and Latinx households tend to own only a fraction of the wealth of White households (Asanthe-Muhammed et al. 2017; Bhutta et al. 2020; Dettling et al. 2017). African-American and Latinx households are much less likely than White households to own their own house, a retirement account, or a business (Hanks, Solomon, and Weller 2018; Solomon and Weller 2018). Evidence also shows that wealth is more unevenly distributed among Asian Americans than among Whites, largely because (relative to Whites) there is much less wealth among Asian-American households at the bottom of the wealth distribution (Weller and Thompson 2018). Also, even when they own these assets, the size of such assets is usually smaller for people of color, often reflecting systemic racism in labor, housing, and credit markets (Hamilton et al. 2015; Hanks, Solomon, and Weller 2018).

RISK EXPOSURE, PSYCHOLOGICAL STRESSES, AND LOW SAVINGS

Household wealth serves not only as a financial buffer in an emergency, but also as a means for economic mobility and as a pathway to a secure retirement. Since such wealth is a stock of assets accumulated over time, it includes what economists call precautionary savings—income saved so it will be available to meet an unanticipated need. The COVID-19 pandemic highlighted the importance of precautionary savings and overall wealth in times of emergencies.

The pandemic forced individuals and households to make difficult choices—choices that were often wrenchingly difficult for those without emergency savings. Many workers faced the choice of continuing to work and risking their health or not working and finding themselves unable to pay their living expenses. In contrast, sufficient emergency savings allowed others to stay home and protect the health of themselves and their family members. In fact, those with even more wealth were able to move to new locations that offered more space for social distancing, thus lowering their chances of illness. Older workers, people who are generally at greater risk of becoming seriously ill from the coronavirus than their younger counterparts, faced an especially difficult choice, and only those with sufficient wealth could opt to leave the labor force to reduce their risk of illness.

The widespread lack of wealth to draw upon in crises became apparent during the pandemic and associated recession. For example, renters, who typically have much less wealth than homeowners, faced more housing uncertainty as they fell behind on their rent. About 20 percent of renters and approximately 10 percent of homeowners with a mortgage fell behind on rent and mortgage payments during the pandemic (US Census Bureau 2020). Renters also generally had less access to a reliable internet service and electronic devices for their children's remote learning (Francis and Weller 2021). Looking at households more broadly, the combination of limited savings and a severe economic crisis exposed millions of households to housing insecurity, hunger, and poverty (Han, Meyer, and Sullivan 2020; US Census Bureau 2020). Current and future economic uncertainty went hand-in-hand with little or no wealth during the pandemic.

In short, the COVID-19 pandemic demonstrated that many households do not have the wealth, or even the precautionary savings, needed to effectively handle crises. It also showed that many times the people facing the greatest risks—such as low-income healthcare workers, for example—tend to have the least wealth and the fewest opportunities to save more (Weller 2018). Unfortunately, rising wealth inequality has left a large and growing share of households ill-prepared for the future.

Moreover, the adverse consequences of rising inequality are not limited to times of crisis. Rising inequality has meant that more and more households have fewer opportunities to invest in their own future by starting a business, relocating to an area with better employment opportunities, buying a house, and supporting their children's education. These challenges have impeded households' financial security for at least two decades. Even worse, rising costs of housing, healthcare, and care for children and older adults presented households with substantially greater economic risks well before the pandemic (Weller and Newman 2020; Weller and Tolson 2018).

To be clear, the long-term economic forces that have increased US wealth inequality have *simultaneously* shifted the burden of economic risks from companies to workers (examples include replacing long-term employment with gig work and short-term work contracts, and the move from defined-benefit pensions to defined-contribution retirement plans) and left households in a weaker financial position to cope with those growing risks. At the same time, public policy changes and policy inaction at the federal, state, and local levels have often *worsened* the problem by adding to the burden of economic risk borne by individuals and households. For example, a variety of social protections—such as minimum wages, union membership, and social insurance programs—have eroded over the past three decades, as has support for public education (Weller and Newman 2020). That deterioration has left individuals with more precarious income and employment.

Precarious Work and Volatile Incomes

The concept of precarious work goes back to the French sociologist Pierre Bourdieu's (1998) idea of *précarité*. According to Bourdieu, who closely observed working conditions after 1980, precariousness is everywhere and influences almost everything from industry to institutions of cultural production (Bourdieu 1998). Similarly, Arne Kalleberg (2009) defines precarious work as "employment that is uncertain, unpredictable, and risky from the point of view of the worker" (Kalleberg 2009, 2). British economist Guy Standing argued that new labor market conditions after the 1980s created a new working class, termed the precariat (Standing 2011). Standing shifted precarity from Bourdieu's description of labor conditions to "precarious workers as a socio-economic category or class" (Millar 2017, 3).[4]

Precarious work and income volatility have become more evident since the 1970s in the US (Kalleberg 2009). According to Kalleberg (2009, 2), the economic crisis of the early 1970s and the ensuing period of slow growth and falling profits gave rise to a reorganization of labor institutions amid growing global competition. Several public policies contributed to the rise of precarious work. These include erosion of the minimum wage, deunionization, and deregulation, all of which increased corporate power. For example, the minimum wage has been eroding for decades, offering less and less security to workers. By the early 1990s, an employee working full time at the federal minimum wage received less than what she would have needed to have an income above the federal poverty line (Bernstein and Schmitt 2000; Luce 2017). The federal minimum wage has subsequently lost ground further, as Congress last adjusted its value to $7.25 per hour in 2009, but has made no further adjustments to account for inflation or productivity gains since then.

Moreover, workers have faced increasingly worsening conditions since the mid-1970s as employers and the public sector attacked unions. This has resulted in a steady decline of workers protected by collective bargaining agreements since the early 1980s (Kalleberg 2011). The federal government also deregulated key industries and cut the budgets of public agencies that monitor labor regulations. For example, the Reagan administration reduced the monitoring and regulatory functions of institutions such as the Occupational Safety and Health Administration (OSHA) and the Equal Employment Opportunity Commission (EEOC). Meanwhile, as a result of lax enforcement of (and loopholes in) existing protective labor legislation, employers could avoid their legal obligations to workers by increasingly hiring people as independent contractors (Kalleberg 2011; Luce 2014).

Precarious workers often lack other job options and alternatives (McKay et al. 2012). In the United States, there have always been such workers. Today, the difference is that fewer and fewer workers have access to what were once considered "standard employment relations," which Leah Vosko (2010, 1) describes as "a full-time continuous employment relationship, where the worker has one employer, works on the employer's premises under direct supervision, and has access to comprehensive benefits and entitlements."

David Weil's (2014) notion of the "fissured workplace" captures many of the workplace changes associated with the spread of labor-market precariousness. According to Weil, the three main forces that have fractured standard employment relations are increased employment subcontracting, franchising, and supply-chain globalization. All three are driven by the same motivation: to reduce labor costs and shield employers from responsibility for employees' working conditions by transferring that responsibility to individual workers or third parties (such as subcontractors or employment agencies). As a result, workers and work become commodified, resulting not only in slower wage growth, but also greater instability in employment and earnings for the affected employees.[5]

Widespread precarious work also translates into both slower income growth and greater income volatility for households. To increase income in the face of sluggish wage gains and the rising cost of household expenses such as housing, healthcare, and education, workers need to work more hours, work additional jobs, or have more family members join the labor force. Since well-paying, stable jobs with benefits have fallen as a share of labor force employment, much of this additional work also occurs in precarious jobs (Jacobs and Gerson 2004). As a result, while many households have gained income on average, that income has often become increasingly unstable.

Instability in earnings has many sources, but chief among them are irregular work schedules, unemployment spells, and contingent pay such as tips, bonuses, and commissions (Board of Governors 2014). Employment by retailers and restaurants, which grew prior to the pandemic (Golden 2015; Morduch and Schneider 2017) and is likely to recover slowly afterward, is particularly prone to this erratic earnings pattern. However, workers in others sectors have also increasingly experienced negative earnings-related shocks over the past several decades. In addition, the observed trend toward shorter periods of employment with a given employer likely reflects involuntary instabilities, not voluntary increases in job mobility (Weller 2018).

Increasing income volatility has been a key characteristic of households' economic experience as precarious jobs have proliferated. For example, Karen Dynan, Douglas Elmendorf, and Daniel Sichel (2012) find that income volatility has grown since the 1970s. Just prior to the Great Recession, households had a 12 percent chance of income drops that were greater than 50 percent of their income, compared with a 7 percent chance for households in the 1970s (Dynan, Elmendorf, and Sichel 2012). Hardy and Ziliak (2014) similarly find increasing income volatility, at both the bottom and the top of the income distribution. Underlying changes in income volatility appear to be increases in earnings volatility, especially for men (Dahl, DeLeire, and Schwabish 2007; Gottschalk et al. 1994; Haider 2001; Shin and Solon 2011; Ziliak, Hardy and Bollinger 2011), but also for women (Ziliak, Hardy, and Bollinger 2011).

Short-term Instability and Long-term Insecurity

Families that experience greater income instability also generally have less wealth available to ensure a secure future. This link between short-term and long-term economic insecurity results from several factors; four are mentioned here. First, families experiencing more income volatility must more often dip into savings—or borrow—to pay their bills than families without such volatility. That reduced savings or increased borrowing then becomes a long-term drag on household finances.

Second, families with more income volatility save less because they are less likely to qualify for a retirement or healthcare plan at work or even to work for an employer that offers one. Part of the problem here is that employees experiencing income volatility might also have short work tenures and therefore fail to qualify for certain workplace benefits (as opposed to those with more time on the job). But the growth of precarious work also has made it hard for many workers to gain access to such benefits regardless of work tenure, since more and more jobs (such as so-called "gig economy" jobs) do not offer those benefits. Workers without such benefits also usually have less income available to save because their out-of-pocket expenses (such as for healthcare, for example) are higher than for workers in standard work arrangements (Keith, Harms, and Long 2020; Larsson and Sabolova 2020).

Third, households with high income volatility can ill afford risky but potentially high-return investments, such as stocks (Gollier and Pratt 1996; Kimball 1993; Pratt and Zeckhauser 1987). Instead, they tend to take a cautious approach to investing that focuses on protecting their savings (Cagetti 2003; Carroll and Samwick 1998; Gourinchas and Parker 2001; Guiso, Jappelli and Terlizzese 1992; 1996; Hochguertel 2003). In short, their savings grow more slowly because of greater risk exposure in other parts of their lives.[6]

Fourth, the uncertainty that accompanies more negative income shocks often creates anxiety that interferes with savings decisions. Research finds that people experiencing substantial uncertainty, as in the case of income volatility, experience more stress (Peters, McEwen, and Friston 2017; Rohde et al. 2016; Sinclair and Cheung 2016). This leads to a greater reliance on heuristics, including status quo bias, and often results in limited exploration of financial options and fewer active financial decisions, including those that involve saving for the future (Bernartzi and Thaler 2007; Porcelli and Delgado 2009). In fact, uncertainty often results in worse outcomes, as a consequence of stress and an inability to make decisions, than the certainty of negative outcomes (De Berker et al. 2016; Peters, McEwen, and Friston 2017).

The Need for—and Lack of—Savings

The need for an emergency buffer or financial support for economic mobility has not diminished as wealth has decreased for most households. On the contrary, less stable incomes have increased the need for more precautionary savings.

In the face of precarious work, income volatility, and decreased wealth, households could benefit from more risk protections such as pooled social insurance programs. This is especially true in the case of protections for retirement security. However, since the 1980s, the shift from retirements supported by defined-benefit pensions and Social Security to those supported by individualized savings—such as individual retirement accounts (IRAs) and 401(k)s—has moved the risk burden in the opposite direction (Weller 2016). Regular attacks on unions and collective bargaining rights have made it harder for workers to access defined-benefit pensions both in the private and public sectors. Moreover, the unwillingness of policymakers to raise taxes on higher-income earners has meant greater pressure on programs such as Social Security. Congress has not updated Social Security's benefits to address increasing risks such as mounting caregiving needs (Weller and Hamilton 2018). Instead, initial benefits relative to lifetime earnings have declined as the age of eligibility for full benefits has increased from 65 years to 67 years.

To offset the decline of defined-benefit pensions and Social Security, households need to save more on their own. Yet, individualized forms of saving are highly inefficient and increase households' risk exposure even further. Households face greater financial risk exposure with these savings plans than with social insurance programs such as Social Security (Weller 2016; Weller and Newman 2020). Moreover, Congress has offered tax incentives that are complex and heavily skewed towards higher-income earners (Weller 2016; Weller and Ghilarducci 2015). In fact, higher-income earners, especially those with stable incomes, are more likely to make use of such retirement savings plans (Weller 2016; 2018). As a result, the current system's emphasis on individualized savings adds to economic insecurity for most households and further exacerbates wealth inequality.

The COVID-19 Pandemic: A Closer Look

The need for and lack of emergency savings amid widespread risks became readily apparent during the pandemic of 2020. Many low- and middle-income households lacked sufficient financial cushions for an emergency such as job losses, higher childcare costs, or additional healthcare expenses—and the pandemic threatened many families with all of these. With little savings to fall back on, many households fell behind on rent and mortgage payments (US Census Bureau 2020; Weller 2020a). For example, one-in-seven renters with family incomes from $35,000 to $100,000 were not current on their rent in November 2020, and 79.9 percent of these renters expected to face eviction within two months. At the same time, among homeowners with a mortgage, one in ten were not current on their mortgage, and 56.1 percent expected a foreclosure within two months.[7]

Because of the pandemic, many people left the labor force to care for children and other family members. This was especially true for women, particularly women of color (Kashen, Glynn, and Novello 2020). In November 2020, for instance, 14.2 percent of non-retired people living in families with incomes between $35,000 and $100,000 did not work because they took care of children or other family members, and another 13.7 percent stayed away from work because of health worries. The pandemic only highlighted the stark choices that people must often make between earning income and caring for themselves, children, and other family members; many of these difficult choices already existed, owing to insufficient and unaffordable child-care options (Malik et al. 2018) and limited support for those caring for older relatives (Weller and Tolson 2020). The recession of 2020 merely illustrated (in an extraordinarily vivid manner) the financial insecurity of many US households.[8]

While the pandemic highlighted the need for policies supporting those families in the most precarious financial situations, congressional action fell short of what was needed. For instance, only about 30 percent of workers in the pandemic had the privilege of working from home (Gould and Shierholz 2020); at the same time, many of those who could not work remotely failed to receive protective equipment and pay supplements that would have enhanced their physical safety and financial security. This was particularly true among direct care workers who were pivotal in protecting the lives of others (Weller 2020d; Weller, Cohen, and Stone 2020; Weller et al. 2020). In early 2020, Congress enacted the CARES Act to counter the economic and public health effects of the pandemic, but it did not directly provide for hazard pay for those most at risk (Kinder, Stateler, and Du 2020) and much of its added financial assistance to struggling workers ran out by that summer. Public policy had put many workers in a precarious situation before the pandemic, and then Congress offered too little assistance when it was needed most.

HOUSEHOLD DEBT, SLOW GROWTH, AND FINANCIAL INSTABILITY

Households with little or no savings often turn to debt, not just to make investments in the future (such as purchasing a home or starting a business), but also to cover emergencies, including the need to continue paying for daily living expenses in the face of an unexpected drop in income. For example, many middle-income households borrowed during the pandemic to pay for their regular expenses. In November 2020, more than one-third of households with incomes between $35,000 and $100,000 borrowed from friends or family or used loans (including credit card debt) to pay their current expenses.[9]

The recession of 2020 highlighted the importance of informal lending as a way to get households through difficult times. According to the US Census Bureau (2020), 13.1 percent of all households borrowed money from family or friends to pay their expenses in November 2020, up from 11.4 percent in August 2020 (see Figure 5.2). This type of debt is much more widespread among Black and Latinx families, younger families, and those without a college degree (Figure 5.2). For example, 24.6 percent of households without a high school degree borrowed money from family or friends (Figure 5.2).

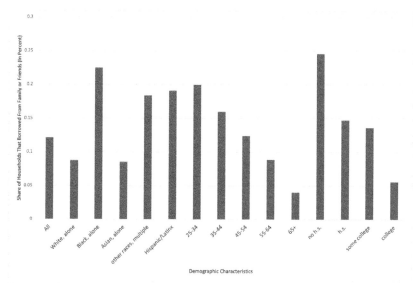

Source: Authors' calculations based on US Census Bureau (2020).

Figure 5.2   *Share of households that borrowed from family or friends to pay for expenses from August to November 2020, by demographics*

New household debt during the pandemic extended a longer-term trend of borrowing money to bridge a widening gap between household financial resources and expenses. For example, indebtedness has grown for three decades among older households about to enter retirement (Lusardi, Mitchell, and Oggero 2018). In addition, household debt, especially in the form of mortgages and home equity lines of credit, increased startlingly for several years before the Great Recession. Then, amid tightening credit standards following the financial and economic crisis from 2007 to 2009, mortgages, home equity lines, and credit card debt became harder to acquire. Auto loans and student debt filled the void, reaching record highs prior to the pandemic recession of 2020 (Board of Governors 2020c; Weller 2020b) (see Figure 5.3).

When the recession hit in early 2020, those formal types of debt were not enough, especially as banks tightened lending. Many households did not have the resources needed to pay their expenses or make important investments, such as those necessary to support their children's online learning (Francis and

Weller 2021). As a result, many households had to rely on informal networks for financial help.

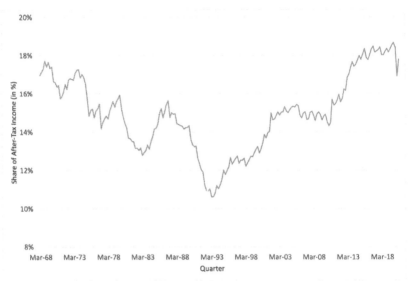

Note: Consumer debt in Board of Governors (2020c) is allocated to non-revolving credit in the same proportion reported in Board of Governors (2020f).
Source: Authors' calculations based on Federal Reserve research (Board of Governors 2020c; 2020f).

Figure 5.3   Non-revolving consumer debt to after-tax income, 1968–2020

From Higher Debt to Slower Growth

The combination of massive wealth inequality and continued high debt levels raises the specter that household difficulties will lead to slower growth across the entire economy. For example, slower growth may result from reduced business investment in response to concerns over widespread consumer debt (Dutt 2006; Palley 1994; 2009). Firms know the level of debt, and thus the level of debt service, that consumers have to repay. Thus, they also understand that households' debt burden will depress demand in the future, since that burden means those households will be less able to make future purchases. This reduces the incentive for firms to invest (Dutt 2006; Palley 1994; 2009).

Heavy debt burdens also make it harder for households to receive financing for other ventures. For example, banks will consider unsecured debt levels when making decisions about new loan applications. Thus, households that have taken on large loans to cover expenses will find it harder to make other large investments: they will be less able to access the financial resources needed for purposes such as buying a house or starting (or growing) a business.[10] In the absence of such investments, economic growth will be less robust.

From Indebtedness to Instability

In addition to leading to slower economic growth, household indebtedness can also spread financial insecurity and instability to other sectors of the economy. This can occur through at least two channels.

One channel involves informal borrowing through social networks. As we have already observed, households with little or negative wealth often rely on friends or family for financial assistance (O'Brien 2012; Pugliese, Le Bourdais and Clark 2020). But borrowers often struggle to repay that debt, and unrepaid loans reduce the financial security of lending households.

Data from the Federal Reserve (Board of Governors 2020b) provide some insight into the magnitude of financial support that households provide to friends or family. In 2019, 14.5 percent of households financially supported family or friends with an average of $9,337 that year. This totaled about $173 billion in payments between family or friends at a time when unemployment was low and incomes were rising in general. The data also show that lending households are often in shaky financial situations themselves. One-quarter of households that financially supported others in 2019 had less than $37,670 in income; such households loaned an average of $3,000.[11]

Often those amounts will not be repaid because they were meant as a gift or because of the borrowers' inability to repay. This directly lowers the financial security of the lenders, who themselves are often financially insecure. Estimates suggest, for example, that financial interrelationships between family members tend to correlate with financial instability and substantially contribute to the wealth gap between White and Black families (Chiteji and Hamilton, 2000; 2002; Toney and Hamilton, 2020). Economic insecurity then proliferates through already economically insecure households and depresses demand.

The other channel linking indebtedness to instability emerges when heavily indebted households fall behind on their debt repayments for formal debt such as mortgages. The growth of delinquent and ultimately defaulted-on debt can have two negative consequences for economic growth. For one, banks become more cautious in extending credit, even as just loan delinquencies increase. Starting in April 2020, banks quickly tightened lending standards for mortgages and other consumer loans (Board of Governors 2020d). By July 2020, more than half of all banks reported that they tightened standards for non-subprime mortgages and for all types of consumer loans, for instance (Board of Governors 2020d). As a result, households will have a harder time purchasing durable goods and buying a house, reducing aggregate demand and longer-term growth. Moreover, banks can fail if loan defaults become substantially large, although increased capital requirements have considerably reduced this possibility in the aftermath of the Great Recession. Yet, banks reported that 2.81 percent of all residential mortgages were delinquent in the third quarter of 2020, up from 2.34 percent at the end of 2019 and the highest delinquent share since the end of 2018 (Board of Governors 2020e). The quality of mortgages quickly deteriorated in the recession, but remained in the range of the prior years.

Consequences of Unequal Access

The lack of access to capital for future investments is unevenly distributed. African-American, Latinx, and many Asian-American households already have higher levels of consumer indebtedness than White households (Hanks, Solomon, and Weller 2018; Solomon and Weller 2018; Weller and Thompson 2018). They will find it especially difficult to secure additional financing for new investments.

This racial and ethnic inequality has two consequences that will indirectly slow growth. First, if current trends continue, the lack of affordable financing for people of color to invest in their own future will make it harder for them to increase their wealth. Wealth inequality by race and ethnicity, already at or near record high levels, will thus become worse and perpetuate financial insecurity for a large proportion of the population. As discussed above, such financial insecurity slows economic growth. Second, people of color are a growing share of the US population. As people of color on average have more debt than White households, an increasing share of American households will find it difficult to make productive, long-term investments, which means growth will be constrained even further.

DISCUSSION AND CONCLUSION

Wealth inequality has grown over the past four decades, reaching persistently high levels for much of the past decade. The lack of wealth for many households has left a large section of the population ill-prepared for emergencies and with few means to invest for the future. At the same time, households have faced increasing exposure to economic risk in a number of ways, most notably through the proliferation of precarious jobs, which offer low pay, little income stability, and few benefits. As a result, the combination for many families of very little wealth and high risk exposure further cemented wealth inequality since such households have often needed to go deeper into debt. Widespread, high, and growing household debt burdens also slow economic growth and raise the possibility of more financial instability: microeconomic insecurity translates into weaker overall economic performance and threatens macroeconomic stability.

Our chapter counters the Neoclassical economists' argument that households respond to more short-term financial insecurity by building up precautionary savings. On the contrary, the available evidence shows that increasing economic risk exposure contributes to increasing wealth inequality. The risks are concentrated among middle-income and lower-income households, who have the least room for increased savings from the outset. Wealth and economic risk exposure are also unequally distributed by race, ethnicity, and gender, often leaving people of color and women most vulnerable.

As inequality has widened and the challenges and economic risks confronting US households have increased, public policies, especially at the federal level, have often made matters worse for struggling workers and their families. Some aspects of this difficulty have been mentioned in our chapter, especially with regard to minimum wages, unions, and social insurance. But the policy challenges are even greater than we have had an opportunity to address above. For example, Congress has failed to provide paid family and medical leave to assist households with caregiving responsibilities for children and other family members. Policymakers have also repeatedly attacked Medicaid, even though it is one of the key sources of financial assistance to households that require long-term care due to illness or disability. In a similar way, conservative congressional majorities and the Trump administration attacked the Affordable Care Act, which offered households some protections from healthcare risks that would not be available in the absence of that law.

Worsening inequality and mounting household risk exposure are social problems; as such, public policy can address them. The pathway forward towards more wealth equality, greater economic security for households, and thus a foundation for stronger economic growth will have to rely on large-scale and sustained policy interventions. As the discussion in this chapter shows, lower-income and middle-income households, African-Americans and Latinx households, single women, and other vulnerable groups will not be able to build more wealth rapidly, and on a sustained basis, without substantial policy changes.

One set of key policy interventions will need to focus on giving all workers equal access to well-paying, stable jobs with strong career opportunities and decent health insurance and retirement benefits. Higher minimum wages, more opportunities for workers to join a union, and universal healthcare and retirement benefits are all important first steps in this direction.

Other policy interventions will need to reduce economic risks to families. This requires a variety of policy steps, including: broadening the circle of workers eligible for unemployment insurance benefits; raising unemployment insurance benefits; making healthcare more affordable (so that workers will face lower out of pocket expenses); investing in a progressive family care infrastructure; making college education debt-free; and expanding Social Security benefits. A wide range of policies will also need to target systemic discrimination against people of color and women—especially women of color—in labor, housing, credit, and other markets.

Moreover, simply making sure that people have enough money to save will not be enough to substantially shrink and possibly reduce wealth inequality. Additional and systemic reforms to reduce inequality and boost wealth creation will need to be considered and crafted alongside those changes. In particular, Congress will need to find ways to rectify decades, centuries even, of systemic oppression and exploitation of people of color, especially African-Americans, but also Native Americans. Because of these past historic injustices, previous generations were often robbed of the opportunity to build wealth. They could not pass on wealth to the same degree that White households could. Wealth inequality persisted and, without institutional reforms, will continue to persist across generations. Targeted wealth transfers to members of those groups that historically have been harmed will have to be part of any realistic agenda to eliminate massive wealth inequality by race and ethnicity.

Widespread household debt slows economic growth. It depresses economic demand and increases financial instability. Microeconomic insecurity translates into macroeconomic instability. Congress needs to have the willingness to tackle this generational challenge with serious and sustained policy interventions.

ACKNOWLEDGMENTS

Charles Whalen provided extensive and insightful feedback on earlier versions of this chapter. We are also very grateful to Olugbenga Ajilore and Oren Levin-Waldman for helpful comments on an earlier draft. All remaining errors are our sole responsibility.

NOTES

1. The authors' calculations based on Federal Reserve research (Board of Governors 2020b).
2. The authors' calculations based on Federal Reserve research (Board of Governors 2020b).
3. To be sure, median wealth for many quintiles in 2007 was relatively high due to inflated housing values, but median wealth in 2019 was also below levels recorded during the late 1990s and early 2000s.
4. The rising precariousness of work corresponds with the rising economic insecurity that Hyman Minsky and Charles Whalen (1996–1997) associated with

the emergence of money manager capitalism in the early 1980s. According to Whalen (2020, 189–190), the rise of money manager capitalism and the spread of worker insecurity and economic inequality are two sides of the same coin.

5. The workplace fissuring is part of a series of changes in the structures, strategies, and practices of corporations beginning in the 1970s. Corporate executives, often driven by the growing influence of institutional investors (Minsky and Whalen 1996–1997), gained more incentives to pursue short-term profits (Lazonick 2014). The search for such profits meant that workers increasingly became residual claimants to corporate earnings. Corporate restructurings accelerated to trim labor costs, often through the downsizing, outsourcing, and offshoring of jobs (Lazonick 2014). As a result, workers saw jobs and incomes disappear. Meanwhile, firms sought to increase profits and maintain profitability, even in recessions (Bivens and Weller 2006). In this context, companies eliminated labor protections and reduced employer responsibility (Weil 2014). In the end, workers ended up with lower and less stable incomes and benefits, while the growth of corporate profits accelerated, signaling a substantial shift in economic risks.

6. For related research on how households with high income volatility are relatively less willing to invest their money for the longer term, see, for example, Benito (2006); Gonyea (2007); Orel, Ford, and Brock (2004); and Weller (2018).

7. All figures (data) in this paragraph are the authors' calculations based on US Census Bureau (2020).

8. Healthcare is another area that presented an economic risk to US households even before the pandemic. In 2019, for example, 59.8 percent of households that experienced large, unexpected health expenses and had no health insurance ended up with medical debt (Hanlon, Vinelli, and Weller 2020). Among households with health insurance, 38.2 percent still had medical debt (Hanlon, Vinelli, and Weller 2020). Health insurance reduces the chance of medical debt, but it does not eliminate it, leaving many households across the United States indebted as a consequence of necessary medical procedures (Weller 2020c).

9. All figures in this paragraph are the authors' calculations based on US Census Bureau (2020).

10. Banks will be especially reluctant to lend when delinquent loans and debt defaults are on the rise. Moreover, unpaid loans further dampen growth by limiting lenders' ability to lend, spend, and invest.

11. All figures in this paragraph are the authors' calculations based on Board of Governors (2020b).

REFERENCES

Asanthe-Muhammed, Dedrick, Chuck Collins, Josh Hoxie, and Emanuel Nieves. 2017. *The Road to Zero Wealth: How the Racial Wealth Divide Is Hollowing Out America's Middle Class*. Washington, DC: Prosperity Now and Institute for Policy Studies. http://tinyurl.com/sp6fkpr9. Accessed February 8, 2021.

Benito, Andrew. 2006. "Does Job Insecurity Affect Household Consumption?" *Oxford Economic Papers* 58 (1): 157–181.

Bernartzi, Shlomo and Richard Thaler. 2007. "Heuristics and Biases in Retirement Savings Behavior." *Journal of Economic Perspectives* 21 (3): 81–104.

Bernstein, Jared and Schmitt, John. 2000. "The Impact of the Minimum Wage." Economic Policy Institute Briefing Paper. Washington, DC: Economic Policy Institute.

Bhutta, Neil, Andrew C. Chang, Lisa J. Dettling, and Joanne W. Hsu. 2020. "Disparities in Wealth by Race and Ethnicity in the 2019 Survey of Consumer Finances." *FEDS Notes*, September 28. Washington, DC: Federal Reserve.

Bivens, Josh and Christian Weller. 2006. "The Job-Loss Recovery: Not New, Just Worse." *Journal of Economic Issues* 51 (3): 603–628.

Board of Governors, Federal Reserve System. 2014. *Report on the Economic Well-Being of US Households in 2013*. Washington, DC: Federal Reserve.

Board of Governors, Federal Reserve System. 2020a. *Distributional Financial Accounts*. Washington, DC: Federal Reserve.

Board of Governors, Federal Reserve System. 2020b. *Survey of Consumer Finances, 1989–2019*. Washington, DC: Federal Reserve.

Board of Governors, Federal Reserve System. 2020c. *Release Z.1, Financial Accounts of the United States*. Washington, DC: Federal Reserve.

Board of Governors, Federal Reserve System. 2020d. *Senior Loan Officer Opinion Survey on Bank Lending Practices, October 2020*. Washington, DC: Federal Reserve.

Board of Governors, Federal Reserve System. 2020e. *Charge-Off and Delinquency Rates on Loans and Leases at Commercial Banks*. Washington, DC: Federal Reserve.

Board of Governors, Federal Reserve System. 2020f. *Release G.19 Consumer Credit*. Washington, DC: Federal Reserve.

Bourdieu, Pierre. 1998. *Acts of Resistance: Against the Tyranny of the Market*. New York: The New Press.

Bricker, Jesse, Sarena Goodman, Kevin B. Moore, and Alice H. Volz. 2020. "Wealth and Income Concentration in the SCF: 1989–2019." *FEDS Notes*, September 28. Washington, DC: Federal Reserve.

Bureau of Economic Analysis. 2020. *National Income and Product Accounts*. Washington, DC: Bureau of Economic Analysis.

Cagetti, Marco. 2003. "Wealth Accumulation Over the Life Cycle and Precautionary Savings." *Journal of Business & Economic Statistics* 21 (3): 339–353.

Carroll, Christopher D. and Andrew A. Samwick. 1998. "How Important is Precautionary Saving?" *Review of Economics and Statistics* 80 (3): 410–419.

Chiteji, Ngina and Darrick Hamilton. 2000. "Family Matters: Kin Networks and Asset Accumulation." CSD Working Paper No. 2000-06. St. Louis, MO: Center for Social Development, Washington University.

Chiteji, Ngina and Darrick Hamilton. 2002. "Family Connections and the Black-White Wealth Gap Among Middle-Class Families." *Review of Black Political Economy* 30 (1): 9–28.

Dahl, Molly, Thomas DeLeire, and Jonathan Schwabish. 2007. *Trends in Earnings Variability over the Past 20 Years*. Washington, DC: Congressional Budget Office.

De Berker, Archy O., Robb B. Rutledge, Christoph Mathys, Louise Marshall, Gemma F, Cross, Raymond J. Dolan, and Sven Bestmann. 2016. "Computations of Uncertainty Mediate Acute Stress Responses in Humans." *Nature Communications* 7 (10996): 1–15.

De La Cruz-Viesca, Melany, Zhenxiang Chen, Paul M. Ong, Darrick Hamilton, and William A. Darity Jr. 2016. "The Color of Wealth in Los Angeles." San Francisco:

Federal Reserve Bank of San Francisco. http:// tinyurl.com/3py82ptw. Accessed February 8, 2021.

Dettling, Lisa J., Joanne W. Hsu, Lindsay Jacobs, Kevin B. Moore, and Jeffrey P. Thompson. 2017. "Recent Trends in Wealth-Holding by Race and Ethnicity: Evidence from the Survey of Consumer Finances." *FEDS Notes*, September 27. Washington, DC: Federal Reserve.

Dutt, Amitava K. 2006. "Maturity, Stagnation and Consumer Debt: A Steindlian Approach." *Metroeconomica* 57 (3): 339–364.

Dynan, Karen, Douglas Elmendorf, and Daniel Sichel. 2012. "The Evolution of Household Income Volatility." *The BE Journal of Economic Analysis and Policy* 12 (2): 1–42.

Francis, Dania and Christian Weller. 2021. "Economic Inequality, the Digital Divide and Remote Learning During COVID-19." *Review of Black Political Economy*. Published online May 26, 2021. https://doi.org/10.1177/00346446211017797. Accessed July 28, 2021.

Golden, Lonnie. 2015. "Irregular Work Scheduling and its Consequences." Briefing Paper, No. 394. Washington, DC: Economic Policy Institute.

Gollier, Christian and John W. Pratt. 1996. "Risk Vulnerability and the Tempering Effect of Background Risk." *Econometrica* 64 (5): 1109–1123.

Gonyea, Judith G. 2007. "Improving the Retirement Prospects of Lower-Wage Workers in a Defined-Contribution World." *Families in Society* 88 (3): 453–462.

Gould, Elise and Heidi Shierholz. 2020. "Not Everybody Can Work from Home." Economic Policy Institute Working Economics Blog, March 19. http://tinyurl.com/pkvmqz9z. Accessed February 8, 2021.

Gourinchas, Pierre-Olivier and Jonathan A. Parker. 2001. "The Empirical Importance of Precautionary Saving." *American Economic Review* 91 (2): 406–412.

Gottschalk, Peter, Robert Moffitt, Lawrence F. Katz, and William T. Dickens. 1994. "The Growth of Earnings Instability in the US Labor Market." *Brookings Papers on Economic Activity* 1994 (2): 217–272.

Guiso, Luigi, Tullio Jappelli, and Daniele Terlizzese. 1992. "Earnings Uncertainty and Precautionary Saving." *Journal of Monetary Economics* 30 (2): 307–337.

Guiso, Luigi, Tullio Jappelli, and Daniele Terlizzese. 1996. "Income Risk, Borrowing Constraints, and Portfolio Choice." *American Economic Review* 86 (1): 158–172.

Haider, Steven J. 2001. "Earnings Instability and Earnings Inequality of Males in the United States: 1967–1991." *Journal of Labor Economics* 19 (4): 799–836.

Hamilton, Darrick, William Darity Jr., Anne E. Price, Vishnu Sridharan, and Rebecca Tippett. 2015. "Umbrellas Don't Make it Rain: Why Studying and Working Hard Isn't Enough for Black Americans." Durham, NC: Duke University, Center for Social Equity http://tinyurl.com/yczkm8tp. Accessed February 8, 2021.

Han, Jeehoon, Bruce D. Meyer, and James X. Sullivan. 2020. "Real-time Poverty Estimates During the COVID-19 Pandemic through November 2020." Harris School Working Paper. Chicago, IL: Harris School of Public Policy at the University of Chicago.

Hanks, Angela, Danyelle Solomon, and Christian Weller. 2018. "Systematic Inequality: How America's Structural Racism Helped Create the Black-White Wealth Gap." Washington, DC: Center for American Progress, February 21. http://tinyurl.com/1vd19yf3. Accessed February 8, 2021.

Hanlon, Seth, Andres Vinelli, and Christian E. Weller. 2020. "Repealing the ACA Would Put Millions at Risk While Giving Big Tax Cuts to the Very Wealthy."

Washington, DC: Center for American Progress, September 29. http://tinyurl.com/etrt78po. Accessed February 9, 2021.

Hardy, Bradley and James P. Ziliak. 2014. "Decomposing Trends in Income Volatility: The "Wild Ride" at the Top and Bottom." *Economic Inquiry* 52 (1): 459–476.

Hochguertel, Stefan. 2003. "Precautionary Motives and Portfolio Decisions." *Journal of Applied Econometrics* 18 (1): 61–77.

Jacobs, Jerry A. and Kathleen Gerson. 2004. *The Time Divide: Work, Family, and Gender Inequality*. Cambridge, MA: Harvard University Press.

Kalleberg, Arne L. 2009. "Precarious Work, Insecure Workers: Employment Relations in Transition." *American Sociological Review* 74 (1): 1–22.

Kalleberg, Arne L. 2011. *Good Jobs, Bad Jobs: The Rise of Polarized and Precarious Employment Systems in the United States, 1970s to 2000s*. New York: Russell Sage Foundation.

Kashen, Julie, Sarah Jane Glynn, and Amanda Novello. 2020. "How COVID-19 Sent Women's Workforce Progress Backward." Washington, DC: Center for American Progress, October 30. http://tinyurl.com/vkhk44a1. Accessed February 8, 2021.

Keith, Melissa, Peter D. Harms, and Alexander C. Long. 2020. "Worker Health and Well-Being in the Gig Economy: A Proposed Framework and Research Agenda." In *Research in Occupational Stress and Well-Being*, 18th edition, edited by Pamela L. Perrewé, Peter D. Harms, and Chu-Hsiang Chang, 1–34. Bingley, UK: Emerald Publishing.

Kimball, Miles S. 1993. "Standard Risk Aversion." *Econometrica* 61 (3): 589–611.

Kinder, Molly, Laura Stateler, and Julia Du. 2020. "The COVID-19 Hazard Continues, But the Hazard Pay Does Not: Why America's Essential Workers Need a Raise." Brookings Report. Washington, DC: Brookings Institution.

Larsson, Anthony and Dominika Sabolova. 2020. "'Gig Patients': Health and Dental Care in the Gig Economy." In *The Digital Transformation of Labor: Automation, the Gig Economy and Welfare*, edited by Robin Tiegland and Anthony Larsson, 174–184, New York, NY: Routledge.

Lazonick, William. 2014. "Profits without Prosperity." *Harvard Business Review* 92 (9): 46–55.

Luce, Stephanie. 2014. *Labor Movements: Global Perspective*. Cambridge, UK: Polity Press.

Luce, Stephanie. 2017. "Living Wages: A US Perspective." *Employee Relations* 39 (6): 863–874.

Lusardi, Annamaria, Olivia Mitchell, and Noemi Oggero. 2018. "The Changing Face of Debt and Financial Fragility at Older Ages." *American Economic Review* 108 (5): 407–411.

Malik, Rasheed, Katie Hamm, Leila Schochet, Cristina Novoa, Simon Workman, and Steven Jessen-Howard. 2018. "America's Child Care Deserts in 2018." Washington, DC: Center for American Progress, December 6. http://tinyurl.com/4htv3d5z. Accessed February 8, 2021.

McKay, Sonia, Steve Jeffreys, Anna Paraskevopoulou, and Janoi Keles. 2012. *Final Report: Study on Precarious Work and Social Rights*. Carried out for the European Commission. London: Working Lives Research Institute, London Metropolitan University.

Millar, Kathleen M. 2017. "Toward a Critical Politics of Precarity." *Sociology Compass* 11 (6): 1–11.

Minsky, Hyman P. and Charles J. Whalen. 1996–1997. "Economic Insecurity and the Institution Prerequisites for Successful Capitalism." *Journal of Post Keynesian Economics* 19 (2): 155–170.

Morduch, Jonathan and Rachel Schneider. 2017. *The Financial Diaries: How American Families Cope in a World of Uncertainty.* Princeton, NJ: Princeton University Press.

O'Brien, Rourke. 2012. "Depleting Capital? Race, Wealth and Informal Financial Assistance." *Social Forces* 91 (2): 375–396.

Orel, Nancy A., Ruth A. Ford, and Charlene Brock. 2004. "Women's Financial Planning for Retirement: The Impact of Disruptive Life Events." *Journal of Women and Aging* 16 (3–4): 39–53.

Palley, Thomas. 1994. "Debt, Aggregate Demand, and the Business Cycle: An Analysis in the Spirit of Kaldor and Minsky." *Journal of Post Keynesian Economics* 16 (3): 371–390.

Palley, Thomas. 2009. "The Simple Analytics of Debt-Driven Business Cycles." PERI Working Paper No. 200. Amherst, MA: Political Economy Research Institute.

Peters, Achim, Bruce S. McEwen, and Karl Friston. 2017. "Uncertainty and Stress: Why It Causes Diseases and How It is Mastered By the Brain." *Progress in Neurobiology* 156, 164–88.

Piketty, Thomas, Emmanuel Saez, and Gabriel Zucman. 2017. "Distributional National Accounts: Methods and Estimates for the United States." *Quarterly Journal of Economics* 133 (2): 553–609.

Porcelli, Anthony J. and Mauricio R. Delgado. 2009. "Acute Stress Modulates Risk Taking in Financial Decision Making." *Psychological Science* 20 (3): 278–283.

Pratt, John W. and Richard Zeckhauser. 1987. "Proper Risk Aversion." *Econometrica* 55 (1): 143–154.

Pugliese, Maude, Celine Le Bourdais and Shelley Clark. 2020. "Credit Card Debt and the Provision of Financial Support to Kin in the US." *Journal of Family and Economic Issues.* Published online, November 6, 2020. https://link.springer.com/article/10.1007/s10834-020-09731-7. Accessed July 27, 2021.

Rohde, Nicholas, K.K. Tang, Lars Osberg, and Prasada Rao. 2016. "The Effect of Economic Insecurity on Mental Health: Recent Evidence from Australian Panel Data." *Social Science and Medicine* 151 (February): 250–258.

Shin, Donggyun, and Gary Solon. 2011. "Trends in Men's Earnings Volatility: What Does the Panel Study of Income Dynamics Show?" *Journal of Public Economics* 95 (7–8): 973–982.

Sinclair, Robert R. and Janelle H. Cheung. 2016. "Money Matters: Recommendations for Financial Stress Research in Occupational Health Psychology." *Stress and Health* 32 (3): 181–193.

Solomon, Danyelle and Christian Weller. 2018. "When a Job Is Not Enough: The Latinx-White Wealth Gap." Washington, DC: Center for American Progress, December 5. http://tinyurl.com/2mcvp6gt. Accessed February 9, 2021.

Standing, Guy. 2011. *The Precariat: The New Dangerous Class.* London: Bloomsbury Academic.

Toney, Jermaine and Darrick Hamilton. 2020. "Economic Insecurity in the Family Tree and the Racial Wealth Gap." SSRN Working Paper, January. http://tinyurl.com/4nc5xh53. Accessed February 9, 2021.

US Census Bureau. 2020. "Household Pulse Survey: Measuring Social and Economic Impacts during the Coronavirus Pandemic." Washington DC: Census Bureau. http://tinyurl.com/1atag1p5. Accessed February 9, 2021.

Vosko, Leah. 2010. *Managing the Margins: Gender, Citizenship, and the International Regulation of Precarious Employment.* Oxford: Oxford University Press.

Weil, David. 2014. *The Fissured Workplace: Why Work Became So Bad for So Many and What Can Be Done to Improve It.* Cambridge, MA: Harvard University Press.

Weller, Christian E. 2016. *Retirement on the Rocks: Why Americans Can't Get Ahead and How New Savings Policies Can Help.* New York: Palgrave Macmillan.

Weller, Christian E. 2018. "Working Class Families are Getting Hit From All Sides." Washington, DC: Center for American Progress, July 26. http://tinyurl.com/43s9x8as. Accessed February 9, 2021.

Weller, Christian E. 2020a. "Debt, Evictions, Job Losses: America's Hollowed Out Middle Class Needs More Help." *Forbes.* December 22. https://tinyurl.com/ru5dwr64. Accessed July 27, 2021.

Weller, Christian E. 2020b. "It Is Not Healthy When Middle-Class Families Drown in Debt in a Growing Economy." *Forbes.* February 3. https://tinyurl.com/798f79xy. Accessed, July 27, 2021.

Weller, Christian E. 2020c. "ACA Repeal by the Supreme Court Will Be Robin Hood in Reverse." *Forbes.* October 3. https://tinyurl.com/2twsxsfj. Accessed, July 27, 2021.

Weller, Christian E. 2020d. "Home Care Aides Keep Working Amid Massive Health Risks." *Forbes.* July 15. https://tinyurl.com/3rua3f5y. Accessed July 27, 2021.

Weller, Christian E., Beth Almeida, Marc Cohen, and Robyn Stone. 2020. "Making Care Work Pay." Washington, DC: LeadingAge. http://tinyurl.com/xz2oegi3. Accessed February 9, 2021.

Weller, Christian E., Marc Cohen, and Robyn Stone. 2020. "Who Cares for Those Most Vulnerable to COVID-19? 4 Questions about Home Care Aides Answered." *The Conversation*, March 25. http://tinyurl.com/7hf8w33a. Accessed February 9, 2021.

Weller, Christian E. and Teresa Ghilarducci. 2015. "The Inefficiencies of Existing Retirement Savings Incentives." Washington, DC: Center for American Progress, October 30. http://tinyurl.com/zj3y6mri. Accessed February 8, 2021.

Weller, Christian E. and Darrick Hamilton. 2018. "More Retirement Stability in an Unstable World: Expanding Qualifying Credit Options for Social Security Benefits." *Public Policy and Aging* 28 (1 Supplement): S46–S54.

Weller, Christian E. and Katherine Newman. 2020. "Increasing Risks, Costs, and Retirement Income Inequality." *Annual Review of Gerontology and Geriatrics* 40 (1): 69–103.

Weller, Christian E. and Jeffrey P. Thompson. 2018. "Wealth Inequality More Pronounced Among Asian Americans than Among Whites." *Challenge* 61 (2): 183–202.

Weller, Christian E. and Michele E. Tolson. 2018. "Do Unpaid Caregivers Save Less for Retirement?" *Journal of Retirement* 6 (2): 61–73.

Weller, Christian E. and Michele E. Tolson. 2020. "The Retirement Savings Penalty Borne by Women." *Challenge* 63 (4): 201–218.

Whalen, Charles J. 2020. "Understanding Financialization: Standing on the Shoulders of Minsky." In *Alternative Approaches to Economic Theory*, edited by Victor A. Beker, 185–206. London: Routledge.

Wolff, Edward N. 2017. "Household Wealth Trends in the United States, 1962 to 2016: Has Middle Class Wealth Recovered?" NBER Working Paper No. 24085, Cambridge, MA: National Bureau of Economic Research. https://www.nber.org/papers/w24085. Accessed February 9, 2021.

Ziliak, James P., Bradley Hardy, and Christopher Bollinger. 2011. "Earnings Volatility in America: Evidence from Matched CPS." *Labour Economics* 18 (6): 742–754.

6. Labor-market institutions matter: inequality, wage policy, and worker well-being

Oren M. Levin-Waldman

INTRODUCTION

Isaac Newton's famous law of motion states that every action produces an equal and opposite reaction. This would also appear to be true in politics and economics. An idealized model of ever-competitive markets and economy-wide equilibrium, which has found expression in a range of neoliberal policies over the past few decades, can be viewed as a reaction to the Keynesian welfare-state model that, during the 1970s, could not address the contradiction of high unemployment and inflation.

Since at least the early 1980s, economic policies in the United States (and many other countries) have been driven mainly by the notion of market self-regulation, resulting in increased capital mobility, greater hostility to workers and labor unions, reduced spending on social programs, and increased income inequality (Friedman and Friedman 1980; Goldfield 1987). Those arguing for this course claimed that the traditional welfare state had gone too far and was interfering with economic growth, productivity, and efficiency. For example, they insisted that the pursuit of efficiency and competitiveness in a global economy required the elimination of labor rights that were believed to interfere with wage flexibility. However, consistent with Newton's law, the adverse consequences of globalization on the middle class may now be dictating a return to some of the worker rights and labor market institutions we abandoned (Levin-Waldman 2018a).[1]

With each new phase in the evolution of capitalism has come a corresponding evolution of the state and the role of government and policy. In the late-nineteenth century, industrial capitalism led to the development of a regulatory state, partly in an attempt to smooth out bumps in the business cycle and protect firms from hostile takeovers by their competitors (Kolko 1963; Lustig 1982; Weinstein 1968). Later, the Great Depression led to the

New Deal's more expansive regulatory and welfare state, including efforts to boost and sustain aggregate demand. With that welfare state came new labor protections, such as the minimum wage, and (partly because strife between labor and management was considered disruptive to the economy) the right of workers to form unions and bargain collectively with employers.

Following World War II, the nation has seen the advent of money manager capitalism (Minsky and Whalen 1996), a stage of capitalist development that parallels the emergence of the neoliberal, market-driven approach to public policy. Driven by the goal of increasing shareholder value, money manager capitalism has resulted in catastrophic consequences for workers and communities. While the nation may debate the merits of green energy, free college tuition, Medicare for all, and higher taxes on the wealthy to redress rising inequality, we must recognize that all of these proposals are in large part a reaction to the consequences of money manager capitalism.

Yet attention to money manager capitalism alone means our diagnosis of the economic ailments of the United States—and of what it will take to address them through constructive policy action—only scratches the surface. Today, many analysts recognize a sharp political polarization in the United States and attribute it to the divergent views of conservatives and liberals; in fact, that polarization is rooted in the existence of two different economies within a single nation. The economies of what we refer to as "blue" states and "red" states are not the same, and neither are their respective labor markets. The results of the presidential and congressional elections in 2016 and 2020 showed the country to be deeply polarized along these blue and red lines. Some have remarked that it is as though these states were located in parallel universes; and that's nearly the case. The ideological and cultural differences that constitute the blue state/red state dichotomy are rooted in different economies.

In this chapter, I argue that money manager capitalism, which has resulted in greater inequality, a deterioration of the middle class, and erosion of democratic governance, has also contributed much to the political polarization of recent years. I also argue that the consequences of money manager capitalism have necessitated the strengthening of labor market institutions for the sake of worker well-being. In fact, if capitalism is once again to be saved from itself (as it was by the New Deal in the 1930s), there needs to be greater coordination between the public and private sectors in ways that not only increase economic opportunity for struggling workers, but also protect working families and shore up the middle class.[2]

At the same time, the data will show that the consequences of money manager capitalism are more visible in blue states than red states, consequences which appear to have made blue-state residents generally more open to pro-worker public policy reforms than red-state residents. As a result, although blue-state residents may have experienced a greater increase in economic insecurity in recent decades, red-states residents may be experiencing greater anxiety—as a result of concerns not only about where the economy of their state is heading, but also about the prospect of policy changes that do not yet seem as inevitable to them as to many blue-state residents. A unified policy approach has the potential to reduce economic polarization in red states and blue states, but because each grouping faces unique economic and political realities, residents of red states may not be as accepting of such an approach as residents of blue states.

CAPITALIST EVOLUTION

Joseph Schumpeter ([1942] 1975) famously observed that dynamic capitalist economies are characterized by creative destruction, whereby old and obsolete industries, organizations, and institutions are replaced by those that are new and more technologically advanced. Far from labeling this a problem, Schumpeter considered it a mark of progress. To be sure, creative destruction means job loss for many workers, but most economists have usually just assumed that workers will be reabsorbed, sooner or later, by new or surviving parts of the economy. In general, the creative destruction view of the economy says nothing about displacement, nothing about consequences for the middle class, and nothing about the possibility that such dynamism will exacerbate economic inequality.

Many who write about creative destruction suggest it is natural or inevitable. However, the writings of Hyman Minsky, whose doctoral work was supervised by Schumpeter at Harvard University, offer a different perspective. According to Minsky (1986, 7; 1991, 10), economic systems are social systems—created by the decisions of individuals, private organizations, and policymakers—not natural systems, and nothing about their shape is preordained. In fact, Minsky often stressed that capitalism can and does come in many varieties.

From Minsky's perspective, much of the creative destruction that took place in the US economy since World War II can be traced to the transition from *managerial* capitalism, grounded in the institutions established during the New Deal, to *money manager* capitalism, grounded in the rise of institutional investors, a focus on the maximization of shareholder value, labor-market changes that aimed to slash labor costs, and public policies (such as trade liberalization and deregulation) consistent with the market-oriented neoliberal agenda. Building on that viewpoint, Minsky and Whalen (1996) divide postwar US economic performance into two periods. The first, from 1945 until about 1970, was a generally successful period characterized by robust economic growth, rising wages, and declining inequality. It was also a period in which cyclical instability was controlled and human resource development (human capital) and public investments were supported by the federal government. The second period, however, turned out to be the opposite. The economy suffered from mounting financial instability, debilitating inflationary booms, increasingly serious recessions, stagnant family incomes, a neglect of public infrastructure and human-capital investments, rising inequality, and spreading workforce insecurity.

The Mask of Globalization

It has become commonplace to attribute the postwar evolution of US capitalism to globalization. In fact, though, globalization is both an effect of money manager capitalism and its mask. References to the "forces of globalization" effectively obscure the deliberateness of money manager capitalism, which became a reality during the 1980s as institutional investors, holders of the largest share of corporate stocks and bonds by the end of that decade, began to exert their influence on financial markets and business enterprises (Whalen 2000).

In the era of money manager capitalism, financial markets and arrangements are dominated by institutional fund managers, whose sole objective is the maximization of shareholder value as measured by the total return on investment assets and investments (Minsky and Whalen 1996; Lazonick and Shin 2020). The situation is quite different than in the initial era of capitalism, known as commercial capitalism, when outside financing was principally used to facilitate commerce by financing goods in process or in transit, or later in industrial capitalism, when financing aimed to enable the rise of factories and industrial expansion. Because of the growing influence of the current era's institutional investors, business leaders were forced to focus more than ever on quarterly profits and the stock-market value of their corporations; maximization of shareholder value has also caused employers to insist on lower labor costs and greater workplace flexibility (Whalen 2017).

All of this has resulted in more capital flight to areas around the globe where wage rates have been lower. Money manager capitalism's need to increase shareholder value requires the suppression of workers' wages, which has been conveniently masked under the guise of globalization. In short, creative destruction has been aided and abetted by a willful desire to maximize share value at the expense of workers and their communities.

Kathleen Thelen (2001) suggests that while all of this has happened under the rubric of globalization, the combined effect in advanced capitalist countries has been a reorienting of labor politics, away from labor's traditional distributional agenda and towards employers' firm-level preoccupation with productivity and efficiency. The widespread nature of that preoccupation resulted in employers pushing for even more flexibility to respond to changing market conditions, including the heightened competitive pressures of increasingly integrated international markets, and in many cases that drive for flexibility has been linked to efforts to weaken labor unions and push for more decentralized wage bargaining. With globalization, the balance of economic and political power shifted towards capital, and the full-employment focus of previous decades was replaced by an emphasis on wage restraint, labor market flexibility, and production issues.

The Rise of Money Manager Capitalism

The era of managerial capitalism that existed in the United States (US) following World War II was a period in which corporate managers dominated the economic scene. In most major industries, a few large, vertically integrated firms controlled the market and set prices to cover labor costs (and other production expenses), provide for their reinvestment needs, and ensure a target rate of return for stockholders. Because such firms did not face intense competition, managers could offer workers rising wages and benefits, which were often determined directly via collective bargaining or indirectly by benchmarking to other firms' collective agreements. They also could generally keep stockholders satisfied by combining corporate control over prices with steady business growth. The federal government played a supporting role by providing not only a policy framework (on labor relations, business regulation, and social insurance, for example) that complemented the private sector's institutional structure, but also a commitment to using monetary and fiscal policy to sustain robust aggregate demand.

Over time, however, US corporations faced increasing competition from companies based in Europe and Asia, where nations had rebuilt and refocused their economic systems following massive wartime damage. This had consequences not only for US enterprises, but also for the American economy overall. At the enterprise level, the competition put a squeeze on corporate profits, which peaked in the mid-1960s and then stagnated for more than a decade (Harrison and Bluestone 1988, 7–11); and at the macroeconomic level, attempts to contain inflation through conventional policy tools resulted only in both inflation and unemployment occurring together (in addition to greater strain on the social safety net). At the same time, a narrative emerged within the financial community that insisted the problem facing large US corporations was that their managers built empires "for their personal aggrandizement" and forgot that corporations exist to serve the interests of their owners (Lazonick and Shin 2020, 63).

In response to those developments, business and government in the United States pursued what Bennett Harrison and Barry Bluestone (1988) described as a "great U-turn." For business, that meant a drive not simply to restore short-term profits, but to boost such profits as much as possible so as to maximize shareholder value, consistent with the demands of institutional investors and shareholder activists (who were, in fact, often fund managers) (Harrison and Bluestone 1988, 53–75). It also meant "zapping labor," by attacking unions, sending jobs offshore, and slashing labor costs, especially by cutting worker benefits (Harrison and Bluestone 1988, 21). Looked at more broadly, the U-turn in corporate strategies, which began in the early 1970s and accelerated in the 1980s, aimed to regain control over an increasingly competitive environment by establishing more flexible arrangements with employees, subcontractors, governments, and even customers (Harrison and Bluestone 1988, 11). Meanwhile, for government (at the federal, state, and local levels), the great U-turn, which began in the late 1970s but also accelerated in the 1980s, meant (economic, social and labor-market) deregulation, privatization, corporate tax cuts, tight money, new business subsidies, and even military spending that underwrote and supported the new approach pursued by American corporations (Harrison and Bluestone 1988, 76–108).

ECONOMIC CONSEQUENCES OF MONEY MANAGER CAPITALISM

Among the many economic consequences of money manager capitalism, three are worth special attention: a shift in businesses' focus from value creation to value extraction; rising worker insecurity; and increasing income inequality.

Value Extraction

Value creation is the process that generates high quality, low-cost goods that are the essence of productivity growth. In contrast, value extraction is the process of appropriating portions of value that already have been created. According to William Lazonick (2019, 5), money manager capitalism's maximization of shareholder value—"incentivized by the stock-based pay of senior corporate executives"—has involved "massive distributions of corporate cash to shareholders" and "legitimized predatory value extraction from US business corporations." In turn, the shift from value creation to value extraction has "undermined innovative business enterprise." While the corporate executives of managerial capitalism aimed to "retain-and-reinvest" corporate earnings, the executives of money manager capitalism are instead driven to "downsize (total employment and the scale of business operations)-and-distribute" corporate earnings.

MIT's Suzanne Berger shares Lazonick's assessment. According to Berger (2014), financial market pressures since the 1980s have transformed US corporations, emphasizing their need to pursue activities that promise short-term profitability and reducing their ability to research, innovate, make large capital outlays, and bring new products or services to market. This has contributed not only to the gutting of US manufacturing, but also to a wider slowdown of business productivity growth after 1973 (compared with 1947 through 1973) (US Bureau of Labor Statistics 2020).

Worker Insecurity

Rising worker insecurity is another major consequence of the emergence and development of money manager capitalism. Lazonick and Shin (2020, 5) identify three trends that have eliminated increasing numbers of middle-class employment opportunities in the United States since the late 1970s: rationalization, marketization, and globalization. Rationalization, the earliest of these trends to appear, involves plant closures, resulting in the elimination of jobs for blue-collar workers with a high school education, most of whom were also unionized. Marketization began in the early 1990s, and ended the employment-relations norm of companies providing workers with career-long employment; this structural change put in jeopardy the job security of middle-age, white-collar workers, many of whom were college educated. Then globalization became the dominant trend starting in the early 2000s, and has been characterized by the offshoring of employment to lower-wage countries. This has left the American worker vulnerable to displacement regardless of educational attainment.

Other aspects of rising worker insecurity in the United States are highlighted in research by David Weil (2014) on what he calls the "fissured workplace." Weil identifies several fissures to the stable employment-relations system that most middle-class workers enjoyed in the age of managerial capitalism. For example, the fissured workplace of the current era of (money manager) capitalism is characterized not only by arrangements that put intense downward pressure on wages and benefits, but also by employment instability, union avoidance, and business practices that shield corporations from responsibility for working conditions. These new employment-relations realities have been brought about by labor subcontracting (as growing numbers of corporations narrowed their in-house operations and shed activities deemed peripheral to their core business), heavy corporate reliance on franchising, and supply-chain globalization (facilitated by the internet and information technology).

Income Inequality

Increasing US income inequality is a third major consequence of money manager capitalism. In the 26 years between 1947 and 1973, real family income for those in the bottom fifth of the income distribution grew by 117 percent, more rapidly than for any other income quintile; in fact, during that period, real family income grew slowest for the top quintile, though still by 88.3 percent. In contrast, over the 27 years between 1973 and 2000, real family income for the lowest quintile grew only 11.2 percent, more slowly than any other income quintile (growth in those other quintiles ranged from 17.4 percent for the second quintile to 65.5 percent for the top quintile) (Mishel, Bernstein, and Shierholz 2009, 59).

Increasing inequality is also evident in more recent data. In 2019, according to the most recent estimates from the US Census Bureau (2020), the share of total US income received by the two lowest-earning quintiles was 11.4 percent, compared to 14.1 percent for the middle quintile, 22.7 percent for the fourth quintile, and 51.9 percent for the top quintile. Except for the top quintile, which saw its share rise from 43.3 percent in 1970, all other quintiles saw a decrease in the total income share received since 1970 (US Census Bureau 2020). In addition, decades of rising income inequality have made the distribution of wealth increasingly unequal as well (Saez and Zucman 2020).

Moreover, income growth associated with the transition from managerial to money manager capitalism has been most rapid at the very top of the income distribution. In 1947, the average income of families in the top five percent of the income distribution was 14 times that of families in the bottom income quintile; then, by 1979, that ratio had fallen to 11.4 times. However, the gap began to widen thereafter, with the top 5 percent earning nearly 20 times that of families in the bottom quintile in 2007 (Mishel, Bernstein, and Shierholz 2009, 60).

Meanwhile, families within the top 1 percent of the income distribution received 60 percent of the income gains generated between 1979 and 2007, while families at the bottom 90 percent of the income distribution received only about 9 percent of the period's income gains (Belman and Wolfson 2014). More recent data indicate these trends toward widening inequality have continued. Not surprisingly, tax records also show that most of the people at the very top "are not media stars or celebrity athletes, but corporate and financial executives"—including, of course, Wall Street's money managers (Hacker and Pierson 2020, 45).

CONSEQUENCES FOR POLITICAL ECONOMY

Money manager capitalism has also brought political as well as economic consequences. One political consequence is erosion, as a result of rising worker insecurity and increasing inequality, of the individual autonomy necessary for an effective system of democratic governance. Another is a political polarization, the roots of which appear to lie in labor markets.

Erosion of Democratic Governance

An effective democratic system requires that individuals participate in democratic governance as equals. However, wide disparities in the distribution of income and wealth can adversely affect the autonomy of individuals with low income and little or no wealth, thereby eroding democratic governance. In other words, societies with a high degree of economic inequality do not merely put many people in a position to be exploited in the labor market; they also generate unequal access to political and policy officials, excluding many citizens from participation in civic life and from an opportunity to have their voices heard.

When income and wealth are concentrated, those at the top are in a better position than others to achieve their political and other ideological objectives, and that's precisely what we find in the United States today (Bachrach and Botwinick 1992, 4–5; Hacker and Pierson 2020). Numerous studies find that legislative bodies are most responsive to their affluent constituents (Bartels 2008; Gilens 2012; Volscho and Kelly 2012). Using that influence, those at the top of the income distribution are able to not only limit redistribution to others, but also tilt the rules of the game in their favor (Stiglitz 2012). Even the Earned Income Tax Credit, which is provided to workers, represents an *upward* redistribution because it serves to subsidize the profits of employers who pay low wages (unlike a higher minimum wage); low wages cost the nation an estimated $152.8 billion a year in social supports (Jacobs, Perry, and MacGillvary 2015).

A highly unequal society provides large numbers of working families with neither the time nor the resources to exert individual autonomy and participate in civic engagement. A market-driven, capitalist economy is, by definition, one of control. Workers are effectively exploited by their employers precisely because of asymmetrical power relations (see, e.g., Prasch 1995). David McNally (2011), for instance, argues that workers are perpetually disciplined in capitalist markets by the need to provide labor in exchange for wages that enable them to live. As globalization exerts intense downward pressure on wages and requires slashing social programs to attract business investment and economic growth, the effect is to discipline workers even more. They are forced to conform to the dictates of those who control the means of production, or face the uncertainty that comes with unemployment and eventual poverty (Braekkan and Sowa 2015). The result for most workers is greater economic insecurity (even as people often work more hours and multiple jobs) and less involvement in community and political life. In short, widespread inequality and worker insecurity combine to diminish community engagement, reduce social capital, and erode democratic governance (Putnam 2020, 358–360; Wisman 2011, 890).

Political Polarization

In addition to eroding democratic governance via rising inequality and worker insecurity, money manager capitalism has produced an economic divide that has contributed to the political polarization of America. In the era of money manager capitalism, a close look at US labor markets in red states and blue states reveals a tale of two economies.

The analysis here is based on data from the IPUMS Current Population Survey for the years 1992, 2000, 2008, and 2016.[3] In particular, I look at full-time workers between the ages of 18 and 65, and use the same blue state/red state distinction widely adopted by US news organizations. A blue state is one in which the majority of voters typically cast ballots for the Democratic candidate in a presidential election, and where Democrats typically hold a majority of seats in the state legislature; in contrast, red states typically favor Republican presidential candidates and state legislators.[4] Because the crucial elements of this analysis are skill levels and industrial and occupational features of labor markets, I examine educational attainment and job characteristics, not demographics such as age, gender, race, and ethnicity. Also, because the focus is on full-time labor market participants, I look only at wage inequality, rather than at the larger category of household wealth and income inequality.[5]

Wage inequality in red and blue states

When states are divided along these lines, we see some clear labor market differences. For example, Table 6.1 shows levels of wage inequality according to 90/10, 90/50, and 50/10 percentile ratios and the top-to-bottom quintile ratios.

The data in Table 6.1 show distinct patterns across the red/blue divide. In 1990 and 2008, there was greater wage inequality in red states on all measures except the 90/50 percentile measure in 1990. But in 2000 and 2016, there was greater wage inequality in the blue states on all measures except the 90/50 percentile. Between 1990 and 2016, on all measures except the 90/50 measure, wage inequality decreased in both blue states and red states, but more so in red states; on the 90/50 percentile measure, wage inequality increased 4.8 percent more in red states than in blue states. Over that same period, according to the top-to-bottom quintile ratio, wage inequality in red states decreased by 26.3 percent, whereas it only decreased by 8.5 percent in blue states, a difference of 209.4 percent. The data suggest that a widening gap in blue states between earners at the top and the bottom helps account for relatively greater overall wage inequality decreases in red states between 1990 and 2016.

Table 6.1   Wage inequality in blue states and red states, percentile ratios

	Blue				Red				Blue/Red Differential			
	90/10 percentile ratio	90/50 percentile ratio	50/10 percentile ratio	Top-to-bottom Quintile ratio	90/10 percentile ratio	90/50 percentile ratio	50/10 percentile ratio	Top-to-bottom Quintile ratio	90/10 percentile ratio	90/50 percentile ratio	50/10 percentile ratio	Top-to-bottom Quintile ratio
1990	15.7	2.4	6.7	16.4	18.4	2.3	7.9	17.9	14.0<	4.3>	17.9<	9.1<
2000	12.1	2.3	5.2	15.6	11.5	2.4	4.8	14.4	5.0>	4.3<	8.3>	8.3>
2008	10.0	2.4	4.1	13.4	11.1	2.5	4.4	14.3	11.0<	15.0<	6.8<	6.3<
2016	11.2	2.6	4.4	15.0	10.0	2.5	4.0	13.2	12.0>	4.0>	10.0>	13.6>
Percent Change	-28.7	+8.3	-34.3	-8.5	-45.7	+8.7	-49.4	-26.3	59.2<	4.8<	44.0<	209.4<

Source: Author's calculations using data from Ruggles et al. (2020).

A closer look

To further explore the smaller decrease in wage inequality in blue states than in red states, we must look at differences in industrial and occupational composition as well as in educational attainment. Michael Lind (2020) suggests that American society divides into two categories: the managerial elites, who are well educated and employed in high paying occupations (often in the finance and information-technology sectors), and everybody else, including many workers who do not possess an abundance of skills. The managerial elites have not only discretionary income to spend on luxury goods; they also have resources available to influence political leaders. As a result, they are the citizens to whom the political class is most responsive (Bartels 2008).

In an effort to approximate Lind's classification, I examine workers across three broad occupational groups: Professional/Managerial, Skilled, and Unskilled. Examples of Professional/Managerial occupations include jobs in finance and real estate; corporate executives; and many occupations in the information and communications technology sector. Both Skilled and Unskilled occupations include many blue-collar jobs, including, for instance, craft and related trades workers in the former group, and mining and manufacturing laborers in the latter group. Using this occupational categorization in Tables 6.2 and 6.3, we can further examine differences in inequality across the red/blue divide.

We see from Tables 6.2 and 6.3 that there have been greater decreases in wage inequality in red states than in blue states. It may be that blue states have more skilled workers at the top and more unskilled workers at the bottom, whereas red states may have more of a middle, although it too may be dwindling. A logistic regression analysis can help sort that out. Because the Current Population Survey provides only individual level data, it will only tell us that individual workers with certain characteristics are either more or less likely to be in either a blue or red state. Therefore, two regressions are done, with residing in a blue state as the dependent variable in the first regression, and residing in a red state as the dependent variable in the second regression.

Here's how the regressions were structured. In addition to independent variables for Professional/Managerial, Skilled, and Unskilled jobs, I also use a variety of industry categories as additional independent variables: Manufacturing and Mining (which are better paying industries for blue-collar workers and may well speak to significant differences between red states and blue states), Finance and Real Estate, Business and Repair Services, and Services (which includes information technology jobs). In addition, I include variables for educational attainment, and whether one lives in a state where there is greater wage inequality than in the US as a whole. All variables are dichotomous with values of either 0 or 1. Regression coefficients and their statistical significance can be seen in Tables 6.4 and 6.5. The purpose of pre-

Table 6.2   *Wage inequality in blue states, various occupational categories*

	Professional/Managerial			Skilled			Unskilled
	90/10 percentile ratio	90/50 percentile ratio	50/10 percentile ratio	90/10 percentile ratio	90/50 percentile ratio	50/10 percentile ratio	90/10 percentile ratio
1990	9.1	2.1	4.5	11.4	2.0	5.7	22.8
2000	8.6	2.3	3.7	9.3	2.0	4.6	23.0
2008	6.5	2.3	2.8	9.3	2.0	4.6	17.3
2016	8.0	2.4	3.4	10.0	2.0	5.0	20.0
Percentage Change	-12.1	+14.3	-24.4	-12.3	0	-12.3	-12.3

Source: Author's calculations using data from Ruggles et al. (2020).

Table 6.3   *Wage inequality in red states, various occupational categories*

	Professional/Managerial			Skilled			Unskilled
	90/10 percentile ratio	90/50 percentile ratio	50/10 percentile ratio	90/10 percentile ratio	90/50 percentile ratio	50/10 percentile ratio	90/10 percentile ratio
1990	9.6	2.2	4.4	11.9	2.1	5.6	26.0
2000	7.3	2.3	3.2	10.0	2.0	5.0	19.0
2008	7.5	2.4	3.1	10.8	2.0	5.3	18.0
2016	6.8	2.4	2.9	9.4	2.1	4.5	18.3
Percentage Change	-29.2	+9.1	-34.1	-21.0	0	-19.6	-29.6

Source: Author's calculations using data from Ruggles et al. (2020).

senting both regressions is to demonstrate that blue-state and red-state results are almost mirror images of each other.

The results of Tables 6.4 and 6.5 do indeed move, for the most part, in opposite directions. For example, both tables suggest that, in 1990 and 2016, those living in states with more wage inequality than the nation as a whole were also more likely to be in blue states, which is to say that there was also less wage inequality in red states. Thus, it is indeed possible that blue states have more workers at the top and bottom of the distribution, with fewer in between. This may account for why wage inequality is higher in blue states, and would support the proposition that wage inequality has been about those at the top pulling away from everybody else (Piketty 2014; Stiglitz 2012). The ranks of

Table 6.4   *Regression coefficients and statistical significance (blue states as dependent variable)*

	1990	2000	2008	2016
Professional/Managerial	.169	.120	-.030	.138
	.000	.000	.000	.000
Skilled workers	.046	-.041	.045	-.077
	.000	.000	.000	.000
Unskilled workers	.104	.040	-.002	.028
	.000	.000	.672	.000
Higher Wage Inequality than the US as a whole	1.844	.959	-1.055	1.351
	.000	.000	.000	.000
Manufacturing	.134	.127	.106	-.163
	.000	.000	.000	.000
Mining	-.920	--1.325	-.-358	-1.422
	.000	.000	.000	.000
Business and Repair Services	.172	.155	-.019	.060
	.000	.000	.017	.000
Graduate and/or Professional Degree	.216	.254	-.092	.309
	.000	.000	.000	.000
High School Degree	016	-.000	.011	-.008
	.000	.882	.001	.010
Finance and Real Estate	.289	.183	-.016	-.080
	.000	.000	.004	.000
Services	.030	.019	-.080	.199
	.005	.043	.000	.000
Constant	-.160	.349	.302	.772
	.000	.000	.000	.000

Source: Author's analysis using data from Ruggles et al. (2020).

the high-income earners appear to be greater in blue states than in red states. Moreover, because there is less dispersion in red states, red-state residents may not consider inequality to be as serious a problem as blue-states residents.

The regression coefficients would appear to confirm a tale of two economies. For example, almost the entire data series indicates that those with advanced university degrees are more likely to be found in blue states (the exception being in 2008) and less likely to be found in red states. This is an important variable for at least two reasons. First, advanced degrees serve as a good (albeit imperfect) proxy for additional skills. Second, advanced degrees speak to the presence of a managerial/professional class; the fact that the coefficient for

Table 6.5   *Regression coefficients and statistical significance (red states as dependent variable)*

	1990	2000	2008	2016
Professional/Manager	.015	.000	-.014	-.138
	.001	.905	.000	.000
Skilled workers	.137	.170	.028	.077
	.000	.000	.000	.000
Unskilled workers	.095	.095	.003	-.028
	.000	.000	.425	.000
Higher Wage Inequality than the US as	--1.583	-.836	---.093	-1.351
a whole	.000	.000	.000	.000
Manufacturing	-.068	-.086	.008	.163
	.000	.000	.125	.000
Mining	.917	1.321	.615	1.422
	.000	.000	.000	.000
Business and Repair Services	-.096	-.120	-.066	-.060
	.000	.000	.000	.000
Graduate and/or Professional Degree	-.133	-.199	-.011	-.309
	.000	.000	.032	.000
High School Degree	.094	.076	-.061	.008
	.000	.000	.000	.010
Finance and Real Estate	-.154	-.105	.013	.080
	.000	.000	.018	.000
Services	.022	.006	-.116	-.199
	.042	.548	.018	.000
Constant	.533	-.148	.546	-.772
	.000	.000	.000	.000

Source: Author's analysis using data from Ruggles et al. (2020).

such degrees tends to become stronger over time in blue states suggests the growth of this managerial/professional class. At the same time, having a high school diploma as the highest level of educational attainment is not statistically significant in blue states in 2000 and 2008, and the effects are small in the other years, as though it is a given that most workers have a minimum of a high school degree. And yet, a high school degree as the highest level of educational attainment appears to be more significant in red states, which might suggest that workers have more opportunities with only a high school education in red states than they do in blue states. The change of that coefficient in blue states and its decrease in size in red states may reflect what Goldin and Katz (2008) refer to as the decline of the high school premium, which they consider an important factor contributing to rising inequality.

In general, professional and managerial jobs have a positive correlation with living in a blue state, whereas working in manufacturing has been increasingly correlated with working in red states. Here is a summary of some other results from Tables 6.4 and 6.5:

- Working in a professional/managerial job has positive effects for being in a blue state (except in 2008), but is either not statistically significant or negative in red states.
- Working in finance and real estate has strong positive effects for being in a blue state in 1990 and 2000, but it has little effect in 2008 and a negative effect in 2016. In red states, that effect is negative in 1990 and 2000, but begins to have a small positive effect by 2008 and 2016.
- Working in services (including information technology) has little effect for being in a blue state, but by 2016 it does have a relatively stronger effect than in the earlier years, whereas in red states it has little effect in 1990 and 2000, but becomes negative by 2008 and 2016.
- In both 2000 and 2016, being a blue-collar skilled worker has negative effects for being in a blue state; it has positive effects for being in a red state. Also, with the exception of 2008, being an unskilled worker has a small positive effect for being in a blue state. In red states, however, the effect for unskilled workers is positive beginning in 1990, but its effect weakens and turns negative by 2016.
- Working in manufacturing has a positive effect for being in a blue state beginning in 1990, but becomes negative in 2016, which may speak to a greater decline in manufacturing in blue states than in red states, whereas its effects for being a red state are positive in 2008 and 2016, which may suggest a greater presence of manufacturing in red states.
- Working in business and repair services has a positive effect for being in a blue state, with the exception of 2008. In red states, however, it is negative throughout.

Wage structures in red and blue states
To shed even more light on labor market differences between red and blue states, we turn finally to the wage structures on each side of the red/blue divide; see Table 6.6. The overall wage structure has historically been lower in the South than in the North (Schulman 1991): both median and mean wages have been considerably higher in blue states than in red states. To be sure, some of this difference reflects the historically lower cost of living in red states. Still, differences in wage structure provide a prism through which workers in particular states view a wide range of issues.

Table 6.6   Median and mean wages by occupational category, 2016 dollars

	Blue								Red							
	Professional/Manager		Skilled		Unskilled		Other		Professional/Manager		Skilled		Unskilled		Other	
	Median	Mean	Median	Mean	Median	Mean	Median	Mean	Median	Mean	Median	Mean	Median	Mean	Median	Mean
1990	53658	64057	37006	40085	23661	28657	31455	37890	46257	55788	31455	34965	19428	23774	27754	33033
2000	56473	73622	38112	42280	26428	32143	34774	44369	48684	60073	34635	38208	22673	27629	30601	37652
2008	55761	72979	35687	40073	25650	30248	33457	43583	55761	64220	35687	40245	24535	30162	33457	45392
2016	68000	88194	39600	43829	27200	34895	38500	52293	55000	72000	36000	40463	24000	28964	33000	43248
Percent Change	+26.7	+37.7	+7.0	+9.3	+15.0	+21.8	+22.4	+38.0	+18.9	+29.1	+14.4	+15.7	+23.5	+21.8	+18.9	+30.9

Source: Author's analysis using data from Ruggles et al. (2020).

It becomes clear from Table 6.6 that median and mean wages of those in the professional/managerial class are higher in blue states than they are in red states, and that their percentage increase from 1990 to 2016 was also greater in blue states. Although mean and median wages for skilled blue-collar workers is higher in blue states than in red states, their percentage increase over the period analyzed was greater in red states than in blue states. The same was true for unskilled workers, at least when it came to median wages. Still, greater wage inequality in blue states can be accounted for by median and mean wages of those in the professional/managerial class increasing faster than those of unskilled workers (Gottschalk 1997), whereas in red states there appears to be less dispersion.

In short, the labor markets of blue and red states appear to be significantly different. The professional/managerial class, which includes money managers, appears to be more predominant in blue states where the wage gap between the top and bottom is indeed wider. Meanwhile, there are more skilled workers in red states and in industries that appear to have disappeared in blue states.

Polarization rooted in the economic divide

The analysis above suggests that America's political polarization is rooted in the existence of two different labor markets. While further investigation is certainly warranted, including focus groups and interview-based studies, some working hypotheses can be offered from what we know currently.

One hypothesis is that residents of red states have a vantage point on the economic consequences of money manager capitalism that has caused them to double down on their traditional political philosophy. Residents of red states have long supported limited government regulation, low taxes, and restrained public spending. Observing the consequences of money manager capitalism, first in blue states then even closer to home, may have reinforced their distrust of government.[6]

Driven by an emphasis on shareholder value, the managerial elites predominant in blue states have already exported millions of (blue-state) jobs under the guise of an increasingly globalizing economy. Residents in red states are likely concerned that a similar loss of jobs could happen in their states as well, and to the extent that it has already begun to occur they may even hold partly responsible the professional and managerial elites residing in blue states. In short, although the adverse consequences of money manager capitalism appear to have so far affected blue states more than red states, red-state residents might actually be much more anxious than blue-state residents about possible future economic changes.

Given that anxiety, it is understandable that red-state residents have doubled down in support of political candidates who aren't viewed as imposing elitist or big government solutions (such as globalization, government regulation, or income redistribution). After all, more than a generation of political rhetoric has linked the Democratic Party, fairly or unfairly, to: Wall Street financiers and business executives who are believed to favor globalization over saving US jobs; labor unions that are thought to have priced US workers out of the global marketplace; regulations that are said to have made American businesses uncompetitive; and redistributive fiscal policies that are supposed to have overburdened the public sector and discouraged many people from working. Red-residents may believe it is still possible to protect their communities from the ravages of globalization.[7] Moreover, a genuine belief in independence, autonomy, and personal responsibility may accompany red states' relatively higher concentration of skilled blue-collar jobs.

Another working hypothesis is that residents of blue states have also doubled down on their traditional political viewpoint, which is that government has a constructive role to play in the economy. As we have seen, labor market structures in blue states have become increasingly polarized, contributing to growing insecurity for many workers—especially those without advanced university degrees—and to widening income inequality. Given that these consequences of money manager capitalism are already unmistakable in blue states, it is not surprising that many residents of such states would believe that government has a responsibility to assist those left behind by a changing economy.

A third hypothesis accounts for the several blue states that flipped red in 2016, giving Donald Trump an electoral victory. Most of the anti-establishment voters who supported Trump in 2016 (and, in many cases, in 2020 as well) resided in red states. However, in 2016, they were joined by enough anxious voters outside that block, especially blue-collar workers, to flip some other key states and elect Trump. The willingness of anxious blue-collar workers to vote Republican is no aberration, nor is the reason a mystery. Rather, it reflected the anxiety of such workers that they are headed toward what Michael Sandel (2020) calls obsolescence: their apprehension is that, because of how US capitalism has evolved, society may no longer need the skills they have to offer, and that this evolution may have been hastened by public policies often associated with business and academic elites (such as policies in support of globalization).

LABOR MARKET INSTITUTIONS AND PUBLIC POLICY

Increasing worker insecurity and inequality threaten both our economic and political systems. If capitalism is once again to be saved from itself, there needs to be greater coordination between the public and private sectors in ways that increase economic opportunity for struggling workers, protect working families, and revitalize the middle class.[8] Moreover, since many of our economic and political challenges can be traced to the labor market, labor market institutions in the United States need strengthening for the sake of democratic governance as well as economic performance and worker well-being. Five types of public policies that can contribute constructively to that end are mentioned briefly below.

The Right to Organize and Bargain Collectively

The right of workers to join together and bargain collectively with their employer is an important way for workers to improve employment terms and conditions. Labor unions also allow workers to collaborate with employers in ways that creatively solve enterprise problems and generate innovations that can serve as a source of competitive advantage. However, US laws governing workers' right to organize and bargain collectively are weak, have usually been feebly enforced, and have not been updated to reflect workplace and economy-wide changes.

The right of workers to organize and bargain with employers needs to be bolstered by means of federal labor law reform (for a variety of policy details, see, e.g., Block and Sachs 2020; Kochan 2020). With the emergence of money manager capitalism, many corporations in blue states sought to avoid unions, sometimes moving jobs initially to red states—where so-called "right-to-work" laws make union organizing difficult—and then out of the country. But capital flight motivated by a "race to the bottom" on wages and benefits is not a sustainable solution for enterprises or for job-sending and job-receiving nations. The only sensible alternative is labor law reform that respects the human rights of workers to organize and bargain collectively, combined with both domestic policy inducements that encourage firms to compete by treating labor as a valuable resource (not a cost to be minimized) as well as international support for labor rights abroad.[9]

Wage Policy

For the purposes of helping to level the playing field in employment relations and ensuring a viable labor force, collective bargaining is a valuable labor market institution. But the right to organize and bargain collectively is not the only policy element needed to bolster and protect worker incomes; it is only one component of a broader wage policy. A wage floor is also needed.

Traditionally, wage floors assumed the form of federal and state minimum wage legislation, but in recent years they have often assumed the form of "living wage" ordinances at the local level, as well as broader proposals for basic and/or minimum incomes (Levin-Waldman 2011). Local ordinances are useful to address geographic differences in the cost of living, and minimum income proposals certainly warrant public discussion. Nevertheless, a higher federal minimum wage (and more comprehensive coverage, since some workers are excluded from current law), which peaked in value in 1968, is a vital first step toward a more robust wage policy (Economic Policy Institute 2021). As this chapter is being written, the federal minimum wage is $7.25 per hour, and has lost 22 percent of its value to inflation since it was last raised in 2009. Raising the minimum wage to $15 and allowing it to rise each year with the cost of living (and perhaps occasionally adjusting it further upward to reflect economy-wide productivity increases) would benefit not only low-wage workers, but also the middle class through its effect on wage contours (Levin-Waldman 2018a).

Workforce Development

The United States must also bolster its workforce development policies so those in the workforce and those preparing for the workforce have the education and training needed to succeed in a dynamic, knowledge-driven economy. The need for aggressive workforce development policies, created with input from educators, business leaders, and organized labor, is even greater today than in the era of managerial capitalism, not only because of the rapid pace of economic change in the restless, digital era of money managerial capitalism, but also because employer-provided training and long-term employment relationships are no longer the norm.

Suitable jobs skills are important, but so are basic education, critical thinking, and lifelong learning. Unfortunately, policy initiatives in the area of job training, even for dislocated workers, have long tended to be out of date and woefully underfunded (Glover and King 2010). General education also has not kept pace with technological advances, and may account for the decline in the high school wage premium (Goldin and Katz 2008). There are best-practice examples in the United States and abroad that can be used benchmarks, and what the United States needs most of all in this policy area is a sound and coherent system of education and training standards, assessments, and curricula (Marshall 2010).

Stakeholder Voice

Public policy must also aim to redirect corporate governance from an exclusive focus on shareholder value to a broader consideration that protects the interests of workers and their communities. David Zalewski (2003), for example, suggests combining "triple bottom line" reporting requirements (that is, attention to profits, workers, and the environment) with tax changes that promote worker well-being and ecological sustainability. Moreover, stakeholder considerations are not always in conflict with business needs. Environmental destruction is ultimately in nobody's interest; and low wages are inefficient when employees can't adequately sustain themselves, reducing not only worker morale but also productivity (Webb 1912).

Another constructive policy possibility is to put workers (and perhaps also community members) on corporate boards. This has long been a recommendation of Institutionalists (see, e.g., Marshall 1987). The voice of labor has much to contribute to all areas of economic decision-making, and with greater worker input employee rights are more likely to be guaranteed and less likely to be suppressed in the face of shocks to the system (Altman 2008).

Ensuring greater attention to worker interests might also require a redefinition of property rights to include a genuine right to work at a living wage, or even a universal basic income. With a true right to work, unemployment and payment of subsistence wages would be akin to encroaching upon workers' property rights. It would, in short, amount to a form of theft (Zatz 2009). Institutionalists and Post Keynesians have long called for such a right—and for government to back it up by serving as an employer of last resort (Minsky 1986, 308–313)—and today such employment could be combined with the need to address community and environmental needs that have gone unaddressed for far too long (Whalen 2019). Moreover, the emergence of artificial intelligence and the spread of automation underscore the need to seriously consider a policy that would ensure a basic income for all (Levin-Waldman 2018b).

Antitrust Action

A final policy area involves vigorous antitrust action against employers who exert monopoly power over the labor market, making them the primary (or only) purchaser of particular kinds of labor, especially within a certain community or region. Such employers—monopsonists—use that power to drive wages below what they would be in a more competitive labor market (Bahn 2019; Muehleman, Ryan, and Wolter 2013). Antitrust laws could be used to break up such monopsonies (Litwinski 2001).

Political Philosophy as an Obstacle to Constructive Policy Action

The various policies mentioned above would help support the middle class and counteract rising income inequality and worker insecurity. They would offer constructive change in both red and blue states. But that doesn't mean that residents of red states would embrace this agenda. Red-states residents might be open to more forceful antitrust action and workforce development, but the other initiatives suggested here are likely to be seen as conflicting too much with the dominant political philosophy of small government and laissez-faire (even though, in fact, there is very little about contemporary economic policy that is actually small or laissez-faire in red-states or anywhere else in the capitalist world). Yes, it is true John Kenneth Galbraith (1958, 21–22) long ago observed that "the enemy of the conventional wisdom is not ideas, but the march of events." But he also admitted that the conventional wisdom "dies but does not surrender." Thus, an important implication of the analysis presented in this chapter is that a large portion of the nation might not yet be ready for the policies that will be necessary to address some of America's most serious and pressing economic difficulties.

CONCLUSION

In the name of increasing shareholder value, money managers have effectively assaulted workers and created a cycle that has resulted in an ever-widening income gap, rising worker insecurity, and erosion of the middle class. New institutional arrangements that consider the well-being of the middle class are needed to redress these issues. The economy can only become more efficient and inclusive when the rights of workers are placed on a par with those of money managers, who have imposed upon the economy a single-minded focus on shareholder value.

The nation needs a new policy direction. And yet, the political polarization gripping the nation might also make it more difficult to achieve the institutional changes we need to move in that new direction. That's because, as this chapter has shown, residents of red states and blue states do not necessarily view the US economy in quite the same way.

To be sure, there is common ground to be found by looking at the economic facts. In both red states and blue states, the most pressing problems point to a clear need to strengthen labor market institutions. In the age of money manager capitalism, the experience of blue states is a bellwether for the rest of the nation. Over time (without a change in direction), the worker obsolescence and insecurity now pervasive in blue states will ultimately reach red states. But red-state residents might hold fast to their traditional political views until that happens—and perhaps even longer. Deep-seated political realities are as formidable as economic reality.

Strengthening labor market institutions is not the same as adopting what might be considered, especially among red-state residents, the standard blue-state response of income redistribution. That fact points to America's need for a fresh look at the science and art of politics and public policy—and provides hope for finding policies that benefit working families in all states. But the starting point for that sort of scholarship and practice must begin with recognition of the realities and consequences of money manager capitalism, including its divergent consequences for red and blue states over the past several decades, as described in this chapter.

ACKNOWLEDGMENTS

The author thanks Christian Weller, Charles Whalen, and Timothy Wunder for helpful comments and suggestions.

NOTES

1. Heterodox economists will recognize a similarity between Newton's law of motion and Karl Polanyi's notion of a "protective response" to the consequences of a market-driven society (see Stanfield 1980).
2. It is important to recall that the emergence of the US middle class was not inevitable. It came about by means of worker struggles via a union movement that fought for living wages, which afforded low-skilled, assembly-line workers not only economic security but also dignity in their jobs (Glicksman 1997).
3. IPUMS is an interdisciplinary research center based at the University of Minnesota. IPUMS began as an acronym for Integrated Public Use Microdata Series, but the scope of the center's work has subsequently expanded beyond public use and microdata.
4. Using presidential election results, red and blue states are somewhat fluid categories; with states identified as follows:
    - Red states in 1992: Alabama, Alaska, Arizona, Florida, Idaho, Indiana, Kansas, Mississippi, Nebraska, North Carolina, North Dakota, Oklahoma, South Carolina, South Dakota, Texas, Utah, Virginia, Wyoming. All other states (and the District of Columbia) were blue states. Note that 1992 red/blue electoral results are applied to the 1990 data in this analysis.
    - Red states in 2000: Alabama, Alaska, Arizona, Arkansas, Colorado, Florida, Georgia, Idaho, Indiana, Kansas, Kentucky, Louisiana, Mississippi, Missouri, Montana, Nebraska, Nevada, New Hampshire, North Carolina, North Dakota, Ohio, Oklahoma, South Carolina, South Dakota, Tennessee, Texas, Utah, Virginia, West Virginia, Wyoming. All other states (and the District of Columbia) were blue states.
    - Red states in 2008: Alabama, Alaska, Arizona, Arkansas, Georgia, Idaho, Kansas, Kentucky, Louisiana, Mississippi, Missouri, Montana, Nebraska, North Dakota, Oklahoma, South Carolina, South Dakota, Tennessee, Texas, Utah, West Virginia, Wyoming. All other states (and the District of Columbia) were blue states.
    - Red states in 2016: Alabama, Alaska, Arizona, Arkansas, Florida, Georgia, Idaho, Indiana, Iowa, Kansas, Kentucky, Louisiana, Michigan, Mississippi, Missouri, Montana, Nebraska, North Carolina, North Dakota, Ohio, Oklahoma, Pennsylvania, South Carolina, South Dakota, Tennessee, Texas, Utah, West Virginia, Wisconsin, Wyoming. All other states (and the District of Columbia) were blue states.
5. Because the data focuses on wages among full-time workers, which allows comparisons in the wage structure of red and blue states, decreases in wage inequality

will be observed in some groups of states over certain time periods even as other measures, such as total household income (which includes all sources of income, not just full-time wages), have pointed to increasing income or wealth inequality.

6. To be sure, this chapter does not mean to suggest that residents of red states—or any states—would recognize money manager capitalism by that name. However, many would certainly recognize it by its features (such as an extreme focus on near-term shareholder value and the outsized influence of private equity firms and other institutional investors) and economic consequences (such as corporate downsizing and restructurings, increased globalization of production, erosion of employer-provided benefits for much of the work force, and more precarious employment relationships for most workers).

7. As mining is more prevalent in red states (see Table 6.5), there is also likely to be much less interest in green energy in red states than in blue states. In the absence of abundant job alternatives with comparable wages and benefits in other industries, many red-state residents will likely seek to retain their existing extractive industries.

8. According to Post-Keynesian Institutionalists, institutional adjustment provides the balancing wheel of the economy. Thus, institutional change is required when economic performance falters (Minsky and Whalen 1996). In the field of political science, a similar view—especially on the need for institutional adjustments to coordinate private and public economic activity—is held by scholars working in the tradition known as "varieties of capitalism" (Hall and Soskice 2001).

9. There are successful real-world alternatives to the US approach to labor law. Germany, where there is much labor-management co-determination, offers one example.

BIBLIOGRAPHY

Altman, Morris. 2008. "Toward a Theory of Induced Institutional Change: Power, Labor Markets, an Institutional Change." In *Alternative Institutional Structures: Evolution and Impact*, edited by Sandra S. Batie and Nicholas Mercuro, 300–329. London: Routledge.

Bachrach, Peter and Aryeh Botwinick. 1992. *Power and Empowerment: A Radical Theory of Participatory Democracy*. Philadelphia: Temple University Press.

Bahn, Kate. 2019. "How Monopsony Impacts Older Women Workers." *Generations— Journal of the American Society on Aging* 43 (3): 90–92.

Bartels, Larry M. 2008. *Unequal Democracy: The Political Economy of the New Gilded Age*. Princeton: Princeton University Press.

Belman, Dale and Paul J. Wolfson. 2014. *What Does the Minimum Wage Do?* Kalamazoo, MI: W.E. Upjohn Institute for Employment Research.

Berger, Suzanne. 2014. "How Finance Gutted Manufacturing." *Boston Review* April 1. https://tinyurl.com/9vxz90j0. Accessed February 17, 2021.

Block, Sharon and Benjamin Sachs. 2020. "Clean Slate for Worker Power: Building a Just Economy and Democracy." Labor and Worklife Program, Harvard Law School. https://tinyurl.com/1x1bv7fx. Accessed February 17, 2021.

Braekkan, Kristian, and Victoria Sowa. 2015. "Exploitation by Economic Necessity: Using the Marxist Conceptualization of Exploitation to Investigate the Impact of Workplace Violations." *Journal of Workplace Rights* 5 (4): 1–10.

Economic Policy Institute. 2021. "Why the US Needs a $15 Minimum Wage." Fact Sheet. January 26. https://tinyurl.com/zzrl17ch. Accessed February 17, 2021.

Friedman, Milton and Rose D. Friedman. 1980. *Free to Choose: A Personal Statement.* Orlando, FL: Harcourt.

Galbraith, John K. 1958. *The Affluent Society.* Boston: Houghton Mifflin.

Gilens, Martin. 2012. *Affluence & Influence: Economic Inequality and Political Power in America.* Princeton: Princeton University Press.

Glicksman, Lawrence B. 1997. *A Living Wage: American Workers and the Making of Consumer Society.* Ithaca, NY: Cornell University Press.

Glover, Robert W. and Christopher T. King. 2010. "Sectoral Approaches to Workforce Development: Toward an Effective US Labor-Market Policy." In *Human Resources Economics and Public Policy*, edited by Charles J. Whalen, 215–252. Kalamazoo, MI: W.E. Upjohn Institute.

Goldfield, Michael. 1987. *The Decline of Organized Labor in the United States.* Chicago: University of Chicago Press.

Goldin, Claudia and Lawrence F. Katz. 2008. *The Race Between Technology and Education.* Cambridge, MA: Belknap Press of Harvard University Press.

Gottschalk, Peter. 1997. "Inequality, Income Growth, and Mobility: The Basic Facts." *Journal of Economic Perspectives* 11 (2): 21–40.

Gramm, Warren S. 1981. "Property Rights in Work: Capitalism, Industrialism, and Democracy." *Journal of Economic Issues* 15 (2): 363–375.

Hacker, Jacob S. and Paul Pierson. 2020. *Let Them Eat Tweets: How the Right Rules in an Age of Extreme Inequality.* New York: W.W. Norton.

Hall, Peter A. and David Soskice. 2001. "An Introduction to Varieties of Capitalism." In *Varieties of Capitalism: The Institutional Foundations of Comparative Advantage*, edited by Peter A. Hall and David Soskice, 1–70. Oxford: Oxford University Press.

Harrison, Bennett and Barry Bluestone. 1988. *The Great U-Turn: Corporate Restructuring and the Polarizing of America.* New York: Basic Books.

Jacobs, Ken, Ian Perry, and Jenifer MacGillvary. 2015. "The High Cost of Low Wages." University of California Center for Labor Research and Education. Research Brief (April). Berkeley, CA.

Kochan, Thomas A. 2020. "Worker Voice, Representation, and Implications for Public Policies." Research Brief, MIT Task Force on Work of the Future. July 8, 2020. https://tinyurl.com/mfp84hrv. Accessed February 17, 2021.

Kolko, Gabriel. 1963. *The Triumph of Conservatism: A Reinterpretation of American History, 1900–1916.* New York: The Free Press.

Lazonick, William. 2019. "Innovative Enterprise and Sustainable Prosperity." January 18. https://tinyurl.com/2ltwbs3a. Accessed February 17, 2021.

Lazonick, William and Jang-Sup Shin. 2020. *Predatory Value Extraction: How the Looting of the Business Corporation Became the U.S. Norm and How Sustainable Prosperity Can be Restored.* Oxford: Oxford University Press.

Levin-Waldman, Oren M. 2011. *Wage Policy, Income Distribution, and Democratic Theory.* London: Routledge.

Levin-Waldman, Oren M. 2018a. *Restoring the Middle Class Through Wage Policy: Arguments for a Middle Class.* London: Palgrave Macmillan.

Levin-Waldman, Oren M. 2018b. "The Inevitability of a Universal Basic Income." *Challenge* 61 (2): 133–155.

Lind, Michael. 2020. *The New Class War: Saving Democracy from the Managerial Elite.* New York: Penguin Books.

Litwinski, John A. 2001. "Regulation of Labor Market Monopsony." *Berkeley Journal of Employment and Labor Law* 22 (1): 49–98.

Lustig, R. Jeffrey. 1982. *Corporate Liberalism: The Origins of Modern American Political Theory, 1890–1920.* Berkeley: University of California Press.

McNally, David. 2011. *Global Swamp: The Economics of Politics of Crisis and Resistance.* Oakland, CA: PM Press.

Marshall, Ray. 1987. *Unheard Voices.* New York: Basic Books.

Marshall, Ray. 2010. "Learning Systems for a Globalized Economy." In *Human Resources Economics and Public Policy*, edited by Charles J. Whalen, 187–214. Kalamazoo, MI: W.E. Upjohn Institute.

Minsky, Hyman P. 1986. *Stabilizing an Unstable Economy.* New Haven: Yale University Press.

Minsky, Hyman P. 1991. "The Transition to a Market Economy: Financial Options." Working Paper No. 66, Annandale-on-Hudson, NY: Levy Economics Institute of Bard College.

Minsky, Hyman and Charles J. Whalen. 1996. "Economic Insecurity and Institutional Prerequisites for Successful Capitalism." *Journal of Post-Keynesian Economics* 19 (2): 155–170.

Mishel, Lawrence, Jared Bernstein, and Heidi Shierholz. 2009. *The State of Working America 2008/2009.* Ithaca, NY: ILR Press.

Muehleman, Samuel, Paul Ryan, and Stefan C. Wolter. 2013. "Monopsony Power, Pay Structure, and Training." *Industrial Labor Relations Review* 66 (5): 1097–1114.

Piketty, Thomas. 2014. *Capital in the Twenty-First Century.* Cambridge, MA: Belknap Press of Harvard University Press.

Prasch, Robert E. 1995. "Toward a 'General Theory' of Market Exchange." *Journal of Economic Issues* 29 (3): 807–828.

Putnam, Robert D. 2020. *Bowling Alone: Revised and Updated.* New York: Simon and Schuster.

Ruggles, Steven, Sarah Flood, Ronald Goeken, Josiah Grover, Erin Meyer, Jose Pacas, and Matthew Sobek. 2020. IPUMS USA: Version 10.0 [dataset]. Minneapolis, MN: IPUMS. https://doi.org/10.18128/D010.V10.0, Files 1992, 2000, 2008, and 2016. Accessed January 4, 2021.

Saez, Emmanuel and Gabriel Zucman. 2020. "The Rise of Income and Wealth Inequality in America: Evidence from Distributional Macroeconomic Accounts." *Journal of Economic Perspectives* 34 (4): 3–26.

Sandel, Michael J. 2020. *The Tyranny of Merit: What's Become of the Common Good?* New York: Farrar, Straus and Giroux.

Schumpeter, Joseph A. (1942) 1975. *Capitalism, Socialism and Democracy.* New York: Harper and Row.

Schulman, Bruce J. 1991. *From Cotton Belt to Sunbelt: Federal Policy, Economic Development, and the Transformation of the South, 1938–1980.* Oxford: Oxford University Press.

Stanfield, J. Ron. 1980. "The Institutional Economics of Karl Polanyi." *Journal of Economic Issues* 14 (3): 593–614.

Stiglitz, Joseph E. 2012. *The Price of Inequality.* New York: W.W. Norton.

Thelen, Kathleen. 2001. "Varieties of Labor Politics in the Developed Democracies." In. *Varieties of Capitalism: The Institutional Foundations of Comparative Advantage*, edited by Peter Hall and David Soskice, 71–103. Oxford: Oxford University Press.

US Bureau of Labor Statistics. 2020. "Labor Productivity and Costs: Productivity Change in the Nonfarm Business Sector, 1947–2020." https://www.bls.gov/lpc/prodybar.htm. Accessed February 14, 2021.

US Census Bureau. 2020. Table H-2. "Share of Aggregate Income Received by Each Fifth and Top 5 Percent of All Households, 1967–2019." https://tinyurl.com/1pfjd5zz. Accessed February 14, 2021, showing data last revised September 8, 2020.

Volscho, Thomas W. Jr. and Nathan J. Kelly. 2012. "The Rise of the Super-Rich: Power Resources, Taxes, Financial Markets, and the Dynamics of the Top 1 Percent, 1949–2008." *American Sociological Review* 77 (5): 679–699.

Webb, Sidney. 1912. "The Economic Theory of a Legal Minimum Wage." *The Journal of Political Economy* 20 (10): 973–998.

Weil, David. 2014. *The Fissured Workplace: Why Work Became So Bad for So Many and What Can be Done to Improve It.* Cambridge, MA: Harvard University Press.

Weinstein, James. 1968. *The Corporate Ideal in the Liberal State: 1900–1918.* Boston: Beacon Press.

Whalen, Charles J. 2000. "Integrating Schumpeter and Keynes: Hyman Minsky's Theory of Capitalist Development." *Journal of Economic Issues* 35 (4): 805–823.

Whalen, Charles J. 2017. "Understanding Financialization: Standing on the Shoulders of Minsky." *E-Finance: Financial Internet Quarterly* 12 (2): 45–60.

Whalen, Charles J. 2019. "Institutional Economics and Chock-Full Employment: Reclaiming the 'Right to Work' as a Cornerstone of Progressive Capitalism." *Journal of Economic Issues* 53 (2): 321–340.

Wisman, Jon D. 2011. "Inequality, Social Respectability, Political Power, and Environmental Devastation." *Journal of Economic Issues* 45 (4): 877–900.

Zalewski, David. 2003. "Corporate Objectives—Maximizing Social versus Private Equity." *Journal of Economic Issues* 37 (2): 503–509.

Zatz, Noah D. 2009. "The Minimum Wage as a Civil Rights Protection: An Alternative to Antipoverty Arguments?" *University of Chicago Legal Forum* 2009 (1): article 3. https://tinyurl.com/yoy93b3j. Accessed February 17, 2021.

PART III

Concepts and methods

7. Social capital and public policy: the role of civil society in transforming the state

Asimina Christoforou

INTRODUCTION

This chapter focuses on the concepts of social capital and civil society. Social capital includes social norms and networks of reciprocity, trust, and cooperation. Civil society encompasses non-governmental, not-for-profit self-governing organizations, and informal groups. In the past three decades, the concepts of social capital and civil society have received much academic and public interest. Social capital appeared to enhance the ability of civil society to cultivate cooperation and solidarity, influence public policy, and promote democratic ideals and social welfare. The public debate on these concepts reminded economists that markets are socially embedded, and in many cases shifted their attention to the social factors required to improve the functioning of economies on a global, national, and subnational scale.

Concepts of social capital and civil society are not merely topics of scientific investigation and discussion. By the start of the new millennium, they were put to the test as they found their way into policy reports and social welfare programs across developed and less developed countries; development programs for the eradication of poverty by international organizations, such as the World Bank and the United Nations; the common policies and the economic governance systems of supranational institutions, such as the European Union (EU); and alternative frameworks for local development in both rural and urban areas (with the coordination of national and supranational institutions). These projects and studies claimed to restore the social dimensions of economies and public policy by accounting for the ways social groups and their underlying norms and networks can contribute to economic and political objectives.

However, under the influence of Third Way politics and the post-Washington Consensus, those initiatives most often reproduced dominant rational-choice principles and neoliberal agendas (e.g. Fine 2010, 98, 111). They overshadowed the "dark side" of social capital, and the role of powerful groups operating at the expense of broader social objectives.[1] They reduced social capital and civil society to a mere means for serving market objectives of profit and competition, which reproduce social inequalities and power structures. Nonetheless, there are studies in social capital research that employ these concepts with an aim of unraveling those conditions under which individuals and groups can *build norms and networks of cooperation and mobilize social forces to scrutinize and challenge the social injustices and inequalities created by power relations, market competition, and undemocratic states.*

Post-Keynesian Institutionalism (PKI) recognizes that the active contribution and collaboration of states and citizens are essential in addressing the abuses of private power and creating a civilized life and a good society founded on values of equality, security, and fairness (Whalen 2020). However, little has been said about the dynamics and complexities related to the formation and evolution of the social institutions that enable us to determine and pursue social transformation and welfare. Institutionalists have yet to unravel questions regarding how values, institutions, and behaviors for social welfare, justice, and equality come about and evolve, especially in a market society where values of profit and competition prevail. Also, they have all too seldom sketched out the ways in which social groups organize and mobilize collectively to voice social needs and concerns; make state officials accountable and responsive; take part in the provision of public goods and services by applying cooperative and democratic principles and practices of labor and production; challenge and resist powerful groups, which pursue particularized interests via clientelistic networks with state officials and policymakers; and develop synergistic relations with the state and promote norms of generalized trust in order to support broader social welfare objectives.

Moreover, economic policy debates usually evolve around the market-state dualism—more market and less state, or less market and more state. This is seldom the case in Institutionalism, Post Keynesianism, and PKI, which recognize the creative role of the state (e.g., see Ayres 1967, 101; Larson 2002; and Whalen 2008, respectively). Those traditions understand that the state has the power to make legislative, administrative, and judicial decisions, which define and legitimize rights and freedoms and thus determine the form of the economy and its relations with the government. They also understand that conflicting economic classes and interests compete in the political field to legitimize their rights and freedoms, and consolidate their power to shape the social order through the state apparatus. This raises important questions with regard to the form state action takes as well as the type of interests it serves. Nevertheless, even in PKI little attention has been given to the non-market and non-state institutions that comprise the civil society and contribute to the formation of the social norms and networks that specify not only society's relations with the market and the state, but also the means and objectives of public policy.

This chapter seeks to fill that void by explaining how social capital and civil society can develop the social values and institutions that make markets and governments accountable, and that promote public policies for social welfare. We argue that, according to the social capital literature, social transformation and welfare require synergistic relations across diverse groups and with the state, as well as generalized norms and networks of reciprocity, cooperation, and trust. We take the argument further by exploring the concepts and processes of participatory and deliberative democracy and the commons, and their potential to provide the basis for creating the synergistic relations and generalized norms for social justice and equality.

We begin by conceptualizing social capital and its relations with civil society. Then we discuss the relations of social capital and civil society with the state and the critical role they can play in public policy. In the penultimate section, we further explore how social capital and civil society can build values and institutions to promote social participation and welfare by connecting this literature with studies on processes of participatory and deliberative democracy and the commons. We conclude by stressing that PKI has much to gain by engaging with these ideas and delving deeper into the development of those social institutions that will enable us to define and achieve change for social welfare.

SOCIAL CAPITAL AND CIVIL SOCIETY

Social capital includes social norms and networks of cooperation, reciprocity, and trust that facilitate collective action for a mutual benefit. Since the late twentieth century, social capital has been associated with the social resources that enable individuals and groups to promote cooperation and participation, and to improve the institutional effectiveness of markets and states. Mainstream economic approaches to social capital are influenced by Neoclassical assumptions of individualism, instrumentalism, and functionalism. Hence, they view social norms and networks of cooperation and trust either as a means to enhancing individual utility or as an outcome of individual investment decisions (Becker 1996; Glaeser et al. 2000; 2002). These assumptions are reproduced in the theoretical models and experimental games used by New Institutional economics to study the formation and evolution of social capital as cooperative behavior and trust (see, for instance, Keefer and Knack 2008). As a result, these approaches largely ignore the impact of contextual factors—such as governance structures, power relations, and social inequalities—on cooperation, trust, and economic behavior (Fine 2001; 2010).

This chapter adopts an alternative approach to social capital whereby social norms and networks are not subject to the reductionist confines of the utility-maximization and capital-accumulation framework of Neoclassical economics. According to this approach (for instance, see van Staveren 2001; Christoforou 2011), elements of social capital do not solely constitute an instrumental means for improving one's personal socioeconomic status; they are pursued for their intrinsic value, which reflects people's social, political, and moral considerations (non-instrumental approach). In addition, elements of social capital are not simply an outcome of individual biological/psychological predispositions; they also derive from social, political, and moral processes of individual agency that create common identities, needs, and demands (non-individualist approach). Furthermore, they do not respond only to one's personal preferences or strategic choices; they express people's commitment to shared values and institutions of trust, cooperation, and reciprocity (non-preference-based approach). Finally, they are not primarily formed to minimize transaction costs from state and market imperfections; they inspire responsibility and concern toward others (non-consequentialist approach). Overall, the underlying idea is that human beings are not primarily and naturally guided by their egotistical instincts and impulses, rather they have naturally and historically evolved to equally consider altruistic and cooperative motivations in their behavior.[2]

We distinguish two traditions in the theoretical and empirical social capital literature, namely the Putnamian and Bourdieusian traditions (Christoforou 2017). The Putnamian tradition identifies with the work of the American political scientist Robert Putnam, whose work in the 1990s triggered renewed interest, among scholars and policymakers alike, regarding the role of social relations in improving the effectiveness of market and state institutions. It adopts a more macro-social perspective by stressing the importance of social capital for social cohesion and political integration. Measures of social capital are typically derived from survey data, which focus on individuals' perception of and participation in a variety of social and political activities, and are aggregated to compare aspects of generalized trust and civic engagement across regions or countries. An indicative list of relevant measures includes: the number of group memberships, club meetings, elections or referenda in which individuals participate, or the hours they do volunteer work; frequency of attendance in public meetings on community issues; frequency of spending time visiting friends or entertaining them at home; and the share of individuals claiming that most people can be trusted, are honest, fair, and helpful, or engage in acts of civic behavior (e.g. pay taxes, keep public spaces clean). However, it has been argued that this tradition suffers from a historical and cultural determinism that overlooks the impact of human agency in shaping institutional factors; a functionalism that regards institutional factors as an outcome of rational choice decisions or an exogenously-determined factor, with disregard to alternative social, political, and moral motivations and considerations in decision-making; and a reductionism that not only oversimplifies the complex and evolutionary dynamics of the interactions between agency and structure, but also underestimates the role of social inequalities and power relations in the formation of social capital.

The Bourdieusian tradition derives from French sociologist Pierre Bourdieu. Although it preceded the work of Putnam, it received relatively less attention in the broader social capital literature, perhaps due to its critical stance toward rational choice approaches to human behavior (Fine 2010). Here social capital becomes important because it grants individuals access to a set of material and non-material resources possessed by the members of their networks, be they personal (family, kin, friends, and neighbors) or professional (at the workplace, in professional organizations, and within shared fields of activity or business). However, social structures are characterized by the unequal distribution of capital and power, and thus differentially affect individuals' capacity to invest in the various types of capital, including economic, cultural, and social capital. In the Bourdieusian tradition, the rather understudied notions of conflict and struggle, as well as the interactions between agency and structure, are reinstated in the analysis of social capital. This sheds further light on the dark side of social capital, which can be used to consolidate social inequalities and power structures. To empirically assess social capital, Bourdieu applied social network analyses in order to distinguish: the number of links and nodes; the degree of network closure or openness toward other groups and networks; the flow of economic and non-economic resources among members; and the structure of hierarchical and vertical relations. Thus, the value of individuals' social capital depends not only on the connections they have, but also on the economic, cultural, and social capital resources they can access through their connections.

Both traditions can be combined to obtain a more holistic and relational interpretation of social capital by highlighting not only its structural and cognitive aspects, but also the impact of individual and institutional factors. It must be stated, however, that all these methods and measures can only provide proxies to capturing dimensions of social capital. As van Staveren (2001) notes, values express commitments that are intrinsically valuable and incommensurable; they are at the same time economic, social, political, and moral, so they are subject to multiple considerations and motivations of human behavior; and they have unintended consequences across different value domains in the economy, the state, and our interpersonal relationships. Thus, norms and networks are characterized by a multiplicity of motives, conditions, and social outcomes, which reflect different perceptions of individual members and groups on issues of development and redistribution, efficiency, and fairness.

Our focus is to unravel those conditions, particularly the collective processes of association and political participation, whereby state-society synergistic relations will cultivate generalized norms and networks of cooperation and reciprocity. We return to this argument in subsequent sections.

Social capital is often identified with the notion of civil society (for an overview, see Keane 1998; Edwards 2014). Civil society generally includes non-governmental, not-for-profit self-governing organizations, voluntary associations, and informal groupings and networks, which act collectively in a public sphere to express their interests and pursue collective values and goals. Discussions regarding the relations between citizens and the state trace back to the philosophies of the Ancient civilizations of the Mediterranean Basin (such as Aristotle's concept of the *polis*, or city-state, as a civil community; see also Adloff 2021). These issues were reinvigorated in social capital research in the twentieth century. Whether one adopted a communitarian approach (emphasizing cohesion, integration, and social harmony) or a more critical stance (highlighting power, conflict, and social change), most would see social norms and networks of cooperation, reciprocity, and trust as the elements which have enabled the organizations and collectives that comprise civil society to cultivate values of social participation, democracy, and welfare, and thus to play a critical role in the formation of public policy.

Although the revival of civil society in the late twentieth century highlighted the critical role of participation and democracy, in some cases it tended to overlook the power relations and social injustices that hinder individuals' capacity to partake in democratic deliberations. The civil society revivalists also attributed the weakening of civil society and social capital to individuals' moral decline: distance from traditional values of family, respect for authority, and personal responsibility (Roberts 2000; see also Edwards 2014). However, by focusing on the history of the racial exclusion of Blacks in the United States, Roberts (2000) reminds us that social injustices, not moral decline, have prevented people from participating in the nation's economic and political life and co-creating a sense of common humanity. These injustices emanate from institutional barriers, such as the lack of public assistance; social and spatial segregation; the violation of human rights to freedom, justice, association, and self-determination; limited access to education and employment; and the social and scientific justification of racial hierarchy.[3]

Radical approaches to civil society perceive it as a source of social resistance and transformation. While imprisoned by the Italian Fascist regime in 1926, Antonio Gramsci introduced the concept of hegemony as a form of domination, which relied on the expansion of the state, including the ways it extends into the complex institutions and organizations of civil society. Yet he also envisioned a civil society where an alternative moral and intellectual order, what he termed the counter-hegemony, would emanate from the collective efforts of the working class, intellectuals, and social organizations, in order to transform economies and societies (see Gramsci 1971). As we discuss in the following section, the economic and political impact of social capital and civil society depends largely on their relationship with the state and public policy.

SOCIAL CAPITAL, CIVIL SOCIETY, THE STATE, AND PUBLIC POLICY

In the past decades, many theoretical and empirical studies have emerged concerning the relationship between social capital and the state. Most find that social capital and the state mutually influence one another in the formation of public policy. Before identifying social relations conducive to social welfare, we summarize the kinds of questions those studies raise regarding state-society relations in public policy.

Often social capital has been associated with programs for state-building, conflict resolution, local development, social regeneration, and targeted social provisioning in various regions across the globe. Supranational organizations and national governments have funded these programs conditional upon the utilization or creation of social capital, especially in what is called the social economy (or the voluntary sector or the third sector of the economy), where public-private partnerships are forged to provide welfare services and goods to those who face social exclusion or displacement.[4] In these settings, less privileged social groups of local communities would be invited to actively and collectively partake in the determination of those social norms and networks that were needed to govern collaborative relations within and among communities in a polycentric system of governance developed at the supranational, national, and subnational levels (Ostrom 2010). However, by focusing on rational-choice principles and incentive-based mechanisms to alter individual behavior, these initiatives tended to overlook the impact of contextual factors, such as the unequal distribution of resources, the capture of powerful groups, and welfare state retrenchment, which prevented other social groups from exploiting opportunities for social participation, empowerment, and the provision of welfare goods and services (e.g. Fine 2001, 123). Eventually, the state is absolved from its own duties for redistribution and welfare, concealing the interests and acts of powerful groups.

In other studies, social capital underscores the kind of civic behavior needed for people to respond to their obligations as citizens and honor their commitment to the state by, among other things, paying taxes and avoiding bribery (Andriani 2016); protecting the environment and respecting human rights (Jones et al. 2009; Marbuah 2019); and supporting social protection (against poverty, unemployment, disability) and welfare programs (Schneider 2006). In debates among social groups on citizens' obligations, human rights, and social protection, the government may step in to act as a coordinator of discussions and exchanges among these groups (capital and labor, for example), or as a broker enabling parties to reach a consensus and to honor their commitments as partners in a social agreement. However, it could be argued that the government may simply be mediating to ameliorate citizens' and social partners' collective resistance against certain policies which serve the particularized interests of powerful groups. A case in point is fiscal austerity applied after the recent financial crises, when national economies were already experiencing deep recession. In this context, social resistance would often be relegated to an illogical and imprudent reaction toward state policy and social consensus (reflecting weak social capital and civil society), rather than a resounding protest by the unprivileged and the unheard against the rolling back of the state and the violation of human rights to participation, welfare, equality, and justice (signifying a strong sense of social capital and civil society).

Another strand of literature focuses on the kinds of evaluation systems governments establish, namely public and social accounting and auditing techniques, for measuring and assessing the social norms and networks and governance structures in development programs and social economy organizations (e.g. European Commission 2014; 2017). Though evaluation methods now appreciate the impact of social networks and governance structures on economic, social, and political processes and outcomes,[5] they seem to underestimate and exclude important relational and contextual dimensions of social capital: the critical role of informal networks in responding to social needs and concerns, especially in times of crisis; the inequalities and power relations in society; and the importance of inclusiveness and democracy in decision-making processes. Further insights can be gained on these aspects of social capital by introducing alternative evaluation methods, which incorporate institutional-historical analyses, social network analyses, and process-based techniques (in conjunction with almost exclusively-used output-based evaluation) (cf. Pisani et al. 2017).

Ultimately, the underlying question throughout the literature is: Can top-down initiatives via legislation and public policy foster or debilitate bottom-up initiatives for solidarity, state accountability, and social welfare? The dominant view, supported by international organizations, policy authorities, and social scientists, was that social capital and civil society provide an additional social means to fulfilling market objectives of profit, competitiveness, and growth. That perspective saw the development of norms and networks as a process of social *investment* rather than social *transformation*. International and national public bodies would stress the importance of social capital and citizens' collective support for ensuring good governance, which was perceived as the state's commitment to cost-benefit analyses in policy-making, efficiency-enhancing public management, and the individualization and marketization of welfare.[6] Hence, both civil society and government become restricted and frugal in pursuing social values and controlling markets.

However, other studies acknowledge social capital and civil society as expressions of active citizenry, participatory and deliberative democracy, and social transformation. Some claim that social capital had enormous appeal in the late twentieth century, precisely because it coincided with general disillusionment toward Western market-oriented neoliberal regimes and Eastern centrally-planned communist regimes, and because it offered valuable insights on new forms of politics and governance structures, where civil society would play a central role in the struggle for social welfare (Evans 1996a; Bowles and Gintis 2002). More recent work on third sector organizations stresses that social capital is conducive to the transition of the social economy from one related to "*good* governance," with its neoliberal overtones, toward one founded on "*democratic* governance," with emphasis on plurality, participation, deliberation, and self-organization (Laville and Salmon 2015). In this context, third sector organizations are seen as a result of the "re-embeddedness" of the economy à la Polanyi, as the civil society activates to restrict the detrimental effects of individualization and marketization. Moreover, they reflect a hybridization of the different poles of the economy designated by Polanyi, namely exchange (market), redistribution (state), and reciprocity (civil society), because they take part in market exchange (e.g. social enterprises, cooperatives) as well as public policy. This is consistent with conceptions of social capital that emerged in the late nineteenth century to confront the negative consequences of capitalism and promote democratic participation, community action, and social movements (Christoforou 2013; Farr 2014).

Certain studies observe that social participation and welfare can be achieved when social capital develops synergistic relations across diverse groups and with the state (Andriani and Christoforou 2016; Christoforou 2017; Evans 1996b; Rothstein and Stolle 2003; Woolcock 1998). Woolcock (1998) introduces two concepts that refer to distinct but complementary forms of social capital, namely "embeddedness" and "autonomy." "Embeddedness" emphasizes the importance of what we refer to as "bonding" social capital, while "autonomy" stresses the importance of "bridging" social capital. Forms of "bonding" social capital are necessary to support intra-group ties in order to pursue collective goals. To avoid the exclusion, introversion, and discrimination by intra-group ties serving particularized interests, more generalized forms of social capital that transcend local or special-interest groups and *bridge* ties across multiple, diverse groups must be established. In other words, embedded social relations need to be combined with autonomous social ties. At the micro level, autonomy enables members of local groups to create links with diverse groups outside their own locality, in order to explore different opportunities and capabilities, including job positions, access to educational and health facilities, as well as new ideas, visions, and practices of collective action, participation, and welfare. At the macro level, autonomy enables local groups to create generalized norms and networks of cooperation and solidarity and thus overcome the impact of powerful (public and private) groups, which serve particularized interests and function as vehicles of corruption, nepotism, and exploitation. In this manner, government officials and policymakers become accountable to broader social welfare objectives.

The dynamics and complexities of the relationships between the state and social capital are also addressed in studies investigating how trust in public institutions and the type of welfare state regimes, such as Esping-Andersen's (1990) categorization, may affect structural or cognitive aspects of social capital (cf. Christoforou 2010; Kumlin and Rothstein 2005; Rothstein and Stolle 2003). These studies contend that, compared to more universal systems, selective welfare systems are susceptible to discrimination and fraud, and thus reduce confidence in public institutions, which in turn adversely affects norms and networks of cooperation and trust within society. On the one hand, selective public services are provided to individuals only after they are proved to meet a number of more or less specific conditions to qualify for benefits and services (such as poor income and health). On the other hand, universal welfare systems ensure access to many social programs that are less targeted to specific groups and instead cover a wider segment of the population without considering their particular status. This may explain why the social democratic countries of Scandinavia, where universal systems prevail, portray relatively higher levels of trust among citizens and toward public institutions, as well as higher levels of membership in a diverse set of associations, compared to the neoliberal systems of Anglo-Saxon countries, where selective welfare systems have been established. In fact, the universal welfare systems of Scandinavian countries were the outcome of a history of social struggles among groups and organizations representing conflicting interests in view of the expansion of markets and the need to preserve social welfare.

Questions may arise with regard to the potential of civil society to build synergistic relations within a context of authoritarian governance and sectarian societies. However, there are studies which evidence the capacity of social capital to mediate between conflicting interests and develop synergistic relations with the state in order to produce social change (see, for instance, Evans 1996a; 1996b). It is argued that in such societies the real key to synergy is translating social ties from engines of parochial loyalties into vehicles for more encompassing forms of organization through political activity and debate. To achieve this transformation, citizens need to foster the consolidation of representative and autonomous social organizations; forge an objective alliance between social movements and reformists; and promote structures of bureaucratic organization on the basis of impartiality, transparency, and cred-ibility (Evans 1996a; 1996b; Harriss 2002). In this manner, social struggles and conflict, rather than stifling social capital, may contribute to the creation of social capital, as power relations shift and new social groups and networks take form to pursue collective goals (Paterson 2001). For example, in response to financial crisis and the fiscal consolidation policies, a series of new informal networks emerged in Greece ranging from self-help neighborhood groups, to second-hand shops, social kitchens, even local currencies and barter economy institutions, all aiming to respond to society's needs and concerns, which con-ventional, formal organizations operating in the market, state, and civil society were unable to satisfy (Sotiropoulos and Bourikos 2014).

Therefore, state-society relations are influenced by institutional factors, conflicting interests, and incommensurable values across social groups. Karl Polanyi uses the term "re-embeddedness" to explain the ways in which the state and the civil society work in synergy to promote values and institutions of redistribution and reciprocity against the social "dis-embeddedness" imposed by unregulated markets (Adaman and Madra 2002; Polanyi 1944). To avoid the patron-client relations, rent-seeking, and corruption that could arise from unchecked reciprocal exchanges in dealings with the state, van Staveren (2001) suggests that the value domains of freedom (exchange), justice (redis-tribution), and care (reciprocity) become accountable to one another, and eco-nomic actors invest in all virtues of each of the domains. In this manner, actors would compete in exchange, agree on a legitimate distribution, and incorporate others' contingent needs in the economic process on the basis of broader social welfare objectives of justice and equality. Put differently, according to Klimina (2020), a reasonable market capable of weakening power elites and building economic and political democracy should be founded on universal values of ownership empowerment and equal opportunity, and supported by impartial state regulations, an unbiased judiciary, and liberalized impersonal exchanges, alongside personal reciprocal relations.

Overall, we accept that social capital and civil society have the poten-tial to generate social awareness, mobilize groups, develop institutions of state-society synergy relations, and cultivate values of responsibility and solidarity, equity, and justice. However, the question remains: how can we strengthen this potential to achieve social transformation? We think the key lies in values and institutions of participatory democracy and "commoning." We take up this issue in the following section.

REBUILDING SOCIAL CAPITAL AND MOBILIZING CIVIL SOCIETY FOR SOCIAL TRANSFORMATION

To discuss how social capital and civil society can develop the capacity for social transformation and public welfare, we introduce concepts of participatory and deliberative democracy and the commons, and examine how the ideas and structures of cooperation they promote can become the basis for social norms and networks of synergistic relations and generalized trust, which will transform economies and societies toward the social goals of equality and justice.

Mainstream economics focuses mainly on competitive modes of democracy, which emphasize voting as a mechanism for aggregating political preferences, and choosing representatives and leaders (Enjolras and Steen-Johnson 2015). Yet little attention has been given to participatory and deliberative modes of democracy: on the one hand, participatory democracy stresses the direct involvement of all those affected by certain activities in processes of political discourse and decision-making; on the other hand, deliberative democracy highlights rational discussion and deliberation in the public space in order to solve conflicts of interest by means of transformation rather than preference aggregation (Enjolras and Steen-Johnson 2015). Mainstream economics fails to explain collective acts of participation and deliberation due to its reductionist view of economic behavior: it excludes the social and moral values of commitment and solidarity toward the needs and concerns of others, values which constitute the quintessential elements of democracy (Sen 1999).

For Post Keynesians, the aim of economic policy is primarily the development of an open, democratic, and civilized society, by appealing to the social and moral values upheld by individuals and groups in their economic transactions and social relationships, namely loyalty, responsibility, the pursuit of excellence, love, and compassion (Marangos 2000). Post Keynesians claim that a civilized society cannot prosper on efficiency considerations alone; it must eradicate social inequalities and injustices by harmoniously blending civic values with self-interested behavior. Similar views are found among American Institutionalists. For instance, John R. Commons focuses on the concept of "collective democracy," which draws our attention not only to the social outcomes produced by democratic participation, but also to the processes themselves, where all affected parties form groups of common interests (like representatives of labor and capital in industrial relations) and partake in collective bargaining and negotiated problem-solving (Commons 1950; see also Whalen 2022). Wilber and Jameson (1983) note that, inspired by Institutionalism, PKI focuses on mediating structures, such as family, church, voluntary associations, neighborhood, and subculture, which operate beyond the market and the state, and cultivate ethics of cooperation and stewardship against hedonism and quietism, and thus enable societies to fulfill the economic goals of life-sustenance, freedom of choice, esteem, and fellowship. The authors argue that these structures should take an active role in economic planning through public policies which promote decentralization (e.g. application of the subsidiarity principle in governance structures) and institutions of participatory, democratic decision-making within firms (e.g. worker ownership) and communities (e.g. formal and informal neighborhood associations).

Generally, Post Keynesians and Institutionalists focus on state intervention (including the judicial system) as the central means for coordinating the conflicting interests of social groups, especially representatives of capital and labor, and for regulating markets on the basis of civic values. PKI leaves unresolved some of the tensions discussed in previous sections: How can we ensure that social goals of cooperation and participation do not devolve into a mere means for economic goals? Does focus on traditional moral and familial values overshadow the impact of social inequalities and injustices? Can bottom-up initiatives be stifled by top-down actions? Here we argue that civil society can play a more active role in creating the social values and prefigurative relations that will transform economies and societies and promote participation and democracy.

To ensure the conditions for a truly participatory and deliberative democracy, a three-way relationship is suggested between representative bodies, administrative structures, and self-governing groups of civil society (Boje 2017; Devine 1988). This is reminiscent of Gramsci's (1971) concept of counter-hegemony and Polanyi's (1944) idea of the social re-embeddedness of the economy, where civil society challenges market domination and restores human values of social and environmental protection. A case in point is the application of participatory budgeting within firms, social organizations, or the broader community. These methods have already been implemented in various forms around the globe, manifesting their ability to enhance public participation and democratic decision-making.[7] At the heart of these processes is the involvement of all interested parties, including community residents and government officials, in order to share and discuss proposals for projects; to vote and decide on the allocation of available funds among the different proposals; to monitor and assess the results of these projects and the effective use of funds; and to reflect on, and improve for the future, procedures of resource allocation and democratic participation.

Values and practices of participatory and deliberative democracy are related to the commons and "commoning." The commons is understood as a pool of resources that groups of people manage for individual and collective benefit (Akbulut 2017; van Laerhoven and Ostrom 2007). Ostrom (1990) challenged the view that states and markets provide the sole solution to Hardin's tragedy of the commons, and introduced the possibility of community-based management of resources. Though these ideas generated a series of policy reports by international organizations and national governments, which shifted attention to community-based collective initiatives for development programming, these policies perceived the commons as a means to promote market objectives of capital accumulation and competition, again in the spirit of Third Way politics and the post-Washington Consensus. We endorse an alternative understanding of the commons as a social sphere of life, which mainly challenges market dominance and protects against social injustices and inequalities. Thus, the commons is not perceived as an existing, pre-defined entity, but as a process of social interaction, struggle, and transformation, or as a process of *commoning*, where production and reproduction take place under collective labor, equal access to resources, and egalitarian forms of decision-making (Akbulut 2017; Fournier 2013; Wainwright 2013).

Commoning goes beyond the distribution of rights to access commonly produced and preserved resources; it incorporates social duties and responsibilities for organizing work in the provision of common goods (Fournier 2013). For example, in a community garden, the commons may be open to those who preserve the natural and social environment in a way that they fulfill everyone's needs for food, leisure, knowledge, and association. Generally, as Wainwright (2013) argues, commoning requires a shift from an instrumental logic to a prefigurative one, that is, toward a logic whereby we act in the present according to the social values we are trying to envision and apply in our daily lives in the future. Our capacity to labor, or to create, is understood as a commons, not as a commodity, because it is not only *for* the good life, it is itself *part of* the good of life. Hence, we are in want of building alternative frameworks for reflection and decision-making in production, evaluation, and collective bargaining, which go beyond standard practices of individualized wage and income maximization, and take account of values of participatory democracy, social and environmental accounting, and the abolition of social segregation and inequalities (Wainwright 2013).

The question is how we envision and apply the values and practices enabling us to move beyond conventional institutions of civil society and public policy. According to Gibson-Graham (2003; 2006), these values and practices *already exist*. Beneath the systems of formal market transactions, wage labor, and capitalist enterprise, we encounter a myriad of submerged but sustaining alternative forms of labor and production, which interact with one another to form a diverse economy characterized by multiplicity, interdependence, and potentiality. It is within this diverse economy that we can discover alternative, non-capitalist subjectivities, rationalities, and imaginaries, and learn how to create collective modes of production and community economies founded on values and practices of participatory and deliberative democracy. In other words, social interaction and collective learning are essential elements of the commoning process, which raise awareness of social injustices and teach us how to mobilize and organize collectively to restore social welfare.

Adaman and Devine (2002) discuss the benefits of a participatory economic system in relation to the production and allocation of material and non-material resources, and to the implementation of inclusive and democratic processes of participation and decision-making. They define a participatory economic system as an interlocking network of social relationships and institutions, where the values and interests of people in the different aspects of their lives interact and shape one another in a discursive process of decision-making through negotiation and cooperation. Generalized norms and networks of participation constitute a crucial element of this economic system: all those with either a relevant input to contribute or a legitimate interest in the outcome, i.e. all those who are affected by an activity and operate in the market, the state, or the civil society, are actively involved on an equal footing.

Researchers and academics can play a critical part in this process of learning and co-transformation. Gibson-Graham and Roelvink (2009) introduce what they term "hybrid research collectives," where researchers and academics collaborate with all community members whose interests are affected by a certain activity—including workers, pensioners, students, local producers, and administrators—in order to discuss and resolve socioeconomic problems on the basis of social welfare objectives. Researchers and community members engage in a discursive process, based on participatory democratic principles and practices, and are jointly mobilized and re-constituted to embody a new "econo-sociality" (Gibson-Graham and Roelvink 2009), which cultivates collaborative possibilities and subjectivities, and ethical considerations of justice and equality (Christoforou and Adaman 2018). In this process, civil society organizations may contribute to the creation of transformational and prefigurative relations toward alternative economies by envisioning and experimenting with new ideas and practices for labor and production on the basis of collective and democratic values.

CONCLUSIONS

In this chapter, we discussed how social capital and civil society can impact public policy and transform the state. Contrary to the instrumentalist and individualist interpretations of social capital and civil society in mainstream economics, which emphasizes their extrinsic value as a (social) means for enhancing market efficiency and economic growth, we argue for forms of social capital and civil society which enhance social participation and cooperation in scrutinizing and challenging the injustices and inequalities created by power relations, market competition, and undemocratic states.

To explore the conditions under which state-society relations develop the potential to promote social welfare, justice, and equality, we connected the literature on social capital and civil society with studies on the concepts of participatory and deliberative democracy and the commons. We contend that social capital and civil society can play a critical role in public policy for social welfare and the transformation of the state by promoting social values of justice and equity on the basis of principles and practices of participatory and deliberative democracy and processes of commoning. Conditions of democracy and the commons are necessary to ensure that social capital and civil society organizations will be employed to prevent capture from powerful groups and particularized interests, and to cultivate social responsibility and solidarity, social justice and equality, state-society synergy, and generalized norms and networks of cooperation, reciprocity, and trust. In short, the chapter has investigated social capital and civil society and their relations with public policy and the state, in order to shed further light on the complex interactions between social organizations, the market, and the state, and to determine the ways they affect economic and political outcomes and processes, particularly the ways they can restore values and institutions of social welfare, equity, and justice.

PKI can inform and enrich its theories, methods, practices, and policies by studying the institutional and historical analyses of civil society organizations, and by examining the emergence and evolution of non-capitalist economies and forms of commons and commoning. Within these diverse economies, PKI can discover the transformational and prefigurative relations which already exist and foster alternative rationalities and subjectivities, influencing forms of labor and production, as well as policymaking processes and outcomes aimed at promoting social change and welfare. Ultimately, the key questions we need to address are not *how much* state, but *what kind* of state we want, and what needs to be done to transform it.

In closing, we should bear in mind that through these processes of participation, transformation, and commoning, our conceptions, relations, and structures of coordination and governance in society (including the market, the state, and the civil society) will evolve and change. Indicatively, the state-dominated welfare regimes of the Fordist era in the previous century gave way to new forms of governance characterized by the co-production of private and public initiatives and the hybridization of civil society organizations, which now also partake in commercial activities and public policy. This can be seen as the outcome of two opposing forces: on the one hand, there has been the dismantling of the welfare state, the privatization of social provisioning, and the dominance of values of efficiency and profit in the private and public sectors; and on the other hand, new social groups and movements have emerged to respond to these trends and counteract the attack on social justice and equality. To be sure, the challenges are great. For example, recent years have witnessed a number of troubling developments, including: serious restrictions on the civic space following violations of fundamental rights such as the freedom of association, peaceful assembly, and expression; withdrawal from international initiatives and treaties for social and environmental protection; and violence against social groups of a different gender, race, religion, or ethnicity (CIVICUS 2019). Thus, the aim is to mobilize and organize social forces that can reflect on and respond to these changes so as to protect social values of participation, democracy, welfare, equality, and justice *for all*.

ACKNOWLEDGMENTS

I would like to thank my dear friends Fikret Adaman, Anna Klimina, and Charles Whalen for their invaluable comments on the chapter.

NOTES

1. Examples of the dark side of social capital include, among others, local, national, and global economic and political elites; groups supporting acts of discrimination, nepotism, and racism; patron-client networks with the government; and criminal organizations.
2. By now a vast literature versed in the Institutionalist and Post Keynesian traditions explains how economic behavior is socially embedded and motivated by considerations beyond the narrowly-defined instincts of *homo economicus*. See Wrenn and Waller (2018) for an analysis of the ways mainstream economics has distorted the social and ethical dimensions of human behavior.
3. Moreover, disenfranchised groups are similarly rendered responsible not only for their own deprivations, but also for disrupting civil life when they organize collectively to protest against social degradation. However, according to Jessica Gordon Nembhard (2014) and Caroline Hossein (2018), Black people have learned to master the creation of collectives and community-based inclusive cooperatives in order to pool resources, deal with constant crises, and help one another in safe ways.
4. An example would be the much-celebrated microfinance institutions and networks.
5. They have typically used measures of social capital introduced in the Putnamian tradition; see the previous section ("Social Capital and Civil Society").
6. This is reminiscent of a Foucauldian understanding of neoliberalism as a mode of governmentality, whereby the social is organized through economic incentives and political power is organized on the competitive logic of markets (Madra and Adaman 2014).
7. See, for instance, Participatory Budgeting Project (2021); and Lodewijckx (2021).

REFERENCES

Adaman, Fikret, and Pat Devine. 2002. "A Reconsideration of the Theory of Entrepreneurship: A Participatory Approach." *Review of Political Economy* 14 (3): 329–355.

Adaman, Fikret, and Yahya M. Madra. 2002. "Theorizing the 'Third Sphere': A Critique of the Persistence of the 'Economistic Fallacy.'" *Journal of Economic Issues* 36 (4): 1045–1078.

Adloff, Frank. 2021. "Capitalism and Civil Society Revisited or: Conceptualizing a Civil, Sustainable and Solidary Economy." *International Journal of Politics, Culture, and Society* 34 (2): 149–159.

Akbulut, Bengi. 2017. "Commons." In *Routledge Handbook of Ecological Economics: Nature and Society*, edited by Clive L. Spash, 395–403. London: Routledge.

Andriani, Luca. 2016. "Tax Morale and Prosocial Behavior: Evidence from a Palestinian Survey." *Cambridge Journal of Economics* 40 (3): 821–841.

Andriani, Luca, and Asimina Christoforou. 2016. "Social Capital: A Roadmap of Theoretical and Empirical Contributions and Limitations." *Journal of Economic Issues* 50 (1): 4–22.

Ayres, Clarence E. 1967. "Ideological Responsibility." *Journal of Economic Issues* 1 (1–2): 3–11.

Becker, Gary S. 1996. *Accounting for Tastes*. Cambridge: Harvard University Press.

Boje, Thomas P. 2017. "Concluding Essay: Social Activism against Austerity–the Conditions for Participatory and Deliberative Forms of Democracy." *Journal of Civil Society* 13 (3): 349–356.

Bowles, Samuel, and Herbert Gintis. 2002. "Social Capital and Community Governance." *Economic Journal* 112 (483): F419–F436.

Christoforou, Asimina. 2010. "Social Capital and Human Development: An Empirical Investigation across European Countries." *Journal of Institutional Economics* 6 (2): 191–214.

Christoforou, Asimina. 2011. "Social Capital: A Manifestation of Neoclassical Prominence or a Path to a More Pluralistic Economics?" *Journal of Economic Issues* 45 (3): 685–701.

Christoforou, Asimina. 2013. "On the Identity of Social Capital and the Social Capital of Identity." *Cambridge Journal of Economics* 37(4): 719–736.

Christoforou, Asimina. 2017. "Social Capital: Intuition, Precept, Concept and Theory." In *Social Capital and Local Development: From Theory to Empirics*, edited by Elena Pisani, Giorgio Franceschetti, Laura Secco, and Asimina Christoforou, 23–41. New York: Palgrave Macmillan.

Christoforou, Asimina, and Fikret Adaman. 2018. "Democratization of Economic Research and Policy by Building a Knowledge Commons: Inspiration from Cooperatives." *Forum for Social Economics* 47 (2): 204–213.

CIVICUS. 2019. *State of Civil Society Report 2019*. https://www.civicus.org/index.php/state-of-civil-society-report-2019. Accessed August 20, 2020.

Commons, John R. 1950. *The Economics of Collective Action*, edited by Kenneth H. Parsons. New York: Macmillan.

Devine, Pat. 1988. *Democracy and Economic Planning: The Political Economy of a Self-Governing Society*. Cambridge: Polity Press.

Edwards, Michael. 2014. *Civil Society*, third edition. Cambridge: Polity Press.

Enjolras, Bernard, and Kari Steen-Johnson. 2015. "Democratic Governance and Citizenship." In *Civil Society, the Third Sector and Social Enterprise: Governance and Democracy*, edited by Jean-Louis Laville, Dennis R. Young, and Paul Eynaud, 191–204. London: Routledge.

Esping-Andersen, Gøsta. 1990. *The Three Worlds of Welfare Capitalism*. Cambridge: Polity Press.

European Commission. 2014. *Proposed Approaches to Social Impact Measurement*. Luxembourg: Publications Office of the European Union.

European Commission—DG for Agriculture and Rural Development—Unit C. 4. 2017. *Guidelines: Evaluation of LEADER/CLLD*. Brussels.

Evans, Peter. 1996a. "Introduction: Development Strategies across the Public–Private Divide." *World Development* 24 (6): 1033–1037.

Evans, Peter. 1996b. "Government Action, Social Capital and Development: Reviewing the Evidence on Synergy." *World Development* 24 (6): 1119–1132.

Farr, James. 2014. "The History of 'Social Capital.'" In *Social Capital and Economics: Social Values, Power and Social Identity*, edited by Asimina Christoforou and John B. Davis, 15–37. London: Routledge.

Fine, Ben. 2001. *Social Capital versus Social Theory—Political Economy and Social Science at the Turn of the Millennium*. London: Routledge.

Fine, Ben. 2010. *Theories of Social Capital: Researchers Behaving Badly*. London: Pluto Press.

Fournier, Valérie. 2013. "Commoning: On the Social Organization of the Commons." *M@n@gement* 16 (4): 433–453.

Gibson-Graham, Julie-Katherine. 2003. "Enabling Ethical Economies: Cooperativism and Class." *Critical Sociology* 29 (2): 123–161.

Gibson-Graham, Julie-Katherine. 2006. *A Postcapitalist Politics*. Minneapolis, MN: University of Minnesota Press.

Gibson-Graham, Julie-Katherine, and Gerda Roelvink. 2009. "An Economic Ethics for the Anthropocene." *Antipode* 41 (S1): 320–346.

Glaeser, Edward L., David Laibson, and Bruce Sacerdote. 2002. "An Economic Approach to Social Capital." *Economic Journal* 112 (483): F437–F458.

Glaeser, Edward L., David Laibson, José A. Scheinkman, and Christine L. Soutter. 2000. "Measuring Trust." *Quarterly Journal of Economics* 115 (3): 811–846.

Gordon Nembhard, Jessica. 2014. *Collective Courage: A History of African American Cooperative Economic Thought and Practice*. University Park, PA: Penn State University Press.

Gramsci, Antonio. 1971. *Selections from the Prison Notebooks*. New York: International Publishers.

Harriss, John. 2002. *Depoliticizing Development: The World Bank and Social Capital*. London: Anthem Press.

Hossein, Caroline S. ed. 2018. *The Black Social Economy in the Americas: Exploring Diverse Community-Based Markets*. New York: Palgrave Macmillan.

Jones, Nikoleta, Costas M. Sophoulis, Theodoros Iosifides, Iosif Botetzagias, and Konstantinos Evangelinos. 2009. "The Influence of Social Capital on Environmental Policy Instruments." *Environmental Politics* 18 (4): 595–611.

Keane, John. 1998. *Civil Society: Old Images, New Visions*. Cambridge: Polity Press.

Keefer, Philip, and Stephen Knack. 2008. "Social Capital, Social Norms and the New Institutional Economics." In *Handbook of New Institutional Economics*, edited by Claude Ménard and Mary M. Shirley, 701–725. Berlin and Heidelberg: Springer.

Klimina, Anna. 2020. "Defining and Defending a Progressive Market Square: Bringing Institutionalist Development Discourse in line with the Reality of Post-Soviet Transition Experiences." *Journal of Economic Issues* 54 (2): 384–391.

Kumlin, Staffan, and Bo Rothstein. 2005. "Making and Breaking Social Capital: The Impact of Welfare-State Institutions." *Comparative Political Studies* 38 (4): 339–365.

Larson, Sven R. 2002. *Uncertainty, Macroeconomic Stability and the Welfare State.* London: Routledge.

Laville, Jean-Louis, and Anne Salmon. 2015. "Rethinking the Relationship between Governance and Democracy: The Theoretical Framework of the Solidarity Economy." In *Civil Society, the Third Sector and Social Enterprise: Governance and Democracy*, edited by Jean-Louis Laville, Dennis R. Young, and Paul Eynaud, 145–162. London: Routledge.

Lodewijckx, Ilona. 2021. "8 Steps to Participatory Budgeting." Citizen Lab. January 18, 2021. https://www.citizenlab.co/blog/civic-engagement/steps-to-effective -participatory-budgeting/. Accessed July 13, 2021.

Madra, Yahya M., and Fikret Adaman. 2014. "Neoliberal Reason and its Forms: De-politicization through Economization." *Antipode* 46 (3): 691–716.

Marangos, John. 2000. "A Post Keynesian View of Transition to Market Capitalism: Developing a Civilized Society." *Journal of Post Keynesian Economics* 23 (2): 301–311.

Marbuah, George. 2019. "Is Willingness to Contribute for Environmental Protection in Sweden Affected by Social Capital?" *Environmental Economics and Policy Studies* 21 (3): 451–475.

Ostrom, Elinor. 1990. *Governing the Commons: The Evolution of Institutions for Collective Action.* Cambridge: Cambridge University Press.

Ostrom, Elinor. 2010. "Polycentric Systems for Coping with Collective Action and Global Environmental Change." *Global Environmental Change* 20 (4): 550–557.

Participatory Budgeting Project. 2021. Website of the Participatory Budgeting Project. https://www.participatorybudgeting.org. Accessed July 13, 2021.

Paterson, Lindsay. 2001. "Civil Society and Democratic Renewal." In *Social Capital: Critical Perspectives*, edited by Stephen Baron, John Field, and Tom Schuller, 39–55. Oxford: Oxford University Press.

Pisani, Elena, Giorgio Franceschetti, Laura Secco, and Asimina Christoforou. eds. 2017. *Social Capital and Local Development: From Theory to Empirics.* New York: Palgrave Macmillan.

Polanyi, Karl. 1944, *The Great Transformation: The Political and Economic Origins of our Time.* Mattituck, NY: Amereon House.

Roberts, Dorothy E. 2000. "The Moral Exclusivity of the New Civil Society." *The Chicago-Kent Law Review* 75 (2): 555–582.

Rothstein, Bo, and Dietlind Stolle. 2003. "Social Capital, Impartiality and the Welfare State: An Institutional Approach." In *Generating Social Capital: Civil Society and Institutions in Comparative Perspective*, edited by Marc Hooghe and Dietlind Stolle, 191–209. New York: Palgrave Macmillan.

Schneider, Jo Anne 2006. *Social Capital and Welfare Reform: Organizations, Congregations, and Communities.* New York: Columbia University Press.

Sen, Amartya K. 1999. *Development as Freedom.* Oxford: Oxford University Press.

Sotiropoulos, Dimitris A., and Dimitris Bourikos. 2014. "Economic Crisis, Social Solidarity and the Voluntary Sector in Greece." *Journal of Power, Politics & Governance* 2(2): 33–53.

van Laerhoven, Frank, and Elinor Ostrom. 2007. "Traditions and Trends in the Study of the Commons." *International Journal of the Commons* 1 (1): 3–28.

van Staveren, Irene. 2001. *The Values of Economics: An Aristotelian Perspective.* London: Routledge.

Wainwright, Hilary. 2013. "Doing Away with 'Labor': Working and Caring in a World of Commons." Report of the Labor Discussion Stream. *Transnational Institute,* https://www.tni.org/en/briefing/doing-away-labour. Accessed August 28, 2018.

Whalen, Charles J. 2008. "Toward 'Wisely Managed' Capitalism: Post-Keynesian Institutionalism and the Creative State." *Forum for Social Economics* 37(1): 43–60.

Whalen, Charles J. 2020. "Post-Keynesian Institutionalism: Past, Present, and Future." *Evolutionary and Institutional Economics Review* 17 (1): 71–92.

Whalen, Charles J. 2022. "Reasonable Value: John R. Commons and the Wisconsin Tradition." In *Institutional Economics: Perspectives and Methods in Pursuit of a Better World,* edited by Charles J. Whalen, 49–77. London: Routledge.

Wilber, Charles K., and Kenneth P. Jameson. 1983. *An Inquiry into the Poverty of Economics.* Notre Dame, IN: University of Notre Dame Press.

Woolcock, Michael. 1998. "Social Capital and Economic Development: Toward a Theoretical Synthesis and Policy Framework." *Theory and Society* 27 (2): 151–208.

Wrenn, Mary V., and William Waller. 2018. "The Pathology of Care." *Oeconomia* 8 (2): 157–185.

8. Constructing an economically democratic society in the former Soviet Union: Post-Keynesian Institutionalist insights in historical perspective

Anna Klimina

INTRODUCTION: PROGRESSIVE REFORM OF PREDATORY CAPITALISM

Building on the work of Institutional economists such as Thorstein Veblen, Post-Keynesian Institutionalists have long recognized that advanced capitalist economies are dominated by the concentrated economic and political power of business corporations, which control most national industrial and financial assets and influence societal choices in their own interest (Peterson 1989, 381–382).[1] To counter the deleterious socioeconomic effects of corporate control, they have also long argued that it is crucial to progressively restructure economic relations along more equitable and inclusive lines, which is to say to make them more economically democratic. The work of such scholars has resulted in a framework for research with international significance and applicability.[2]

Using the framework of Post-Keynesian Institutionalists, this chapter outlines a program for progressively reforming authoritarian and oligarchic market societies in post-Soviet transition. It focuses most directly on how to remedy the deeply elitist and profoundly unjust economies of Russia and Ukraine, the largest and most heavily industrialized countries of the former Soviet Union (FSU).

There is an urgent need for such a progressive program to address the economic difficulties that global neoliberalism has produced on several continents. The political decision to dissolve the Union of Soviet Socialist Republics (USSR) and build a "free market" order in its culturally and economically diverse republics has led to the emergence of a variety of "national neoliberalisms" with different institutional facades. That surface diversity resulted from the differing ways in which national elites and other influential social groups modified and reconstructed the newly imposed neoliberal policies, not only to align with institutional and economic legacies of the past, but also to suit their own visions of socioeconomic development. Yet, despite these apparent differences, the modern economic order in most states of the FSU fully conforms to the toxic neoliberal ideology of unrestricted market freedom, and thus it is commonly characterized by corporate, financial, and labor market deregulation; acceptance of great inequality in income and opportunity; aggressive anti-unionism; lack of democratic decision-making, and deep de-socialization.[3] Moreover, neoliberal privatization of state-owned property at the start of post-Soviet transition has led to a particular variety of neoliberal capitalism in Russia and Ukraine: oligarchic capitalism. Both countries are characterized by the highly concentrated private ownership of equally concentrated productive assets, previously controlled by the socialist state, and both nations are dominated by business tycoons known as oligarchs.[4]

Russian and Ukrainian oligarchic capitalism generally favors unrestricted market freedoms for its oligarchic class and allows oligarchs to "manipulate politicians and shape institutions" in the course of appropriating the national wealth for themselves (Hellman, Jones, and Kaufmann 2003, 752). Among former Soviet economies, oligarchic capitalism in Russia and Ukraine is closest to the "predatory" type of contemporary Western corporate capitalism described by Post-Keynesian Institutionalist James Galbraith in his book on the "predator state" (Galbraith 2008, 130–132). Because unchecked predatory economic behavior is neither acceptable in the short term nor sustainable over time, it becomes important to review the Post-Keynesian Institutionalist vision of progressive reform and apply it to these countries.[5]

A key point of this chapter is that many Soviet reform scholars of the 1960s to the 1980s reached similar conclusions to those of the early Institutionalists as well as more recent Post-Keynesian Institutionalists. In particular, the work of those Soviet and Western economists emphasizes the need for a comprehensive democratization in the parts of the economy where one finds concentrated economic and political power, which in the case of Soviet-type state socialism appeared in the form of monopolistic state ownership of societal productive assets and dictatorial political control of society. Of course, we are all a product of our times, and the Soviet reform scholars' proposals for decentralizing and democratizing the Soviet command economy reflect the experience, history, and vision of Soviet citizens at the time. For example, those scholars recognized that proper economic motivation is required for any functioning economy and can emerge only through marketization, but also retained due emphasis on construction of an equitable, participatory, and viable economic order. In this chapter, we recognize both the importance of historically grounded insight and the emergence of common themes across Western and Soviet scholarship—themes that include the importance of establishing a more equitable market economy on the foundation of comprehensive democratization of the relations of large-scale productive property, progressive regulation of industry by the democratic state, and wide-ranging use of participatory processes throughout the national economy.

The narrative of the chapter is presented in three broad stages. The first stage focuses on the foundation of a Post-Keynesian Institutionalist vision for the construction of economically democratic markets in advanced industrial society, which was developed in the pioneering work of original Institutionalists. The second stage discusses the continued preference for fostering democratic processes throughout the economy, as further developed in the work of John Kenneth Galbraith, one of the original Post-Keynesian Institutionalists, as well as contemporary Institutionalists and Post Keynesians. The third stage focuses on the ideas developed in the Soviet Union during the economic reforms from the 1960s to the 1980s, and underlines useful lessons from Mikhail Gorbachev's Perestroika (1985–1991) movement.[6] It also discusses economic developments in Russia and Ukraine since the 1990s to illustrate in some detail the argument of this chapter—that insights from a distinctive theoretical tradition of Post-Keynesian Institutionalism (PKI), concerning the construction of economically democratic society in developed industrial capitalism, are best suited for remedying the neoliberal economies of the post-Soviet region.

To begin then, we need to review the key elements of the Post-Keynesian Institutionalist understanding of the crucial role that more equitable distribution of economic power in society plays in progressively reforming economic relations in developed capitalist economies. As important as is the seminal work of John Kenneth Galbraith and his followers on the subject, many ideas that they built on can be traced to Veblen, John R. Commons, and other Institutionalist forerunners of the Post-Keynesian Institutionalist approach to progressive development.

PROGRESSIVELY REFORMING INDUSTRIAL CAPITALISM: INSIGHTS FROM FORERUNNERS OF PKI

The best place to begin is with Veblen's analysis of vested interests of concentrated ownership and control of industry. Veblen was the first among Institutionalists to acknowledge the inevitable growth of "large wealth, large-scale industry and large-scale commerce and credit" (Veblen 1919a, 160) owing to the technological triumphs and associated progressive increases in per-unit productivity in scale economies. Despite recognizing the unfairness of the existing dictatorship of "vested rights of [concentrated] property and privilege" (Veblen 1921, 83) that resulted from the capture of the development of a large-scale industrial economy by pecuniary business interests, Veblen did not endorse a "reversion to the [old] system of free competition [among small-scale traditional owners-employers]," arguing instead that going backward in economic evolution "might involve great waste ... and might seriously retard the advance of the [human] race toward something better than our present condition" (Veblen 1891, 73). He considered the path of economic modernization toward a highly productive, large-scale industrial economy an important prerequisite for successfully moving market-based economies toward an economically abundant and socially just future.

Hence, in his response to both the inevitability and progressive potential of large-scale development, Veblen argued that predatory business interests of "concentrated power" (Veblen 1921, 83) could be "ousted," and "economic respectability" among "actual producers" re-established through "carrying democracy and majority rule over into [the] domain of [modern] industry" (Veblen 1919b, 175). Veblen foresaw that providing industrial workers and engineers with greater control and decision-making rights (Veblen 1921, 168) would not only increase worker participation and democratization of the workplace (Veblen 1919c, 374), but also foster comprehensive economic and political changes in the society (Veblen 1904, 160; 1921, 76, 158–159). Veblen considered trade unions and worker councils as inherently progressive forms of decentralized governance and argued that union members endeavour, "under the compulsion of the machine process, to construct an institutional scheme on the lines imposed by the [progressive] new exigencies of the machine process" (Veblen 1904, 160).

Overall, Veblen's belief in the progressive potential of democratically reorganized large-scale industrial development set the stage for two important conclusions made by Post-Keynesian Institutionalist scholars. The first is that breaking up large companies to curtail concentration of economic power is often inadvisable (see, e.g., Galbraith 1967, 23–26, 39–41); the second is that it is possible to counter the negative effects of monopolistic market power through strengthening industrial democracy and promoting broader democratic participation in all spheres of political and social life (Dugger 1987, 89–93; Tool 1979, 144–146). At present, many Institutionalist scholars consider "broad democratic participation in the economy and society" as indispensable for resisting the predatory value system of a pecuniary capitalist culture (Ayres 1961, 282; Brown 1992, 294–297).

Equally influential are the insights of Commons, another early contributor to Institutionalism. Commons also regarded the emergence of concentrated large-scale industrial production as an inevitable result of economic modernization and its "sociological law of centralization" (Commons [1899–1900]

1965, 168). However, in contrast to Veblen, Commons did not anticipate that progressive economic changes would be brought about primarily as a result of grassroots incentives and decentralized decision-making (Commons [1934] 1964, 51); rather, he believed that progressive changes can be implemented by combining such incentives and decision-making with the actions of governmental and judicial authorities (Commons [1924] 1968, 387; [1934] 1961, 751, 759).

Commons, in fact, expected progressive economic change to develop through the continuing processes of "collective bargaining" and "conflict resolution," which involve "law-givers and law-interpreters" (such as "courts, legislatures, government executives") as well as organized interested groups such as worker unions and political parties (Commons 1921, 90; [1924] 1968, 378; [1934] 1964, 51, 751,759). Above all, Commons emphasized the important role of worker unions and the public sector in establishing processes of negotiation for resolving otherwise inevitable conflicts between capital and labor, conflicts that would become only more intense in the age of large-scale industrial dominance (Commons [1924] 1968, 306, 363; [1934] 1961, 5, 109, 673; 1950, 237).

Commons defined the legal outcome of these extensive processes of negotiation and dispute resolution as an "artificial" (purposeful) selection of best practices and institutions and emphasized that "artificial selection" is always aimed at reconciling conflicting interests in society (Commons [1924] 1968, 120; [1934] 1961, 636). It is through such processes of "artificial selection" that economic power in society is redesigned, new practices and working rules are developed, and necessary changes in law, backed by the sovereign power of the state, are implemented.

Two important insights from Commons's analysis of progressive economic change through "artificial selection" deserve special emphasis in this discussion of the Post-Keynesian Institutionalist approach to the purposeful construction of an economically democratic society.

The first relates to Commons's acknowledgement of the ameliorative nature of human volition, viewed as "survival of good customs and punishment of bad customs" that is purposefully enforced by "the visible hand of ... courts" as well as of governments on "refractory individuals" (Commons [1934] 1961, 162) or "attached to property and contract" (Commons [1924] 1968, 318–321). This artificial selection signifies "Purpose, Futurity, Planning, injected into and greatly controlling the struggle for life" (Commons [1934] 1961, 636). Among the "most fundamental wishes of mankind" to be created through legislation and guaranteed by the authorities, Commons regarded "security, liberty, and equality" (Commons [1934] 1961, 706) as the most important, and of these three, it is "security for [their] expectations" that people "crave" the most, since "without the feeling of security" they "could not act at all as rational being(s)" (Commons [1934] 1961, 705).[7]

A second and closely related insight is Commons's perspective on the crucial role that the sovereign state is expected to play in progressively reshaping the course of economic development and directing it toward greater social efficiency and justice.[8] Commons considered this role essential and explained that in democratic market society it is the state that, through "a concerted action under the name of Political Parties," selects and gains "control of the hierarchy of legislative, executive, and judicial personalities" in order to shape and reshape the structure of the national economy by establishing "the laws of the land," controlling and changing the regulation of large-scale "property and contract," and proportioning "the factors [of production] over which it has control" (Commons 1909, 79; [1924] 1968, 318–321, 387; [1934] 1961, 751, 752). Institutional regulatory economics, which called for a sufficient rearrangement of concentrated market power by the democratic state to increase common welfare and serve all members of society, had its origin in this Commonsian approach to institutionalism (Miller 1990; Trebing 1974).

In contemporary PKI, Commons's constructivist vision of the role of the state is thus largely interpreted as an indication of both the state's ability and its obligation to design, impose, and nurture institutions that will correct economic injustices, channel business activities in a socially desirable direction, and guide economic development toward a market order that is equitable, democratic, and humanist (see, e.g., Ayres 1961; Klimina, 2014; Pressman 2006; Samuels 1997; Stanfield 1992; Whalen 2008; 2013; and Wilber and Jameson 1983). When we thus combine insights from Institutionalist scholarship, we see the unmistakable outline of a Post-Keynesian Institutionalist approach to constructing an economically democratic society: democratization of the relations of large-scale productive property through the encouragement of industrial democracy, all-encompassing democratic participation in all spheres of social life, and progressive regulation of the economy by a democratic state and its judiciary system.[9]

These foundational insights were further developed by John Kenneth Galbraith in his important and manifestly insightful theory of progressive convergence that first and foremost raised questions about how to use more assertively the constructivist role of the government and other authoritative agencies for promoting—in different but technologically still compatible societies—a new kind of modern industrial order, an order that will be more democratic, humanist, transparent, and civilized. That discussion needs to be revisited and analyzed, so that lessons can be learned, and potential applications of the theory can be explored.

MATURATION OF PKI'S VISION OF ECONOMICALLY DEMOCRATIC SOCIETY: SIGNIFICANCE OF THE PROGRESSIVE CONVERGENCE HYPOTHESIS

The concept of convergence among the characteristics and structure of the industrial systems of all highly developed technological societies, often generalized as convergence between market capitalism and command socialism, appeared in Western economic thought at the end of the 1950s (Sorokin 1960, 143–147; Tinbergen 1961, 333–335). Its core idea is that differences between market and collectivist industrial orders would undoubtedly become smaller and smaller because similar patterns of technological progress would result in increased compatibility between their organizational-economic relations, especially in the correlation between concentrated industrial production and an equally concentrated control over an economy's industrial assets (Meyer 1965, 208–209; Tinbergen 1961, 335–336). At the same time, most Western theorists viewed the liberal market as an organizing principle of that projected joint industrial system, and maintained that the private ownership of industrial property, despite its "increasing concentration as a result of technological advances," must in fact be retained and, if anything, strengthened (Goldman 1963, 510–512). In 1964, Zbigniew Brzezinski and Samuel Huntington openly acknowledged that "most convergence theories [at that time] in reality postulate not convergence but [pragmatic] absorption of the opposing system" (Brzezinski and Huntington 1964, 491). What seemed to be at stake in the minds of many Western convergence scholars was not actually convergence toward a new industrial system, but assimilation of command socialism into unfettered market capitalism.

It was John Kenneth Galbraith, Institutionalist and social democrat, who, "being influenced by early institutionalists" (Adkisson 2008, 1), was the first to argue that a convergence between two economic systems (capitalist and socialist) could actually produce not a predominantly unrestricted market society, but a reasonable market economy built on progressive values and democratic principles. Convergence could be progressive and lead to a better future in both economic systems (Galbraith 1967, 389, 391, 398–399). It is that hopeful vision of a progressive convergence that constitutes an important step in the development of the Post-Keynesian Institutionalist approach to the construction of an economically democratic society.[10]

Most notably, Galbraith fearlessly emphasized the importance of state intervention for progressive management of the economy. In fact, the starting point for Galbraith's analysis of convergence was in complete accord with Commons's belief in the state's essential role in harmonizing capitalism through government legislation. His main questions became not how ideologically and culturally diverse the economic systems of capitalism and socialism were, but how hospitable any particular economic system was to the emergence and nurturance of Commonsian "good customs" and institutions beneficial to promoting social justice and common good. If economic systems are not hospitable, what legislative actions of the reformist state are then required to enable the cultivation of such progressive "customs" and "beliefs" (Galbraith 1967, 176–177, 320, 345–346, 349–351; 1973b, 221; 228–232; 250–251)?

Galbraith discussed in detail the rise of corporate power under capitalism and acknowledged, again very much in line with Commons, that the state and its judicial system could be "captured by powerful corporations" which "exercise an influence or control over the larger economic, political, and social context that far exceeds anything available to the entrepreneurial firm" and, therefore, act as "the executive committee of the great corporation and its planning system" (Galbraith 1973a, 10; cf. Galbraith 1988, 373). Galbraith, who identified himself as a Post Keynesian (as well as an Institutionalist) when that camp emerged in the 1970s (Galbraith 1978, 8), further explained that, given John Maynard Keynes's recognition that economic agents must act in a world of fundamental uncertainty, the only reasonable response to "unpredictable markets in the technological era" is to take control over markets through the kind of global and detailed planning that only large corporations can achieve (Galbraith 1967, 16, 20, 23–26, 31–33, 39–41, 60–65, 171–173). It is thus inevitable that corporations must replace the individual entrepreneur as the center of power in modern economic society (Galbraith 1967, 60–61).

However, despite his recognition of such "promiscuous exercise of power in modern economic life by the large enterprise" (Galbraith 1988, 374), Galbraith was also convinced that the state could be "emancipated" from corporate control and further "retrieved for the public purpose" by being placed "at the disposal of the public through the electoral process" (Galbraith 1973b, 221–222). Then, after the establishment of competent and trustworthy democratic leadership, the state would be in a position to nurture the "reasonable" market and provide for public goods and benefits (Galbraith 1973a, 10; 1973b, 218–220; 242–244). Galbraith thus based his hope for liberation from the hegemony of corporate control and for optimum human development on the countervailing power and "responsibility" of the democratic state. In his thinking, "despite the conjunction of state and corporate power," necessary "remedial action"—such as "restriction of excessive resource use, organization to offset inadequate resource use, controls, actions to correct systemic inequality, protection of the environment, [and] protection of the consumer"—still "lies with the state" (Galbraith 1973a, 11; 1973b, 242; 1988, 376). In the 1990s, acknowledging "the [continually] diminishing role of the trade union in the modern industrial society" (Galbraith 1988, 374; cf. James Galbraith 2008, 115–120), Galbraith was passionate in his urgent reminders to economists about the "increased importance of the state" in correcting market failures and providing "fully independent" government regulation of corporate management. Without such government regulation, it was highly unlikely that the public good would be served, social justice created, and economic democracy enhanced (Galbraith 1996, 31–32, 75–81).

In this regard, it is interesting to point out that some contemporary Institutionalists go even further and, for cases when "regulated corporations avoided or fought the regulations, captured many of the regulators, and/or had themselves deregulated," suggest nationalizing corporations and placing them under direct public control (Dugger 2010, 442; cf. Melman 1970). Thus, with regard to electric utilities, William Dugger proposes replacing corporate-owned utilities "with a network of municipally-owned utilities connected by a national power grid owned and operated by the federal government" (Dugger 2010, 442). This proposal, very much in line with the Soviet Perestroika model of shared ownership that will be discussed below, confirms Galbraith's point, with which I concur, that the role of the democratic state in restructuring concentrated economic power is indispensable.[11]

The obvious conclusion here is that Galbraith's economic theory of progressive convergence calls for state-led democratic regulation of large-scale production in mature industrial societies, both market-based and collectivist. His theory is built on the economic need to retain yet democratize large-scale firms in the process of progressive modernization. Especially helpful in this respect are Galbraith's considerations about the important role that large-scale companies could have in alleviating market uncertainties, stabilizing the economy, and promoting investment spending (Galbraith 1967, 16, 20, 23–26, 29–30, 39–41; cf. Eichner 1976, 17–25; Shapiro 2005, 542–544). Consequently, Galbraith argued that reforms of large-scale productive property should not be conducted through the forcible division of large enterprises into smaller companies. Instead, large companies should be independently regulated by reputable government agencies within a national system to make certain that the following outcomes would be guaranteed: better equalization of economic power; adequate, even generous, provision of social services; equality of return between oligopolistic and competitive systems (based on an enhancement of return to workers and entrepreneurs in the competitive realm); an inter-industry coordination, of which the corporate sector is incapable; and, above all, a strict control of public expenditures to ensure that only public purposes are served (Galbraith 1973b, 250–251, 270–273).

Admittedly, Galbraith's constructivist theory of progressive convergence, developed in the United States of the 1960s, was rather visionary and well ahead of his time. In the Soviet Union, however, the timing of his theory was so much better that it had a profound impact on the Soviet economic reformers. It is unfortunate that the subsequent innovative Soviet approach to social-democratic reforms was sidelined by predatory oligarchic capitalism and its resultant misery and neoliberal despair. To understand the impact of Galbraith's theory on Soviet reformers, subsequent developments, and its current relevance, some historical context is required. The next section will— very briefly—present that 50-year story.

TWO STEPS FORWARD, THREE STEPS BACK: SOVIET ATTEMPTED REFORMS AND POST-SOVIET ATAVISTIC RELAPSE

The Need for—and Theoretical Contribution of—Soviet Reforms

After the Bolshevik (socialist) Revolution of 1917 and their winning of the Russian civil war of 1918–1920, the Bolsheviks' plans for building a workable collectivist society in a predominantly backward country were implemented.[12] In particular, centralized state control of the economy on behalf of the proletariat was established, and all industrial property was nationalized and placed under state control (Lenin [1917] 1974: 402–410). From that point on, the advancement of socialism came to be exclusively associated with expansion of state ownership of property, and, consequently, with expansion of state power over the economy (Lewin 1974, 83).

At the end of the 1920s, Stalin, who succeeded Lenin in 1924 as the leader of the Soviet Union, accelerated the Soviet industrialization program, which was intended to create a modern industrial structure and transform a backward Soviet economy into a large industrial power.[13] That industrial structure, built in the USSR by the end of the 1930s, was characterized by large-scale production, capital-intensive industries, a high degree of industrial concentration, extreme specialization, and the dominance of heavy and extractive industries (Gregory and Stuart 1986, 142–144).

By the end of the 1950s, Soviet economic growth, based on extensive expansion of inputs of production, began to decelerate. The urgent need to restore economic growth by reorienting it toward an "intensive pattern, driven by increases in factor productivity and efficiency in production" (Aganbegyan 1984, 3–5) led to the emergence of Soviet reform economics. For Soviet reform scholars, it had become clear that to achieve an increase in efficiency, deep changes were required in the way in which the economy was managed, enterprises operated, enterprise and industry performance assessed, prices formed, and workplace incentives structured.

Given that the time of reform coincided with the Khrushchev thaw, when more congenial relations between the USSR and the West were established, reform scholars were permitted, briefly, to sidestep the usual automatic denigration of Western views.[14] Hence, they were able to discuss, more positively, Galbraith's convergence ideas about a potential increase in similarities of organizational forms of economic management between capitalism and socialism and, consequently, consider some pro-market reforms, aimed at democratizing economic relations within the Soviet state-industrial complex (Bregel 1968, 15–20; Kozlova 1968, 142–144; Menshikov 1964). Those reform measures included: the use of shadow prices in optimal planning and "cost-accounting" systems in the assessment of enterprise results; a shift to multi-level models of rolling, indicative planning; the establishment of inter-enterprise contracting for materials and product flows; and the use of enterprise profitability as a decision-making criterion (Katsenelinboigen, Lackman, and Ovsienko 1969; Petrakov 1971).

It is during this time of Soviet economic reform that the concept of multi-leveled state ownership of large industrial assets, envisioned as a working template for the democratic restructuring of large-scale productive property, was originally introduced (Kornienko 1966).[15] Here is a clear beginning for the carrying-out of Galbraith's vision, but unfortunately the promise of change was short-lived. At the end of the 1960s, especially after the 1968 uprising in Prague, the nascent Soviet reform economics was basically stopped, and anti-Western rhetoric regained its dominance in Soviet economic discourse. The comprehensive reform process was resumed, in its fullness, only during Gorbachev's 1985–1991 Perestroika, which at that time was perceived in certain Soviet academic and political circles as an actual realization of "the process of [economic] convergence" with the democratic West (Karpinski 1989, 18; Shishkov 1989, 33–41; cf. Zweynert 2017, 21–34).

On the one hand, the economic program of Perestroika was undoubtedly inspired by the Galbraithian concept of democratic convergence discussed above (see, e.g., Galbraith and Menshikov 1988, 127–175). On the other hand, it can also be seen as an original contribution of Soviet reform scholars to the Post-Keynesian Institutionalist discourse on deliberate construction of an economically democratic society. In particular, Perestroika reformers creatively combined PKI's approach to the public regulation of large-scale corporations (through legislation and European social-democratic practices of worker co-determination and participation in management) with their own vision for the wide-ranging reorganization of large-scale production through establishing a tripartite (or "shared") model of large-scale ownership of pro-ductive property.

According to this model, there are three co-dependent, co-existing levels of ownership: the state level, the enterprise (firm) level, and the worker (employee) level (Mereste 1987, 22–34; Starodubrovskaya 1990, 31–37; Zaslavskaya 1986b, 35–37). Without being entirely transformed into the prop-erty of worker collectives or turned over into private hands, such a tripartite version of large-scale ownership offered possibilities for worker co-ownership and co-decision-making of enterprise plans, allocation of resources, election of managers, and profit (revenue) sharing, all of which would increase the economic motivation of workers and promote workplace democracy (Zaslavskaya, 1986a, 5–9). In a similar vein, Perestroika scholars explained that multi-level co-ownership of the means of production within an enterprise, which provides workers with significant control and decision-making rights, would better address the diverse economic interests in a workplace, moderate their potential conflicts, and reduce worker alienation (Ryvkina and Yadov 1989, 247–248). Some researchers also pointed out that for small- and medium-size enterprises, both in industry and agriculture, the development of worker cooperatives would result in increased worker commitment and involvement (Abalkin 1987, 7–11; Mereste 1987, 30–34; Kurashvili 1989, 21–44).[16]

The vision of Perestroika reformers for a new economic order to be constructed in the Soviet Union was very much in line with Galbraith's theory of progressive convergence on a more democratic, humane, and civilized society. This new (envisioned) society, which this chapter calls an economically democratic market order, included: the construction of a state-guided, mixed economy based on transparent and impartial public regulation of large-scale production; strengthened economic power of the public, vital for popular checks on bureaucratized management and the polity; support of labor-owned small and medium-sized enterprises, including worker-run cooperatives; a secure flow of income to all economic participants; wide-ranging welfare programs; and disarmament and peaceful coexistence (Gorbachev 1987).

Unfortunately, the Soviet Union as a united country did not have enough time to implement these reforms, let alone see the long-term outcomes of its progressivist Perestroika policies. The "centrifugal forces of nationalism and regionalism" (Nove 1992, 419), combined with external pressure for reform radicalization, brought about economic disintegration and made it impossible to continue the intended reform processes. In the summer of 1990, under the conditions of an accelerated breakdown of the country and worsening economic situation, a group of pro-market economists (S. Shatalin, G. Yavlinsky, E. Yasin, N. Petrakov and others) drafted the "500 Day Program" for a decidedly radical transition to an alternative, free-market system, a program that envisaged large-scale privatization, radical price liberalization, and total deregulation of the economy (Shatalin et al. 1991, 27–47). After the collapse of the USSR in 1991, that essentially neoliberal 500 Day Program was implemented, with minor changes, and led to a total replacement of the economic system. The subsequent neoliberal privatization of the 1990s made the notion of shared ownership and democratic tripartite control of large-scale enterprises largely irrelevant.

Neoliberal Disaster and Its Aftermath: A New Hope

The dynamics of neoliberal reforms in post-socialist Russia and Ukraine, the most heavily industrialized states of the FSU, are cases in point that illustrate the direct correlation between the neoliberal rolling-back of the regulatory capacity of the interventionist state and the rapid privatization, advocated by officials of the International Monetary Fund, of highly concentrated state ownership of industrial assets.[17] On the eve of the transition, Ukraine had the highest share of large-scale enterprises and was the second largest industrial producer among the FSU countries after Russia. With 3 percent of USSR territory and 18 percent of its population, Ukraine produced 16.7 percent of the USSR's industrial output (Boss 1993, 3–4). In Russia, even in 2012, 60 percent of Russian gross domestic product was produced by "the 100 largest enterprises," while the average four-firm concentration ratio in Russia's industries has remained virtually unchanged at between 45 and 47 percent since 1992 (OECD 2013, 28). Unquestionably, the unrestricted and profoundly opaque large-scale privatization in these countries led to the creation of highly concentrated private equity ownership controlled by selected (and openly favored) business clans.[18] In both countries, the end of the 1990s saw the emergence of a neoliberal, "wildcat capitalism," the entire "oligarchizing" of the economy, and "chaos, and deep division of society" (Gorbachev 2006, 52).

Then, in the early 2000s, Russian President Vladimir Putin's authoritarian actions reasserted state control over strategic industries, including natural resources, and deprived many oligarchs of their economic power. As I explain elsewhere (see Klimina 2018), the state under Putin "has focused on accumulating authority, not on fulfilling urgent tasks" (Inozemtsev 2009, 45). Moreover, its increased power has not been directed "to ensure that citizens receive the social benefits guaranteed by the Constitution" (Inozemtsev 2009, 45), but primarily to "concentrate key assets in an ever smaller circle of state-owned companies, most of them controlled by individuals close to the Kremlin and indeed to Putin himself" (Gustafson 2012, 435). In Putin's Russia, power is once again concentrated at the top as leading state bureaucrats now hold "the positions of oligarchs" (Lipman 2016, 39), while the people remain alienated from power over the production and distribution of the nation's wealth, a power they have never had historically.

During the same time in oligarchic Ukraine, a few clans used their enormous economic power to capture the state's legislative, executive, judicial, and regulatory apparatuses to such a degree that even after two pro-democratic and essentially anti-oligarchic revolutions (the Orange Revolution of 2004, which brought power only to a set of competing oligarchic clans, and the Euromaidan Revolution of 2014, which essentially did the same), Ukraine's politico-administrative organization still remains firmly in the grip of oligarchic vested interests and is widely considered to be profoundly corrupt (Csaky 2020, 5–6; cf. Klimina 2015).

When we juxtapose Russia with Ukraine, it matters little whether the majority of productive wealth is controlled by top-ranking bureaucrats as in state-capitalist Russia, or by a few private large-scale owners as in openly oligarchic Ukraine. In both cases, the result has been an increasing concentration of income and wealth in the upper strata of society, entrenched power distribution, growing workers' alienation, and marginalization of trade unions. This is the current disagreeable reality of not only the Ukrainian but also the Russian economy (Klimina 2015; 2018; Olimpieva 2011, 2). As long as people remain economically powerless and alienated from control over the economy's productive assets, both countries continue to be deeply elitist and profoundly unjust. State capitalism, while seemingly logical and fair in its re-nationalization of unfairly appropriated state assets, is clearly not a panacea for unjust and non-democratic oligarchic development; it should not remain an end in itself if the goal is to change the neoliberal nature of the economy and move toward a more equitable and inclusive society.

However, as a transitory condition, as a tool to divest oligarchs of their often unlawfully acquired economic power and to subordinate them (e.g., as state-hired managers of large-scale productive assets) to formal regulation, state capitalism is definitely a step in the right direction and as such, should be implemented in Ukraine. Then, after establishing trustworthy and competent democratic leadership and placing former oligarchic property under state control, the predatory neoliberal orders in state-capitalist Russia and Ukraine must be progressively reformed.

The best possible blueprint for such reforms has already been laid out in the tenets of Post-Keynesian Institutionalism, as has been presented in this chapter in the form of insights from both Western Post-Keynesian Institutionalist scholars and Soviet reform economists. Let me summarize again: to divest the vested interests of modern large business enterprises of their economic power and establish instead an adequate citizen control over the social order, there is but one workable route. It is to establish, democratically, a competent and trustworthy leadership, under which a progressive market order can be deliberately implemented. Through state regulation and state-encouraged comprehensive restructuring of large-scale ownership of productive property, possibilities for worker co-ownership and joint decision-making can be offered, including workers' shared ownership of enterprise assets and participation in determining enterprise plans. The concept of multi-level state ownership, developed thoroughly in the years of Perestroika, can become a working template for democratic restructuring of large-scale state capitalist property. All these measures would promote economic democracy and reduce alienation. Thereafter, as part of a larger program of nurturing democratic and participatory processes throughout the economy, "new property" in social investment can and should be created, through state-supported access to jobs, state-guaranteed income programs, and a state-funded system of social benefits, to secure more equitable sharing of economic surplus and "upward chances for all" (Galbraith 1996, 31–32).

CONCLUSION

Using the Post-Keynesian Institutionalist approach to the construction of an economically democratic market in advanced industrial societies—which Post-Keynesian Institutionalist scholars, ahead of other economists, recognized were dominated by concentrated economic power in both production and finance and were thus in need of the comprehensive democratic restructuring of their economic relations in order to become more equitable and fair— this chapter has outlined a framework for progressively reforming neoliberal capitalist orders in the emerging markets of the FSU. It has explained that since post-Soviet economies are still at a stage of industrial capitalism, they should thus be treated accordingly. This necessity makes especially relevant the insights from Post-Keynesian Institutionalist scholarship concerning the progressive restructuring of developed industrial markets. The chapter has focused most directly on how to remedy the deeply elitist and profoundly unjust economies of state capitalist Russia and manifestly oligarchic Ukraine.

The template outlined in this chapter for progressive reforms in these countries includes the comprehensive democratization of the relations of large-scale productive property, but without the forced fragmentation of its enterprises. Given the important role of large companies in alleviating market uncertainties, stabilizing the economy, and promoting investment spending, the path toward necessary reform requires the progressive regulation of industry by a trustworthy democratic state, and the nurturing of all-encompassing participatory processes throughout the national economy. It also involves offering state-supported access to jobs, state-guaranteed income programs, and a state-funded comprehensive system of social benefits. The ability to pursue such comprehensive policies can and will determine the success of progressive reforms in post-Soviet transition.[19]

ACKNOWLEDGMENTS

The author thanks Oren Levin-Waldman and Asimina Christoforou for reviewing an early draft and Charles Whalen for reviewing drafts and offering comments and suggestions.

NOTES

1. Post-Keynesian Institutionalism emerged as a separate strand of economic thought in the 1980s (see, e.g., Wilber and Jameson 1983). It represents a synthesis of Post Keynesian economics, which emerged in the mid-1970s (Mata 2004, 250) and traditional Institutionalism, which originated in the work of Thorstein Veblen (1857–1929) and John Commons (1862–1945) (Whalen 2013, 15–17). The Post-Keynesian Institutionalist vision of economically democratic society in mature industrial capitalism is rooted in traditional Institutionalism.

2. To date, most Post-Keynesian Institutionalism has focused on advanced capitalist economies. From the end of the nineteenth century until the middle of the twentieth century, big business enterprises in such economies were primarily industrial corporations; since the end of World War II, they have often operated as industrial-financial corporations or (increasingly) as financial corporations (Jo and Henry 2015; Minsky 1996).

3. The exceptions are the Baltic states (and the Western part of modern Ukraine). The non-Baltic states of the FSU were part of the pre-World War I Russian Empire, which even at the start of the twentieth century remained "the most backward of the major European countries" and was characterized by an autocratic and anti-proprietary cultural matrix, bureaucratic tyranny, and the absence of vital civil liberties (Gregory 1994, 35). In contrast, the Baltic states—Latvia, Estonia, and Lithuania—more closely resemble the transition countries of Eastern and Central Europe (in terms of both their pre-socialist history and their post-socialist transition performance); these nations joined the European Union in 2004 as part of the European Union expansion, their market models resembling the European model of a social market economy and welfare state, rather than neoliberal unfettered capitalism.

4. The form of capitalism found in Russia and Ukraine is not merely the result of early privatization. Both areas have long been characterized by a highly concentrated industrial structure. In the Russian Empire, large-scale industries started to emerge between the late 1880s and 1917, as part of the Russian state-led industrialization that favored the development of heavy industries and the highly concentrated production of capital goods in what had been a mostly rural, underdeveloped country (Gerschenkron 1963, 152–153). After the October 1917 Bolshevik Revolution, the socialist government continued to prioritize the development of highly concentrated, heavy industries in the USSR; central planners emphasized the construction of gigantic industrial plants and considered small-scale production to be economically inefficient (Gregory and Stuart 1986, 142–144).

5. While it is possible to apply elements of the Post-Keynesian Institutionalist vision of democratic society to Russia and Ukraine, it is also clear that these countries have not moved through the stages of capitalist development described by Hyman Minsky (1993) in an analysis he fashioned mainly on the experience of the United States. The oligarchic, industrial capitalism in Russia and Ukraine is its own variety of capitalism (in fact, each is its own variety, as will be briefly discussed later in this chapter). Of course, Minsky understood that capitalism comes in many varieties; in fact, he stressed this when writing about economic options for former socialist countries at the start of the post-Soviet transition (see Minsky 1991, 9–10). As it happens, the capitalism evident today in Russia

and Ukraine includes several features found in the United States early in the twentieth century; thus, insights from early Institutionalists (such as Veblen) and originators of Post-Keynesian Institutionalism (such as John Kenneth Galbraith) are relevant to analyzing those post-Soviet economies.

6. The literal meaning of Perestroika is comprehensive restructuring.

7. Notably, Commons was among the first Institutionalists not only to acknowledge the unfavorable impact of uncertainty on all market participants but also to emphasize that it is through the deliberate provision of laws and regulation by the authorities that the "new" social conditions of security are created (Commons [1924] 1968, 296, 305–307).

8. The fact that the state in many market-based economies does not always satis-factorily manage the economy for public benefit does not negate the state's huge potential for accomplishing good (cf. Mayhew 2001, 244).

9. An especially detailed and thoughtful Post-Keynesian Institutionalist discussion of the vital elements of an economically democratic society is provided by Wilber and Jameson (1983, 230–263).

10. Although Galbraith explicitly discussed the convergent tendencies of industrial societies in his 1967 book, *The New Industrial State* (Galbraith 1967), elements of his argument, including the need for establishing a "workable" economy and the importance of countervailing power and social balance, can be found in his popular books of the 1950s, *American Capitalism* (Galbraith 1952) and *The Affluent Society* (Galbraith 1958).

11. Minsky, another pioneering Post-Keynesian Institutionalist, also thought that certain large-scale, capital intensive industries should be placed under public control (Minsky 1986, 311).

12. The Russian February 1917 revolution dismantled the Tsarist feudal autocracy and established a pro-market Provisional Government, which was overturned by Vladimir Lenin during the October 1917 Bolshevik revolution.

13. The Soviet Union was officially established in December 1922 with the union of the Russian, Ukrainian, Byelorussian, and Transcaucasian Soviet republics, each ruled by local Bolshevik parties. Early Soviet industrialization debates have been thoroughly addressed in economic literature concerning Soviet economic thought of the 1920s (Erlich 1960; Nove 1992, 78–158).

14. The "Khrushchev thaw" was a distinct period of relative freedom and cultural liberalization from the time of Stalin's death in 1953 to the 1965 reversal of Khrushchev's policies of "de-Stalinization" by Leonid Brezhnev, Nikita Khrushchev's successor as leader of the Soviet Union.

15. This multi-level concept (a shared model of large-scale ownership) is discussed further below.

16. The Post-Keynesian Institutionalist vision of Wilber and Jameson (1983, 7–8, 241–248)—which contains democratic economic decision-making by and within government, enterprises, and workplaces—is remarkably similar to the multi-level model of Soviet reformers.

17. For details see Boycko, Shleifer, and Vishny (1995, 11, 83).

18. From 1998 through 2006, the average fraction of capital held by the principal shareholder in the Russian corporate sector was approximately 50 percent (Vanteeva and Hickson 2012, 188). For a discussion of how the oligarchy was created in Russia, see Goldman (2008); and for the case of Ukraine, see Kuzio and Wilson (1994).

19. To be sure, achieving the vision outlined in this chapter is complicated by the increasingly globalized nature of what Minsky (1996) called money manager capitalism, but carefully examining that challenge is beyond the scope of this chapter and must be tackled in a follow-up analysis—as must the consequences of Russia's invasion of Ukraine, which began just as this chapter's proofs arrived for review.

REFERENCES

Abalkin, Leonid. 1987. "Market in Economic System of Socialism" (in Russian). *Problems of Economy* 53 (7): 3–12.

Adkisson, Richard. 2008. "Introduction to Symposium: John Kenneth Galbraith and Institutional Economics." *Journal of Economic Issues* 42 (1): 87–99.

Aganbegyan, Abel. 1984. "Important Positive Changes in the Economic Life of the Country" (in Russian). *EKO: Economics and Organization of Industrial Production* 15 (6): 3–16.

Ayres, Clarence. 1961. *Toward a Reasonable Society: The Values of Industrial Civilization*. Austin: University of Texas Press.

Boss, Helen. 1993. *Ukraine's Economy in Sectoral and Regional Perspective*. Vienna: Vienna Institute for Comparative Economic Studies.

Boycko, Maxim, Andrei Shleifer, and Robert W. Vishny. 1995. *Privatizing Russia*. Cambridge, MA: The MIT Press.

Bregel, Enokh. 1968. "The Theory of Convergence of Two Economic Systems" (in Russian). *World Economy and International Relations* 12 (1): 15–28.

Brzezinski, Zbigniew and Samuel P. Huntington. 1964. *Political Power: USA/USSR*. New York: Viking Press.

Brown, Doug. 1992. Review of *The Political Economy of Participatory Economics*, by Michael Albert and Robin Hahnel. *Journal of Economic Issues* 26 (1): 294–297.

Commons, John R. (1899–1900) 1965. *A Sociological View of Sovereignty*. New York: Augustus M. Kelley.

Commons, John R. 1909. "American Shoemakers, 1648–1895: A Sketch of Industrial Evolution." *Quarterly Journal of Economics*. 24 (1): 39–84.

Commons, John R. 1921. "The Webbs' Constitution for the Socialist Commonwealth." *American Economic Review* 11 (1): 82–90.

Commons, John R. (1924) 1968. *Legal Foundations of Capitalism*. Madison: University of Wisconsin Press.

Commons, John R. (1934) 1961. *Institutional Economics* Madison: University of Wisconsin Press.

Commons, John R. (1934) 1964. *Myself*. Madison: University of Wisconsin Press.

Commons, John R. 1950. *The Economics of Collective Action*. New York: Macmillan.

Csaky, Zselyke. 2020. *Nations in Transit: Dropping the Democratic Facade*. Washington, DC: Freedom House.

Dugger, William M. 1987. "Democratic Economic Planning and Worker Ownership." *Journal of Economic Issues* 21 (1): 87–99.

Dugger, William M. 2010. "Progressive Alternatives to Re-Regulation." *Journal of Economic Issues* 2: 441–447.

Eichner, Alfred S. 1976. *The Megacorp and Oligopoly*. Armonk, NY: M.E. Sharpe.

Erlich, Alexander. 1960. *The Soviet Industrialization Debate, 1924–1928*. Cambridge, MA: Harvard University Press.

Galbraith, James K. 2008. *The Predator State: How Conservatives Abandoned the Free Market and Why Liberals Should Too.* New York: Free Press.

Galbraith, John Kenneth. 1952. *American Capitalism: The Concept of Countervailing Power.* Boston: Houghton Mifflin.

Galbraith, John Kenneth. 1958. *The Affluent Society.* Boston: Houghton Mifflin.

Galbraith, John Kenneth. 1967. *The New Industrial State.* Boston: Houghton Mifflin.

Galbraith, John Kenneth. 1973a. "Power and the Useful Economist." *American Economic Review* 63 (1): 1–11.

Galbraith, John Kenneth. 1973b. *Economics and the Public Purpose.* Boston: Houghton Mifflin.

Galbraith, John Kenneth. 1978. "On Post Keynesian Economics." *Journal of Post Keynesian Economics* 1 (1): 8–11.

Galbraith, John Kenneth. 1988. "Time and the New Industrial State." *American Economic Review* 78 (2): 373–376.

Galbraith, John Kenneth. 1996. *The Good Society: The Humane Agenda.* Boston: Houghton Mifflin.

Galbraith, John Kenneth and Stanislav Menshikov. 1988. *Capitalism, Communism and Coexistence: From the Bitter Past to a Better Prospect.* Boston: Houghton Mifflin.

Gerschenkron, Alexander. 1963. "The Early Phases of Industrialization in Russia: Afterthoughts and Counterthoughts." In *The Economics of Take-off into Sustained Growth*, edited by W.W. Rostow, 151–169. New York: Palgrave Macmillan.

Goldman Marshall I. 1963. "Economic Controversy in the Soviet Union." *Foreign Affairs* 41 (3): 498–512.

Goldman, Marshall I. 2008. *Petrostate: Putin, Power, and the New Russia.* New York: Oxford University Press.

Gorbachev, Mikhail. 1987. *Perestroika: New Thinking for Our Country and the World.* New York: HarperCollins.

Gorbachev, Mikhail. 2006. "Twenty Years since the Start of Perestroika." In *The Road We Traveled, the Challenges We Faced. Speeches, Articles, Interviews*, edited by Mikhail Gorbachev, 50–58. Moscow: Gorbachev Foundation.

Gregory, Paul R. 1994. *Before Command: An Economic History of Russia from Emancipation to the First Five-Year Plan.* Princeton: Princeton University Press.

Gregory, Paul R. and Robert C. Stuart. 1986. *Soviet Economic Structure and Performance*, 3rd edition. New York: Harper & Row.

Gustafson, Thane. 2012. *Wheel of Fortune: The Battle for Oil and Power in Russia.* Cambridge, MA: Harvard University Press.

Hellman, Joel, Geraint Jones, and Daniel Kaufmann. 2003. "'Seize the State, Seize the Day': State Capture and Influence in Transition Economies." *Journal of Comparative Economics* 31 (4): 751–773.

Inozemtsev, Vladislav. 2009. "The Nature and Prospects of the Putin Regime." *Russian Social Science Review* 50 (1): 40–60.

Jo, Tae-Hee and John Henry. 2015. "The Business Enterprise in the Age of Money Manager Capitalism." *Journal of Economic Issues* 49 (1): 23–46.

Karpinski, Len. 1989. "The Essence of Perestroika" (in Russian). *Twentieth Century and Peace* 23 (1): 3–24.

Katsenelinboigen, Aron, Igor Lackman, and Yuri Ovsienko. 1969. *Optimality and Commodity-Monetary Relations* (in Russian). Moscow: Nauka.

Klimina, Anna. 2014. "Finding a Positive Vision for State Capitalism." *Journal of Economic Issues* 48 (2): 421–429.

Klimina, Anna. 2015. "The Role of Economic Class in Understanding Social Provisioning Processes in the Post-Soviet Transition: The Case of Ukraine." *Journal of Economic Issues*, 2: 541–550.

Klimina, Anna. 2018. "An Unfortunate Alignment of Heterodoxy, Nationalism, and Authoritarianism in Putin's Russia." *Journal of Economic Issues* 52 (2): 517–526.

Kornienko, Vladimir. 1966. "The Main Features of Ownership under Socialism" (in Russian). *Economy of Soviet Ukraine* 9 (3): 13–20.

Kozlova, Kama. 1968. "New Industrial State of John Galbraith" (in Russian). *World Economy and International Relations* 12 (1): 142–150.

Kurashvili, Boris. 1989. "Restructuring and the Enterprise." In *Perestroika and the Economy: New Thinking in Soviet Economics*, edited by A. Jones and W. Moskoff, 21–44. Armonk, NY: M.E. Sharpe.

Kuzio, Taras and Andrew Wilson. 1994. *Ukraine: Perestroika to Independence.* London: Palgrave Macmillan.

Lenin, Vladimir. (1917) 1974. "War and Revolution." In *Lenin's Collected Works*, Volume 24, edited by Bernard Isaacs, 398–421. Moscow: Progress Publishers.

Lewin, Moshe. 1974. *Political Undercurrents in Soviet Economic Debates: From Bukharin to the Modern Reformers*. Princeton: Princeton University Press.

Lipman, Maria. 2016. "How Putin Silences Dissent: Inside the Kremlin's Crackdown." *Foreign Affairs* 95 (3): 38–44.

Mata, Tiago. 2004. "Constructing Identity: The Post-Keynesians and the Capital Controversies." *Journal of the History of Economic Thought* 26 (2): 241–259.

Mayhew, Anne. 2001. "Human Agency, Cumulative Causation, and the State: Remarks upon Receiving the Veblen-Commons Award." *Journal of Economic Issues* 35 (2): 239–250.

Menshikov, Stanislav. 1964. *The Economic Policy of the Kennedy Administration, 1961–1963* (in Russian). Moscow: Mysl.

Melman, Seymour. 1970. "Industrial Efficiency Under Managerial versus Cooperative Decision-Making." *Review of Radical Political Economics* 2 (1): 9–34.

Mereste, Uno. 1987. "The Theory of Property and Improvement of the Economic Mechanism." *International Journal of Sociology* 17 (4): 23–44.

Meyer, Alfred G. 1965, *The Soviet Political System: An Interpretation.* New York: Random House.

Miller, Edythe. 1990. "On Public and Private Control in a 'Reasonable Society.'" *Journal of Economic Issues* 24 (1): 239–248.

Minsky, Hyman P. 1986. *Stabilizing an Unstable Economy.* New Haven: Yale University Press.

Minsky, Hyman P. 1991. "The Transition to a Market Economy: Financial Options." Working Paper 66, November 1991. The Levy Economics Institute of Bard College, Annandale-on-Hudson, NY.

Minsky, Hyman P. 1993. "Schumpeter and Finance." In *Market and Institutions in Economic Development: Essays in Honor of Paolo Sylos Labini*, edited by Salvatore Biasco, Alessandro Roncaglia, and Michele Salvati, 103–115. New York: St. Martin's Press.

Minsky, Hyman P. 1996. "Uncertainty and the Institutional Structures of Capitalist Economies: Remarks Upon Receiving the Veblen-Commons Award." *Journal of Economic Issues* 39 (2): 357–368.

Nove, Alec. 1992. *An Economic History of the USSR: 1917-1991.* London: Penguin Books.

OECD. 2013. "Russia: Modernizing the Economy." *Better Policy Series.* April 2013. http://www.oecd.org/russia/Russia-Modernising-the-Economy-EN.pdf.   Accessed July 21, 2021.

Olimpieva, Irina. 2011. "'Free' and 'Official' Labor Unions in Russia: Different Modes of Labor Interest Representation." *Russian Analytical Digest* No. 104 (October 27): 2–6.

Peterson, Wallace C. 1989. "Market Power: The Missing Element in Keynesian Economics." *Journal of Economic Issues* 2: 379–391.

Petrakov, Nikolay. 1971. *Economic Reform: Plan and Economic Independence* (in Russian). Moscow: Mysl.

Pressman, Steven. 2006. "A Post-Keynesian Theory of the State." In *Alternative Theories of the State,* edited by Steven Pressman, 113–138. New York, NY: Palgrave Macmillan.

Ryvkina, Rosalina and Vladimir Yadov. 1989. *Social Mechanism of Organization and Development of Production* (in Russian). Moscow: Nauka.

Samuels, Warren J. 1997. "Instrumental Valuation." In *The Economy as a Process of Valuation,* edited by Warren J. Samuels, Steven G. Medema, and A. Allan Schmid, 1–71. Cheltenham, UK: Edward Elgar.

Shapiro, Nina. 2005. "Competition and Aggregate Demand." *Journal of Post-Keynesian Economics* 27 (3): 541–549.

Shatalin, Stanislav, Nikolai Petrakov, Sergey Aleksashenko, Grigory Yavlinsky, and Boris Fedorov. 1991. *500 Days: Transition to the Market: The Concept and Program.* New York: St. Martin's Press.

Shishkov, Yuri. 1989. "Perestroika and the Phantom of Convergence" (in Russian). *Working Class and Modern World* 19 (1): 31–41.

Sorokin, Pitirim A. 1960. "Mutual Convergence of the United States and the USSR to the Mixed Sociocultural Type." *International Journal of Comparative Sociology* 1 (2): 143–176.

Stanfield, James Ronald. 1992. "The Fund for Social Change." In *The Economic Surplus in Advanced Economies,* edited by John B. Davis, 130–148. Brookfield, VT: Edward Elgar.

Starodubrovskaya, Irina. 1990. "Foundations of Antimonopoly Policy" (in Russian). *Problems of Economy.* 56 (6): 31–37.

Tinbergen, Jan. 1961. "Do Communist and Free Economies Show a Converging Pattern?" *Soviet Studies* 12 (4): 333–341.

Tool, Marc R. 1979. *The Discretionary Economy: A Normative Theory of Political Economy.* Santa Monica, CA: Goodyear.

Trebing, Harry M. 1974. "Realism and Relevance in Public Utility Regulation." *Journal of Economic Issues* 8 (2): 209–233.

Vanteeva, Nadia and Charles Hickson. 2012. "Whither Corporate Russia?" *Comparative Economic Studies* 54 (1): 173–201.

Veblen, Thorstein. 1891. "Some Neglected Points in the Theory of Socialism." *The Annals of the American Academy of Political and Social Science* 2 (3): 57–74.

Veblen, Thorstein. 1904. *The Theory of Business Enterprise.* New York: Charles Scribner's Sons.

Veblen, Thorstein. 1919a. *The Vested Interests and the Common Man.* London: Allen &Unwin.

Veblen, Thorstein. 1919b. "Bolshevism is a Menace–to Whom?" *The Dial* 66 (February 22): 174–179.

Veblen, Thorstein. 1919c. "Bolshevism and the Vested Interests in America." *The Dial* 67 (November 1): 373–380.

Veblen, Thorstein. 1921. *The Engineers and the Price System*. New York: The Viking Press.

Whalen, Charles J. 2008. "Toward 'Wisely Managed' Capitalism: Post-Keynesian Institutionalism and the Creative State." *Forum for Social Economics* 37 (1): 43–60.

Whalen, Charles J. 2013. "Post-Keynesian Institutionalism after the Great Recession." *European Journal of Economics and Economic Policies: Intervention* 10 (1): 12–27.

Wilber, Charles K. and Kenneth P. Jameson. 1983. *An Inquiry into the Poverty of Economics*. Notre Dame, IN: University of Notre Dame Press.

Zaslavskaya, Tatyana. 1986a, "Creative Activity of the Masses: Social Reserves of Growth" (in Russian). *EKO: Economics and Organization of Industrial Production* 17 (1): 3–25.

Zaslavskaya, Tatyana. 1986b, "Social Justice and the Human Factor in Economic Development" (in Russian). *Communist* 57 (13): 61–73.

Zweynert, Joachim. 2017. *When Ideas Fail: Economic Thought, the Failure of Transition, and the Rise of Institutional Instability in Post-Soviet Russia*. London: Routledge.

9. A Post-Keynesian Institutionalist perspective from Latin America: the monetary circuit across stages of development

Alicia Girón

INTRODUCTION

Understanding the historical process and challenges of economic development is a central issue in Latin American economic thought. This chapter traces some important theoretical and methodological contributions of heterodox Latin American economists to the study of such development. Their research has long contained elements compatible with aspects of Institutional and Post Keynesian economics, and more recently it has converged with Post-Keynesian Institutionalism (PKI) through a focus on financial crises and financialization.

The chapter links the region's economic heterodoxy to a historical analysis of Latin American and Caribbean economic development, which is placed in the context of capitalist development worldwide. In particular, that analysis is divided into three stages and focuses on the integration of the region's spaces of production and monetary and financial exchange into a global economy, as well on as the expansion of financial capital. The first stage covers the insertion of Latin America into the global economy from the conquest era to the independence era and the eventual erosion of the dominance of British capital between the two world wars; the second covers the rise and decline of United States (US) capital hegemony from the end of World War II until the late 1970s; and the third considers international finance capital since the late 1970s, an era in which the Washington Consensus has exposed multiple contradictions regarding profitability and recurring economic and financial crises.

Special attention is given to the contributions of José Carlos Mariátegui, Agustín Cueva, Raúl Prebisch, and Celso Furtado, which reflect influences ranging from Karl Marx through John Maynard Keynes and contain key features compatible with Institutional and Post Keynesian economics. Their work highlights the monetary circuit, but also draws attention to prevailing and changing modes of production within countries, inequalities in terms of trade, the class struggle, the formation and shape of leading economic groups, the policies of governments and government-led organizations, and the lack of technological innovation and of an industrialization project of national scope. The chapter also shows that more recent contributions by the region's heterodox economists, such as Eugenia Correa, have brought a Post-Keynesian Institutionalist perspective to the region's challenges, which has simultaneously enhanced PKI's view of the emergence and consequences of money manager capitalism.

FROM JOSÉ CARLOS MARIÁTEGUI TO AGUSTÍN CUEVA

Pioneering work by José Carlos Mariátegui and Agustín Cueva provide important contributions to understanding the first stage of the development of capitalism in Latin America and the Caribbean, a period reaching from the conquest era to the independence era and ending between the two world wars. The theoretical-methodological body of development theory has its roots in explorations of the development of capitalism worldwide. Since global production determines a methodological indivisibility between the countries of the North and the South, it is essential to analyze the integration between pre-capitalist and capitalist modes of production to understand the importance of the development of capitalism in Latin American societies from the conquest to the present day.

For Mariátegui ([1928] 2005), the origin of the region's capitalist development is found in the moment the Spaniards arrived as colonizers. They did not arrive with large bands of pioneers like those who came to New England. Instead, colonizers in Latin America used a labor force comprised of natives and dedicated themselves to exploiting gold and silver in Mexico and Peru. Therefore, the region's capitalist economic bases developed out of the Spanish conquest and the later establishment of colonies, which served as economic and political spaces integrated into Spain.

The Viceroyalties of Peru and New Spain (Mexico) became independent from the Spanish Empire during the first decades of the nineteenth century. At the same time, the Industrial Revolution in Europe made necessary the expansion of new territorial spaces. British finance capital found an interest for its growth in the newly independent countries. Thus, the new republics were born to independent life, but also simultaneously intertwined with the international monetary circuits commanded by England.

The characterization of the current capitalist development of Latin America has its roots in the way in which Spain approached and managed the colonization process, which was unlike that which occurred in the British colonies of New England. On the one hand, the declining power of the Spanish Empire resulted in a weak transition from an ecclesiastical and feudal military structure toward an economy commanded by an expanding bourgeoisie and based on the discovery and exploitation of mines and the production of gold and silver. On the other hand, the expansion of the capitalism of the British Empire required spaces for the export of its financial capital. In the evolution from Spanish colonization to the construction of independent countries, the Latin American region came to depend on the financial circuits commanded by the British banks. As Mariátegui writes:

> Mr. [George] Canning, faithful interpreter and agent of England's interests, recognized [Latin Americans] and thereby justified their right to separate from Spain and, in addition, to organize themselves democratically. And even before Mr. Canning, the bankers of London—no less timely and effective for being usurers—had financed the formation of the new republic. (Mariátegui [1928] 2005, 23)[1]

The independent life of those new Latin American countries was subject to the expansion needs of British industrial and financial capitalism. For example, the export of rubber, gold, silver, guano, and saltpeter was a source of foreign exchange in Peru. The Latin American countries, independent from Spain, became integrated with the financial capital of the British Empire.

Then, starting in the period between the two world wars, British capital in the region ceased to predominate, gradually fading as US finance capital gained strength. At the same time, the Panama Canal (which opened in 1914) made it easier for products to reach the United States and Europe from Peru and Latin America's Southern Cone, which spurred the growth of industries in that region. Meanwhile, a nascent capitalist class, integrated to British and American finance capital, was shaping loan decisions for the area.

In addition to the relevance of his work to Latin America's first stage of capitalist development, Mariátegui's contributions also contain insights that remain applicable to contemporary Latin America. Even today, there are segments of the region in which the development of capitalism has not created solid markets and where the labor force is subject to ancestral cultural relations. Writing on Peru in the 1920s, Mariátegui ([1928] 2005, 30) observed the following, which remains true for much of Latin America: "The elements of three different economies coexist in Peru today. Underneath the feudal economy inherited from the colonial period, vestiges of the indigenous communal economy can still be found in the sierra. On the coast, a bourgeois [but underdeveloped] economy is growing in feudal soil."[2] Contemporary Latin America is a heterogeneous region with very particular specificities for each country, but, in general, there is modern capitalism along the coast (where the most dynamic sectors integrate into the global financial system), an economy with feudal and colonial roots in areas where colonizers established mines and exploited native people, and pre-capitalist subsistence communities in the Amazon.

For Agustín Cueva, the combining of Latin America's different modes of production with the international accumulation process accounts for the economic, political, and social development of each country. The result is heterogeneity and diversity in the countries of the region, which implies different economic policies. Moreover, the development of capitalism cannot happen without its contradictions, most evident in the emergence of class struggle.

Cueva's description of development in Latin America is worth quoting at some length. He writes:

> The very analysis of the development of capitalism in Latin America depends on a correct understanding of its articulation with pre-capitalist modes of production. For it is obvious that capitalism did not develop in a social vacuum and that, for example, its initial phase, the so-called "outward expansion," was also and necessarily the stage of an "inward" development, in which the original accumulation process marked the fundamental pattern of the relationship between the different modes of production. It was the beginning of a long process of the implantation of capitalism in our societies, with insufficiently studied phases and modes of transition either because the pan-capitalism thesis took it for granted since the 16th century, or because dependency theory—not detached from the previous thesis— saw in this whole process nothing more than the mechanical reflection of an external determination. (Cueva 1975, 34)

Cueva also offers suggestions for more constructive analyses. In particular, he identifies three examples of matters that not only merit systematic investigation, but also rest on more solid (and historically grounded) foundations than earlier analyses. Those three subjects are: (1) "the process and ways of development of capitalism in the countryside" (which he describes as "an unfinished process in many areas of the continent"); (2) "the constitution of the truly capitalist State after the 'anarchic' and 'oligarchic' phases of transition;" and (3) "the evolution of the ideological [and] cultural instance of our societies" (Cueva 1975, 34).

Cueva's work extends Mariátegui's line of thought by connecting the interrelation of certain production modes to class struggle, thus making the class structure more comprehensible. It is class struggle that reveals the articulation of the different modes of production to the international accumulation process. Moreover, that struggle accounts simultaneously for the diversity within Latin America as well as for the unity of the region's financial organizations and central banks in the struggle for profitability.

In short, the expansion of the accumulation of capitalist development and its reproduction in the meeting of two worlds (pre-capitalist and capitalist) is what laid the foundation for creating capitalist development in Latin America and the Caribbean as well as for the region's entry into the orbit of international capitalist reproduction. Exchange relations of social reproduction, and consequently monetary relations, created intertwined monetary circuits between the hegemonic countries and the peripheral economies. Therefore, principles of monetary theory were established that include not only a simple accumulation process, but also one of expanded, global, and hegemonic accumulation.

The economic, political, and social development process of capitalism depends on institutions, the power of dominant groups, and past economic development. It is a unique and particular process in which the development of productive forces, the relations of production, and the formation of the class struggle will be decisive in determining the region's exchange relations and its relationship with world circuits. Applied to today, the work of Mariátegui and Cueva suggests the need for institutional changes (via public policy reforms) to achieve more equitable development in the region, and we will return to this later in the chapter.

From our perspective, the stage of Latin American development described in this section corresponds to the first phase of financialization in Latin America and the Caribbean.[3] The export of the financial and productive capital of the British Empire, within the framework of global development of capitalism, gained momentum during the nineteenth century until its increasing displacement by the United States. In this first stage, financialization involved both an expansion of loans from the British banks to newly independent governments and an upsurge in direct foreign investment in the interest of the capitalist accumulation process. It also involved appropriation of agricultural and mining production, which large British companies financed in the recently independent countries to satisfy world demand. This nascent capitalism was also accompanied by a combination of low wages and feudal conditions for countless workers.

RAÚL PREBISCH AND CELSO FURTADO

The contributions of Raúl Prebisch and Celso Furtado on matters of development policy explain the second stage of the monetary circuit in the development of Latin American capitalism. This stage corresponds to the second phase of financialization, characterized by US economic hegemony and financial and industrial capital organized under the Bretton Woods accord. It was during this second stage that Latin American thought began to question the conventional notion of "stages of capitalist development" and to focus even more on troublesome aspects of relations between center countries and the periphery.

Raúl Prebisch is one of the most important exponents of the structuralist current of heterodox thought. His pioneering work in the 1950s and 1960s focused on the problems of the region by questioning the economic theories from developed countries. According to Prebisch (1963), the capitalist development in center countries is not comparable to that of the Latin American region; the path to economic development, as described by American economist Walter Rostow, for example, is not adaptable to the Latin American situation. Prebisch added: "[A]fter a while, we also discovered in Latin America that Keynes's genius was not universal, but that his analyses were limited to the economic phenomena of large centers and did not take into account the problems of the periphery" (Prebisch 1963, xii).

Prebisch called on Latin American economic scholars to find solutions to the region's problems. In particular, he stressed the need to "continue examining the development process, not only as an economic phenomenon but also as something that has deep social and political significance" (Prebisch 1963, xvi). The region's scholars had already come to recognize that the key to understanding Latin American development lies in studying the origins of that development and the way in which countries inserted themselves into the world economy through international trade. But Prebisch also shed light on the absence of reciprocity in international trade, and on the increasing gap between development in center countries and those in the periphery, which have been mainly producers of raw materials. In addition, he stressed the impossibility of understanding phenomena such as inflation or external economic imbalances "without considering in-depth structural factors" (Prebisch 1963, xiii).

In the early 1960s, Prebisch wrote (1963, 3), "A century ago our economies [in Latin America] were articulated with the international economy and half of the population still vegetates in precapitalist ways incompatible with their growing economic and social aspirations." Looking for improvement, he emphasized the importance of industrialization aimed toward advancing the region's own industries. In particular, he thought that state protections for industries should move from merely subsidizing the production of substitutes for imported goods and advance to providing support for "the substitution of intermediate goods or durable consumer or capital goods that, being complex in manufacture, require a market of much larger dimensions than the national ones" (Prebisch 1963, 84). In other words, he offered a vision that looked beyond important substitution and toward export-oriented growth.

Thus, Prebisch (1963) believed the only way to strengthen the economy of underdeveloped countries was through a series of policies. That includes an industrialization policy accompanied by a plan through which the public sector increases private sector investment. It also includes state participation in capital formation, in conjunction with fiscal reform that compresses high-income groups' consumption and allows for a redistributive policy that functions as the axis of economic development. In addition, public policy must aim (as mentioned above) to reduce the import of manufactured goods and move from exporting raw materials to exporting manufactured goods, using temporary international resources (facilitated by organizations such as the World Bank) to achieve that end.[4]

Celso Furtado points out that development has a historical dimension; the behavior of the world economy undergoes a radical transformation through the historical process. Furtado focuses on "the causal genetic factors of growth, which become endogenous to the economic system," but also on a particular aspect of those factors: "the imperative of technological advance, which resulted in the intimate articulation of the capital formation process with the development of experimental science" (Furtado 1964, 151). In addition, he stresses the historical importance of openness to finance capital and large foreign investors, which are fundamental and decisive in the international division of labor and the deepening and expansion of the world market.

Furtado emphasizes that this development has been far from perfect—and more than a transitory stage. He writes:

> [The expansion of financial circuits linking Latin America to the center economies produced] capitalist expansion on archaic structures ... which ... varied depending on the region, driven by local circumstances, the type of capitalist penetration, and its intensity. The result was almost always the creation of hybrid structures, one part of which tended to behave like a capitalist system and the other to remain within the pre-existing structure. (Furtado 1964, 165)

Thus, Furtado concludes that the heterogeneity and differentiation of real-world capitalist development led to "underdevelopment as an autonomous historical process, and not a stage through which economies that had already reached a higher degree of development went through" (Furtado 1964, 165).

In short, the second stage of Latin American capitalist development is associated with a phase of financialization that developed from the expansion of transnational business and financial corporations, which were mainly North American. For Latin American countries, accompanying that expansion was the process of external indebtedness as well as the continued subordination of the region's currencies to the dominant international currency, which in this case was the US dollar.[5] Meanwhile, the financial policies of the US Federal Reserve mainly favored US financial institutions. For Prebisch and Furtado, meaningful regional development requires autonomous development based on an autonomous industrial project and regionally oriented monetary, fiscal, and financial policies that allow such economic expansion. The near-term vision was not one of regional financial and fiscal independence; rather, it was one in which the region's industrial project was successfully linked to expansion of foreign capital and the financing of the development of large transnational companies.

WASHINGTON CONSENSUS, MONEY CIRCUITS, AND FINANCIALIZATION

The third stage of Latin American economic heterodoxy began in the late 1970s, in the wake of the unraveling of the Bretton Woods arrangements. In this stage, the region's economists confront the hegemonic thought of the Washington Consensus, which emerged in the 1980s and has been closely associated with the stabilization and adjustment plans of the International Monetary Fund (IMF). Features of this third stage include the influence on policymakers of market-focused economists such as Milton Friedman and neoliberal thinkers; the breakdown of external financing from mainly US commercial banks to Latin American governments; and the consequent moratoriums and multiple renegotiations of Latin American foreign debt, which plunged the region into a so-called "lost decade" (in the 1980s) until financing became available to the region from institutional investors. As a result, from the late 1970s to the present, recurring crises have created an amalgam of Latin American countries inserted into the development of capitalism without being able to promote autonomous economic development. Moreover, the influence and interference of the IMF in monetary, fiscal, and financial policies, together with the weight of the interests of institutional investors, have intensified regional political conflicts and created confrontations between citizens and the region's governments, deepening the economic contradictions that reveal themselves as social movements demand better living conditions and alternative development plans.

For Latin Americanists, the process of Latin American development is based implicitly on the theory of a monetary economy of world production. Thus, central to that theory are "the circuits of money" needed for reproduction and globalization (Girón 2007, 36). It is not by chance that capitalist history in the middle of the last century included both the penetration of large foreign banks into the independent life of Latin American countries and the creation of international financial organizations. That need for reproduction and globalization continues: the speculative movements from the 1970s until the present decade show the powerful influence exerted by the interests of hedge funds and other non-banking financial entities, whose growth has been exponential for the last forty years.

The stages of capitalist development identified in this chapter show how the money circuit is decisive for the different phases of social reproduction of capital in the region, to such a degree that the independence of colonies was a result of the need for the realization of capital itself.[6] In the first stage, the insertion of Latin American countries into the international financial orbit allowed foreign investment to expand. Moreover, newly created governments used capital flows to expand roads and highways and to create public works. In the second stage, the state encouraged the expansion of consumption by creating aggregate demand to expand the production circuit and, in turn, circulation for the appreciation of capital. Meanwhile, financial capital has been decisive from the mining stage, through the expansion of guano and nitrate, to today's enclaves such as automotive maquiladoras and the export of oil and agricultural products. The organic construction of the bourgeoisie also continuously adapts, along with the state, to the needs of the international accumulation process. All of that brings us to the current era (the region's third stage of development), where national and international interests collide, and that conflict defines both the existing political processes and the future direction of underdeveloped capitalism.

In recent years, the work of several Latin American economists has converged with the work of Post-Keynesian Institutionalists. From the perspective of Eugene Correa (2012; 2014) and other Latin Americanists who have been influenced by—and contributed to—PKI, the evolution of capitalism in Latin America and the Caribbean since the 1970s involves the transition from a regulated international financial system (under the Bretton Woods accord) to a deregulated monetary and financial system characterized by financialization and recurrent, severe financial crises.[7]

The current third stage of Latin American development coincides with the global emergence of an era Post-Keynesian Institutionalists call "money manager capitalism" (Correa 2014, 324). Consistent with that emergence, capital account opening and other forms of financial deregulation and liberalization in Latin America have contributed to the rise of institutional investors (such as mutual funds and pension funds) as the main international economic actors, and, in turn, they have fueled a process of financialization through an intense focus on the value of corporate stocks and the maximization of near-term returns. This process has not only discouraged long-term productive investments, but it has also resulted in risky financial innovations and rising consumer indebtedness (owing to increasing worker insecurity and inequality), all of which have increased the likelihood and severity of financial and economic crises.[8] These various trends are clearly evident in the privatization of financial systems and the banking crises of Latin America (Girón 2006).

Government fiscal and monetary policies have also been affected by this capitalist evolution. For example, austerity policies and privatization of state services have accompanied market liberalization and financialization; the so-called "fiscal discipline" of public-sector austerity has prevented regional efforts at sustained development—and reduced the policy space available for addressing economic crises (see, e.g., Girón and Correa 2021; Vidal and Correa 2021).[9] In fact, when democratic and "center-left" governments emerge and try to advance policies that generate employment (consistent with existing modes of production) and aim toward a more equal distribution of income, financial markets step in to impose their desired degree of profitability through pressure on the central bank and other policymakers. The dispute over profitability between finance capital and the state produces confrontations that are regular occurrences in Latin America.

According to François Chesnais (2000, 46), the current capitalist regime is far-reaching in that it "has arisen from liberalization and deregulation in the triple sphere of the financial scene, commercial exchanges and productive investments."[10] He also finds that the regime is global. At the same time, however, he writes: "[L]et us not forget that this globalization is selective and hierarchical, and the previous economic and social trajectories of the countries have given rise to varied forms of integration."[11] Mariátegui could not have said it better.

CONCLUSIONS

This chapter has traced some important contributions of heterodox Latin American economic thought to the study of economic development, linking those ideas to a historical analysis of Latin American and Caribbean economic development in the context of capitalist development worldwide. Tracing capitalism's development in Latin America through three stages, the chapter gives special attention to the contributions of José Carlos Mariátegui, Agustín Cueva, Raúl Prebisch, and Celso Furtado, followed by insights from the work of more recent Latin Americanists such as Eugenia Correa. The work of the earlier writers highlight a number of elements, including unequal exchange relations and contradictions among social classes, and the more recent work adds—and augments—Post-Keynesian Institutionalist insights on financial crises and financialization.

A central element across all three stages of Latin American development is the monetary circuit. Today it is indisputable that the US dollar, the dominant currency (also referred to as the hegemonic "general equivalent") for nearly a century, has spread through the circuit of money worldwide as part of commercial and everyday financial transactions. In fact, however, since the days of the Latin American conquest, there has been a dominant currency from outside the region, and Latin America and the Caribbean have been integrated into a money circuit extending to all corners where commercial exchange was established as the priority process for global capital accumulation.

The concept of the monetary circuit provides a vital link between Latin American economics and a long heterodox tradition that includes Institutionalists and Post Keynesians (as well as Joseph Schumpeter and Marx, among others). Instead of the conventional economists' emphasis on money as a medium of exchange, this heterodox tradition emphasizes money as a means of payment, which means that credit-debit relations are at the heart of what we consider money; in the ever-changing real world, money is a flow as well as a stock. In other words, money enters as part of an economic process that occurs over time: production precedes exchange, and financing precedes production. Thus, the notion of the monetary circuit corresponds to the dynamics behind the monetary theory of production found in the work of Keynes and the Institutionalists (which closely parallels the core idea of Marx's M-C-M' formula of money circulation), and it leads to an endogenous view of the money supply, which reverses the mainstream (ahistorical) beliefs that saving creates investment and deposits create loans.[12] At the same time, the Latin American perspective emphasizes that the region's money circuits can only be understood as part of a global network shaped by centuries of hegemonic accumulation and unequal financial relationships.

The more recent Latin American research reviewed in this chapter shows a convergence with PKI, especially with respect to the study of financial crises and financialization. Scholars like Correa have found PKI indispensable for analyzing such crises and understanding the institutional changes they have produced in Latin American countries, including those changes that have "cleared the way for money manager capitalism" in the region (Correa 2014, 323). At the same time, the work of such scholars in Latin America has enhanced PKI's view of the emergence and consequences of this investor-driven stage of capitalism, which has until recently been examined most often by scholars from the United States and Western Europe. Moreover, the three-stage analysis in this chapter augments the long-term historical description of capitalist development that the pioneering Post-Keynesian Institutionalist Hyman Minsky (1990; 1996) offered largely on the basis of his familiarity with the United States. Today, global capitalism is a central reason why "life itself is at risk globally" (Vidal and Correa 2021, 432); thus, an international convergence of heterodox research on economic development—bringing together scholars from both the North and the South—has come not a moment too soon.

ACKNOWLEDGMENTS

The author thanks Marcia Solorza (Postgraduate Program in Economics at UNAM), Roberto Soto (University of Zacatecas), Daniel Mirón (scholar of the UNAM's Economic Postgraduate Program), and Charles Whalen (University at Buffalo) for their thoughtful observations on this chapter. This work is part of the Project PAPIIT IN300921 "Credit and Investment: The Problems of the Post-Crisis State."

NOTES

1. Canning served twice as British Foreign Secretary in the nineteenth century; at the end of his life, he served briefly as Prime Minister of the United Kingdom. For the English translation, by Marjory Urquidi, of Mariátegui's "Outline of the Economic Evolution," see Mariátegui ([1928] 1971, Essay One).
2. This English translation also comes from Mariátegui ([1928] 1971, Essay One).
3. While many scholars describe financialization as a particular stage of capitalism that emerged in the 1970s, this chapter sees three phases of financialization from a Latin American perspective. The first phase is consistent with what many, following Rudolf Hilferding ([1910] 1981) call "finance capitalism" (see, e.g. Minsky 1990, 67). The second phase is consistent with what many from the United States call "managerial capitalism," an era that takes on a different appearance when viewed from Latin America. The third phase is consistent with what Post-Keynesian Institutionalists call "money manager capitalism," an era driven by shareholder value, which many refer to as the age of financialization.
4. For more on Prebisch and his policy ideas, see, for example, Love (1980); Sikkink (1988); and Street (1987).
5. The subordination of Latin American currencies to a dominant currency outside the region has been a continuing, central feature of its economic history since the arrival of the Spanish. In the colonial period, Spanish money was the official currency; in the early years of independence, regional currencies integrated themselves into an international economy dominated by the British pound. Since World War II, the dominant currency—or "international general equivalent" (Girón 2012, 511)—has been the US dollar.
6. As discussed in an earlier section, Mariátegui points out that the independence of the colonies was a product of—in fact, it facilitated—the expansion of British capital.
7. According to Correa (2014, 323), "[T]o understand what really happens during financial crises and the changes in overall economic activity that they produce, a Post-Keynesian Institutionalist approach is essential." For related work on Latin America, see Arza and Español (2010); Correa and Vidal (2012); Cruz and Walters (2010); Girón (2012; 2015); Girón and Correa (2021); Girón and Solorza (2015); Levy-Orlik (2010); Ventimiglia and Tavasci (2010); Vidal and Correa (2021).
8. For Post-Keynesian Institutionalist perspectives from outside the region, see Minsky (1996) and Whalen (2020). For a related discussion—from the perspective of regulation theory—of how financialization has affected business organizations, production, and the relationship of employees with the means of production, see Boyer (1986).
9. For a Post-Keynesian Institutionalist discussion of reduced policy space within emerging economies during the era of financialization, see Liang (2011). Meanwhile, it is important to recognize that financial investors "have succeeded in getting governments to apply policies that guarantee high interest rates and security in collecting all loan-related income" (Chesnais 2000, 46).
10. Like Boyer, Chesnais's work is grounded in the regulation theory perspective. For a similar view grounded in PKI, see Vidal and Correa (2021, 433–435), which also gives attention to the labor realm.

11. Chesnais (2000) also observes that the current era is not merely dominated by finance; it is also an era during which the degree of financial concentration has intensified.
12. The notion of a monetary theory of production is mentioned in the previous section of this chapter as a "theory of a monetary economy of world production." For discussions of the monetary circuit and a monetary production economy and their usefulness as concepts in economic analysis, see, for example, Dillard (1980), Lavoie (2006, 54–82), and Seccareccia and Correa (2018), which also suggest that the heterodox theory of money and monetary circulation (because of its focus on money as a means of payment) can even apply to pre-capitalist economies.

REFERENCES

Arza, Valeria and Paula Español. 2010. "Dealing with Financial Crises the Latin American Way: The Argentinean, Brazilian, and Mexican Experiences." In *Minsky, Crisis and Development,* edited by Daniela Tavasci and Jan Toporowski, 275–293. London: Palgrave Macmillan.

Boyer, Robert. 1986. *La Théorie de la régulation*. Paris: La Découverte.

Chesnais, François. 2000. ¿Crisis financieras o indicios de crisis económicas características del régimen de acumulación actual?, en Las Trampas de las Finanzas Mundiales, Coordinado por Chesnais. François y Dominique Plihon. Madrid: Akal.

Correa, Eugenia. 2012. "Fiscal Policies and the World Financial Crisis: Understanding the Experience of Three Major Latin American Countries." *International Journal of Political Economy* 41 (2): 82–97.

Correa, Eugenia. 2014. "Institutional Changes in Financial Crises: Lessons from Latin America." *Journal of Economic Issues* 48 (2): 323–330.

Correa, Eugenia and Gregorio Vidal. 2012. "Financialization and Global Financial Crisis in Latin American Countries." *Journal of Economic Issues* 46 (2): 541–548.

Cruz, Moritz and Bernard Walters. 2010. "Dealing with Financial Crises the Latin American Way: The Argentinean, Brazilian, and Mexican Experiences." In *Minsky, Crisis and Development,* edited by Daniela Tavasci and Jan Toporowski, 294–301. London: Palgrave Macmillan.

Cueva, Agustín. 1975. "El uso del concepto de modo de producción en América Latina: algunos problemas teóricos" en *Historia y Sociedad Revista Latinoamericana de Pensamiento Marxista* (México: Segunda época) N° 5, Primavera, pp. 20–36.

Dillard, Dudley. 1980. "A Monetary Theory of Production: Keynes and the Institutionalists." *Journal of Economic Issues* 14 (2): 255–273.

Furtado, Celso. 1964. *Desarrollo y Subdesarrollo*. Buenos Aires: Editorial Universitaria de Buenos Aires EUDEBA.

Girón, Alicia. 2006. "Obstáculos al desarrollo: el paradigma del financiamiento en América Latina" en *Reforma financiera en América Latina,* coordinado por Alicia Girón y Eugenia Correa. Buenos Aires, Argentina: IIEc-UNAM y CLACSO.

Girón, Alicia. 2007. "Circuito monetario y actores del orden económico internacional" en *Sur hacia el Norte. Economía Política del Orden Económico Internacional Emergente,* coordinado por Alicia Girón y Eugenia Correa, 35–44. Argentina, Buenos Aires: Publicaciones Cooperativas, CLACSO. http://bibliotecavirtual.clacso .org.ar/ar/libros/sursur/giron_correa/04Giron.pdf. Accessed June 25, 2021.

Girón, Alicia. 2012. "Crisis, Dollar, and Shadow Financial System." *Journal of Economic Issues* 46 (2): 511–518.

Girón, Alicia. 2015. "Women and Financialization: Microcredit, Institutional Investors, and MFIs." *Journal of Economic Issues* 49 (2): 373–396.

Girón, Alicia and Eugenia Correa. 2021. "Fiscal Stimulus, Fiscal Policies, and Financial Instability." *Journal of Economic Issues* 55 (2): 552–558.

Girón, Alicia and Marica Solorza. 2015. "The European Crisis and Lessons from Latin America through the Glass of Financialization and Austerity Measures." *International Journal of Political Economy* 44 (1): 32–50.

Hilferding, Rudolf. (1910) 1981. *Finance Capital. A Study of the Latest Phase of Capitalist Development*, edited by Tom Bottomore. London: Routledge & Kegan Paul.

Lavoie, Marc. 2006. *Introduction to Post-Keynesian Economics*. London: Palgrave Macmillan.

Levy-Orlik, Noemi. 2010. "Minsky's Financial Instability Hypothesis in the New Financial Institutional Framework: What are the Lessons for Developing Countries?" In *Minsky, Crisis and Development*, edited by Daniela Tavasci and Jan Toporowski, 155–167. London: Palgrave Macmillan.

Liang, Yan. 2011. "Money-Manager Capitalism, Capital Flows, and Development in Emerging Market Economies." In *Financial Instability and Economic Security after the Great Recession*, edited by Charles J. Whalen, 179–201. Cheltenham, UK: Elgar.

Love, Joseph L. 1980. "Raul Prebisch and the Origins of the Doctrine of Unequal Exchange." *Latin American Research Review* 15 (3): 45–72.

Mariátegui, José Carlos. (1928) 1971. *Seven Interpretive Essays on Peruvian Reality*. https://www.marxists.org/archive/mariateg/works/7-interpretive-essays/index.htm. Accessed June 25, 2021.

Mariátegui, José Carlos. (1928) 2005. "Esquema de la Evolución Económica" en *Siete ensayos de interpretación de la realidad peruana*. Buenos Aires: Gorka: 17–45.

Minsky, Hyman P. 1990. "Schumpeter: Finance and Evolution." In *Evolving Market Technology and Market Structure: Studies in Schumpeterian Economics*, edited by Arnold Heertje and Mark Perlman, 51–74. Ann Arbor: University of Michigan Press.

Minsky, Hyman P. 1996. "Uncertainty and the Institutional Structure of Capitalist Economies." *Journal of Economic Issues* 30 (2): 357–368.

Prebisch, Raúl. 1963. *Hacia una dinámica del desarrollo.* Fondo de Cultura Económica, Distrito Federal, México.

Seccareccia, Mario and Eugenia Correa. 2018. "Rethinking Money as an Institution of Capitalism and the Theory of Monetary Circulation: What Can Modern Heterodox Economists/Institutionalists Learn from Karl Polanyi?" *Journal of Economic Issues* 52 (2): 422–429.

Sikkink, Kathryn. 1988. "The Influence of Raul Prebisch on Economic Policy-Making in Argentina, 1950–1962." *Latin American Research Review* 23 (2): 91–114.

Street, James H. 1987. "Raul Prebisch, 1901–1986: An Appreciation." *Journal of Economic Issues* 21 (2): 649–659.

Ventimiglia, Luigi and Daniela Tavasci. 2010. "Money Manager Capitalism in Primary Commodity-Dependent Developing Countries." In *Minsky, Crisis and Development,* edited by Daniela Tavasci and Jan Toporowski, 275–293. London: Palgrave Macmillan.

Vidal, Laura and Eugenia Correa. 2021. "New Limits of the Neoliberalism: Society and Market." *Journal of Economic Issues* 55 (2): 432–438.

Whalen, Charles J. 2020. "Post-Keynesian Institutionalism: Past, Present, and Future." *Evolutionary and Institutional Economics Review* (2020) 17 (1): 71–92.

10. What do economists really mean? Post-Keynesian Institutionalists as economic translators

Timothy A. Wunder

INTRODUCTION

Mainstream economics has a lexicon of words and phrases that are used in specific ways and often convey something very different from what the terms mean to non-economists. Even "economics" has a meaning among mainstream economists that is at odds with what most other people mean when using that word. Mainstream (aka conventional) economists are taught that economics is the study of how scarce resources are allocated in a world of unlimited human wants; therefore, to those so trained, economics is understood as the study of how people choose. In contrast, most others view economics as the study of a system ("the economy") that fosters the production and distribution of the goods and services people need to survive and enjoy life.

The mainstream vision of the economy leads those economists to explore issues such as how people rationally choose mates, when parents choose to have children to maximize happiness, and even how individuals may rationally choose to become addicted to a narcotic.[1] In contrast, most non-economists are more likely to see the economy as a system that produces the means and opportunities to entertain a potential spouse during courtship, the housing and goods required to raise a family, and even the products that can trap people in a black hole of dependency. Conventional economists and the general population are talking past each other because they are using the same words differently. This communication divide would mean little were it not for the fact that such economists are often given positions that enable them to exert great influence on how a society is structured; as a result, the misunderstanding can conceal a huge gulf between the sort of structure preferred by economists and the sort preferred by most of the rest of society.

This chapter stresses the vital work of Post-Keynesian Institutional economists and other non-mainstream economists as economic translators.[2]

Post-Keynesian Institutionalists and their intellectual forebears have long served as translators of mainstream pronouncements on the economy and public policy, using their broad training in economics and related disciplines to clarify mainstream assumptions and highlight the implications of mainstream policy guidance.[3] Moreover, in the wake of the global COVID-19 pandemic—as was the case following the global financial crisis a decade earlier—such work takes on even greater significance than usual. This chapter looks at the privileged place of economists in policy discussions and then explores three concepts that clearly call for this type of translation: rationality, scarcity, and small government. In each case, there is a vast gulf between what the concept means to conventional economists and what it means to other people.

THE OUTSIZED ROLE OF ECONOMISTS IN POLICY DISCUSSIONS

Economists have a disproportionate impact on public policy compared to scholars in most other academic disciplines. Economists are given a voice in the making of all sorts of policies, ranging from local matters such as school busing (Hafner, Stepanek, and Troxel 2017) to national and international matters such as the COVID-19 pandemic (IGM Forum 2020) and global climate change. In fact, policymakers seek economists' input on just about every proposed project, statute, or regulation. With the possible exception of lawyers, the policy influence of no other group of professionals comes close to that of economists.

It is a fair question to ask why economists, and most often *mainstream* economists, are given such a privileged policy position. Do they really add value to policy discussions? Does society truly benefit from giving their considerations a key role in public decision-making? Those are, of course, important questions; but they are seldom asked. The fundamental reason economists are usually given a hearing has little to do with such thoughtful questions, even as it reveals an important gap between the public's perception of the economics profession and the actual work of economists: economics is seen as the study of money, and, as the saying goes, "Money makes the world go around." Moreover, since conventional economists hold dominant positions in most major university economics departments and policy think tanks, mainstream voices are those most often heard in policy discussions.

This outsized role in policy discussions is what makes mainstream economists powerful when it comes to the shaping of societies. Their training and thinking has a major impact on which policy choices are widely perceived as "economically" viable. Unfortunately, a pool of like-minded economists, all with similar training and experience, results in a set of policy prescriptions that are limited in scope and vision. The training and thinking of the economics discipline limits not only the research agenda of the discipline, but also the scope of solutions offered to address society's problems.

To understand the thinking of mainstream economists, one first must be trained by, and associate with, its practitioners. The training required to become a professional economist is extensive, and it takes a long time to understand their way of thinking. Going through such training, and being exposed to such thinking for a long while, will inevitably affect a student's worldview. Like an initiate to a religious order, the student will find it difficult to be surrounded by a way of thinking for extended periods of time without internally accepting at least some, and usually most, of the ideas of the group. Individuals highly critical of the group's ideas are likely to leave before completing the ritualized training—and may even be ejected for failing to understand "The Truth."

The result is that a group of ideologically pure economists serves as the advisors who shape policy discussions. These practitioners use the same language and jargon-laden shorthand, have similar ways of valuing things, and employ common methods of analysis. Yet these similarities mean that any effective criticism of their opinions will have to come from outside the camp of orthodox believers.

Critics who wish to challenge the mainstream body of thought must first be trained in it. They must not only understand mainstream premises, but also be able to point out where those premises fail. In addition, such critics must be willing to endure belittlement as a consequence of challenging the profession's unifying faith. Critics of this sort—with the necessary training, critical insight, and will—are hard to find, and economists with those characteristics usually manage to stay in the profession largely by forming or joining groups with other critical economists. These groups are given the name "heterodox" (unorthodox) schools of economic thought and practice. Post-Keynesian Institutionalists make up one such school of outsiders.

Conventional economists like to dismiss heterodox schools, but Post-Keynesian Institutional economists are fully trained in the methods used by the mainstream. They draw on that training not only to criticize mainstream methods and theories, but also to develop alternative theories that better reflect observations that can be made by the general citizen.[4] The next three sections of this chapter use their insight to explain what mainstream economists actually mean when they talk about rational individuals, scarcity, and small government, respectively.

THE RATIONAL INDIVIDUAL

The mainstream economic vision of the individual is that she/he is a decision-maker who optimizes choices in the face of constraints generated by a world of scarcity. This vision is sometimes referred to as *homo-economicus*.

Thorstein Veblen, one of the intellectual forerunners to Post-Keynesian Institutionalism (PKI), had a great time making fun of this vision of the individual. As Veblen put it:

> The hedonistic conception of man is that of a lightning calculator of pleasures and pains, who oscillates like a homogeneous globule of desire of happiness under the impulse of stimuli that shift him about the area but leave him intact ... He is an isolated, definitive human datum, in stable equilibrium except for the buffets of the impinging forces that displace him in one direction or another. Self-poised in elemental space, he spins symmetrically about his own spiritual axis until the parallelogram of forces bears down on him, whereupon he follows the line of the resultant. (Veblen 1898, 389)

This vision of the economic actor, as a decision-maker who calculates pleasure and pain in order to maximize individual well-being, plays a primary role in mainstream economics.

For example, in a 1984 *Journal of Political Economy* article, Boulier and Rosenzweig (1984) use a maximizing model to look at how people optimize decision-making during a "spouse search." They write: "Assume also that the lifetime welfare maximized by the offspring who live Ω years is the weighted sum of per-period utilities in the post-school, unmarried and married states" (Boulier and Rosenzweig 1984, 716). Clearly these authors are hopeless romantics; the *Journal of Political Economy*, one of the world's top-ranked mainstream economics journals, is a gold mine of this sort of understanding on the subject of human courtship.

The predominance of such "optimizing" in decision-making can be seen in the fact that Gary Becker won The Sveriges Riksbank Prize in Economic Sciences in Memory of Alfred Nobel for just such work.[5] Becker's contribution was "for having extended the domain of microeconomic analysis to a wide range of human behavior and interaction, including nonmarket behavior" (Nobel Foundation n.d.). One of Becker's most famous contributions was to "develop a theory of rational addiction, in which rationality means a consistent plan to maximize utility over time" (Becker and Murphy 1988, 675).

In response to the Great Recession, Paul Krugman (2009) wrote an article (published with the title "How Did Economists Get It So Wrong?") highlighting the errors that prevented mainstream economists from seeing the oncoming global financial crisis. According to Krugman, mainstream models "turned a blind eye to the limitations of human rationality that often lead to bubbles and busts; to the problems of institutions that run amok; to the imperfections of markets—especially financial markets—that can cause the economy's operating system to undergo sudden, unpredictable crashes." Krugman concluded that the concept of rationality needs to be reassessed in economics.[6]

Yet, a decade later a simple search of the "top" economics journals gives little doubt that the optimizing view of the individual is still alive and well in mainstream economics. One can quickly find several articles in such journals on courting within "marriage markets" (see, e.g., Pollak 2019; Persson 2019). It is equally easy to find articles that assume optimizing behavior on the part of addicted individuals (such as Galenianos and Gavazza 2017). Like a comfortable blanket, mainstream economists long for the warmth of a world in which individuals optimize their decisions to maximize personal pleasure.

This is where Post-Keynesian Institutionalists can help in the translation between mainstream economists and non-economists. Merriam-Webster defines *rational* as "having reason or understanding," which seems a laudable trait for individuals making decisions. Given that definition, most people are rational when making choices. However, as implied above, what mainstream economists define as rational should instead be referred to as *optimizing*. Reasoning through a problem and optimizing are two very different mental activities. A person may not be able to optimize due to many variables or lack of information. There are multiple reasons a person may not optimize, but optimization and being rational are not the same thing. A person in a situation where they are not optimizing may be acting perfectly rationally, and to conflate rationality with optimization is problematic. Further, a person may optimize their behavior but do so not in a manner that maximizes their personal pleasure and pain matrix. They may optimize in a way to try to help others and this too would be quite different from what mainstream economists define as optimization. The mainstream conflation of reasoning with optimization, and optimization with utility maximizing, creates communication issues that Post-Keynesian Institutionalist translators can clarify.

The vision of individuals as optimizing decision-makers—both as an image of what sensible people do (whether they actually realize it or not) and what, therefore, all people should do—plays a large role in mainstream economic thinking, even though there exists strong evidence that such individuals are empirical anomalies. In a study of wealthy suburban Tokyo citizens, for example, it was found that only a tiny fraction of people demonstrated *homo-economicus* behavior (Yamagishi et al. 2014). The same study showed a correlation between demonstrating such behavior and exhibiting the traits of a sociopath.

In addition to assuming that individuals are hedonistic optimizing decision-makers, mainstream economists dispense with all questions about the motivations and influences that lie behind an individual's wants. As a result, the role of the individual in mainstream models is reduced to a utility function that exists outside of time and place. In such economics, an individual's tastes and preferences are taken as given; they are beyond the scope of inquiry. In this way of thinking, the child wants a candy bar; *what* the child wants, and *why* the child wants a candy bar is irrelevant to the economist. The CEO wants a personal jet; *what* the CEO wants, and *why* the CEO wants a jet is irrelevant. Such wants are simply taken as the given starting point for an optimization analysis.

This mainstream vision of "economic man" is not really a definition of what it means to be an individual.[7] Heterodox economist John B. Davis put it this way: stripping away all social influences and psychological considerations results in mainstream economic theory lacking "an adequate conception of the individual" (Davis 2003, 17). Nevertheless, mainstream economics places that individual at the center of its analyses. In fact, such individuals and their given preferences are the origin of the concept of consumer demand and the related "demand curve" of mainstream microeconomics.

The centrality to conventional economics of its vision of individuals can be explained as follows. According to the mainstream, an individual, who is optimizing under a budget constraint, chooses differing goods to maximize her/his utility. This maximizing behavior, combined with the assumption of diminishing marginal utility, leads to people choosing to buy a greater quantity of an item as its price drops. Thus, the "law of demand" comes directly from the mainstream's optimizing vision—and, of course, the laws of supply and demand are the cornerstones of mainstream market analysis, the heart of mainstream economic theory.

Since optimizing behavior does not represent general individual behavior, and utility functions fail to represent a coherent vision of individuality, then the mainstream economic vision is built upon a weak foundation. But that departure from reality also means mainstream economics is misleading in its description of how people behave and its prescriptions for how they ought to. A quick example involving two supermarket shoppers helps illustrate how the mainstream perspective is out of touch with real life.

Chris walks into a supermarket and begins the weekly ritual of buying food. Chris starts in the produce section, picks up a head of lettuce and quickly analyzes how many units of satisfaction it would give versus the price. Chris then picks up a bundle of broccoli and calculates the satisfaction versus price. Next, Chris compares the satisfaction-to-price ratio of the broccoli to the ratio of the lettuce and determines that lettuce gives less satisfaction per unit of money and therefore puts back the lettuce. Then Chris picks up an apple and does a quick analysis of satisfaction per price and determines that broccoli still grants greater satisfaction per unit and thus puts the apple back down. In a similar manner, Chris goes through each product in the store, calculating satisfaction per price and only buys products in such a manner that the shopping budget is expended to maximize Chris's overall satisfaction.[8]

Then Pat enters the same supermarket. Upon reaching the snacks section, Pat's eyes come to rest upon a puffed corn product covered in a powdery cheese substance. Upon seeing this product, Pat, in a blissful childlike manner, places the product in a shopping cart, saying, "I love Cheesy Poofs!" Pat then proceeds to travel the rest of the store, choosing products that have a habitual attraction or that tickle Pat's fancy at the moment. Pat is motivated by a series of impulses far outside the realm of optimization.

While the shopping behavior of Pat might be too embarrassingly close to reality for some people, Pat's behavior is probably the closer of the two descriptions when it comes to the reality of how most people make their actual decisions. In fact, if forced, most mainstream economists would probably also admit that human behavior is most often closer to that of Pat. However, to the mainstream economist, how people *actually* decide—on a conscious level—is irrelevant to the models used to describe economic behavior. In conventional economic models, people are assumed to act like Chris, the optimizing shopper, whether they realize they are acting that way or not.

Moreover, the mainstream economist is likely to add that people "should" behave like Chris. Since optimization represents the "economics way of thinking," the profession's distinctive terminology substitutes for the dictionary definition of rationality—and it is this moral proposition (that all consumers should behave like the optimizing shopper) that gives light to the actual preferences held by mainstream economists. Their vision of *homo-economicus* is not a vision of how people actually behave—indeed, how and why people behave the way they actually do is really not of interest to the economic mainstream—rather, theirs is a moral vision of how people *ought to* behave.

For many economists, there is appeal to the moral vision that people should make decisions with the goal of maximizing their own personal gain. It is attractive to think that consumers should weigh alternatives and choose on the basis of what will make them most happy. In the example above, Chris's optimizing seems morally laudable, while Pat's impish behavior seems to deserve moral approbation. However, on closer examination, it can be easily shown that Chris's method of decision-making is not necessarily a morally superior method. To show this, we must merely continue to observe our two shoppers.

With Cheesy Poofs in the cart, Pat accidentally bumps into a store worker who is stocking breakfast cereals, knocking a few boxes off the shelf. Pat reacts by taking a few minutes to help the worker pick up the boxes, and they engage in a brief conversation about the weather. Pat then moves on to other aisles.

After five hours of calculating the value ratios of all products in the produce area, Chris has moved on to another aisle and bumps into the same worker in the cereal aisle, causing another spill of boxes. Unlike Pat, however, Chris makes a quick calculation about the satisfaction to be received from helping to pick up the boxes, concluding that providing help would lead to a negative amount of satisfaction; besides, the worker is paid to deal with such situations.

Our optimizing shopper further realizes that a conversation would only serve to increase lost time. As a result, Chris continues shopping, with nothing said to the worker, and begins to calculate the satisfaction-to-cost ratio of Uber Sugar Charms cereal.

Most reasonable people would probably be appalled by Chris's behavior in this circumstance. The cold optimization of Chris is on par with what a sociopath would do. Most mainstream economists would probably also agree that such actions are morally inappropriate as social behavior. But as *economic* behavior, our optimizing shopper made the "right" decisions.

Of course, some mainstream economists would argue that the scenario just described disregards mainstream economists' full view with respect to utility functions. In particular, they might argue that utility functions of individuals can and do take into consideration a person's interaction with others. In other words, the mainstream vision of the individual recognizes that social interactions affect a person's utility; thus, our optimizing shopper would need to take into consideration the possibility of negative consequences associated with simply walking away from the store employee.

However, such mainstream additions to the maximization position seem weak at best. What if the shopper was only visiting that store once, and would never see the worker again? In that case, why should the shopper speak to or assist the worker? Perhaps Chris's utility function incorporates judgment by a moral overlord, a God that rewards courtesy and punishes bad behavior. Thus, helping to pick up the boxes would actually represent utility maximization.

All these arguments are likely to be part of the discussion of optimizing behavior when talking to a mainstream economist. Yet they add complexities that move the mainstream recognition of reality far outside the realm of anything that conventional economists actually put in their models. The bottom line is clear: Individuals are generally *not* optimizing creatures, and models using such optimization should not be treated as providing either realistic accounts of "what is" or sensible recommendations for "what ought to be." Moreover, optimization and rationality are not the same thing; mainstream economists should not conflate the terms.

After more than a century of being criticized for putting forth a false narrative of the optimizing individual, a number of mainstream economists have begun to take seriously the need to examine how individuals actually behave. This group has been given the name "behavioral economists." Some of the work done by behavioral economists has been excellent, even if much of their work is only now discovering what other social sciences learned decades ago.

Yet even behavioral economists are enamored with hedonistic optimization in their own way. Much of the popularity of the behavioral school is the result of policy prescriptions offered by such economists to address cases in which people are not behaving in an optimizing manner. For example, a key contribution of Richard Thaler (another Sveriges Riksbank Prize winner) and Shlomo Benartzi points out that many workers, when offered a 401(k) plan by employers, have usually opted out because opting out was the default choice. If the default is changed to "opt in," many more people choose to save in such plans. In fact, Thaler and Benartzi (2004) see this "Libertarian Paternalism" as providing part of the solution to the problem Americans are facing in the era in which defined-contribution retirement plans have replaced defined-benefit pensions.[9]

It is also interesting to note that Thaler and Benartzi (2004) do more than lay out their "opt in" plan. They also identify many reasons why individuals make poor decisions on a regular basis. For example, they point to lack of knowledge, procrastination, and lack of self-control. Given such poor decision-making, it would seem important to explore how well people will tend to their new 401(k) savings. Will they notice the service fees they pay to 401(k) managers? Will they pay attention to the dividends paid by the firms in which they own shares? Will they worry about outlandish pay packages for executives? Thaler and Benartzi do not explore or mention any of these questions.

A complete accounting of the issues with behavioral economics would take far more space than is available here. However, an excellent source that offers further discussion is *Individuals and Identity in Economics*, by Davis (2011), which provides a close look at the conceptual flaws that behavioral economists do not address. The bottom line for Davis: mainstream and behavioral economists fail to properly define how people actually behave because their economics remains grounded in a vision of individuals who exists *outside* a social context.

Individuals are rational, but rational is not the same thing as optimizing. Further, individuals may optimize towards goals that are not self-serving, which is not what mainstream economics implies when they use optimizing in their models. Mainstream economic models usually assume optimization to maximize personal utility, which is a morally loaded position. The person optimizing to maximize another person's joy is still optimizing, yet such people are generally outside of mainstream consideration. By conflating the concepts, mainstream economists, at best, obfuscate what is meant by rational; at worst, they are being duplicitous.

The emphasis that mainstream economists place on optimization is closely aligned with the vision that we live in a world of scarcity. When a society does not have enough material goods to meet all the needs of its citizens, then choices have to be made. Of course, it makes sense that in such a world we should prioritize the allocation of goods to their most valued use; thus optimization becomes a laudable goal. However, the next section will call into question the mainstream vision of scarcity that underpins the fascination with optimization.

SCARCITY

Universal scarcity is one of the generally accepted precepts within mainstream economics. Many conventional economists even place the study of scarcity at the heart of their definition of economics. The issue of optimizing behavior addressed in the preceding section comes out of the notion that the world is defined by a confluence of unlimited human wants and a world with limited resources. This section will clarify what mainstream economists mean by scarcity. It also explores the origin of their definition; criticizes that approach to scarcity; and examines how scarcity relates to making choices.

Mainstream economics places extreme emphasis on the importance of scarcity with respect to economic activity. The assumption of universal scarcity permeates conventional economic research on all fronts, yet finding an explicit statement in peer-reviewed articles about the definition of scarcity is difficult. In fact, trying to find articles in mainstream economic journals that explore the reality of the mainstream's scarcity assumption is nearly impossible.

To find a general statement about this assumption, one must turn to conventional economists instructing new initiates on the tenets of the mainstream faith. As economist Steven Horwitz (2019) writes,

> Almost every introductory economics course begins with the fact that we live in a world of omnipresent scarcity. For economists, scarcity is not a physical concept—it is not the same as 'rarity' … Scarcity means that people can imagine more possible ways in which they can put a good to use than there are goods that can be used.

This mainstream vision of scarcity arises from two opposing forces: on one side, there exists a finite world with a limited amount of resources; on the other side, there are unbounded human desires.

Further evidence about the primacy of place that scarcity holds in mainstream economics can be found by looking at the opening chapters of most mainstream economics texts. Backhouse and Medema (2009a) take a look at the definition of economics offered in the most widely used mainstream texts and show that the definition varies. Some authors subscribe to the scarcity definition, but others define economics more broadly.

However, even economists who don't explicitly define economics in scarcity terms still give a primacy of place in their thinking to scarcity. For example, Paul Krugman is listed as not having an explicitly scarcity-oriented definition by Backhouse and Medema, yet upon looking more closely, the primacy of scarcity can clearly be found. In the text *Krugman's Economics for AP*, the first line of the preface reads: "Economics is the study of choice and scarcity" (Ray and Anderson 2011). In the Krugman and Wells (2009) introductory (university) microeconomics text, the first section of the book centers on the assumption that choice and scarcity are the heart of economics. On page 5, a section called "Individual Choice: The Core of Economics" starts, and its first subsection is "Resources are Scarce." Such emphasis on scarcity permeates the opening catechism of mainstream economics teaching; it also dominates the mainstream's research agenda.

The origin of the emphasis on scarcity did not arise with the foundations of political economy; early definitions of economics often centered on the production of wealth and goods for survival. It is true that classical economics included a broad discussion of the subsistence wage, but the classical definition focused on material goods creation, not simply scarcity. In classical political economy, scarcity was a concern, but it was not the sole focus. Scarcity only emerged as the central focus starting in the 1930s with the work of Lionel Robbins (1932), and even then it met with opposition.[10] According to Backhouse and Medema (2009a, 225):

> The Robbins definition of economics was criticized both for being too broad and too narrow. It was considered too broad in that it failed to divide economics sufficiently from other social sciences. But it was also said to be overly narrow in that it was too heavily tilted toward theory and left little, if any, room for empirical analysis, history, and institutions—and essentially wrote ethics out of economics.

The true dominance of scarcity as the central tenet of conventional economics did not occur until the 1960s and 1970s (Backhouse and Medema 2009b). Its acceptance in that period corresponds with the rise in stature of optimizing analysis. In the 1970s, mainstream economics transitioned away from Keynesian analysis and began to embrace a vision more closely aligned with pre-Keynesian analysis, in particular a Malthusian perspective. Acceptance of the scarcity definition accompanied the need to justify why economists were analyzing topics more typically covered by anthropologists and psychologists.

In the wake of the transition to the scarcity definition, economics was no longer about a topic; it was about emphasizing a way of thinking. To this way of thinking, scarcity is all pervasive and optimization is the best way to deal with scarcity. If potential spouses are scarce, then choosing a spouse can be framed as an optimization problem and is within the bounds of mainstream economic analysis. To the conventional economist, the scarcity definition is not about limiting the scope of economics; it is about expanding the reach of optimizing analysis.

Real scarcity exists, and it is irrefutable that some people live in what realistically should be labeled poverty. Research on poverty shows that coping with impoverishment produces extreme mental distress and impedes cognitive functioning (Shah et al. 2018; Mani et al. 2013). Such research suggests there is a clear difference between actual material scarcity and the mainstream definition of economic scarcity. It would be difficult to argue that a CEO has her/his mental faculties diminished by the scarcity that forces a choice between two corporate jets, yet an impoverished farmer can indeed suffer cognitive impairment from the stress of deciding how to use extremely limited resources so as to avoid death.

Research in anthropology demonstrates that the scarcity mindset is a cultural condition. Marshall Sahlins explored the conditions facing hunter-gatherers, concluding that hunter-gatherers found material possessions to be a burden. While the common perception of a hunter-gatherer society is one in which starvation was always close at hand, Sahlins argues that the average hunter-gatherer worked three to four hours a day gathering food. Sahlins writes that the "food quest is so successful that half the time people seem not to know what to do with themselves" (Sahlins 1972, 11). Anthropologists continue to discuss these observations and present evidence demonstrating hunter-gatherer abundance (Dyble et al. 2019). The mainstream economics advocate would be quick to disregard the hunter-gatherer society, arguing that they represent a small part of the modern world; yet to do so would be problematic. Hunter-gatherer societies account for the vast majority of human history, so it would not seem extreme to suggest that unlimited wants is the exception to human experience rather than the rule.[11]

Post-Keynesian Institutional economists have their own history of pointing out the *cultural* nature of the concept of scarcity. Well before scarcity became a foundational element in conventional economics, Veblen argued that conspicuous consumption is based on the desire to obtain social acceptance, rather than the result of an inborn trait (Veblen [1899] 1953). In short, the mainstream economic notion that *everything* is scarce—just because humans have the ability to think of unlimited different uses for objects—is as flawed as the rationality assumption examined in the previous section.

For the economic mainstream, scarcity is what leads to choice. But that is actually easy to refute. We do so by introducing the mainstream concept of "opportunity cost." That concept refers to the foregone best alternative that was available when choosing one option over others.

Imagine a mainstream economics instructor offering a student two candy bars and telling the student that they may only choose one. Bar A is the Outrageous Chocolate Cocoa Chip bar and bar B is the Honey O'Crunch bar. The student chooses bar A, which causes the instructor to point out that, in choosing bar A, the student is making a sacrifice of bar B; thus, in mainstream economic terms, bar B represents the opportunity cost of choosing bar A. Building on this example, mainstream economists can demonstrate how a scarcity view of the world applies to all areas of life in which choice occurs.

However, scarcity is not the only source of choices, as can be shown by a smart student. Suppose the student presents a different demonstration to the instructor. The student offers the instructor an Outrageous Chocolate Cocoa Chip bar. In this case, since no choice must be made (except, of course, to accept or refuse the offer), the cost to the instructor of accepting the bar would be zero: there is no opportunity cost because no second-best alternative exists. Now suppose the student pulls out a second Outrageous Chocolate Cocoa Chip bar and forces the instructor to choose between the two bars. The instructor must now decide to choose either bar one or bar two, and the student then asks: what is the cost to the selection? In the mainstream vision, the act of choosing either bar now involves an opportunity cost represented by the other bar.

The reader of this example would properly ask why the student is being so cruel to the instructor. In presenting two bars instead of one, the student is introducing an opportunity cost that wouldn't have existed if the student had merely offered a single bar. By adding a greater amount of resources to the scenario, the student is adding a cost to the instructor. In other words, by adding resources the student is creating the need for choice—the choice is caused by adding *abundance*, not by scarcity. If economics is the study of choice, then abundance is equally responsible for the need to choose as is scarcity.

This example of abundance creating choice was made clear by economic anthropologist Karl Polanyi (1977). Post-Keynesian Institutional economists have been using this type of analysis to critique conventional economics for nearly half a century. Thus, the premise that scarcity alone forces choice (and therefore, choice is what economists should be analyzing) is false. Since scarcity and increased abundance may each force individuals to make choices, arguing that any choice comes with a cost is to truly misinterpret the notion of cost.

Cost would be better defined as something causing actual harm, leading to negative emotional or physical circumstances. The existence of multiple jets that a CEO has to choose between is the result of abundance, whereas a poor mother choosing which bill to pay is truly a demonstration of scarcity. The mother is facing a real cost, whereas it is difficult to argue that the CEO is facing a hardship. In fact, an honest analysis of the human condition in a developed country would be hard pressed to prove that scarcity is the cause of human misery. In the United States, food is plentiful but nearly 20 percent of children face hunger; there are vacant houses in numbers enough to give every homeless person a place to live; and there is healthcare in abundance (and there could be even more abundance were it not for salary-boosting limits on the availability of qualified medical professionals), yet every year tens of thousands die due to lack of access.

For a further look at this, let's return to the student-instructor example. Suppose that the student, in order to make the demonstration, took the second chocolate bar from a homeless person for whom the bar would have been the only food for the day. Now there is a real economic cost in this scenario, but the instructor is not paying the cost (she/he merely chooses between bar one or bar two); instead, it is the homeless person who pays the cost. More importantly, that homeless person is not paying a cost due to a lack of chocolate bars (scarcity); the homeless person is paying a cost because of the action of the student. Neither a scarcity of bars nor the student's presentation of a choice to her/his instructor is what imposes a cost in this example: a cost is imposed because of human action that has nothing to do with either the production of candy bars or the quantity produced.

The real problem in the above scenario is that the ownership of the resources leaves one person to pay a cost so that other people can have an academic argument over what economics is about. There are more than enough means to satisfy all the needs in the system (that is, a meal for one person and a course lesson for two others, since even stones could be used for the classroom exercise); however, the student and instructor are using more of the means than needed. It is not *scarcity* that leads to the need for choice; it is the *choices* of some that lead to actual scarcity for others. Distribution, not scarcity, is the major economic problem in developed economies and mainstream economics offers little in the way of analysis on how to deal with this fundamental problem. In our example, the instructor is not facing a "cost" when choosing between the two bars, and to pretend the instructor does minimizes the real harm to millions caused by poor distribution.

In the actual world, this example is made real when the issue of private property is considered. The real issue of economic scarcity (that is, poverty) in developed countries is not about a lack of goods; it is about the *allocation* and *distribution* of goods. Many mainstream economists are committed to a narrow vision of capitalist ownership and are convinced that limited government is the best way to run an economy. According to many conventional economists, the role of government should be small—a role limited to enforcing property rights. The next section looks at this vision of "small government" and explores what its conception of property rights actually entails.

SMALL GOVERNMENT

Mainstream economic analysis places a strong emphasis on the argument that government should be "small." Yet the concept of *small* in this case is once again a redefinition based on a specific way of thinking. To the conventional economist, the size of the government is about the amount of resources a government uses. That may be measured by the amount of gross domestic product (GDP) going through government hands, or perhaps by the number of workers the government employs. To such an economist, government spending and taxation determine the size of government; yet this is a confusing consideration seeing that, for most people, the size of government is much more about the impact government has on their personal lives, and the extent to which government is a constructive force is usually more important than the size of GDP it commands. This section first looks at the emphasis mainstream economics places on this concept of small government; then it looks at how this emphasis misses the real impact of government as the definer and enforcer of property rights.

President Ronald Reagan infamously stated, "Government is not the solution to our problem: government is the problem" (Reagan 1981). President Bill Clinton surrendered to this notion in 1996 when he said, in his State of the Union Address, "The era of big government is over" (Clinton 1996). These political statements did not arise out of a popular, cultural uprising; rather, they were an extension of the mainstream economic consensus, rooted in a return to pre-Keynesian economic theory. The economic advisors to both presidents gave preferential voice to redefining the government's role with respect to the economy. Milton Friedman, who advised Reagan, was notoriously anti-government, and Larry Summers, who advised Clinton, was responsible for overseeing the dismantling much of the regulatory regime that was created in response to the Great Depression.

The ideas of Friedman and Summers each influenced their political counterparts. Friedman had a clear disdain for most government policies and went so far as to reanalyze history in an attempt to blame the Great Depression on the government (Friedman and Schwarz 1963). While Summers does not have as negative a view of the government, some of his views have been similar to those of Friedman. On the occasion of Friedman's death, Summers wrote: "[L]ike many others I feel that I have lost a hero—a man whose success demonstrates that great ideas convincingly advanced can change the lives of people around the world" (Summers 2006).

Mainstream research on the efficacy of small government continues. Whether it involves measuring the size of government in relation to its population (Krieger and Meierrieks 2020) or in relation to economic growth (Asimakopoulos and Karavias 2016), such research emphasizes the "optimal" amount of economic resources that should be dedicated to governmental use (note the continuing theme of optimization). In the mainstream way of thinking, there is the government and its resource use, and the rest of the economy. In this way of thinking, the government and the rest of the economy are separate entities, intersecting only where the government appropriates resources from the economy (through taxation or spending, the latter of which is believed to "crowd out" private spending).

This conventional way of thinking implies that the government's role is that of a consumer of resources, rather than maker of public investments (education, healthcare, infrastructure, etc.) or creator of the institutional network within which the economy operates. In fact, though, as Post-Keynesian Institutionalists emphasize (see, e.g., Whalen 2008) the government's role in an economy is pervasive, and affects the actions of every civilian daily. Yes, the business owner bristles at government regulations, and the worker decries the taxes taken from a paycheck; but the impact of government goes far beyond these small inconveniences—into the shaping and stabilizing of markets, and even into the definition of private property.

To be sure, the mainstream economist might point to the importance of public services in their models (conventional economics can recognize a role for government in providing public goods and services such as well-maintained city streets, lighthouses, and a national military force); they also argue that government plays a major role in protecting property rights. Some mainstream economists would even argue there is a place in the system for government redistribution to deal with income and wealth inequalities. Yet this mainstream vision of the limited nature of the government misses the largely unlimited and hidden role that the government plays, not just in advanced economies, but always and everywhere (with the exception, of course, of countries that have fallen into "anarchy," which only underscores the need for government in a capitalist society).

For example, the mainstream economist recognizes the role of government in enforcing property rights, but glosses over the actual impact that such enforcement implies. The enforcement of property rights sounds like a simple proposition, but we offer a short illustration to demonstrate that this role is actually one of the driving forces behind most economic activity.

Consider person X, who lives in an apartment but suddenly decides she/he is going to live a life free from the constraints of holding down a job. Along comes the first of the month, and the landlord demands that X makes a rent payment. Person X states to the landlord that she/he does not have the money, and has no intention of paying. At this point (or after some reasonable due process), the landlord would call upon the power of the state, in the form of the local police, to forcefully compel the person from the apartment. In such a situation, the police are authorized to use force, up to and including deadly force, to compel the tenant to leave.

Person X, upon eviction, might remain committed to a nontraditional role within the economy, deciding to build a cabin or shack in the city park. Upon completion of this new home, the police are called to have X removed from the park. Person X may then decide to build a shelter in the parking lot of the local S-mart, only to once again have the police evict her/him. The same thing could happen again and again, perhaps on vacant agricultural land, and even on national forest property. These instances would eventually convince X that the need to have a place to live cannot be achieved without first finding money to buy or rent property. Since this person has no resources to trade, X's only option is to provide wage labor to get the money needed to afford a place to live.

In a developed economy, such as the United States, nearly all working-age citizens may be able to (in some sense) choose an employer, but very few can choose not to work. They may work for others, or they may start their own business; but either way they lack the option of not working. The only way a person can have the option of not working (except for those eligible for disability support, social security, or other public assistance, all of which may be challenged by the mainstream call for "small" government) is to have ownership of extensive resources. If those resources include rental property, ownership of such resources allows the owner to use the state to compel other people to work for the property owner.

Consider the landlord in the above scenario, who could demand payment because she/he is able to call upon the power of the state when payment is not given. Now consider that this landlord and others like him/her own millions of apartments in the United States, all of which can be used to compel rental payments. Across the world's developed countries, this form of property ownership compels billions to work in order to simply have a place to exist, and failure to work will bring the quick use of force by the government. This private property system is the ultimate income redistribution tool—redistribution compelled by the state's use of force.

Mainstream economists like to believe the relationship between the property owner and the renter, as well as between worker and employer, are the result of private economic choices. To the mainstream economist, the person working and the landlord having places to rent are all private-sector activities, yet it seems apparent that much of this type of activity is clearly compelled by government action. The implicit threat of government force is so pervasive that individuals usually work and pay bills without considering the state's role in compelling their compliance. Mainstream economists enable this vision by creating a narrative in which these activities are based upon private choices, even though it is the state's threat of force that ultimately compels a person's activities.[12]

The Post-Keynesian Institutionalist way of thinking emphasizes the important role that the state-run institution of private property entails. Veblen (1923) clarified the importance of this role of the government in his discussion of *Absentee Ownership*. The reason that the landlord can force rent payments is *not* due to scarcity, rather it is due to the ability of the landlord to call upon state force to compel payment or force eviction. The reason people are homeless is not that there are too few homes; instead, it is because use of homes by people with no money is curtailed through state violence.

This type of *created scarcity* permeates developed economic systems. The production of life-saving drugs is limited by companies who call upon the state in the enforcement of patents. The state prohibits the reproduction of movies and television programs in order to enforce copyrights. The creation of scarcity through state sabotage in the name of property is extensive, yet the conventional economist often seems to disregard the massive role property rights play in all aspects of the economy. A state that enforces an extensive private property regime should not be labeled *small* government. Friedman applauded a limited government focused mostly on enforcing property rights, a society in which people would be "free to choose" their role within the economy. However, the enforcement of property rights, and the presence of absentee ownership, means that a person may be free to choose who to serve, but still must be a servant.

CONCLUDING REMARKS

This chapter has offered a glimpse into what mainstream economists really mean when they make key economic statements and policy pronouncements. Mainstream economists use the terms *rationality, scarcity,* and *small government* in ways that differ substantially from what non-economists mean by them—and the mainstream meanings actually obscure key insights about how the economy really works. Moreover, those meanings conceal the profoundly anti-social, narrowly conceived, and financially stratified society that economists have in mind as their (often tacit) ideal.

Here is a short translation of the aforementioned terms. When the conventional economist argues that people decide rationally, what she/he really means is that people should be optimizing their preference satisfaction where these preferences are conceived of essentially egoistically. When the conventional economist emphasizes the role of scarcity (and choice), her/his emphasis often hides the fact that the real source of scarcity is most often allocation and distribution, not scarcity per se. When the conventional economist calls for small government, she/he is really emphasizing an opinion that government should have only one main, yet all-powerful role, the creation and enforcement of private property rights. Moreover, unlimited wants, scarcity, and government protection of private property combine to create a partially decentralized system of coercion that ensures that most of the population will work all or nearly all of their adult life.

When these three mainstream positions are brought together, a clear picture emerges: conventional economics is creating a narrative. This mainstream story argues that the natural condition of humans is to optimize limited resources to address unlimited wants. Because people naturally have unlimited wants, according to this worldview, scarcity and choice are the prime questions in economics. The final part of this narrative argues that the best way to deal with this scarcity is to allow people to make free choices, constrained only by limited government.

Post-Keynesian Institutionalists can help make these mainstream assumptions clear, and they can also show that the assumptions are not based upon observable facts. Thinking rationally is not the same thing as hedonistic optimizing; the truth is that optimizing, as understood by mainstream economists, is not how most people behave. Scarcity is not the only thing that brings about choice; in fact, it is actually abundance that often compels choice—and scarcity and poverty can most often be traced to human decisions, not limited resources. State enforcement of property rights allows property owners to create scarcity and reorder allocation; the state's role as property enforcer is pervasive, contradicting the enabling myth of "small" government in the mainstream narrative.

This chapter finishes with a final note on finding solutions to the problems of our current economic system, problems hidden—and often exacerbated—by the recommendations of mainstream economics. Post-Keynesian Institutionalists do not agree on the how to solve our current problems. For example, some economists associated with PKI would move the economy away from capitalism, whereas others would oppose such a move. Some might even suggest abandoning, or severely curtailing, our private property regime, whereas others would certainly not. Unlike conventional economists, Post-Keynesian Institutionalists do not share a universal narrative about how the economy should be fashioned.[13] However, such economists *do* agree that the mainstream paradigm is based on observably false premises, and that translating economic jargon into plain English, to expose those premises for what they are, is the first step to a better world. As John Kenneth Galbraith (1973, 223) wrote, "The emancipation of belief is the most formidable of the tasks of reform, one on which all else depends."

ACKNOWLEDGMENTS

The author would like to thank Tom Kemp and Kenneth Williford for extensive comments that improved this chapter. The author would also like to thank Charles Whalen for patient editorial work. Any remaining errors are my own.

NOTES

1. This vision of the economy is most readily observable in economics textbooks. Some might argue that the textbook version doesn't represent actual mainstream economics; why then do so many "top" economists continue to author these texts? Further, the key concepts from these texts clearly can be seen in the research that permeates the "top" journals. If the "top" journals and "top" economists espouse the ideas analyzed in this chapter, it would seem proper to refer to their ideas as the "mainstream" ideas. If, however, an economist would like to argue that most economists really don't hold these ideas, then perhaps a major restructuring of the field would be in order. During such a restructuring, Post-Keynesian Institutionalist criticisms should be more valuable than ever.

2. Consistent with the role of non-mainstream economists as translators, Joan Robinson (1978, 75) writes: "The purpose of studying economics is not to acquire a set of ready-made answers to economic questions, but to learn how to avoid being deceived by economists."

3. Some Post-Keynesian Institutional economists consider themselves to be exclusively Post-Keynesian Institutionalists, while others feel at home in more than one non-mainstream camp.

4. For example, James K. Galbraith is a heterodox economist broadly compatible with Post-Keynesian Institutionalism and has written an excellent book on these issues entitled *The Predator State: How Conservatives Abandoned the Free Market and Why Liberals Should Too.* Of course, the contributions to this *Modern Guide* also illustrate the work of such economists.

5. Often referred to as a Nobel prize, the award was in fact created in the 1960s and some descendants of Alfred Nobel have criticized the creation of the prize in economics. For example, Peter Nobel has argued that Alfred would likely not have wanted an award given in economics and that the prize is a "public relations coup by economists to improve their reputation" (quoted in "Nobel Descendant Slams Economics Prize" 2005).

6. It is interesting to note that Krugman believed the parties responsible for the 2008 collapse were acting irrationally. Were they? Is it really irrational (according to either economists or ordinary people) to ramp up loans to people who can't pay them back when you receive massive bonuses for doing so? Was irrationality the problem, or was it just a combination of rational, financially motivated behavior and widespread fraud? The latter (rational behavior) interpretation shines a more critical light on mainstream economics, since it dispenses with the argument that the mortgage run-up and collapse would not have happened if only people in the real world behaved as they are assumed to behave in mainstream economic models. Either way, mainstream economics faces a serious problem.

7. One might be troubled by the gendered nature of the mainstream term "economic man" were it not such a distorted view of all humans.

8. Of course, Chris might have used calculations from a previous shopping experience to draw up a shopping list in advance, as many people do. However, prices and product features do change, so that is not a perfect substitute for a full recalculation.

9. Thaler and Benartzi call their idea the Save More Tomorrow™ plan, designed to help low-wage workers save more. While this may be a laudable goal, it is a point of interest to note that the authors make sure to emphasize the trademark on the

name (and yes, there are "self-help" plans based on this model). This 24-page "adverresearch" is published in the *Journal of Political Economy*. Perhaps other researchers should consider this type of activity to boost their incomes. For example, one envisions a libertarian educators' plan, called "General Revenue voucher Education Directive," which could be shortened to the GReED™ plan.

10. According to Robbins (1932, 15), "Economics is the science which studies human behavior as a relationship between ends and scarce means which have alternative uses."

11. Modern humans have existed for somewhere between 100,000 to 300,000 years. Modern agricultural "civilization" is perhaps 10,000 years old. Put those facts together and it is clear that over 90 percent of human existence is represented by hunter-gatherer societies that did not have a social predisposition to unlimited material wants.

12. Comparing a modern worker's life to a feudal peasant's life offers an interesting thought experiment. The peasant was born into his economic role and failure to do as the role required would quickly bring down the lord's wrath. The modern worker has the ability to choose their role and who they will serve, but failure to choose a lord will still result in the state's use of violence. So the difference between a modern worker and a peasant is that the worker is free to choose, but neither is really very free in any robust sense.

13. While all Post-Keynesian Institutionalists do not agree on policy details and do not share a universal narrative on how the economy should be fashioned, this *Modern Guide* also demonstrates the existence of a widely shared and broadly conceived Post-Keynesian Institutionalist vision of a more economically democratic society.

REFERENCES

Asimakopoulos, Stylianos and Yiannis Karavias. 2016. "The Impact of Government Size on Economic Growth: A Threshold Analysis." *Economic Letters* 139 (February): 65–68.

Backhouse, Roger E. and Steven G. Medema. 2009a. "Retrospectives: On the Definition of Economics." *Journal of Economic Perspectives* 23 (1): 221–234.

Backhouse, Roger E. and Steven G. Medema. 2009b. "Defining Economics: The Long Road to Acceptance of the Robbins Definition." *Economica* 76 (Supplement 1): 805–820.

Becker, Gary S. and Kevin M. Murphy. 1988. "A Theory of Rational Addiction." *Journal of Political Economy* 96 (4): 675–700.

Boulier, Brian L. and Mark R. Rosenzweig. 1984. "Schooling, Search, and Spouse Selection: Testing Economic Theories of Marriage and Household Behavior." *Journal of Political Economy* 92 (4): 712–732.

Clinton, William Jefferson. 1996. State of the Union Address, January 23, 1996. https://clintonwhitehouse4.archives.gov/WH/New/other/sotu.html. Accessed June 16, 2020.

Davis, John B. 2003. *The Theory of the Individual in Economics: Identity and Value.* London: Routledge.

Davis, John B. 2011. *Individuals and Identity in Economics.* Cambridge: Cambridge University Press.

Dyble, Mark, Jack Thorley, Abigail E. Page, Daniel Smith, and Andrea Bamberg Migliano. 2019. "Engagement in Agricultural Work Is Associated with Reduced Leisure Time among Agta Hunter-Gatherers." *Nature Human Behavior* 3 (8): 792–796.

Friedman, Milton and Anna J. Schwarz. 1963. *A Monetary History of the United States: 1867–1960*. Princeton: Princeton University Press.

Galbraith, James K. 2008. *The Predator State: How Conservatives Abandoned the Free Market and Why Liberals Should Too*. New York: Free Press.

Galbraith, John Kenneth. 1973. *Economics and the Public Purpose*. Boston: Houghton Mifflin.

Galenianos, Manolis and Gavazza Alessandro. 2017. "A Structural Model of the Retail Market for Illicit Drugs." *American Economic Review* 107 (3): 858–896.

Hafner, Marco, Martin Stepanek, and Wendy M. Troxel. 2017. "Later School Start Times in the U.S.: An Economic Analysis." RAND Research Report. https://www.rand.org/pubs/research_reports/RR2109.html. Accessed June 16, 2020.

Horwitz, Steven. 2019. "Costs, Cancer, and Making Better Choices." The Library of Economics and Liberty, a website of the Liberty Fund. January 7, 2019. https://www.econlib.org/library/Columns/y2019/Horwitzcosts.html. Accessed June 16, 2020.

IGM Forum. 2020. "Policy for the COVID-19 Crisis." IGM Forum of the University of Chicago Booth School of Business. http://www.igmchicago.org/surveys/policy-for-the-covid-19-crisis/. Accessed June 16, 2020.

Krieger, Tim and Daniel Meierrieks. 2020. "The Population and the Size of Government." *European Journal of Political Economy* 61 (January): Article 101837. https://www.sciencedirect.com/science/article/abs/pii/S0176268019304859. Accessed July 28, 2021.

Krugman, Paul. 2009. "How Did Economists Get It So Wrong?" *New York Times Magazine,* September 2. https://www.nytimes.com/2009/09/06/magazine/06Economic-t.html. Accessed June 16, 2020.

Krugman, Paul and Robin Wells. 2009. *Microeconomics*, second edition. New York: Worth.

Mani, Anandi, Sendhil Mullainathan, Eldar Shafir, and Jiaying Zhao. 2013. "Poverty Impedes Cognitive Function." *Science* 341 (6149): 976–980.

"Nobel Descendant Slams Economics Prize." 2005. *The Local, SE* (Swedish edition). September 28. https://www.thelocal.se/20050928/2173-3. Accessed June 16, 2020.

Nobel Foundation. n.d. "Gary Becker Facts." https://www.nobelprize.org/prizes/economic-sciences/1992/becker/facts/. Accessed June 16, 2020.

Persson, Petra. 2019. "Social Insurance and the Marriage Market." *Journal of Political Economy* 128 (1): 252–300.

Polanyi, Karl. 1977. *The Livelihood of Man*. New York: Academic Press.

Pollak, Robert A. 2019. "How Bargaining in Marriage Drives Marriage Market Equilibrium." *Journal of Labor Economics* 37 (1): 297–321.

Ray, Margaret and David Anderson. 2011. *Krugman's Economics for AP*. New York: Worth.

Reagan, Ronald. 1981. Inaugural Address, January 20, 1981. https://www.reaganfoundation.org/media/128614/inaguration.pdf. Accessed June 16, 2020.

Robbins, Lionel. 1932. *An Essay on the Nature & Significance of Economic Science*. London: Macmillan & Co. Limited.

Robinson, Joan. 1978. *Contributions to Modern Economics*. New York: Academic Press.

Sahlins, Marshall. 1972. *Stone Age Economics*. New York: Aldine De Gruyter.

Shah, Anuj K. Jiaying Zhao, Sendhil Mullainathan, and Eldar Shafir. 2018. "Money in the Mental Lives of the Poor." *Social Cognition* 36 (1): 4–19.

Summers, Lawrence H. 2006. "The Great Liberator." 2006. *New York Times*, November 19, 2006. https://www.nytimes.com/2006/11/19/opinion/19summers.html. Accessed June 16, 2020.

Thaler, Richard H. and Shlomo Benartzi. 2004. "Save More Tomorrow™: Using Behavioral Economics to Increase Employee Saving." *Journal of Political Economy* 112 (1): 164–187.

Veblen, Thorstein. 1898. "Why Is Economics Not an Evolutionary Science?" *Quarterly Journal of Economics* 12 (4): 373–397.

Veblen, Thorstein. (1899) 1953. *Theory of the Leisure Class*. New York: Macmillan.

Veblen, Thorstein. 1923. *Absentee Ownership and Business Enterprise in Recent Times: The Case of America*. New York: B.W. Huebsch.

Whalen, Charles J. 2008. "Toward Wisely Managed Capitalism: Post-Keynesian Institutionalism and the Creative State." *Forum for Social Economics* 37 (1): 43–60.

Yamagishi, Toshio, Yang Li, Haruto Takagishi, Yoshie Matsumoto, and Toko Kiyonari. 2014. "In Search of Homo Economicus." *Psychological Science* 25 (9): 1699–1711.

11. Stock-flow consistent macroeconomic modeling and Post-Keynesian Institutionalism

Marc Lavoie

INTRODUCTION

The stock-flow consistent (SFC) approach to macroeconomic modeling is ever more popular among young Post-Keynesian economists. It has also attracted the attention of other heterodox economists, in particular scholars engaged in Ecological economics or Socio-ecological economics. Stock-flow consistency, as it will be defined below, is also progressively becoming a requirement of agent-based models, at least those constructed by scholars in the heterodox tradition and who are thus aware of Post-Keynesian economics. Carnevali et al. (2019, 228) argue that "the stock-flow consistency of models is now regarded as a *conditio sine qua non* for publication by many heterodox economics journals." Indeed, the *Cambridge Journal of Economics* goes so far as to have devoted a virtual special issue on its website to "stock-flow consistent macroeconomics," with a paper explaining the foundations of SFC macroeconomics (Shipman 2019), along with a list of papers published in that journal that could be said to be in this tradition.[1]

Some readers may wonder whether there is a link between this SFC modeling approach and Post-Keynesian Institutional economics. Charles Whalen (2013, 23) argues that the foundations of Post-Keynesian Institutionalism (PKI) "would benefit from further attention to methodology (or philosophical grounding) and to methods," adding that "insight on methods can be found in the system dynamics literature and in Wynne Godley's pioneering work on stock-flow consistent modeling." Indeed, there are substantial similarities between system dynamics and the stock-flow consistent approach.

In what follows, I shall first briefly explain and illustrate the SFC approach. I will then show that its origins can be linked to Institutionalists and to the work of Post-Keynesian authors who can be associated with PKI. Finally, I will provide three examples, based on stock matrices, of how the SFC approach can be helpful in describing the role played by various institutions and sectors of an economy.

WHAT IS THE SFC APPROACH?

I see the SFC approach as a method that allows economists to fully integrate the real economy with the financial system. As Nikiforos and Zezza (2017, 1213) put it, "[I]n SFC models, decisions made by the agents of the economy on debt, credit and assets and liabilities allocation have an impact on the determination of the real variables and vice versa." They define stock-flow consistent models as based on four principles that underline accounting consistency:

(1)   There is *flow* consistency, meaning that every transaction flow must come from somewhere and must go somewhere; there cannot be any black holes. Flow consistency is ensured by the construction of a transactions-flow matrix, which integrates the standard national income and product accounts with the financial accounts (or flow-of-funds accounts).

(2)   There is *stock* consistency, meaning that to every financial liability issued by some sector there must correspond a financial asset held by other sectors. Only tangible assets (such as fixed capital, homes or inventories) have no counterpart. Stock consistency is ensured by the construction of a stock matrix, also called the balance-sheet matrix.

(3)   There is *stock-flow* consistency, meaning that stocks at the end of the current period must be the sum of past stocks, plus the current flows plus current capital gains or capital losses. There must be thus, at least implicitly or in the equations, the equivalent of a revaluation matrix, and one may build a full-integration matrix that collects all that information.

(4)   There is *quadruple book-keeping*, meaning that any one transaction generates changes in at least four entries of the transactions-flow matrix. This is the quadruple entry principle.

As Carnevali et al. (2019, 228) mention, "the use of the label 'stock-flow consistent' is quite controversial." That is because the label, for the last 15 years or so, has been associated with SFC Post-Keynesian models with demand-led specifications and endogenous money. One might think that all models do or ought to fulfill all these accounting consistent requirements. My own view on this question is that all models fulfill stock accounting, but that very few fulfill all four of the above requirements. For instance, dynamic stochastic general equilibrium (DSGE) models often lack flow consistency as bank reserves often seem to arise from nowhere. Thus, while it is true that accounting consistency and the matrices that are used to ensure this consistency can no doubt be applied just as well to Neoclassical models, the reality is that this is rarely the case as a consequence of the modern Neoclassical obsession with microeconomic foundations rooted in optimization.

Models, however, are made of more than accounting equations. They also incorporate behavioral equations that give rise to different closures, depending on how the equations are set up. A key feature of SFC models, as they are now called, is that they rely on behavioral equations based on Post-Keynesian theory. As claimed earlier, SFC models are demand-led, as they are based on Keynesian and Kaleckian strictures. Agents are imbedded with procedural rationality and can make forecast mistakes; firms take production, costing, pricing, and financial decisions, and banks play a crucial role in providing credit and setting some of the interest rates; and except for a few financial markets, prices are not the adjusting variable, as quantities are the main signaling device. Most importantly, *SFC models provide a fully explicit traverse towards the stationary or steady-growth state.* These models can show visually, through simulations, how flows and stocks gradually change in line with each other through time—hence in the short, medium, and long run—as the consequence of a change in any parameter. These SFC models are a true illustration of Kalecki's (1971, 165) statement to the effect that "the long-run trend is but a slowly changing component of a chain of short-period situations."

The first paper fully written in this SFC tradition was by Godley (1996), and a substantially different version was published in a journal three years later (Godley 1999a).[2] Carnevali et al. (2019, 228) say that the "Bible of SFC modelers" became the book by Godley and Lavoie (2007). While the book by Godley and Cripps (1983) did entertain the accounting consistency and the Post-Keynesian behavioral assumptions mentioned above, it did not deal with a multiplicity of financial assets and did not integrate portfolio choice and its adding-up conditions. These were to be integrated in Godley's analysis years later, by making use of the work pursued by James Tobin from the late 1960s to the early 1980s. Dos Santos (2006) has underlined the similarities between the work that Tobin pursued then with Godley's work in the 1970s and 1980s and the models that he built later, inspired in particular by the transactions-flow matrix found in Backus et al. (1980).[3] Yet Tobin, despite all of his Keynesian credentials, still held tight to the Neoclassical tradition, first by not entertaining any of the behavioral assumptions mentioned in the previous paragraph, and second by considering that banks were a financial intermediary like all the others, thus minimizing the specific credit-creating ability of banks (Lavoie 2021). Thus, while Tobin's work was a major inspiration for Godley when launching the current vogue for SFC models, and though Tobin's models are certainly stock-flow consistent in a broad sense, they do not belong to the SFC tradition in the modern meaning of the word.[4]

Dos Santos (2021, 68–69) suggests that an extensive description of the approach of Godley and of his SFC followers could have been "stock-flow consistent models of capitalist economies with realistic government institutions and developed financial markets which are closed in a Keynesian way and whose dynamics are carefully analysed by means of computer simulations." While this is a correct description, it is rather long; obviously *SFC* sounds better! Carnevali et al. (2019, 232) suggest that SFC models "are not just stock-flow *consistent*, but also stock-flow *relevant*," meaning that in addition they are realistic. Nikiforos and Zezza (2017, 1229) conclude that "it is true that the name 'SFC' is misleading and sometimes confusing for what the post-Keynesian SFC approach wants to convey," but also that "it is probably too late to change the name."

TRANSACTION-FLOW AND BALANCE-SHEET MATRICES

To illustrate the concept of accounting consistency, here is an example of the transactions-flow matrix and the balance-sheet matrix. The two matrices shown are taken from the model *DIS*, for disequilibrium, found in Godley and Lavoie (2007, chapter 9). The model is very simple, as it describes a closed economy without government or a central bank.

Starting with the balance-sheet matrix of Table 11.1, note that the convention is that assets take a plus sign while liabilities take a negative sign. The institutions of this model could not be simpler. Firms have no fixed capital, but they hold inventories as production takes time and because all that is produced within a time period is not necessarily sold. These inventories are entirely financed by bank loans. There is only one kind of financial institution—banks. Households can only hold one kind of financial asset—bank deposits—and hence as the own funds of both firms and banks are assumed away (meaning that all profits are distributed to households, as in a cooperative), bank deposits and bank loans must, by necessity, be equal to each other. The last column of Table 11.1 illustrates that financial assets must have a counterpart liability, and hence that each row of financial assets must sum to zero. This is not the case for inventories, since these are a tangible asset for the firms.

Table 11.2 illustrates how the national income and product accounts can be combined with the flow-of-funds accounts. Once again, all the rows must sum to zero, ensuring that everything that goes somewhere comes from somewhere. The columns reflect the budget constraints of each set of agents. As is the tradition with flow-of-funds analysis, sources of funds carry a positive sign, while uses of funds carry a negative sign. For each agent, sources must exactly equal uses of funds. Thus, for instance, households receive wages, dividends, and interest payments on their deposits (held at the end of the previous period).

Table 11.1   Balance sheet of model DIS

	Households	Production firms	Banks	Σ
Money deposits	$+M$		$-M$	0
Loans		$-L$	$+L$	0
Inventories		$+IN$		$+IN$
Balance (net worth)	$-V_h$	0	0	$-V_h$
Σ	0	0	0	0

Source: Godley and Lavoie (2007, 285). Reproduced with permission of the licensor through PLSclear.

Table 11.2   The transactions-flow matrix of model DIS

	Households	Production firms		Banks		Σ
		Current	Capital	Current	Capital	
Consumption	$-C$	$+C$				0
Change in the value of inventories		$+\Delta IN$	$-\Delta IN$			0
Wages	$+WB$	$-WB$				0
Interest on loans		$-r_{l-1}.L_{-1}$		$+r_{l-1}.L_{-1}$		0
Entrepreneurial profits	$+F$	$-F$				0
Bank profits	$+F_b$			$-F_b$		0
Interest on deposits	$+r_{m-1}.M_{-1}$			$-r_{m-1}.M_{-1}$		0
Change in loans			$+\Delta L$		$-\Delta L$	0
Change in deposits	$-\Delta M$				$+\Delta M$	0
Σ	0	0	0	0	0	0

Source: Godley and Lavoie (2007, 285). Reproduced with permission of the licensor through PLSclear.

What they don't use for consumption expenditure must thus be used as additions to their money balances. While this is an addition to their bank deposits, the term carries a negative sign as it is a use of funds.

Looking at their current account, firms receive funds from their sales of goods to households. When production surpasses sales, there is an increase in inventories ($+\Delta IN$). The accounting convention is that the increased inventories are considered as a sale to the capital account of the firm that occurs at the production cost of the good, which explains the plus sign in the column of the current account. This can be seen when assuming that none of the produced goods have been sold to consumers. In that case, the wage bill would need to be exactly equal to the change in the value of inventories: $WB = \Delta IN$. Paid wages, interest payments on loans, and profits are uses of funds and carry a negative sign. In this simple model, there are no retained earnings, as all profits are distributed. Looking now at the capital account of firms, the sources of funds are the additions to the loans granted by banks, while the funds are used for the implicit purchase of the additional inventories.

Naturally, models and matrices that are much more complicated can be built, as we shall see later. Matrices quickly become much bigger when open-economy models are constructed. While one can simply add a column representing the rest of the world, this could only be valid when assessing a small open economy that has virtually no feedback effect on the rest of the world, as done by Raza et al. (2019). In general, if dealing with two large countries, then an economist would need to have a two-country model, with the size of the matrix thus being multiplied by two. Godley (1999b) provided the first such model—a closed model of an open economy. There are now three- and four-country SFC models, with quite varying specifications (Mazier 2020).

THE SFC APPROACH AND INSTITUTIONALISM

Post-Keynesian Institutionalists

One can argue that there are five branches of Post-Keynesian economics (Lavoie 2014): the Fundamentalist branch, associated mostly with Paul Davidson and closest to the spirit of John Maynard Keynes; the Kaleckian branch, associated of course with Michał Kalecki and Josef Steindl; the Sraffian branch, associated with Piero Sraffa, Pierangelo Garegnani, and other neo-Ricardians; the Kaldorian branch, associated with Nicholas Kaldor and Anthony Thirlwall; and the Institutionalist branch, with authors such as Frederic Lee as well as advocates of modern monetary theory (MMT), whose policy recommendations rest on detailed analyses of monetary institutions. While there are differences of emphasis between these various branches, one could argue that they all agree about the principle of effective demand and the importance of historical time.

The SFC approach is usually associated with the Kaldorian branch, since Godley was a long-time friend of Kaldor and had been brought to the University of Cambridge by Kaldor. Moreover, Godley's ideas on monetary economics, international trade, and pricing theory were all very close to those of Kaldor, and his views on the balance-of-payment constraints were similar to those of Thirlwall, who was also considered a Kaldorian economist as he had been influenced by Kaldor's views on regional economics and technical progress.

It is possible to argue, however, that Godley's economics and his stock-flow consistent approach also fit well within the Institutionalist branch of Post-Keynesian economics. First, Godley's views of pricing were heavily influenced by those of P.W.S. Andrews, who was his tutor at Oxford University. Godley himself published on pricing theory (Coutts, Godley, and Nordhaus 1978), entertaining views of cost-plus pricing and normal-cost pricing that are in the spirit of Institutionalist Post-Keynesians such as Lee (1998). In addition, the analysis of flow-of-funds accounts is part of the Institutionalist tradition and was emphasized by some Post-Keynesian authors close to the Institutionalist tradition.

While some scholars would put Minsky in the Fundamentalist camp, Whalen (2013) places him within the Institutionalist branch, insisting that his own view of PKI draws heavily on the contributions of Minsky. But Minsky, because of his concern with the details of the financial system, has also shown on several occasions that he paid attention to the stock-flow consistency most closely associated with the Kaldorian camp. One can provide a long list of statements to that effect, including the following:

- "One way every economic unit can be characterized is by its portfolio: the set of tangible and financial assets it owns and the financial liabilities on which it owes." (Minsky 1975, 70)
- "Inasmuch as the effective demand for current output by a sector is determined not only by the current income flows and current external finance but also by the sector's cash-payment commitments due to past debt, the alternative interpretation can be summarized by a theory of the determination of the effective budget constraints. The economics of the determination of the budget constraints logically precedes and sets the stage for the economics of the selection of particular items of investment and consumption." (Minsky 1975, 132)
- "An ultimate reality in a capitalist economy is the set of interrelated balance sheets among the various units. Items in the balance sheet set up cash flows." (Minsky 1975, 118)
- "The structure of an economic model that is relevant for a capitalist economy needs to include the interrelated balance sheets and income statements of the units of the economy. The principle of double entry book-keeping, where financial assets are liabilities on a balance sheet and where every entry on a balance sheet has a dual in another balance sheet, means that every transaction in assets requires four entries." (Minsky 1996, 77)

The last quote above underlines the quadruple-entry principle that was identified earlier as the fourth accounting feature of the SFC approach. All these quotes show that Minsky was concerned with an adequate understanding of the relationship between the flow of payments arising from the accumulated stocks of assets and debts. He was fully aware of the budget constraints and the constraints imposed by the relationships between the various balances. A key insight of Minsky, besides the claim that banks and other agents get euphoric after a period of tranquility, was that balance sheets are interrelated and give rise to cash commitments; this can best be represented within an explicit SFC framework.

It is fitting that many SFC models purport to represent and illustrate Minsky's financial fragility hypothesis, since the SFC approach allows integration of the real and financial systems. Minsky himself sets up a complete balance-sheet matrix in Delli Gatti, Gallegati and Minsky (1994). One may wonder if he had been influenced at the time by Godley's work, since Minsky and Godley were then together at the Levy Economics Institute. But the interest in balance-sheet relations was already there (as indicated by the quotes from the 1970s above). In fact, it was at Minsky's encouragement that his student, L. Randall Wray, who was to become the main advocate of MMT and whose work has also long been associated with the Institutionalist and Post-Keynesian traditions, made extensive use of balance sheets in a chapter of his doctoral thesis, which was later published as *Money and Credit in Capitalist Economies* (Wray 1990).

Another Post-Keynesian and Institutionalist author who was clearly concerned with stock-flow consistency is Alfred Eichner, whose work is unfortunately often overlooked. In his synthesis of Post-Keynesian economics, Eichner (1987, chapter 12) presents the endogeneity of money, the creation of loans, as well as clearinghouse and central bank operations through a balance-sheet approach, where he makes a distinction between the financial sector and two non-financial sectors. Eichner explicitly ties his approach to the flow-of-funds approach and to the work of Godley and Cripps (1983). That Eichner (1976) was also within the Institutionalist tradition is obvious from his work on pricing theory and the megacorp, for which he is best known; in addition, it can be ascertained from the subtitle of his book of essays, *Essays in Post-Keynesian and Institutionalist Theory* (Eichner 1986).

Eichner insisted that one must go beyond the standard national income and product accounts, by adding flow-of-funds accounts and the analysis of balance sheets. Flow-of-funds analysis is presented as early as chapter 2 of his monumental 1987 book, right after an introduction to national income accounts. In that book, Eichner (1987, 810–838) devotes nearly 30 pages to flow-of-funds analysis, with more than a dozen tables reproducing the consequences of various decisions by economic agents. The very first of these tables (Eichner 1987, 811) illustrates the quadruple accounting entry principle. The intent of Eichner in presenting this method is clear. He wants to convince his readers that "the amount of funds available to finance investment depends far more on the lending policies of the banks, including the central bank, than on the willingness of households to forego consumption" (Eichner 1987, 138). In his assessment of Eichner's work on monetary theory, Davidson (1992, 189) points out that Eichner "almost alone among economists—recognized that the flow-of-funds approach provides a much more useful analytical tool for explaining economic processes than the national income accounts."

The Link with Earlier Institutionalists

In his recommended readings, Eichner (1987, 108) refers to the research of Morris Copeland (1952) and that of Jacob Cohen (1972)—the latter assessing how the work of Copeland had stood the test of time. This confirms that Eichner was attempting to put together a synthesis of Cambridge Keynesian economics and Institutionalist economics, as we shall now see.

It is well-known that the study of flow of funds in the United States (US) started with the work of Copeland, which he called moneyflows. What is perhaps less known is that Copeland considered himself to be an Institutionalist, perhaps in the tradition of Wesley Clair Mitchell. As James Millar (1996, 83) puts it, "Copeland and Mitchell clearly belong to the same broad branch of American Institutionalist thought of the twentieth century, and they have been parallel influences in the development of a more quantitative and scientific economics." Most American proponents of financial-flows analysis were heterodox economists, associated more or less closely with (original) Institutionalism.[5] For instance, in the preface to his huge handbook on flow-of-funds analysis, John Dawson (1996, xxix), who was a student of Copeland, says that "the book will reveal me as an institutionalist, practical in orientation, and skeptical of economic doctrine." Dawson (1996, 5) criticizes Neoclassical economics, claiming that it "behaves as if the way toward improved economic understanding is to combine more and more theory with less and less fact." Dawson (1996, 5) further points out that "the acceptance of ... flow-of-funds accounting by academic economists has been an uphill battle because its implications run counter to a number of doctrines deeply embedded in the minds of economists," and he adds that Copeland, who is considered to be the inventor of flow-of-funds accounts, "was at pains to show the incompatibility of the quantity theory of money with flow-of-funds accounting."

Similarly, Millar (1996, 85) claims that "Copeland always proudly proclaimed his commitment to institutionalism. For this reason, and because of his unswerving adherence to a neutral science point of view, Copeland has never been fully accepted into the mainstream of economics. Ironically, neither is Copeland fully recognized today as an institutionalist." Indeed, the subtitle of Copeland's (1958) collected papers is *The Testament of an Institutionalist.* Copeland could also almost be recognized as an early radical Post-Keynesian. First, Copeland had a full-scale battle against the equation of exchange and the quantity theory of money, just like Post-Keynesians, including Kaldor, went to war against monetarism and the assumption of exogenous money. In addition, Copeland argued that Keynes's *General Theory* was more of a *reformation* than a *revolution* and that "the changes Keynes introduced represented modifications of neoclassicism, not its rejection." Millar (1996, 90) also recalls that "in the late 1950s Copeland frequently suggested in his graduate course at Cornell University that Keynes was being brought back into the neoclassical church." This assessment is nearly identical to the one made by Kaldor (1982, 21) many years later, when he argued that Keynes's solution "was a *modification* of the quantity theory of money, not its *abandonment.*"

There are, no doubt, several other links between flow-of-funds analysis and Institutionalists or PKI. One link I know of is the work of James Earley, from the University of California, Riverside. I was in touch with Earley in the mid-1980s, as a consequence of my analysis of endogenous money. Earley sent me some of his writings, including a 1976 paper he published with Robert Parsons and Fred Thompson, which was reproduced in the flow-of-funds handbook edited by Dawson. As well expressed in their introduction,

> [T]he major theses of this paper are two: First, in a modern financial economy such as the US, changes in credit flows are the primary financial variables causing changes in total money spending on goods and services. Second, in such an economy changes in the money stock as commonly defined play only a secondary role. (Earley, Parsons, and Thompson 1996, 156)

This was clearly an attack on monetarism, and relied on the use of a flow-of-funds analysis.[6]

INSTITUTIONAL EXEMPLARS OF THE SFC APPROACH

Macedo e Silva and Dos Santos (2011, 106) claim that

> institutionally rich stock-flow consistent (SFC) models—i.e. models that identify economic agents with the main social categories/institutional sectors of actual capitalist economies, thoroughly describe these agents' short period behaviour, and consistently model the "period by period" balance sheet dynamics implied by the latter—are ... a crucial contribution to the consolidation of the broad post-Keynesian research programme.

At the time, Macedo e Silva and Dos Santos feared that many Post-Keynesians remained skeptical about the worth of SFC models despite their observation that the SFC approach was an active area of research in Post-Keynesian economics. This section attempts to provide some additional arguments to those who would still show some reluctance to accept the worth of this approach. To do so, we shall only provide exemplars of the balance-sheet matrix, assessing how financialization has affected the representation of the financial system and its relationship with the real economy. This seems to be an appropriate goal because, in his review of Godley and Lavoie (2007), Taylor (2008, 643–644) questioned whether the SFC approach could handle the main features of financialization and its financial innovations, which became known as the shadow banking system.

While it is always easier to propose a balance-sheet matrix that takes into account the main financial institutions than it is to actually build the corresponding SFC model and get it to run, the design of the appropriate stock matrix is not necessarily an obvious task. Different scholars have come up with different setups, depending on their understanding of the mechanisms underneath the various institutions of the shadow banking system. Indeed, as long as one does not yet try to get a full model going, one can create as complicated a balance-sheet matrix as one wishes.

A First Attempt following the Subprime Financial Crisis

Right after the subprime financial crisis, I tried to design a simple stock-matrix representation of the financial system that had led to the crisis. Table 11.3 reproduces exactly the balance sheet matrix that can be found in Lavoie (2009) and that was presented at the Berlin Keynesian conference in October 2008, organized by the Forum for Macroeconomics and Macroeconomic Policies.

At the time, I benefitted from the balance-sheet matrix posted by Gennaro Zezza (2008), who introduced housing and mortgages in an SFC model, but with two classes of households. Recall that assets carry a positive sign, while liabilities carry a negative sign. The peculiarity of my stock matrix compared to that of Zezza's as well as all previous ones is that I consider two sets of financial institutions—commercial banks and investment banks, the latter, the reader may recall, having run into all kinds of trouble during the subprime financial crisis. The investment banks in this representation are the shadow banking system. Investment banks don't grant loans or mortgages, in contrast to commercial banks.

The households column shows that while they take on mortgages (MO) to finance their homes, they hold demand deposits and term deposits. The investment bank column shows that investment banks purchase mortgage-based securities (MBS), s sets of such securities, each carrying the market-determined price p_s. To finance these MBS, investment banks are assumed to attract term deposits from households, presumably at some desirable interest rate. It is assumed, however, that the funds so drawn are insufficient to finance all the MBS desired by the investment banks, which are thus forced to engage in repo operations (R) with the banks, which grant them funds based on the MBS collateral offered by the investment banks.

Table 11.3   A balance-sheet matrix with mortgage-based securities

	Households	Firms	Commercial banks	Investment banks	Central bank	Σ
Productive capital		$+K_f$				$+K_f$
Homes	$+p_h.h_h$					$+K_h$
Cash			$+HPM_b$		$-HPM$	0
Advances			$-A$		$+A$	0
Deposits	$+D_h$		$-D$			0
Term deposits	$+TD_h$			$-TD$		
Loans		$-L_f$	$+L$			0
Repos			$+R$	$-R$		
Mortgages	$-MO_h$		$+MO$			0
Mortgage-based securities			$-p_s.s$	$+p_s.s$		0
Net worth	$-NW_h$	$-NW_f$	$-NW_b$	$-NW_{ib}$	0	$-K_h-K_f$
Σ	0	0	0	0	0	0

Source: Lavoie (2009).

Commercial banks constitute the category that has the most complex design. On the asset side, banks hold reserves (HPM_h) at the central bank, make loans to firms, provide mortgages to households, and furnish collateralized loans (repos) to the investment banks. On the liability side, besides the deposits of households, it is assumed that banks take advances from the central bank so as to hold enough reserves. Banks are assumed to issue mortgage-based securities, which, in this setup, remain on their balance sheet.

The Analysis of Botta, Caverzasi, and Tori

Another way to represent the shadow banking system is found in the work by Alberto Botta, Eugenio Caverzasi, and Daniele Tori (2020).[7] They provide an assessment of the macroeconomics of shadow banking from a Post-Keynesian perspective, starting from an alternative balance-sheet matrix, shown here in Table 11.4. An obvious difference from the previous stock matrix is that the household sector is split into two categories—the workers and the rentiers. As in Table 11.3, there are two kinds of financial institutions, which Botta and his co-authors call commercial banks and financial firms, the latter taking the role of investment banks. There are also many other similarities. For example, commercial banks make collateralized loans (the repos) to the investment

Table 11.4   An alternative balance-sheet matrix

	Workers	Rentiers	Firms	Commercial banks	Investment banks	Central bank	Σ
Capital			$+K_f$				$+K_f$
Homes	$+p_h h_h$						$+K_h$
Cash				$+HPM_b$	$+HPM_{ib}$	$+HPM$	0
Deposits	$+D$			$-D$			0
Mortgages	$-MO$			$+(1-z)MO$	$+zMO$		0
Loans			$-L$	$+L$			0
CDO		$+CDO_r$	$+CDO_f$		$-CDO$		0
Repos				$+R$	$-R$		0
Equities		$+E$		$-E_b$	$-E_{ib}$		0
Net worth	$-NW_w$	$-NW_r$	$-NW_f$	$-NW_b$	$-NW_{ib}$	$-NW_{cb}$	$-K_h$ $-K_f$
Σ	0	0	0	0	0	0	0

Source: Botta, Caverzasi, and Tori (2020, 168), notation adapted by the author. Reproduced with permission of the licensor through PLSclear.

banks; working households hold deposits at commercial banks; and both kinds of banks hold reserves at the central bank.

The main interesting institutional feature of Botta, Caverzasi, and Tori's (2020) stock matrix is the way securitization has been handled. They assume that a proportion z of the mortgages is being passed on to the investment banks (the financial institutions), thus reducing by a percentage $1-z$ the amount of mortgages left on the balance sheet of commercial banks. This representation is more faithful to the way securitization proceeded before the subprime financial crisis than what was shown in Table 11.3, since the main purpose of financialization was for banks to reduce their capital adequacy requirements by removing assets with high capital requirements—the mortgages. In Table 11.4, the mortgage-based securities are replaced by collateralized debt obligations (CDOs), which in addition to mortgages could be based on other kinds of loans, such as car loans, other consumer loans, credit card loans or corporate loans. Here the CDOs are issued by the investment banks, and it is assumed that they are purchased by the rentier households and by firms, which are both looking for assets with high rates of return.

Botta, Caverzasi, and Tori (2020) also assume that both commercial and investment banks issue stock market equities (E), which are purchased by rentiers. They could have assumed as well that production firms also issue shares. This is a minor issue. There is a more puzzling anomaly in their stock matrix:

while the central bank has the reserves of banks on its liability side, the asset side is empty. Central banks hold no assets! With the government absent from the matrix, as it also was in Table 11.3, the authors should have assumed that the central bank provides advances to commercial banks, so as to close their matrix in a proper way.

Beyond Botta, Caverzasi, and Tori

As Botta, Caverzasi, and Tori (2020, 167) themselves recognize, their model and balance-sheet matrix do not incorporate some institutions that played a role in the 2008 debacle. In particular, there are no special purpose vehicles (SPVs), no structured investment vehicles (SIVs), no hedge funds, and no money market funds (MMFs).[8] However, as long as we don't intend to produce a full-scale SFC model and get it running, we can certainly build a balance-sheet matrix that could include all, or at least most, of the actors of the shadow banking system. Table 11.5 shows how such a stock matrix could look, in an attempt to provide an institutionally rich balance sheet of the economy.[9]

The matrix keeps the innovations introduced by Botta, Caverzasi, and Tori (2020), that is, the fact that a proportion z_1 of the mortgages that have been granted are being dispatched to an SPV, along with a proportion z_2 of other kinds of loans, such as consumer loans or corporate loans (L). All these dispatched loans are then securitized and issued as asset-based securities (*ABS*) or collateralized debt obligations (CDOs). The SPVs could also transform the loans into short-term securities, but this has mostly been done by SIVs, or conduits, thus acting as pure financial intermediaries by financing their purchases of ABS and CDOs by issuing asset-based corporate paper (ABCP), the rate of return of which is lower than that of the longer-term ABS. The ABCP was purchased mainly by money market funds and firms disposing of excess liquidity and in search of higher yields than those of government treasury bills. The shadow banking system is thus based on an appropriate structure of interest rate differentials.

The appearance of money market funds is an innovation of Table 11.5 relative to previous stock matrices. They attract funds provided by firms and households; hold a series of assets (bank deposits, treasury bills, corporate paper issued by firms in need of funding, and asset-based corporate paper); and provide repos (R) to investment banks. Also, in contrast to previous stock matrices, the balance sheet matrix of Table 11.5 includes the government sector, which issues treasury bills. These, being safe assets, are purchased by most financial institutions and by producing firms. Finally, we can see that the central bank also holds government bonds and provides advances to the commercial banking system; on its liability side, the central bank provides deposit

Table 11.5 An extended balance-sheet matrix incorporating the shadow banking system

	Households	Firms	Commercial banks	Investment banks	SPV	SIV conduits	Money market funds	Central bank	Govt	Σ
Tangible Capital	$+K$									$+K$
Inventories		$+IN$								$+IN$
Homes	$+p_h h_h$									$+p_h h_h$
Cash	$+HPM_h$		$+HPM_b$					$-HPM_{cb}$	$+HPM_g$	0
Deposits	$+D_h$		$-D$	$+D_{ib}$			$+D_{mmf}$			0
MM funds	$+MMF_h$	$+MMF_f$					$-MMF$			0
Mortgages	$-MO$		$+(1-z_1)MO$		$+z_1 MO$					0
Loans	$-L_h$	$-L_f$	$+(1-z_2)L$		$+z_2 L$					0
ABS/CDO				$+ABS_{ib}$	$-ABS$	$+ABS_{siv}$				0
ABCP		$+ABCP_f$				$-ABCP$	$+ABCP_{mmf}$			0
Repos			$+R_b$	$-R_{ib}$			$+R_{mmf}$			0
Corporate paper		$-CP$	$+CP_b$				$+CP_{mmf}$			0
Equities	$+p_e e_h$	$-p_e e_f$	$-p_e e_b$	$-p_e e_{ib}$						0
T-bills		$+TB_f$	$+TB_b$	$+TB_{ib}$			$+TB_{mmf}$	$+TB_{cb}$	$-TB$	0
Advances			$-A$					$+A$		0
Net worth	$-NW_h$	$-NW_f$	$-NW_b$	$-NW_{ib}$	$-NW_{spv}$	$-NW_{siv}$	$-NW_{mmf}$	$-NW_{cb}$	$-NW_g$	$-(K+IN$ $+p_h h_h)$

Source: Author.

accounts to the government and to commercial banks, on top of providing cash to the household sector. This shows that it is not overly difficult to build a relatively complex balance-sheet matrix, which provides a detailed institutional picture. The challenge would be to create and run an SFC model based on such a large number of assets and liabilities.

CONCLUSION

In this chapter, I have described the main characteristics of the stock-flow consistent (SFC) approach advocated by Godley (1999a) and Godley and Lavoie (2007). I have provided a short history of the approach and reviewed some of the controversies that the name of this approach has generated. I have discussed how the SFC approach is related to a number of Post-Keynesian writers, in particular those who have a connection with PKI, through their use of flow of funds. I have further argued that flow-of-funds analysis was endorsed and even created by *original* Institutionalist authors, and hence one could argue that the SFC approach ought to enhance PKI. I have further provided examples of how a specific institutional feature of modern economies—the shadow banking system—has been described in different ways through the balance-sheet matrix, and how several additional institutional details could be incorporated in that matrix. In short, SFC modeling provides a method of macroeconomic analysis fully in line with the Post-Keynesian Institutionalist perspective and its aim of better understanding the role of financial institutions in real-world capitalist economies.

ACKNOWLEDGMENTS

I wish to thank Louis-Philippe Rochon, Charles Whalen and Michael Radzicki for their numerous comments and suggestions.

NOTES

1. See *Cambridge Journal of Economics* (n.d.).
2. Dos Santos (2006) and Godley and Lavoie (2007) recall previous works that could be said to have been in this tradition.
3. Whalen (2013, 18) also recalls that Tobin, just like Godley, emphasized the need to check the balance sheets of households, firms, and the government.
4. The same could be said about numerous SFC models constructed by Peter Flaschel and his many collaborators, as they contain Neoclassical assumptions, such as exogenous money. Some of their models, however, are barely distinguishable from Post-Keynesian models.
5. By *original* Institutionalism, I mean Institutional economics in the tradition of Thorstein Veblen, John R. Commons, Wesley Mitchell, Walton Hamilton, John M. Clark, and other early Institutionalists, a tradition that differs consid-

erably from much of today's more mainstream-oriented "New" Institutional economics, which often traces its roots to the work of Douglass North and Oliver Williamson.

6. Earley had some influence on Robert Pollin, a young colleague at the time, and a radical Post-Keynesian, who cited Earley's papers of the 1980s. As an aside, it should be said that Earley did not fully manage to get rid of the orthodox view of the money supply process, still believing that reserves were a constraint on the creation of bank loans, thus explaining money endogeneity through financial innovation and the existence of liability management instead of reverse causation, as would Kaldor and Godley. This modification of exogenous money theory was called structural endogeneity by Pollin (1991) and it initiated the structuralist versus horizontalist controversy on the money supply process among Post-Keynesians.

7. Sawyer and Veronese Passarella (2017) have a similar balance-sheet matrix, but with a simplified list of assets.

8. Caverzasi, Botta, and Capelli (2019), however, do include special purpose vehicles and mutual funds to commercial banks and investment banks.

9. The conception of the matrix has benefitted from extensive discussions with Mehmet Uluğ, a visiting doctoral student from the University of Siena.

REFERENCES

Backus, David, William C. Brainard, Gary Smith and James Tobin. 1980. "A Model of U.S. Financial and Nonfinancial Economic Behavior." *Journal of Money, Credit, and Banking* 12 (2): 259–293.

Botta, Alberto, Eugenio Caverzasi, and Daniele Tori. 2020. "The Macroeconomics of Shadow Banking." *Macroeconomic Dynamics* 24 (1): 161–190.

Cambridge Journal of Economics. n.d. "Stock Flow Consistent Macroeconomics." https://academic.oup.com/cje/pages/sfc_macro_economics. Accessed August 11, 2021.

Carnevali, Emilio, Matteo Deleidi, Riccardo Pariboni, and Marco Veronese Passarella. 2019. "Stock-Flow Consistent Dynamic Models: Features, Limitations, and Developments." In *Frontiers of Heterodox Macroeconomics*, edited by Philip Arestis and Malcolm Sawyer, 223–276. Basingstoke, UK: Palgrave Macmillan.

Caverzasi, Eugenio, Alberto Botta, and Clara Capelli. 2019. "Shadow Banking and the Financial Side of Financialisation." *Cambridge Journal of Economics* 43 (4): 1029–1051.

Cohen, Jacob. 1972. "Copeland's Moneyflows after Twenty-Five Years: A Survey." *Journal of Economic Literature* 10 (1): 1–25.

Copeland, Morris A. 1952. *A Study of Moneyflows in the United States.* New York: Bureau of Economic Research.

Copeland, Morris A. 1958. *Fact and Theory in Economics: The Testament of an Institutionalist*, edited and with an introduction by Chandler Morse. Ithaca, NY: Cornell University Press.

Coutts, Ken, Wynne Godley and William D. Nordhaus. 1978. *Industrial Pricing in the United Kingdom.* Cambridge: Cambridge University Press.

Davidson, P. 1992. "Eichner's Approach to Money and Macrodynamics." In *The Megacorp and Macrodynamics: Essays in Memory of Alfred Eichner*, edited by William Milberg, 185–192. Armonk, New York: M.E. Sharpe.

Dawson, John C. (ed.). 1996. *Flow-of-Funds Analysis: A Handbook for Practitioners*. Armonk, New York: M.E. Sharpe.

Delli Gatti, Domenico, Mauro Gallegati and Hyman P. Minsky. 1994. "Financial Institutions, Economic Policy and the Dynamic Behaviour of the Economy." Jerome Levy Economics Institute, Working Paper No. 126.

Dos Santos, Claudio H. 2006. "Keynesian Theorising During Hard Times: Stock-Flow Consistent Models as an Unexplored Frontier of Keynesian Macroeconomics." *Cambridge Journal of Economics* 30 (4): 541–565.

Dos Santos, Claudio H. 2021. "A Passionate Craftsman and His Craft: Reflections on Wynne Godley's Work and Legacy." *Journal of Post Keynesian Economics* 44 (1): 46–56.

Earley, James S., Robert J. Parsons, and Fred A. Thompson. (1976) 1996. "Source and Use Analytics." In *Flow-of-Funds Analysis: A Handbook for Practitioners*, edited by John C. Dawson, 156–182. Armonk, New York: M.E. Sharpe.

Eichner, Alfred S. 1976. *The Megacorp and Oligopoly*. Cambridge: Cambridge University Press.

Eichner, Alfred S. 1986. *Toward a New Economics: Essays in Post-Keynesian and Institutionalist Theory*. London: Macmillan.

Eichner, Alfred S. 1987. *The Macrodynamics of Advanced Market Economies*. Armonk, New York: M.E. Sharpe.

Godley, Wynne. 1996. "Money, Finance and National Income Determination: An Integrated Approach." Jerome Levy Economics Institute, Working Paper No. 167.

Godley, Wynne. 1999a. "Money and Credit in a Keynesian Model of Income Determination." *Cambridge Journal of Economics* 23 (4), 393–411.

Godley, Wynne. 1999b. "Open Economy Macroeconomics Using Models of Closed Systems." Jerome Levy Economics Institute, Working Paper No. 281.

Godley, Wynne and Francis Cripps. (1983). *Macroeconomics*. Oxford: Oxford University Press.

Godley, Wynne and Marc Lavoie. (2007). *Monetary Economics: An Integrated Approach to Credit, Money, Income, Production and Wealth*. Basingstoke, UK: Palgrave Macmillan.

Kaldor, Nicholas. 1982. *The Scourge of Monetarism*. Oxford: Oxford University Press.

Kalecki, Michał. 1971. *Selected Essays on the Dynamics of the Capitalist Economy*. Cambridge: Cambridge University Press.

Lavoie, Marc. 2009. "Towards a Post-Keynesian Consensus in Macroeconomics: Reconciling the Cambridge and Wall Street Views." In *Macroeconomic Policies on Shaky Foundations – Wither Mainstream Economics?*, edited by Eckhard Hein, Torsten Niechoj, and Engelbert Stockhammer, 75–99. Marburg, Germany: Metropolis Verlag.

Lavoie, Marc. 2014. *Post-Keynesian Economics: New Foundations*. Cheltenham, UK: Edward Elgar.

Lavoie, Marc. 2021. "Godley Versus Tobin on Monetary Matters." *Review of Keynesian Economics* 10 (1): 1–24.

Lee, Frederic S. 1998. *Post Keynesian Price Theory*. Cambridge: Cambridge University Press.

Macedo e Silva, Antonio C. and Claudio H. Dos Santos. 2011. "Peering Over the Edge of the Short-Period? The Keynesian Roots of Stock-Flow Consistent Macroeconomic Models." *Cambridge Journal of Economics* 35 (1): 105–124.

Mazier, Jacques. 2020. *Global Imbalances and Financial Capitalism: Stock-Flow-Consistent Modelling*. London: Routledge.

Millar, James R. 1996. "Institutionalist Origins." In *Flow-of-Funds Analysis: A Handbook for Practitioners*, edited by John C. Dawson, 83–92. Armonk, New York: M.E. Sharpe.

Minsky, Hyman P. 1975. *John Maynard Keynes*. New York: Columbia University Press.

Minsky, Hyman P. 1996. "The Essential Characteristics of Post Keynesian Economics." In *Money in Motion: The Post Keynesian and Circulation Approaches*, edited by Ghislain Deleplace and Edward J. Nell, 70–88. London: Macmillan.

Nikiforos, Michalis and Gennaro Zezza. 2017. "Stock-Flow Consistent Macroeconomics Models: A Survey." *Journal of Economic Surveys* 31 (5): 1204–1239.

Pollin, Robert. 1991. "Two Theories of Money Supply Endogeneity." *Journal of Post Keynesian Economics* 13 (1): 366–396.

Raza, Hamid, Bjorn R. Gudmundsson, Gylfi Zoega, and Mikael R. Byrialsen. 2019. "Crises and Capital Controls in Small Open Economies: A Stock-Flow Consistent Approach." *European Journal of Economics and Economic Policies: Intervention* 16 (1): 94–133.

Sawyer, Malcolm and M. Veronese Passarella. 2017. "The Monetary Circuit in the Age of Financialisation: A Stock-Flow Consistent Model with a Twofold Banking Sector." *Metroeconomica* 68 (2): 321–353.

Shipman, Alan. 2019. "Stock-Flow Consistent Macroeconomics—The Foundations." https://academic.oup.com/cje/pages/sfc_macro_economics

Taylor, Lance. 2008. "A Foxy Hedgehog: Wynne Godley and Macroeconomic Modelling." *Cambridge Journal of Economics* 32 (4): 639–663.

Whalen, Charles J. 2013. "Post-Keynesian Institutionalism and the Great Recession." *European Journal of Economics and Economic Policies: Intervention* 10 (1): 12–27.

Wray, L. Randall. 1990. *Money and Credit in Capitalist Economies: The Endogenous Money Approach*. Aldershot, UK: Edward Elgar.

Zezza, Gennaro. 2008. "US Growth, the Housing Market, and the Distribution of Income." *Journal of Post Keynesian Economics* 30 (3): 375–401.

PART IV

Theories and syntheses

12. The market for labor in Post-Keynesian Institutionalism: a theoretical framework

Eduardo Fernández-Huerga

INTRODUCTION

Labor economics has occupied an important place within Institutional economics since that tradition's earliest days. Drawing on Kaufman (2004), it is possible to identify four generations within labor Institutionalism, broadly defined. The first generation includes authors such as Beatrice and Sidney Webb, Richard Ely, Selig Perlman, Wesley Mitchell, John R. Commons, and Thorstein Veblen, who often brought a historical perspective to their work and occupied a prominent place in economic thought through the 1930s. The second generation, which focused mainly on the "web of rules" that structure labor market outcomes, dominated the scene during the 1940s and 1950s, and included Richard Lester, John Dunlop, Clark Kerr, Lloyd Reynolds, Charles Myers, Lloyd Fisher, Arthur Ross, and Robert Livernash. The third generation, of the 1960s and 1970s, explored structural unemployment, crafted employment and training policies, developed dual labor market theory, and highlighted overlaps with Post Keynesian economics; it includes economists such as Charles Killingsworth, Ray Marshall, Michael Piore, Peter Doeringer, Barry Bluestone, and Eileen Appelbaum (for more on that generation's work on dual labor markets, see Ramstad 1993). Finally, the fourth generation, which has developed since the 1980s, includes various authors including Deborah Figart, Oren Levin-Waldman, Paul Osterman, and Thomas Kochan, whose work has often intersected with gender studies, political science, industrial and labor relations, organizational studies, and human resources management.

Although it is possible to find various common elements of methodology and content in the work of the four generations, the idea still persists—especially among mainstream economists—that the main link within and across the generations lies in the rejection of orthodox economic theory, not in the development of Institutional theory. Taking a more sanguine view,

Kaufman (2004) argues that labor Institutionalists are united by shared normative commitments on how theory should be constructed. To be sure, Kaufman acknowledges Institutionalists' rejection of the traditional microeconomic model of demand and supply in competitive markets, but he also identifies six other intellectual links that connect the four generations: (1) emphasis on the analysis of persistent "imbalances," such as involuntary unemployment or wage and occupational differences; (2) acceptance of the view (held by Keynes as well as the Institutionalists) that the labor market is not self-balancing, and that its function is not to set a single wage rate that determines the level of employment; (3) the idea that an alternative theory must start from models of the behavior of individuals and companies that are more realistic than the orthodox models; (4) the idea that any theory about the labor market should emphasize identifying the institutions that determine what happens in the labor market; (5) the belief that an alternative theory must be multidisciplinary; and (6) commitment to a humanistic set of welfare criteria that includes efficiency but also other ethical goals.

Employment and unemployment also occupy a central place in Post Keynesian economics, but Post Keynesians have not devoted much attention to developing a consistent framework for labor market analysis. In large part, that is because Post Keynesians have focused on the study of employment from the *macroeconomic* level, leaving in the background microeconomic labor-market issues (King 2002). In fact, for many Post Keynesians *the labor market* "does not truly exist" (Lavoie 2015, 275), by which they mean that it is "not a true market" (Appelbaum 1979, 39) in the sense that wages and employment levels are not determined simultaneously by a process of price adjustment. According to the Post Keynesian approach, employment and wages are influenced by different considerations and determined separately (King 1990).

Despite some Post Keynesian skepticism about the notion of a labor *market*, efforts to integrate Institutionalist and Post Keynesian approaches to the study of labor and employment are not new. In fact, Appelbaum (1979) pointed in the direction of a Post-Keynesian Institutionalist labor framework several decades ago when she proposed combining the basic principles of Post Keynesian economics in the field of labor demand with the Institutionalists' contributions on labor supply via their theory of labor market segmentation. It is also possible to find research publications that could easily be classified as labor economics from a Post-Keynesian Institutionalist perspective. For example, although no express reference was made to Post-Keynesian Institutionalism (PKI), the "anthropogenic" or "human development" approach to labor economics proposed by Eichner (1979) can be considered—with respect to both methodology and content—one of the first and most solid contributions in this ambit. Moreover, Seccareccia (1991) explicitly outlined a Post-Keynesian Institutionalist model of the labor market, which relies on the Institutionalists' segmentation approach on the labor demand side and Eichner's (1979) anthropogenic approach on the labor supply side.

Today, growing interest in PKI underscores the value of building a Post-Keynesian Institutionalist framework for the labor market. Thus, this chapter seeks to sketch the main elements of such a framework. Because such a theoretical construction must be consistent with the ontological and epistemological foundations of PKI, its starting point must be a holistic, organic vision of reality. There must also be recognition that fundamental uncertainty is ever-present, and that reality is transmutable (evolutionary), owing to such factors as human agency, conflict, and power (Brazelton and Whalen 2011; Lawson 1994). In this context, the goal of theorizing is to find the causal mechanisms (associated with the tendencies or powers that govern the flow of events in an open system, not with universal laws) that underlie the observed phenomena and can explain their existence and evolution. Moreover, in the search for causal explanations, special attention should be paid to the interaction between institutions and human agency.

Given that what happens in the labor market—and in the workplace in general—implies a relationship between individuals and employers, especially corporations, the Post-Keynesian Institutionalist labor market framework must include a model of the behavior of those economic agents that fits with the foundations of PKI. For example, the behavior model of human beings must recognize that individuals have limited cognitive and reasoning capacities and that they act and make their decisions in a world subject to the presence of uncertainty. Similarly, an alternative approach to business enterprise is necessary—one that not only fits with the Post-Keynesian Institutionalist vision of human beings, but that also highlights firms' internal organizational structure and recognizes the diversity of activities that firms undertake in an uncertain environment.

The rest of this chapter develops a Post-Keynesian Institutionalist conception of the labor market along the lines just described. At the same time, the exposition is organized in a manner that parallels how such an analysis is usually approached in conventional economics. In other words, we examine labor supply, labor demand, and then the labor market as a whole.

LABOR SUPPLY

The Relationship between Human Motivation and the Conception of Work

We begin by examining what motivates people to offer their labor and what they receive in return. The Neoclassical model approaches labor supply decisions within a framework guided by a single purpose: utility maximization. In pursuit of that end, humans are confronted by *work* that is believed to generate a loss of utility (Budd 2011), but that also provides *income*, which enables a gain of utility through future consumption.

The construction of an alternative vision of labor supply should be based on a more realistic concept of human beings and their motivation, along with a more complete vision of what work can contribute to individual well-being (Fernández-Huerga et al. 2017). PKI is associated with a more complex motivation model (Fernández-Huerga 2008; Hodgson 1988; Lavoie 2015). It recognizes that human behavior is directed toward the *satisfaction* (in contrast to maximization) of several *differentiated*—and more or less hierarchical—*goals*, which are linked to the full range of human needs and wants (Lutz and Lux 1979; Hodgson 1988; Lavoie 2015). Because goals are driven by various purposes and values, they might not be substitutable and are often difficult to compare, especially in any rigorous and quantitative manner (Lutz and Lux 1979; Reisman 2002; Lavoie 2015). Further, individuals identify needs and wants—and determine what is satisfactory—by means of *cognitive processes* that are conditioned by their socio-institutional environment (Hodgson 1988; Simon 1979). Some human aims are of a material nature (i.e., their satisfaction implies the consumption of goods and services), but others are of a non-material nature, both personal and social (Eichner 1979; Lutz and Lux 1979; Maslow 1954; Reisman 2002). The latter are not satisfied through consumption, but through some kind of action, that is, by means of "doing" or "interrelating" with others.

Thus, PKI conceives of work as something that can bring various returns to an individual (Budd 2011; Eichner 1979; Fernández-Huerga et al. 2017; Kaufman 1998; Spencer 2006; 2011). It provides an income and, therefore, a means of meeting material needs. In addition, it can satisfy non-material needs, such as personal development, self-esteem, social belonging, purposeful activity (which connects with the Veblenian notion of "instinct of workmanship"), and approval or appreciation from others. It also provides a way to use and maintain acquired capabilities, as well as to develop new ones (Appelbaum 1979; Eichner 1979; Spencer 2006).

The Individual Contribution to Work

Another dimension of labor supply is what a worker actually contributes when performing work activity. Perhaps the most obvious contribution of a worker is his/her *time*. But PKI does not assume that this contribution is a result of choices made freely and voluntarily, guided by personal desires, and situated in a context in which one has full discretion (Spencer 2015). To the contrary, in the real world the length of the working day, like any other feature of a work relation, is the result of some type of "negotiation" (explicit or implicit) between an employer and employee, conditioned on the distribution of power and the prevailing institutional environment (Lavoie 2015; Robinson 1937; Spencer 2006). The institutional framework conditions the process of determining the working day; it shapes choices on the length of the working day by determining what is legal, acceptable, normal, and legitimate, and what is not.

Individuals engaged in work also contribute their knowledge and skills—in other words, they contribute their *competences* and productive capabilities. This may seem similar to the idea put forward in the theory of human capital, according to which individuals contribute their skills. However, both the origin and nature of these capabilities are different from those assumed by orthodox economics.[1] The competences that individuals provide can be of different types but, in general, they are usually a matter of knowledge as well as intellectual and practical skills (Eichner 1979; Nelson and Winter 1982). Thus, PKI must consider how the cognitive process develops in the real world. In a world characterized by the presence of fundamental uncertainty and humans' cognitive limitations, the formation of knowledge and the learning process are—at least in part—social acts, which require habits of thinking as well as interpretations conditioned by the institutional environment (Hodgson 1997). In this context, individuals form knowledge and acquire competencies through social affiliation (such as family, school, and employment organizations) (Eichner 1979; Hodgson 1998a; 2003).

An additional type of work contribution is *effort*. In orthodox economics, effort is often seen through the lens of a narrow conception of both human motivation and the content of work: work provides disutility and motivation appears to be guided by the selfish principles that define moral risk or opportunism. This leads to a portrayal of workers as necessarily lazy, spiteful beings (Spencer 2011), who will surely shirk in the absence of adequate control mechanisms. In contrast, PKI highlights three observations. First, it is a distortion of reality to believe that workers will always strive to reduce their efforts or that they will behave spitefully (Spencer 2011); we cannot even assume that workers' goals will necessarily conflict with those of the firm. Second, although wages can play an important role in uniting worker and employer interests, remuneration is not the only external incentive, and external stimuli are not the only engines of human motivation (Eichner 1979). Third, both an individual's needs and wants and their aspirational intensities are products of cognitive, culturally conditioned processes (Hodgson 1988; Kaufman 1989); this opens the possibility that a business, through its web of institutions, can not only establish the effort level considered appropriate for a given job, but also influence worker motivation and, consequently, shape work effort (Hodgson 1988; Kaufman 1989; Lavoie 2015; Nelson and Winter 1982; Seccareccia 1991). In fact, shirking is meaningless and cannot occur without the existence of work rules and norms (Fleetwood, 2017).

The Process of Decision-making Regarding Labor Supply

Just as consumption decisions cannot be addressed without reference to the available goods and services, labor supply decisions cannot be addressed without reference to the available jobs. Individuals offer their "work" (time, competences, and effort) in exchange for certain benefits encapsulated in jobs. The attributes and benefits of employment have various dimensions that may affect, in different ways, a person's needs and wants. For example, in addition to remuneration, work hours, and the effort required, these attributes may include opportunities to achieve personal growth, forge social relations, and acquire and develop new skills (Spencer 2015).

This multidimensional nature of jobs should be linked to the human motivation structure. However, as we have noted, each individual has a set of differentiated needs and wants, some of which are given a higher priority than others at any moment in time, and endeavors to satisfy them through work and other activities. Thus, there is normally no simple and direct relation between what an individual seeks and what can be offered by different jobs; instead, there is a much more complex interrelation.

PKI points out that these decisions tend to be made using some kind of lexicographic criteria (Lavoie 2015; Lutz and Lux 1979); that is, each attribute is evaluated more or less separately and sequentially, according to the order derived from the structure of priorities that characterizes the motivation of the individual. This order should not be considered perfect, consistent, or stable; after all, identifying priorities is a cognitive process, conditioned by the limitations of the human being. Furthermore, the individual constructs for each job attribute a level of aspiration that allows him/her to distinguish what is satisfactory from what is not (Hodgson 1988; Lavoie 2015; Simon 1979). Since these levels of aspiration depend on the evolving knowledge that individuals develop about what is desirable or achievable, they are not exogenous or static. Rather, they have an adaptive nature and depend, for example, on an individual's previous experiences and on the results obtained by other individuals in one's reference groups (Hodgson, 1988; Kaufman 1989; Lavoie 2015; Simon 1979).

In the case of labor-supply decisions, the wage rate is usually considered a high-priority job attribute. One of the first aims of a labor-supply decision is generally to obtain a satisfactory level of remuneration. Once a particular job provides a satisfactory wage, it may be that an individual would then turn his/her attention to other job attributes. This is not to say that the individual does not want a higher wage; it simply means that the ranking of this attribute within his/her list of priorities has been overtaken by attributes that fulfill other needs.

Another relevant issue is that labor supply decisions are subject to the presence of fundamental uncertainty. Post-Keynesian Institutionalists recognize that individuals do not know all the available jobs, the full range of job attributes, or how such attributes will evolve in the future. Furthermore, individuals also do not have perfect knowledge about their own needs and wants and how they will change over time.

The presence of uncertainty has multiple consequences for labor-supply decisions, of which we will mention three. First, these decisions depend not only on knowledge that has been constructed, but also on the trust placed in an individual's knowledge and expectations (Dequech 1999; Fernández-Huerga 2008; Keynes 1936). This assumes that the origin or source of knowledge is important for decision-making. Second, any decision-making process is accompanied by a certain degree of doubt, which must be overcome (or at least temporarily put aside) for a decision to be adopted (Dequech 1999; Fernández-Huerga 2008; Keynes 1936). This fact leads us to recognize that individuals' psychological features and emotions play an important role in labor-supply decisions (just as they do in the case of investment decisions) so that, for example, there may be some individuals more predisposed than others to changing jobs. The third consequence is that the presence of fundamental uncertainty is ontologically linked to an open conception of reality. In this context, a recognition that reality is transmutable and that the future is yet to be created means incorporating the possibility that economic agents will be creative and even try to influence their environment (Dequech 2006). In other words, individuals are not necessarily limited to offering their work and choosing among available job options; they can also try to create new options or modify existing ones, either by taking action on their own or by seeking to alter the existing institutional framework.

Finally, it is necessary to note that human beings are not constantly making calculations and decisions with regard to their labor supply, nor do they constantly offer their work (that is, seek new job opportunities) with the same level of intensity. Indeed, normally an individual only "offers himself/herself" on the job market, at least in an active way, under certain circumstances, such as when he/she is unemployed or when his/her needs or aspiration levels change. Ultimately, people offer their labor when the work-related part of their needs and wants is not fulfilled in a satisfying way. In addition, we may consider that an individual sometimes "offers himself/herself" for certain jobs in a passive way; this often takes place in internal labor markets, where, according to the internal rules and procedures that govern the assignment of individuals to jobs, simply occupying a particular job can be interpreted as a worker's availability for jobs higher in the organizational hierarchy (Fernández-Huerga et al. 2017).

LABOR DEMAND

The Firm as a Combination of Competences

A Post-Keynesian Institutionalist analysis of labor demand should explain the causal processes and determinants of employers' decisions about seeking and hiring workers. Since most of those decisions are adopted in organizational environments, particularly in firms, it is necessary to begin with a theoretical approach to the firm consistent with the fundamentals of PKI. In particular, competences-based theories of the firm provide a useful theoretical framework. The compatibility between such theories—associated with the so-called "capabilities approach" to firms—and several branches of non-mainstream economics (specially Institutional, Evolutionary, and Post Keynesian economics) has been emphasized recently by several studies (Dunn 2000; Foss 1997; Hodgson 1998b). Further, this view of the firm—which places knowledge and the learning process at the heart of the characterization of the organization— connects with the anthropogenic approach proposed by Eichner (1979), as well as with a proposal by Piore (1979; 1995) that calls for grounding labor market analysis in cognitive psychology, and with efforts to use labor market segmentation theory to explain real-world training processes (Gray and Chapman 2004).

According to the capabilities approach, a firm can be considered a systematically arranged combination of competences or productive capabilities of different types (Foss 1993; Hodgson 1998b; Nelson and Winter 1982; Teece 2007). One part of these competences consists of the capabilities contributed by the individuals who work for the firm; another part is contributed by the "institutional content" of the firm; and a third part is contributed by the organization's physical capital. All of these productive competences are interrelated and interdependent (Nelson and Winter 1982).

The competences that individuals contribute may be of many kinds, but most of them are a matter of knowledge and skills, both practical and intellectual (Nelson and Winter 1982; Teece 2007), which supposes that the generation of these competences is conditioned by the institutional environment working in conjunction with individuals' cognitive systems. A part of this knowledge and skills is acquired by individuals outside the firm—mainly through the educational system and the socialization process to which they have been exposed. But there is another part of the competences which is acquired in the enterprise itself, through experience, learning by doing, and interaction within the organization with other individuals and with the group as a whole (Teece and Pisano 1994).

A firm's full system of competences constitutes the ensemble of factors at its disposal to carry out its activities. Some of these activities are "external" in the sense that they involve other agents and the environment, but other activities are of an "internal" nature, given that they affect the elements that form part of the firm itself. Among the latter, perhaps the most significant is the endeavor to acquire, improve, adapt, and coordinate the firm's productive competences (Hodgson 1998b; Teece and Pisano 1994). All of those activities are carried out in real time and in an environment that is transmutable and subject to fundamental uncertainty. This means that taking control is highly important, whence comes the need to plan *strategically* (Dunn 2002). Strategic planning involves not merely choosing between the different courses of action available, but also creating new ones and preparing oneself to face and control the impact of unforeseeable events (Dunn 2002).

Starting from this conception of the firm, we identify four basic principles or ideas that can characterize the analysis of the demand for labor from PKI (Fernández-Huerga 2019), each of which will be examined in turn. They are:

1. Labor demand decisions are linked to the firm's strategic plans and conditioned by the nature and characteristics of the activities to be carried out (in particular by the level of uncertainty);
2. Labor demand appears to be associated with a demand for productive competences or capabilities;
3. The competences associated with the demand for labor are embedded in human beings, which has various consequences; and
4. The labor demand decision-making process is largely independent of the wage-setting process.

The Link between Labor Demand and a Firm's Strategic Plans

Labor demand decisions must be made before starting or changing production (or engaging in other enterprise activities) and decision-making and production take (real, historical) time. Therefore, labor demand decisions are generally linked to a company's strategic plans, which are normally established by the organization's management team and designed in an environment subject to uncertainty. This implies, among other things, that the content of these plans (and, therefore, labor demand decisions) are conditioned by the competences and psychological traits—which evokes the concept of "animal spirits" (Dequech 1999; Keynes 1936)—of those who develop them, as well as by their own objectives. Strategic plans also depend on the historical trajectory that each company (and/or management team) has followed, since they are constructed through a dynamic process dependent upon past experience.

Labor demand decisions are also conditioned by the nature and characteristics of the enterprise activities to be carried out. That means the level of uncertainty plays a key role in planning and gives special importance to a firm's capacity to acquire control over the different factors that could influence its activities. Since such control is vital to reducing uncertainty, it is not surprising that the aim of acquiring control over such factors influences (and is reflected in) a firm's labor demand.[2] For example, gaining some control over the demand for the firm's product makes it possible to plan the volume of labor demand, thereby reducing labor demand variability; gaining control over prices reduces the impact of variations in labor costs, thereby giving firms more opportunity to set high wages and offer wage increases as necessary to attract good workers; and gaining control of innovation assists in planning for the productive competences of workers that will be required to carry out the firm's activities.

Labor Demand and Demand for Productive Competences

To carry out strategically planned activities, firms require different productive competences, some of which are contributed by individuals. Hence, labor demand appears to be associated with a demand for productive capabilities. Most of these competences are of a cognitive nature (knowledge and skills, acquired through some type of learning), and therefore their acquisition is conditioned by the social and institutional environment (Hodgson 1998a; 2003) and has a certain context-specific character (Teece and Pisano 1994). Further, individual competences tend to expand through use, experience, and learning by doing, and to depreciate or disappear altogether if unused (Foss 1993; Hodgson 1998b; Seccareccia 1991).

Some of the competences that firms need can be acquired by individuals outside the organization, but there are others which—owing to the nature of the cognitive process and the context-specific character of some competences—must be created and transmitted internally (Foss 1993; Hodgson 1998b; Teece and Pisano 1994; Penrose 1959). This is so because much knowledge cannot easily be codified or communicated through the use of language, which means its transmission and learning cannot be based upon a process of formal teaching. Instead, it is produced through constructed knowledge and imitation generated by participation in—and interaction with—the other individuals and with the institutional content of the organization (Hodgson 1988), or in a process of learning by doing; in other words, this is tacit knowledge. Meanwhile, the specialization and dispersion of productive knowledge mean that it must be coordinated; in this regard, the set of institutions that are part of the firm can prove very useful not just in generating this knowledge, but also in coordinating it (Hodgson 1988; Teece and Pisano 1994).

All of this suggests that a great deal of productive activity within a company is directed toward the creation, improvement, and coordination of productive competences. This is a process with uncertain outcomes and which takes time, a fact that calls for the creation of internal configurations (such as systematic configurations of job positions, with more or less organized relationships between them) that are capable of producing and passing on these competencies. This idea played an important part in the earliest theoretical explanations of internal labor markets and labor market segmentation, which highlighted the role of training (and its connections with technology and with uncertainty and variability in product demand) as one of the main elements causing segmentation (Doeringer and Piore 1971; Gray and Chapman 2004; Piore 1975, 1980b; Thurow 1975).[3]

Finally, if a large proportion of the competences that individuals bring to work are created or developed through the learning that occurs in performing their working activities, this means that the "quality of the labor supply" is also interrelated with the number and characteristics of jobs in an economy (Eichner 1979). This supports the idea that the supply and demand of labor are interdependent.

Competences Embedded in Human Beings

The fact that competences are incorporated into human beings has three main consequences. The first is that the firm must design (and, over time, redesign) its demand for competences (and the work activities to be carried out) and link them to jobs, which may then be assigned to individual employees. In other words, the firm becomes an organized system of job positions, each of which is associated with one or more tasks or activities to be carried out by the employee. The design of the system of job positions is a decision for the senior management of the organization, and so it is conditioned by the competences of the individuals who work at the management level and is dependent on the past.

This design generates a series of relationships among the various job positions in the organization and among the positions and the firm's physical capital. Some of these relations are more or less fixed, which imposes a certain indivisibility on the productive activity and connects with the view that most enterprises tend to be affected by the prevalence of (quasi-)fixed technical coefficients of production. Further, the move from a demand for competences to a demand for individuals is another source of indivisibility (as an individual may have many competences) and can contribute to the accumulation of an inventory of competences that gives rise to surplus capacities within the firm (Penrose 1959). This connects with the idea that firms frequently operate with unused productive capacities.

A second consequence of the fact that competencies are possessed by human beings is that some "effort" is required for the competencies to be deployed. An essential element that differentiates "labor" from other goods is that it cannot be separated from the individuals who provide it, who bring with them their own goals, interests, psychological traits, self-awareness, capacity for reflection, values, norms of justice, past, etc. (Seccareccia 1991; Prasch 2004). Although PKI does not view workers as beings who will shirk whenever possible, it also recognizes the possibility of conflict arising between objectives of individuals and employers. This gives rise to the need to set up control instruments that permit the firm to align workers' interests with its own, which can be achieved, for example, by designing the wage system and/or the system of job positions and the rules, procedures, and conventions that guide mobility between these positions. It also must be recognized (as we have already noted) that the firm, through its institutional content, can influence the setting of the level of effort considered normal or acceptable, and can influence the ordered configuration of workers' aims, in order to bring employee behavior and aims more closely in line with the interests of the organization.[4] This connects with the concept of bureaucratic control, which has developed within some branches of labor market segmentation theory (Edwards 1979; Gordon et al. 1982).

The third consequence of this embedding is that labor demand decisions require the selection and assignment of specific individuals to jobs. Such decisions are taken in a context subject to fundamental uncertainty. Indeed, managers responsible for making these decisions do not know all the available individuals, their capabilities, and their drive. Thus, such decision-making tends to rely on the use of formal rules, informal rules, and norms that make it possible to assign workers to jobs despite the fact that knowledge is imperfect.

The presence of uncertainty also means selecting workers depends not only on knowledge that can be built up about those individuals, but also on the confidence decision-makers have in their knowledge. This means that both the source of managerial knowledge and the way it has been constructed will influence the decision-making process and its outcomes (Dequech 1999; 2006). For instance, if the person responsible for making job assignment decisions is faced with a choice between different individuals about which he/she knows very little, the manager might choose one worker over another simply because the information available comes from personal experience (such as the case in which one candidate is already employed by the firm in another position) or from persons he/she trusts, such as friends or family members. In fact, the opportunity to develop this kind of knowledge and trust is one of the arguments favoring long-lasting labor relations and the construction of internal labor markets.

The Independence of Labor Demand and Wage Setting

Since labor demand decisions are linked to a firm's action plans, those decisions are generally required only when such plans are formed for the first time and when the plans change. Managers responsible for such decisions are usually not continually making calculations and evaluating possible new hires. On the contrary, these decisions are generally taken only at certain times and have a relatively lasting effect. Apart from when vacancies arise in an existing job position, such decisions tend to arise in a going concern only when changing enterprise plans require more, fewer, or different productive capabilities— that is, because of a change in the content or, perhaps more often, in the volume of a firm's activities. Because such business changes are frequently linked to variations in expectations about product demand, changes in labor demand are commonly associated with the principle of effective demand. According to that principle—a fundamental element of Post Keynesian economics—the level of employment depends not on the market-clearing power of wage changes, but instead on the level of aggregate economic activity.

This fact does not mean that wages and wage variation do not play some part in labor demand decisions, but it does mean that they do not play the predominant role that is attributed to them in Neoclassical economics (Appelbaum 1979; King 1990; Fleetwood 2006, 2014b; Lavoie 2015; Seccareccia 1991). In large part, this is because wages in the real world are not determined in an impersonal market in conjunction with the amount of labor, as we will demonstrate further in the next section. On the contrary, wage setting is the result of a process of (formal or informal) negotiation of some kind, contingent upon the distribution of power between the parties and the influence of the institutional framework (Appelbaum 1979; Robinson 1937; Woodbury 1987). Thus, setting wage levels occurs in accordance with its own set of "rules of the game" and is distinct from determining labor demand.

THE LABOR MARKET: A CONCEPTION CONSISTENT WITH PKI

In PKI, there is no clear mathematical relationship between wages and the coordination of labor supply and labor demand (Fleetwood 2006). On the contrary, the underlying decision-making mechanisms in these areas are much more complex and are necessarily conditioned by the institutional environment. This fact dislodges the cornerstone of the Neoclassical conception of interplay between labor supply and demand (Fleetwood 2006; 2014b), which is that the interaction between those supplying and demanding labor can be reduced to an impersonal relationship focused solely on wages. In fact, in reality there is not one all-encompassing labor market; rather, there are labor "markets" with no market-clearing price mechanism and in which complex supply and demand interrelationships occur.

From the perspective of PKI, the activities and interrelationships found within labor markets are conditioned, regulated, and organized through a diverse set of institutions with which labor-market participants interact consciously or unconsciously. Further, in the course of their activities, the participants contribute to reproducing and/or transforming those institutions. To be sure, labor markets cannot be dissociated from their institutional content (Fernández-Huerga 2013; Fleetwood 2006; 2011; 2014a; 2017).[5] But that doesn't mean that the labor market is exactly the institutions that constitute it, in the sense of being reducible to them. As Fleetwood (2014a; 2017) points out, a labor market *emerges* from the institutions that constitute it, becoming a *specific* systematic configuration of those institutions—and that configuration is subject to change over time. Further, the institutions of a labor market are not independent from the rest of the institutions of the economic and social environment; on the contrary, they are built on, interact with, and evolve from those other socioeconomic institutions.

Taking as a starting point the definitions developed by Fleetwood (2014a, 253; 2017, 99), it can be said that labor markets are specific and systematic configurations of institutions, which govern the set of activities and interrelations that occur around the exchange of the (quasi-)commodity labor force for a wage (among other elements), and upon which the agents that operate in them have to draw (consciously or unconsciously) to develop those activities and interrelationships (thereby contributing to reproducing and/or transforming those institutions, as well as themselves as agents that act in those markets).

In this context, any attempt to theorize about the labor market has to be focused on explaining the activities and relationships that occur in the market as well as the interaction between the agents and the market institutions, placing emphasis on how these institutions are created, reproduced, and/or transformed (Fleetwood 2006; 2011). Moreover, these institutions can arise in, and develop their influence on, different areas: within a company, in a type of occupation, within a productive sector or industry, in a specific geographic area, etc.

Given that any institution has a context-specific character, and therefore may vary from one environment to another, the objective of constructing a theoretical analysis of the labor market that is fully generalizable loses part of its meaning. On the contrary, the area to which the analysis is directed (the labor market of a company, a type of occupation, an industry, a country, etc.) determines the degree of specificity or generality with which the essential features that characterize this phenomenon can be identified (the same is true for the identification of differences across time, space, or area of analysis). In short, the objectives of labor-market research, and in particular the area to which the analysis is directed, condition the theorizing about the labor market that is the object of study.

In PKI, the method of analysis is causal-explanatory, and rests on the utility of finding (through retroduction or abduction) "demi-regularities" (Lawson 1994; 1997) or stylized facts/"ideal types" (Hodgson 1998a) that characterize the essence of phenomena, as well as on developing conjectures or hypotheses (Hodgson 1998a; Lawson 1994; Lawson 1997; Tauheed 2013) about the structures, interactions, and (deep) underlying mechanisms that explain observed results. Thus, it would be useful to have a "guide" to help identify the characteristic features of each labor market. To that end, we can ask what relationships take place in the labor market and what institutions are necessary for the development of these relationships. We can also organize our thinking on the matter by drawing a distinction between vertical relationships (those that occur between potential employers and employees) and horizontal relationships (among different potential employees or among employers).

Vertical Relationships in the Labor Market

The main relationship that occurs in the labor market, and the one that gives meaning to the existence of any type of market (Fourie 1991; Jackson 2019), is the exchange relation. For that reason, it is useful to begin by asking what is being exchanged. As a first approximation, the exchange implies the transfer of a "labor service," or, using Fourie's (1991) terminology, of some kind of "right of use." This leads to recognizing the need for a set of institutions, both legal and otherwise, that help determine what exactly is being exchanged and that specify and cover the existence and transfer of rights involved. These institutions are not independent of the rest of the institutions of the economic and social environment. In fact, the integration of individuals in the labor force is shaped from birth, progressively, by the set of social environments in which they participate (Eichner 1979; Seccareccia 1991). As Fleetwood (2011, 19) points out:

> Workers are born into a pre-existing world replete with, inter alia, social structures of class, laws, rules and discourses governing the legitimate and acceptable exchange of labor services for wages. These (and other) socioeconomic phenomena ensure that laboring activity is a quasi-commodity. And this quasi-commodity, labor, is traded in labor markets.

Time, competences and effort

The contribution of individuals at work (or what they "deliver" in exchange) focuses mainly on three elements: time, competences, and effort. All these contributions are conditioned by the institutions of the labor market.

The first thing workers contribute is a part of their time. This contribution is strongly influenced by the institutional framework of the market, since it conditions the power of each of the parties in setting the working day and contributes to establishing what can and cannot be chosen in that area. Legal institutions often play an important role in determining working hours in many countries; however, in some areas it may be that non-legal institutions are more relevant, even prevailing over existing laws. For example, some companies or work environments may operate under customs that establish that it is normal to work ten hours a day, even though the law may permit and perhaps even encourage a shorter work day. These institutions are not invariable or independent of the actions of labor market participants; in fact, the actions of individuals contribute to reproducing and/or transforming existing institutions.

The contribution of productive competences is also conditioned by the full set of (legal and other) labor-market institutions. In fact, this occurs in two ways. First, the institutional environment affects (as discussed previously) the creation and content of competences. Second, institutions help to identify and delimit what capabilities or competences, of all those available to individuals, can be used by employers (and in what way) and which ones cannot be used. In other words, the institutional environment helps define the rights of use that are transferred in the labor exchange process. For example, an individual may be skilled at performing cleaning tasks, but this does not mean that the employer automatically has the right to use these competences in the development of the work activity.

Finally, the contribution of effort is also conditioned by the institutional environment at least in two ways that we have already mentioned. First, the institutional environment conditions the determination of the level of "effort" considered "normal," "acceptable," or "desirable." Second, that environment can influence both the identification of the needs and wants of each individual and the establishment of aspiration levels considered satisfactory.

Wage determination

The realization of an exchange through the labor market requires that the employer provide compensation to the worker, and that it includes, in addition to other possible elements, a monetary transfer associated with a wage. This makes it possible to differentiate the exchange that takes place in the labor market from other types of activities, such as the development of a volunteer activity. This means that the labor market exchange relationship entails a process of determining wages in particular and the attributes and rewards of work more broadly.

A wide variety of processes are available for determining wages, including some involving formal mechanisms of negotiation and dispute resolution. In each labor market, the institutional framework helps to determine the process used, the role different agents have in that process, and how the process takes place. The framework also influences the considerations that enter into wage determination. For example, wages are at least somewhat dependent on past practices; they also contain a certain idiosyncratic character that reflects a particular company, occupation, or industry; and, of course, wages are conditioned by the distribution of power and by the broader socio-institutional environment (Robinson 1937; Appelbaum 1979; Woodbury 1987; Greenwood 2016).

The fact that wages are, at least in part, a consequence of decisions made by those on both the supply and demand sides of the market (decisions developed in a context of explicit or implicit negotiation) makes it necessary to take into consideration the various elements that mobilize their behavior. On the workers' side, the wage is not the only end that they seek through work; and the wage objective is usually to obtain a satisfactory level of remuneration, not some optimal, maximum wage. This is a cognitive and adaptive construction, the fixation and evolution of which depends on, among other aspects, the wage received in the past and on the remuneration received by other individuals belonging to the same reference groups. All of this gives relevance to relative wages and to worker wage profiles that (tend to) trend upward over time.

On the side of firms, wage decisions are generally not made to maximize profits. In a world subject to the presence of fundamental uncertainty, optimization is not a viable option in most situations (Hodgson 1988, 1997; Lavoie 2015), profit cannot be considered the only goal that guides company decisions (Simon 1979), and all costs and revenues generated by each worker cannot be known in advance. All this leads to rejection of the theory of marginal productivity as the basis for wage determination (Appelbaum 1979; Eichner 1979; Gray and Chapman 2004; Greenwood 2016). Instead, wage decisions, like the other choices made by companies, can be considered strategic decisions (Shapiro and Sawyer 2003), adopted in the pursuit of a set of higher-level enterprises goals. From the perspective of PKI, the design of the internal wage structure of each company is conditioned by the past and by the routines of the organization, as well as by that structure's influence on the effort extraction process and on the process of on-the-job training and acquisition of competences (Eichner 1979; Piore 1975; 1980a; 1980b). In addition, a firm's wage structure is also conditioned by the influence of external references, mainly from other jobs with which there is a relationship within the same occupation, industry, or geographic area (Dunlop 1957). Finally, decisions on wages are not independent of the possibilities of the company to manipulate the prices of its products or to manage the rest of the costs. In fact, the determination of nominal and real wages is subject to different influences, since the latter depend on forces operating in the goods market, in particular on the ability of firm to set profit margins and manipulate prices (Appelbaum 1979; Eichner 1979; Seccareccia 1991).

This conception of the process of wage determination is consistent with the relative rigidity that wages present in the real world. Once established, wages acquire a certain legitimacy or "authority" and tend to remain relatively stable over time. This stability helps reduce uncertainty and helps agents to plan and make other decisions. This is not to say that wages do not change. In fact, the institutional environment also conditions the procedures for wage adjustments, regulating when they can be raised and what practices and variations are considered normal, fair, or acceptable and which ones are not. But, in the end, wages are not designed to adjust to "clear" the market, and even flexible wages do not necessarily lead to full employment or even a market "equilibrium."

Other job attributes and relationships

Of course, the wage is not the only relevant attribute of a job. For example, each job incorporates possibilities for the maintenance, development, and acquisition of productive competences by the worker, and offers a scope that can also satisfy other human needs, both individual and social (Eichner 1979; Reisman 2002; Seccareccia 1991; Spencer 2006). As in the case of work hours and wages, the institutional environment similarly conditions these job features. Further, the institutional environment determines what agents seek in these areas. For example, what each worker considers satisfactory in the field of social needs is conditioned by his/her past and by the rest of his/her social affiliations; therefore, the set of individuals' previous affiliations tends to channel them towards certain affiliations in the workplace (Eichner 1979; Seccareccia 1991; Piore 1975; 1980a).

All the above elements influence what employers and workers deliver in the exchange relationship. However, labor markets usually also involve other types of relationships and perhaps even additional parties. For example, the parties could become embroiled in a dispute; as a result, additional relationships may emerge as third parties help resolve such disputes and/or monitor workers' or managers' compliance with the terms of their employment agreement. A care relationship could also emerge from concerns about health and safety at work (Prasch 2004). And, of course, parties could also develop affective or emotional relationships, resulting in bonds such as loyalty and trust.

Assigning workers to jobs

Decisions about assigning workers to jobs tend to be made by employers. But that is not always true; workers sometimes play an important role in making these decisions, especially when there is a labor organization that gives them power and an institutional environment that permits them to play such a role. Either way, labor market allocation is institutionally conditioned, and decisions are affected by not only formal and informal rules, but also by the unavoidable reality of uncertainty and power dynamics.

There are two main ways for workers to be assigned to jobs—through the use of internal labor markets or through external hiring. When decision-makers use an internal labor market, what normally happens is that there is a set of "administered rules" (which includes both formal and informal rules) that conditions and guides decision-making in this area and that constitutes the firm's "system of promotions or mobility" (Doeringer and Piore 1971). When decision-makers hire from outside their organization, they usually do not have direct knowledge of the competences and characteristics of the available candidates. As a result, decision-makers evaluate the work-related credentials of job applicants, sometimes supplementing their evaluation with job interviews or skills tests. Personal traits of candidates are also sometimes considered, even traits (such as age, sex, and race) that may be illegal to consider in a given jurisdiction. In any event, the value judgments underlying both internal and external hiring decisions are conditioned not only by the institutional framework within the hiring organization, but also by the sociocultural environment of the community in which the firm is located (Fleetwood 2011).

In short, workers are selected and assigned to jobs through a "filtering" process that rarely adjusts wages to coordinate labor supply and demand (Dugger 1989; Thurow 1975). Instead, the credentials or characteristics required to fill job positions are most often adjusted to ensure that essential positions get filled. All this means that individuals do not compete for jobs through wages, but rather on the basis of their skills, past behavior, credentials, contacts, and sometimes even personal characteristics.

Horizontal Relationships in the Labor Market

In the Neoclassical conception of the labor market, horizontal relationships are reduced to wage competition. There are no other horizontal relationships between the agents involved, and no institutions that regulate those relationships; in fact, any type of additional relationship would be an "imperfection." On the contrary, the conception presented here leads to a different—and broader—vision of the horizontal relationships among agents. Indeed, each of the vertical relationships that we described in the previous section constitutes a space in which workers and/or firms could try to outperform other labor market participants.

Horizontal relationships entail, in their very essence, some degree of rivalry or competition since, once the exchange is made, other suppliers or applicants are excluded. However, this rivalry does not have to occur with the same intensity in all cases; in fact, in many areas there are common interests within the same group of agents (suppliers and demanders), which can give rise to agreements among them (such as the formation of labor unions or trade associations).

Furthermore, in the real world it is common for this exclusion to be more relevant among workers (suppliers of labor), mainly for two reasons. First, since work is usually a necessary and irreplaceable mechanism to meet basic needs, the possibility of waiting or leaving the market is not always an option valid for suppliers of labor (Prasch 2000). Second, it is normally easier to find substitutes on the part of demanders than among the suppliers, partly because there is usually some unemployment in the economy and because firms can often attract people into the labor force if the need for workers is sufficiently strong (automation, which substitutes machinery for workers, or some other adjustment of production processes could also be an option).

In any case, given that workers contribute time, skills, and effort to the exchange, and that employers contribute a series of attributes (wage and others) associated with the job, each of these elements can be used to compete and try to outperform the rest of the suppliers or demanders. Each agent can try to contribute more than others to the exchange or show a willingness to receive less in return. In addition, the presence of uncertainty opens the possibility that labor market rivalry can also be exercised in other ways as well. For example, suppliers of labor might find ways to enhance the credibility associated with the content of their work. This could include reliance on credentials, accreditations, certificates, and letters of recommendation, but it could also include the establishment of personal relationships with potential employers.

As in the case of vertical relationships, horizontal relationships are conditioned by the institutional environment, which helps determine what can or cannot be done by both workers and firms. Thus, institutions (formal and informal) may establish that some practices are prohibited and/or that others are preferred. The institutionalized rules of the game may even determine that the best way for agents to compete is not by competing directly with each other, but by maintaining a cooperative relationship with the rest of the agents; this happens, for example, in some internal labor markets, in which cooperative behavior is considered a valuable attribute and can lead to worker advancement. There is also the possibility that workers or firms can gain an advantage over others by taking steps to modify or control the institutional environment that conditions labor market interrelationships.

CONCLUSION

The broad vision presented here incorporates contributions from Institutional and Post Keynesian economics, and offers one more step toward construction of a Post-Keynesian Institutionalist conception of the labor market. This vision treats the presence of different outcomes across labor markets (and within labor markets over time) as a normal occurrence, not as an anomaly or imperfection. Analytically, these differences could come from the coexistence of different institutional settings or from the heterogeneity of the processes underlying both the supply and demand for labor. In practice, however, the setting and processes of labor markets are closely interrelated and constantly interact with each other.

ACKNOWLEDGMENTS

The author wishes to thank Deb Figart, Steve Fleetwood, and Charles Whalen for helpful comments and suggestions.

NOTES

1. Human capital theory assumes that most of the skills of individuals are acquired in the "market" and that this acquisition is approached as any investment decision. Furthermore, it is assumed that skills are similar to any physical asset, ignoring the distinctive features associated with their origin and evolution (including the consequences of use and disuse).
2. This idea was already present in the first contributions of the theory of labor market segmentation, which highlighted that the uncertainty and variability of product-market demand—and, as a consequence, of the demand for labor as well—were among the main generators of segmentation in the labor market (Piore 1980a; 1980b).
3. One of the causes of segmentation is the fact that some companies make significant investments in the training of their workers, especially investments that generate specific qualifications (Piore 1975; 1980a; Thurow 1975). Once these investments are made, workers become a quasi-fixed factor of production, similar to capital, and therefore employers have incentives to avoid their loss. Thus, it is no surprise that labor market structures are influenced by the characteristics of the work that employees must carry out. In fact, Piore (1980b) even hypothesized that the various segments of the labor market are ultimately an expression of different modes of learning and understanding work.
4. This is not to say that the rules and norms that govern effort and shirking are exactly what firms determine, nor that, once they exist, firms can simply impose them on workers. These rules and norms exist prior to any particular cohort of agents and condition their thinking and action, but at the same time they are transformed and/or reproduced by the actions of the agents acting under their influence (Fleetwood, 2014a; 2017).
5. Labor markets are not unique in that they cannot be dissociated from their institutional content; this is, of course, true of all other markets as well.

REFERENCES

Appelbaum, Eileen. 1979. "Post-Keynesian Theory: The Labor Market." *Challenge* 21 (6): 39–47.

Brazelton, W. Robert, and Charles J. Whalen. 2011. "Towards a Synthesis of Institutional and Post Keynesian Economics." In *Financial Instability and Economic Security after the Great Recession*, edited by Charles J. Whalen, 28–52. Cheltenham, UK and Northampton, MA, USA: Edward Elgar.

Budd, John. 2011. *The Thought of Work*. Ithaca, NY: Cornell University Press.

Dequech, David. 1999. "Expectations and Confidence under Uncertainty." *Journal of Post Keynesian Economics* 21 (3): 415–430.

Dequech, David. 2006. "The New Institutional Economics and the Theory of Behaviour under Uncertainty." *Journal of Economic Behavior and Organization* 59 (1): 109–131.

Doeringer, Peter, and Michael Piore. 1971. *Internal Labor Markets and Manpower Analysis*. Lexington, MA: DC Heath and Co.

Dugger, William. 1989. "Instituted Process and Enabling Myth: The Two Faces of the Market." *Journal of Economic Issues* 23 (2): 607–615.

Dunlop, John. 1957. "The Task of Contemporary Wage Theory." In *New Concepts in Wage Discrimination*, edited by George Taylor and Frank Pierson, 117–139. New York: McGraw-Hill.

Dunn, Stephen. 2000. "Fundamental Uncertainty and the Firm in the Long Run." *Review of Political Economy* 12 (4): 419–433.

Dunn, Stephen. 2002. "A Post Keynesian Approach to the Theory of the Firm." In *Post Keynesian Econometrics, Microeconomics and the Theory of the Firm: Beyond Keynes, Volume One*, edited by Sheila C. Dow, 60–80. Cheltenham, UK and Northampton, MA, USA: Edward Elgar.

Edwards, Richard. 1979. *Contested Terrain*. New York: Basic Books.

Eichner, Alfred. 1979. "An Anthropogenic Approach to Labor Economics." *Eastern Economic Journal* 5 (4): 349–366.

Fernández-Huerga, Eduardo. 2008. "The Economic Behavior of Human Beings: The Institutional/Post-Keynesian Model." *Journal of Economic Issues* 42 (3): 709–726.

Fernández-Huerga, Eduardo. 2013. "The Market Concept: A Characterization from Institutional and Post-Keynesian Economics." *American Journal of Economics and Sociology* 72 (2): 361–385.

Fernández-Huerga, Eduardo. 2019. "The Labor Demand of Firms: An Alternative Conception Based on the Capabilities Approach." *Cambridge Journal of Economics* 43 (1): 37–60.

Fernández-Huerga, Eduardo, Jorge García-Arias, and Ana Salvador. 2017. "Labor Supply: Toward the Construction of an Alternative Conception from Post Keynesian and Institutional Economics." *Journal of Post Keynesian Economics* 40 (4): 576–599.

Fleetwood, Steve. 2006. "Re-thinking Labor Markets: A Critical Realist-Socioeconomic Perspective." *Capital and Class* 30 (2): 59–89.

Fleetwood, Steve. 2011. "Sketching a Socio-Economic Model of Labor Markets." *Cambridge Journal of Economics* 35 (1): 15–38.

Fleetwood, Steve. 2014a. "Conceptualizing Future Labor Markets." *Journal of Critical Realism* 13 (3): 233–260.

Fleetwood, Steve. 2014b. "Do Labor Supply and Demand Curves Exist?" *Cambridge Journal of Economics* 38 (5): 1087–1113.

Fleetwood, Steve. 2017. "From Labor Market Institutions to an Alternative Model of Labor Markets." *Forum for Social Economics* 46 (1): 78–103.

Foss, Nicolai. 1993. "Theories of the Firm: Contractual and Competence Perspectives." *Journal of Evolutionary Economics* 3 (2): 127–144.

Foss, Nicolai. 1997. "The Resource-Based Perspective: An Assessment and Diagnosis of Problems." *Danish Research Unit for Industrial Dynamics*. Working Paper No. 97-1.

Fourie, Frederic. 1991. "The Nature of the Market: A Structural Analysis." In *Rethinking Economics: Markets, Technology and Economic Evolution*, edited by Geoffrey M. Hodgson and Ernesto Screpanti, 40–57. Cheltenham, UK and Northampton, MA, USA: Edward Elgar.

Gordon, David, Richard Edwards, and Michael Reich.1982. *Segmented Work, Divided Workers*. Cambridge: Cambridge University Press.

Gray, Jerry, and Richard Chapman. 2004. "The Significance of Segmentation for Institutionalist Theory and Public Policy." In *The Institutionalist Tradition in Labor Economics*, edited by Dell P. Champlin and Janet T. Knoedler, 117–130. New York: Sharp.

Greenwood, Daphne. 2016. "Institutionalist Theories of the Wage Bargain: Beyond Demand and Supply." *Journal of Economic Issues* 50 (2): 406–414.

Hodgson, Geoffrey. 1988. *Economics and Institutions. A Manifesto for a Modern Institutional Economics*. Polity Press: Cambridge.

Hodgson, Geoffrey. 1997. "The Ubiquity of Habits and Rules." *Cambridge Journal of Economics* 21 (6): 663–684.

Hodgson, Geoffrey. 1998a. "The Approach of Institutional Economics." *Journal of Economic Literature* 36 (1): 166–192.

Hodgson, Geoffrey. 1998b. "Evolutionary and Competence-Based Theories of the Firm." *Journal of Economic Studies* 25 (1): 25–56.

Hodgson, Geoffrey. 2003. "The Hidden Persuaders: Institutions and Individuals in Economic Theory." *Cambridge Journal of Economics* 27 (2): 159–175.

Jackson, William. 2019. *Markets: Perspectives from Economic and Social Theory*. London: Routledge.

Kaufman, Bruce. 1989. "Models of Man in Industrial Relations Research." *Industrial and Labor Relations Review* 43 (1): 72–88.

Kaufman, Bruce. 1998. "Regulation of the Employment Relationship: The "Old" Institutional Perspective." *Journal of Economic Behavior & Organization* 34 (3): 349–385.

Kaufman, Bruce. 2004. "The Institutional and Neoclassical Schools in Labor Economics." In *The Institutionalist Tradition in Labor Economics*, edited by Dell P. Champlin and Janet T, Knoedler, 13–38. New York: Sharp.

Keynes, John M. 1936. *The General Theory of Employment, Interest and Money*. Royal Economic Society.

King, John. 1990. *Labor Economics*, 2nd edition. London: Macmillan.

King, John. 2002. "Some Elements of a Post Keynesian Labor Economics." In *Keynes, Uncertainty and the Global Economy. Beyond Keynes. Volume Two*, edited by Sheila C. Dow and John Hillard, 68–87. Cheltenham, UK and Northampton, MA, USA: Edward Elgar.

Lavoie, Marc. 2015. *Post-Keynesian Economics. New Foundations*. Cheltenham, UK and Northampton, MA, USA: Edward Elgar.

Lawson, Tony. 1994. "The Nature of Post Keynesianism and its Links to Other Traditions." *Journal of Post Keynesian Economics* 16 (4): 503–538.

Lawson, Tony. 1997. *Economics and Reality*. London: Routledge.

Lutz, Mark, and Kenneth Lux. 1979. *The Challenge of Humanistic Economics*. Menlo Park, CA: The Benjamin/Cummings Publishing Company.

Maslow, Abraham. 1954. *Motivation and Personality*. New York: Harper and Row.

Nelson, Richard, and Sidney Winter. 1982. *An Evolutionary Theory of Economic Change*. Cambridge: Harvard University Press.

Penrose, Edith. 1959. *The Theory of the Growth of the Firm*. Oxford: Basil Blackwell.

Piore, Michael. 1975. "Notes for a Theory of Labor Market Stratification." In *Labor Market Segmentation*, edited by Richard Edwards, Michael Reich, and David M. Gordon, 125–150. Lexington, MA: D.C. Heath and Co.

Piore, Michael. 1979. "Unemployment and Inflation: An Alternative View." In *Unemployment and Inflation: Institutionalist and Structural Views*, edited by Michael J. Piore, 1–16. New York: M. E. Sharpe.

Piore, Michael. 1980a. "Dualism as a Response to Flux and Uncertainty." In *Dualism and Discontinuity in Industrial Societies*, edited by Michael J. Piore and Suzanne Berger, 23–54. Cambridge, MA: Cambridge University Press.

Piore, Michael. 1980b. "The Technological Foundations of Dualism and Discontinuity." In *Dualism and Discontinuity in Industrial Societies*, edited by Michael J. Piore and Suzanne Berger, 55–81. Cambridge, MA: Cambridge University Press.

Piore, Michael. 1995. *Beyond Individualism*. Cambridge, MA: Harvard University Press.

Prasch, Robert. 2000. "Reassessing the Labor Supply Curve." *Journal of Economic Issues* 34 (3): 679–692.

Prasch, Robert. 2004. "How is Labor Distinct from Broccoli? Some Unique Characteristics of Labor and their Importance for Economic Analysis and Policy." In *The Institutionalist Tradition in Labor Economics*, edited by Dell P. Champlin and Janet T. Knoedler, 146–158. New York: Sharp.

Ramstad, Yngve. 1993. "Institutional Economics and the Dual Labor Market Theory." In *Institutional Economics: Theory, Method, Policy*, edited by Marc R. Tool, 173–243. Dordrecht: Springer.

Reisman, David. 2002. *The Institutional Economy: Demand and Supply*. Cheltenham, UK and Northampton, MA, USA: Edward Elgar.

Robinson, Joan. 1937. *Essays in the Theory of Employment*. London: Macmillan.

Seccareccia, Mario. 1991. "An Alternative to Labor-Market Orthodoxy: The Post-Keynesian/Institutionalist Policy View." *Review of Political Economy* 3 (1): 43–61.

Shapiro, Nina, and Malcolm Sawyer. 2003. "Post Keynesian Price Theory." *Journal of Post Keynesian Economics* 5 (3): 355–365.

Simon, Herbert. 1979. "Rational Decision Making in Business Organizations." *American Economic Review* 69 (4): 493–513.

Spencer, David. 2006. "Work for All Those Who Want It? Why the Neoclassical Labor Supply Curve is an Inappropriate Foundation for the Theory of Employment and Unemployment." *Cambridge Journal of Economics* 30 (3): 459–472.

Spencer, David. 2011. "Work is a Four-Letter Word: The Economics of Work in Historical and Critical Perspective." *American Journal of Economics and Sociology* 70 (3): 563–586.

Spencer, David. 2015. "Developing an Understanding of Meaningful Work in Economics: The Case for a Heterodox Economics of Work." *Cambridge Journal of Economics* 39 (3): 675–688.

Tauheed, Linwood. 2013. "A Critical Institutionalist Reconciliation of "Contradictory" Institutionalist Institutions: What Is an Institution?" *Journal of Economic Issues* 47 (1): 147–168.

Teece, David. 2007. "Explicating Dynamic Capabilities: The Nature and Microfoundations of (Sustainable) Enterprise Performance." *Strategic Management Journal* 28 (13): 1319–1350.

Teece, David, and Gary Pisano. 1994. "The Dynamic Capabilities of Firms: An Introduction." *Industrial and Corporate Change* 3 (3): 537–156.

Thurow, Lester. 1975. *Generating Inequality.* New York: Basic Books.

Woodbury, Stephen. 1987. "Power in the Labor Market: Institutionalist Approaches to Labor Problems." *Journal of Economic Issues* 21 (4): 1781–1807.

13. The cyclical evolution of financial regulation: a theoretical explanation

Samba Diop

INTRODUCTION

The global financial crisis of 2007–2009 demonstrated the adverse and widespread consequences of regulatory and supervisory weaknesses that led to increasingly complex financial products and risk-management shortcomings by financial institutions. Thus, it is not surprising that the crisis led to the implementation of restrictive rules to regulate financial activities, including the Dodd-Frank Act (in the United States), the Banking Union (in the European Union), and Basel III (a global framework). However, history also shows that, over time, public authorities tend to gradually unravel the mechanisms put in place to regulate financial activities. For example, the Trump administration eased Dodd-Frank restrictions barely ten years after the crisis (and Republican Party efforts to roll back its restrictions actually began shortly after the law was passed). In short, financial regulation appears to have a fundamentally cyclical dimension: periods of tranquility are usually accompanied by significant financial deregulation, symbolizing a desire to reduce the regulatory constraints on financial institutions, while periods of financial crisis tend to produce major reforms aimed at providing a stricter framework for the activities of such institutions.

This chapter provides a theoretical explanation for the cyclical nature of financial regulation. To this end, we draw on Hyman Minsky's work on institutional change. At the heart of that explanation is Minsky's notion of a barrier of "financing orthodoxy" (Minsky [1986] 2008, 236, n. 15). According to Minsky, profit seeking by bankers and other financial-sector participants means they are always aiming to stay on the frontier of acceptable financial practices—and are constantly looking for financial innovations that will allow a profit advantage. It is only the "subjective preferences" of business leaders, bankers, and policymakers—their views of what's "acceptable"—that keep such practices and innovations in check: the constraining force of that collective sentiment is what Minsky called the barrier of financing orthodoxy

(Minsky [1986] 2008, 236–237). Of course, financing orthodoxy changes over time, causing that barrier to fall during economic expansions and rise during periods of financial crisis. Analysis of the factors that determine these movements will make it possible to propose a theoretical explanation for the cyclical nature of financial regulation.

The first section of this chapter provides an Institutionalist reading of Minsky's work on financial instability. That section begins by reviewing the most common interpretation of his *financial instability hypothesis* (FIH), an interpretation focusing on the gradual reduction of safety margins. Then we show that a less common reading of financial instability is possible—one that insists on the institutional dimension. To this end, we emphasize Minsky's career-long interest in institutions, which was particularly evident in his decision to devote most of the last decade of his life to the study of institutional change in capitalist economies.

The interpretation of the FIH that focuses on institutional change not only explains the business cycle as an endogenous feature of capitalism but also accounts for the cyclical nature of financial regulation through the upward or downward movement of the barrier of financial orthodoxy. According to this institutionally oriented interpretation, finding the determinants of the movement of the financial orthodoxy barrier is crucial for analyzing the cyclical tendency of financial regulation. We actually find two types of determinants: psychological factors and power struggles between different economic participants. Together, those factors help account not only for systemic economic tendencies, but also for the specific regulatory outcomes observed at any particular time and place.

The second section of the chapter then examines how real-world patterns of regulation fit into this cyclical framework. It briefly reviews the Great Depression, the Asian financial crisis, and the subprime-driven global financial crisis, demonstrating the usefulness of our theoretical explanation of the regulatory pendulum. The second section is followed by a brief conclusion, which underscores the importance of integrating Minsky's cyclical work on financial instability with his structural analyses of capitalist evolution.

INTERPRETING MINSKY'S FINANCIAL INSTABILITY HYPOTHESIS

Unlike approaches that analyze capitalist economies in terms of equilibrium and optimized allocation of resources, Minsky insisted on a view of these economies as fundamentally unstable. From his perspective, the concept of equilibrium is incompatible with the nature of capitalist economies; rather, they are ever-evolving and prone to booms and downturns (Minsky 1986; Minsky [1986] 2008; Minsky and Campbell 1988). For that reason, Minsky preferred thinking in terms of periods of tranquility rather than equilibrium. He developed the FIH to account for the dynamic process that leads the economic system from tranquility to panic and financial disaster. After a brief review of the main results of the financial interpretation of Minsky's analysis, we present an institutional reading of the FIH (that is, an interpretation focused on institutions and institutional change) and discuss how it helps us understand the cyclical nature of financial regulation.

The Financial Reading of Capitalist Instability

Most readings of Minsky's FIH stress his emphasis on analyzing the role of finance when seeking to understand capitalist instability. That feature of Minsky's thought goes against the view of mainstream economists, which results from a tradition of seeing money as neutral. The "real business cycle" (RBC) theory perfectly illustrates that mainstream approach.

According to RBC theory, the shocks that affect the economy are "real"— not financial in nature and origin—and generally stem from significant random fluctuations in technological progress (Kydland and Prescott, 1982; Long and Plosser 1983).[1] More precisely, changes in relative prices following such shocks are believed to cause the economy's fully "rational" actors to change their behavior (including, for example, their consumption, investment, and work offers) such that economic fluctuations are the result of optimal conduct within the economic system. Despite that framework's influence in economics, it has clear limitations when thinking about the subprime-driven crisis and other real-world economic crises.[2]

In contrast to conventional economics, Minsky's perspective sees no separation between the real and financial spheres. In fact, at the heart of his conception of capitalist economic instability is the centrality of financial relations that result from investment decisions made by actors in the context of radical uncertainty. According to the FIH, the proportion of an economy's different debt structures (which Minsky called *hedge*, *speculative*, and *Ponzi* finance) defines its degree of fragility and its propensity for slipping into crisis as financing conditions deteriorate.[3] In short, the financial dimension exerts a tremendous influence on instability and on crisis dynamics—and existing debt structures define the ability of economic actors to function in the face of declining financial conditions. That said, there are different variants of the financially oriented interpretation of the FIH, each emphasizing particular variables.

Some economists interpreting the FIH insist on the anesthetizing effect of euphoria on the perception of risk and on crisis dynamics. A period without crisis, during which predictions come to fruition, has a reinforcing effect on lenders and borrowers; it also greatly reduces their risk aversion. The longer the period of calm, the greater the sense of confidence on the part of entre-preneurs and banks, and the more likely each is to tolerate ever-greater risk.[4] This, in turn, leads to fragility in the financial system. Hence the paradox of tranquility.

Such a reading of the FIH finds support in Minsky's statement that "success breeds a disregard of the possibility of failure." He continued: "[T]he absence of serious financial difficulties over a substantial period leads to the develop-ment of a euphoric economy in which increasing short-term financing of long positions becomes a normal way of life" (Minsky [1986] 2008, 237). In such a euphoric situation, radical suspension of disbelief brings new investors into the market despite increases in asset prices.

Another financially oriented reading of the FIH highlights the importance of a long-term dynamic. This view insists on the role played by the current phase of capitalism, which Minsky called "money manager capitalism" (MMC), in the financial fragility of contemporary capitalist economies (Whalen 2017). In particular, the emphasis here is on a certain number of aggravating factors associated with MMC, including the principle of shareholder value and the expansion of international competition among financial institutions. These factors influence the financial system and contribute to its instability.

The subprime-driven global crisis of 2007–2009 offered a chance to demonstrate the pertinence of such an interpretation of the FIH. According to this interpretation, factors playing a role in the crisis of 2007–2009 included highly leveraged funds that, in order to increase shareholder value, attempted to maximize yield in a general context of underestimation of risk (Wray 2007). This perspective allows us to highlight the importance of financial innovations such as securitization and derivatives in the long process that led to that crisis.

While interesting, those interpretations of Minsky's modeling of financial instability do not allow us to account for the totality of his contribution to understanding crisis dynamics. Although Minsky himself helped to promote a mainly financial reading (see, for example, Minsky 1992a), it is also pos-sible to identify a more deeply Institutionalist perspective in his work. We agree with Palley (2011, 31) that restricting Minsky to a strictly financial interpretation is tantamount to making him "a narrow theorist of financial business cycles." A full understanding of Minsky requires going beyond the financial level of interpretation to consider the part of his work devoted to the institutional dynamics at play in financial instability. That reading highlights the Institutionalist foundation of FIH, and thus most closely aligns Minsky's economics with the tradition of Post-Keynesian Institutionalism (Whalen 2011; 2020).

An Institutional Approach to Financial Instability

The analysis of institutions was always an important part of Minsky's work. For example, in an article in the 1950s, he presented institutional changes as responses to tightening monetary policy that contribute to greater financial instability (Minsky 1957). A dozen years later, he wrote: "[M]onetary economics cannot escape being institutional economics" (reprinted in Minsky 1982, 280). In addition, less than a year before his death, Minsky (1996) grounded his own work in the intellectual proximity of John Maynard Keynes and Institutionalist John R. Commons. In fact, institutional dynamics took center stage in Minsky's research during the last decade of his life (Ferri and Minsky 1992; Minsky 1996; Minsky and Whalen 1996). We propose an institutional interpretation of FIH that draws heavily on that decade of work.

Institutions as thwarting mechanisms

The institutional interpretation of Minsky's model flows from the role he assigns to institutions. Emphasizing the constructive role of institutions in stabilizing an economy, Ferri and Minsky (1992 80) wrote: "Institutions and interventions thwart the instability breeding dynamics that are natural to market economies by interrupting the endogenous process and 'starting' the economy again with non-market determined values as 'initial conditions.'" That message was underscored two years later: "Endogenous interaction can lead to incoherence and the impact of institutions and interventions aim to contain these thrusts towards incoherence" (Delli Gatti, Gallegati and Minsky 1994, 3).

Minsky highlighted two roles for institutions in maintaining financial stability: they can "prevent perverse feedback" (for example, they can attenuate risk-taking during an economic expansion); and they can "impose new initial conditions within which the structure will generate an alternative, presumably more satisfactory, future" (they can, for instance, interrupt a downward economic spiral when a crisis emerges) (Minsky 1992a, 12). Unlike analyses in which the behavior of the economy reflects first and foremost the mechanisms of the market, Minsky's analysis relies on a model in which market behavior is shaped by "institutions, conventions and policy interventions [that] contain and dominate the endogenous economic reactions that, if left alone, breed instability" (Ferri and Minsky 1992, 80). In another work, he clarifies his position by highlighting that it is the "aptness" of the institutions that determine whether an economy's path moves toward turbulence or tranquility (Delli Gatti, Gallegati and Minsky 1994, 8). The mere existence of institutions does not guarantee a stable financial system. As Sinapi (2011, 7) reminds us, instability depends on institutional effectiveness.

For Minsky, we might even say that the occurrence of a deflation crisis can be explained by the lack of an adequate institutional structure. That structure "at any date reflects legislation, administrative actions, and the evolution of institutions and usages that are due to the past behavior of market participants" (Delli Gatti, Gallegati and Minsky 1994, 7). An effective institutional structure acts as the guarantor of stability by warning against risky financial behaviors and serving as a circuit breaker capable of establishing maxima and minima over economic variables. It is in this way that laws and regulations governing financial activity, along with other aspects of the economy's institutional structure, play a decisive role in preserving the stability of the financial system.

Institutional dynamics and financial regulation
When we keep in mind the role of institutions as thwarting mechanisms in Minsky's work, we are better equipped to understand that their suppression, disappearance, or absence paves the way for a situation of fragility or even financial instability. Therefore, institutions cannot be left aside when it comes to understanding the dynamics described by the FIH. This is precisely the meaning of the analysis proposed by Arestis and Glickman (2002).

Focusing on the role that financial innovations play in risk taking and in increasing financial fragility, Arestis and Glickman (2002, 240) draw on Minsky to observe that even if bankers are always seeking new financial instruments and practices, "orthodoxy and conservatism can form a barrier to the assimilation of innovation." They also stress Minsky's emphasis on the endogenously dynamic nature of that barrier. Quoting Minsky, they write: "[A] period of success of the economy ... will lead to a lowering of the financial innovation barrier, whereas a period of bankruptcies ... has the potential for raising [it]" (ibid.).

But the barrier of financing orthodoxy affects more than innovation. A long period of tranquility reduces overall financial conservatism. In addition to prompting more financial innovation, it causes financial institutions to increase their offers, non-financial corporations to increase their requests for financing, and policymakers to adopt a more permissive approach to financial regulation. In contrast, a financial crisis tends to result in greater financial conservatism and tighter regulation. In fact, from a Minskyan perspective, deregulation is the embodiment of institutional easing, while stricter regulation means increased reliance on institutions as thwarting mechanisms.[5]

What is the economic agent that orients administrative and legislative interventions towards more or less strict regulations? For Minsky, the government plays a crucial role, since it is "a source of change in financial market usages and institutions, [and] operates by way of legislation and decrees or interventions by authorities, such as central banks" (Minsky [1986] 2008, 220). More generally, it is political decision-makers who, according to the prevailing economic dynamics, adopt economic perspectives that respond to the regulatory and deregulatory needs warranted by the economic situation.[6]

Thus, the more firmly that euphoria takes hold of the economic system, the more likely it is that an economic perspective calling for financial regulation will be disregarded. Thwarting mechanisms become weaker, and imprudent lending and borrowing practices become more and more common. The key point is that political decision-makers and regulators are not immune to the dominant climate of economic performance and expectations; like financiers and business leaders, policymakers can also become intoxicated by a period of robust economic success. This pushes them toward more permissive regulatory provisions even when stricter regulation would produce greater economic stability. As Minsky (1986, 16) writes: "[I]t is very difficult to set up a regime of regulation which long remains effective. This is particularly true as the regulators live in the same environment as the regulated. The decrease in risk aversion by financiers is accompanied by greater permissiveness by regulators."

If we also recognize the validity of the Keynesian precept which says that the current performance of the economy exerts influence over the model of the economy that actors use to shape their expectations, we can easily see why Minsky considers that the laws and regulations are a reflection of economic theory: "Legislated changes, such as the reforms that took place during the Roosevelt years and the deregulation mania of the late 1970s and 1980s, reflect some theory" (Minsky [1986] 2008, 221). Several years later, Minsky broadened the scope of this idea: "The behavior of the economy depends not only upon endogenous dynamic processes, institutional structures, and interventions by the authorities, but also upon the model of the economy that guides the authorities" (Delli Gatti, Gallegati and Minsky 1994, 8). Thus, the economic views "held by our rulers and their court intellectuals" (Minsky [1986] 2008, 220) shape legislation, decrees, and interventions intended to regulate the practices of the banking system and prevent the economy from slipping into financial fragility and economic crisis.

In short, when the economic theories and perspectives chosen by government leaders celebrate the virtues of market self-regulation, a tendency toward regulatory easing will be observed; and when governments immerse themselves in analyses grounded in an endogenous view of financial instability, the tendency will be reversed—toward stricter financial regulation. Minsky ([1986] 2008, 221) even pushes his analysis further by arguing that when the dominant theory that inspires legislative reform is not able to propose a satisfactory explanation of economic phenomena, the resulting legislative changes can be dangerous and destabilizing. More precisely, on the question of financial regulation, in order for the influence that economic theories exert over laws and regulations to be constructive, it is imperative that these theories are able to explain the endogenous instability of capitalist economies and don't rely only on seeing this instability as anomalous or external in origin.

The application of the above-mentioned Keynesian precept explains why pro-regulatory ideas lose influence in a well-performing economy, especially as one gets further away from a period of crisis. A regulatory system put into place to curb the effects of a crisis appears less and less valid the longer the period of tranquility. In such an economic climate, theories that postulate the stability of the economic system gain ground to the detriment of those that postulate the inherent instability of capitalist economies. The self-regulation hypothesis of financial markets appears self-evident in times of stability, contributing to the de-legitimation of discourse on the necessity of financial regulation. The weakening of the intellectual underpinnings of regulatory discourse is rooted in the experience of a long period without major crisis. At the same time, deregulation mania ends up getting the better of legislation and the regulatory institutions it created.

This cyclical dimension to economic thinking is undoubtedly one of the keys to understanding how financial regulation evolves over time. As Delli Gatti, Gallegati and Minsky (1994, 8) write: "[I]nitial conditions are not set once and for all, but are imposed from time to time as institutional usages become binding or the authorities react to their view of the state of the economy and its future." But there is also another regulatory dynamic: regulation is continuously shaped not only by the economic setting, but also by the evasion strategies used by those being regulated. The economy's financial actors are essentially engaged in a perpetual process of adaptation that allows them to work around the regulatory constraints in place. That means the financial regulation must be constantly updated to preserve a certain level of effectiveness amidst constant innovation. The result is a reinforcement of the dynamic nature of financial regulation.

Of course, even financial regulation aimed at updating the regulatory system occurs against the backdrop of a particular state of the economy, so the cyclical dynamic generated by business conditions is powerful. In fact, although Minsky never explicitly incorporated into his analyses a nation's elected legislators and its electorate, it is possible to see how their actions are also consistent with the cyclical nature of financial regulation. Just as regulators are not immune to the optimism or pessimism of the economic climate of the moment, legislators also can be influenced by the economic euphoria or distress of the moment. When it comes to both crafting and voting on legislative proposals, lawmakers may be more inclined to ease institutional constraints during a phase of tranquility and stiffen them in times of economic crisis. By the same token, we can understand that citizens—who are also borrowers, consumers, workers, and entrepreneurs—might be more receptive to anti-regulatory political programs when memories of crisis are dim, and more receptive to pro-regulatory proposals during periods of economic turbulence.

In summary, the prolongation of economic tranquility produces a relaxing effect on regulatory constraints and is a powerful factor in reducing risk aversion on the part of borrowers and lenders. Regulators, legislators, and voters also get caught up in the euphoria, making regulatory easing a widely agreed-upon option. The relaxing of constraints facilitates the taking of risks and fuels financial innovation. The proportion of entities with fragile debt structures increases to the threshold of financial fragility. At that point, any adverse evolution of financing conditions can set off a financial crisis.

In response to such a crisis, economic participants tend to sharply change both their expectations and their behavior. Borrowers and lenders become much more cautious; regulators engage in stricter supervision and oversight; and voters tend to back legislators whose platforms are more favorable to financial regulation. The dominant economic theories of the day also change as the economy evolves: theories that see the economy as self-regulating tend to be ascendant when the economy is tranquil and prosperous; theories that emphasize financial instability gain popularity during crises and downturns.

Toward a deeper analysis of institutional change

Although the institutional approach to financial instability described above is more thorough than financial interpretations, it remains nonetheless an approach that places great importance on psychological factors. As discussed above, the euphoria generated during periods of tranquility and the stress produced by crises have a significant impact on institutional structure. On that note, it is interesting to point out that Robert Skidelsky, in his monumental biography of Keynes, finds a shortcoming in Keynes's treatment of psychological factors. In fact, analyzing the reasons why institutions are neglected in *The General Theory*, Skidelsky (1992, 543) underlines that: "The psychological 'propensities' are data. They are the equipment which 'agents' bring to their decisions. Their roots in events or social systems are unexplored. There is no mention of ... the changing balance between capital and labor ... which might plausibly be called [one of the] causes of the [G]reat [D]epression."

To a large extent, Skidelsky's critique also can be applied to the institutional interpretation of the FIH. In Minsky, there is often no attention given to the underlying mechanisms that determine psychological variables. To be sure, the institutional analysis proposed above offers a lens through which crises can be read: During pre- and post-crisis periods, two forms of institutional change—deregulation and regulation—are explained by the expectational consequences of periods of tranquility and financial instability, respectively. Yet we are also left wondering about the *roots*, to use Skidelsky's term, of the key psychological variables.

An explanation of financial instability and cyclical institutional change based solely on psychological considerations (working via their influence on economic expectations) is inadequate. Driven only by the prevailing mood of optimism or pessimism, capitalist regimes would alternate between expansions and contractions like clockwork. Yet history indicates that has not been the case: sometimes the push for deregulation comes soon after a crisis; sometimes it does not come for quite some time.

However, a closer look at Minsky reveals several elements that caution against a mechanistically repetitive conception of institutional change. For example, Minsky liked to quote Heraclitus: "You cannot step twice in the same river" (for instance, see Minsky 1987, 1). This is a comment on the singularity of each event and the evolving and unique character of the prevailing conditions that precede each crisis. Minsky (1991) also stressed that crises have both common, systemic elements and their own idiosyncratic elements. Thus, he accounted for the financial instability of the early 1990s by combining a discussion of the financial structure's evolution from robustness to fragility with "special characteristics of the present situation," including the economic legacy of the monetarism of the late-1970s and early 1980s, and the emergence of MMC (Minsky 1991, 19–20).

In short, a truly Minskyan analysis necessitates factoring in elements that are specific to a particular time and place. According to Minsky (1991, 18), "Each period of increased indebtedness has unique elements." What happens next also depends on unique, situational characteristics: "The transformation of a downturn from a recession cycle to a depression cycle depends upon the details of the institutional structure and the pattern and efficacy of interventions" (ibid.). This aspect of Minsky's work underscores the benefit of complementing attention to psychological factors with a consideration of situational factors that permit a deeper analysis of institutional change.

Incorporating power struggles into the financial instability hypothesis
One way to incorporate situational factors into the FIH is to draw on insights from French Regulation Theory (FRT) (Diop 2016). According to the approach to institutional change in FRT, institutions carry the mark of their judicial, political, and sociological history, and their evolution is the result of transformations in the balance of power, specifically the shift of objectives and strategies of the most powerful actors (Boyer 2003; Lordon 2008).[7] In other words, the easing of the barrier of financing orthodoxy is not solely the result of an anesthetizing euphoria—and its tightening a sign of mobilizing pessimism—but it equally points to a power struggle between economic interests, such as corporate managers, bankers, and regulators; that is, between the principal actors in industry, finance, and the state (government). Yes, all of those actors (one could also include legislators and the public) share the same

expectational climate, but their interests are not always identical and power struggles do emerge between (and sometimes even among) various groups.

Because institutions are interwoven into economic activities and are the manifestation of social relations, studying them becomes inseparable from looking at the conflicts and the power plays unfolding in the society as a whole. Thus, far from being ahistorical creations, institutions are a reflection of power relations at a particular time and in a specific context. With this conception of institutions, it becomes possible to place the notion of power at the heart of Minsky's analysis—and this takes us further in our understanding of the evolution of regulation, the instability of capitalism, and the persistence of its financialized form.[8]

With the hypothesis of the evolution of regulation under the effect of a balance of power, there is a place for the role of the state and for political decisions coming from the domain of law and jurisprudence (Boyer 2003). The laws that govern financial practices, shape the surveillance of financial inno-vations, and more generally contribute to raising the barrier of financing ortho-doxy, are in fact nothing more than the legislative incarnation of a resolution of power struggles. Thus, the process of forming laws—including lobbying and other interventions by influential economic actors that occur before legislation is adopted—must be integrated into the analysis of power relations between the financial and regulatory sectors.[9]

Thus, by considering not only the influence of (fading or vivid) memories of financial crisis, but also the struggle for power between regulators and regu-lated (and similar struggles among other actors), one arrives at an understand-ing of the de-regulationist or regulationist ideas that prevail at any particular time and place. Next, we will use this lens to analyze the cyclical nature of financial deregulation in three financial crises.

REAL-WORLD FINANCIAL CRISES AND CYCLICAL REGULATION

Over the past century, several financial crises have left their mark on the evolution of capitalist economies, thereby demonstrating capitalism's inherent instability. In this section, we present an analysis of three of these crises in light of the arguments developed above. In particular, we show the links in the sequential and cyclical pattern involving deregulation, financial instability, and crisis.

The Great Depression

The political consequences of the Great Depression in the United States (US) are well known. The national election of 1932 brought about a transition marked by the coming to power of the Democratic Party. The victory of Franklin Roosevelt, with nearly 57 percent of the popular vote and a comfortable majority of Democratic legislators in both the House and Senate, initiated a long period of 22 years during which the Democrats held the US presidency. For many people, the result of the 1932 election was the consequence of an evolution in the understanding of the role of the state in regulating economic activity, and Roosevelt's arrival in the White House was considered a major change in managing the economic crisis that began in 1929.[10]

However, to account for shifts in the barrier of financing orthodoxy related to the Great Depression, it is necessary to look at the evolution of financial regulation not only before the start of the crisis, but also afterward. The Federal Reserve Act of 1913 established the Federal Reserve. Over time, partly to attract banks to the new system, the Federal Reserve reduced reserve requirements, lifted restrictions on real estate loans, and enhanced member banks' access to discount window loans (White 1982).

The passage of the Federal Farm Loan Act in 1916 allowed for the creation of joint stock and federal land banks. With that law and the subsidies that came with it, farmers, who had a history of being deemed too risky for bank loans, would now have greater access to mortgage loans (Dagher 2018). The difficulties they faced getting loans would be circumvented by support in the form of subsidies. Also, with this law, national banks could offer loans guaranteed by any type of real estate for up to one year. This law greatly increased the number of real estate loans advanced by joint stock land banks over the course of the 1920s, contributing to a dramatic increase in the farm foreclosure rate and the rise of regional bank failures in the late 1920s.

Another development in the decades prior to the Great Depression was the emergence of large commercial and industrial firms with financial needs that could not be met by banks because of regulatory limits placed on long-term bank loans. This led to the development of the securities market and risk-avoidance strategies by the banking sector. Thus, although most banks were forbidden from trading in securities, many financial institutions put into place securities affiliates, and the number of such affiliates increased significantly over the course of the 1920s (White 1986; 1990).

With the Great Depression, deregulation mania gave way to the inverse. Nudged by the Roosevelt administration, a set of regulatory acts was enacted in 1933, for example, to reinforce the stability of the banking sector and facilitate the accumulation of capital. The creation of the Federal Deposit Insurance Corporation (FDIC) was the main response to the problem of securing bank deposits and avoiding outbursts of panic that could lead to mass deposit withdrawals. The Glass-Steagall Act erected firewalls between capital markets and deposit banks with the goal of separating money markets from the risky capital markets.[11] In addition, Regulation Q aimed to establish an upper limit on the interest rates on deposits. That initiative was taken to contain the competition between banks and to ensure low rates on loans.

A cyclical dimension to financial regulation is clearly evident from a look at the pre-crisis and crisis periods of the Great Depression. The legacy that the crisis left on regulation was consequential and the mark it left on financial activities in the post-Great Depression period was long-lasting. But the prolonged absence of another crisis, coupled with the prevalence of economic theories hostile to financial regulation, gradually led to a push toward deregulation which would slowly bear fruit, culminating in the era of MMC and regulatory rollbacks right up to the start of the subprime-driven financial crisis of 2007.

The Asian Financial Crisis of 1997

The Asian Financial Crisis—which affected a number of countries including Thailand, Philippines, Malaysia, South Korea, and Indonesia—marked an economic turning point in several ways. It shattered an extended period of growth in a part of the world that had long been considered by the Bretton Woods institutions to be a model for developing countries. It spread by means of financial contagion, once again illustrating the instability of capitalism and the international dimension of financial crises. It also led many analysts to see the need for a regulatory system that better supports—or perhaps even curbs—the process of financial globalization.[12]

The analysis presented here is distinct from other interpretations of the Asian crisis. For example, interpretations that emphasize moral hazard (Corsetti et al. 1999; Krugman 1998) and multiple equilibria (Chang and Velasco 1998; Radelet and Sachs 1998) fail to fully account for the structural dimension of the crisis. We also go beyond other Minsky-inspired readings (Cozzi and Toporowski 2006; Dymski 1999; Kregel 1998; Mayer 1998) by examining the case of South Korea to illustrate (1) the role of financial deregulation in triggering the crisis; and (2) the post-crisis regulatory dynamic that aimed to reinforce the underlying robustness of affected financial systems.

From the 1970s to the outbreak of the Asian crisis, South Korea recorded three decades of exceptional economic growth, averaging 7 percent a year. That long period of tranquility, seen as an Asian miracle by the Bretton Woods institutions, led to changes—in the direction of financial liberalization or deregulation—that planted the seed of the subsequent crisis. As a result, the crisis was the consequence of a series of developments that gradually eroded the stability of the banking sector.

In addition, a subtle slowing of South Korean economic activity at the beginning of the 1990s brought about political initiatives to restart investment. The choice was made to deregulate the financial and industrial sectors with measures such as the liberalization of the commercial paper market in 1994, the reversal of credit controls on the large conglomerates known as chaebols, and the transformation of 24 financially weak short-term financing companies into commercial banks. Those measures, presented as concrete variants of the process of financial liberalization, led to a considerable increase in the level of investment and the volume of credit distributed. Yet documented problems with influence trafficking, along with the financial scandals that followed the rise in investment and credit, attest to the fragile foundation on which these changes were built. The financing of investment projects with low profitability put the banking system over the edge, first into a fragile situation and then into crisis as financing conditions deteriorated and capital ebbed.

Once the crisis broke out, the party in power undertook initiatives to restore the confidence of investors. In November 1997, only several months after the devaluation of the Thai baht, which was the first in a chain of events leading to the crisis, a South Korean reform aiming to set up a Financial Supervisory Board was discussed. That board would oversee the consolidation of existing regulatory agencies (Haggard 2000). While the reform was never adopted, the mere fact of its discussion attests to a change in perspective regarding the role of financial regulation.[13]

In December 1997, national elections brought into power the National Congress for New Politics (NCNP), quickly resulting in 13 new financial laws aiming at overhauling the financial system.[14] Those laws sought to fund a restructuring and recapitalization of viable financial institutions, reduce the influence of the chaebols, impose a minimum capital requirement ratio as of April 1998 (Crotty and Lee 2002), and reinforce the infrastructure of financial supervision by replacing a fragmented financial supervision system with a single Financial Supervisory Service empowered to control all compartments of the financial sector.

Kim Dae-Jung's presidency, from 1998 to 2003, began with financial re-regulation led by the Korean government, but this active role of the state was short-lived. Very quickly—in fact, in mid-1998—a change of direction in favor of financial deregulation was undertaken. For reasons as varied as the conversion of public opinion to the mainstream explanation of the crisis, the increased power of foreign capital, and the preservation of the power of the chaebols (Lee, 2010), measures in favor of greater financial liberalization were undertaken. The relaxation or even abolition of foreign investment regulations, the authorization of hostile mergers and acquisitions for foreign investors, and the completion of the liberalization of the derivatives market were effective in June 1998. And in April 1999, the "two-phase financial opening" was launched: Korea definitively turned its back on the ephemeral regulatory phase that followed the crisis.

The Subprime Crisis

The cyclical nature of financial regulation is also evident in the US financial crisis of 2007, which was driven in large part by widespread issuance and securitization of subprime mortgages, and which triggered a severe global financial crisis. If we examine the politics surrounding the regulation of the real estate and financial markets in the United States, it appears that two sets of mechanisms worked together to trigger disaster: (1) those incentivizing real estate investment; and (2) those related to the deregulation of financial instruments. Together they created one of the greatest financial disasters since the Great Depression. In short, the subprime-driven financial crisis was the result of a progressive deregulation of financial markets. Then, once the crisis broke out, there was a shift in direction toward regulation.

The political consequences of the crisis are hard to refute. The Republican Party, in power when the crisis hit, lost the presidential election and a significant number of seats in Congress. To be sure, the crisis may not have been the sole driver of that political transition, but (as in the other cases discussed above) it certainly played a role. The electoral gains of the Democratic Party signaled a clear and widespread desire to contain the excesses of financial institutions and clean up Wall Street.

To understand what led to the Subprime Crisis, it is useful to begin with developments following passage of the Glass-Steagall Act of 1933. Although that legislation separated deposit banks and investment banks, which prevented the former from underwriting equities or engaging in brokerage activities, it was quickly circumvented by bank holding companies and brokerage companies. Very quickly, the Federal Reserve began allowing commercial banks to offer investment loans as long as their amount did not exceed 10 percent, and then 25 percent, of total bank revenue. Brokerage firms also engaged in offering traditional deposit accounts through money market mutual funds and cash management accounts.

The loosening of limits set by Glass-Steagall was followed by other changes. For example, in the interests of fighting inflation, the Treasury-Fed Accord of 1951 freed the central bank from its commitment to keeping interest rates low. In addition, the Community Reinvestment Act of 1977 introduced the possibility of banks loaning to entities with low credit-worthiness.

Additional changes in the direction of deregulation occurred in the 1980s. The Depository Institutions Deregulation and Monetary Control Act of 1980 made it possible for financial institutions to impose elevated interest rates and high commissions onto customers. Other laws passed in the early 1980s allowed banks to make adjustable-rate mortgage loans and permitted the use of variable interest rates and "balloon" payments for other loans. In addition, the Tax Reform Act of 1986 ended the tax deductibility of interest paid on consumer loans, but not on real estate loans, which provided an incentive for greater use of the latter.

Still more deregulation occurred in the 1990s. For example, the Gramm-Leach-Bliley Act of 1999 ended the separation put in place by Glass-Steagall. The argument was that the change would give American banks the ability to compete with foreign banks, which were becoming quite large. Passed with the support of Republican Fed Chairman Alan Greenspan, Democratic President Bill Clinton and his Treasury Secretary Robert Rubin, and a comfortable majority in both chambers of Congress, Gramm-Leach-Bliley allowed for the merging of traditional banking and financial activities, thereby leading to the consolidation of financial services. In retrospect, the end of Glass-Steagall's separation is an important reason why the top five US investment banks (Bear Stearns, Goldman Sachs, Morgan Stanley, Lehman Brothers, and Merrill Lynch) eventually found themselves at the center of the Subprime Crisis.

The importance of this series of regulatory changes in accounting for the Subprime Crisis cannot be ignored. They not only transitioned the American banking system toward greater permissiveness in credit operations, but also paved the way for the invention and development of high-risk real estate loans. These laws fashioned a more permissive regulatory environment that provided incentives for developing risky innovations and pursuing financial practices with a strong speculative dimension.

All of those changes happened under the banner of financial modernization. In fact, however, the driving force appears to have been the increasingly distant the memory of the Great Depression. But regardless of how it was presented, the result was that legislators and regulators tore up the framework inherited from the New Deal era and replaced it with faith in both a "great moderation" of economic fluctuations and the idea that crises were a thing of the past.

Then, in 2007, reality set in. The first tensions were reported in the stalling real estate market at the end of the first quarter of 2007, and, along with difficulties encountered by certain financial institutions, were a stark contrast with the position represented by the "efficient market" hypothesis, which had become the cornerstone of modern finance (Fama 1970). Soon, it became clear that what was occurring was no temporary correction; instead, it was a crisis threatening both the United States and the global economy. The crisis quickly brought into general acceptance the idea that quick action and broad reforms were necessary to save the financial system. It also contributed (as a result of the presidential election of 2008) to a change in the political party controlling the White House.

In response to the crisis, the US Congress passed the Dodd-Frank Act in 2010, the most comprehensive reform in the domain of US financial regulation since the Great Depression. It included the following: (1) a rethinking of the oversight of financial institutions; (2) a new mechanism for resolving problems at major financial institutions; (3) strict minimum leverage and reserve requirements for banks; and (4) oversight of credit rating agencies. Another aspect of this law was an attempt to better manage the demand for consumer credit, and for that reason the Consumer Financial Protection Bureau (CFPB) was established in 2011. The goal of the CFPB was to provide consumers with assistance and education about financial institutions and services.

As it turns out, the chorus of those complaining about excess regulation and its adverse effects on economic growth—voices that had not fully disappeared even during the acute phase of the crisis—began to regain strength just as the CFPB started to operate. In fact, the Republican Party called for the repeal of Dodd-Franks during the presidential election of 2012. While its candidate, Mitt Romney, was not elected, deregulation became more and more attractive as the crisis became a more distant memory and the economy continued to improve. In 2016, the election of Donald Trump, while certainly not explainable solely by the swinging of the regulatory pendulum, nonetheless marked a turning point on this front.

In May of 2017, significant legislation was passed—with bipartisan support—in the direction of a dismantling of the Dodd-Frank regulatory framework. Then two other developments the next month left no doubt as to the desire of the new administration and its allies in Congress to turn their backs on financial regulation. First, the Republican-controlled House of Representatives voted in favor of a bill that would have further weakened Dodd-Frank regulations (it was not passed by the Senate); and second, just a few days later, the Treasury Department issued a report that aimed to loosen bank regulations. The deregulatory phase had indeed begun.

CONCLUSION: TOWARD AN INTEGRATION OF CYCLICAL AND STRUCTURAL ANALYSES

Drawing on Minsky's FIH and his work on institutional change, this chapter has provided a theoretical explanation for not only the endogenous nature of business cycles, but also the cyclical nature of financial regulation. At the heart of that explanation is Minsky's notion of an ever-evolving barrier of financing orthodoxy, driven both by a systemic evolution traceable to the psychological effects of memories of economic crisis (which tend to produce stricter regulation when crisis memories are fresh and looser regulation as such memories fade) and by the less predictable outcome of economic and political power struggles between competing economic interests. Thus, the evolution of financial regulation has systemic tendencies, but also depends on the special—or idiosyncratic—characteristics of a particular time and place. In the end, our theoretical explanation is not merely an analysis of business cycles and institutional dynamics, but actually a broader analytical perspective on the political economy of financial regulation.

The chapter has also examined how real-world patterns of regulation fit into our cyclical framework. A look at events surrounding the Great Depression, the Asian Financial Crisis, and the Subprime Crisis indicate that historical experience is indeed compatible with our theory of the cyclical evolution of financial regulation, including our position that such evolution never moves like clockwork. The speed and intensity of such evolution varies with time and place, and is never fully predictable.

There are also periods that seem to defy the regulatory movement that we describe in this chapter. For example, the long period of US economic experience from the end of World War II to the Subprime Crisis was characterized by an overall trend toward financial deregulation despite the appearance of a number of financial crises. In part, this is because those crises were resolved, often by the Federal Reserve's action as a lender of last resort, before there was much harm done to the overall economy. But that does not appear to be the whole story, as Minsky recognized in various works written between the mid-1980s and his death in 1996.

In that last decade of his life, Minsky sought a deeper look at the resilience of capitalism and the nature of its ongoing evolution (see, e.g., Minsky 1990). The result was his sketch of stages of US capitalism, with a focus on the transition from an era he called "managerial capitalism," which ran from the New Deal through the end of the 1970s, to the era of MMC that came next and eventually spread globally. Minsky's analysis of the emergence and spread of MMC helps account for the continued push toward deregulation in the decades leading up to the Subprime Crisis, the persistent resistance to regulation in the face of that crisis, and the aggressive steps taken by Republican officials once that party regained control of the White House in 2017.

The key element added here by Minsky's analysis of capitalism's stages is that MMC is an era driven by finance in general and by institutional investors (money managers) in particular. Their drive for maximization of shareholder value has shifted the balance of power away from the managers of industrial corporations, whose voices were dominant in the era of managerial capitalism. In fact, MMC's short-term-oriented financialization has shaped not only industry and finance but also public policy. As Gerald Epstein writes, "Financialization refers to the increasing importance of financial markets, financial motives, financial institutions, and financial elites in the operation of the economy and its governing institutions, both at the national and international level" (Epstein 2002, 1). Since the early 1980s, state power has responded to crises (including the COVID-19 pandemic in which the world finds itself as this chapter is being written) with at least as much of a focus on rescuing the financial sector (including enabling it to offload or insulate itself from risk) as on protecting the economy and the public.

Thus, a central conclusion of this chapter is the need to integrate Minsky's work on stages of capitalism with his work on cycles and financial instability. In other words, understanding the current era of capitalism, not only in the US but also in the overall global economy, requires integrating Minsky's cycle-oriented FIH and his structural analysis of MMC. Moreover, the possibility of such an integration comes most clearly into view when we adopt an institutionally oriented reading of the FIH. Properly viewed, both the FIH and MMC are evolutionary and institutionally grounded analytical concepts.

Despite this chapter's focus on an underlying cyclical tendency and a postwar historical movement toward economic and political dominance by the US financial sector, it is possible to end on a note that contains some hope. At bottom, Minsky's fundamental policy message is the same as that of Keynes and a long line of Institutionalists: "Our economic destiny is controllable" (Minsky [1986] 2008, 8). Thus, we should not view cycles as a reason for fatalism and for thinking that regulatory frameworks are inevitably condemned to a short lifespan, but rather as an invitation to look for institutions and processes that could allow us to initiate a new phase of capitalism—a more regulated capitalism in which public authorities have the power, will, and endurance to resist the siren song of deregulation.

ACKNOWLEDGMENTS

The author thanks Faruk Ülgen, Jan Toporowski, and Charles Whalen for helpful comments and suggestions. He also thanks Maison Européenne des Sciences de l'Homme et de la Société for financial assistance to translate the text into English.

NOTES

1.   Some contributions within the RBC framework admit the possibility of a relationship between the level of production and money. The work of King and Plosser (1984), for example, explores this relationship, but exclusively in the sense of causality that runs from production to money.
2.   At the time of writing, the crisis sparked by the COVID-19 pandemic, which has resulted in a reduction in supply and demand worldwide, has not yet delivered all its consequences. The available projections, however, point to a reduction in economic activity that is undoubtedly significant enough to place it at the forefront of the economic crises that have recently shaken world capitalism.
3.   Ponzi finance is named after financial schemer Charles Ponzi.
4.   Kregel insists on the importance of cushions of safety, which cover the margin of error on the expected returns in an investment project, in order to understand how the normal functioning of capitalist economies produces instability (Kregel

2008). From that point of view, an increase in financial fragility derives from the progressive erosion of cushions of safety that occurs as risk aversion decreases.

5. Minsky confirms the perspective described above when he maintains that the transition from robustness to institutional easing does not happen in a vacuum, but is instead determined by a series of institutions and rules themselves determined by the legislative and administrative interventions of governments and central banks (Minsky [1986] 2008, 219). See also Sinapi (2011).

6. Minsky ([1986] 2008, 3) stressed that economic institutions "are not ordained by nature." In fact, he emphasized: "Economic systems are not natural systems. An economy is a social organization ... [and] policy can change both the details and the overall character of the economy" (Minsky [1986] 2008, 7).

7. In Regulation Theory, attention to balances of power is a consequence of the influence of Karl Marx. While the influence of Marx does not appear explicitly in Minsky's work, others have highlighted important commonalities shared by Marx and Minsky; see, for example, Crotty (1986; 1990) and Keen (2001).

8. Although power does not enter into Minsky's discussion of the FIH, it is part of his analysis of stages of capitalist development. In particular, the balance of power between economic actors is part of what distinguishes one stage from another (Minsky 1990, 66). Thus, power struggles are implicitly part of the contextual backdrop for Minskyan financial instability.

9. This element is very well documented in Chavagneux and Philipponnat (2014), particularly in the case of the European Commission.

10. While Roosevelt certainly offered a different approach to the Great Depression than his predecessor, Minsky notes that the "bank holiday" that followed soon after the presidential inauguration in 1933—and helped transfer the problem of illiquid and insolvent banks to the federal government—"was forced on Roosevelt" by bank closures in 30 states. Minsky also notes that the Reconstruction Finance Corporation (RFC), created in early 1932 at the initiative of President Herbert Hoover, played a "central role" in resolving the financial crisis, though the expanded powers and additional funds the RFC needed to make a significant difference did not occur until after Roosevelt took office (Minsky 1993, 1–2).

11. For Minsky, the Glass-Steagall Act introduced a greater transparency of financial activities. He writes:
   The scope of permissible activities by a depository institution was to be limited to what examiners and supervisors could readily understand. This objective of examinability and supervisability supported the separation of investment and commercial banking. It was not so much the differences in riskiness as it was the ease of understanding the operations that led to the separation of investment and commercial banking. (Minsky 1995, 5)

12. Until the Asian crisis, globalization was presented as an opportunity to push growth worldwide, but the 1997 crisis highlighted the fact that globalization also links the economic cycles of different countries.

13. Studies on this issue reveal that the failure to pass the law to create a Financial Supervisory Board is related to the political costs it would have imposed on the ruling party (Haggard and Mo 2000).

14. It took about ten days for president-elect Kim Dae-Jung to enact the new financial laws. He was elected on December 18 and the laws came into effect on December 29, 1997.

REFERENCES

Arestis, Philip and Murray Glickman. 2002. "Financial Crisis in Southeast Asia: Dispelling Illusion the Minskyan Way." *Cambridge Journal of Economics* 26 (1): 237–260.

Boyer, Robert. 2003. "Les Analyses Historiques Comparatives du Changement Institutionnel: Quels Enseignements Pour la Théorie de la Régulation." *L'année de la Régulation* n°7, 167–204.

Chang, Roberto and Andrés Velasco. 1998. "The Asian Liquidity Crisis." Working Paper 98-11, Federal Reserve Bank of Atlanta.

Chavagneux, Christian and Thierry Philipponnat. 2014. *La Capture*. Paris: Editions La Découverte.

Corsetti Giancarlo, Paolo Pesanti, and Nouriel Roubini. 1999. "What Caused the Asian Currency and Financial Crisis?" *Japan and the World Economy* 11 (3): 305–373.

Cozzi, Giovanni and Jan Toporowski. 2006. "The Balance Sheet Approach to Financial Crisis in Emerging Markets." Working Paper 485, Levy Economics Institute of Bard College.

Crotty, James R. 1986. "Marx, Keynes and Minsky on the Instability of the Capitalist Growth Process and the Nature of Government Economic Policy." In *Marx, Schumpeter, Keynes: A Centenary Celebration of Dissent*, edited by Suzanne W. Helburn and David F. Bramhall, 297–324. Armonk, NY: M.E. Sharpe.

Crotty, James R. 1990. "Owner-manager Conflict and Financial Theories of Investment Instability: A Critical Assessment of Keynes, Tobin and Minsky." *Journal of Post Keynesian Economics* 12 (4): 519–540.

Crotty, James R. and Kang-Kook Lee. 2002. "A Political-Economic Analysis of the Failure of Neo-Liberal Restructuring in Post-Crisis Korea." *Cambridge Journal of Economics* 26 (5): 667–678.

Dagher, Jihad. 2018. "Regulatory Cycles: Revisiting the Political Economy of Financial Crises." IMF Working Paper 18-8.

Delli Gatti, Domenico, Mauro Gallegati, and Hyman P. Minsky. 1994. "Financial Institutions, Economic Policy and the Dynamic Behavior of the Economy." Working Paper 126, Levy Economics Institute of Bard College.

Diop, Samba. 2016. "Minsky's Analysis of Capitalist Development: A Critical Assessment and Perspectives." *Review of Radical Political Economics* 48 (2): 201–216.

Dymski, Gary A. 1999. "Asset Bubbles and Minsky Crises in East Asia: A Spatialized Minsky Approach." University of California, Riverside, Department of Economics, Research Paper. April 1999.

Epstein, Gerald. 2002. "Financialization, Rentier Interests, and Central Bank Policy." Paper prepared for PERI Conference on "Financialization of the World Economy." December 7–8, 2001, University of Massachusetts, Amherst. Version 1.2, June 2002. https://tinyurl.com/yb2lwrx7. Accessed December 31, 2020.

Fama, Eugene F. 1970. "Efficient Capital Markets: A Review of Theory and Empirical Work." *Journal of Finance* 25 (2): 383–417.

Ferri, Piero and Hyman P. Minsky. 1992. "Market Processes and Thwarting Systems." *Structural Change and Economic Dynamics* 3 (1): 79–91.

Haggard, Stephan. 2000. *The Political Economy of the Asian Financial Crisis*. Washington, DC: Institute for International Economics.

Haggard, Stephan and Jongryn Mo. 2002. "The Political Economy of the Korean Financial Crisis." *Review of International Political Economy* 7 (2): 197–218.

Keen, Steve. 2001. "Minsky's Thesis: Keynesian or Marxian?" In *Financial Fragility and Investment in the Capitalist Economy: The Economic Legacy of Hyman Minsky, Volume I*, edited by Riccardo Bellofiore and Piero Ferri, 106–122. Cheltenham, UK: Edward Elgar.

King, Robert G. and Charles I. Plosser. 1984. "Money, Credit, and Prices in a Real Business Cycle." *American Economic Review* 74 (3): 363–380.

Kregel, Jan A. 1998. "Yes, 'It' Did Happen Again: A Minsky Crisis Happened in Asia." Working Paper 234, Levy Economics Institute of Bard College.

Kregel, Jan A. 2008. "Minsky's 'Cushions of Safety,' Systemic Risk and the Crisis in the Subprime Mortgage Market." *Finance & Bien Commun* 31–32 (2): 51–59.

Krugman, Paul. 1998. "What Happened to Asia?" Department of Economics, MIT. http://web.mit.edu/krugman/www/DISINTER.html. Accessed December 26, 2020.

Kydland, Finn and Edward Prescott. 1982. "Time to Build and Aggregate Fluctuations." *Econometrica* 50 (6): 473–491.

Lee Kang-Kook. 2010. *The Post-Crisis Changes in the Financial System in Korea: Problems of Neoliberal Restructuring and Financial Opening After 1997.* TWN Global Economy Series 20, Financial Crisis and Asian Developing Countries, Penang, Malaysia: Third Word Network.

Long, John B. and Charles I. Plosser. 1983. "Real Business Cycles." *Journal of Political Economy* 91 (1): 39–69.

Lordon, Frédéric. 2008. *Conflits et Pouvoirs Dans les Institutions du Capitalisme*, Paris: Presses de Sciences Po.

Mayer, Martin. 1998. "The Asian Disease: Plausible Diagnoses, Possible Remedies." Working Paper 232, Levy Economics Institute of Bard College.

Minsky, Hyman P. 1957. "Central Banking and Money Market Changes." *Quarterly Journal of Economics* 71 (2): 171–187.

Minsky, Hyman P. 1982. *Can It Happen Again? Essays in Finance and Instability.* Armonk, NY: M.E. Sharpe.

Minsky, Hyman P. 1986. "Global Consequences of Financial Deregulation." Hyman P. Minsky Archive, Paper 378.

Minsky, Hyman P. (1986) 2008. *Stabilizing an Unstable Economy.* New York: McGraw Hill.

Minsky, Hyman P. 1987. "Securitization." Hyman P. Minsky Archive, Paper 15. http://digitalcommons.bard.edu/hm_archive/15. Accessed December 26, 2020.

Minsky, Hyman P. 1990. "Schumpeter: Finance and Evolution." In *Evolving Technology and Market Structure: Studies in Schumpeterian Economics*, edited by Arnold Heertje and Mark Perlman, 51–74. Ann Arbor: University of Michigan Press.

Minsky, Hyman P. 1991. "Financial Crises: Systemic or Idiosyncratic." Working Paper 66, Levy Economics Institute of Bard College.

Minsky, Hyman P. 1992a. "The Financial Instability Hypothesis." Working Paper 74, Levy Economics Institute of Bard College.

Minsky, Hyman P. 1992b. "The Capital Development of the Economy and the Structure of Financial Institutions." Working Paper 72, Levy Economics Institute of Bard College.

Minsky, Hyman P. 1993. "Finance and Stability: The Limits of Capitalism." Working Paper 93, Levy Economics Institute of Bard College.

Minsky, Hyman P. 1994. "Financial Instability and the Decline (?) of Banking: Public Policy Implications." Hyman P. Minsky Archive, Paper 88, Levy Economics Institute of Bard College.

Minsky, Hyman P. 1995. "Reforming Banking in 1995: Repeal of the Glass Steagall Act—Some Basic Issues." Hyman P. Minsky Archive, Paper 59, Levy Economics Institute of Bard College.

Minsky, Hyman P. 1996. "Uncertainty and the Institutional Structure of Capitalist Economies." *Journal of Economic Issues* 30 (2): 357–368.

Minsky, Hyman P. and Claudia Campbell. 1988. "Getting Off the Back of a Tiger: The Deposit Insurance Crisis in the United States." Hyman P. Minsky Archive, Paper 67.

Minsky, Hyman P. and Charles J. Whalen. 1996. "Economic Insecurity and the Institutional Prerequisites for Successful Capitalism." *Journal of Post Keynesian Economics* 19 (2): 155–170.

Orléan, André. 1999. *Le Pouvoir de la Finance*, Paris: Odile Jacob.

Palley, Thomas I. 2010. "The Limits of Minsky's Financial Instability Hypothesis as an Explanation of the Crisis." *Monthly Review* 61 (11): 28–43.

Palley, Thomas I. 2011. "A Theory of Minsky Super-Cycles and Financial Crises." *Contributions to Political Economy* 30 (1): 31–46.

Papadimitriou, Dimitri B. and L. Randall Wray. 1998. "The Economic Contributions of Hyman Minsky: Varieties of Capitalism and Institutional Reform." *Review of Political Economy* 10 (2): 199–225.

Radelet, Steven and Jeffrey Sachs. 1998. "The Onset of the East Asian Financial Crisis." Harvard Institute for International Development, March 30.

Sinapi, Christine. 2011. "Institutional Prerequisites of Financial Fragility within Minsky's Financial Instability Hypothesis: A Proposal in Terms of Institutional Fragility." Working Paper 674, Levy Economics Institute of Bard College.

Skidelsky, Robert. 1992. *John Maynard Keynes. The Economist as Saviour: 1921–1937*, London: Macmillan.

Whalen, Charles J. 2011. *Financial Instability and Economic Insecurity after the Great Recession.* Cheltenham, UK: Edward Elgar.

Whalen, Charles J. 2017. "Understanding Financialization: Standing on the Shoulders of Minsky." *Financial Internet Quarterly* 13 (2): 45–61.

Whalen, Charles J. 2020. "Post-Keynesian Institutionalism: Past, Present, and Future." *Evolutionary and Institutional Economics Review* 17 (1): 71–92.

White, Eugene N. 1982. "The Political Economy of Banking Regulation, 1864–1933." *Journal of Economic History* 42 (1): 33–40.

White, Eugene N. 1986. "Before the Glass-Steagall Act: An Analysis of the Investment Banking Activities of National Banks." *Explorations in Economic History* 23 (1): 33–55.

White, Eugene N. 1990. "The Stock Market Boom and Crash of 1929 Revisited." *Journal of Economic Perspectives* 4 (2): 67–83.

Wray, L. Randall. 2007. "Lessons from the Subprime Meltdown." Working Paper 522, Levy Economics Institute of Bard College.

14. From Public Choice to Minskyan collective action: the case for macro rationality-based financial regulation

Faruk Ülgen

INTRODUCTION

As this chapter is being written (in early 2021), economies around the world face extraordinary uncertainty. Despite the harmful consequences of the global financial crisis of 2007–2009, the limited nature of post-crisis regulatory reform (and, indeed, a recent trend toward deregulation in some nations over the past several years) means that serious financial crises remain a threat to economic stability worldwide.[1] Moreover, economic distress generated by the COVID-19 pandemic has made socioeconomic life all the more precarious.

Faced with that uncertainty and precarity, questions about the organization and management of the economy are emerging both within and outside academia. These questions partly relate to the characteristics of our monetary and financial systems. The search for ways to control the evolution of an economic situation that could become collectively dangerous and humanly unacceptable necessarily raises questions about the functioning of financial markets and the sustainability of debt relations that are at the heart of all economic operations in market-based capitalist economies. In a broader sense, the challenges we face include both the propensity of today's capitalist economies to generate recurrent systemic instabilities and insufficient societal awareness of the crucial role of collective/public mechanisms and regulatory institutions in fighting against such a tendency and achieving a more stable and prosperous society.

This chapter focuses on the endogenous financial instability of capitalist economies and seeks to assess and highlight the relevance of a regulatory framework that is different from market-centered self-regulation. Drawing on the work of Hyman Minsky and other contributors to the Institutionalist and Post Keynesian literature—which regards the working of the economy as a whole and not as a mere sum of individual decisions—the chapter develops a systemic (holistic) view of contemporary capitalism. The originality of the current analysis is that it supplies a relevant framework on financial stability by using theoretical approaches that do not immediately seem compatible with each other, namely the economic approaches of Public Choice (PC) and Post-Keynesian Institutionalism (PKI).

Although PC is usually related to microeconomic rationality hypotheses and PKI is generally associated with the primacy of macroeconomic coherence over individual rationality, both perspectives aim at dealing with public-decision/collective-action issues to improve the functioning of capitalist economies. The difference is PC maintains that the decisions of public officials cannot be relied upon to rise above narrow self-interest and serve the public interest, while PKI (a branch of the Institutionalist tradition situated at the cross-roads of the economics of Keynes, Post Keynesianism, and Institutionalism) stresses that market self-regulation cannot ensure macroeconomic stability. The purpose of this analysis is not to suggest micro-foundations to conduct a macroeconomic analysis or vice versa; nor is it to suggest that PC is either fully or in all circumstances relevant to PKI scholarship. Rather, this chapter argues that the PC may be regarded as a relevant departure point for the study of systemic stability in a capitalist economy.

The main explanation put forward in this chapter is that a natural bridge between micro-rational individual behavior and macro-rational systemic stability is not provided through market mechanisms. Systemic stability is a society-wide issue that requires—despite the challenges—society-wide measures and actions, while the micro-rational behavior of PC provides only action driven by separate and individual goals and judgments. Thus, this chapter rejects the notion of market self-regulation and calls instead for transforming the *microeconomic* rationality-based logic of the PC approach into a *macroeconomic* approach focusing on collective rationality. A clear separation between private and public decisions and interests is a necessary condition when it comes to systemic stability. Put simply: financial regulation and supervision require a framework based in macroeconomics and collective action.

The rest of the chapter proceeds as follows. First, we focus on the convergence between Institutionalist and Post Keynesian visions of a monetary capitalist economy, highlighting the pitfalls of the neoliberal, free-market approach that has dominated economics and public policy for several decades. Second, we review the PC approach and argue not only that its assumptions about self-interested policymakers *can* be amended, but also that they *must* be amended to have any relevance in a world with financial markets—because such markets give rise to systemic problems that cannot be resolved without collective action. The assumptions of the PC approach are right with regard to the incentives that drive individual market participants in their decisions and strategies; the trouble is that such incentives often lead to outcomes widely recognized as societally inefficient and unstable. Third, we adapt the PC approach to address the financial-market realities highlighted by PKI. Since financial markets require public regulation and supervision, that section calls for transforming the micro-rationality-based logic of the PC approach into a macroeconomic reasoning—that is, into an approach focusing on collective rationality. A final section concludes.

PKI: THE ECONOMICS OF A MONETARY ECONOMY AND FINANCIALIZATION

In mainstream (Neoclassical) economics, the underlying image of the economy is that of a real exchange (non-monetary) economy (Minsky 1975, 57). To be sure, money can be added to the analysis under some ad hoc assumptions without providing a deeper understanding of economic reality. Once real equilibrium is achieved under competitive market assumptions, in the long run, money only affects nominal prices, not real variables such as output and employment (Minsky 1975, 8). Thus, it is no surprise that such economics cannot adequately explain the recurrent monetary and financial instabilities of capitalist economies.

PKI insists that economics must not ignore these instabilities. As a result, it offers an alternative vision rooted in two positions that contrast sharply with mainstream economics. One is that capitalism is a *monetary* economy: financial relations play a central role in its evolutionary dynamics. In fact, Minsky (1975, 57–58) argued that the proper alternative to the barter paradigm (underlying conventional economics) is a Wall Street paradigm: "the image is of a banker making his [sic] deals on a Wall Street." The other core position is that capitalism's internal dynamics endogenously generate systemic instability that threatens the viability of the whole system; thus, those dynamics engender the need for a public hand in the form of government regulation. In other words, PKI maintains that collective action is required to establish an institutional environment that sustains economic activity and provides a stabilizing force in the face of capitalism's destabilizing tendencies.[2]

Contemporary PKI is the economics of a monetary economy. But it is also the economics of financialization. That's because PKI emphasizes the core role played by money and financial institutions in capitalist development, which in recent decades has led to an era that Minsky called money manager capitalism (Minsky 1993a; Whalen 2012; 2020). Analyses of a monetary economy and financialization both point to the need for public intervention.

The Money Economy

Looking at capitalism as a monetary economy enables us to recognize and study the significance of its ongoing evolution. More than three decades ago, Arestis and Eichner (1988) pointed to the close links between Institutional and Post Keynesian economics, which they traced to the fact that John Maynard Keynes, Thorstein Veblen, and others inspired by them worked on the monetary theory of production, wherein money is an endogenous and core variable allowing capitalism to evolve through an accumulation path. Indeed, Institutionalists like Veblen, Wesley Mitchell, and John R. Commons, each highlighted the monetary characteristics of capitalism and the links between those characteristics and the systemic instabilities observed over the course of its history.[3] In more recent work, Ülgen (2016; 2017; 2018) shows that the Institutionalist approach offers a relevant analysis of capitalism as a "money economy" in which the characteristics of money and the behavior of financial systems are central to capitalist evolution.

Two important theoretical constructs can be found at the intersection of Institutional and Post Keynesian economics: a monetary theory of production, and the hypothesis of endogenous money.[4] Working at the crossroads of Institutional and Post Keynesian economics—but within a tradition that encompasses not only Keynes, Michał Kalecki, and Nicholas Kaldor, but also Joseph Schumpeter—Dudley Dillard (1987, 1623) highlighted what he called an Institutionalist monetary theory of production. His theory stresses the central role of money in the economic process, and points to perhaps the central weaknesses of mainstream economics, which is it overlooks the fact that "the production of goods and services by which we live is a byproduct of the expectation of businessmen [sic] to 'make money.'" Minsky's (1975; 1986) investment theory of endogenous business cycles—which explicitly highlights not only the need for countercyclical macroeconomic policy, but also government regulation to bring some stability to an inherently unstable economy—rests on such a monetary theory of production.

The hypothesis of endogenous money (see Lavoie 2014) stresses that a capitalist economy works through continuous and expansive debt relations, which provide the means of financing decentralized and private economic decisions without any central planning and public oversight. A capitalist economy is inherently a debt economy, and, as a consequence, it needs viable and sustainable public (extra-market) rules to ensure the society-wide validity of the process of circulation and repayment of debts.[5] Such a process allows for wealth accumulation on a large scale.

The endogenous money approach is implicit in Minsky's (1986) work on financial and macroeconomic instability, but also in L. Randall Wray's (2002) sectoral balances approach to macroeconomic analysis. Wray's analysis focuses on the macro structure of debt relations and points to the crucial role played by the institutions of the system of payments. Wray, who was a doctoral student of Minsky, actually wrote his dissertation on endogenous money. That work demonstrates that the endogeneity of money and the need for public regulation of financial operations are two sides of the same coin (Wray 1990).[6]

Money Manager Capitalism

PKI's attention to money manager capitalism is part of Institutionalism's longstanding interest in the stages of capitalist evolution. Writing in the 1920s, Veblen (1921, 34–38) observed that the rise of industrial capitalism in the latter half of the nineteenth century meant that corporate finance had become "the controlling factor in industry." Commons (1950, 61) went further—but still with a focus on finance—and identified three stages: merchant capitalism, industrial capitalism, and financial capitalism, using the latter designation to highlight the dominant economic role of investment bankers in the early twentieth century.[7] Minsky (1993a), drawing on a similar approach to capitalist development that he learned from Schumpeter (his dissertation adviser), then extended Commons's analysis by adding two more stages: managerial capitalism, which began with the New Deal and reached its peak in the first two decades after World War II, and the current stage (which took shape around 1980) that he called money manager capitalism.

PKI argues that much of the dynamism in capitalism in any era can be traced to the financial system, where profit-seeking lenders, investors, and executives are always looking for institutional innovations that will provide them with an edge over others (Minsky and Whalen 1996, 156). Moreover, since finance proceeds production (which, of course, is a key insight of any monetary theory of production), finance is always an important driver of economic activity. But the present period, like the earlier stage of financial capitalism, is notable because financial actors—in this case, institutional investors (who manage pension funds, hedge funds, and other large financial portfolios)—play a dominant role, not the entrepreneurs, industrialists, and business leaders who were dominant in several other stages (ibid., 158).

Instead of financing productive activities, most financial relations in the era of money manager capitalism focus on maximizing near-term financial profitability. In fact, because maximization of shareholder value over the short run is the key aim, attention is heavily oriented toward speculative operations that often involve increasing systemic risks. Writing in the wake of the global financial crisis of 2007–2009, Wray (2012, 6) notes that the new practices stemming from such financial innovations generally serve "no social purposes beyond making top management and financial institutions incredibly rich." He adds: "At the same time, the structure of incentives and rewards was changed [over the course of several decades] such that risky bets, high leverage ratios, and short-term profits were promoted over long-term firm [enterprise] survival and returns to investors."

The now decades-long focus on shareholder value and on short-term financial gains is what many today describe as financialization, which is really just another way of describing what Minsky called the emergence of money manager capitalism.[8] Elements of financialization were identified by the Financial Crisis Inquiry Commission (FCIC), established by the United States (US) Congress, as a factor contributing to the global financial crisis. In particular, the FCIC (2011) highlighted various aspects of the evolution of financial markets between the early 1980s and the start of the crisis, including the oversizing of financial activities, the growth and asset concentration of investment banks, the increasing role of shadow banking, the growth of derivatives, and the increasing gap in compensation between financial and non-financial sectors.[9]

Leading up to the crisis of 2007–2009, such a long-term financial evolution was permitted and even supported by regulatory changes. Restrictive public oversight was removed or loosened to encourage financial innovations and market openness. The regulatory framework was also changed in favor of market-centered self-regulation models that relied not only on credit rating agencies, which were often paid for by the issuers of the products being rated, but also on banks' own risk calculations (a method called the "internal ratings-based approach" to credit risk). Until the crisis hit, many policymakers and regulators, such as Federal Reserve Board chairman Alan Greenspan, were enthusiastic supporters of such a reform process—even when the increasing risks related to this transformation began to worry financial industry practitioners.[10]

Free-Market Pitfalls and the Need for Public Action

By focusing on both the cyclical and structural dimensions of the current era, PKI highlights the pitfalls of free markets and the need for public action. According to PKI, private institutions are vital because they allow individuals and enterprises to undertake profit-seeking economic activities via decentralized credit-debt relations. But this is also where cycles enter the picture: when local disequilibria accumulate within those credit-debt relations—as is bound to happen owing to an endogenous tendency toward riskier practices during expansions (Minsky 1986)—crises break out and public institutions are usually required to restore financial-sector confidence and stabilize the economy (Delli Gatti, Gallegati, and Minsky 1994). PKI also stresses that pursuit of maximum shareholder value and other features of the current financialized era—including a general emphasis on market-oriented, neoliberal policies—exacerbate capitalism's core tendency toward periods of financial expansion and contraction. In addition, money manager capitalism generates and intensifies worker insecurity and economic inequality (Minsky and Whalen 1996; Whalen 2020).

From the perspective of Post-Keynesian Institutionalists, it is clear that a new approach to public action in financial markets is needed—beyond market self-regulation, but also beyond dependence on bailouts in periods of crisis. Indeed, in the aftermath of the global financial crisis of 2007–2009, it was clear the biggest gains from public action went to financial institutions, whose profits (boosted by low interest rates and access to low-cost government borrowing) rebounded within two years of the start of the crisis (FCIC 2011, 401). What is needed is a macroprudential preventive approach that recognizes the public as well as private dimensions of finance and stability.

MICROECONOMIC RATIONALITY, COLLECTIVE RATIONALITY, AND THE GOAL OF FINANCIAL STABILITY

Recognizing that there are public and private dimensions to finance and stability means admitting that monetary economies present us with social dilemmas—that is, conflicts between what is optimal from an individual (microeconomic) perspective and from a societal (macroeconomic) vantage point. The PC approach accepts the need for some sort of coordination of individual decisions; indeed, it accepts the need for some type of regulation. However, it concludes that such coordination should emerge from within the private sector—and that the most efficient form of regulation is market-based, self-regulation (Buchanan 2003). This section reviews that approach's assumptions, which, we argue, must be amended to reflect the realities of a monetary economy.

The PC Approach and Microeconomic Rationality

PC builds on the hard-core assumptions of Neoclassical economics—such as methodological individualism, rational choice, and "politics as exchange" (which means individuals secure mutual gains by "contracting" for a constitution)—and concludes that what motivates the behavior of both public and private decision-makers is the process of rational, self-interested decision-making at the microeconomic level of individuals and enterprises. Recognizing the existence of market failures, PC also aims at establishing conditions for efficient allocation in the presence of such failures, which leads to "the study of nonmarket procedures for revealing individual preferences in these situations" (Mueller 1976, 396). Although considered a critique of the public regulation of markets, one of the most important contributions of PC is to show the impossibility of determining the conditions of an optimal equilibrium that would result from a collective choice process, whether based on market mechanisms or public action.

Within some limits, the assumptions of the PC approach are right with regard to the incentives that could drive people in their decisions and strategies. Especially in the case of public goods, a relevant decision process for goods allocation is not obvious.[11] More generally, PC maintains that although markets (the private invisible hand) do not work at optimum, government (the public visible hand) does not always effectively correct market failures. In fact, PC maintains that public bureaucracies tend to grow, apparently without limit and without connection to initially promised functions (Buchanan 2003).

Because of the difficulties the PC approach associates with revealing individual preferences and determining an optimal economic equilibrium, James Buchanan and Gordon Tullock (1962) argue that a collective decision in the public interest has to be supported unanimously by all the voters, whereas majority decisions may be unfair. However, Steven Croley (2008) maintains that the PC theory rests on an incomplete and undertheorized understanding of regulatory government. In particular, he argues that it is possible to produce regulatory outcomes that promote the public interest by means of existing legal-procedural mechanisms. With a more specific focus on the characteristics of a monetary economy, one can also argue that, in their usual form, the assumptions of PC about the individualistic micro-rationality of self-interested policymakers are not relevant with regard to the issues generated by the workings of financial markets.

Private Interests, the Public Good, and Collective Rationality

The workings of financial markets give rise to systemic problems that cannot be resolved without collective action, and market incentives often lead to social outcomes widely recognized as unacceptable and inefficient. A distinction between private interests and the public good must be established. Adam Smith's invisible hand does not work in a monetary economy: private and public interests do not converge toward the same outcome.

Given that PC aims at dealing with collective (public) action in the case of market failures, it would be suitable to transform the logic of the microeconomic, individual rationality-based PC approach into a macroeconomic reasoning, based on a *collective* rationality. Because of the divergence of individual private interests and the public good, it would not be logically consistent to think that financial regulation and supervision would be achievable through the self-regulation of decentralized market mechanisms. The monetary and financial characteristics of contemporary capitalist economies—and the disequilibria and instabilities they endogenously generate—require a different methodological and conceptual approach than is usual in PC: they require a theory of collective action based on macroeconomic reasoning. Such a theory must allow rational decision-making at the *societal* level; it must consider financial regulation for the common good.

Since micro-oriented PC economics does not address systemic instabilities and provides no avenue for encouraging private entities to pursue strategies that foster macroeconomic stability, the search for an alternative approach to financial regulation—that is, an approach based in collective action and focused on preventive public oversight—points us in the direction of PKI (Phillips 1997; Whalen 2011). This alternative is not intended to inhibit financial-market innovation and dynamism. It rather seeks to redirect market dynamics toward economically and societally sustainable activities. Furthermore, such an alternative would enable financial regulation to address other socioeconomic challenges—including poverty, worker insecurity, widening inequality, threats to public health, environmental degradation, and global warming—through a collectively coherent organization of financial markets.

The Macroprudential Approach of PKI

This macroprudential approach—necessitated by the fact that markets do not work in a socially efficient way—offers coordination by a visible (public) hand that could put collective interests ahead of individual interests. From such a perspective, the role of public intervention, regulation, and oversight of markets is to correct, reframe, and sanction actors' behavior, providing incentives that rest on collective goals and that (with those goals in mind) fix the limits of acceptable individual behavior. Since the rules of the game are common coordination devices, the aim of this regulatory approach is mainly to rely on institutions (including the organization of markets and extra-market institutions), thereby shaping individual strategies according to "the common good" in ways that cannot be achieved by relying entirely on private information and individual plans and actions.[12]

Financial regulation takes on systemic importance since a smooth functioning of markets requires the continuous and sustainable provision of financial stability. Systemic financial stability is, thus, a public good to be provided by appropriate mechanisms—and cannot rest on market self-regulation. Nevertheless, a mix of micro (private) and macro (public) regulation may have a political and ideological attraction for policymakers and private corporations. It might also be attractive as a practical matter: there are certainly private dimensions to financial markets. In fact, from the perspective of PKI, it turns out that the dilemma of how voluntary associations could be made to pursue public interest—highlighted several decades ago by Mancur Olson (1965)—

can be seen as a matter of providing the right institutional environment such that the consistency of each micro-level alternative depends on specific conditions and predefined public goals.[13]

PUBLICNESS OF FINANCIAL STABILITY AND MACRO-COHERENT FINANCIAL REGULATION

Provision of financial stability is not something that can be left to the private sector. Financial operations generate externalities—both positive and negative in nature—that affect the whole of society, whether or not individuals are directly involved in those operations. But, as indicated in the previous section, the matter goes beyond externalities: financial stability must be considered a public good since it is a systemic need that cannot be met by market mechanisms.[14] In fact, because economic relations rest on the feasibility of continuous payment and settlement operations, monetary and financial services can be viewed as part of the vital infrastructure of a capitalist economy.

Appreciating and Reforming the Basic Infrastructure of Capitalism

Many economists recognize the central bank as part of the economy's basic infrastructure because it acts as a rule-maker and rule-keeper. But that infrastructure includes the entire legal and regulatory framework that enables the central bank and various government agencies to stabilize the economy by means of rules, regulations, and oversight (Minsky 1964). In a capitalist society, the monetary system is a society-wide payments system that determines how economic relations take place among individuals and organizations. The system consists of rules and practices that define, govern, and support the process of debt creation, circulation, and repayment. These debts, also known as money, finance individual and organizational decisions across the economy and are the common denominator of capitalist accumulation; debt financing is also the fundamental linkage between the real and financial sector (Kregel 2010a).[15] The monetary structure allows private decision units to make their economic plans effective without any collective plan but according to some common rules. At the same time, financial stability is a societal concern that links the viability of the whole to the consequences of the monetary and financial decisions of a few. Thus, the financial system displays the features of a basic infrastructure common to the whole of society, and financial stability displays those of a public good.

In the wake of the global financial crisis, several regulatory reforms have been discussed; some have even been implemented.[16] However, the core of financial regulation in the United States and elsewhere still relies on self-regulatory schemes and has not been modified to give a larger place to procedures and tools centered on collective action and aimed at anticipating and preventing economic catastrophes. Endogenous fragilities and the fundamental weaknesses of liberal financial regulation yield recurrent crises and call for a thoroughgoing transformation of supervision mechanisms by means of extra-market public oversight.

The first goal of such reform is to break financialized capitalism's "doom loop," whereby the system evolves through a boom-bust-bailout financial cycle that leads to recurrent economic crises. When markets are loosely regulated, risky investments and dangerous financial practices gain ground and initially lead to increased growth and profit. However, such a boom is soon counterbalanced by a slump that puts markets under the pressure of an uncertain future and pushes the financial sector toward collapse. In the face of generalized difficulties and the threat of systemic panic, collective action takes the superficial form of a bailout, which calms markets without addressing the system's fundamental flaws.

Preventive and prudential regulation and supervision, organized and managed by an extra-market/public power, is required to break the doom loop. A macroprudential framework regards the financial sector's evolution toward instability as endogenously determined and assumes that a system-wide economic failure is not an accident but a normal outcome of the working of free markets—an outcome with widespread societal consequences. Thus, the aim of macroprudential regulation must be to oversee systemic risk and limit the likelihood of a generalized systemic failure. Market-related self-regulation and micro-prudential risk management are insufficient because they lack a global view. That insufficiency is evident not only in the euphoric period prior to a crisis, when it makes sense for individual firms to make increasingly risky moves, but also in a downturn, which is when it becomes obvious that financial institutions are not able to internalize the costs imposed on society as many firms shrink their assets at the same time (Hanson, Kashyap, and Stein 2011). There is then a rationale for the macroprudential organization of the economy regarding its sustainability conditions.

Some Rules and Challenges

Since a key macro objective is financial stability over time, two general regulatory rules can be put forward. One is that regulators need to supervise balance sheets and cash flows with an eye to identifying solvency threats and preventing an increase of systemic risk (see, e.g., Phillips 1997). The other is that when gains are private, losses must not be socialized. In line with this rule, and given the societal criticalness of financial operations in a capitalist society, financial responsibility of the market deciders (for instance, chief executives) must also be linked to effective criminal responsibility such that the punishment should be proportional to the damages caused by unfair speculative operations.[17] The aim is to reduce, by all means, the likelihood of hazardous strategies that could generate systemic consequences. This is not a moral statement; rather, it aims to encourage prudent business decision-making and reduce the social costs of private failures.

Macroprudential regulation also requires the supervision of regulators to ensure their work stays focused on the public interest. Regulators should be civil servants, beyond the influence of those being regulated. They must also issue reports to the public on a regular basis. Of course, no human system is perfect, so there will certainly be room for improvement over time. But the main current challenge is not to achieve something close to institutional perfection. Rather, it is to forge firm national and international commitments to moving financial regulation in the macroprudential direction.

CONCLUSION

This chapter has argued that a major source of economic imbalances and systemic crises since the 1980s is the transformation of capitalist economies into speculation-based financialized machines that are overseen by insufficient extra-market public regulation. In fact, the past several decades have seen a general trend toward liberalization of finance and market-self regulation of the financial sector. There has even been a "commodification" of financial regulation, resulting from often heavy reliance on rating agencies to assess the default risk of organizations and the credit risk of specific debt securities (including new, untested financial innovations).

The chapter has also argued that Institutionalist and Post Keynesian research offers valuable insight relevant to designing the collective action framework required to reshape financial markets and ensure systemic stability. Fashioning such a framework is a matter of designing institutions for regulation and supervision, and is closely linked to the broader matter of social dilemmas and the challenges of public decision-making. Thus, financial regulation can also be studied with the PC approach and public goods literature. However, PC methodology, based on the micro-dynamics of markets, cannot capture the systemic roots of financial instabilities that are part of macroeconomic dynamics and that, therefore, need to be addressed at the level of the economy as a whole, beyond the perspective of individual financial institutions.

Although one might maintain that policymakers can be regarded as micro-rational decision units that may seek to maximize their own interests even when they are expected to serve the public interest, a collective action framework of financial regulation cannot be considered a mere tool of private-interest satisfaction. The challenges of financial regulation are macroeconomic and extend beyond the scope of individual behavior. To be sure, as Gary Dymski (2010, 253) states, "[T]he ability to control instability, which Minsky so prized, depends on institutional arrangements that are, in the end, themselves fragile and unstable." Yet that does not lead to the conclusion that micro-rationality-based market self-regulation is better than public regulation.[18] As this chapter has emphasized, the problem of endogenous financial instability, inherent in a (capitalist) monetary economy, makes it necessary to frame financial regulation at the systemic level—beyond or outside market relations. Thus, the appropriate questions are: how to forge national and international commitments to macroprudential supervision and regulation; and how to devise (and then update) frameworks that would reduce the risk of conflicts of interest in the exercise of public power?

The publicness of financial stability renders self-regulation mechanisms inadequate as a means of ensuring economy-wide financial stability. The stability of the financial system cannot be produced and managed by decentralized market mechanisms. The gap between micro-rational efficiency and macro-rational systemic stability cannot be bridged by the invisible hand of the price mechanism and market incentives.

Nearly three decades ago, Minsky (1993b) described two opposing models of capitalism. One is an interventionist, big-government capitalism (that is, an economy with government big enough to stabilize aggregate profits in downturns), aimed at sustaining welfare-generating activities. The other is a laissez-faire capitalism, wherein the public hand seeks to loosen public oversight and regulation over markets, intervening only in emergencies and in ways that primarily socialize the financial losses of large organizations. The latter model, which has provided the standard for most economic activity in the industrialized world since the 1980s, has led to an exuberant growth of speculative finance at the expense of industrial development and social improvement, as well as to large and recurrent financial crises, rising worker insecurity, and extraordinary inequalities of income and wealth—all of which call into question the sustainability of such an approach to economic organization.

Unfortunately, nations still seem to beat around the bush on this issue and avoid cutting to the chase and getting to what really counts. The sooner that market-centered regulation is replaced by collective action-based regulation, the sooner we will have economies that are stronger and more stable over the long term. The serious worldwide downturn caused by the COVID-19 pandemic could have served as the decisive reminder of the need for collective action to ensure the stability of financial markets. However, current developments do not bode well for those seeking a fundamental change in financial regulation; the current health crisis seems to largely have obscured the underlying economic problems that no vaccine can solve.

ACKNOWLEDGMENTS

The author wishes to thank Samba Diop, Lyubov Klapkiv, Wesley Marshall, and Charles Whalen for reviewing and commenting on the previous drafts of this chapter. According to the usual politeness formula, I bear sole responsibility for any remaining errors, even if this is only partially true, since any research work is the result of efforts shared by those who participate directly or indirectly!

NOTES

1. See the chapter in this volume by Diop (Chapter 13) for an illustrative discussion of how policymakers in the United States began to loosen financial regulation as memory of the global financial crisis began to fade.
2. While PKI highlights the compatibility of the economics of Keynes, Post Keynesians, and Institutionalists, it is called Post-Keynesian *Institutionalism* because it is, most fundamentally, *Institutional* economics. Yes, this strand of Institutionalism is informed by the common ground it shares with (and the insight contained within) Keynes and Post Keynesians, but PKI begins and ends as a branch of Institutionalism on a par with, for example, the Veblen-Ayres and Commons traditions. While Keynes and the Post Keynesians offer important insights and contributions, Institutionalism has always gone beyond both of them in its emphasis not only on the fundamental importance of the institutional character of economies in general, but also on the crucial role of monetary features in capitalist economies in particular. Indeed, this is what attracted Minsky to Institutionalism (see, e.g., Minsky 1982, 280; and Whalen 2008a, 251).
3. Indeed, Mitchell (1916, 157), maintained that money "is the root of economic science" and envisioned a theory of the "money economy" as the ultimate goal of his research on business cycles (see Dillard 1987, 1629).
4. For a comprehensive presentation of different strands of Post Keynesian analyses, see Lavoie (2014); for a similar look at Institutional economics, see Whalen (2022).
5. A debt not built on generally accepted and legally reinforced rules is of limited value because it cannot be used as a socially asserted means of financing.
6. I owe the above observations on endogenous money in Minsky and Wray to Charles Whalen.
7. In *Institutional Economics*, Commons (1934, 763–773, 789) even used the term "banker capitalism" to refer to what he (and others) later called financial (or finance) capitalism.
8. According to Epstein (2005, 3), "[F]inancialization means the increasing role of financial motives, financial markets, financial actors and financial institutions in the operation of the domestic and international economies."
9. In 2009, annual average compensation was $102,069 in the US financial sector (which includes finance and insurance) and $58,666 in the non-financial sector (FCIC 2011, 62).
10. According to the FCIC (2011, 20), "Even those who had profited from the growth of nontraditional lending practices said they became disturbed by what was happening." The report continues:

Herb Sandler, the co-founder of the mortgage lender Golden West Financial Corporation, which was heavily loaded with option ARM [i.e., adjustable rate mortgage] loans, wrote a letter [in 2006] to officials at the Federal Reserve, the FDIC, the OTS, and the OCC warning that regulators were "too dependent" on ratings agencies and "there is a high potential for gaming when virtually any asset can be churned through securitization and transformed into a AAA-rated asset, and when a multi-billion dollar industry is all too eager to facilitate this alchemy."

11. For a comprehensive presentation of the related issues, see Mueller (1976).
12. The above discussion is one illustration of Minsky's (1982, 280) observation that "monetary economics cannot escape being institutional economics."
13. For an excellent discussion of the need for public policy to establish (and constantly update) an institutional environment that can contain capitalism's endogenous tendency toward instability, see Ferri and Minsky (1992), which emphasizes the need for institutional "containing or thwarting" mechanisms "that make observed values of variables different from what they would have been if each economic agent pursued 'only his [sic] own gain'" (ibid., 79, 84).
14. For further discussion of financial stability as a public good, see Ülgen (2021).
15. This again harkens back to our discussion of the monetary theory of production at the heart of PKI.
16. For discussions of reform ideas from the viewpoint of PKI and related perspectives, see, for example, Epstein and Crotty (2013); Keen (1995); Kregel (2010a; 2010b); Palley (2009); Rosser, Rosser, and Gallegati (2012); Whalen (2008b); Wray (2011; 2012); and Wolfson (2002).
17. I owe this remark to Lyubov Klapkiv.
18. Indeed, Minsky clearly recognized that the economic stability produced by policy-driven institutional arrangements would always be transitory at best (see, e.g., Ferri and Minsky 1992, 84).

REFERENCES

Arestis, Philip and Alfred S. Eichner. 1988. "The Post-Keynesian and Institutionalist Theory of Money and Credit." *Journal of Economic Issues* 22 (4): 1003–1021.
Buchanan, James M. 2003. "Public Choice: The Origins and Development of a Research Program." Center for Study of Public Choice, George Mason University.
Buchanan, James M. and Gordon Tullock. 1962. *The Calculus of Consent. Logical Foundations of Constitutional Democracy.* Ann Arbor: University of Michigan Press.
Commons, John R. 1934. *Institutional Economics.* New York: Macmillan.
Commons, John R. 1950. *The Economics of Collective Action,* edited by Kenneth H. Parsons. New York: Macmillan.
Croley, Steven P. 2008. *Regulation and Public Interests: The Possibility of Good Regulatory Government.* Princeton, NJ: Princeton University Press.
Delli Gatti, Domenico, Mauro Gallegati, and Hyman P. Minsky. 1994. "Financial Institutions, Economic Policy and the Dynamic Behavior of the Economy." The Jerome Levy Economics Institute of Bard College Working Paper No. 126.
Dillard, Dudley. 1987. "Money as an Institution of Capitalism." *Journal of Economic Issues* 21 (4): 1623–1647.
Dymski, Gary A. 2010. "Why the Subprime Crisis is Different: A Minskyan Approach." *Cambridge Journal of Economics* 34 (2): 239–255.

Epstein, Gerald. 2005. "Introduction." In *Financialization and the World Economy*, edited by Gerald Epstein, 3–16. Cheltenham, UK: Edward Elgar.

Epstein, Gerald and James Crotty. 2013. "How Big Is Too Big? On the Social Efficiency of the Financial Sector in the United States." University of Massachusetts Amherst, Political Economy Research Institute Working Paper Series Number 313.

Ferri, Piero and Hyman P. Minsky. 1992. "Market Processes and Thwarting Systems." *Structural Change and Economic Dynamics* 3 (1): 79–91.

Financial Crisis Inquiry Commission. 2011. *Financial Crisis Inquiry Report, Final Report of the National Commission on the Causes of the Financial and Economic Crisis in the United States*, February 25, 2011. https://www.govinfo.gov/content/pkg/GPO-FCIC/pdf/GPO-FCIC.pdf. (Accessed March 5, 2020.)

Hanson, Samuel G., Anil K. Kashyap, and Jeremy C. Stein. 2011. "A Macroprudential Approach to Financial Regulation." *Journal of Economic Perspectives* 25 (1): 3–28.

Keen, Steve. 1995. "Finance and Economic Breakdown: Modeling Minsky's 'Financial Instability Hypothesis.'" *Journal of Post Keynesian Economics* 17 (4): 607–635.

Kregel, Jan. 2010a. "What Would Minsky have Thought of the Mortgage Crisis?" In *The Elgar Companion to Hyman Minsky*, edited by Dimitri B. Papadimitriou and L. Randall Wray, 31–46. Cheltenham, UK: Edward Elgar.

Kregel, Jan. 2010b. "Is This the Minsky Moment for Reform of Financial Regulation?" The Jerome Levy Economics Institute of Bard College Working Paper No. 586.

Lavoie, Marc. 2014. *Post-Keynesian Economics: New Foundations*. Cheltenham, UK: Edward Elgar.

Minsky, Hyman P. 1964. "Financial Crisis, Financial Systems, and the Performance of the Economy." In *Private Capital Markets: A Series of Research Studies Prepared for the Commission on Money and Credit*, edited by Irvin Friend, 173–380. Englewood Cliffs, NJ: Prentice Hall.

Minsky, Hyman P. 1975. *John Maynard Keynes*. New York: Columbia University Press.

Minsky, Hyman P. 1982. *Can "It" Happen Again? Essays in Instability and Finance*. Armonk, New York: M.E. Sharpe.

Minsky, Hyman P. 1986. *Stabilizing an Unstable Economy*. New Haven: Yale University Press.

Minsky, Hyman P. 1993a. "Schumpeter and Finance." In *Market and Institutions in Economic Development: Essays in Honor of Paolo Sylos Labini*, edited by Salvatore Biasco, Alessandro Roncaglia, and Michele Salvati, 103–115. New York: St. Martin's Press.

Minsky, Hyman P. 1993b. "Finance and Stability: The Limits of Capitalism." The Jerome Levy Economics Institute of Bard College Working Paper No. 93.

Minsky, Hyman P. and Charles J. Whalen. 1996. "Economic Insecurity and the Institutional Prerequisites for Successful Capitalism." *Journal of Post Keynesian Economics* 19 (2): 155–170.

Mitchell, Wesley C. 1916. "The Role of Money in Economic Theory." *American Economic Review* 6 (1): 140–161.

Mueller, Dennis C. 1976. "Public Choice: A Survey." *Journal of Economic Literature* 14 (2): 395–433.

Olson, Mancur. 1965. *The Logic of Collective Action: Public Goods and the Theory of Groups*. Cambridge, MA: Harvard University Press.

Palley, Thomas I. 2009. "A Theory of Minsky Super-Cycles and Financial Crises." Macroeconomic Policy Institute Working Paper 5/2009, Hans Böckler Stiftung.

Phillips, Ronnie J. 1997. "Rethinking Bank Examinations: A Minsky Approach." *Journal of Economic Issues* 31 (2): 509–516.

Rosser, J. Barkley Jr., Marina V. Rosser, and Mauro Gallegati. 2012. "A Minsky-Kindleberger Perspective on the Financial Crisis." *Journal of Economic Issues* 46 (2): 449–458.

Ülgen, Faruk. 2016. "Financial Liberalization as a Process of Flawed Institutional Change." *Journal of Economic Issues* 50 (2): 485–493.

Ülgen, Faruk. 2017. "Financialization and Vested Interests: Self-Regulation versus Financial Stability as a Public Good." *Journal of Economic Issues* 51 (2): 332–340.

Ülgen, Faruk. 2018. "Collective Action and the Institutionalist Approach to Financial Regulation." *Journal of Economic Issues* 52(2): 541–549.

Ülgen, Faruk. 2021. "Public Good, Collective Action and Financial Regulation." *Annals of Public and Cooperative Economics* 92 (1): 147–167.

Veblen, Thorstein. 1921. *The Engineers and the Price System.* New York: Huebsch.

Whalen, Charles J. 2008a. "A Minsky Moment: Reflections on Hyman P. Minsky (1919–1996), *Journal of Economic Issues* 42 (1): 249–253.

Whalen, Charles J. 2008b. "The Credit Crunch: A Minsky Moment." *Studi e Note di Economia* 13 (1): 3–21.

Whalen, Charles J., ed. 2011. *Financial Instability and Economic Security after the Great Recession.* Cheltenham, UK: Edward Elgar.

Whalen, Charles J. 2012. "Post-Keynesian Institutionalism after the Great Recession." Levy Economics Institute of Bard College Working Paper No. 724.

Whalen, Charles J. 2020. "Post-Keynesian Institutionalism: Past, Present, and Future." *Evolutionary and Institutional Economics Review* 17 (1): 71–92.

Whalen, Charles J., ed. 2022. *Institutional Economics: Perspectives and Methods in Search of a Better World.* London: Routledge.

Wolfson, Martin H. 2002. "Minsky's Theory of Financial Crises in a Global Context." *Journal of Economic Issues* 36 (2): 393–400.

Wray, L. Randall. 1990. *Money and Credit in Capitalist Economies: The Endogenous Money Approach.* Aldershot, UK: Edward Elgar.

Wray, L. Randall. 2002. "What Happened to Goldilocks? A Minskian Framework." *Journal of Economic Issues* 36 (2): 383–391.

Wray, L. Randall. 2011. "Minsky Crisis." Levy Economics Institute of Bard College Working Paper No. 659.

Wray, L. Randall. 2012. "Global Financial Crisis: A Minskyan Interpretation of the Causes, the Fed's Bailout, and the Future." Levy Economics Institute of Bard College Working Paper No. 711.

15. Women's work and its conceptualization in Post-Keynesian Institutionalism

Anna Zachorowska-Mazurkiewicz

INTRODUCTION

The situation of women in the economy is affected by the roles they play in society. Women's work illustrates how culture defines the economic situation. Women's engagement in care labor defines their position in the labor market, not only in terms of their participation, but also the remuneration they receive for their work compared with that of men. The mechanism that creates this difference in pay is the main focus of the chapter. The main objective is to explain why women's work is valued less than that of men. In particular, we consider the problem from a Post-Keynesian Institutionalist perspective, drawing, along the way, on vital insight from Feminist economics.

The chapter begins by presenting some manifestations of women's contemporary economic status. The data presented show the time people devote to paid and unpaid work, as well as the difference in pay that women receive for their work relative to men. Then women's work is discussed from the perspective of Institutional economics, focusing on the gender division of paid and unpaid work. Next, the Post Keynesian attention to the monetary production process is presented, shedding light on the necessity of paid employment in modern capitalist economies. The last part of the chapter (followed by a brief conclusion) offers a Post-Keynesian Institutional perspective that discusses women's remuneration by linking the gender and monetary processes. It is this last part—informed by crucial insights from Feminist economics—that provides the full picture of women's subordination through work in contemporary societies.

WOMEN AT WORK: ALLOCATION OF TIME AND THE GENDER PAY GAP

When writing about women's work, what is considered "work" needs to be precisely defined. Work can be analyzed in a narrow or broader sense. The narrow meaning of the term is connected to paid employment; indeed, that is also the concept's most common contemporary meaning. Work in this narrow sense consists of activities performed for remuneration, which means that work refers to activities that are sold in the market. Here the function of work is to produce marketable goods and services, and in this way the work one does provides for one's livelihood.

However, work might also be defined in a broader sense than just paid activities. A broader definition describes activities tied to effort, time, and opportunity cost. For example, Margaret Reid (1934, 11) writes that work includes all activities to which a "third-person criterion" could be used. According to this criterion, if one *can* hire a third person to perform the activities (such as cleaning, ironing, or cooking, for example), then those activities are "work," regardless of whether they *are* performed for pay.

But there are still other types of work to which the third-person criterion cannot be applied, such as unpaid care labor performed in order to develop, sustain, or deepen a relationship—labor we can classify as a relational work. To be sure, people can be paid—and many are—to provide childcare and adult care, but in such cases the person who hires another to provide that care is not building their own personal relationship with the person receiving the care. When the purpose of unpaid care labor is to develop or maintain a relationship, such work cannot be performed by a third person.

Referring to a report by the United Nations (UN), Margaret Snyder (2007, 13) describes work broadly as the participation of people in productive activities for which they either receive a (monetary or in-kind) payment or are unpaid because the activities are undertaken free of charge for the benefit of a family (or community) member or enterprise. For example, such work may include housework, childcare, volunteer work, looking after elderly family members, providing labor to a family business enterprises, or constructing and repairing owner-occupied buildings (UN 2000, 109). The International Labor Organization (ILO) also proposes a definition that includes unpaid activities in the concept of work. In the ILO definition, all activities that generate products and services—whether or not they are later sold in the market—should be seen as work (Campillo 2003, 11).

Therefore, there is a strong case for "work" to be conceived broadly, indeed, for defining it to include the full range of activities necessary for survival, reproduction, and personal development (Standing 2009, 7). But, of course,

Table 15.1   *Minutes of work daily—paid and unpaid—by gender, region,*
                   and income group

Region	Unpaid care work		Paid work		Total work	
	Women	Men	Women	Men	Women	Men
World	265	83	183	322	448	404
Low-income countries	262	89	193	290	455	378
Middle-income countries	267	66	192	346	460	412
High-income countries	257	135	154	249	411	384

Note: Unpaid care work and paid work may not add up to total work due to rounding.
Source: Data from Addati et al. (2018, 56).

that provides only a starting point for studying and analyzing work. In the next step, we should recognize that opportunities for engaging in paid employment are influenced by decisions concerning the unpaid work done in one's household. Thus, it becomes necessary to analyze paid and unpaid activities jointly.

We must also introduce an awareness of gender. Brenda Spotton Visano (2017, 4) recognizes that gender awareness raises important questions about the nature of *what* and *how* we know. In the case of work, gender awareness not only expands our inquiry into such domains as unpaid household activity, it also encourages disaggregation of marketed labor and income variables.

The distribution of paid work and unpaid care work between women and men in different regions of the world is presented, according to average minutes of work per day, in Table 15.1. The data come from an ILO report in which care work "is broadly defined as consisting of activities and relations involved in meeting the physical, psychological and emotional needs" of people of any age, regardless of whether the work is provided within households or elsewhere in the community (Addati et al. 2018, 6).

The findings presented in Table 15.1 illustrate a gender division of work, in which women are primarily responsible for unpaid care work, while men do more paid work. Women are also involved in paid work more than men in unpaid care work; as a result, women do more work in total than men. In addition, there are some differences between regions divided according to level of income. In low-income countries, the gap in total work performed by men relative to women is largest: 77 minutes daily. Women in middle-income countries perform unpaid care work the longest—267 minutes per day—while men in these countries spent only 66 minutes doing such work daily.

The data presented point to the gender division of work as a worldwide phenomenon. Women work longer hours than men, but they are mainly involved in unpaid work, not receiving monetary rewards for their efforts. Moreover, the allocation of time across these two activities is connected. Among women, 41.6 percent of those not employed report that the reason is their involvement

Table 15.2   *Mean and median gender pay gaps by region and income:*
                 hourly wages and monthly earnings

Region	Hourly wages		Monthly earnings	
	Mean gender pay gap	Median gender pay gap	Mean gender pay gap	Median gender pay gap
High-income countries	16.2	15.7	25.6	24.9
Upper-middle income countries	15.1	17.3	19.2	20.2
Lower-middle income countries	16.2	14.8	15.8	22.3
Low-income countries	14.6	22.7	28.2	31.7
World	15.6	16.6	20.5	21.8

Source: Data from ILO (2018, 24–25).

in unpaid care work. This means that 606 million women are not employed because they are taking care of other people and are not remunerated for it. In contrast, only 5.8 percent of men—41 million—report that they are not employed because they are providing unpaid care work (Addati et al. 2018, xxxi–xxxii).

In addition to the gender *work* gap (gender division of work), there is also a gender *pay* gap. Table 15.2 presents ILO (2018) data on pay for women and men across the world. In all regions, women earn less than men.[1]

Both mean and median gender pay gaps are substantial. In the case of hourly wages, the difference in the mean pay gap across regions is not substantial (with gaps ranging from 14.6 to 16.2 percent); the difference in the median gap is much larger, and women experience a 22.7 percent median pay gap in low-income countries. In the case of monthly earnings, the pay gaps are generally even larger than for hourly wages. The largest monthly gender pay gaps are found in low-income countries (it does not matter if we look at median or mean results), but the second largest are in high-income countries. In terms of monthly earnings, both the mean and median gender pay gaps for the world overall exceed 20 percent.

INSTITUTIONAL INSIGHT ON WOMEN'S WORK: THE GENDER DIVISION OF WORK

What accounts for the gender division of work and the gender pay gap? Economists have generally focused on the pay gap, which seems linked to the valuation of women's work in terms of sectors and occupations. While other features that contribute to the gender pay gap have diminished over time, such as differences in education, gender differences in the sorting between and within occupations and industries remain important in explaining the gap (Boll, Rossen, and Wolf 2017; Blau and Kahn 2017).

Ariane Hegewisch and Heidi Hartmann (2014, 16) suggest there is a clear financial penalty for working in female-dominated occupations. Women dominate in jobs that resemble their traditional gender roles and are linked to care and services (Zachorowska-Mazurkiewicz 2016). Considering the actual salaries received by caregivers, it seems clear that the human and societal value of care exceeds the market value calculated according to the services performed.

The reason the market undervalues care is that the monetary value assigned to care work accounts only for those aspects of caregiving for which substitutes can be found in the market (Campillo 2003, 106). Since the personal and relational aspects of care do not have market equivalents, they are difficult to valuate—and their value often goes uncalculated (Folbre 2001; Sikoska 2003). However, this is exactly what matters most in the care relationship—the caregiver's positive attention to the person receiving care. That attention involves the creation and keeping of a personal relationship (van Staveren 2015, 45), which is precisely the part of care work that becomes difficult to value monetarily. Additionally, a paid caregiver can perform many activities that are usually done as part of unpaid household work. This is the case with nurses, for those providing care to the elderly and young children, and is also true of some work performed in other professions such as teaching or therapy. As a result, employed women often compete with women who do not receive a monetary reward for their work.

According to Claudia Goldin (2014, 1093), "[R]elative earnings often signify how individuals are valued socially and economically." Paying women less sends a message that society regards women as having less economic and social worth. The gender division of work and the gender pay gap could be analyzed separately, but deserve to be discussed together because they are closely linked and because they are both grounded in cultural influences that shape the role of women in society.

Insights from Institutional economics effectively serve the purpose of exploring the connection between the involvement of women in unpaid work and care work (Zachorowska-Mazurkiewicz 2015). Institutionalism strives to explain the real world by means of theories that represent observed reality as accurately as possible (see, e.g., Whalen 1996, 88).[2] Moreover, Thorstein Veblen, originator of Institutional economics, produced pioneering work that recognized gender norms as important institutions in the economy; in recent years, other Institutionalists have followed his lead.

Institutional economists recognize that producers, workers, and consumers are largely cultural products (Whalen 1996, 96). For that reason, an Institutionalist interpretation of economic behavior examines the various cultural influences shaping that behavior. Many cultural categories exist to label groups of people with some similarity on the basis of that commonality. The commonality may or may not affect each person in any meaningful way and, in fact, it may not signify any substantial difference between those inside or outside the group, but the cultural label treats that common characteristic as having social significance and values it either positively or negatively in the particular culture. The creation of any category is, hence, at the same time the creation of a value category (Waller 2005, 331). Thus, Institutional economics begins its analysis by looking at cultural processes rather than an isolated individual.[3] A consequence of this approach is Institutionalism's strong resistance to the notion that any significant portion of human behavior is private in the sense of being untouched by cultural norms and values (Zachorowska-Mazurkiewicz 2015).

One categorization that serves as a criterion to build such cultural labels and hierarchies is gender. Gender is a set of cultural categories that use biological sex as the element of commonality to assign value in our culture to people and the activities they perform, including work. Gender, like all cultural categories, assigns attributes, roles, and behavioral norms to each person based on the category in which they are placed (Waller 2005, 331).

Veblen often gave attention to the norms that valued the position of men and degraded the position of women in society (van Staveren 2010a, 21). In two groundbreaking articles (Veblen 1894; 1899), he recognized gender norms as exemplary for how historical and cultural patterns influence the economic process of provisioning. Moreover, Veblen stressed the fact that pecuniary activities, those of buying and selling, were not synonymous with social provisioning (Mayhew 1999, 480). The market represents one important way that people organize themselves collectively to make a living, but social provisioning can also occur within the household or via the state (Power 2004). For example, the work of women that takes place without remuneration within households, including caring for others, is a vital element of social provisioning. In fact, according to Zdravka Todorova (2015, 426), that work is simultaneously production and reproduction.

The concept of care work focuses on the gendered character of social norms that shape the division of work in both the family and the market. The gender division of work was established in a historical process that started with the industrial revolution. Social norms that link being female to caring for others developed as part of this historical process. The consequences of those norms have been extensive and significant, contributing to gender inequality within both the household and the labor market (Badgett and Folbre 1999).

Before the industrial revolution, work in most countries occurred in the household or in agriculture. After industrialization, the definition of work evolved to focus on activities performed outside the home or farm, which influenced the perception of jobs undertaken by women and men in different ways (Coleman 1999, 503). At the end of the eighteenth century, women whose work consisted mainly of taking care of the family were considered productive workers. That view changed with the development of the market economy, which is when production for personal use—rather than for the market—began to be equated with the responsibilities of women (Folbre 1991, 466).

Thus, in the second half of the nineteenth century, the division of labor became established in the leading industrialized economies. In many households, only men took up employment in the labor market as long as their families could afford it. (In low-income households, both women and men were often compelled to work out of economic necessity.) The activity of women within the household did not provide any basis for measuring their work against that of men (and women) in the monetized part of the economy. Earning money became primarily the domain of men, while performing household work the domain of women—a realm more often described using moral rather than economic terminology (Gornick and Meyers 2009, 7; Himmelweit 1995, 7).

During the census carried out in England in 1851, women working for their own household were recognized as a separate category; by the census of 1881, however, they were added to the category of people working without a specific occupation. Then, at the end of the nineteenth century, a special parliamentary committee took into account Alfred Marshall's suggestion to adopt the German tradition and transfer women working for their own household without pay into the category of *dependent persons* (Folbre 2009, 252–253).

Antonella Picchio (1992) argues that the separation of production and reproduction that took place during the industrial revolution explains why macroeconomics was not structured to consider the unpaid and care work women provide for households. Consequently, this considerable part of the economy—consisting of unpaid activities, often carried out within households, and primarily undertaken by women—remains invisible (van Staveren 2010b, 1132). But outside of economic analysis, in the economy of the real world, unpaid housework does not take place independently from the general capitalist structure. Such work instead conditions the reproduction of the labor force, and is an important part of the overall culture of capitalist production (Todorova 2009, 52).

In short, the private realm of households is a product of particular historical and geopolitical circumstances. According to Todorova (2009, 86–87), it is a product of gender and monetary processes, which form what Veblen called a "pecuniary culture." Todorova further writes that the Victorian period saw a development in the gender process that is specific to a pecuniary culture and best manifests the ideological notion of the household as a separate, autonomous, and feminine sphere. Households acquired a position of remoteness from the public sphere, which was deemed masculine, and they consequently became the ideological embodiment of the feminine domain. However, this separation is, of course, a fiction. This fictional autonomy of the household as a distinct arena for women "is revealed by its economic dependence on the public sphere" (Todorova 2009, 96).

The data presented in the first part of this chapter show that women are not only devoted to their care duties but are also active in the public realm. This contributes to long hours of women's work. Todorova (2009, 122–123) uses the concept of "ceremonial encapsulation" to explain the puzzle of long hours that women work. In particular, ceremonial encapsulation involves a situation in which a social innovation is both ceremonially and instrumentally feasible, and it is through ceremonial encapsulation that the ceremonial aspects of a given institution—those linked to myths, mores, and arbitrary distinctions of status and rank—are left undisrupted.[4] With respect to households and the economic activity of women, ceremonial encapsulation accounts for the "double burden" of work represented by the innovation of women entering the labor force, while continuing with their homemaking responsibilities.[5] It is predominately women's time that is stretched between work in the unpaid and paid economies. The innovation in household relations is allowed only under the condition of preserving the dominance of a woman's role as a homemaker, mother, and wife (Todorova 2009, 122–123).

Popular conceptions of women's appropriate roles have shifted since Veblen's time, but differential economic outcomes for women and men remain linked to distinctions between market and familial activities (Jennings 1994, 559). In their analyses, Institutionalists view the concept of power as involving "multifaceted systems of status and hierarchy" (Waller and Jennings 1990, 620) that can be of use when discussing the relation between market and household activities. The hierarchical gender relations that characterize our contemporary societies are a manifestation of that power, resulting in public-private bifurcation, a hierarchical valuation of economic activities, and the gender division of work (Todorova 2009, 86).

POST KEYNESIAN INSIGHT: EMPLOYMENT AND THE SIGNIFICANCE OF MONEY

The main aim of Post Keynesian economics is to provide a clear understanding of how the economy works, thereby relating economic analysis to real economic problems (Arestis 1996, 112). According to Wallace Peterson (1977), that aim is, in fact, one of many features that Post Keynesian economics (which he called the "economics of Keynes") shares with Institutionalism. Other commonalities identified by Peterson include the recognition that pecuniary criteria matter in capitalist reality, and an appreciation of the role of the following as significant aspects of economic reality (all of which were addressed in Keynes's (1936) *The General Theory of Employment, Interest, and Money*): uncertainty, economic instability, the institutions of money (and finance) and wage determination, and culturally and institutionally grounded human behavior.

Keynes (1937, 215) wrote that money serves two principal purposes. By acting as a unit of account, it facilitates exchanges without being a substantive object. In this respect, it is a convenience, leading some economists to refer to money as "a veil" (which merely shrouds the underlying transactions of actual goods and services).[6] In the second place, it is a store of wealth, and in this respect it is a barometer of the degree of our distrust in our own calculations and conventions concerning the future (Keynes 1937, 216). But Keynes also showed that real and monetary phenomena are inextricably linked in an economy in which participants face uncertainty over the possible outcomes of future events, an economy Post Keynesians call a monetary production economy (Todorova 2009, 26).

People make active, thoughtful, and socially embedded efforts to make their own futures (Danby 2004, 59), and money provides a necessary link between the present and the future (Peterson 1977, 217). In Post Keynesian economics, by holding cash, individuals (and firms) become better equipped to face unexpected events (Danby 2004, 59).[7] While the future is unmade, it is being made (Danby 2004, 60).

Post Keynesians have much to say about money, production, and employment in a monetary production economy, but of particular relevance to the analysis in this chapter is how the Post Keynesian perspective links to gender and Feminist theory. According to Marc Lavoie (2003) there are some commonalities between Post Keynesian economics and Feminist economics, including that both traditions are more interested in production (and distribution) rather than exchange. But in Post Keynesian theorizing, money and finance are necessarily integrated with the "real" economy from the start of the analysis (Arestis 1996, 118). In addition, Colin Danby (2004, 61) observes that the Post Keynesian literature tends to see the "economic" as that which is monetized, and thus to ignore non-monetized transactions and production. In such a case, there is no place for the unpaid work performed in households.

In fact, Irene van Staveren (2010b, 1124) takes a different view from that of Lavoie. According to van Staveren, Post Keynesianism has traditionally exhibited little concern for Feminism and shows limited recognition that the major Post Keynesian concerns may matter differently for women and men. The strong connection between the economy, the market, and money in Post Keynesian economics appears to exclude attention to non-market and non-monetary production and to reinforce a strict dividing line between markets and society (Danby 2004; van Staveren 2010b, 1128).

The difference between Post Keynesian and Feminist economics is well illustrated by their approach to the concept of social reproduction. In the Post Keynesian tradition, the label of social reproduction is often concerned with material well-being generated through markets (and public goods), hence through paid labor. Thus, Post Keynesians generally ignore institutions beyond the market (and market-centered institutions such as the corporation and labor union) and the state—institutions such as kinship or gender or ethnic solidarity, all of which may be performing important roles in organizing or structuring economic activity (Danby 2004, 63).

In contrast, social reproduction in Feminist economics has always referred to women's unpaid work in a patriarchal system. According to van Staveren (2010b) the very term social reproduction has been replaced in Feminist economics by notions of unpaid work and caring. The "blind spot for unpaid work and caring in Post Keynesian economics" implicitly assumes that these categories are separate from the monetized economy and do not affect it (van Staveren 2010b, 1133). In fact, Feminist Institutionalist Ann Jennings (1994) notes that monetary theories of production recognize the social power of money, but also fail to explore the implications of this social power on women, families, and other gender issues (see also Waller 1999, 627).[8]

However, gender relations often manifest themselves in unpaid housework, which in the monetary production economy cannot be performed without inputs purchased with money (Todorova 2009, 65). As this chapter has already made clear, many goods and services produced within households contribute appreciably to peoples' livelihoods but do not generate income. Yet the production of such nonmarket goods and services requires the purchase of commodities (Todorova 2013, 63). For the purposes of social reproduction, households must obtain money through participation in the market process.

Consumption expenditures are necessary for the biological survival of workers, but also for the social cohesion of the household as well as for its cohesion in relation to other households (Todorova 2009, 64). Thus, households are not self-sufficient: they need money to buy goods and services, and to pay their tax obligations. Households rely on market-based output, income, and employment; they also rely on money as a link between the present and the future.

This brings us back to Post Keynesianism, which gives much attention to dimensions of the employment relationship, especially the money wage. In Post Keynesian analyses, the money wage assumes an important role not just because it is the fundamental determinant of the price level (Robinson 1969) and is the most widely utilized contract in the entrepreneurial system where money is used (Arestis 1996, 113). Rather, the fundamental importance of the money wage comes from a recognition that it is primarily through employment that individuals obtain the income necessary for purchasing products that are crucial to their survival (Todorova 2009, 36–37).

But Post Keynesianism also looks beyond the money wage. According to the pioneering Post Keynesian work of Alfred Eichner (1979), which clearly and self-consciously straddled the Institutionalist and Post Keynesian traditions, it is vital to remember that the labor market involves human beings, and that many people spend a large portion of time within employment relations. Thus, Eichner called for an "anthropogenic approach" to labor economics, an approach that views work as affiliation, not just a contract. According to that approach, because work functions as a milieu for social interactions, employment provides opportunities for broadening people's options in life (Eichner 1979, 354, 363).

Thus, Post Keynesian economics provides important economic insight. Money is a form of wealth that matters in capitalism (Jennings 1994, 556). From such a perspective, money is no longer an innovation that simply facilitates market transactions; monetary production economies cannot be reduced to "money-using" systems. Money signifies value and social relations, and the acceptance of the money unit as an invariable measure of value and standard of wealth is a convention that permeates the whole culture (Todorova 2009, 22, 41).

The Post Keynesian attention to money also underscores the connection of that tradition to Institutionalism—and an unmistakable conclusion from looking at that connection is that attention to gender must be a common focus of both traditions. After all, it was Veblen (1891, 350) who wrote more than a century ago that the value of human beings may also be presented in terms of money:

> When we say that a man is "worth" so many dollars, the expression does not convey the idea that moral or other personal excellence is to be measured in terms of money, but economic success is the most widely accepted as well as the most readily ascertainable measure of esteem.

Thus, money has consequences for the material provisioning of households, and cannot be separated from other social relations, including gender (Todorova 2009, 58).

POST-KEYNESIAN INSTITUTIONALISM: GENDER AND MONETARY ISSUES

In addition to highlighting the significance of money, Post Keynesian economics points to the need for employment. According to Hyman Minsky (1986, 9), providing employment opportunities for all who seek them is a key to social justice; which rests "on individual dignity and independence from both private and political power centers." But the gender division of labor and the gender wage gap suggest that employment opportunities are not the same for women and men. Thus, we integrate Post Keynesian and Institutional economics—in light of the engagement of both traditions with Feminist economics—to fashion a Post-Keynesian Institutionalist analysis regarding women's employment opportunities and remuneration.

The significance of a Post-Keynesian Institutional analysis of women's work and pay relative to men, especially analysis informed by the literature of Feminist economics, is that it enables a more comprehensive explanation than individual traditions provide on their own. Institutional economics, as we have seen above, introduces culture and culturally generated gender categories to shed light on the connection between the involvement of women in unpaid work and paid care work. We have also seen that Post Keynesian economics focuses more on paid employment; Post Keynesians recognize that all work may provide human affiliation, but they also stress that paid work generates income that is indispensable in capitalism. Thus, it isn't surprising that Post Keynesianism has more to say about the gender pay gap than the gender work gap (gender division of labor). In particular, Post Keynesians tend to explain observed differences in the pay received by women relative to men by referring to segmentation into typically "male" and "female" jobs (van Staveren 2010b, 1137), without questioning where this stereotyping comes from. In contrast, Feminist economists often explain the gender wage gap by referring to intangible gender institutions, such as shared ideas among labor market participants about appropriate pay differences between men (often seen as breadwinners) and women (often considered secondary earners) (van Staveren 2010b, 1137). The aim of Post-Keynesian Institutional analysis is to provide a more unified account of observed patterns of work and pay.

As indicated above, Institutionalism and Post Keynesianism have much in common. In addition to a commitment to realistic theories and the recognition of uncertainty, economic instability, institutions, culture, and the pecuniary focus of capitalist economies, both *power* and *distribution of income and wealth* are at the heart of Post Keynesian and Institutional analyses. In both traditions, individual choice "is heavily influenced by income, class, and the technical conditions of production" and a major object of economic analysis is to shed light on "income distribution amongst social classes" (Arestis 1996, 112).

Of course, each tradition also has its own particular emphases. For example, coercion and power are the central facts of economic life in Institutionalism. Uncertainty occupies this role in Keynes (Peterson 1977, 215). In a world of uncertainty, Keynes (1936, 147–164) emphasized the "precariousness" of "conventions" and the possibility of a violent and cumulative change in "mood" and "expectations." Hence, the economic system is not "self-balancing;" rather, it is a "cumulative unfolding" process (Arestis 1996, 114). Of course, Institutionalists have reached the same conclusion about the economic process, and what's striking to those familiar with both traditions is that, even with different initial emphases, Keynes and the Institutionalists reach common conclusions again and again.[9]

Integrating Post Keynesian economics and Institutional economics to fashion Post-Keynesian Institutionalism (PKI) is not new. Charles K. Wilber and Kenneth P. Jameson (1983) crafted and used PKI to analyze the stagflation of the 1970s and early 1980s. Charles J. Whalen (2011) and David Zalewski (2019) are among those using PKI more recently. According to Whalen (2020, 78), PKI builds on the following foundations: (1) Post-Keynesian Institutionalists are interested in analysis built on realistic assumptions rather than on the construction of formal models; (2) people act in a world of uncertainty, and, in the process of dealing with that uncertainty, they rely heavily on habits and social conventions; and (3) PKI concentrates on institutions, not impersonal forces or universal laws of nature, as crucial for shaping the economy.[10]

What is relatively new, however, is focusing PKI on issues involving gender. As has already been discussed, gender has generally not received serious attention within Post Keynesian economics and has largely been treated as unimportant for the advancement of a monetary theory of production, which, according to Todorova (2009, 1), restricts the explanatory power of that framework. In contrast, in Institutional economics, gender analysis was present from the very beginning (in the previously cited articles published by Veblen). Therefore, adopting a Post-Keynesian Institutionalist perspective allows for Feminist-oriented economic analysis.

The scope and pre-analytic vision of PKI is certainly capable of incorporating Feminist economists' understanding of the economy as a realm that includes unpaid work and caring. As outlined by Wilber and Jameson (1983, 155), PKI is a "holistic, systemic, and evolutionary" approach that emphasizes the impact of socioeconomic change on social provisioning and economic welfare. That is surely broad enough to encompass not only social reproduction and provisioning outside the marketplace (involving unpaid work), but also cultural influences and economic consequences relating to gender.

By drawing on Post Keynesianism's focus on monetary institutions, Institutionalism's emphasis on history and culture, and Feminist economics' attention to gender and gendered socioeconomic institutions, PKI helps to explain both the gender division of work and the pay gap. A starting point for such an analysis is provided by Post Keynesian economist Joan Robinson (1972, 9), who stresses that "everyone can see" that their relative earnings depend on the bargaining power of the group of workers to which they belong. Building on that observation, Peterson (1977, 210) maintains that Institutionalism and Post Keynesianism come together in recognizing not only that "the distribution of income and wealth is an economic mirror which reflects the power struggles of society," but also that "power relationships work through institutions." Peterson (1977, 210) also emphasizes that money is an especially important institution in our world, since "capitalism is essentially a pecuniary order."

Jennings (1994, 558) then adds to Peterson's insight. Drawing on a background in both Feminist economics and Institutionalism, Jennings writes not only that money is asymmetrical in market exchange—that is, it is harder to sell for money than it is to buy—but also that women's labor has been socially constructed as less saleable than men's labor. William Waller (1999, 626), who identifies as both a Feminist and Post-Keynesian Institutionalist, explains that this means that if money is a veil over productive activity, then the activities that yield monetary gain are socially valuable and those that do not yield a monetary gain are not. In other words, in contemporary capitalist society we find (as did Veblen in his era) *pecuniary* criteria rather than industrial criteria at the center of evaluating the worthiness of an occupation (Todorova 2009, 93–94). The highest incomes appear (according to conventional economics as well as society's dominant cultural beliefs) to result from the greatest productive contribution to society. Following this argument, unpaid activities must then also be equated with *non*-productivity and devalued (Jennings 1994, 559). Money in such a case is not a veil, but rather a social prerogative.

The gender analysis of PKI then moves from money to employment. In contemporary economies, employment supports the provision of care in the household and the purchase of care-related services (Danby 2010, 1163). At the same time, however, access to livelihood through paid employment is impeded by care work due to time constraints (Todorova 2015, 430). The concept of unpaid housework does not necessarily imply that these activities ought to be paid; it simply underscores that the monetary production economy provides no compensation "for the time and effort spent in such household activities" (Todorova 2009, 52)—even as the time and resources that enable a household to provide unpaid care can only occur when the household is supported by some form of income stream. In short, the household is economically dependent on the public (market) sphere.

Of course, the public sphere is also dependent on households for a supply of labor inputs. Nevertheless, the wages paid by business enterprises do not completely compensate for "the full maintenance of labor inputs," much of which occurs within the home (Todorova 2009, 59). Business enterprises are "exempt" from considerations of care because households are conceptualized as a peaceful feminine realm that functions away from the market. Care work has been socially constructed to take place "naturally" within the realm of households and primarily under the obligations and guidance of women (Todorova 2009, 96). One result of this is the observed worldwide gender division of work.

PKI also accounts for the gender pay gap. Paid work is treated as valuable, while unpaid work is considered to be of much less value. Since women are delegated to unpaid work at home, this unpaid activity affects the valuation of the work that women perform in the labor market. Thus, at the heart of the explanation for the pay gap is that women's work is paid less because it mirrors the work women do for free within their households.

But that's not the entire story. Care implies a relationship of dependency. Within a pecuniary culture, dependency within the household is considered virtuous, while dependency on others outside the household is considered pathological—especially when it involves the state in pecuniary terms (Todorova 2009, 110). But households, in order to provide unpaid care work, *need* monetary support, and that support can come from either the market, through employment, or from the state (or both).[11] Households, the state, and the business enterprise do not belong to separate spheres; rather their interaction collectively constitutes a pecuniary culture (Todorova 2009, 115). And this culture devalues women's work, be it in the household or in the market, resulting in the prevailing gender pay gap in capitalist economies.

CONCLUSION

The observed gender division of work and the gender pay gap are best explained jointly with a Post-Keynesian Institutional analysis. Such an analysis, bolstered by insight from Feminist economics, paints the picture of women's subordination by drawing not only on the patriarchal segregation of women's work described by Institutional economists, but also on the monetary production processes explained by Post Keynesian economists. Women are primarily responsible for providing unpaid work within households. But in a capitalist society they are also dependent, one way or another, on money wages, and women most often receive lower pay in the labor market than men. PKI demonstrates that the observed patterns of work and pay are interconnected.

In the course of cultural evolution—that is, as a consequence of social forces driving historical development, not inherent differences between women and men—women were delegated to unpaid and care work. This accounts for the gender division of work, but is also a starting point for analyzing the gender pay gap. Much care work can be performed within households, without monetary rewards, or it can be performed in the market and remunerated. But some aspects of care work, such as those involving a relationship between the caregiver and recipient of care, cannot be translated into monetary terms, and thus are left unremunerated. Since women are associated with unpaid work, this is a reference point resulting in a gender pay gap that characterizes all paid activities performed by women. In the market, women do not compete merely with other employees, but also with their own unpaid work—and much of the work they do in the labor market mirrors work women do for free in the household. This helps account for women's lower pay relative to men.

Since households are not self-sufficient, and performing care work is dependent on purchasing products and services in the market, it is necessary to obtain money wages (or a stream of income from the state that is widely considered a redistribution of money wages). Additionally, employment is an affiliation and a condition of economic independence. However, women have limited opportunities to participate in the labor market for two reasons: (1) they have less time available because of their responsibility for providing unpaid work in their households; and (2) their paid work is accorded less value than men's work. Both these reasons contribute to sustaining the hierarchical gender structure in the economy and society.

Limiting access to money wages influences women's ability to successfully perform unpaid care work, and that affects the quality of care in society. At the same time, care provides social ties; and social ties are vital to human survival. As Danby (2010, 1159) observes, it is not just that our social existence in the present is heavily influenced by our ties to others; it is also true that our ability to construct the future rests on how we and others shape those ties. In the case of women's work, that observation forces us to ask whether we truly want to shape our ties with others through the existing (socially constructed) hierarchical system; it also compels us to seriously consider how that hierarchy influences our construction of the future. Social ties can indeed be reshaped; but, in the meantime, construction of the future is already underway.

ACKNOWLEDGMENTS

The author wishes to thank Charles Whalen, William Waller, and Zdravka Todorova, who read and commented on early versions of the chapter.

NOTES

1. In Table 15.2, pay (wages and earnings) refers to "total gross remuneration including regular bonuses received by employees during a specified period of time" (ILO 2018, 102). "Mean gender pay gap" compares the average of the pay distribution of women to that of men, while "median gender pay gap" compares the value located in the middle of those pay distributions. Using hourly wages to estimate the gender pay gap has the advantage of disentangling earnings from working time. Conversely, monthly measures can reflect differences not only in

hourly pay but also in the number of hours worked over an analyzed period of time (ILO 2018, 21–22).

2.   Post Keynesian economics also aims to construct theories relevant to observed reality. For example, see Arestis (1996), which not only offers this perspective on economic theory, but also underscores the interrelatedness of Institutional economics and Post Keynesianism.

3.   It is not only Institutionalism that notices the tendency to categorize people or events based on observed similarities and then to make judgments based on those categorizations. Keynes (quoted in Arestis 1996, 117) writes: "Knowing that our individual judgement is worthless, we endeavor to fall back on the judgement of the rest of the world which is perhaps better informed. That is, we endeavor to conform with the behavior of the majority or the average."

4.   In such situations, myths can obtain the status of knowledge claims, but they still remain distinct from instrumentally-warranted knowledge based in problem-solving, experience, and tools (Todorova 2013, 68).

5.   Hochschild (1989) uses the term "stalled revolution" to describe this situation, in which a higher women's employment rate is not followed by an increase in men's responsibility for domestic work. Another term used to describe this phenomenon of increasing numbers of women who are income earners, yet at the same time continue to perform their traditional roles as household managers and care providers, is the "second shift" (Lynch, Baker, and Lyons 2009, 19).

6.   For the origins of the notion of money as a veil, see Patinkin and Steiger (1989); but see also Jennings (1994), who criticizes this view from a Feminist Institutionalist perspective, arguing that money is instead "a social prerogative," not a veil. From Jennings's perspective, money is only a veil in that it conceals the underlying reality of economic and social power.

7.   However, as Danby (2004, 59) rightly observes, the same could be achieved by cultivating kinship ties.

8.   Despite finding a "blind spot" regarding unpaid and care work in Post Keynesian economics, van Staveren (2010b, 1133) also writes that this can be overcome by recognizing the relationships between unpaid care work and the monetized economy. Moreover, van Staveren (2010b, 1135) finds three key features of Post Keynesianism—attention to uncertainty, market power, and endogenous economic dynamics (including circular cumulative causation)—that she believes Feminist economists might benefit from using to advance gendered economic analyses. The bottom line of the article by van Staveren (2010b, 1140) is that elements within each of these traditions can inform (indeed have already constructively informed) the work of the other; and she concludes by expressing hope that the mutual learning among Feminist and Post Keynesian scholars will intensify in the years ahead.

9.   For an example of the observation that Institutionalists and Post Keynesians reach common conclusions, see Peterson (1977). Writing about uncertainty in the economics of Keynes and its similarity to elements found in Institutionalism, Peterson stresses that uncertainty pervades economic life and that economic activity "cannot be separated from history" because the economy exists in real time (Peterson 1977, 215). The system moves on; it is not static, and the (uncertain) future is always different from the past. In both economics traditions, a process—"a movement through time"—is underlined (Peterson 1977, 216).

10. Whalen (2020, 74) also surveys the literature that finds commonality and compatibility in terms of the Post Keynesian and Institutionalist traditions on matters

ranging from the economic significance of time, money, and power to a shared interest in real-world wage and price determination.

11. Interestingly the state through its policies may actually institutionalize gender roles (Zachorowska-Mazurkiewicz 2009).

REFERENCES

Addati, Laura, Umberto Cattaneo, Valeria Esquivel, and Isabel Valarino. 2018. *Care Work and Care Jobs for the Future of Decent Work.* Geneva: International Labour Organization.

Arestis, Philip. 1996. "Post-Keynesian Economics: Towards Coherence." *Cambridge Journal of Economics* 20 (1): 111–135.

Badgett, M.V. Lee, and Nancy Folbre. 1999. "Assigning Care: Gender Norms and Economic Outcomes." *International Labour Review* 138 (3): 311–326.

Blau, Francine D., and Lawrence M. Kahn. 2017. "The Gender Wage Gap: Extent, Trends, and Explanations." *Journal of Economics Literature* 55 (3): 789–865.

Boll, Christina, Anja Rossen, and André Wolf. 2017. "The EU Gender Earnings Gap: Job Segregation and Working Time as Driving Factors." *Journal of Economics and Statistics* 237 (5): 407–452.

Campillo, Fabiola. 2003. "Unpaid Household Labour: A Conceptual Approach." In *Macro-Economics: Making Gender Matter: Concepts, Policies and Institutional Change in Developing Countries*, edited by Martha Gutierrez, 106–121. London and New York: Zed Books.

Coleman, Margaret S. 1999. "Labour Market Participation." In *The Elgar Companion to Feminist Economics*, edited by Janice Peterson and Margaret Lewis, 499–505. Cheltenham, UK: Edward Elgar.

Danby, Colin. 2004. "Toward a Gendered Post Keynesianism: Subjectivity and Time in a Nonmodernist Framework." *Feminist Economics* 10 (3): 55–75.

Danby, Colin. 2010. "Interdependence Through Time: Relationships in Post-Keynesian Thought and the Care Literature." *Cambridge Journal of Economics* 34: 1157–1171.

Eichner, Alfred S. 1979. "'An Anthropogenic' Approach to Labor Economics." *Eastern Economic Journal* 5 (3): 349–366.

Folbre, Nancy. 1991. "The Unproductive Housewife: Her Evolution in Nineteenth-Century Economic Thought." *Signs: Journal of Women in Culture and Society* 16 (3) (Spring): 463–484.

Folbre, Nancy. 2001. *The Invisible Heart: Economics and Family Values.* New York: The New Press.

Folbre, Nancy. 2009. *Greed, Lust and Gender: A History of Economic Ideas.* Oxford: Oxford University Press.

Goldin, Claudia. 2014. "A Grand Convergence: Its Last Chapter." *American Economic Review* 104 (4): 1091–1119.

Gornick, Janet C., and Marcia K. Meyers. 2009. "Institutions that Support Gender Equality in Parenthood and Employment." In *Gender Equality: Transforming Family Divisions of Labor*, edited by Janet C. Gornick, and Marcia K. Meyers, 3–66. London: Verso.

Hegewisch, Ariane, and Heidi Hartmann. 2014. "Occupational Segregation and the Gender Wage Gap: A Job Half Done." Institute for Women's Policy Research Report. Washington DC: Institute for Women's Policy Research.

Himmelweit, Susan. 1995. "The Discovery of 'Unpaid Work:' The Social Consequences of the Expansion of Work." *Feminist Economics* 1 (2): 1–19.

Hochschild, Arlie. 1989. *The Second Shift. Working Parents and the Revolution at Home.* New York: Viking.

International Labour Organization. 2018. *Global Wage Report 2018/19. What Lies Behind Gender Pay Gaps.* Geneva: International Labour Organization.

Jennings, Ann. 1994. "Toward a Feminist Expansion of Macroeconomics: Money Matters." *Journal of Economic Issues* 28 (2): 555–565.

Keynes, John M. 1936. *The General Theory of Employment, Interest, and Money.* London: Macmillan.

Keynes, John M. 1937. "The General Theory of Employment." *Quarterly Journal of Economics* 51 (2): 209–223.

Lavoie, Marc. 2003. "The Tight Links Between Post-Keynesian and Feminist Economics." In *The Crisis in Economics*, edited by Edward Fullbrook, 189–192. London: Routledge.

Lynch, Kathleen, John Baker, and Maureen Lyons. 2009. *Affective Equality: Love, Care and Injustice.* Basingstoke, UK: Palgrave Macmillan.

Mayhew, Anne. 1999. "Institutional Economics." In *The Elgar Companion to Feminist Economics*, edited by Margaret Lewis and Janice Peterson, 479–486. Cheltenham, UK: Edward Elgar.

Minsky, Hyman P. 1986. *Stabilizing an Unstable Economy.* New Haven: Yale University Press.

Patinkin, Don and Otto Steiger. 1989. "In Search of the 'Veil of Money' and the 'Neutrality of Money:' A Note on the Origin of Terms." *Scandinavian Journal of Economics* 91 (1): 131–146.

Peterson, Wallace C. 1977. "Institutionalism, Keynes, and the Real World." *Journal of Economic Issues* 11 (2): 201–221.

Picchio, Antonella. 1992. *Social Reproduction: The Political Economy of the Labour Market.* Cambridge: Cambridge University Press.

Power, Marilyn. 2004. "Social Provisioning as a Starting Point for Feminist Economics." *Feminist Economics* 10 (3): 3–19.

Reid, Margaret. 1934. *Economics of Household Production.* New York: John Wiley.

Robinson, Joan. 1969. "Introduction." In Michał Kalecki, *Studies in the Theory of Business Cycles: 1933–1939.* London: Basil Blackwell.

Robinson, Joan. 1972. "The Second Crisis of Economic Theory." *American Economic Review* 62 (1/2): 1–10.

Sikoska, Tatjana. 2003. "Measurement and Valuation of Unpaid Household Production: A Methodological Contribution." In *Macro-Economics: Making Gender Matter*, edited by Martha Gutierrez, 122–145. London: Zed Books.

Snyder, Margaret. 2007. "Gender, the Economy and the Workplace: Issues for the Women's Movement." In *Unpacking Globalization: Markets, Gender, and Work*, edited by Linda E. Lucas, 11–20. Lanham, MD: Lexington Books.

Spotton Visano, Brenda. 2017. "Gendering Post-Keynesian Macroeconomics. A Contribution to the Debate." Paper delivered at the Allied Social Science Associations Annual Meeting, Chicago, IL, January 6, 2017.

Standing, Gary. 2009. *Work after Globalization: Building Occupational Citizenship.* Cheltenham, UK: Edward Elgar.

Todorova, Zdravka. 2009. *Money and Households in a Capitalist Economy: A Gendered Post Keynesian-Institutional Analysis.* Cheltenham, UK: Edward Elgar.

Todorova, Zdravka. 2013. "Connecting Social Provisioning and Functional Finance in a Post-Keynesian-Institutional Analysis of the Public Sector." *European Journal of Economics and Economic Policies: Intervention* 10 (1): 61–75.

Todorova, Zdravka. 2015. "Economic and Social Classes in Theorizing Unpaid Household Activities Under Capitalism." *Journal of Economic Issues* 49 (2): 425–431.

United Nations. 2000. *The World's Women 2000.* New York: United Nations.

van Staveren, Irene. 2010a. "Feminist Economics, Setting out the Parameters." In *Feministische Kritik der Politischen Ökonomie*, edited by Christine Bauhardt, and Gülay Çağlar, 18–48. Wiesbaden, Germany: VS Verlag für Sozialwissenschaften.

van Staveren, Irene. 2010b. "Post-Keynesianism Meets Feminist Economics." *Cambridge Journal of Economics* 34: 1123–1144.

van Staveren, Irene. 2015. *Economics after Crisis: An Introduction to Economics from a Pluralist and Global Perspective.* Abingdon, UK: Routledge.

Veblen, Thorstein. 1891. "Some Neglected Points in the Theory of Socialism." *Annals of the American Academy of Political and Social Sciences* 2(3): 345–362.

Veblen, Thorstein. 1894. "The Economic Theory of Woman's Dress." *Popular Science Monthly* 46 (2): 198–205.

Veblen, Thorstein. 1899. "The Barbarian Status of Women." *American Journal of Sociology* 4 (4): 503–514.

Waller, William. 1999. "Post Keynesian Economics." *The Elgar Companion to Feminist Economics*, edited by Janice Peterson and Margaret Lewis, 622–628. Cheltenham, UK: Edward Elgar.

Waller, William. 2005. "Accidental Veblenian, Intentional Institutionalist, and Inevitable Feminist." *Journal of Economic Issues* 39 (2): 327–334.

Waller, William, and Ann Jennings. 1990. "On the Possibility of a Feminist Economics: The Convergence of Institutional and Feminist Methodology." *Journal of Economic Issues* 24 (2): 613–622.

Whalen, Charles J. 1996. "The Institutional Approach to Political Economy." In *Beyond Neoclassical Economics: Heterodox Approaches to Economic Theory*, edited by Fred E. Foldvary, 83–99. Cheltenham, UK: Edward Elgar.

Whalen, Charles J. 2011. *Financial Instability and Economic Security after the Great Recession.* Cheltenham, UK: Edward Elgar.

Whalen, Charles J. 2020. "Post-Keynesian Institutionalism: Past, Present, and Future." *Evolutionary and Institutional Economics Review* 17 (1): 71–92.

Wilber, Charles K., and Kenneth P. Jameson. 1983. *An Inquiry into the Poverty of Economics.* Notre Dame: University of Notre Dame Press.

Zachorowska-Mazurkiewicz, Anna. 2009. "Role of Macroeconomic Policy in Reinforcing Gender Inequality—A Case Study of Poland in the European Union." *Journal of Economic Issues* 43 (2): 503–511.

Zachorowska-Mazurkiewicz, Anna. 2015. "The Concept of Care in Institutional and Feminist Economics and Its Impact on Public Policy." *Journal of Economic Issues* 49 (2): 405–413.

Zachorowska-Mazurkiewicz, Anna. 2016. *Praca kobiet w teorii ekonomii – perspektywa ekonomii głównego nurtu i ekonomii feministycznej.* Kraków: Jagiellonian University Press.

Zalewski, David A. 2019. "Uncertainty and the Economy of Exclusion: Insights from Post-Keynesian Institutionalism." *American Journal of Economics and Sociology* 78 (4): 955–972.

16. Toward real sustainability: incorporating insight from Ecological economics into Post-Keynesian Institutionalism

Charles J. Whalen

INTRODUCTION

Post-Keynesian Institutionalism (PKI) is a strand of the Institutionalist research tradition that builds on Institutionalism's compatibility and complementarity with Post Keynesian economics.[1] According to Charles K. Wilber and Kenneth P. Jameson (1983, 155), PKI is "holistic, systemic, and evolutionary" in its orientation toward economic activity. They also characterize it as giving attention to economic power and conflict, culturally conditioned human behavior, and real-world problem solving.[2] At the heart of that problem solving is PKI's decades-long work to achieve sustainable and broadly shared prosperity nationally and internationally (Whalen 2008).

The sustainability at the center of attention in PKI has most often involved sustaining macroeconomic (and transnational economic) expansions. In particular, the main aim has usually been to eradicate involuntary unemployment, ensure a decent standard of living for all, and prevent—or at least contain—financial crises and other sources of recessions and economic depressions. PKI has given much less attention to environmental sustainability.

Today, however, macroeconomic (or global economic) sustainability is not enough. The world faces a climate change crisis that threatens not only our economic system, but also the very survival of humanity. Moreover, the climate crisis can be traced back in large part to human economic activity. Thus, we have no choice but to expand the scope of what we mean by sustainability so that it includes environmental as well as economic sustainability.

This chapter seeks to point the way toward a genuine, more comprehensive sustainability for PKI. It does so by suggesting the incorporation of insight from Ecological economics into PKI. Although PKI has not devoted much attention to Ecological economics, it should be well-positioned to do so:

Institutionalism has long been better able than conventional economics to recognize and accommodate the issue of ecological sustainability, and the relentless and single-minded drive for shareholder value at the heart of the current
era of money manager capitalism represents perhaps the greatest challenge to
moving toward real sustainability.

The chapter is structured as follows. We begin with a brief overview of
Ecological economics. Next, we look at two articles that appeared in the
Institutionalists' *Journal of Economic Issues* in the 1970s, not only to illustrate
that Institutional economics has long been able to accommodate vital aspects
of Ecological economics, but also to demonstrate that Institutionalism has
long recognized the importance of environmental issues and that its insight
on such issues remains relevant. Then we draw attention to the work of some
Post-Keynesian Institutionalists who have given attention to the environment;
identify (from our literature review) some lessons and suggestions for advancing the research agenda of PKI; and highlight the relationship between climate
change and money manager capitalism, a relationship that provides a logical
starting place for incorporating Ecological economics into contemporary PKI.
The chapter closes with a brief summary and conclusion.

ECOLOGICAL ECONOMICS

According to Ecological economist Arild Vatn (2009, 120), "Ecological economics is concerned with the interrelations between the economic system and
the ecological or biophysical processes on which it is based."[3] It grew out of
the work of ecologists and economists seeking interdisciplinary cooperation
to address concerns about resource limits, environmental degradation, and
environmental sustainability. Recognizing that the field continues to evolve,
Vatn (2009, 119) identifies the years between the end of World War II and
the mid-1980s as the period during which Ecological economics emerged,
owing to increased interest in environmental and resource issues as well as to
advances ranging from the development of systems ecology to the formation of
general systems theory and its application to the physical sciences.[4]

Boulding's "Spaceship Earth"

In the mid-1960s, Evolutionary economist Kenneth Boulding (1966) wrote an
essay that many identify as the starting point for modern Ecological economics.[5] In that essay, "The Economics of the Coming Spaceship Earth," Boulding
describes an ongoing and fundamental shift in the image humans have of
the world around them. According to Boulding (1966, 3), humans have long
considered themselves inhabitants of a limitless plain: "[T]here was always
someplace else to go when things got too difficult, either by reason of the dete-

rioration of the natural environment or a deterioration of the social structure in places where people happened to live." The new image, which did not begin to receive wide acceptance until the mid-twentieth century, is that humanity inhabits a closed sphere, into which sunlight and solar energy are essentially the only inputs from outside "spaceship earth" (Boulding 1966, 3–9).

At the same time that he stressed the largely "closed system" nature of our planet, Boulding (1966, 4) also emphasized the "open system" nature of living organisms, human societies, and economic activity. In each case, inputs are received from the earth, atmosphere, and waters, while outputs are later returned to those same places. Thus, his article hints at a tremendous irony in conventional economics, which seems to have these perspectives backwards: the economic mainstream (mistakenly) tends to study human production and consumption (and income and expenditures) as essentially a closed system with a perpetual circular flow, while also providing an intellectual home to those in the profession who have shown the greatest difficulty transitioning to a closed earth conception of the world ecosystem (Boulding 1966, 4).

In short, Boulding (1966, 9) maintains that humanity is an integral part of the world ecosystem, which itself is a predominantly closed system: "a single spaceship, without unlimited reservoirs of anything, either for extraction or for pollution." Thus, humanity must find its place within that largely cyclical ecological system (Boulding 1966, 9). Of course, the energy input provided by the sun is vital to humanity and to the sphere of human economic activity that Boulding called the "econosphere," but he stresses that once we deplete the "stored-up sunshine" of fossil fuels—assuming we don't destroy the environment in the process—humans will need to retreat to living within the bounds of what is possible using the sun's current energy (Boulding 1966, 7–8).[6]

Boulding never uses the word "sustainability," but the need to live sustainably on "spaceship earth" is the central implication of the shift from viewing the planet as an endless, wide-open frontier to a closed spaceship stocked with finite amounts of matter. One way to live more sustainably in such a world would be to recycle outputs from consumption into inputs for future production, though Boulding (1966, 7) admits that recycling itself requires energy.[7] What's necessary to ensure truly sustainable living is more far-reaching: a major rethinking of our attitude toward consumption and production is in order, insists Boulding (1966, 9–11), and that means jettisoning the idea that the size (not to mention the growth) of national output is an "adequate measure of economic success." In particular, Boulding (1966, 10) calls for policymakers to focus on improving human well-being, rather than on expanding what we today call gross domestic product; to that end, he also argues for bolstering and maintaining the quality of our capital stock—broadly conceived to include material, people, and knowledge—rather than increasing flows such as output and income.

The Worldview of Ecological Economics

Today's Ecological economics adopts a pluralistic perspective toward economic outlook and methods. But what distinguishes that tradition from "environmental economics" and "resource economics" is that these two fields have traditionally been associated with Neoclassical economics, while much of Ecological economics has generally involved looking beyond the economic mainstream. That is evident in the worldview underlying Ecological economics as well as in its research directions and contributions, which can be summarized as follows.

Ecological economics begins with recognition of Boulding's essentially "closed system" or "spaceship earth" perspective of the world.[8] It views the econosphere as situated within that global biosphere; thus, the economic realm—which Institutionalists call the realm of human social provisioning—is conceived as a complex, open system inextricably linked to the biophysical world and replete with interdependencies (Vatn 2009, 125–126). Ecological economics also views both the biosphere and econosphere as in a constant state of flux: it adopts an evolutionary perspective of both natural and human systems (and their interrelations), and their evolution may head in the direction of order or chaos, but may also cycle between different states. Time, meanwhile is recognized as irreversible; Ecological economists emphasize "real or historic time and path-dependency" (Vatn 2009, 121).

The worldview of Ecological economics also emphasizes real-world complementarities, rather than resource substitution, and highlights uncertainty, rather than probabilistic risk. In the 1970s, Ecological economists' concerns about natural limits to economic growth were met by the economic mainstream's response that there are "no fundamental scarcity problems"—since there is "always the opportunity" for using technology to substitute human-made capital for natural resources.[9] In contrast, Ecological economists emphasize "substitutability thresholds" (that is, limited substitutability) and non-substitutability, and focus on complementarity "as the dominant aspect of biophysical systems," owing to the econosphere's technical and biological interdependencies (as well as its limitations). Ecological economists also stress that the concept of risk is insufficient for capturing either ecological or economic evolution because future situations always involve novelty.[10] Thus, such economists generally support both the "precautionary principle" (which recommends minimum interference when long-term effects cannot be predicted and change may be irreversible) and the use of inclusive, participatory processes when assessing the consequences of alternative policies (Vatn 2009, 120–121, 123, 126).[11]

Ecological economists also distinguish between prices and values. In part, this relates to their rejection of the mainstream economists' emphasis on substitutability. Even the mainstream acknowledges that markets do not provide prices that fully reflect the benefits of environmental preservation and the costs of environmental degradation, but Ecological economists argue that the challenge is not simply to get the prices right (via taxes and tradable permits, for example) and then use market signals to affect tradeoffs on the margin. In addition to non-substitutability, relying on prices alone also overlooks important interdependencies (where "the actions of one influence opportunities for others"), the endogeneity of preferences, and, more broadly, how existing institutions, rights, and power relations influence price estimates and resource access (Vatn 2009, 121–122).

To be sure, prices provide one form of valuation mechanism, but according to Vatn (2009, 122), Ecological economists stress that "the way valuation is undertaken"—that is, the choice of value-articulating institutions—influences both the values emphasized and the form in which they are expressed. Richard P.F. Holt and Clive L. Spash (2009, 3) complement Vatn's observation by writing that Ecological economists believe economics "cannot and should not be separated from ethical judgments, particularly in regard to the impact of those living today on future generations and the health of the planet." Holt and Spash (2009, 3) also highlight the following: Ecological economists question the conventional (and usually implicit) value that more economic growth "is always better;" and such economists consider nature to have "an intrinsic value."[12]

Research Directions and Contributions

Ecological economics is problem oriented. That explains its interdisciplinary orientation and pluralistic approach to methods. As Holt and Spash write, such economists hold that "*problems* should be the focus of concern rather than *techniques* which restrain the type and form of concepts used in analysis" (Holt and Spash 2009, 5, emphasis in original).

As suggested by Boulding's notion of "spaceship earth," Ecological economics began with a focus on "its own type of 'macroeconomics'" (Vatn 2009, 122). According to that approach, economic sustainability is not only a matter for individual nations but also—and more importantly—a planetary aim, which recognizes the earth's resource constraints and regenerative capacity as well as their implications for the growth of humanity's population and artifacts (Courvisanos 2009, 282; Holt and Spash 2009, 3). Moreover, the concerns are not narrowly economic; limits to sustainability are recognized to have social, economic, and ecological consequences (Holt and Spash 2009, 3). At the same time, considerations within the scope of the conventional domain of economics—especially all of the subject matter relating to economic growth—still remain important, if only because, as Holt and Spash (2009, 3) write, "Endless economic growth is unsustainable both socially and environmentally." The scope of Ecological economics is certainly broader, but much of the domain is the same as in standard economics; what has changed most fundamentally is the context and the point of view.

A key early contributor to Ecological economics' effort to "link economics to its biophysical basis" was Herman Daly, whose work has focused on seeking to establish a "steady-state economy" (Daly 1991; Vatn 2009, 119). Daly's steady state centers on a scale of production that "balances material and energy throughputs into the economy, and maintains flows from the ecosystem at a constant and sustainable level" (Courvisanos 2009, 282). According to Daly's vision, innovations allow the economy to continue to develop, but that development would center on improving "the quality of society" without distorting the biophysical equilibrium (Courvisanos 2009, 282). In short, like Boulding, Daly emphasizes humanity's interaction with the processes of the biosphere, and the need to match the scale of the economy with its ecological base (Vatn 2009, 120).

Because of the work of early contributors such as Boulding and Daly, Ecological economics has always given much attention to flows of matter in the econosphere.[13] For example, Vatn (2009, 120) identifies two products of such work: indicators that measure the physical impact of human consumption, such as the concept of the "ecological footprint" (a measure that connects flows of matter to depletion of stocks); and the notion of "social metabolism," which "links matter flows to the organization and dynamics of socioeconomic systems" (Vatn 2009, 120). Thus, matter flows are a key component of Ecological economists' focus on "the interplay between ecological and economic systems" (Vatn 2009, 123).

Another research direction in Ecological economics centers around the concept of resilience. The focus here is on the adaptive nature of ecological systems—that is, on the capacity of socioecological systems to withstand many external pressures as well as to reorganize "in the face of more fundamental challenges" (Vatn 2009, 121). According to Ecological economist Carl Folke (2006, 259), socioecological resilience focuses on "adaptive capacity, transformability, learning, [and] innovation."[14]

There is also Ecological economics at the microeconomic level, especially in a "still developing" field called the "Ecological economics of consumption" (Vatn 2009, 122). This involves the intersection of Ecological economics and the sort of microeconomics found in Behavioral, Institutional, and Post Keynesian economics. In particular, that work examines motivation and behavior as they relate to issues such as the importance of institutions and the fashioning of environmental policy (Soderbaum 1994; Vatn 2008; 2009, 122). The microeconomic branch of Ecological economics also explores how power relations "influence access to resources and the distribution of risk" (Vatn 2009, 123).

EARLY INSTITUTIONALIST ENGAGEMENT WITH ENVIRONMENTAL ISSUES

Institutional economists have addressed environmental issues for at least a half century. This section highlights that attention by focusing on two articles that appeared in the Institutionalists' *Journal of Economic Issues* in the 1970s. The first is by American economist Harold Wolozin; the second is by German-American economist K. William Kapp.

Wolozin

Wolozin's article, "Environmental Controls at the Crossroads," is based on a paper he presented at the annual meeting of the Institutional economists' Association for Evolutionary Economics in December of 1970. That was the same month in which President Richard Nixon signed into law the Clean Air Act of 1970 (a substantial amendment to legislation enacted in 1963), and less than a year after the enactment of the National Environmental Policy Act and creation (by executive order) of the United States (US) Environmental Protection Agency (EPA). The *Journal of Economic Issues*—launched only a few years earlier—published Wolozin's essay, along with brief comments from Anatol Murad, in early 1971 (Murad 1971; Wolozin 1971).

Wolozin opens his article by describing his view of the environmental problem facing the United States and the world. Acknowledging measurement inadequacies, huge gaps in existing human knowledge, and the certainty of unpredictable "surprises" beyond our current horizon, Wolozin stresses the widespread evidence of serious and worsening pollution, deterioration of the environment, depletion of the planet's natural resources, and a rising toll on our quality of life. Describing the situation as an "environmental crisis" and a "supreme challenge" to human society, he is blunt: "The prognosis for environmental quality is not good" (Wolozin 1971, 26–27, 29–31).[15]

Wolozin's article maintains not merely that humanity has given insufficient attention to the environmental problem, but also that conventional public-policy approaches and the concepts of law and economics on which they are based are inadequate for addressing the problem. Thus, he calls for both a fresh approach to policy and a fundamental reappraisal of its existing foundations. In particular, he focuses on the United States (while recognizing, of course, that much of the environmental crisis knows no national boundaries) and identifies four elements he considers essential for moving toward adequate environmental protection (Wolozin 1971, 27, 39).

First, Wolozin argues that the nation's environmental authority (the EPA) needs broad authority, ample resources for research as well as regulation, the teeth required to accomplish its mission and enforce its actions, and the ability to avoid being controlled by polluters. On the need for broad authority, he writes, "Emphasis on the pervasiveness of [negative] externalities and the importance of interdependencies must be faced up to in environmental research, planning, and control; and this can only be done by effective control at the federal level" and must include "a hard look" not just at production and consumption systems that generate and dispose of waste, but also at energy, transportation, and growth policies (Wolozin 1971, 38–39). While he expresses hope that appropriations (and, implicitly, a professional staff) would be sufficient to keep the agency independent, Wolozin admits that regulatory capture by special interests is a concern, and indeed the article pointed to evidence suggesting that most state-level pollution control agencies were under the sway of major polluters (Wolozin 1971, 27).[16]

Wolozin also calls for "redefining and expanding the role of law" so as to give those seeking to protect the environment "more effective legal recourse" (Wolozin 1971, 27). This is the second of the four elements he identifies as necessary to protect the environment. In particular, he calls for moving beyond compensating people for damages under existing property rights and nuisance laws, which are piecemeal solutions and often put the burden of proof on those seeking damages, and proposes instead a constitutional right to a clean environment, which he described as an "Environmental Bill of Rights."[17] According to Wolozin, this would not only shift the burden of proof in litigation, but also change the policy emphasis "from narrow quantitative values in environmental planning, regulation and litigation to broad concerns ... [aimed at fostering] a healthy and wholesome environment" (Wolozin 1971, 39).[18]

Third, Wolozin argues there is a need for "a searching reappraisal of the relevancy" of the economic models and concepts applied to problems of environmental quality control. In his view, much of economists' work relating to environmental management has been "fruitless" and its concepts are so narrow that, as constructed, they warrant "only a very limited role in overall environmental policy" (Wolozin 1971, 27, 33). For example, many proposed efforts at environmental control aim to take "a fee and incentive approach," relying on effluent charges and tradable pollution rights. But Wolozin argues that such approaches rely on two highly questionable assumptions: (1) policymakers have (or can easily acquire) full and accurate knowledge of environmental costs, enabling fees and other incentives to be properly calibrated; and (2) businesses and individuals will be driven to make socially optimal decisions in the normal course of seeking to maximize profit and utility. Even if the first were true (which, Wolozin maintains, it is not), the second is too much of a reach to use in making policy, he insists, since it fails to hold in real-world conditions characterized by market power, complex economic interdependencies (involving various aspects of production, consumption, and pollution), and producer and consumer uncertainty (Wolozin 1971, 33, 35, 38). In fact, Wolozin (1971, 36–38) even explains that economists' conception of individuals and organizations as "maximizers" does not conform to reality because business behavior is often affected by multiple influences and consumption is shaped by advertising and a variety of cultural factors.[19]

Wolozin's (1971, 27, 39) fourth element calls for broadening the concept of social costs and benefits. Efforts to identify the costs of pollution and environmental damage are used in litigation as a way to decide awards that aim to compensate for such costs. Similar efforts to identify the costs and benefits of human behavior—indeed, benefit-cost analyses—are also at the root of market-based environmental management policies. In both judicial and public-policy settings, the underlying aim is to internalize the external costs of production or consumption; there is also an underlying assumption that externalities are an exceptional case and (especially in court proceedings) often affect only one third party. However, externalities, including those with widespread and even global impact, are a normal and inherent part of production and consumption—"a significant accompaniment of economic activity" (Wolozin 1971, 30, 32, 39). Moreover, Wolozin (1971, 33) argues that "the mere summing of measurable, individual external costs does not give an adequate or true measure of social costs as they should be conceived in our modern, interdependent society."

Thus, what Wolozin (1971, 39) envisions as the basis for his Environmental Bill of Rights is a concept of social costs and benefits "far wider than we have hitherto been willing to accept." His broader conceptualization of the social costs of environmental degradation begins with recognizing the psychological as well as physical effects of environmental damage upon humans, agriculture, and the rest of the natural world. It requires recognition that some costs involve problems that are acute and immediate, while others—which public policy often doesn't take into account—may be hidden initially, yet show up later as problems that are extremely serious and chronic, or may involve long-term exposure to what at first appear to be insignificant levels of pollutants but eventually prove to have irreversible or even toxic effects. It also requires recognition of interactions among pollutants, which means that pollution—and even environmental media (such as air and water)—can't be properly addressed in isolation; and it necessitates recognition that environmental damage and costs are usually nonlinear—they often grow exponentially with economic activity (Wolozin 1971, 29–31, 38–39).[20]

Wolozin's approach also requires accepting that not all social costs and benefits can be quantified, regardless of whether the measurement is dollars, lives, or some other unit. In part, this is because "dependable cause and effect relationships" have yet to be established with respect to many types of pollution and because aspects of our knowledge in this area are evolving so quickly that it's possible that "present knowledge would be out of date before we are able to feed it into any policy model" (Wolozin 1971, 31). But that's not the whole story. As Murad (1971, 44) writes, "[I]t is clearly impossible to assign unambiguous market values to health, esthetics, noise, and so on."[21] In fact, that's a key reason why Wolozin stresses the limited role of internalizing external costs and focuses instead on shifting environmental policy from narrow quantitative values to broader concerns associated with the right to a healthy environment and its role in enabling humans to improve their quality of life.

Kapp

Like Wolozin, Kapp—who emigrated to the US in the 1930s—was also an Institutionalist whose post-World War II research exhibited a special interest in environmental issues and the problem of social costs. In fact, he is often considered an early pioneer in Ecological economics, on the basis of publications such as *The Social Costs of Private Enterprise*, published in 1950 by Harvard University Press (Kapp 1950). Toward the end of 1975, and only months before his death, Kapp delivered a paper in Kyoto, Japan, at the International Congress of Scientists on the Human Environment. In 1977, that paper appeared in the *Journal of Economic Issues* as "Environment and Technology: New Frontiers for the Social and Natural Sciences" (Kapp 1977).

In that paper, Kapp argues that environmental degradation presents a fundamental challenge to both scientists and society. The challenge to scientists is that the content and evolution of scientific research in the social and natural sciences must be aimed at helping society formulate and implement environmental norms consistent with human needs and well-being (Kapp 1977, 537–539). The challenge to society is that it must rethink core institutions and processes that not only adversely affect the conditions and quality of human life, but also endanger social and economic reproduction (Kapp 1977, 534–537).

Most of Kapp's article outlines what he calls the "substantive" nature of the problem of environmental disruption—an institutionally and historically grounded description of the problem in which social costs play a central role. Before we get to social costs, however, he introduces us to the setting, which involves "the manifold interdependencies between socioeconomic and ecological-physical systems," and simultaneously highlights the ecological and human dimensions of the environmental problem as well as its interdisciplinary nature (Kapp 1977, 528). This interdisciplinarity is also evident in Kapp's (1977, 531) discussion of the "complex and cumulative character of the causation of environmental disruption."[22]

According to Kapp, environmental damage is just one of various social costs generated in the course of economic activity; such costs are "anything but exceptions or minor side effects" (Kapp 1977, 529). Moreover, the threat to the environment from such costs are particularly great in our market-driven system, where the overriding objective of producers is to maximize returns and minimize costs; thus, their aim is to "internalize" only monetary benefits and "externalize" environmental disruption and other social costs "as far as possible within the existing institutional and legal framework" (Kapp 1977 532). As a rule, Kapp adds, as long as there is air, land, or water to pollute freely, and as long as enterprises feel some amount of market pressure to maximize profits, less environmentally harmful techniques and processes won't even be explored. In short, market systems have a "built-in" tendency toward environmental disruption—and entrepreneurial optimization is "a pseudo-optimization," at least from society's vantage point, because it fails to take total costs into account (Kapp 1977, 532–533).[23]

As did Wolozin, Kapp rejects relying on market-based approaches to provide an effective solution to the environmental problem. While admitting (but with an expression of wariness) that taxes, tradeable rights, and awards for damages might be able to play some limited constructive role, Kapp (1977, 534) concludes that protecting human health and safeguarding the environment for future generations require more active public policy measures. These include: (1) introducing strict, science-based standards to control the use of harmful production inputs and the disposal of dangerous residuals; (2) exploring, developing, promoting, and requiring production methods and technologies with a low ecological impact; (3) increasing the natural environment's "capacity to assimilate residuals" (such as by water aeration or treatment of wastes before they are discharged); and (4) making public investments to find "new ways of recovering and reusing waste materials" (Kapp 1977, 534–535). Kapp also underscores that reducing environmental destruction is good for the economy: Toward the end of his article, he emphasizes both that economic activity does not require uncontrolled environmental disruption (it all depends on the amount and composition of input and output) and that, over time, such disruption and depletion of natural resources actually constrain economic activity (Kapp 1977, 535–536). In other words, both Wolozin and Kapp are pointing toward a genuinely sustainable economy.

POST-KEYNESIAN INSTITUTIONALISTS AND ECOLOGICAL CONCERNS

The previous section's look at two Institutionalist articles from the 1970s shows that Institutionalism has indeed long been able to accommodate vital aspects of Ecological economics. While the holism of Institutional economics has traditionally focused on how the economy interacts, in complex ways, with culture and other aspects of human society, Wolozin and Kapp demonstrate that an even more complex economic interaction with the rest of the biosphere likewise fits within—indeed, must be part of—the perspective of Institutionalism. Their essays, despite having been written a half-century ago, also show a solid grasp of issues and challenges that are unmistakable today, including the limited effectiveness of market-based solutions, the resistance of vested interests, and the threat of irreversible climate change "with far-reaching consequences" (Kapp 1977, 529; Wolozin 1971, 30).[24] In addition, although the work of these Institutionalists predates widespread use of the notion of the "precautionary principle" (which began roughly in the 1990s), it is clear that a precautionary approach to environmental management is consistent with their attention to unmistakable climate dangers, considerable gaps of knowledge, and an uncertain tomorrow.

The current section considers the work of some Post-Keynesian Institutionalists who have turned their attention to environmental concerns. In particular, we focus on John Kenneth Galbraith's discussion of such issues in several publications, including chapters on the environment in *Economics and the Public Purpose* (Galbraith 1973a, 275–282) and *The Good Society* (Galbraith 1996, 82–88), and Wilber and Jameson's discussion of environmental matters in *An Inquiry into the Poverty of Economics* (hereinafter referred to as *The Poverty of Economics*) (Wilber and Jameson 1983).

Galbraith

Recognized as both an Institutionalist and Post Keynesian, Galbraith was in many ways the first Post-Keynesian Institutionalist. In 1958, Galbraith's *The Affluent Society* described environmental damage as part of American society's failure to achieve a "social balance" between the interests of private economic activity (which encompasses production and consumption, both of which he traced back to producing corporations and their army of advertising firms that molded consumer demand) and the public sector's need to protect the public interest. The result was a nation characterized to a large extent by "private opulence and public squalor," a society in which "the private goods have full sway." Polluted water and air could be found in communities from one end of the country to the other, as were litter-filled cities, congested roadways, and scenic vistas blighted by roadside billboards (Galbraith 1958, 251–258).

In *Economics and the Public Purpose*, Galbraith identifies two ways to protect the environment.[25] One is for the public sector to spend the money necessary to clean up past damage and to protect resources and public areas (waterways, city streets, parks, etc.) from future damage. Of course, this is the sort of expenditure "against which the modern economy systematically discriminates, because there has long been a presumption in favor of economic growth and the prerogatives of private enterprise," but Galbraith (1973a, 276) insists that the role of the state must be to protect the public interest. The other way the state can protect the environment is to set boundaries that define the permissible environmental damage associated with production and consumption. This would not prohibit economic growth, but instead provide a legislatively determined assessment of when private interests are outweighed by those of society overall. Moreover, observing that production and consumption are already shaped by large corporations, Galbraith stresses that his approach is merely "public guidance and planning" in place of "private guidance and planning" (Galbraith 1973a, 275–280).[26]

Other relevant publications by Galbraith include his presidential address to the American Economic Association (Galbraith 1973b); his essay "On Post Keynesian Economics," which appeared in the inaugural issue of the *Journal of Post Keynesian Economics* (Galbraith 1978); and his chapter on the environment in *The Good Society* (Galbraith 1996, 82–88). In his presidential address, Galbraith makes a number of the same points found in *Economics and the Public Purpose*, but he also warns proponents of economic growth that there might be no growth at all in decades to come without a policy strategy that confines growth "within parameters" protecting the public interest—not merely because of environmental destruction, but also because other voices argue that "growth itself is the villain" and "are seeking its extinction" (Galbraith 1973b, 9). In the *Journal of Post Keynesian Economics*, Galbraith stresses that the market—controlled by huge corporations and no longer impersonal and unplanned—has lost "its authority as a regulatory force," and that Post Keynesian economics centers on accepting the decline of the market and working to best ensure that modern economic life "can be made socially acceptable to as many people as possible" (Galbraith 1978, 8, 11).[27]

While a call for social balance can be viewed as implicit in all the works of Galbraith discussed in this section, he not only makes that point explicit, but also places it at the center of his discussion of the environment in *The Good Society*. In particular, Galbraith argues that a central task of any "good society" is to find a balance between (on the one hand) the production and consumption needs of the present and (on the other hand) the adverse consequences of that activity, which appear not only in the present but also over the long term. Since corporate interests, motivated by near-term economic reward (profit), are fervent advocates on the side of current economic activity (that is, business as usual), social balance requires some other segment of society to champion protection of the environment and to speak up for future generations, and the principal instrument of that protection is the state (Galbraith 1996, 82–88).

Galbraith does not hide the fact that his perspective gives the state responsibility for both protecting the environment (which is an advocacy role) and achieving "a compromise between the current financial and longer-range public interests" (which is a dispute-resolution role). But current economic power (the business community) is at no great disadvantage because, as Galbraith observes, business interests have money, lobbyists, and plenty of political power on their side. Besides, the compromise that Galbraith describes as "essential and inevitable" is one he believes must, "as broad rule, ... favor the larger community interests and the interests of those to come" (Galbraith 1996, 87).

Wilber and Jameson

The Poverty of Economics (Wilber and Jameson 1983) is the first volume to outline an explicitly Post-Keynesian Institutionalist analysis. Consistent with Institutionalism's longstanding attention to practical problems, Wilber and Jameson focus on the stagflation that caused economic hardship and perplexed policymakers in the United States throughout the 1970s and into the early 1980s.[28] To be sure, there is attention to business cycles and the need for macroeconomic stabilization, but much of the book probes deeper, drawing on a rich and diverse literature (both in terms of perspectives and methods) to highlight the US economy's post-World War II emphasis on economic growth and mass consumption.

Wilber and Jameson stress that a market-based emphasis on growth, especially in an economy dominated by powerful mega-corporations, is both self-perpetuating and self-destructive. It's self-perpetuating because consumer demand becomes insatiable in an economy in which competition rests on product differentiation and business advertising, production centers on stylistic and physical obsolescence, and consumption—elevated to the status of a virtue more important than thrift—focuses on "positional" goods. It's self-destructive because much growth is "based on profligate use of natural resources," and the market, at best, reflects the current cost of obtaining such resources; market-based activity largely ignores environmental pollution and assumes technology will find a solution to resource exhaustion (Wilber and Jameson 1983, 2, 217–220).[29]

The conclusion of Wilber and Jameson is not that economic growth or market-based activity must end; rather, they argue that we must judge economic performance by its ability to meet human needs—including not just life-sustenance (physiological needs), but also psychic needs, such as esteem and fellowship (a sense of worth, dignity, and belonging), and the need for genuine choices and avenues of meaningful participation for consumers, workers, and citizens (Wilber and Jameson 1983, 4–8, 230–263). To address life-sustenance, they propose that the concept of *stewardship* offers a guiding principle, which they describe as the right to use property for private purposes "only as long as it does not result in harm to the common good" (Wilber and Jameson 1983, 239–240).

Wilber and Jameson (1983, 240) write that a key implication of the moral cannon of stewardship is that "society has responsibility for the resources which are at its disposal, and they must be used well." They also write that their perspective is all encompassing: "the whole earth is held under stewardship." Thus, as part of meeting human needs for life-sustenance, Wilber and Jameson insist on the need for energy and resource conservation as well as on various forms of civic engagement and collaborative decision-making (throughout the economy) to ensure the planet's resources are protected (Wilber and Jameson 1983, 240–241).[30] In short, the concept of stewardship leads Wilber and Jameson to the same need to temper or even override market-based drives that Galbraith described as the need to achieve social balance.

Galbraith and Wilber and Jameson are certainly not the only Post-Keynesian Institutionalists to recognize the need for environmental protection. For example, Hyman Minsky emphasized the importance of devoting more expenditures and attention to the provision, upkeep, and quality of public goods and services (offering national parks and forests as examples) as well as schools and educational programs, public health services, and community recreational facilities.[31] In fact, he explicitly argued that expenditures aimed at a more humane and civilized society were warranted even at the expense of some near-term market efficiency or aggregate income. Minsky also advocated linking a government job-guarantee initiative to modern versions of programs such as the Civilian Conservation Corps and Works Progress Administration, with the aim of not only enhancing public resources, but also achieving environmental improvements.[32] Nevertheless, PKI has undoubtedly focused much less on environmental stability than on macroeconomic stability, and it is to a discussion of ways to improve that situation that we now turn.

LESSONS AND SUGGESTIONS

The literature examined in the previous sections points to several lessons and suggestions for incorporating insight from Ecological economics into PKI.

Lessons

The first lesson is that PKI is indeed well positioned to recognize and accommodate the issue of ecological sustainability and other vital aspects of Ecological economics. The worldview of both traditions have much in common: in addition to sharing a holistic, systems oriented, and evolutionary perspective toward economic activity, they also emphasize limited substitutability, uncertainty, historical time and its irreversibility (resulting in path dependence), and cultural influences upon individual and organizational behavior (all while not diminishing the driving force of the profit motive in contemporary capitalist societies such as that found in the United States). Both traditions also recognize the importance of power relations, social conflict (rather than focusing narrowly on voluntary exchanges), a pluralistic approach to methods, and a focus on real-world problems.[33]

The second lesson, which flows from the first, is that the key to accommodating the central concerns of Ecological economics into PKI is for the latter to incorporate Boulding's "spaceship earth" perspective, including its recognition of complex interrelations between human economic activity and a biosphere that has limited resources and assimilative capacities. Through its look at not only the Institutional economics of Wolozin and Kapp, but also the PKI of Galbraith and Wilber and Jameson, this chapter has demonstrated that Boulding's perspective, a core element of Ecological economics, indeed can be incorporated into Institutionalism in general and PKI in particular. Wolozin, Kapp, Galbraith, and Wilber and Jameson may have focused more on environmental protection than on "ecological sustainability," but, as mentioned above, Boulding's groundbreaking article never even uses the term "sustainability," and a common focus on "quality of life" (rather than merely economic growth) and the interests of future generations reflects these economists' shared "spaceship earth" viewpoint. The current task is to make that perspective a foundational element in all contemporary PKI.

Another lesson also derives from the shared worldview of Ecological economics and PKI: the importance of inclusive, participatory processes of policy decision-making. Evidence of this third lesson was highlighted above in Vatn's (2009, 121) overview of Ecological economics, and in Wilber and Jameson's (1983, 7) discussion of the importance of meaningful citizen participation at all policy levels. But the need for public engagement and genuine stakeholder participation in decision-making is also found in the work of the other economists reviewed above (see, e.g., Galbraith 1996, 84; Kapp 1977, 539; Wolozin 1971, 27) and has been a key element of Post-Keynesian Institutionalism from the very start (Whalen 1992, 61–74; 2008, 46).

A fourth lesson is that the authors examined in this chapter have already cleared a shared path for Ecological economics and PKI with regard to the limited usefulness of the market as a measure of human well-being. None of the writers discussed in this chapter wish to eliminate market-based transactions, but their writings offer a catalogue of important reasons to be skeptical of using the market as a mechanism for all economic allocation and social provisioning. Thus, they also see a limited role for market-based environmental policies that aim to internalize external diseconomies, even as their work underscores the pervasiveness of social costs and the importance of taking an expansive view of such costs and benefits of economic activity.

A fifth lesson is that there is much that can be done to address environmental disruption. It begins with recognizing and strengthening the state's responsibility to protect the public interest by stepping in when private activities are outweighed by society's interests. This can be backed by an expanded Bill of Rights, as proposed by Wolozin, combined with a regulatory body with broad authority, science-based boundaries on permissible environmental damage (based, for example, on the environment's ability to assimilate waste), policies that require adoption of "low ecological impact" methods of production and consumption, and environmental considerations that are factored into all aspects of public policy (energy policy, transportation policy, etc.). Of course, those policy steps are not comprehensive (indeed, as Wilber and Jameson indicated, environmental protection requires action from the local level to the international level) and they will always meet obstacles and challenges. Nevertheless, the point is that PKI has a sizeable body of policy ideas to build upon when seeking to protect the environment.

There is also an important sixth lesson that underscores the whole aim of protecting the environment as part of PKI. It's implicit in Boulding's conception of "spaceship earth," but warrants emphasis. The lesson is that the literature surveyed in this chapter demonstrates that environmental destruction threatens all of our economic activity—and, indeed, humanity itself. Thus, protecting the environment is, in large part, about ensuring that future generations will have any economy at all. The literature reviewed in this chapter, especially when combined with what we now know about the current state of climate change (Intergovernmental Panel on Climate Change 2018; 2021), makes it clear that PKI's longstanding attention to economic sustainability can no longer continue in any meaningful way without also incorporating ecological sustainability. The environmental crisis was a "supreme" or "fundamental" challenge in the eyes of Institutionalists in the 1970s; it is clearly an *existential threat* to humanity today.

Suggestions

The literature reviewed in this chapter suggests a number of concepts that could be useful to Post-Keynesian Institutionalists. An example is the precautionary principle, which seems to make more sense than ever in the context of the projected consequences and irreversibilities associated with climate change as well as the growing evidence of long-term harm associated with many of today's chemicals and pollutants. That principle is also consistent with PKI research on policy-generated institutions (ceilings and floors on permissible economic activity) that act as circuit breakers to stabilize the macroeconomy and prevent complex, nonlinear systems from experiencing chaotic dynamics or outright collapse.[34] Other useful concepts include stewardship, social balance, and (broadly defined) social costs and benefits.

The above discussion also suggests that PKI would benefit from giving attention to Boulding's focus on the stocks, rather than merely the flows, of the econosphere, as well as to Daly's notion of a steady-state economy. Boulding's essay on "spaceship earth" emphasizes society's (broadly conceived) capital stock, which bears some resemblance to Minsky's (1986, 300) notions of resource creation and public capital assets; and hints at a balance-sheet approach to economic activity, which is also found in the work of Minsky and other Post-Keynesian Institutionalists (Whalen 2013, 18). Indeed such an approach can be found in Boulding's writings on macroeconomics (Wray 1997). Meanwhile, Daly's contributions draw attention not only to a bio-physical equilibrium consistent with economic and ecological balance, but also to the broader quality-of-life considerations found in the work of the Institutionalists and Post-Keynesian Institutionalists discussed above.[35]

In the past two decades, much environmentally oriented research and practice has focused on the notion of industrial ecology and the related per-spective of a circular economy, which aims to replace the "linear" notion of "take, make, and dispose," with a more cyclical approach to production and consumption (Whalen and Whalen 2018). That work, inspired to a large extent by Boulding's "spaceship earth" essay, also deserves the attention of PKI. Industrial ecology aims to apply not only recycling but also biomimicry (redesigning industrial systems along biological lines) to achieve a more eco-logically sustainable, circular economy, and PKI can benefit from that litera-ture's emphasis on the environment and resource use in an economic context. Meanwhile, PKI can help dispel some of the misconceptions of the circular economy literature (which in several cases can be traced to its inattention to the fallacy of composition) as well as underscore the essential role for public policy often overlooked by industrial ecologists (Whalen and Whalen 2020).

An increasingly prominent feature of the circular economy literature is discussion of the usefulness of indicators of "economic circularity," measures of the extent to which circular economy considerations (such as product dura-bility and recyclability) are adopted by enterprises, communities, or nations as a foundation for economic activity. PKI would certainly benefit from considering ways of incorporating such indicators into their own analyses and policy-oriented research. The same is true of related work on the "triple bottom line," which seeks to encourage—or perhaps even compel—corporations to consider social and environmental goals in addition to their traditional eco-nomic objectives. An example of such work is an article by David Zalewski (2003), which recommends linking measures of triple-bottom-line perfor-mance to the US tax code, thus providing enterprises with an incentive that brings the pursuit of profits into closer alignment with the broader public interest.

Other contemporary Post-Keynesian Institutionalists follow Minsky (and Institutionalists such as Gordon 1980, 320–339) in calling for linking a federal job guarantee to environmental clean-up and protection. For example, Pavlina Tcherneva (2018) proposes public jobs related to care for the environment (such as flood control, environmental surveys, and weatherization projects) as one of three broad categories of government-provided work for the unemployed (the other categories are care for one's community and care for people). In a similar manner, Whalen (2019, 333–334) envisions a public employment program working in an integrated fashion with a national economic strategy and a national investment initiative focused on addressing climate change (with special attention to the development and adoption of clean energy in place of fossil fuels).[36] This is a promising area for further policy-oriented PKI research, especially as the reality, costs, and dangers of climate change begin to sink in among policymakers and the general public.[37]

The literature reviewed in this chapter also leads me to suggest that Post-Keynesian Institutionalists would benefit from looking at the work of the late A. Allan Schmid, who studied at the University of Wisconsin under students of the pioneering Institutional economist John R. Commons and taught agricultural and resource economics at Michigan State University for over four decades (retiring in 2006). Schmid's (2008) "Institutional law and economics" approach to the environment stresses that "economic value is not independent of law." That approach, and Schmid's Institutionalism in general, provides an excellent bridge between Ecological economics, which emphasizes that institutions, rights, and power relations influence access to resources and the distribution of risk (Vatn 2009, 121), and PKI, which recognizes that "property is not an absolute right and never has been" (Wilber and Jameson 1983, 240).[38]

Yet another suggestion is for PKI to incorporate Ecological economists' recognition of the intrinsic value of nature and other species. Since publication of the Wolozin and Kapp essays discussed above, the intrinsic value of nature has been reflected in the writing of a number of Institutionalists.[39] However, a similar recognition has generally not entered the literature of PKI in a significant way; thus, this represents an area where Ecological economics can appreciably broaden the worldview of Post-Keynesian Institutionalists.

Going further on the subject of values, a broader suggestion can also be made. Scholars may be convinced that changing conditions warrant changes to public policy and other social institutions, but such changes do not occur without an adjustment of social beliefs. Thus, Post-Keynesian Institutionalists must aim for a better understanding of why people hold certain social beliefs, how those beliefs are rooted in deep-seated cultural values, and how those values and beliefs can and do change over time (for more on this as it relates to environmental problems, see Adkisson 2022). Such knowledge is essential to addressing the challenge for scholars that Kapp identified decades ago: helping society fashion and make use of environmental norms consistent with human well-being.[40]

A final suggestion for contemporary PKI is to find ways to apply Kapp's insight that market capitalism has a built-in tendency toward environmental disruption in that it seeks to offload costs as much as possible and internalize only monetary gains. Early Post-Keynesian Institutionalists such as Galbraith and Wilber and Jameson echoed Kapp's observations, noting not only corporations' efforts to shift costs, risks, and other burdens onto the community at large, but also the tremendously destructive nature of that process when left unchecked. Today, this dynamic can be examined by recognizing and exploring the interrelations of climate change and money manager capitalism. In fact, such an exploration may provide the most logical starting place for incorporating insight from Ecological economics into PKI, and it's for that reason that we give the matter a brief look before bringing this chapter to a close.

CLIMATE CHANGE AND MONEY MANAGER CAPITALISM

Since real-world problem solving is the focus of both Ecological economics and PKI, it's appropriate that efforts to incorporate insight from the former into the latter should begin with the top problems confronting these traditions—climate change in the case of Ecological economics, and money manager capitalism in the case of PKI. Of course, "money manager capitalism" is merely the name Minsky (1993) gave to the current, investor-driven stage of capitalism that emerged in the United States during the early 1980s, replacing the business-driven "managerial" stage fashioned in the wake of the Great Depression. But the current era is recognized as a problem because it is associated with a number of serious economic difficulties, including widespread worker insecurity, rising income inequality, persistent financial fragility, increased macroeconomic instability, slowed technological progress, and erosion of manufacturing capacity (Whalen 2020).[41] Money manager capitalism also appears to exacerbate the climate-change problem (for reasons discussed below), thus it poses a threat to ecological sustainability as well as to Post-Keynesian Institutionalists' longstanding goals of macroeconomic sustainability and broadly shared prosperity. This is a matter that deserves to be at the top of the research agenda of PKI—especially as money manager capitalism has become an increasingly global phenomenon.

The driving force of money manager capitalism is the maximization of shareholder value. In this stage of capitalist development, institutional investors seek to maximize short-term returns for their fund holders, which translates into corporate executives' relentless focus on profits and the stock-market value of their firm. Maximization of shareholder value also leads to corporate mergers, break-ups, restructurings, and stock buybacks; fuels the introduction of risky financial innovations; encourages downsizing, outsourcing, offshoring, and union busting; and undermines worker wages and benefits (Minsky and Whalen 1996; Whalen 2022). The result is the set of economic difficulties listed above.

Even without bringing in the problem of climate change, it is easy to see how Kapp's discussion of business's tendency to socialize costs can apply to the era of money manager capitalism. This is especially true with regard to workers, who often find they are on their own in bearing retirement, healthcare, education, and other costs in the current era.[42] In fact, many corporations subcontract large portions of their workforce, freeing them from any obligations to workers at all. And, of course, "gig economy" enterprises such Uber and Lyft take this offloading of risk upon workers to the extreme and consider most of their workers "independent contractors" (Whalen 2022).[43]

PKI needs to introduce the climate change crisis into its discussion of money manager capitalism from both an economic and human perspective; current economic activity is on a path to self-destruction of the economy and the planet's ability to sustain human life. But Ecological economics also needs to examine money manager capitalism because that system's single-minded focus on shareholder value poses perhaps the greatest challenge to achieving ecological sustainability. For example, money manager capitalism pits nations against each other in a race to the bottom on environmental regulation (or at least resistance to the elevation of national and international standards); it stands as an obstacle to the development and use of environmentally friendly energy innovations and clean technologies; it demands low taxes that make governments reluctant to undertake necessary public investments; and it generates economic inequality and insecurity that draws public attention away from the mounting environmental threat.[44]

Another way to look at the ecological problem posed by money manager capitalism is that at the heart of this stage of capitalism is the process of *financialization*, which Gerald Epstein (2005, 3) defines as "the increasing role of financial motives, financial markets, financial actors and financial institutions in the operation of the domestic and international economies."[45] Embedded in that definition is the notion that financialization is an economic and a political process, both of which impede the attainment of any sort of Galbraithian social balance.[46] Instead, profit is pursued without regard for the environment or other aspects of the current and long-term public interest.[47]

While PKI has yet to incorporate a concern for environmental sustainability into its analyses of money manager capitalism, at least one recent paper explores the connection between financialization and sustainability. Jacob

Assa, an economist at the United Nations, identifies and considers a number of direct and indirect ways that financialization exacerbates climate change. For example, adverse direct effects include financial firms' disruption of the solar energy industry and the introduction of financial instruments that reduce the resilience of farming, while adverse indirect effects include weakened support for multinationalism and evidence of global institutions dominated by the interests of financial elites (Assa 2020). The paper by Assa provides a promising beginning for such work; going forward, this is likely be a fruitful and important area of Post-Keynesian Institutionalist research.

SUMMARY AND CONCLUSION: TOWARD REAL SUSTAINABILITY

Until now, PKI has largely ignored ecological sustainability and focused instead on macroeconomic sustainability that involves attenuating business cycle downturns and seeking to foster broadly shared prosperity nationally and internationally. But the current climate change crisis requires that Post-Keynesian Institutionalists give attention to environmental concerns and conduct research that contributes to moving us toward real sustainability—that is, in environmental as well economic terms.[48] This chapter has sought to point toward that genuine, more comprehensive type of sustainability, and it has done so by recommending the incorporation into PKI of insight from Ecological economics.

A good portion of the chapter offered a survey of relevant literature. It began with a brief overview of the origins, worldview, research directions, and contributions of Ecological economics, with particular attention to the work of Boulding. Then, articles from the 1970s by Wolozin and Kapp were examined—to demonstrate Institutionalism's longstanding engagement with environmental issues as well as that engagement's continuing relevance—followed by an overview of similar works by Galbraith and Wilber and Jameson that can be considered early contributions to PKI. The rest of the chapter brought all of that material together in the form of lessons and suggestions for advancing the research agenda of PKI, giving special attention to the opportunity—and pressing need—for analyses of the relationship between climate change and the current, financialized era that Minsky called money manager capitalism. While the chapter identifies a number of ways that insight from Ecological economics can be incorporated into contemporary PKI, the problem-oriented nature of both traditions draws attention in the direction of the interrelations of climate change and today's financialized capitalism.

In *Stabilizing an Unstable Economy*, Minsky (1986, 7) writes: "Economic systems are not natural systems. An economy is a social organization created ... through legislation ... [and] an evolutionary process of invention and innovation. Policy can change both the details and the overall character of the economy." Today, we must use policy not merely to achieve near-term macroeconomic stability, but also to ensure long-term economic and ecological sustainability. However, time is running out; we must move toward real sustainability while we still can.

ACKNOWLEDGMENTS

The author thanks Erik Dean, Nicola Matthews, Jim Peach, Robert Scott, and Linda Whalen for valuable comments and suggestions.

NOTES

1. Drawing on the work of economists such as John Kenneth Galbraith, Joan Robinson, Wallace C. Peterson, Dudley Dillard, Alfred S. Eichner, and Hyman Minsky, PKI emerged in the 1970s with a focus on stagflation, and shifted its gaze to financial instability (and endogenously generated business cycles) in the 1980s. The tradition proved its worth during the global financial crisis of 2007–2009, by analyzing and addressing that period's tumultuous events far better than standard economics. Since then, PKI has focused on the economic evolution that produced the era of "money manager capitalism," a stage of capitalist development characterized by the dominant role of institutional investors, a relentless drive for shareholder value (short-term returns), the financialization of economic activity, rising worker insecurity, and widening economic inequality. For further discussion of PKI, see Charles Whalen's introduction to this volume; see also Whalen (2022).
2. Wilber and Jameson (1983, 155) stress that human behavior often deviates from the "rational" (utility maximizing) decision-making assumed by standard economics. Moreover, the problem-solving focus of PKI results in an interdisciplinary approach that pursues the study of real-world problems (which are themselves interdisciplinary) across academic boundaries as needed.
3. This chapter's overview of Ecological economics relies heavily on Vatn (2009), but interested readers are also encouraged to see Costanza et al. (2015) and Spash (1999).
4. In the mid-1980s, scholars in the field of Ecological economics established both a journal, *Ecological Economics*, and the International Society of Ecological Economics.
5. Although Boulding did not consider himself an Institutional economist, he was a member of the Association for Evolutionary Economics (founded by Institutionalists) and his own view of Evolutionary economics had much in common with Institutionalism. (Commenting on a draft of this chapter, Robert Scott noted that Boulding was also a financial contributor to the establishment of the *Journal of Post Keynesian Economics*.) In addition to Boulding's essay, another important early contribution to Ecological economics is the work of Nicholas Georgescu-Roegen (1971); for an Institutionalist appraisal and extension of that work (and related literature), see Swaney (1985).

6. Boulding (1966, 7–10) acknowledged that technological improvements might forestall that retreat to living within the bounds of the sun's current energy, but he did not count on technology to offer an enduring solution. It should also be emphasized that humans are on track to irreparably damage the environment well before fossil fuels run out (United Nations 2019; Kuo 2019).

7. Developing and relying on more efficient ways to transform solar energy into usable forms, and depending more on renewable resources and less on exhaustible resources, are also ways to live more sustainably, observes Boulding (1966, 8–9).

8. To be sure, the universe may still appear as a nearly limitless frontier, and humans have certainly demonstrated a capacity to explore beyond our own planet, but such explorations do not appear likely to resolve the earth's economic and/or ecological problems anytime soon and are thus beyond the scope of the current discussion.

9. See Vatn (2009, 120), who cites works by conventional economists such as Robert M. Solow. Note also that this reveals yet another irony of conventional economics: the school of thought that organizes itself around the notion that resource scarcity is a dominant force in the world also relies on technological change and resource substitution to avoid confronting the long-term problem of exhaustible resources.

10. Like many conventional economists, some Institutional economists also hold an approach that comes close to denying that there are fundamental scarcity problems. For many Institutionalists, the matter around us (raw materials, plants, etc.) is "neutral stuff," which gets transformed into resources as capabilities emerge when humans interact with that "stuff" on the basis of our ever-changing knowledge (that is, science and technology) (Gordon 1980, 28–30; De Gregori 1987). But even neutral stuff is limited in quantity, and technological change cannot be assumed to always offer timely and environmentally benign solutions to material shortages, nor can humans fully anticipate all side effects and ecosystem disruptions that will emerge over time as a result of introducing new technologies; for a nuanced Institutionalist view of resources and technology, see Swaney (1987; 1989).

11. On the need for participatory processes, Vatn (2009, 121) writes, "In a situation with radical uncertainty [that is, a situation in which probabilistic risk does not apply], expert and citizen evaluations should be combined."

12. Vatn (2009, 122) also underscores Ecological economics' "emphasis on the intrinsic value of other species." Most economics is anthropocentric, with nature's value evaluated according to the economically measurable benefits humans receive from other animals and plants (Costanza and Wainger 1990). In contrast, many preservationists argue "not that we elevate other species to the importance of people, but rather that we extend rights of existence … to all flora and fauna because it is in our own survival interest [in a world of complex ecological interrelations] to do so;" this involves non-mainstream economic thinking in that the perspective looks "far beyond the dictates of pecuniary self-interest" (Swaney 1987, 1744, 1751–1752).

13. To be sure, Boulding (as previously discussed) wanted policymakers to focus on bolstering and sustaining stocks, not flows (such as today's gross domestic product). Nevertheless, Ecological economists must study flows (as well as stocks) because their expansion without regard to environmental damage and resource limits is considered a primary source of ecological problems.

14.   More broadly, Ecological economics has focused on three distinct yet interrelated themes: resilience, vulnerability, and adaptation; see Janssen and Ostrom (2006). While much research on resilience examines how humans affect the adaptability of ecosystems, vulnerability research focuses on the vulnerability of people to environmental change; and adaptation studies focus on adjustment in socioecological systems (by means including, for example, sustainable development initiatives or disaster preparedness programs) "in response to actual, perceived, or expected environmental changes and their impact" (Janssen and Ostrom 2006, 237).

15.   Wolozin saw environmental damage not merely as a threat to the quality of human life, but also as a threat to human survival (Wolozin 1971, 40, n. 1).

16.   Murad's commentary also expresses concern about regulatory capture: "Business will not let itself be regulated, but will itself regulate the regulators, as has been the experience of [many] regulatory agencies ... Whatever teeth there may be [in a national environmental regulatory authority] may well bite the little fellows, not the big polluters" (Murad 1971, 43).

17.   According to Murad (1971, 45–46), an environmental extension of the US Bill of Rights would complement an economic extension of the Bill of Rights proposed by some within the administration of Franklin Roosevelt during the 1940s.

18.   As this chapter is being completed, residents of New York prepare for a statewide ballot measure that would give New Yorkers a constitutional right to clean air and clean water (DeWitt 2021).

19.   Murad (1971, 44) elaborates on Wolozin's critique of a market-based approach to environmental management as follows:
       [T]he fact that everybody wants a car and would be willing to pay for all the measurable environmental damage caused by producing and using it is no proof that people would not be better off and feel better off in a car-free society. The individual's choices are limited and conditioned by the kind of society in which he [sic] lives. His choices do not express his preference for that particular kind of society. In an automobile society, people ... are willing to pay for automobiles because for all practical purposes they cannot live without them. They do not have the option to live in a car-free society.

20.   It is important to note that in addition to environmentally harmful interactions among pollutants, there are even synergistic processes between pollutants and sunlight, which can, for example, create hazardous, ground-level smog.

21.   Murad also challenges the conventional notion that social costs might be calculated as the sum of private costs; see note 19 above.

22.   Much of Kapp's discussion of the complex and cumulative nature of environmental disruption is similar to that found in Wolozin's article. For example, Kapp (1977, 529–531) mentions that: (1) residual waste products and other pollutants come from multiple sources and then react upon one another, often giving rise to toxic combinations; (2) there are important nonlinearities because once critical environmental media reach thresholds of assimilative capacity there can be sudden and catastrophic consequences for health and well-being—and irreversible effects on the environment; and (3) the negative effects of pollution and environmental degradation may take years to become apparent, usually making it impossible to identify a specific source when damages materialize. Readers familiar with Institutional economics will also recognize Kapp's reference to that tradition's principle of *cumulative causation*, which, along with an open-system conception of economic activity (that is, open to an extensive

sphere of social, cultural, and environmental influences), he considers to be at the core of Institutionalism (Kapp 1976).

23. In addition, in a further example of cumulative causation, the worldwide economic expansion following World War II added to the environmental problem—at an accelerating pace—through an expanded use of highly polluting technologies (involving petrochemicals, for example), high rates of obsolescence, and increased reliance on automobiles (Kapp 1977, 533).

24. See Kapp (1977, 538) for his discussion of how vested interests can be expected to obstruct environmental management (including their tendency to "delay and inhibit the successful search for truthful information"); attention to this matter in Wolozin (1971, 27) has been highlighted above.

25. Galbraith also mentions the possibility of internalizing external diseconomies so that producers, and thus ultimately customers, are required to pay to protect the environment, but, like Wolozin and Kapp, he considers that approach to be of limited practical value and effectiveness (Galbraith 1973a, 276–277).

26. Galbraith (1973a, 278) writes, "Effective environmental protection requires explicit and unyielding legal specifications." Then, a few pages later, he adds that his strategy "does not exclude growth .... [Rather,] it undertakes to discipline that growth, align it with public purposes and do this under public auspices" (Galbraith 1973a, 281).

27. Having mentioned Post Keynesian economics above, it is worth noting that Joan Robinson, an originator of Post Keynesianism who often had much in common with Institutionalists, wrote occasionally about environmental issues, often making points similar to those of Wolozin, Kapp, and Galbraith (see, e.g., Robinson 1972, 7; 1980, xiii, 42, 118). Moreover, in addition to chiding economists for their failure to offer society much help on the most important questions of the day, Robinson (1972, 6) admonished them for having nothing to say about the content of employment and the composition of public expenditures: "Keynes did not want anyone to dig holes and fill them;" and Robinson did not want military spending to be the go-to solution for the unemployment problem, expressing concern that "[t]he most convenient thing for a government to spend on is armaments." Robinson's criticisms continue to offer lessons for contemporary Post-Keynesian Institutionalists on the subject of the environment and ecological sustainability.

28. Stagflation was also a problem in other industrial democracies, but the United States was among the nations in which it was especially troublesome, and Wilber and Jameson focus most of their attention on that country.

29. Wilber and Jameson (1983, 218–222) also identify American society's tendency toward individualized consumption (private automobiles, home washing machines, etc.) and self-centered behavior (an erosion of ethical standards and conduct) as both self-perpetuating and, ultimately, self-destructive.

30. Wilber and Jameson also indicate that environmental protection must occur, via stakeholder engagement, at all societal levels—at the workplace, locally (which, for example, can involve weatherizing homes, minimizing pollution discharges, and boosting public transit services), nationally, and internationally (Wilber and Jameson 1983, 8, 241–248, 256).

31. Minsky frequently referred to providing public goods and services as public "resource creation," a process he conceived as encompassing the development of human as well as physical resources, and that he thought was all too often over-

shadowed by attention to private goods and services and to government transfer payments (see, e.g., Minsky 1986, 311–312).

32. For examples of the views of Minsky mentioned above, see Minsky (1986, 293, 300, 310–312; 1996; 2013, 71).

33. The overlapping worldviews of Ecological economics and PKI are not just a matter of (pre-analytic) methodology; this is particularly evident in Vatn's (2009, 122–125) discussion of the links between Ecological, Institutional, and Post Keynesian economics in the realm of microeconomic analysis.

34. See, for example, Ferri and Minsky (1992). Central to their work is the usefulness of taking precautionary steps that anticipate and limit the processes that fuel economic disruption.

35. In addition to Daly (1991), see his much more recent essay: Daly (2019). But also see Peach (2018, 297), which considers Daly's notion of the steady state as unrealistic and a distraction "that takes the focus away from policies that could facilitate economic development [which, consistent with Boulding, Peach sees as distinct from economic growth], alleviate poverty, reduce environmental damage, and help prevent species extinction." (Individual Post-Keynesian Institutionalists will have to make their own judgments on this literature, but I find valuable insight in the work of both Daly and Peach, and a similar view is offered by Swaney (2003).) Post-Keynesian Institutionalists should also look at Ecological economists' research on social metabolism, socioecological resilience, and adaptive systems (for references, see Vatn 2009, 120–121).

36. For another Post-Keynesian Institutionalist discussion on the subject of linking public service to environmental sustainability, see Forstater (2003).

37. For a discussion of costs and risks associated with climate change in the United States, see US Global Change Research Program (2018).

38. See Schmid (1994; 1999a; 1999b; 2008) for examples of his work.

39. See, for example, Swaney (1987), which mentions both the intrinsic value of nature and the value humans receive when other species continue to exist.

40. For the Institutionalist emphasis on continuous appraisal and reappraisal of values, see Gordon (1980, 37–66); that emphasis can serve as a useful component in a PKI approach to environmental sustainability. Also, see Chapter 7 (by Asimina Christoforou) for a discussion of the role of social capital and civil society in helping to shape social beliefs, values, and institutions.

41. The COVID-19 pandemic has made matters worse by underscoring and aggravating all the problems mentioned above (for more on money manager capitalism and the pandemic, see Chapter 4, by Liang and Whalen, in this volume).

42. Several chapters in Part II of this book highlight the nature and consequences of the offloading of costs and risks by corporations in the age of money manager capitalism.

43. It is also worth noting that the offloading of worker-related costs and risks by corporations in the current era—a process that many describe as trying to turn labor into just another spot-market commodity—underscores the common ground of PKI and Ecological economics on how institutions, law, and power relations affect the distribution of risk (Vatn 2009, 122–123).

44. Of course, many companies claim that their products are good for the environment, but much of that is misleading—what environmentalists call "greenwashing" (see, e.g., National Public Radio 2007). Meanwhile, it is true that corporations have long had a predatory side; money manager capitalism has merely nurtured it and allowed it to flourish (Jo and Henry 2015).

45. For a discussion of money manager capitalism and financialization, see Whalen (2020); for a historical perspective, including a discussion of how the evolution of property rights shaped contemporary US capitalism, see Atkinson, Hake, and Paschall (2021).

46. Bringing ecological considerations into the picture also reveals the environmental dimensions of the inequality generated under money manager capitalism. Those who are most economically disadvantaged are also most likely to live in communities exposed to significant environmental hazards.

47. Of course, market solutions, such as carbon taxes combined with emissions trading initiatives, seek to reconcile profit and regard for the environment, but such arrangements (long viewed with caution and skepticism by Ecological and Institutionalists, as indicated above) have also led to "the financialization of nature." Such arrangements have "normalized the exploitation of nature as part of the financial sphere" (Assa 2020, 7).

48. What I refer to here as "real" sustainability is consistent with Swaney's (1986) notion of the sustainable coevolution of both the ecosystem and the socioeconomic system.

REFERENCES

Adkisson, Richard V. 2022. "Environmental Sustainability in Social Context: An Institutionalist Perspective." In *Institutional Economics: Perspectives and Methods in Pursuit of a Better World*, edited by Charles J. Whalen, chapter six. London: Routledge.

Assa, Jacob. 2020. "Liquidating Society and the Planet: Financialization vs. Sustainability." Preprint (September), The New School, USA. https://tinyurl.com/pn3ms73e. Accessed May 3, 2021.

Atkinson, Glen, Eric R. Hake, and Stephen P. Paschall. 2021. *Evolution of the Corporation in the United States: From Social Control to Financialization*. Cheltenham, UK: Edward Elgar.

Boulding, Kenneth. 1966. "The Economics of the Coming Spaceship Earth." In *Environmental Quality in a Growing Economy*, edited by Henry Jarrett, 3–14. Baltimore: Johns Hopkins Press.

Costanza, Robert, John H. Cumberland, Herman Daly, Robert Goodland, Richard B. Norgaard, Ida Kubiszewski, and Carol Franco. 2015. *An Introduction to Ecological Economics*, second edition. London: CRC Press.

Costanza, Robert and Lisa Wainger. 1990. "No Accounting for Nature: How Conventional Economics Distorts the Real Value of Things." *The Washington Post*, September 2. https://tinyurl.com/yv3b6u42. Accessed June 19, 2021.

Courvisanos, Jerry. 2009. "Optimize versus Satisfice: Two Approaches to an Investment Policy in Sustainable Development." In *Post Keynesian and Ecological Economics: Confronting Environmental Issues*, edited by Richard P.F. Holt, Steven Pressman, and Clive L. Spash, 277–298. Cheltenham, UK: Edward Elgar.

Daly, Herman E. 1991. *Steady-State Economics*, second edition. Washington, DC: Island Press.

Daly, Herman E. 2019. "Growthism: Its Ecological, Economic and Ethical Limits." *Real-World Economics Review* Issue No. 87: 9–23.

De Gregori, Thomas R. 1987. "Resources Are Not; They Become: An Institutional Theory." *Journal of Economic Issues* 21 (3): 1241-1263.

DeWitt, Karen. 2021. "Coalition to Promote Clean Air and Water Amendment on November Ballot." New York NOW. https://tinyurl.com/47ufj8ve. Accessed August 4, 2021.

Epstein, Gerald. 2005. "Introduction." In *Financialization and the World Economy*, edited by Gerald Epstein. Cheltenham, UK: Edward Elgar.

Ferri, Piero and Hyman P. Minsky. 1992. "Structural Change and Economic Dynamics." *Structural Change and Economic Dynamics* 3 (1): 79–91.

Folke, Carl. 2006. "Resilience: The Emergence of a Perspective for Social-Ecological Systems Analysis." *Global Environmental Change* 16 (3): 253–267.

Forstater, Mathew. 2003. "Public Employment and Environmental Sustainability." *Journal of Post Keynesian Economics* 25 (3): 385–406.

Galbraith, John Kenneth. 1958. *The Affluent Society*. Boston: Houghton Mifflin.

Galbraith, John Kenneth. 1973a. *Economics and the Public Purpose*. Boston: Houghton Mifflin.

Galbraith, John Kenneth. 1973b. "Power and the Useful Economist." *American Economic Review* 63 (1): 1–11.

Galbraith, John Kenneth. 1978. "On Post Keynesian Economics." *Journal of Post Keynesian Economics* 1 (1): 8–11.

Galbraith, John Kenneth. 1996. *The Good Society: The Humane Agenda*. Boston: Houghton Mifflin.

Georgescu-Roegen, Nicholas. 1971. *The Entropy Law and the Economic Process*. Cambridge, MA: Harvard University Press.

Gordon, Wendell C. 1980. *Institutional Economics: The Changing System*. Austin, TX: University of Texas Press.

Holt, Richard P.F. and Clive L. Spash. 2009. "Post Keynesian and Ecological Economics: Alternative Perspectives on Sustainability and Environmental Science." In *Post Keynesian and Ecological Economics: Confronting Environmental Issues*, edited by Richard P.F. Holt, Steven Pressman, and Clive L. Spash, 1–22. Cheltenham, UK: Edward Elgar.

Intergovernmental Panel on Climate Change. 2018. *Global Warming of 1.5°C: Summary for Policymakers*. IPCC: Switzerland.

Intergovernmental Panel on Climate Change. 2021. *Climate Change 2021: The Physical Science Basis*. Sixth Assessment Report. https://www.ipcc.ch/report/ar6/wg1/downloads/report/IPCC_AR6_WGI_Full_Report.pdf. Accessed August 9, 2021.

Janssen, Marco A. and Elinor Ostrom. 2006. "Resilience, Vulnerability, and Adaptation: A Cross-cutting Theme of the International Human Dimensions Programme on Global Environmental Change." *Global Environmental Change* 16 (3): 237–239.

Jo, Tae-Hee and John F. Henry. 2015. "The Business Enterprise in the Age of Money Manager Capitalism." *Journal of Economic Issues* 49 (1): 23–46.

Kapp, K. William. 1950. *The Social Costs of Private Enterprise*. Cambridge, MA: Harvard University Press.

Kapp, K. William. 1976. "In Defense of Institutionalism." In *Economics and Sociology: Towards an Integration*, edited by T. Huppes, 76–95. Leiden: Martinus Nijhoff.

Kapp, K. William. 1977. "Environment and Technology: New Frontiers for the Social and Natural Sciences." *Journal of Economic Issues* 11 (3): 527–540.

Kuo, Gioietta. 2019. "When Fossil Fuels Run Out, What Then?" Millennium Alliance for Humanity and the Biosphere, Stanford University. May 23, 2019. https://mahb.stanford.edu/library-item/fossil-fuels-run. Accessed July 22, 2021.

Minsky, Hyman P. 1986. *Stabilizing an Unstable Economy*. New Haven, CT: Yale University Press.

Minsky, Hyman P. 1993. "Schumpeter and Finance." In *Market and Institutions in Economic Development*, edited by Salvatore Biasco, Alessandro Roncaglia, and Michele Salvati, 103–115. New York: St. Martin's Press.

Minsky, Hyman P. 1996. "Uncertainty and the Institutional Structure of Capitalist Economies." *Journal of Economic Issues* 30 (2): 357–368.

Minsky, Hyman P. 2013. *Ending Poverty: Jobs, Not Welfare*. Annandale-on-Hudson, New York: Levy Economics Institute.

Minsky, Hyman and Charles Whalen. 1996. "Economic Insecurity and the Institutional Prerequisites for Successful Capitalism." *Journal of Post Keynesian Economics* 19 (2): 155–170.

Murad, Anatol. 1971. "Comments on Murad." *Journal of Economic Issues* 5 (1): 42–46.

National Public Radio. 2007. "Eco-Friendly Product Claims Often Misleading." November 30. https://www.npr.org/templates/story/story.php?storyId=16754919. Accessed May 3, 2021.

Peach, James. 2018. "Habits of Thought and the Process of Economic Development: Remarks Upon Receiving the Veblen-Commons Award." *Journal of Economic Issues* 52 (2): 293–305.

Robinson, Joan. 1972. "The Second Crisis of Economic Theory." *American Economic Review* 62 (1/2): 1–10.

Robinson, Joan. 1980. *What Are the Questions and Other Essays: Further Contributions to Modern Economics*. Armonk, NY: M.E. Sharpe.

Schmid, A. Allan. 1994. "Institutional Law and Economics." *European Journal of Law and Economics* 1 (1): 33–51.

Schmid, A. Allan. 1999a. "Environmental Law and Economics." In *The Elgar Companion to Law and Economics*, edited by Jurgen G. Backhaus, 201–205. Cheltenham, UK: Edward Elgar Publishing.

Schmid, A. Allan. 1999b. "Government, Property, Markets ...In that Order ... Not Government versus Markets." In *The Fundamental Interrelationships between Government and Property*, edited by Nicholas Mercuro and Warren J. Samuels, 237–242. Stamford, CT: JAI Press.

Schmid, A. Allan. 2008. "My Work as an Institutional Economist." Department of Agricultural and Resource Economics, Michigan State University, January 31. https://thecre.com/pdf/20131229_My_work_as_an_Insitutional_Economist.pdf. Accessed May 2, 2021.

Soderbaum, Peter. 1994. "Actors, Ideology, Markets: Neoclassical and Institutional Perspectives on Environmental Policy." *Ecological Economics* 10 (1): 47–60.

Spash, Clive L. 1999. "The Development of Environmental Thinking in Economics." *Environmental Values* 8 (4): 413–435.

Swaney, James A. 1985. "Economics, Ecology, and Entropy." *Journal of Economic Issues* 19 (4): 853–865.

Swaney, James A. 1986. "A Coevolutionary Model of Structural Change." *Journal of Economic Issues* 20 (2): 393–401.

Swaney, James A. 1987. "Elements of a Neoinstitutional Environmental Economics." *Journal of Economic Issues* 21 (4): 1739–1779.

Swaney, James A. 1989. "Our Obsolete Technology Mentality." *Journal of Economic Issues* 23 (2): 569–578.

Swaney, James A. 2003. "Are Democracy and Common Property Possible on Our Small Earth?" *Journal of Economic Issues* 37 (2): 261–290.

Tcherneva, Pavlina R. 2018. "The Job Guarantee: Design, Jobs, and Implementation." Levy Economics Institute, Working Paper No. 902.

United Nations. 2019. "Only 11 Years Left to Prevent Irreversible Damage from Climate Change, Speakers Warn During General Assembly High-Level Meeting." Meetings Coverage, March 28, 2019. https://www.un.org/press/en/2019/ga12131 .doc.htm. Accessed June 22, 2021.

US Global Change Research Program. 2018. *Fourth National Climate Assessment.* Washington, DC: US Global Change Research Program. https://nca2018 .globalchange.gov. Accessed May 2, 2021.

Vatn, Arild. 2008. "Institutions and Rationality." In *Alternative Economic Structures: Evolution and Impact*, edited by Sandra S. Batie and Nicholas Mercuro, 113–139. London: Routledge.

Vatn, Arild. 2009. "Combining Post Keynesian, Ecological and Institutional Perspectives." In *Post Keynesian and Ecological Economics: Confronting Environmental Issues*, edited by Richard P.F. Holt, Steven Pressman, and Clive L. Spash, 112–136. Cheltenham, UK: Edward Elgar.

Whalen, Charles J. 1992. "Schools of Thought and Theories of the State: Reflections of an Institutional Economist." In *The Stratified State*, edited by William M. Dugger and William T. Waller, 55–85. Armonk, NY: M.E. Sharpe.

Whalen, Charles J. 2008. "Toward 'Wisely Managed' Capitalism: Post-Keynesian Institutionalism and the Creative State." *Forum for Social Economics* 37 (1): 43–60.

Whalen, Charles J. 2013. "Post-Keynesian Institutionalism after the Great Recession." *European Journal of Economics and Economic Policies: Intervention* 10 (1): 12–27.

Whalen, Charles J. 2019. "Institutional Economics and Chock-Full Employment: Reclaiming the 'Right to Work' as a Cornerstone of Progressive Capitalism." *Journal of Economic Issues* 53 (2): 321–340.

Whalen, Charles J. 2020. "Understanding Financialisation: Standing on the Shoulders of Minsky." In *Alternative Approaches to Economic Theory*, edited by Victor A. Beker, 185–206. London: Routledge.

Whalen, Charles J. 2022. "Grappling with an Ever-changing Economy: The Evolution of Post-Keynesian Institutionalism." In *Institutional Economics: Perspectives and Methods in Search of a Better World*, edited by Charles J. Whalen, 101–126. London: Routledge.

Whalen, Charles J. and Katherine A. Whalen. 2020. "Circular Economy Business Models: A Critical Examination." *Journal of Economic Issues* 54 (3): 628–643.

Whalen, Katherine A. and Charles J. Whalen. 2018. "The Circular Economy and Institutional Economics: Compatibility and Complementarity." *Journal of Economic Issues* 52 (3): 605–614.

Wilber, Charles and Kenneth Jameson. 1983. *An Inquiry into the Poverty of Economics.* Notre Dame: University of Notre Dame Press.

Wolozin, Harold. 1971. "Environmental Control at the Crossroads." *Journal of Economic Issues* 5 (1): 26–41.

Wray, L. Randall. 1997. "Kenneth Boulding's Reconstruction of Macroeconomics." *Review of Social Economy* 55 (4): 445–463.

Zalewski, David A. 2003. "Corporate Objectives—Maximizing Social versus Private Equity." *Journal of Economic Issues* 37 (2): 503–509.

Index

Printed and bound by CPI Group (UK) Ltd, Croydon, CR0 4YY

16/04/2025

14658380-0002